C000040327

Blackstone's Statute

Public Law & Human Rights

Blackstone's Statutes on
Public Law &
Human Rights

2002/2003

Twelfth Edition

Edited by

Peter Wallington

MA, LLM, Barrister

11 King's Bench Walk Chambers

and

Robert G. Lee

LLB

Professor of Law, ESRC Centre for Business Relationships, Accountability,
Sustainability and Society, Cardiff Law School

OXFORD
UNIVERSITY PRESS

OXFORD
UNIVERSITY PRESS

Great Clarendon Street, Oxford OX2 6DP

Oxford University Press is a department of the University of Oxford.
It furthers the University's objective of excellence in research, scholarship,
and education by publishing worldwide in

Oxford New York

Auckland Bangkok Buenos Aires Cape Town Chennai
Dar es Salaam Delhi Hong Kong Istanbul Karachi Kolkata
Kuala Lumpur Madrid Melbourne Mexico City Mumbai Nairobi
São Paulo Shanghai Taipei Tokyo Toronto

Oxford is a registered trade mark of Oxford University Press
in the UK and in certain other countries

Published in the United States
by Oxford University Press Inc., New York

First published by Blackstone Press

This selection © Peter Wallington and Robert G. Lee 2002

The moral rights of the authors have been asserted
Database right Oxford University Press (maker)

First edition 1988
Second edition 1990
Third edition 1992
Reprinted 1993
Fourth edition 1994
Fifth edition 1995
Sixth edition 1996
Seventh edition 1997
Eighth edition 1998
Ninth edition 1999
Tenth edition 2000
Eleventh edition 2001
Twelfth edition 2002

All rights reserved. No part of this publication may be reproduced,
stored in a retrieval system, or transmitted, in any form or by any means,
without the prior permission in writing of Oxford University Press,
or as expressly permitted by law, or under terms agreed with the appropriate
reprographics rights organizations. Enquiries concerning reproduction
outside the scope of the above should be sent to the Rights Department,
Oxford University Press, at the address above

You must not circulate this book in any other binding or cover
and you must impose this same condition on any acquirer

British Library Cataloguing in Publication Data
Data available

Crown Copyright material is reproduced with the permission of
the Controller of HMSO and the Queen's Printer for Scotland

ISBN 0–19–925535–0

1 3 5 7 9 10 8 6 4 2

Typeset in ITC Stone Serif and ITC Stone Sans
by RefineCatch Limited, Bungay, Suffolk
Printed in Great Britain by
Ashford Colour Press Ltd, Gosport, Hampshire

CONTENTS

PART II   Other Constitutional Materials   519

EDITORS' PREFACE

The adage that Britain has no written constitution, while still technically true, is an increasingly unhelpful and unreal starting point for the study of Constitutional and Administrative Law. As in many other areas of the law, statute has assumed an increasingly pervasive role. In addition, the incorporation of the European Convention on Human Rights promotes a significant constitutional document against which laws must be measured. Other international sources play an increasing part in the regulation of power in the UK, making it important to look for comparison at the constitutional approach of some other jurisdictions. The volume of statutory and analogous material to which students in the field of Public Law need to refer has become such that a separate set of materials is a necessary guide. Hence this book, which has been re-titled to recognise the importance of Human Rights Law within our constitutional framework.

We have assembled here a collection of statutes on all aspects of Constitutional and Administrative Law and Human Rights. It is not intended to replace textbooks or cases and materials books, but to complement them and to provide necessary and quick reference to essential texts. Since it contains no commentary it is suitable—and we hope will be adopted—for reference in examinations in these subjects (but do check with your faculty or department whether this is so). We hope it will also encourage students to become more accustomed to reading and unravelling the language of Parliament—one of the most basic skills of a lawyer.

The selection of materials for a collection of statutes is a matter of sometimes arbitrary editorial judgment. Our selection is based on the knowledge that courses vary in content and an attempt to meet the major needs of a fairly broad range of undergraduate courses. This means the book will contain some material irrelevant to your particular course—but much that is central, or a valuable supplement, to any course in the Public Law area (including important parts of English Legal System courses). The book is designed to be used by English, Welsh and Scottish students. It includes the legislation allowing significant devolution of power within the United Kingdom. The territorial extent of each Act is indicated and where there is parallel English and Scottish legislation we have included both (with exceptions, especially in the field of Local Government). For reasons of space this approach was not possible for Northern Ireland, but we have included those parts of Northern Irish legislation of most interest to students elsewhere in the UK. It should be noted that one consequence of the creation of a Scottish Parliament with legislative powers is that statutes extending to England and Wales and to Scotland may be amended in relation to one of the jurisdictions but not the other; for simplicity we have adopted the version applicable in England and Wales in such cases.

As well as statutes, we include the Bill of Rights amendments to the United States Constitution, the European Convention on Human Rights, parts of the Treaty of Rome (as consolidated by the Amsterdam Treaty), and major extracts from the key Codes of Practice issued under the Police and Criminal Evidence Act 1984 (in their current versions).

The amount of new material in this edition has required, once again, some editing of the previous text. We hope, however, that nothing vital has been lost. As always we are pleased to receive comments concerning the editorial judgments exercised. Because this is a text for students rather than practitioners we have been able to be more selective in cutting material down to a manageable length. Omissions are indicated by a row of asterisks. Provisions as to commencement, etc. have also been omitted. The text is printed, where appropriate, as subsequently amended; new materials are shown by square brackets and repeals by dots. Statutes are printed in chronological order; other material is gathered together in Part II.

Significant legislation in the field of public law has been a defining feature of the Labour Government, and we have attempted to cover the significant provisions of public law as at

1 June 2002. All legislative changes enacted up to that date have been incorporated, whether or not yet in force.

We gratefully acknowledge the help we received from Clive Lewis, who advised on content and carefully checked the manuscript of the first edition, and Wissam Deeb, who assisted with the research for this edition. We are also indebted to Jeremy McBride of the University of Birmingham both for suggestions as to inclusions and for the benefits of collaboration over the years in the internal production of statutory materials for students at Cambridge, Birmingham, Lancaster and Cardiff. Finally our thanks are due to our publishers for their speed and efficiency in production. The responsibility for errors is the editors' alone.

Peter Wallington
Robert G. Lee
June 2002

PART I

Statutes of the UK Parliament and Its Predecessors

Magna Carta
(Statute 25 Edw. 1, 1297)

Territorial extent: England and Wales, Northern Ireland

The Great Charter of the Liberties of England, and of the Liberties of the Forest; confirmed by King Edward, in the Twenty-fifth Year of his Reign.

Edward by the grace of God King of England, Lord of Ireland, and Duke of Guyan, to all archbishops, bishops, &c. We have seen the Great Charter of the Lord Henry sometimes King of England, our father, of the liberties of England in these words:

Henry by the grace of God King of England, Lord of Ireland, Duke of Normandy and Guyan, and Earl of Anjou, to all archbishops, bishops, abbots, priors, earls, barons, sheriffs, provosts, officers, and to all bailiffs, and other our faithful subjects, which shall see this present charter, greeting: Know ye, that we, unto the honour of Almighty God, and for the salvation of the souls of our progenitors and successors Kings of England, to the advancement of holy church and amendment of our realm, of our meer and free will, have given and granted to all archbishops, bishops, abbots, priors, earls, barons, and to all freemen of this our realm, these liberties following, to be kept in our kingdom of England for ever.

Chapter 1   Confirmation of liberties
First, we have granted to God, and by this our present charter have confirmed, for us and our heirs for ever, that the church of England shall be free, and shall have all her whole rights and liberties inviolable. We have granted also, and given to all the freemen of our realm, for us and our heirs for ever, these liberties underwritten, to have and to hold to them and their heirs, of us and our heirs for ever.

Chapters 2–28   . . .

Chapter 29   Imprisonment, etc. contrary to law
No freeman shall be taken or imprisoned, or be disseised of his freehold, or liberties, or free customs, or be outlawed, or exiled, or any other wise destroyed; nor will we not pass upon him, nor condemn him, but by lawful judgment of his peers, or by the law of the land. We will sell to no man, we will not deny or defer to any man either justice or right.

Chapters 30–36   . . .
[Chapter 37 (Escuage) omitted]

Treason Act 1351
(25 Edw. 3 Stat 5, c. 2)

Territorial extent: United Kingdom

Declaration what offences shall be adjudged treason

Item, whereas divers opinions have been before this time in what case treason shall be said, and in what not; the King, at the request of the lords and of the commons, hath made a declaration in the manner as hereafter followeth, that is to say; when a man doth compass or imagine the death of our lord the King, or of our lady his Queen or of their eldest son and heir; or if a man do violate the King's companion, or the King's eldest daughter unmarried, or the wife the King's eldest son and heir; or if a man do levy war against our lord the King in his realm, or be adherent to the King's enemies in his realm, giving to them aid and comfort in the realm, or elsewhere, and thereof be probably attainted of open deed by the people of their condition: . . . and if a man slea the chancellor, treasurer, or the King's justices of the one bench or the other, justices in eyre, or justices of assise, and all other justices assigned to hear and determine, being in their places, doing their offices: and it is to be understood, that in the cases above rehearsed, that ought to be judged treason which extends to our lord the King, and his royal majesty: . . .

Justices of the Peace Act 1361
(34 Edw. 3, c. 1)

Who shall be justices of the peace—Their jurisdiction over offenders; rioters; barrators; and vagabonds—Commissions of general inquiries to end—Fines to be reasonable

Territorial extent: England and Wales, Northern Ireland (in part—see Magistrates' Courts Act (Northern Ireland) 1964. Sch. 2).

First, that in every county of England shall be assigned for the keeping of the peace, one lord, and with him three or four of the most worthy in the county, with some learned in the law, and they shall have power to restrain the offenders, rioters, and all other barrators and to pursue, arrest, take, and chastise them according their trespass or offence; and to cause them to be imprisoned and duly punished according to the law and customs of the realm, and according to that which to them shall seem best to do by their discretions and good advisement; . . . and to take and arrest all those that they may find by indictment, or by suspicion, and to put them in prison; and to take of all them that be not of good fame, where they shall be found, sufficient surety and mainprise of their good behaviour towards the King and his people, and the other duly to punish; to the intent that the people be not by such rioters or rebels troubled nor endamaged, nor the peace blemished, nor merchants nor other passing by the highways of the realm disturbed, nor put in the peril which may happen of such offenders . . .

The Bill of Rights (1688)
(1 Will. & Mar. sess 2, c. 2)

An Act declaring the Rights and Liberties of the Subject and Setleing the Succession of the Crowne

Territorial extent: England and Wales, Northern Ireland (for Scotland see the equivalent Act of the Scottish Parliament, the Claim of Right 1689).

Whereas the lords spirituall and temporall and comons assembled at Westminster lawfully fully and freely representing all estates of the people of this realme did upon the thirteenth day of February in the yeare of our Lord one thousand six hundred eighty eight present unto their Majesties then called and known by the names and stile of William and Mary Prince and Princesse of Orange being present in their proper persons a certaine declaration in writeing made by the said lords and comons in the words following viz

    The heads of declaration of lords and commons, recited—Whereas the late King James the Second by the assistance of diverse evill councillors judges and ministers imployed by him did endeavour to subvert and extirpate the Protestant religion and the lawes and liberties of this kingdome

    Dispensing and suspending power—By assumeing and exerciseing a power of dispensing with and suspending of lawes and the execution of lawes without consent of Parlyament.

    Committing prelates—By committing and prosecuting diverse worthy prelates for humbly petitioning to be excused from concurring to the said assumed power.

    Ecclesiastical commission—By issueing and causeing to be executed a commission under the great seale for erecting a court called the court of commissioners for ecclesiasticall causes.

    Levying money—By levying money for and to the use of the Crowne by pretence of prerogative for other time and in other manner then the same was granted by Parlyament.

    Standing army—By raising and keeping a standing army within this kingdome in time of peace without consent of Parlyament and quartering soldiers contrary to law.

    Disarming Protestants, etc.—By causing severall good subjects being protestants to be disarmed at the same time when papists were both armed and imployed contrary to law.

    Violating elections—By violating the freedome of election of members to serve in Parlyament.

    Illegal prosecutions—By prosecutions in the Court of King's Bench for matters and causes cognizable onely in Parlyament and by diverse other arbitrary and illegall courses.

    Juries—And whereas of late yeares partiall corrupt and unqualifyed persons have beene returned and served on juryes in tryalls and particularly diverse jurors in tryalls for high treason which were not freeholders.

    Excessive bail—And excessive baile hath beene required of persons committed in criminall cases to elude the benefitt of the lawes made for the liberty of the subjects.

    Fines—And excessive fines have beene imposed.

    Punishments—And illegall and cruell punishments inflicted.

    Grants of fines, etc., before conviction, etc.—And severall grants and promises made of fines and forfeitures before any conviction or judgement against the persons upon whome the same were to be levyed.

    All which are uterly and directly contrary to the knowne lawes and statutes and freedome of the realme.

    And whereas the said late King James the Second haveing abdicated the government and the throne being thereby vacant his Highnesse the Prince of Orange (whome it hath pleased Almighty God to make the glorious instrument of delivering this kingdome from popery and arbitrary power) did (by the advice of the lords spirituall and temporall and diverse principall persons of the commons) cause letters to be written to the lords spirituall and temporall being protestants and other letters to the severall countyes cityes universities boroughss and cinque ports for the choosing of such persons to represent them as were of right to be sent to Parlyament to meete and sitt at Westminster upon the two and twentyeth day of January in this yeare one thousand six hundred eighty and eight in order to such an establishment as that their religion lawes and liberties might not againe be in danger of being subverted, upon which letters elections haveing beene accordingly made.

The subject's Rights – And thereupon the said lords spirituall and temporall and commons pursuant to their respective letters and elections being now assembled in a full and free representative of this nation takeing into their most serious consideration the best meanes for attaining the ends aforesaid doe in the first place (as their auncestors in like case have usually done) for the vindicating and asserting their auntient rights and liberties, declare

[1] Suspending power—That the pretended power of suspending of laws or the execution of laws by regall authority without consent of Parlyament is illegall.

Late dispensing power—That the pretended power of dispensing with laws or the execution of laws by regall authoritie as it hath beene assumed and exercised of late is illegall.

Ecclesiastical courts illegal—That the commission for erecting the late court of commissioners for ecclesiasticall causes and all other commissions and courts of like nature are illegal and pernicious.

Levying money—That levying money for or to the use of the Crowne by pretence of prerogative without grant of Parlyament for longer time or in other manner than the same is or shall be granted is illegal.

Right to petition—That it is the right of the subjects to petition the King and all committments and prosecutions for such petitioning are illegal.

Standing army—That the raising or keeping a standing army within the kingdome in time of peace unlesse it be with consent of Parlyament is against law.

Subject's arms—That the subjects which are protestants may have arms for their defence suitable to their conditions and as allowed by law.

Freedom of election—That election of members of Parlyament ought to be free.

Freedom of speech—That the freedome of speech and debates or proceedings in Parlyament ought not to be impeached or questioned in any court or place out of Parlyament.

Excessive bail—That excessive baile ought not to be required nor excessive fines imposed nor cruell and unusuall punishments inflicted.

Juries—That jurors ought to be duly impannelled and returned . . .

Grants of forfeitures—That all grants and promises of fines and forfeitures of particular persons before conviction are illegal and void.

Frequent Parliaments—And that for redresse of all grievances and for the amending strengthening and preserving of the lawes Parlyaments ought to be held frequently.

The said right claimed, tender of the crown, regal power exercised, limitation of the crown, new oaths of allegiance, etc.—And they doe claime demand and insist upon all and singular the premises as their undoubted rights and liberties and that noe declarations judgements doeings or proceedings to the prejudice of the people in any of the said premises ought in any wise to be drawne hereafter into consequence or example. To which demand of their rights they are particularly encouraged by the declaration of his Highnesse the Prince of Orange as being the only meanes for obtaining a full redresse and remedy therein. Haveing therefore an intire confidence that his said Highnesse the Prince of Orange will perfect the deliverance soe farr advanced by him and will still preserve them from the violation of their rights which they have here asserted and from all other attempts upon their religion rights and liberties. The said lords spirituall and temporall and commons assembled at Westminster doe resolve that William and Mary Prince and Princesse of Orange be and be declared King and Queene of England France and Ireland and the dominions thereunto belonging to hold the crowne and royall dignity of the said kingdomes and dominions to them the said prince and princesse dureing their lives and the life of the survivour of them. And that the sole and full exercise of the regall power be onely in and executed by the said Prince of Orange in the names of the said prince and princesse dureing their joynt lives and after their deceases the said crowne and royall dignitie of the said kingdoms and dominions to be to the heires of the body of the said princesse and for default of such issue to the Princesse Anne of Denmarke and the heires of her body and for default of such issue to the heires of the body of the said Prince of Orange. And the lords spirituall and temporall and commons doe pray the said prince and princesse to accept the same accordingly. And that the oathes hereafter mentioned be taken by all persons of whome the oathes of allegiance and supremacy might be required by law instead of them and that the said oathes of allegiance and supremacy be abrogated.

I A B doe sincerely promise and sweare that I will be faithfull and beare true allegiance to their Majestyes King William and Queen Mary

Soe helpe me God

I A B doe sweare that I doe from my heart abhorr, detest and abjure as impious and hereticall this damnable doctrine and position that princes excommunicated or deprived by the Pope or any authority of the see of Rome may be deposed or murdered by their subjects or any other whatsoever. And I doe declare that noe forreigne prince person prelate, state or potentate hath or ought to have any jurisdiction power superiority preeminence or authoritie ecclesiasticall or spirituall within this realme.

Soe help me God

[Note: for the modern version of this effectively obsolete oath see the Accession Declaration Act 1910, Sch.]

Acceptance of the crown, the two Houses to sit, subjects' liberties to be allowed, and ministers hereafter to serve according to the same, William and Mary declared King and Queen, limitation of the crown, papists debarred the crown, every King, etc, shall make the declaration of 30 Car 2, if under 12 years old, to be done after attainment thereof, King's and Queen's assent. Upon which their said Majestyes did accept the crowne and royall dignitie of the kingdoms of England France and Ireland and the dominions thereunto belonging according to the resolution and desire of the said lords and commons contained in the said declaration. And thereupon their Majestyes were pleased that the said lords spirituall and temporall and commons being the two Houses of Parlyament should continue to sitt and with their Majesties royall concurrence make effectuall provision for the settlement of the religion lawes and liberties of this kingdome soe that the same for the future might not be in danger againe of being subverted, to which the said lords spirituall and temporall and commons did agree and proceede to act accordingly. Now in pursuance of the premises the said lords spirituall and temporall and commons in Parlyament assembled for the ratifying confirming and establishing the said declaration and the articles clauses matters and things therein contained by the force of a law made in due forme by authority of Parlyament doe pray that it may be declared and enacted that all and singular the rights and liberties asserted and claimed in the said declaration are the true auntient and indubitable rights and liberties of the people of this kingdome and soe shall be esteemed allowed adjudged deemed and taken to be and that all and every the paritculars aforesaid shall be firmly and strictly holden and observed as they are expressed in the said declaration. And all officers and ministers whatsoever shall serve their Majestyes and their successors according to the same in all times to come. And the said lords spirituall and temporall and commons seriously considering how it hath pleased Almighty God in his marvellous providence and mercifull goodness to this nation to provide and preserve their said Majestyes royall persons most happily to raigne over us upon the throne of their auncestors for which they render unto him from the bottome of their hearts their humblest thanks and praises doe truely firmely assuredly and in the sincerity of their hearts thinke and doe hereby recognize acknowledge and declare that King James the Second haveing abdicated the government and their Majestyes having accepted the crowne and royall dignity as aforesaid their said Majestyes did become were are and of right ought to be by the lawes of the realme our soveraigne liege lord and lady King and Queene of England France and Ireland and the dominions thereunto belonging in and to whose princely persons the royall state crowne and dignity of the said realmes with all honours stiles titles regalities prerogatives powers jurisdictions and authorities to the same belonging and appertaining are most fully and rightfully and intirely invested and incorporated united and annexed. And for preventing all questions and divisions in this realme by reason of any pretended titles to the crowne and for preserveing a certainty in the succession thereof in and upon which the unity peace tranquillity and safety of this nation doth under God wholly consist and depend the said lords spirituall and temporall and commons doe beseech their Majestyes that it may be enacted established and declared that the crowne and regall government of the said kingdoms and dominions with all and singular the premisses thereunto belonging and appertaining shall bee and continue to their said Majestyes and the survivour of them dureing their lives and the life of the survivour of them and that the entire perfect and full exercise of the regall power and government be onely in and executed by his Majestie in the names of both their Majestyes dureing their joynt lives and after their deceases the said crowne and premisses shall be and remaine to the heires of the body of her Majestie and for default of such issue to her royall Highnesse the Princess Anne of Denmarke and the heires of her body and for default of such issue to the heires of the body of his said Majestie And thereunto the said lords spirituall and temporall and commons doe in the name of all the people aforesaid most humbly and faithfully submit themselves their heires and posterities for ever and doe faithfully promise that they will stand to maintaine and defend their said Majesties and alsoe the limitation and succession of the crowne herein specified and contained to the utmost of their powers with their lives and estates against all persons whatsoever that shall attempt any thing to the contrary. And whereas it hath beene found by experience that it is inconsistent with the safety and welfare of this protestant kingdome to be governed by a popish prince or by any King or Queene marrying a papist the said lords spirtuall and temporall and commons doe further pray that it may be enacted that all and every person and persons that is are or shall be reconciled to or shall hold communion with the see or church of Rome or shall professe the popish religion or shall marry a papist shall be excluded and be for ever uncapeable to inherit possesse or enjoy the crowne and government of this realme and Ireland and the dominions thereunto belonging or any part of the same or to have use or exercise any regall power authoritie or jurisdiction within the same And in all and every such case or cases the people of these realmes shall be and are hereby absolved of their allegiance and the said crowne and government shall from time to time descend to and be enjoyed by such person or persons being protestants as should have inherited and enjoyed the same in case the said person or persons soe reconciled holding communion or professing or marrying as aforesaid were naturally dead And that every King and Queene of this realme who at any time hereafter shall come to and succeede in the imperiall crowne of this kingdome shall on the first day of the meeting of the first Parlyament next after his or her comeing to the crowne sitting in his or her throne in the House of Peeres in the presence of the lords and commons therein assembled or at his or her coronation before such person or persons who shall administer the coronation oath to him or her at the time of his or her takeing the said oath (which shall first happen) make subscribe and audibly repeate the declaration mentioned in the Statute made in the thirtyeth yeare of the raigne of King Charles the Second entituled An Act for the more effectuall preserveing the Kings person and government by disableing papists from sitting in either House of Parlyament But if it shall happen that such King or Queene upon his or her succession to the crowne of this realme shall be under the age of twelve yeares then every such King or Queene shall make subscribe and audibly repeate the said declaration at his or her coronation or the first day of the meeting of the first Parlyament as aforesaid which shall first happen after such King or Queene shall have attained the said age of twelve years. All which their Majestyes are contented and pleased shall be declared enacted and established by authoritie of this present

Parliament and shall stand remaine and be the law of this realme for ever And the same are by their said Majesties by and with the advice and consent of the lords spirituall and temporall and commons in Parlyament assembled and by the authoritie of the same declared enacted and established accordingly

2   Non obstantes made void

. . . noe dispensation by non obstante of or to any statute or any part thereof shall be allowed but . . . the same shall be held void and of noe effect except a dispensation be allowed of in such statute . . .

3   . . .

Crown and Parliament Recognition Act 1689
(2 Will. & Mar., c. 1)

An Act for Recognizing King William and Queene Mary and for avoiding all Questions touching the Acts made in the Parliament assembled at Westminster the thirteenth day of February one thousand six hundred eighty eight

Territorial extent: England and Wales, Northern Ireland (effectively extended to Scotland by the Union with Scotland Act 1706, below).

Wee your Majestyes most humble and loyall subjects the lords spirituall and temporall and commons in this present Parlyament assembled doe beseech your most excellent Majestyes that it may be publisehd and declared in this High Court of Parlyament and enacted by authoritie of the same that we doe recognize and acknowledge your Majestyes were are and of right ought to be by the laws of this realme our soveraigne liege lord and lady King and Queene of England France and Ireland and the dominions thereunto belonging in and to whose princely persons the royall state crowne and dignity of the said realms with all honours stiles tiles regalities prerogatives powers jurisdictions and authorities to the same belonging and appertaining are most fully rightfully and intirely invested and incorporated united and annexed. And for the avoiding of all disputes and questions concerning the being and authority of the late Parliament assembled at Westminster the thirteenth day of February one thousand six hundred eighty eight wee doe most humbly beseech your Majestyes that it may be enacted and bee it enacted by the King and Queenes most excellent Majestyes by and with the advice and consent of the lords spirituall and temporall and commons in this present Parlyament assembled and by authoritie of the same that all and singular the Acts made and enacted in the said Parlyament were and are laws and statutes of this kingdome and as such ought to be reputed taken and obeyed by all the people of this kingdome.

The Act of Settlement (1700)
(12 & 13 Will. 3, c. 2)

An Act for the further Limitation of the Crown and better securing the Rights and Liberties of the Subject

Territorial extent: England and Wales, Northern Ireland; effectively extended to Scotland by the Union with Scotland Act 1706.

Whereas in the first year of the reign of your Majesty and of our late most gracious soverign lady Queen Mary (of blessed memory) an Act of Parliament was made intituled (An Act for declaring the rights and liberties of the subject and for setling the succession of the crown)

wherein it was (amongst other things) enacted established and declared that the crown and regall government of the kingdoms of England France and Ireland and the dominions thereunto belonging should be and continue to your Majestie and the said late Queen during the joynt lives of your Majesty and the said Queen and to the survivor and that after the decease of your Majesty and of the said Queen the said crown and regall government should be and remain to the heirs of the body of the said late Queen and for default of such issue to her royall Highness the Princess Ann of Denmark and the heirs of her body and for default of such issue to the heirs of the body of your Majesty And it was thereby further enacted that all and every person and persons that then were or afterwards should be reconciled to or shall hold communion with the see or church of Rome or should professe the popish religion or marry a papist should be excluded and are by that Act made for ever incapable to inherit possess or enjoy the crown and government of this realm and Ireland and the dominions thereunto belonging or any part of the same or to have use or exercise any regall power authority or jurisdiction within the same and in all and every such case and cases the people of these realms shall be and are thereby absolved of their allegiance and that the said crown and government shall from time to time descend to and be enjoyed by such person or persons being protestants as should have inherited and enjoyed the same in case the said person or persons so reconciled holding communion professing or marrying as aforesaid were naturally dead After the making of which Statute and the settlement therein contained your Majesties good subjects who were restored to the full and free possession and enjoyment of their religion rights and liberties by the providence of God giving success to your Majesties just undertakings and unwearied endeavours for that purpose had no greater temporall felicity to hope or wish for than to see a royall progeny descending from your Majesty to whom (under God) they owe their tranquility and whose ancestors have for many years been principall assertors of the reformed religion and the liberties of Europe and from our said most gracious sovereign lady whose memory will always be precious to the subjects of these realms And it having since pleased Almighty God to take away our said sovereign lady and also the most hopefull Prince William Duke of Gloucester (the only surviving issue of her royall Highness the Princess Ann of Denmark) to the unspeakable grief and sorrow of your Majesty and your said good subjects who under such losses being sensibly put in mind that it standeth wholly in the pleasure of Almighty God to prolong the lives of your Majesty and of her royall Highness and to grant to your Majesty or to her royall Highness such issue as may be inheritable to the crown and regall government aforesaid by the respective limitations in the said recited Act contained doe constantly implore the divine mercy for those blessings And your Majesties said subjects having daily experience of your royall care and concern for the present and future welfare of these kingdoms and particularly recommending from your throne a further provision to be made for the succession of the crown in the protestant line for the happiness of the nation and the security of our religion and it being absolutely necessary for the safety peace and quiet of this realm to obviate all doubts and contentions in the same by reason of any pretended titles to the crown and to maintain a certainty in the succession thereof to which your subjects may safely have recourse for their protection in case the limitations in the said recited Act should determine Therefore for a further provision of the succession of the crown in the protestant line we your Majesties most dutifull and loyal subjects the lords spirituall and temporall and commons in this present Parliament assembled do beseech your Majesty that it may be enacted and declared and be it enacted and declared by the Kings most excellent Majesty by and with the advice and consent of the lords spirituall and temporall and commons in this present Parliament assembled and by the authority of the same that

1   The Princess Sophia, Electress and Duchess dowager of Hanover, daughter of the late Queen of Bohemia, daughter of King James the First, to inherit after the King and the Princess Anne, in default of issue of the said princess and his Majesty, respectively; and the heirs of her body, being protestants

the most excellent Princess Sophia Electress and Dutchess dowager of Hanover daughter of the most excellent Princess Elizabeth late Queen of Bohemia daughter of our late sovereign lord King James the First of happy memory be and is hereby declared to be the next in succession in the protestant line to the imperiall crown and dignity of the [said] realms of England France and Ireland with the dominions and territories thereunto belonging after his Majesty and the Princess Ann of Denmark and in default of issue of the said Princess Ann and of his Majesty respectively and that from and after the deceases of his said Majesty our own soveriegn lord and of her royall Highness the Princess Ann of Denmark and for default of issue of the said Princess Ann and of his Majesty respectively the crown and regall government of the said kingdoms of England France and Ireland and of the dominions thereunto belonging with the royall state and dignity of the said realms and all honours stiles titles regalities prerogatives powers jurisdictions and authorities to the same belonging and appertaining shall be remain and continue to the said most excellent Princess Sophia and the heirs of her body being protestants And thereunto the said lords spirituall and temporall and commons shall and will in the name of all the people of this realm most humbly and faithfully submitt themselves their heirs and posterities and do faithfully promise that after the deceases of his Majesty and her royall Highness and the failure of the heirs of their respective bodies to stand to maintain and defend the said Princess Sophia and the heirs of her body being protestants according to the limitation and succession of the crown in this Act specified and contained to the utmost of their powers with their lives and estates against all persons whatsoever that shall attempt any thing to the contrary.

2   The persons inheritable by this Act, holding communion with the church of Rome, incapacitated as by the former Act; to take the oath at their coronation, according to Stat 1 W& M c. 6
Provided always and it is hereby enacted that all and every person and persons who shall or may take or inherit the said crownby vertue of the limitation of this present Act and is are or shall be reconciled to or shall hold communion with the see or church of Rome or shall profess the popish religion or shall marry a papist shall be subject to such incapacities as in such case or cases are by the said recited Act provided enacted and established. And that every King and Queen of this realm who shall come to and succeed in the imperiall crown of this kingdomby vertue of this Act shall have the coronation oath administered to him her or themat their respective coronations according to the Act of Parliament made in the first year of the reign of his Majesty and the said late Queen Mary intituled An Act for establishing the coronation oath and shall make subscribe and repeat the declaration in the Act first above recited mentioned or referred to in the manner and formthereby prescribed.

3   Further provisions for securing the religions, laws, and liberties of these realms
And whereas it is requisite and necessary that some further provision be made for securing our religion laws and liberties from and after the death of his Majesty and the Princess Ann of Denmark and in default of issue of the body of the said princess and of his Majesty respectively Be it enacted by the Kings most excellent Majesty by and with the advice and consent of the lords spirituall and temporall and commons in Parliament and by the authority of the same

That whosoever shall hereafter come to the possession of this crown shall joyn in communion with the Church of England as by law established

That in case the crown and imperiall dignity of this realm shall hereafter come to any person not being a native of this kingdom of England this nation be not obliged to ingage in any warr for the defence of any dominions or territories which do not belong to the crown of England without the consent of Parliament

. . . . .

That after the said limitation shall take effect as aforesaid no person born out of the kingdoms of England Scotland or Ireland or the dominions thereunto belonging (although he be . . . made a denizen (except such as are born of English parents)) shall be capable to be of the privy councill or a member of either House of Parliament or to enjoy any office or place of trust either civill or military or to have any grant of lands tenements or hereditaments from the Crown to himself or to any other or others in trust for him.

. . . . .

That no pardon under the great seal of England be pleadable to an impeachment by the commons in Parliament.

4   The laws and statutes of the realm confirmed
And whereas the laws of England are the birthright of the people thereof and all the Kings and Queens who shall ascend the throne of this realm ought to administer the government of the same according to the said laws and all their officers and ministers ought to serve them respectively according to the same The said lords spirituall and temporall and commons do therefore further humbly pray that all the laws and statutes of this realm for securing the established religion and the rights and liberties of the people thereof and all other laws and statutes of the same now in force may be ratified and confirmed And the same are by his Majesty by and with the advice and consent of the said lords spirituall and temporall and commons and by authority of the same ratified and confirmed accordingly.

Union with Scotland Act 1706
(6 Anne, c. 11)

An Act for an Union of the Two Kingdoms of England and Scotland

Territorial extent: England, Wales and Scotland (by the combined effect of this Act and the equivalent Act of the Parliament of Scotland (APS, XI, 406)); subsequently applied to Northern Ireland.

Most Gracious Sovereign
Whereas articles of union were agreed on the twenty second day of July in the fifth year of your Majesties reign by the commissioners nominated on behalf of the kingdom of England under your Majesties great seal of England bearing date at Westminster the tenth day of April then last past in pursuance of an Act of Parliament made in England in the third year of your Majesties reign and the commissioners nominated on the behalf of the kingdom of Scotland under your Majesties great seal of Scotland bearing date the twenty-seventh day of February in the fourth year of your Majesties reign in pursuance of the fourth Act of the third session of the present Parliament of Scotland to treat of and concerning an union of the said kingdoms And whereas an Act hath passed in the Parliament of Scotland at Edinburgh the sixteenth day of January in the fifth year of your Majesties reign wherein "tis mentioned that the estates of Parliament considering the said articles of union of the two kingdoms had agreed to and approved of the said articles of union with some additions and explanations and that your Majesty with advice and consent of the estates of Parliament for establishing the Protestant religion and Presbyterian Church government within the kingdom of Scotland had passed in the same session of Parliament an Act intituled Act for securing of the Protestant religion and Presbyterian Church government which by the tenor thereof was appointed to be inserted in any Act ratifying the treaty and expresly declared to be a fundamental and essential condition of the said treaty or union in all times coming the tenor of which articles as ratified and approved of with additions and explanations by the said Act of Parliament of Scotland follows.

Article I
The kingdoms united; ensigns armorial—That the two kingdoms of England and Scotland shall upon the first day of May which shall be in the year one thousand seven hundred and

seven and for ever after be united into one kingdom by the name of Great Britain and that the ensigns armorial of the said United Kingdom be such as her Majesty shall appoint and the crosses of St. George and St. Andrew be conjoyned in such manner as Her Majesty shall think fit and used in all flags banners standards and ensigns both at sea and land.

Article II
Succession to the monarchy—That the succession to the monarchy of the United Kingdom of Great Britain and of the dominions thereto belonging after her most sacred Majesty and in default of issue of her Majesty be remain and continue to the most excellent Princess Sophia Electoress and Dutchess dowager of Hanover and the heirs of her body being protestants upon whom the crown of England is settled by an Act of Parliament made in England in the twelfth year of the reign of his late Majesty King William the Third intituled An Act for the further limitation of the crown and better securing the right and liberties of the subject And that all papists and persons marrying papists shall be excluded from and for ever incapable to inherit possess or enjoy the imperial crown of Great Britain and the dominions thereunto belonging or any part thereof and in every such case the crown and government shall from time to time descend to and be enjoyed by such person being a protestant as should have inherited and enjoyed the same in case such papist or person marrying a papist was naturally dead according to the provision for the descent of the crown of England made by another Act of Parliament in England in the first year of the reign of their late Majesties King William and Queen Mary intituled An Act declaring the rights and liberties of the subject and settling the succession of the crown.

Article III
Parliament—That the United Kingdom of Great Britain be represented by one and the same Parliament to be stiled the Parliament of Great Britain.

Article IIII
Trade and navigation and other rights—That all the subjects of the United Kingdom of Great Britain shall from and after the union have full freedom and intercourse of trade and navigation to and from any port or place within the said United Kingdom and the dominions and plantations thereunto belonging and that there be a communication of all other rights privileges and advantages which do or may belong to the subjects of either kingdom except where it is otherwise expressly agreed in these articles.

Article V . . .

Article VI
Regulations of trade, duties, etc.—That all parts of the United Kingdom for ever from and after the union shall have the same allowances encouragements and drawbacks and be under the same prohibitions restrictions and regulations of trade and liable to the same customs and duties on import and export and that the allowances encouragements and drawbacks prohibitions restrictions and regulations of trade and the customs and duties on import and export settled in England when the union commences shall from and after the union take place throughout the whole United Kingdom . . .

★ ★ ★ ★ ★

Article XVIII
Laws concerning public rights; private rights—That the laws concerning regulation of trade customs and such excises to which Scotland is by virtue of this treaty to be liable be the same in Scotland from and after the union as in England and that all other laws in use within the kingdom of Scotland do after the union and notwithstanding thereof remain in the same force as before (except such as are contrary to or inconsistent with this treaty) but alterable by the Parliament of Great Britain with this difference betwixt the laws concerning publick right

policy and civil government and those which concern private right that the laws which concern publick right policy and civil government may be made the same throughout the whole United Kingdom. But that no alteration be made in laws which concern private right except for evident utility of the subjects within Scotland

★ ★ ★ ★ ★

Article XXV
Laws inconsistent with the articles, void—That all laws and statutes in either kingdom so far as they are contrary to or inconsistent with the terms of these articles or any of them shall from and after the union cease and become void and shall be so declared to be by the respective Parliaments of the said kingdoms.

As by the said articles of union ratified and approved by the said Act of Parliament of Scotland relation being thereunto had may appear.

★ ★ ★ ★ ★

5   Cap 8 ante, and the said Act of Parliament of Scotland to be observed as fundamental conditions of the said union; and the said articles and Acts of Parliament to continue the union
And it is hereby further enacted by the authority aforesaid that the said Act passed in this present session of Parliament intituled An Act for securing the Church of England as by law established and all and every the matters and things therein contained and also the said Act of Parliament of Scotland intituled Act for securing the Protestant religion and Presbyterian Church government with the establishment in the said Act contained be and shall for ever be held and adjudged to be and observed as fundamental and essential conditions of the said union and shall in all times coming be taken to be and are hereby declared to be essential and fundamental parts of the said articles and union and the said articles of union so as aforesaid ratified approved and confirmed by Act of Parliament of Scotland and by this present Act and the said Act passed in this present session of Parliament intituled an Act for securing the Church of England as by law established and also the said Act passed in the Parliament of Scotland intituled Act for securing the Protestant religion and Presbyterian Church government are hereby enacted and ordained to be and continue in all times coming the complete and intire union of the two kingdoms of England and Scotland.

★ ★ ★ ★ ★

Metropolitan Police Act 1839
(2 & 3 Vict., c. 47)

An Act for further improving the Police in and near the Metropolis

Territorial extent: Metropolitan Police Area and City of London

★ ★ ★ ★ ★

52   Commissioners may make regulations for the route of carriages, and persons, and for preventing obstruction of the streets during public processions, etc., or in the neighbourhood of public buildings, etc.
. . . It shall be lawful for the commissioners of police from time to time, and as occasion shall require, to make regulations for the route to be observed by all carts, carriages, horses, and

persons, and for preventing obstruction of the streets and thoroughfares within the metropolitan police district, in all times of public processions, public rejoicings, or illuminations, and also to give directions to the constables for keeping order and for preventing any obstruction of the thoroughfares in the immediate neighbourhood of her Majesty's palaces and the public offices, the High Court of Parliament, the courts of law and equity, the [magistrates' courts], the theatres, and other places of public resort, and in any case when the streets or thoroughfares may be thronged or may be liable to be obstructed.

★ ★ ★ ★ ★

Parliamentary Papers Act 1840
(3 & 4 Vict., c. 9)

An Act to give summary Protection to Persons employed in the Publication of Parliamentary Papers

Territorial extent: United Kingdom

[1] Proceedings, criminal or civil, against persons for publication of papers printed by order of Parliament to be stayed upon delivery of a certificte and affidavit to the effect that such publication is by order of either House of Parliament

. . . It shall and may be lawful for any person or persons who now is or are, or hereafter shall be, a defendant or defendants in any civil or criminal proceedings commenced or prosecuted in any manner soever, for or on account or in respect of the publication of any such report, paper, votes, or proceedings by such person or persons, or by his, her, or their servant or servants, by or under the authority of either House of Parliament, to bring before the court in which such proceeding shall have been or shall be so commenced or prosecuted, or before any judge of the same (if one of the superior courts at Westminster), first giving twenty-four hours notice of his intention so to do to the prosecutor or plaintiff in such proceeding, a certificate under the hand of the lord high chancellor of Great Britain, or the lord keeper of the great seal, or of the speaker of the House of Lords, for the time being, or of the clerk of the Parliaments, or of the speaker of the House of Commons, or of the clerk of the same house, stating that the report, paper, votes, or proceedings, as the case may be, in respect whereof such civil or criminal proceeding shall have been commenced or prosecuted, was published by such person or persons, or by his, her, or their servant or servants, by order or under the authority of the House of Lords or of the House of Commons, as the case may be, together with an affidavit verifying such certificate; and such court or judge shall thereupon immediately stay such civil or criminal proceeding, and the same, and every writ or process issued therein, shall be and shall be deemed and taken to be finally put an end to, determined, and superseded by virtue of this Act.

2 Proceedings to be stayed when commenced in respect of a copy of an authenticated report, etc.

. . . In case of any civil or criminal proceeding hereafter to be commenced or prosecuted for or on account or in respect of the publication of any copy of such report, paper, votes, or proceedings, it shall be lawful for the defendant or defendants at any stage of the proceedings to lay before the court or judge such report, paper, votes, or proceedings, and such copy, with an affidavit verifying such report, paper, votes, or proceedings, and the correctness of such copy, and the court or judge shall immediately stay such civil or criminal proceedings, and the same, and every writ or process issued therein, shall be and shall be deemed and taken to be finally put an end to, determined, and superseded by virtue of this Act.

3   In proceedings for printing any extract or abstract of a paper, it may be shown that such extract was bona fide made
. . . It shall be lawful in any civil or criminal proceeding to be commenced or prosecuted for printing any extract from or abstract of such report, paper, votes, or proceedings, to give in evidence . . . such report, paper, votes or proceedings, and to show that such extract or abstract was published bona fide and without malice; and if such shall be the opinion of the jury, a verdict of not guilty shall be entered for the defendant or defendants.

4   Act not to affect the privileges of Parliament
Provided always . . . that nothing herein contained shall be deemed or taken, or held or construed, directly or indirectly, by implication or otherwise, to affect the privileges of Parliament in any manner whatsoever.
Note: Sch. 20, para. 1 to the Broadcasting Act 1990 provides that s. 3 above is to have effect as if the reference to printing included a reference to inclusion in a programme service (as defined in that Act).

Customs Consolidation Act 1876
(39 & 40 Vict., c. 36)

An Act to consolidate the Customs Laws

Territorial extent: United Kingdom

AS TO THE IMPORTATION, PROHIBITION, ENTRY, EXAMINATION, LANDING, AND WAREHOUSING OF GOODS

. . .

42   Prohibitions and restrictions
The goods enumerated and described in the following table of prohibitions and restrictions inwards are hereby prohibited to be imported or brought into the United Kingdom . . .

A TABLE OF PROHIBITIONS AND RESTRICTIONS INWARDS

Goods prohibited to be imported

Indecent or obscene prints, paintings, photographs, books, cards, lithographic or other engravings, or any other indecent or obscene articles.

★ ★ ★ ★ ★

Riot (Damages) Act 1886
(49 & 50 Vict., c. 38)

An Act to provide compensation for Losses by Riots

Territorial extent: England and Wales. (For Scotland see the Riotous Assembly (Scotland) Act 1822.)

1 Short title

This Act may be cited for all purposes as the Riot (Damages) Act 1886.

2 Compensation to persons for damage by riot

(1) Where a house, shop, or building in [a police area] has been injured or destroyed, or the property therein has been injured, stolen, or destroyed, by any persons riotously and tumultuously assembled together, such compensation as herein-after mentioned shall be paid out of [the police fund] of [the area] to any person who has sustained loss by such injury, stealing, or destruction; but in fixing the amount of such compensation regard shall be had to the conduct of the said person, whether as respects the precautions taken by him or as respects his being a party or accessory to such riotous or tumultuous assembly, or as regards any provocation offered to the persons assembled or otherwise.

(2) Where any person having sustained such loss as aforesaid has received, by way of insurance or otherwise, any sum to recoup him, in whole or in part, for such loss, the compensation otherwise payable to him under this Act shall, if exceeding such sum, be reduced by the amount thereof, and in any other case shall not be paid to him, and the payer of such sum shall be entitled to compensation under this Act in respect of the sum so paid in like manner as if he had sustained the said loss, and any policy of insurance given by such payer shall continue in force as if he had made no such payment, and where such person was recouped as aforesaid otherwise than by payment of a sum, this enactment shall apply as if the value of such recoupment were a sum paid.

Note: Section 10 of the Public Order Act 1986 provides that "riotous" and "riotously" in this Act are to be construed in accordance with the definition of "riot" in that Act.

Public Meeting Act 1908
(8 Edw. 7, c. 66)

An Act to prevent disturbance of Public Meetings

Territorial extent: England and Wales, Scotland

1 Penalty on endeavour to break up public meeting

(1) Any person who at a lawful public meeting acts in a disorderly manner for the purpose of preventing the transaction of the business for which the meeting was called together shall be guilty of an offence [and shall on summary conviction be liable to imprisonment for a term not exceeding six months or to a fine not exceeding [level 5 on the standard scale] or to both] . . .

(2) Any person who incites others to commit an offence under this section shall be guilty of a like offence.

[(3) If any constable reasonably suspects any person of committing an offence under the foregoing provisions of this section, he may if requested so to do by the chairman of the meeting require that person to declare to him immediately his name and address and, if that person refuses or fails so to declare his name and address or gives a false name and address he shall be guilty of an offence under this subsection and liable on summary conviction thereof to a fine not exceeding [level 1 on the standard scale], . . .

[(4) This section does not apply as respects meetings to which section 97 of the Representation of the People Act 1983 applies.]

Official Secrets Act 1911
(1 & 2 Geo. 5, c. 28)

An Act to re-enact the Official Secrets Act 1889, with Amendments

Territorial extent: United Kingdom. See also s. 10(1).

Note: Printed as amended by the Official Secrets Act 1920; section 2 was repealed by the Official Secrets Act 1989 (below).

1 Penalties for spying

(1) If any person for any purpose prejudicial to the safety or interests of the State—

(a) approaches [inspects, passes over] or is in the neighbourhood of, or enters any prohibited place within the meaning of this Act; or

(b) makes any sketch, plan, model, or note which is calculated to be or might be or is intended to be directly or indirectly useful to an enemy; or

(c) obtains, [collects, records, or publishes,] or communicates to any other person [any secret official code word or pass word, or] any sketch, plan, model, article, or note, or other document or information which is calculated to be or might be or is intended to be directly or indirectly useful to an enemy;

he shall be guilty of felony . . .

(2) On a prosecution under this section, it shall not be necessary to show that the accused person was guilty of any particular act tending to show a purpose prejudicial to the safety or interests of the State, and, notwithstanding that no such act is proved against him, he may be convicted if, from the circumstances of the case, or his conduct, or his known character as proved, it appears that his purpose was a purpose prejudicial to the safety or interests of the State; and if any sketch, plan, model, article, note, document, or information relating to or used in any prohibited place within the meaning of this Act, or anything in such a place [or any secret official code word or pass word], is made, obtained, [collected, recorded, published], or communicated by any person other than a person acting under lawful authority, it shall be deemed to have been made, obtained, [collected, recorded, published] or communicated for a purpose prejudicial to the safety or interests of the State unless the contrary is proved.

2 . . .

3 Definition of prohibited place

For the purposes of this Act, the expression "prohibited place" means—

(a) any work of defence, arsenal, naval or air force establishment or station, factory, dockyard, mine, minefield, camp, ship, or aircraft belonging to or occupied by or on behalf of His Majesty, or any telegraph, telephone, wireless or signal station, or office so belonging or occupied, and any place belonging to or occupied by or on behalf of His Majesty and used for the purpose of building, repairing, making, or storing any munitions of war, or any sketches, plans, models, or documents relating thereto, or for the purpose of getting any metals, oil, or minerals of use in time of war];

(b) any place not belonging to His Majesty where any [munitions of war], or any [sketches, models, plans] or documents relating thereto, are being made, repaired, [gotten] or stored under contract with, or with any person on behalf of, His Majesty, or otherwise on behalf of His Majesty; and

(c) any place belonging to [or used for the purposes of] His Majesty which is for the time being declared [by order of a Secretary of State] to be a prohibited place for the purposes of this section on the ground that information with respect thereto, or damage thereto, would be useful to an enemy; and

(d) any railway, road, way, or channel, or other means of communication by land or water (including any works or structures being part thereof or connected therewith), or any place used for gas, water, or electricity works or other works for purposes of a public character, or any place where any [munitions of war], or any [sketches, models, plans] or documents relating thereto, are being made, repaired, or stored otherwise than on behalf of His Majesty, which is for the time being declared [by order or a Secretary of State] to be a prohibited place for the purposes of this section, on the ground that information with respect thereto, or the destruction or obstruction thereof, or interference therewith, would be useful to an enemy.

4, 5 . . .

6 Power of arrest
Any person who is found committing an offence under this Act . . . or who is reasonably suspected of having committed, or having attempted to commit, or being about to commit, such an offence, may be apprehended and detained . . .

7 ★ ★ ★ ★ ★

8 Restriction on prosecution
A prosecution for an offence under this Act shall not be instituted except by or with the consent of the Attorney-General:

. . . . .

9 Search warrants
(1) If a justice of the peace is satisfied by information on oath that there is reasonable ground for suspecting that an offence under this Act has been or is about to be committed, he may grant a search warrant authorising any constable . . . to enter at any time any premises or place named in the warrant, if necessary, by force, and to search the premises or place and every person found therein, and to seize any sketch, plan, model, article, note, or document, or anything of a like nature or anything which is evidence of an offence under this Act having been or being about to be committed, which he may find on the premises or place or on any such person, and with regard to or in connexion with which he has reasonable ground for suspecting that an offence under this Act has been or is about to be committed.

(2) Where it appears to a superintendent of police that the case is one of great emergency and that in the interests of the State immediate action is necessary, he may by a written order under his hand give to any constable the like authority as may be given by the warrant of a justice under the section.

10 Extent of Act and place of trial of offence
(1) This Act shall apply to all acts which are offences under this Act when committed in any part of His Majesty's dominions, or when committed by British officers or subjects elsewhere.

★ ★ ★ ★ ★

Parliament Act 1911
(1 & 2 Geo. 5, c. 13)

An Act to make provision with respect to the powers of the House of Lords in relation of the House of Commons, and to limit the duration of Parliament

Territorial extent: United Kingdom

Note: The words in square brackets in s. 2 were substituted by the Parliament Act 1949, and are included without prejudice to the suggestions of some writers that the 1949 Act (itself passed under the procedure of the 1911 Act) is not a valid Act of Parliament.

Preamble

Whereas it is expedient that provision should be made for regulating the relations between the two Houses of Parliament:

And whereas it is intended to substitute for the House of Lords as it at present exists a Second Chamber constituted on a popular instead of hereditary basis, but such substitution cannot be immediately brought into operation:

And whereas provision will require hereafter to be made by Parliament in a measure effecting such substitution for limiting and defining the powers of the new Second Chamber, but it is expedient to make such provision as in this Act appears for restricting the existing powers of the House of Lords:

1   Powers of House of Lords as to Money Bills

(1) If a Money Bill, having been passed by the House of Commons, and sent up to the House of Lords at least one month before the end of the session, is not passed by the House of Lords without amendment within one month after it is so sent up to that House, the Bill shall, unless the House of Commons direct to the contrary, be presented to His Majesty and become an Act of Parliament on the Royal Assent being signified, notwithstanding that the House of Lords have not consented to the Bill.

(2) A Money Bill means a Public Bill which in the opinion of the Speaker of the House of Commons contains only provisions dealing with all or any of the following subjects, namely, the imposition, repeal, remission, alteration, or regulation of taxation; the imposition for the payment of debt or other financial purposes of charges on the Consolidated Fund, [the National Loans Fund] or on money provided by Parliament, or the variation or repeal of any such charges; supply; the appropriation, receipt, custody, issue or audit of accounts of public money; the raising or guarantee of any loan or the repayment thereof; or subordinate matters incidental to those subjects or any of them. In this subsection the expressions "taxation", "public money" and "loan" respectively do not include any taxation, money, or loan raised by local authorities or bodies for local purposes.

(3) There shall be endorsed on every Money Bill when it is sent up to the House of Lords and when it is presented to His Majesty for assent the certificate of the Speaker of the House of Commons signed by him that it is a Money Bill. Before giving his certificate, the Speaker shall consult, if practicable, two members to be appointed from the Chairmen's Panel at the beginning of each Session by the Committee of Selection.

2   Restriction of the powers of the House of Lords as to Bills other than Money Bills

(1) If any Public Bill (other than a Money Bill or a Bill containing any provision to extend the maximum duration of Parliament beyond five years) is passed by the House of Commons [in two successive sessions] (whether of the same Parliament or not), and, having been sent up to the House of Lords at least one month before the end of the session, is rejected by the House of Lords in each of those sessions, that Bill shall, on its rejection [for the second time] by the House of Lords, unless the House of Commons direct to the contrary, be presented to His Majesty and become an Act of Parliament on the Royal Assent being signified thereto, notwithstanding that the House of Lords have not consented to the Bill: Provided that this provision shall not take effect unless [one year has elapsed] between the date of the second reading in the first of those sessions of the Bill in the House of Commons and the date on which it passes the House of Commons [in the second of those sessions].

(2) When a Bill is presented to His Majesty for assent in pursuance of the provisions of

this section, there shall be endorsed on the Bill the certificate of the Speaker of the House of Commons signed by him that the provisions of this section have been duly complied with.

(3) A Bill shall be deemed to be rejected by the House of Lords if it is not passed by the House of Lords either without amendment or with such amendments only as may be agreed to by both Houses.

(4) A Bill shall be deemed to be the same Bill as a former Bill sent up to the House of Lords in the preceding session if, when it is sent up to the House of Lords, it is identical with the former Bill or contains only such alterations as are certified by the Speaker of the House of Commons to be necessary owing to the time which has elapsed since the date of the former Bill, or to represent any amendments which have been made by the House of Lords in the former Bill in the preceding sesion, and any amendments which are certified by the Speaker to have been made by the House of Lords [in the second session] and agreed to by the House of Commons shall be inserted in the Bill as presented for Royal Assent in pursuance of this section:

Provided that the House of Commons may, if they think fit, on the passage of such a Bill through the House [in the second session], suggest any further amendments without inserting the amendments in the Bill, and any such suggested amendments shall be considered by the House of Lords, and, if agreed to by that House, shall be treated as amendments made by the House of Lords and agreed to by the House of Commons; but the exercise of this power by the House of Commons shall not affect the operation of this section in the event of the Bill being rejected by the House of Lords.

3   Certificate of Speaker

Any certificate of the Speaker of the House of Commons given under this Act shall be conclusive for all purposes, and shall not be questioned in any court of law.

4   Enacting words

(1) In every Bill presented to His Majesty under the preceding provisions of this Act, the words of enactment shall be as follows, that is to say:–

"Be it enacted by the King's most Excellent Majesty, by and with the advice and consent of the Commons in this present Parliament assembled, in accordance with the provisions of [the Parliament Acts 1911 and 1949], and by authority of the same, as follows."

(2) Any alteration of a Bill necessary to give effect to this section shall not be deemed to be an amendment of the Bill.

5   Provisional Order Bills excluded

In this Act the expression "Public Bill" does not include any Bill for confirming a Provisional Order.

6   Saving for existing rights and privileges of the House of Commons

Nothing in this Act shall diminish or qualify the existing rights and privileges of the House of Commons.

7   Duration of Parliament

Five years shall be substituted for seven years as the time fixed for the maximum duration of Parliament under the Septennial Act, 1715.

Official Secrets Act 1920
(10 & 11 Geo. 5, c. 75)

An Act to amend the Official Secrets Act 1911

Territorial extent: United Kingdom

1   Unauthorised use of uniforms; falsification of reports, forgery, personation, and false documents

(1) If any person for the purpose of gaining admission, or of assisting any other person to gain admission, to a prohibited place, within the meaning of the Official Secrets Act 1911 (hereinafter referred to as "the principal Act"), or for any other purpose prejudicial to the safety or interests of the State within the meaning of the said Act—

(a) uses or wears, without lawful authority, any naval, military, air-force, police, or other official uniform, or any uniform so nearly resembling the same as to be calculated to deceive, or falsely represents himself to be a person who is or has been entitled to use or wear any such uniform; or

(b) orally, or in writing in any declaration or application, or in any document signed by him or on his behalf, knowingly makes or connives at the making of any false statement or any omission; or

(c) ... tampers with any passport or any naval, military, air-force, police, or official pass, permit, certificate, licence, or other document of a similar character (hereinafter in this section referred to as an official document), ... or has in his possession any ... forged, altered, or irregular official document; or

(d) personates, or falsely represents himself to be a person holding, or in the employment of a person holding office under His Majesty, or to be or not to be a person to whom an official document or secret official code word or pass word has been duly issued or communicated, or with intent to obtain an official document, secret official code word or pass word, whether for himself or any other person, knowingly makes any false statement; or

(e) uses, or has in his possession or under his control, without the authority of the Government Department or the authority concerned, any die, seal, or stamp of or belonging to, or used, made or provided by any Government Department, or by any diplomatic, naval, military, or air force authority appointed by or acting under the authority of His Majesty, or any die, seal or stamp so nearly resembling any such die, seal or stamp as to be calculated to deceive, or counterfeits any such die, seal or stamp, or uses, or has in his possession, or under his control, any such counterfeited die, seal or stamp;

he shall be guilty of a misdemeanour.

(2) If any person—

(a) retains for any purpose prejudicial to the safety or interests of the State any official document, whether or not completed or issued for use, when he has no right to retain it, or when it is contrary to his duty to retain it, or fails to comply with any directions issued by any Government Department or any person authorised by such department with regard to the return or disposal thereof; or

(b) allows any other person to have possession of any official document issued for his use alone, or communicates any secret official code word or pass word so issued, or, without lawful authority or excuse, has in his possession any official document or secret official code word or pass word issued for the use of some person other than himself, or on obtaining possession of any official document by finding or otherwise, neglects or fails to restore it to the person or authority by whom or for whose use it was issued, or to a police constable; or

(c) without lawful authority or excuse, manufactures or sells, or has in his possession for sale any such die, seal or stamp as aforesaid;

he shall be guilty of a misdemeanour.

(3) In the case of any prosecution under this section involving the proof of a purpose prejudicial to the safety or interests of the State, subsection (2) of section one of the principal Act shall apply in like manner as it applies to prosecutions under that section.

2–4 ★ ★ ★ ★ ★

5 . . .

6 Duty of giving information as to commission of offences

[(1) Where a chief officer of police is satisfied that there is reasonable ground for suspecting that an offence under section one of the principal Act has been committed and for believing that any person is able to furnish information as to the offence or suspected offence, he may apply to a Secretary of State for permission to exercise the powers conferred by this subsection and, if such permission is granted, he may authorise a superintendent of police, or any police officer not below the rank of inspector, to require the person believed to be able to furnish information to give any information in his power relating to the offence or suspected offence, and, if so required and on tender of his reasonable expenses, to attend at such reasonable time and place as may be specified by the superintendent or other officer; and if a person required in pursuance of such an authorisation to give information, or to attend as aforesaid, fails to comply with any such requirement or knowingly gives false information, he shall be guilty of a misdemeanour.

(2) Where a chief officer of police has reasonable grounds to believe that the case is one of great emergency and that in the interest of the State immediate action is necessary, he may exercise the powers conferred by the last foregoing subsection without applying for or being granted the permission of a Secretary of State, but if he does so shall forthwith report the circumstances to the Secretary of State.

(3) References in this section to a chief officer of police shall be construed as including references to any other officer of police expressly authorised by a chief officer of police to act on his behalf for the purposes of this section when by reason of illness, absence or other cause he is unable to do so.]

★ ★ ★ ★ ★

The Statute of Westminster 1931
(22 & 23 Geo. 5, c. 4)

An Act to give effect to certain resolutions passed by Imperial Conferences held in the years 1926 and 1930

Territorial extent: As indicated in the Act (and see note to section 4).

Whereas the delegates of His Majesty's Governments in the United Kingdom, the Dominion of Canada, the Commonwealth of Australia, the Dominion of New Zealand, the Union of South Africa, the Irish Free State and Newfoundland, at Imperial Conferences holden at Westminster in the years of our Lord nineteen hundred and twenty-six and nineteen hundred and thirty did concur in making the declarations and resolutions set forth in the Reports of the said Conferences:

And whereas it is meet and proper to set out by way of preamble to this Act that, inasmuch as the Crown is the symbol of the free association of the members of the British Commonwealth of Nations, and as they are united by a common allegiance to the Crown, it would be in accord with the established constitutional position of all the members of the Commonwealth in relation to one another that any alteration in the law touching the Succession to the Throne or the Royal Style and Titles shall hereafter require the assent as well of the Parliaments of all the Dominions as of the Parliament of the United Kingdom:

And whereas it is in accord with the established constitutional position that no law hereafter made by the Parliament of the United Kingdom shall extend to any of the said Dominions as part of the law of that Dominion otherwise than at the request and with the consent of that Dominion:

And whereas it is necessary for the ratifying, confirming and establishing of certain of the said declarations and resolutions of the said Conferences that a law be made and enacted in due form by authority of the Parliament of the United Kingdom:

And whereas the Dominion of Canada, the Commonwealth of Australia, the Dominion of New Zealand, the Union of South Africa, the Irish Free State and Newfoundland have severally requested and consented to the submission of a measure to the Parliament of the United Kingdom for making such provision with regard to the matters aforesaid as is hereafter in this Act contained:

1 Meaning of "Dominion" in this Act

In this Act the expression "Dominion" means any of the following Dominions, that is to say, the Dominion of Canada, the Commonwealth of Australia, the Dominion of New Zealand, . . . the Irish Free State and Newfoundland.

2 Validity of laws made by Parliament of a Dominion

(1) The Colonial Laws Validity Act 1865 shall not apply to any law made after the commencement of this Act by the Parliament of a Dominion.

(2) No law and no provision of any law made after the commencement of this Act by the Parliament of a Dominion shall be void or inoperative on the ground that it is repugnant to the law of England, or to the provisions of any existing or future Act of Parliament of the United Kingdom, or to any order, rule or regulation made under any such Act, and the powers of the Parliament of a Dominion shall include the power to repeal or amend any such Act, order, rule or regulation in so far as the same is part of the law of the Dominion.

3 Power of Parliament of Dominion to legislate extra-territorally

It is hereby declared and enacted that the Parliament of a Dominion has full power to make laws having extra-territorial operation.

4 Parliament of United Kingdom not to legislate for Dominion except by consent

No Act of Parliament of the United Kingdom passed after the commencement of this Act shall extend, or be deemed to extend, to a Dominion as part of the law of that Dominion unless it is expressly declared in that Act that that Dominion has requested, and consented to, the enactment thereof.

Note: This section has been repealed in relation to Canada by the Canada Act 1982 s. 1, Sch B and in relation to Australia by the Australia Act 1986 s. 12.

Public Order Act 1936
(1 Edw. 8 & 1 Geo. 6, c. 6)

An Act to prohibit the wearing of uniforms in connection with political objects and the maintenance by private persons of associations of military or similar character; and to make further provision for the preservation of public order on the occasion of public processions and meetings and in public places

Territorial extent: England and Wales, Scotland

1   Prohibition of uniforms in connection with political objects

(1) Subject as hereinafter provided, any person who in any public place or at any public meeting wears uniform signifying his association with any political organisation or with the promotion of any political object shall be guilty of an offence:

Provided that, if the chief officer of police is satisfied that the wearing of any such uniform as aforesaid on any ceremonial, anniversary, or other special occasion will not be likely to involve risk of public disorder, he may, with the consent of a Secretary of State, by order permit the wearing of such uniform on that occasion either absolutely or subject to such conditions as may be specified in the order.

(2) Where any person is charged before any court with an offence under this section, no further proceedings in respect thereof shall be taken against him without the consent of the Attorney-General [except such as are authorised by [section 6 of the Prosecution of Offences Act 1979]] so, however, that if that person is remanded in custody he shall, after the expiration of a period of eight days from the date on which he was so remanded, be entitled to be [released on bail] without sureties unless within that period the Attorney-General has consented to such further proceedings as aforesaid.

2   Prohibition of quasi-military organisations

(1) If the members or adherents of any association of persons, whether incorporated or not, are—

(a) organised or trained or equipped for the purpose of enabling them to be employed in usurping the functions of the police or of the armed forces of the Crown; or

(b) organised and trained or organised and equipped either for the purpose of enabling them to be employed for the use or display of physical force in promoting any political object, or in such manner as to arouse reasonable apprehension that they are organised and either trained or equipped for that purpose;

then any person who takes part in the control or management of the association, or in so organising or training as aforesaid any members or adherents thereof, shall be guilty of an offence under this section:

Provided that in any proceedings against a person charged with the offence of taking part in the control or management of such an association as aforesaid it shall be a defence to that charge to prove that he neither consented to nor connived at the organisation, training, or equipment of members or adherents of the association in contravention of the provisions of this section.

(2) No prosecution shall be instituted under this section without the consent of the Attorney-General.

(3), (4) ★ ★ ★ ★ ★

(5) If a judge of the High Court is satisfied by information on oath that there is reasonable ground for suspecting that an offence under this section has been committed, and that evidence of the commission thereof is to be found at any premises or place specified in the information, he may, on an application made by an officer of police of a rank not lower than that of inspector, grant a search warrant authorising any such officer as aforesaid named in the

warrant together with any other persons named in the warrant and any other officers of police to enter the premises or place at any time within one month from the date of the warrant, if necessary by force, and to search the premises or place and every person found therein, and to seize anything found on the premises or place or on any such person which the officer has reasonable ground for suspecting to be evidence of the commission of such an offence as aforesaid:

Provided that no woman shall, in pursuance of a warrant issued under this subsection, be searched except by a woman.

(6) Nothing in this section shall be construed as prohibiting the employment of a reasonable number of persons as stewards to assist in the preservation of order at any public meeting held upon private premises, or the making of arrangements for that purpose or the instruction of the persons to be so employed in their lawful duties as such stewards, or their being furnished with badges or other distinguishing signs.

3, 4, 5, 5A . . .

6   (Amends the Public Meeting Act 1908, printed above as amended).

7   Enforcement

(1) Any person who commits an offence under section two of this Act shall be liable on summary conviction to imprisonment for a term not exceeding six months or to a fine not exceeding [the prescribed sum], or to both such imprisonment and fine, or, on conviction on indictment, to imprisonment for a term not exceeding two years or to a fine . . . or to both such imprisonment and fine.

(2) Any person guilty of [any offence under this Act other than an offence under section 2 . . .] shall be liable on summary conviction to imprisonment for a term not exceeding three months or to a fine not exceeding [level 4 on the standard scale], or to both such imprisonment and fine.

(3) A constable may without warrant arrest any person reasonably suspected by him to be committing an offence under section one . . . of this Act.

8   Application to Scotland

This Act shall apply to Scotland subject to the following modifications:—

(1) Subsection (2) of section one and subsection (2) of section two of this Act shall not apply.

(2) In subsection (3) of section two the Lord Advocate shall be substituted for the Attorney-General and the Court of Session shall be substituted for the High Court.

(3) Subsection (5) of section two shall have effect as if for any reference to a judge of the High Court there were substituted a reference to the Sheriff and any application for a search warrant under the said subsection shall be made by the procurator fiscal instead of such officer as is therein mentioned.

(4) The power conferred on the sheriff by subsection (5) of section two, as modified by the last foregoing paragraph, shall not be exercisable by an honorary sheriff-substitute.

★ ★ ★ ★ ★

9   Interpretation, etc.

(1) In this Act the following expressions have the meanings hereby respectively assigned to them, that is to say:—

. . .

"Meeting" means a meeting held for the purpose of the discussion of matters of public interest or for the purpose of the expression of views on such matters;

"Private premises" means premises to which the public have access (whether on payment or otherwise) only by permission of the owner, occupier, or lessee of the premises;

"Public meeting" includes any meeting in a public place and any meeting which the public or any section thereof are permitted to attend, whether on payment or otherwise;

["Public place" includes any highway and any other premises or place to which at the material time the public have or are permitted to have access, whether on payment or otherwise;]

. . .

★ ★ ★ ★ ★

Bank of England Act 1946
(9 & 10 Geo. 6, c. 27)

An Act to bring the capital stock of the Bank of England into public ownership and bring the Bank under public control, to make provision with respect to the relations between the Treasury, the Bank of England and other banks and for purposes connected with the matters aforesaid   [14 February 1946]

Territorial extent: United Kingdom

1-3 ★ ★ ★ ★ ★

4 Treasury directions to the Bank and relations of the Bank with other banks

(1) The Treasury may from time to time give such directions to the Bank as, after consultation with the Governor of the Bank, they think necessary in the public interest [, except in relation to monetary policy].

(2) . . .

(3) The Bank, if they think it necessary in the public interest, may request information from and make recommendations to bankers, and may, if so authorised by the Treasury, issue directions to any banker for the purpose of securing that effect is given to any such request or recommendation:

Provided that:—

    (a) no such request or recommendations shall be made with respect to the affairs of any particular customer of a banker; and

    (b) before authorising the issue of any such directions the Treasury shall give the banker concerned, or such person as appears to them to represent him, an opportunity of making representations with respect thereto.

(4), (5) . . .

(6), (7) ★ ★ ★ ★ ★

5, 6 ★ ★ ★ ★ ★

Statutory Instruments Act 1946
(9 & 10 Geo. 6, c. 36)

An Act to repeal the Rules Publication Act, 1893, and to make further provision as to the instruments by which statutory powers to make orders, rules, regulations and other subordinate legislation are exercised   [26 March 1946]

Territorial extent: United Kingdom

Note: By virtue of the Scotland Act (Transitory and Transitional Provisions) (Statutory

Instruments) Order 1999 any reference in section 1 below to an Act includes a reference to an Act of the Scottish Parliament and later sections are to be read to apply to the Scottish Parliament. Similarly references to powers exercisable by Ministers of the Crown shall include the Scottish Ministers in accordance with the Order.

1 Definition of "Statutory Instrument"

(1) Where by this Act or any Act passed after the commencement of this Act power to make, confirm or approve orders, rules, regulations or other subordinate legislation is conferred on His Majesty in Council or on any Minister of the Crown then, if the power is expressed—

(a) in the case of a power conferred on His Majesty, to be exercisable by Order in Council;

(b) in the case of a power conferred on a Minister of the Crown, to be exercisable by statutory instrument,

any document by which that power is exercised shall be known as a "statutory instrument" and the provisions of this Act shall apply thereto accordingly.

[(1A) The References in subsection (1) to a Minister of the Crown shall be construed as including references to the National Assembly for Wales.]

(2) Whereby any Act passed before the commencement of this Act power to make statutory rules within the meaning of the Rules Publication Act, 1893, was conferred on any rule-making authority within the meaning of that Act, any document by which that power is exercised after the commencement of this Act shall, save as is otherwise provided by regulations made under this Act, be known as a "statutory instrument" and the provisions of this Act shall apply thereto accordingly.

2 Numbering, printing, publication and citation

(1) Immediately after the making of any statutory instrument, it shall be sent to the King's printer of Acts of Parliament and numbered in accordance with regulations made under this Act, and except in such cases as may be provided by any Act passed after the commencement of this Act or prescribed by regulations made under this Act, copies thereof shall as soon as possible be printed and sold by [or under the authority of] the King's printer of Acts of Parliament.

(2) Any statutory instrument may, without prejudice to any other mode of citation, be cited by the number given to it in accordance with the provisions of this section, and the calendar year.

3 Supplementary provisions as to publication

(1) Regulations made for the purposes of this Act shall make provision for the publication by His Majesty's Stationery Office of lists showing the date upon which every statutory instrument printed and sold by [or under the authority of] the King's printer of Acts of Parliament was first issued by [or under the authority of] that office; and in any legal proceedings a copy of any list so published . . . shall be received in evidence as a true copy, and an entry therein shall be conclusive evidence of the date on which any statutory instrument was first issued by [or under the authority of] His Majesty's Stationery Office.

(2) In any proceedings against any person for an offence consisting of a contravention of any such statutory instrument, it shall be a defence to prove that the instrument had not been issued by His Majesty's Stationery Office at the date of the alleged contravention unless it is proved that at that date reasonable steps had been taken for the purpose of bringing the purport of the instrument to the notice of the public, or of persons likely to be affected by it, or of the person charged.

(3) Save as therein otherwise expressly provided, nothing in this section shall affect any enactment or rule of law relating to the time at which any statutory instrument comes into operation.

4   Statutory instruments which are required to be laid before Parliament

(1) Where by this Act or any Act passed after the commencement of this Act any statutory instrument is required to be laid before Parliament after being made, a copy of the instrument shall be laid before each House of Parliament and, subject as hereinafter provided, shall be so laid before the instrument comes into operation:

Provided that if it is essential that any such instrument should come into operation before copies thereof can be so laid as aforesaid, the instrument may be made so as to come into operation before it has been so laid; and where any statutory instrument comes into operation before it is laid before Parliament, notification shall forthwith be sent to the Lord Chancellor and to the Speaker of the House of Commons drawing attention to the fact that copies of the instrument have yet to be laid before Parliament and explaining why such copies were not so laid before the instrument came into operation.

(2) Every copy of any such statutory instrument sold by [or under the authority of] the King's printer of Acts of Parliament shall bear on the face thereof—

(a) a statement showing the date on which the statutory instrument came or will come into operation; and

(b) either a statement showing the date on which copies thereof were laid before Parliament or a statement that such copies are to be laid before Parliament.

(3) ★ ★ ★ ★ ★

5   Statutory instruments which are subject to annulment by resolution of either House of Parliament

(1) Where by this Act or any Act passed after the commencement of this Act, it is provided that any statutory instrument shall be subject to annulment in pursuance of resolution of either House of Parliament, the instrument shall be laid before Parliament after being made and the provisions of the last foregoing section shall apply thereto accordingly, and if either House, within the period of forty days beginning with the day on which a copy thereof is laid before it, resolves that an Address be presented to His Majesty praying that the instrument be annulled, no further proceedings shall be taken thereunder after the date of the resolution, and His Majesty may by Order in Council revoke the instrument, so, however, that any such resolution and revocation shall be without prejudice to the validity of anything previously done under the instrument or to the making of a new statutory instrument.

(2) ★ ★ ★ ★ ★

6   Statutory instruments of which drafts are to be laid before Parliament

(1) Where by this Act or any Act passed after the commencement of this Act it is provided that a draft of any statutory instrument shall be laid before Parliament, but the Act does not prohibit the making of the instrument without the approval of Parliament, then, in the case of an Order in Council the draft shall not be submitted to His Majesty in Council, and in any other case the statutory instrument shall not be made, until after the expiration of a period of forty days beginning with the day on which a copy of the draft is laid before each House of Parliament, or, if such copies are laid on different days, with the later of the two days, and if within that period either House resolves that the draft be not submitted to His Majesty or that the statutory instrument be not made, as the case may be, no further proceedings shall be taken thereon, but without prejudice to the laying before Parliament of a new draft.

(2) ★ ★ ★ ★ ★

★ ★ ★ ★ ★

Crown Proceedings Act 1947
(10 & 11 Geo. 6, c. 44)

An Act to amend the law relating to the civil liabilities and rights of the Crown and to civil proceedings by and against the Crown, to amend the law relating to the civil liabilities of persons other than the Crown in certain cases involving the affairs or property of the Crown, and for purposes connected with the matters aforesaid   [31 July 1947]

Territorial extent: United Kingdom (ss. 2, 4, 11, 21, 40), England and Wales and Northern Ireland (ss. 1, 17, 25, 28), Scotland (ss. 41, 42, 43, 47).

PART I   SUBSTANTIVE LAW

1   Right to sue the Crown
Where any person has a claim against the Crown after the commencement of this Act, and, if this Act had not been passed, the claim might have been enforced, subject to the grant of His Majesty's fiat, by petition of right, or might have been enforced by a proceeding provided by any stautory provision repealed by this Act, then, subject to the provisions of this Act, the claim may be enforced as of right, and without the fiat of His Majesty, by proceedings taken against the Crown for that purpose in accordance with the provisions of this Act.

2   Liability of the Crown in tort
(1) Subject to the provisions of this Act, the Crown shall be subject to all those liabilities in tort to which, if it were a private person of full age and capacity, it would be subject–

    (a) in respect of torts committed by its servants or agents;

    (b) in respect of any breach of those duties which a person owes to his servants or agents at common law by reason of being their employer; and

    (c) in respect of any breach of the duties attaching at common law to the ownership, occupation, possession or control of property:

Provided that no proceedings shall lie against the Crown by virtue of paragraph (a) of this subsection in respect of any act or omission of a servant or agent of the Crown unless the act or omission would apart from the provisions of this Act have given rise to a cause of action in tort against that servant or agent or his estate.

(2) Where the Crown is bound by a statutory duty which is binding also upon persons other than the Crown and its officers, then, subject to the provisions of this Act, the Crown shall, in respect of a failure to comply with that duty, be subject to all those liabilities in tort (if any) to which it would be so subject if it were a private person of full age and capacity.

(3) Where any functions are conferred or imposed upon an officer of the Crown as such either by any rule of the common law or by statute, and that officer commits a tort while performing or purporting to perform those functions, the liabilities of the Crown in respect of the tort shall be such as they would have been if those functions had been conferred or imposed solely by virtue of instructions lawfully given by the Crown.

(4) Any enactment which negatives or limits the amount of the liability of any Government department [, part of the Scottish Administration] or officer of the Crown in respect of any tort committed by that department [, part] or officer shall, in the case of proceedings against the Crown under this section in respect of a tort committed by that department [, part] or officer, apply in relation to the Crown as it would have applied in relation to that department [, part] or officer if the proceedings against the Crown had been proceedings against that department [, part] or officer.

(5) No proceedings shall lie against the Crown by virtue of this section in respect of anything done or omitted to be done by any person while discharging or purporting to

discharge any responsibilities of a judicial nature vested in him, or any responsibilities which he has in connection with the execution of judicial process.

(6) No proceedings shall lie against the Crown by virtue of this section in respect of any act, neglect or default of any officer of the Crown, unless that officer has been directly or indirectly appointed by the Crown and was at the material time paid in respect of his duties as an officer of the Crown wholly out of the Consolidated Fund of the United Kingdom, moneys provided by Parliament, . . ., or any other Fund certified by the Treasury for the purposes of this subsection or was at the material time holding an office in respect of which the Treasury certify that the holder thereof would normally be so paid.

3 ★ ★ ★ ★ ★

4   Application of law as to indemnity, contribution, joint and several tort-feasors, and contributory negligence

(1) Where the Crown is subject to any liability by virtue of this Part of this Act, the law relating to indemnity and contribution shall be enforceable by or against the Crown in respect of the liability to which it is so subject as if the Crown were a private person of full age and capacity.

(2) . . .

(3) Without prejudice to the general effect of section one of this Act, the Law Reform (Contributory Negligence) Act 1945 (which amends the law relating to contributory negligence) shall bind the Crown.

5–8 . . .

9 ★ ★ ★ ★ ★

10   (Repealed by the Crown Proceedings (Armed Forces) Act 1987) . . .

11   Saving in respect of acts done under prerogative and statutory powers

(1) Nothing in Part I of this Act shall extinguish or abridge any powers or authorities which, if this Act had not been passed, would have been exercisable by virtue of the prerogative of the Crown, or any powers or authorities conferred on the Crown by any statute, and, in particular, nothing in the said Part I shall extinguish or abridge any powers or authorities exercisable by the Crown, whether in time of peace or of war, for the purpose of the defence of the realm or of training, or maintaining the efficiency of, any of the armed forces of the Crown.

(2) Where in any proceedings under this Act it is material to determine whether anything was properly done or omitted to be done in the exercise of the prerogative of the Crown, . . . a Secretary of State may, if satisfied that the act or omission was necessary for any such purpose as is mentioned in the last preceding subsection, issue a certificate to the effect that the act or omission was necessary for that purpose; and the certificate shall, in those precedings, be conclusive as to the matter so certified.

12–16 ★ ★ ★ ★ ★

PART II   JURISDICTION AND PROCEDURE

17   Parties to proceedings

(1) [The Minister for the Civil Service] shall publish a list specifying the several Government departments which are authorised departments for the purposes of this Act, and the name and address for service of the person who is, or is acting for the purposes of this Act as, the solicitor for each such department, and may from time to time amend or vary the said list.

Any document purporting to be a copy of a list published under this section and purporting to be printed under the superintendence or the authority of His Majesty's Stationery Office shall in any legal proceedings be received as evidence for the purpose of establishing what departments are authorised departments for the purposes of this Act, and what person is, or is acting for the purposes of this Act as, the solicitor for any such department.

(2) Civil proceedings by the Crown may be instituted either by an authorised Government department in its own name, whether that department was or was not at the commencement of this Act authorised to sue, or by the Attorney General.

(3) Civil proceedings against the Crown shall be instituted against the appropriate authorised Government department, or, if none of the authorised Government departments is appropriate or the person instituting the proceedings has any reasonable doubt whether any and if so which of those departments is appropriate, against the Attorney General.

(4), (5) ★ ★ ★ ★ ★

18–20 ★ ★ ★ ★ ★

21 Nature of relief

(1) In any civil proceedings by or against the Crown the court shall, subject to the provisions of this Act, have power to make all such orders as it has power to make in proceedings between subjects, and otherwise to give such appropriate relief as the case may require:
Provided that:—

(a) where in any proceedings against the Crown any such relief is sought as might in proceedings between subjects be granted by way of injunction or specific performance, the court shall not grant an injunction or make an order for specific performance, but may in lieu thereof make an order declaratory of the rights of the parties; and

(b) in any proceedings against the Crown for the recovery of land or other property the court shall not make an order for the recovery of the land or the delivery of the property, but may in lieu thereof make an order declaring that the plaintiff is entitled as against the Crown to the land or property or to the possession thereof.

(2) The court shall not in any civil proceedings grant any injunction or make any order against an officer of the Crown if the effect of granting the injunction or making the order would be to give any relief against the Crown which could not have been obtained in proceedings against the Crown.

22–27 ★ ★ ★ ★ ★

PART IV   MISCELLANEOUS AND SUPPLEMENTAL

28, 29, 31–33, 35, 37–8 ★ ★ ★ ★ ★

30, 34, 36, 39 . . .

40 Savings

(1) Nothing in this Act shall apply to proceedings by or against, or authorise proceedings in tort to be brought against, His Majesty in His private capacity.

(2)–(5) ★ ★ ★ ★ ★

PART V   APPLICATION TO SCOTLAND

41 Application of Act to Scotland
The provisions of this Part of this Act shall have effect for the purpose of the application of this Act to Scotland.

42 Exclusion of certain provisions
Section one, Part II (except section thirteen so far as relating to proceedings mentioned in the First Schedule and section twenty-one), Part III (except section twenty-six) and section twenty-eight of this Act shall not apply to Scotland.

43 Interpretation for purposes of application to Scotland

In the application of this Act to Scotland:—

    (a) for any reference to the High Court (except a reference to that Court as a prize court) there shall be substituted a reference to the Court of Session; for any reference to the county court there shall be substituted a reference to the sheriff court; the expression "plaintiff" means pursuer; the expression "defendant" means defender; the expression "county court rules" means Act of Sederunt applying to the sheriff court; and the expression "injunction" means interdict;

    (b) the expression "tort" means any wrongful or negligent act or omission giving rise to liability in reparation, and any reference to liability or right or action or proceedings in tort shall be construed accordingly; and for any reference to Part II of the Law Reform (Married Women and Tortfeasors) Act, 1935, there shall be substituted a reference to section three of the Law Reform (Miscellaneous Provisions) (Scotland) Act, 1940.

44–53 ★ ★ ★ ★ ★

Life Peerages Act 1958
(6 & 7 Eliz. 2, c. 21)

An Act to make provision for the creation of life peerages carrying the right to sit and vote in the House of Lords [30 April 1958]

Territorial extent: United Kingdom

1 Power to create life peerages carrying right to sit in the House of Lords

    (1) Without prejudice to Her Majesty's powers as to the appointment of Lords of Appeal in Ordinary, Her Majesty shall have power by letters patent to confer on any person a peerage for life having the incidents specified in subsection (2) of this section.

    (2) A peerage conferred under this section shall, during the life of the person on whom it is conferred, entitle him–

    (a) to rank as a baron under such style as may be appointed by the letters patent; and

    (b) subject to subsection (4) of this section, to receive writs of summons to attend the House of Lords and sit and vote therein accordingly,

and shall expire on his death.

    (3) A life peerage may be conferred under this section on a woman.

    (4) Nothing in this section shall enable any person to receive a writ of summons to attend the House of Lords, or to sit and vote in that House, at any time when disqualified therefor by law.

Public Records Act 1958
(6 & 7 Eliz. 2, c. 51)

An Act to make new provision with respect to public records and the Public Record Office, and for connected purposes [23 July 1958]

Territorial extent: England and Wales, Scotland

1 General responsibility of the Lord Chancellor for public records

    (1) The direction of the Public Record Office shall be transferred from the Master of the

Rolls to the Lord Chancellor, and the Lord Chancellor shall be generally responsible for the execution of this Act and shall supervise the care and preservation of public records.

(2) There shall be an Advisory Council on Public Records to advise the Lord Chancellor on matters concerning public records in general and, in particular, on those aspects of the work of the Public Record Office which affect members of the public who make use of the facilities provided by the Public Record Office.

The Master of the Rolls shall be chairman of the said Council and the remaining members of the Council shall be appointed by the Lord Chancellor on such terms as he may specify.

(3) The Lord Chancellor shall in every year lay before both Houses of Parliament a report on the work of the Public Record Office, which shall include any report made to him by the Advisory Council on Public Records.

2 ★ ★ ★ ★ ★

3   Selection and preservation of public records

(1) It shall be the duty of every person responsible for public records of any description which are not in the Public Record Office or a place of deposit appointed by the Lord Chancellor under this Act to make arrangements for the selection of records which ought to be permanently preserved and for their safe-keeping.

(2) Every person shall perform his duties under this section under the guidance of the Keeper of Public Records and the said Keeper shall be responsible for co-ordinating and supervising all action taken under this section.

(3) All public records created before the year sixteen hundred and sixty shall be included among those selected for permanent preservation.

(4)–(8) ★ ★ ★ ★ ★

4 ★ ★ ★ ★ ★

5   Access to public records

(1) Public records in the Public Record Office, other than those to which members of the public had access before their transfer to the Public Record Office, shall not be available for public inspection [until the expiration of the period of thirty years beginning with the first day of January in the year next after that in which they were created, or such other period], either longer or shorter, as the Lord Chancellor may, with the approval, or at the request, of the Minister or other person, if any, who appears to him to be primarily concerned, for the time being prescribe as respects any particular class of public records.

(2) Without prejudice to the generality of the foregoing subsection, if it appears to the person responsible for any public records which have been selected by him under section three of this Act for permanent preservation that they contain information which was obtained from members of the public under such conditions that the opening of those records to the public after the period determined under the foregoing subsection would or might constitute a breach of good faith on the part of the Government or on the part of the persons who obtained the information, he shall inform the Lord Chancellor accordingly and those records shall not be available in the Public Record Office for public inspection even after the expiration of the said period except in such circumstances and subject to such conditions, if any, as the Lord Chancellor and that person may approve, or, if the Lord Chancellor and that person think fit, after the expiration of such further period as they may approve.

(3)–(5) ★ ★ ★ ★ ★

6–13 ★ ★ ★ ★ ★

Section 10   FIRST SCHEDULE
                    DEFINITION OF PUBLIC RECORDS

1. The provisions of this Schedule shall have effect for determining what are public records for the purposes of this Act.

Departmental records

2.—(1) Subject to the provisions of this paragraph, administrative and departmental records belonging to Her Majesty, whether in the United Kingdom or elsewhere, in right of Her Majesty's Government in the United Kingdom and, in particular,—

(a) records, of, or held in, any department of her Majesty's Government in the United Kingdom, or

(b) records of any office, commission or other body or establishment whatsoever under Her Majesty's Government in the United Kingdom,

shall be public records.

(2) Sub-paragraph (1) of this paragaph shall not apply—

(a) to records of any government department or body which is wholly or mainly concerned with Scottish affairs, or which carries on its activities wholly or mainly in Scotland, or

(b) to registers, or certified copies of entries in registers, being registers or certified copies kept or deposited in the General Register Office under or in pursuance of any enactment, whether past or future, which provides for the registration of births, deaths, marriages or adoptions, or

(c) except so far as provided by paragraph 4 of this Schedule, to records of the Duchy of Lancaster, or

(d) to records of the office of the Public Trustee relating to individual trusts, [or

(e) to Welsh public records (as defined in the Government of Wales Act 1998).]

* * * * *

Obscene Publications Act 1959
(7 & 8 Eliz. 2, c. 66)

An Act to amend the law relating to the publication of obscene matter; to provide for the protection of literature; and to strengthen the law concerning pornography   [29 July 1959]

Territorial extent: England and Wales

1 Test of obscenity

(1) For the purposes of this Act an article shall be deemed to be obscene if its effect or (where the article comprises two or more distinct items) the effect of any one of its items is, if taken as a whole, such as to tend to deprave and corrupt persons who are likely, having regard to all relevant circumstances, to read, see or hear the matter contained or embodied in it.

(2) In this Act "article" means any description of article containing or embodying matter to be read or looked at or both, any sound record, and any film or other record of a picture or pictures.

(3) For the purposes of this Act a person publishes an article who—

(a) distributes, circulates, sells, lets on hire, gives, or lends it, or who offers it for sale or for letting on hire; or

(b) in the case of an article containing or embodying matter to be looked at or a record, shows, plays or projects it [, or, where the matter is data stored electronically, transmits that data.]

. . .

[(4) For the purposes of this Act a person also publishes an article to the extent that any matter recorded on it is included by him in a programme included in a programme service.

(5) Where the inclusion of any matter in a programme so included would, if that matter were recorded matter, constitute the publication of an obscene article for the purposes of this Act by virtue of subsection (4) above, this Act shall have effect in relation to the inclusion of that matter in that programme as if it were recorded matter.

(6) In this section "programme" and "programme service" have the same meaning as in the Broadcasting Act 1990.]

2   Prohibition of publication of obscene matter

(1) Subject as hereinafter provided, any person who, whether for gain or not, publishes an obscene article [or who has an obscene article for publication for gain (whether gain to himself or gain to another)] shall be liable—

    (a) on summary conviction to a fine not exceeding [the prescribed sum] or to imprisonment for a term not exceeding six months;

    (b) on conviction on indictment to a fine or to imprisonment for a term not exceeding three years or both.

(2) . . .

(3) A prosecution . . . for an offence against this section shall not be commenced more than two years after the commission of the offence.

[(3A) Proceedings for an offence under this section shall not be instituted except by or with the consent of the Director of Public Prosecutions in any case where the article in question is a moving picture film of a width of not less than sixteen millimetres and the relevant publication or the only other publication which followed or could reasonably have been expected to follow from the relevant publication took place or (as the case may be) was to take place in the course of a [film exhibition]; and in this subsection "the relevant publication" means—

    (a) in the case any proceedings under this section for publishing an obscene article, the publication in respect of which the defendant would be charged if the proceedings were brought; and

    (b) in the case of any proceedings under this section for having an obscene article for publication for gain, the publication which, if the proceedings were brought, the defendant would be alleged to have had in contemplation.]

(4) A person publishing an article shall not be proceeded against for an offence at common law consisting of the publication of any matter contained or embodied in the article where it is of the essence of the offence that the matter is obscene.

[(4A) Without prejudice to subsection (4) above, a person shall not be proceeded against for an offence at common law—

    (a) in respect of a [film exhibition] or anything said or done in the course of a [film exhibition], where it is of the essence of the common law offence that the exhibition or, as the case may be, what was said or done was obscene, indecent, offensive, disgusting or injurious to morality; or

    (b) in respect of an agreement to give a [film exhibition] or to cause anything to be said or done in the course of such an exhibition where the commonlaw offence consists of conspiring to corrupt publicmorals or to doany act contrary to public moralsor decency.]

(5) A person shall not be convicted of an offence against this section if he proves that he had not examined the article in respect of which he is charged and had no reasonable cause to

suspect that it was such that his publication of it would make him liable to be convicted of an offence against this section.

(6) In any proceedings against a person under this section the question whether an article is obscene shall be determined without regard to any publication by another person unless it could reasonably have been expected that the publication by the other person would follow from publication by the person charged.

[(7) In this section "film exhibition" has the same meaning as in the Cinemas Act 1985.]

3 Powers of search and seizure

(1) If a justice of the peace is satisfied by information on oath that there is reasonable ground for suspecting that, in any premises in the petty sessions area for which he acts, or on any stall or vehicle in that area, being premises or a stall or vehicle specified in the information, obscene articles are, or are from time to time, kept for publication for gain, the justice may issue a warrant under his hand empowering any constable to enter (if need be by force) and search the premises, or to search the stall or vehicle . . . and to seize and remove any articles found therein or thereon which the constable has reason to believe to be obscene articles and to be kept for publication for gain.

(2) A warrant under the foregoing subsection shall, if any obscene articles are seized under the warrant, also empower the seizure and removal of any documents found in the premises or, as the case may be, on the stall or vehicle which relate to a trade or business carried on at the premises or from the stall or vehicle.

(3) [Subject to subsection (3A) of this section] any articles seized under subsection (1) of this section shall be brought before a justice of the peace acting for the same petty sessions area as the justice who issued the warrant, and the justice before whom the articles are brought may thereupon issue a summons to the occupier of the premises or, as the case may be, the user of the stall or vehicle to appear on a day specified in the summons before a magistrates' court for that petty sessions area to show cause why the articles or any of them should not be forfeited; and if the court is satisfied, as respects any of the articles, that at the time when they were seized they were obscene articles kept for publication for gain, the court shall order those articles to be forfeited:

Provided that if the person summoned does not appear, the court shall not make an order unless service of the summons is proved.

[Provided also that this subsection does not apply in relation to any article seized under subsection (1) of this section which is returned to the occupier of the premises or, as the case may be, to the user of the stall or vehicle in or on which it was found.]

[(3A) Without prejudice to the duty of a court to make an order for the forfeiture of an article where section 1(4) of the Obscene Publications Act 1964 applies (orders made on conviction), in a case where by virtue of subsection (3A) of section 2 of this Act proceedings under the said section 2 for having an article for publication for gain could not be instituted except by or with the consent of the Director of Public Prosecutions, no order for the forfeiture of the article shall be made under this section unless the warrant under which the article was seized was issued on an information laid by or on behalf of the Director of Public Prosecutions.]

(4) In addition to the person summoned, any other person being the owner, author or maker of any of the articles brought before the court, or any other person through whose hands they had passed before being seized, shall be entitled to appear before the court on the day specified in the summons to show cause why they should not be forfeited.

(5)–(8) ★ ★ ★ ★ ★

4 Defence of public good

(1) [Subject to subsection (1A) of this section] a person shall not be convicted of an offence against section two of this Act, and an order for forfeiture shall not be made under the foregoing section, if it is proved that publication of the article in question is justified as being

for the public good on the ground that it is in the interests of science, literature, art or learning, or of other objects of general concern.

[(1A) Subsection (1) of this section shall not apply where the article in question is a moving picture film or soundtrack, but—

    (a) a person shall not be convicted of an offence against section 2 of this Act in relation to any such film or soundtrack, and

    (b) an order for forfeiture of any such film or soundtrack shall not be made under section 3 of this Act,

if it is proved that publication of the film or soundtrack is justified as being for the public good on the ground that it is in the interests of drama, opera, ballet or any other art, or of literature or learning.]

(2) It is hereby declared that the opinion of experts as to the literary, artistic, scientific or other merits of an article may be admitted in any proceedings under this Act either to establish or to negative the said ground.

[(3) In this section "moving picture soundtrack" means any sound record designed for playing with a moving picture film, whether incorporated with the film or not.]

War Damage Act 1965
(1965, c. 18)

An Act to abolish rights at common law to compensation in respect of damage to, or destruction of, property effected by, or on the authority of, the Crown during, or in contemplation of the outbreak of, war   [2 June 1965]

Territorial extent: United Kingdom

1   Abolition of rights at common law to compensation for certain damage to, or destruction of, property

(1) No person shall be entitled at common law to receive from the Crown compensation in respect of damage to, or destruction of, property caused (whether before or after the passing of this Act, within or outside the United Kingdom) by acts lawfully done by, or on the authority of, the Crown during, or in contemplation of the outbreak of, a war in which the Sovereign was, or is, engaged.

(2) . . .

Criminal Law Act 1967
(1967, c. 58)

An Act to amend the law of England and Wales by abolishing the division of crimes into felonies and misdemeanours and to amend and simplify the law in respect of matters arising from or related to that division or the abolition of it; to do away (within or without England and Wales) with certain obsolete crimes together with the torts of maintenance and champerty; and for purposes connected therewith   [21 July 1967]

Territorial extent: England and Wales

PART I   FELONY AND MISDEMEANOUR

1   ★ ★ ★ ★ ★

2   . . . (Repealed by the Police and Criminal Evidence Act 1984)

3   Use of force in making arrest, etc.
(1) A person may use such force as is reasonable in the circumstances in the prevention of crime, or in effecting or assisting in the lawful arrest of offenders or suspected offenders or of persons unlawfully at large.
(2) Subsection (1) above shall replace the rules of the common law on the question when force used for a purpose mentioned in the subsection is justified by that purpose.

★ ★ ★ ★ ★

Parliamentary Commissioner Act 1967
(1967, c. 13)

An Act to make provision for the appointment and functions of a Parliamentary Commissioner for the investigation of administrative action taken on behalf of the Crown, and for purposes connected therewith   [22 March 1967]

Territorial extent: United Kingdom

Note: This Act is printed as extensively amended by the Parliamentary and Health Service Commissioners Act 1987.

The Parliamentary Commissioner for Administration

1   Appointment and tenure of office
(1) For the purpose of conducting investigations in accordance with the following provisions of this Act there shall be appointed a Commissioner, to be known as the Parliamentary Commissioner for Administration.
(2) Her Majesty may by Letters Patent from time to time appoint a person to be the Commissioner, and any person so appointed shall (subject to [subsections (3) and (3A)] of this section) hold office during good behaviour.
(3) A person appointed to be the Commissioner may be relieved of office by Her Majesty at his own request, or may be removed from office by Her Majesty in consequence of Addresses from both Houses of Parliament, and shall in any case vacate office on completing the year of service in which he attains the age of sixty-five years.
[(3A) Her Majesty may declare the office of Commissioner to have been vacated if satisfied that the person appointed to be the Commissioner is incapable for medical reasons—
(a) of performing the duties of his office; and
(b) of requesting to be relieved of it.]
(4), (5) . . .

2   ★ ★ ★ ★ ★

3   Administrative provisions
(1) The Commissioner may appoint such officers as he may determine with the approval of the Treasury as to numbers and conditions of service.
(2), (3) . . .

3A   ★ ★ ★ ★ ★

4   Departments etc. subject to investigation

(1) Subject to the provisions of this section and to the notes contained in Schedule 2 to this Act, this Act applies to the government departments, corporations and unincorporated bodies listed in that Schedule; and references in this Act to an authority to which this Act applies are references to any such corporation or body.

(2) Her Majesty may by Order in Council amend Schedule 2 to this Act by the alteration of any entry or note, the removal of any entry or note or the insertion of any additional entry or note.

(3) An Order in Council may only insert an entry if–

    (a) it relates—
        (i) to a government department; or
        (ii) to a corporation or body whose functions are exercised on behalf of the Crown; or
    (b) it relates to a corporation or body—
        (i) which is established by virtue of Her Majesty's prerogative or by an Act of Parliament or an Order in Council or order made under an Act of Parliament or which is established in any other way by a Minister of the Crown in his capacity as a Minister or by a government department;
        (ii) at least half of whose revenues derive directly from money provided by Parliament, a levy authorised by an enactment, a fee or charge of any other description so authorised or more than one of those sources; and
        (iii) which is wholly or partly constituted by appointment made by Her Majesty or a Minister of the Crown or government department.

[(3A) No entry shall be made if the result of making it would be that the Parliamentary Commissioner could investigate action which can be investigated by the Welsh Administration Ombudsman under Schedule 9 of the Government of Wales Act 1998.]

[(3B) No entry shall be made in respect of—

    (a) the Scottish Administration or any part of it;
    (b) any Scottish public authority with mixed functions or no reserved functions within the meaning of the Scotland Act 1998; or
    (c) the Scottish Parliamentary Corporate Body.]

(4) No entry shall be made in respect of a corporation or body whose sole activity is, or whose main activities are, included among the activities specified in subsection (5) below.

(5) The activities mentioned in subsection (4) above are—

    (a) the provision of education, or the provision of training otherwise than under the Industrial Training Act 1982;
    (b) the development of curricula, the conduct of examinations or the validation of educational courses;
    (c) the control of entry to any profession or the regulation of the conduct of members of any profession;
    (d) the investigation of complaints by members of the public regarding the actions of any person or body, or the supervision or review of such investigations or of steps taken following them.

(6) No entry shall be made in respect of a corporation or body operating in an exclusively or predominantly commercial manner or a corporation carrying on under national ownership an industry or undertaking or part of an industry or undertaking.

(7) Any statutory instrument made by virtue of this section shall be subject to annulment in pursuance of a resolution of either House of Parliament.

(8) ★ ★ ★ ★ ★

5   Matters subject to investigation

(1) Subject to the provisions of this section, the Commissioner may investigate any

action taken by or on behalf of a government department or other authority to which this Act applies, being action taken in the exercise of administrative functions of that department or authority, in any case where—

    (a) a written complaint is duly made to a member of the House of Commons by a member of the public who claims to have sustained injustice in consequence of maladministration in connection with the action so taken; and

    (b) the complaint is referred to the Commissioner, with the consent of the person who made it, by a member of that House with a request to conduct an investigation thereon.

(2) Except as hereinafter provided, the Commissioner shall not conduct an investigation under this Act in respect of any of the following matters, that is to say–

    (a) any action in respect of which the person aggrieved has or had a right of appeal, reference or review to or before a tribunal constituted by or under any enactment or by virtue of Her Majesty's prerogative;

    (b) any action in respect of which the person aggrieved has or had a remedy by way of proceedings in any court of law:

Provided that the Commissioner may conduct an investigation notwithstanding that the person aggrieved has or had such a right or remedy if satisfied that in the particular circumstances it is not reasonable to expect him to resort or have resorted to it.

[(2A) Subsection (2)(a) of this section shall have effect in relation to the right of a person to make a complaint of unlawful discrimination under the Fair Employment and Treatment (Northern Ireland) Order 1998 as if it were such a right of appeal, reference or review as is mentioned in that subsection.]

(3) Without prejudice to subsection (2) of this section, the Commisioner shall not conduct an investigation under this Act in respect of any such action or matter as is described in Schedule 3 to this Act.

(4) Her Majesty may by Order in Council amend the said Schedule 3 so as to exclude from the provisions of that Schedule such actions or matters as may be described in the Order; and any statutory instrument made by virtue of this subsection shall be subject to annulment in pursuance of a resolution of either House of Parliament.

(5) In determining whether to initiate, continue or discontinue an investigation under this Act, the Commissioner shall, subject to the foregoing provisions of this section, act in accordance with his own discretion; and any question whether a complaint is duly made under this Act shall be determined by the Commissioner.

[(5A) For the purposes of this section, administrative functions of a government department to which this Act applies include functions exercised by the department on behalf of the Scottish Ministers by virtue of section 93 of the Scotland Act 1998.

(5B) The Commissioner shall not conduct an investigation under this Act in respect of any action concerning Scotland and not relating to reserved matters which is taken by or on behalf of a cross-border public authority within the meaning of the Scotland Act 1998.]

[(6) For the purposes of this section, administrative functions exercised by any person appointed by the Lord Chancellor as a member of the administrative staff of any court or tribunal shall be taken to be administrative functions of the Lord Chancellor's Department or, in Northern Ireland, of the Northern Ireland Court Service.]

(7)–(9) ★ ★ ★ ★ ★

6 Provisions relating to complaints

(1) A complaint under this Act may be made by any individual, or by any body of persons whether incorporated or not, not being—

    (a) a local authority or other authority or body constituted for purposes of the public service or of local government or for the purposes of carrying on under national ownership any industry or undertaking or part of an industry or undertaking;

(b) any other authority or body whose members are appointed by Her Majesty or any Minister of the Crown or government department, or whose revenues consist wholly or mainly of moneys provided by Parliament.

(2) Where the person by whom a complaint might have been made under the foregoing provisions of this Act has died or is for any reason unable to act for himself, the complaint may be made by his personal representative or by a member of his family or other individual suitable to represent him; but except as aforesaid a complaint shall not be entertained under this Act unless made by the person aggrieved himself.

(3) A complaint shall not be entertained under this Act unless it is made to a member of the House of Commons not later than twelve months from the day on which the person aggrieved first had notice of the matters alleged in the complaint; but the Commissioner may conduct an investigation pursuant to a complaint not made within that period if he considers that there are special circumstances which make it proper to do so.

(4) [Except as provided in subsection (5) below] a complaint shall not be entertained under this Act unless the person aggrieved is resident in the United Kingdom (or, if he is dead, was so resident at the time of his death) or the complaint relates to action taken in relation to him while he was present in the United Kingdom or on an installation in a designated area within the meaning of the Continental Shelf Act 1964 or on a ship registered in the United Kingdom or an aircraft so registered, or in relation to rights or obligations which accrued or arose in the United Kingdom or on such an installation, ship or aircraft.

[(5) A complaint may be entertained under this Act in circumstances not falling within subsection (4) above where—

(a) the complaint relates to action taken in any country or territory outside the United Kingdom by an officer (not being an honorary consular officer) in the exercise of a consular function on behalf of the Government of the United Kingdom; and

(b) the person aggrieved is a citizen of the United Kingdom and Colonies who, under section 2 of the Immigration Act 1971, has the right of abode in the United Kingdom.]

7 Procedure in respect of investigations

(1) Where the Commissioner proposes to conduct an investigation pursuant to a complaint under this Act, he shall afford to the principal officer of the department or authority concerned, and to any person who is alleged in the complaint to have taken or authorised the action complained of, an opportunity to comment on any allegations contained in the complaint.

(2) Every such investigation shall be conducted in private, but except as aforesaid the procedure for conducting an investigation shall be such as the Commissioner considers appropriate in the circumstances of the case; and without prejudice to the generality of the foregoing provision the Commissioner may obtain information from such persons and in such manner, and make such inquiries, as he thinks fit, and may determine whether any person may be represented, by counsel or solicitor or otherwise, in the investigation.

(3), (4) ★ ★ ★ ★ ★

8 Evidence

(1) For the purposes of an investigation under this Act the Commissioner may require any Minister, officer or member of the department or authority concerned or any other person who in his opinion is able to furnish information or produce documents relevant to the investigation to furnish any such information or produce any such document.

(2) For the purposes of any such investigation the Commissioner shall have the same powers as the Court in respect of the attendance and examination of witnesses (including the administration of oaths or affirmations and the examination of witnesses abroad) and in respect of the production of documents.

(3) No obligation to maintain secrecy or other restriction upon the disclosure of information obtained by or furnished to persons in Her Majesty's service, whether imposed by any enactment or by any rule of law, shall apply to the disclosure of information for the purposes of an investigation under this Act; and the Crown shall not be entitled in relation to any such investigation to any such privilege in respect of the production of documents or the giving of evidence as is allowed by law in legal proceedings.

(4) No person shall be required or authorised by virtue of this Act to furnish any information or answer any question relating to proceedings of the Cabinet or of any committee of the Cabinet or to produce so much of any document as relates to such proceedings; and for the purposes of this subsection a certificate issued by the Secretary of the Cabinet with the approval of the Prime Minister and certifying that any information, question, document or part of a document so relates shall be conclusive.

(5) ★ ★ ★ ★ ★

9   Obstruction and contempt

(1) If any person without lawful excuse obstructs the Commissioner or any officer of the Commissioner in the performance of his functions under this Act, or is guilty of any act or omission in relation to any investigation under this Act which, if that investigation were a proceeding in the Court, would constitute contempt of court, the Commissioner may certify the offence to the Court.

(2) Where an offence is certified under this section, the Court may inquire into the matter and, after hearing any witnesses who may be produced against or on behalf of the person charged with the offence, and after hearing any statement that may be offered in defence, deal with him in any manner in which the court could deal with him if he had committed the like offence in relation to the Court.

(3) ★ ★ ★ ★ ★

10   Reports by Commissioner

(1) In any case where the Commissioner conducts an investigation under this Act or decides not to conduct such an investigation, he shall send to the member of the House of Commons by whom the request for investigation was made (or if he is no longer a member of that House, to such member of that House as the Commissioner thinks appropriate) a report of the results of the investigation or, as the case may be, a statement of his reasons for not conducting an investigation.

(2) In any case where the Commissioner conducts an investigation under this Act, he shall also send a report of the results of the investigation to the principal officer of the department or authority concerned and to any other person who is alleged in the relevant complaint to have taken or authorised the action complained of.

(3) If, after conducting an investigation under this Act, it appears to the Commissioner that injustice has been caused to the person aggrieved in consequence of maladministration and that the injustice has not been, or will not be, remedied, he may, if he thinks fit, lay before each House of Parliament a special report upon the case.

(4) The Commissioner shall annually lay before each House of Parliament a general report on the performance of his functions under this Act and may from time to time lay before each House of Parliament such other reports with respect to those functions as he thinks fit.

(5) For the purposes of the law of defamation, any such publication as is hereinafter mentioned shall be absolutely privileged, that is to say—
- (a) the publication of any matter by the Commissioner in making a report to either House of Parliament for the purposes of this Act;
- (b) the publication of any matter by a member of the House of Commons in communicating with the Commissioner or his officers for those purposes or by the

Commissioner or his officers in communicating with such a member for those purposes;

(c) the publication by such a member to the person by whom a complaint was made under this Act of a report or statement sent to the member in respect of the complaint in pursuance of section (1) of this section;

(d) the publication by the Commissioner to such a person as is mentioned in subsection (2) of this section of a report to that person in pursuance of that subsection.

11   Provision for secrecy of information

(1) . . .

(2)–(4) ★ ★ ★ ★ ★

11A, 11B ★ ★ ★ ★ ★

Supplemental

12   Interpretation

(1), (2) ★ ★ ★ ★ ★

(3) It is hereby declared that nothing in this Act authorises or requires the Commissioner to question the merits of a decision taken without maladministration by a government department or other authority in the exercise of a discretion vested in that department or authority.

13, 14 ★ ★ ★ ★ ★

Section 5   SCHEDULE 3
                 MATTERS NOT SUBJECT TO INVESTIGATION

1.   Action taken in matters certified by a Secretary of State or other Minister of the Crown to affect relations or dealings between the Government of the United Kingdom and any other Government or any international organisation of States or Governments.

2.   Action taken, in any country or territory outside the United Kingdom, by or on behalf of any officer representing or acting under the authority of Her Majesty in respect of the United Kingdom, or any other officer of the Government of the United Kingdom [other than action which is taken by an officer (not being an honorary consular officer) in the exercise of a consular function on behalf of the Government of the United Kingdom and which is so taken in relation to a citizen of the United Kingdom and Colonies who has the right of abode in the United Kingdom].

3.   Action taken in connection with the administration of the goverment of any country or territory outside the United Kingdom which forms part of Her Majesty's dominions or in which Her Majesty has jurisdiction.

4.   Action taken by the Secretary of State under the Extradition Act 1870 or the Fugitive Offenders Act 1881.

5.   Action taken by or with the authority of the Secretary of State for the purposes of investigating crime or of protecting the security of the State, including action so taken with respect to passports.

6.   The commencement or conduct of civil or criminal proceedings before any court of law in the United Kingdom, of proceedings at any place under the Naval Discipline Act 1957, the Army Act 1955 or the Air Force Act 1955, or of proceedings before any international court or tribunal.

[6A.   Action taken by any person appointed by the Lord Chancellor as a member of the administrative staff of any court or tribunal, so far as that action is taken at the direction, or on the authority (whether express or implied) of any person acting in a judicial capacity or as a member of the tribunal.]

[6B.   (1) Action taken by any member of the administrative staff of a relevant tribunal so far as that action is taken at the direction, or on the authority (whether express or implied), of any person acting in his capacity as a member of the tribunal.

(2) In this paragraph, "relevant tribunal" has the meaning given by section 5(8) of this Act.]

[6C.   Action taken by any person appointed under section 5(3)(c) of the Criminal Injuries Compensation Act 1995, so far as that action is taken at the direction, or on the authority (whether express or implied) of any person acting as an adjudicator appointed under section 5 of that Act to determine appeals.]

7.   Any exercise of the prerogative of mercy or of the power of a Secretary of State to make a reference in respect of any person to the High Court of Justiciary or the Courts-Martial Appeal Court.

8.   Action taken on behalf of the Minister of Health or the Secretary of State by a [Health Authority, any Special Health Authority], [except the Rampton Hospital Review Board . . . the] [Rampton Hospital Board] [the Broadmoor Hospital Board and the Moss Side and Park Lane Hospitals' Board]], . . . [a Health Board or the Common Services Agency for the Scottish Health Service, [by the Dental Practice Board or the Scottish Dental Practice Board]], or by the Public Health Laboratory Service Board.

9.   Action taken in matters relating to contractual or other commercial transactions, whether within the United Kingdom or elsewhere, being transactions of a government department or authority to which this Act applies or of any such authority or body as is mentioned in paragraph (a) or (b) of subsection (1) of section 6 of this Act and not being transactions for or relating to—

(a)   the acquisition of land compulsorily or in circumstances in which it could be acquired compulsorily;

(b)   the disposal as surplus of land acquired compulsorily or in such circumstances as aforesaid.

10.   (1) Action taken in respect of appointments or removals, pay, discipline, superannuation or other personnel matters, in relation to—

(a)   service in any of the armed forces of the Crown, including reserve and auxiliary and cadet forces;

(b)   service in any office or employment under the Crown or under any authority [(to which this Act applies)]; or

(c)   service in any office or employment, or under any contract for services, in respect of which power to take action, or to determine or approve the action to be taken, in such matters is vested in Her Majesty, any Minister of the Crown or any such authority as aforesaid.

[(2) Sub-paragraph (1)(c) above shall not apply to any action (not otherwise excluded from investigation by this Schedule) which is taken by the Secretary of State in connection with—

(a)   the provision of information relating to the terms and conditions of any employment covered by an agreement entered into by him under section 12(1) of the Overseas Development and Cooperation Act 1980 [or pursuant to the exercise of his powers under Part 1 of the International Development Act 2000] or

(b)   the provision of any allowance, grant or supplement or any benefit (other than those relating to superannuation) arising from the designation of any person in accordance with such an agreement.]

11.   The grant of honours, awards or privileges within the gift of the Crown, including the grant of Royal Charters.

★ ★ ★ ★ ★

Foreign Compensation Act 1969
(1969, c. 20)

An Act to make provision with respect to certain property (including the proceeds thereof and any income or other property accruing therefrom) of persons formerly resident or carrying on business in Estonia, Latvia, Lithuania or a part of Czechoslovakia, Finland, Poland or Rumania which has been ceded to the Union of Soviet Socialist Republics, and to amend the Foreign Compensation Act 1950 [16 May 1969]

Territorial extent: United Kingdom

★ ★ ★ ★ ★

3   Determination of the Foreign Compensation Commission and appeals against such determinations

(1) The Foreign Compensation Commission shall have power to determine any question as to the construction or interpretation of any provision of an Order in Council under section 3 of the Foreign Compensation Act 1950 with respect to claims falling to be determined by them.

(2) Subject to subsection (4) below, the Commission shall, if so required by a person mentioned in subsection (6) below who is aggrieved by any determination of the Commission on any question of law relating to the jurisdiction of the Commission or on any question mentioned in subsection (1) above, state and sign a case for the decision of the Court of Appeal.

(3) In this section "determination" includes a determination which under rules under section 4(2) of the Foreign Compensation Act 1950 (rules of procedure) is a provisional determination, and anything which purports to be a determination.

(4) Where the Court of Appeal decide a question on a case stated and signed by the Commission on a provisional determination in any proceedings, subsection (2) above shall not require the Commission to state and sign a case on a final determination by them of that question in those proceedings.

(5) Any person mentioned in subsection (6) below may, with a view to requiring the Commission to state and sign a case under this section, request the Commission to furnish a written statement of the reasons for any determination of theirs, but the Commission shall not be obliged to state the reasons for any determination unless it is given on a claim in which a question mentioned in subsection (2) above arises.

(6) The person who may make a request under subsection (5) above or a requirement under subsection (2) above in relation to any claim are the claimant and any person appointed by the Commission to represent the interests of any fund out of which the claim would, if allowed, be met.

(7) ★ ★ ★ ★ ★

(8) Notwithstanding anything in section 3 of the Appellate Jurisdiction Act 1876 (right of appeal to the House of Lords from decisions of the Court of Appeal), no appeal shall lie to the House of Lords from a decision of the Court of Appeal on an appeal under this section.

(9) Except as provided by subsection (2) above and subsection (10) below, no determination by the Commission on any claim made to them under the Foreign Compensation Act 1950 shall be called in question in any court of law.

(10) Subsection (9) above shall not affect any right of any person to bring proceedings questioning any determination of the Commission on the ground that it is contrary to natural justice.

(11) Subsection (2) to (10) above shall not apply to a determination of the Commission of which notice was sent by them before the passing of this Act.

(12) Section 4(4) of the Foreign Compensation Act 1950 (which makes provision corresponding to subsection (9) above) shall not apply to a determination of the Commission of which notice is sent by them after the passing of this Act.

★ ★ ★ ★ ★

Courts Act 1971

(1971, c. 23)

An Act to make further provision as respects the Supreme Court and county courts, judges and juries, to establish a Crown Court as part of the Supreme Court to try indictments and exercise certain other jurisdiction, to abolish courts of assize and certain other courts and to deal with their jurisdiction and other consequential matters, and to amend in other respects the law about courts and court proceedings   [12 May 1971]

Territorial extent: England and Wales

1–15   . . .

PART III   JUDGES

16   Appointment of Circuit Judges

(1) Her Majesty may from time to time appoint as Circuit judges, to serve in the Crown Court and county courts and to carry out such other judicial functions as may be conferred on them under this or any other enactment, such qualified persons as may be recommended to Her by the Lord Chancellor.

(2) The maximum number of Circuit judges shall be such as may be determined from time to time by the Lord Chancellor with the concurrence of the Minister for the Civil Service.

(3) No person shall be qualified to be appointed a Circuit judge [unless—

   (a) he has a 10 year Crown Court or 10 year county court qualification within the meaning of section 71 of the Courts and Legal Services Act 1990;

   (b) he is a Recorder; or

   (c) he has held as a full-time appointment for at least 3 years one of the offices listed in Part IA of Schedule 2.]

(4) Before recommending any person to Her Majesty for appointment as a Circuit judge, the Lord Chancellor shall take steps to satisfy himself that that person's health is satisfactory.

   (5) ★ ★ ★ ★ ★

17   Retirement, removal and disqualifications of Circuit judges

[(1) Subject to subsection (4) below and to subsections (4) to (6) of Section 26 of the Judicial Pensions and Retirement Act 1993, a Circuit judge shall vacate his office on the day on which he attains the age of 70.]

   (2), (3) . . .

   (4) The Lord Chancellor may, if he thinks fit, remove a Circuit judge from office on the ground of incapacity or misbehaviour.

   (5), (6) . . .

★ ★ ★ ★ ★

Immigration Act 1971
(1971, c. 77)

An Act to amend and replace the present immigration laws, to make certain related changes in the citizenship law and enable help to be given to those wishing to return abroad, and for purposes connected therewith   [28 October 1971]

Territorial extent: United Kingdom

Note: This Act is printed as extensively amended by the British Nationality Act 1981 and the Immigration and Asylum Act 1999. Provisions formerly in Part II have been replaced by the equivalent provisions of the latter Act.

PART I   REGULATION OF ENTRY INTO AND STAY IN UNITED KINGDOM

1   General principles

(1) All those who are in this Act expressed to have the right of abode in the United Kingdom shall be free to live in, and to come and go into and from, the United Kingdom without let or hindrance except such as may be required under and in accordance with this Act to enable their right to be established or as may be otherwise lawfully imposed on any person.

(2) Those not having that right may live, work and settle in the United Kingdom by permission and subject to such regulation and control of their entry into, stay in and departure from the United Kingdom as is imposed by this Act; and indefinite leave to enter or remain in the United Kingdom shall, by virtue of this provision, be treated as having been given under this Act to those in the United Kingdom at its coming into force, if they are then settled there (and not exempt under this Act from the provisions relating to leave to enter or remain).

(3) Arrival in and departure from the United Kingdom on a local journey from or to any of the Islands (that is to say, the Channel Islands and Isle of Man) or the Republic of Ireland shall not be subject to control under this Act, nor shall a person require leave to enter the United Kingdom on so arriving, except in so far as any of those places is for any purpose excluded from this subsection under the powers conferred by this Act; and in this Act the United Kingdom and those places, or such of them as are not so excluded, are collectively referred to as "the common travel area".

(4) The rules laid down by the Secretary of State as to the practice to be followed in the administration of this Act for regulating the entry into and stay in the United Kingdom of persons not having the right of abode shall include provision for admitting (in such cases and subject to such restrictions as may be provided by the rules, and subject or not to conditions as to length of stay or otherwise) persons coming for the purpose of taking employment, or for purposes of study, or as visitors, or as dependants of persons lawfully in or entering the United Kingdom.

(5) . . .

[2   Statement of right of abode in United Kingdom

(1) A person is under this Act to have the right of abode in the United Kingdom if—
    (a) he is a British citizen; or
    (b) he is a Commonwealth citizen who—
        (i) immediately before the commencement of the British Nationality Act 1981 was a Commonwealth citizen having the right of abode in the United Kingdom by virtue of section 2(1)(d) or section 2(2) of this Act as then in force; and
        (ii) has not ceased to be a Commonwealth citizen in the meanwhile.

(2) In relation to Commonwealth citizens who have the right of abode in the United Kingdom by virtue of subsection (1)(b) above, this Act, except this section and section [(5(2)] shall apply as if they were British citizens; and in this Act (except as aforesaid) "British citizen" shall be construed accordingly.]

[**Note:** Sections 2(1) and 2(2) as in force prior to the commencement of the 1981 Act provided as follows:

"(1) A person is under this Act to have the right of abode in the United Kingdom if—
   (a) he is a citizen of the United Kingdom and Colonies who has that citizenship by his birth, adoption, naturalisation or (except as mentioned below) registration in the United Kingdom or in any of the Islands; or
   (b) he is a citizen of the United Kingdom and Colonies born to or legally adopted by a parent who had that citizenship at the time of the birth or adoption, and the parent either—
      (i) then had that citizenship by his birth, adoption, naturalisation or (except as mentioned below) registration in the United Kingdom or in any of the Islands; or
      (ii) had been born to or legally adopted by a parent who at the time of that birth or adoption so had it; or
   (c) he is a citizen of the United Kingdom and Colonies who has at any time been settled in the United Kingdom and Islands and had at that time (and while such a citizen) been ordinarily resident there for the last five years or more; or
   (d) he is a Commonwealth citizen born to or legally adopted by a parent who at the time of the birth or adoption had citizenship of the United Kingdom and Colonies by his birth in the United Kingdom or in any of the Islands.
(2) A woman is under this Act also to have the right of abode in the United Kingdom if she is a Commonwealth citizen and either—
   (a) is the wife of any such citizen of the United Kingdom and Colonies as is mentioned in subsection (1)(a), (b) or (c) above or any such Commonwealth citizen as is mentioned in subsection (1)(d); or
   (b) has at any time been the wife—
      (i) of a person then being such a citizen of the United Kingdom and Colonies or Commonwealth citizen; or
      (ii) of a British subject who but for his death would on the date of commencement of the British Nationality Act 1948 have been such a citizen of the United Kingdom and Colonies as is mentioned in subsection (1)(a) or (b);
but in subsection (1)(a) and (b) above references to registration as a citizen of the United Kingdom and Colonies shall not, in the case of a woman, include registration after the passing of this Act under or by virtue of section 6(2) (wives) of the British Nationality Act 1948 unless she is so registered by virtue of her marriage to a citizen of the United Kingdom and Colonies before the passing of this Act."]

3 General provisions for regulation and control

(1) Except as otherwise provided by or under this Act, where a person is not [a British citizen]—
   (a) he shall not enter the United Kingdom unless given leave to do so in accordance with [the provisions, or made under] this Act;
   (b) he may be given leave to enter the United Kingdom (or, when already there, leave to remain in the United Kingdom) either for a limited or for an indefinite period;
   [(c) if he is given limited leave to enter or remain in the United Kingdom, it may be given subject to conditions restricting his employment or occupation in the United Kingdom, or requiring him to register with the police, or both.]

(2) The Secretary of State shall from time to time (and as soon as may be) lay before Parliament statements of the rules, or of any changes in the rules, laid down by him as to the practice to be followed in the administration of this Act for regulating the entry into and stay in the United Kingdom of persons required by this Act to have leave to enter, including any rules as to the period for which leave is to be given and the conditions to be attached in different circumstances; and section 1(4) above shall not be taken to require uniform provision to be made by the rules as regards admission of persons for a purpose or in a capacity specified in section 1(4) (and in particular, for this as well as other purposes of this Act, account may be taken of citizenship or nationality).

If a statement laid before either House of Parliament under this subsection is disapproved by a resolution of that House passed within the period of forty days beginning with the date of laying (and exclusive of any period during which Parliament is dissolved or prorogued or during which both Houses are adjourned for more than four days), then the Secretary of State shall as soon as may be make such changes or further changes in the rules as appear to him to be required in the circumstances, so that the statement of those changes be laid before Parliament at least by the end of the period of forty days beginning with the date of the resolution (but exclusive as aforesaid).

(3) In the case of a limited leave to enter or remain in the United Kingdom,—

    (a) a person's leave may be varied, whether by restricting, enlarging or removing the limit on its duration, or by adding, varying or revoking conditions, but if the limit on its duration is removed, any conditions attached to the leave shall cease to apply; and

    (b) the limitation on and any conditions attached to a person's leave [(whether imposed originally or on a variation) shall], if not superseded, apply also to any subsequent leave he may obtain after an absence from the United Kingdom within the period limited for the duration of the earlier leave.

(4) A person's leave to enter or remain in the United Kingdom shall lapse on his going to a country or territory outside the common travel area (whether or not he lands there), unless within the period for which he had leave he returns to the United Kingdom in circumstances in which he is not required to obtain leave to enter; but, if he does so return, his previous leave (and any limitation on it or conditions attached to it) shall continue to apply.

[(4A) For the purposes of subsection (4) above a person seeking to leave the United Kingdom through the tunnel system who is refused admission to France shall be treated as having gone to a country outside the common travel area.]

[(5) A person who is not a British citizen is liable to deportation from the United Kingdom if—

    [(a) having only a limited leave to enter or remain, he does not observe a condition attached to the leave or remains beyond the time limit by the leave; or

    (aa) he has obtained leave to remain by deception; or]

    (b) the Secretary of State deems his deportation to be conducive to the public good; or

    (c) another person to whose family he belongs is or has been ordered to be deported.]

(6) Without prejudice to the operation of subsection (5) above, a person who is not [a British citizen] shall also be liable to deportation from the United Kingdom if, after he has attained the age of seventeen, he is convicted of an offence for which he is punishable with imprisonment and on his conviction is recommended for deportation by a court empowered by this Act to do so.

(7) Where it appears to Her Majesty proper so to do by reason of restrictions or conditions imposed on [British citizens [, British overseas territories citizens] or British Overseas citizens] when leaving or seeking to leave any country or the territory subject to the government of any country, Her Majesty may by Order in Council make provision for prohibiting persons who are nationals or citizens of the country and are not [British citizens] from embarking in the United Kingdom, or from doing so elsewhere than at a port of exit, or for imposing restrictions

or conditions on them when embarking or about to embark in the United Kingdom; and Her Majesty may also make provision by Order in Council to enable those who are not [British citizens] to be, in such cases as may be prescribed by the Order, prohibited in the interests of safety from so embarking on a ship or aircraft specified or indicated in the prohibition.

Any Order in Council under this subsection shall be subject to annulment in pursuance of a resolution of either House of Parliament.

[(7A) Any reference in an Order in Council under subsection (7) above to embarking or being about to embark shall be construed as including a reference to leaving or seeking to leave the United Kingdom through the tunnel system.]

(8) When any question arises under this Act whether or not a person is [a British citizen], or is entitled to any exemption under this Act, it shall lie on the person asserting it to prove that he is.

[(9) A person seeking to enter the United Kingdom and claiming to have the right of abode there shall prove that he has that right by means of either—

    (a) a United Kingdom passport describing him as a British citizen or as a citizen of the United Kingdom and Colonies having the right of abode in the United Kingdom; or

    (b) a certificate of entitlement issued by or on behalf of the Government of the United Kingdom certifying that he has such a right of abode.]

3A, 3B, 3C, 4, 5 ★ ★ ★ ★ ★

6 Recommendations by court for deportation

(1) Where under section 3(6) above a person convicted of an offence is liable to deportation on the recommendation of a court, he may be recommended for deportation by any court having power to sentence him for the offence unless the court commits him to be sentenced or further dealt with for that offence by another court:

    · · · · ·

(2)–(4) ★ ★ ★ ★ ★

(5) Where a court recommends or purports to recommend a person for deportation, the validity of the recommendation shall not be called in question except on an appeal against the recommendation or against the conviction on which it is made; but—

. . . the recommendation shall be treated as a sentence for the purpose of any . . . enactment providing an appeal against sentence; . . .

    (6), (7) ★ ★ ★ ★ ★

7 Exemption from deportation for certain existing residents

(1) Notwithstanding anything in section 3(5) or (6) above but subject to the provisions of this section, a Commonwealth citizen or citizen of the Republic of Ireland who was such a citizen at the coming into force of this Act and was then ordinarily resident in the United Kingdom—

    (a) shall not be liable to deportation under section [3(5)(a)] if at the time of the Secretary of State's decision he had at all times since the coming into force of this Act been ordinarily resident in the United Kingdom and Islands; and

    (b) shall not be liable to deportation under section 3(5)(a), [or (b) or section 10 of the Immigration and Asylum Act 1999] if at the time of the Secretary of State's decision he had for the last five years been ordinarily resident in the United Kingdom and Islands; and

    (c) shall not on conviction of an offence be recommended for deportation under section 3(6) if at the time of the conviction he had for the last five years been ordinarily resident in the United Kingdom and Islands.

(2) A person who has at any time become ordinarily resident in the United Kingdom or in any of the Islands shall not be treated for the purposes of this section as having ceased to be so by reason only of his having remained there in breach of the immigration laws.

(3) The "last five years" before the material time under subsection (1)(b) or (c) above is to be taken as a period amounting in total to five years exclusive of any time during which the person claiming exemption under this section was undergoing imprisonment or detention by virtue of a sentence passed for an offence on a conviction in the United Kingdom and Islands, and the period for which he was imprisoned or detained by virtue of the sentence amounted to six months or more.

(4), (5) ★ ★ ★ ★ ★

8–23 ★ ★ ★ ★ ★

PART III   CRIMINAL PROCEEDINGS

24   Illegal entry and similar offences

(1) A person who is not [a British citizen] shall be guilty of an offence punishable on summary conviction with a fine of not more than [level [5] on the standard scale] or with imprisonment for not more than six months, or with both, in any of the following cases:—

(a) if contrary to this Act he knowingly enters the United Kingdom in breach of a deportation order or without leave;

(b) if, having only a limited leave to enter or remain in the United Kingdom, he knowingly either—
  (i) remains beyond the time limited by the leave; or
  (ii) fails to observe a condition of the leave;

(c) if, having lawfully entered the United Kingdom without leave by virtue of section 8(1) above, he remains without leave beyond the time allowed by section 8(1);

(d) if, without reasonable excuse, he fails to comply with any requirement imposed on him under Schedule 2 to this Act to report to a medical officer of health, or to attend, or submit to a test or examination, as required by such an officer;

(e) if, without reasonable excuse, he fails to observe any restriction imposed on him under Schedule 2 or 3 to this Act as to residence or as to reporting to the police or to an immigration officer;

(f) if he [leaves a train in the United Kingdom] after being placed on board under Schedule 2 or 3 to this Act with a view to his removal from the United Kingdom;

(g) if he [leaves or seeks to leave the United Kingdom through the tunnel system] in contravention of a restriction imposed by or under an Order in Council under section 3(7) of this Act.

[(1A) A person commits an offence under subsection (1)(b)(i) above on the day when he first knows that the time limited by his leave has expired and continues to commit it throughout any period during which he is in the United Kingdom thereafter; but a person shall not be prosecuted under that provision more than once in respect of the same limited leave.]

(2), (3), (4) ★ ★ ★ ★ ★

24A, 25–32 ★ ★ ★ ★ ★

PART IV   SUPPLEMENTARY

33   Interpretation

(1) For purposes of this Act, except in so far as the context otherwise requires—

★ ★ ★ ★ ★

["entrant" means a person entering or seeking to enter the United Kingdom, and "illegal entrant" means a person—

[(a) unlawfuly entering or seeking to enter in breach of a deportation order or of the immigration laws, or

(b) entering or seeking to enter by means which include deception by another person, and includes also a person who has entered as mentioned in paragraph (a) or (b) above;]

"entry clearance" means a visa, entry certificate or other document which, in accordance with the immigration rules, is to be taken as evidence [or the requisite evidence] of a person's eligibility, though not [a British citizen], for entry into the United Kingdom (but does not include a work permit);

"immigration laws" means this Act and any law for purposes similar to this Act which is for the time being or has (before or after the passing of this Act) been in force in any part of the United Kingdom and Islands;

"immigration rules" means the rules for the time being laid down as mentioned in section 3(2) above;

★ ★ ★ ★ ★

"limited leave" and "indefinite leave" mean respectively leave under this Act to enter or remain in the United Kingdom which is, and one which is not, limited as to duration;

"settled" shall be construed in accordance [with subsection (2A) below];

★ ★ ★ ★ ★

"work permit" means a permit indicating, in accordance with the immigration rules, that a person named in it is eligible, though not [a British citizen], for entry into the United Kingdom for the purpose of taking employment.

(2) It is hereby declaredthat, except as otherwise providedin this Act, a personis not to be treated for the purposes of any provision of this Act as ordinarily resident in the United Kingdomor inany of theIslands at a timewhenhe is therein breachof theimmigrationlaws.

[(2A) Subject to section 8(5) above, references to a person being settled in the United Kingdom are references to his being ordinarily resident there without being subject under the immigration laws to any restriction on the period for which he may remain.]

(3), (4) ★ ★ ★ ★ ★

(5) This Act shall not be taken to supersede or impair any power exercisable by Her Majesty in relation to aliens by virtue of Her prerogative.

34–37 ★ ★ ★ ★ ★

Misuse of Drugs Act 1971
(1971, c. 38)

An Act to make new provision with respect to dangerous or otherwise harmful drugs and related matters, and for purposes connected therewith   [27 May 1971]

Territorial extent: United Kingdom

★ ★ ★ ★ ★

Law enforcement and punishment of offences

23   Powers to search and obtain evidence

(1) A constable or other person authorised in that behalf by a general or special order of the Secretary of State . . . shall, for the purposes of the execution of this Act, have power to enter the premises of a person carrying on business as a producer or supplier of any controlled drugs and to demand the production of, and to inspect, any books or documents relating to dealings in any such drugs and to inspect any stocks of any such drugs.

(2) If a constable has reasonable grounds to suspect that any person is in possession of a controlled drug in contravention of this Act or of any regulations made thereunder, the constable may—

(a)   search that person, and detain him for the purpose of searching him;

(b)   search any vehicle or vessel in which the constable suspects that the drug may be found, and for that purpose require the person in control of the vehicle or vessel to stop it;

(c) seize and detain, for the purposes of proceedings under this Act, anything found in the course of the search which appears to the constable to be evidence of an offence under this Act.

In this subsection "vessel" includes a hovercraft within the meaning of the Hovercraft Act 1968; and nothing in this subsection shall prejudice any power of search or any power to seize or detain property which is exercisable by a constable apart from this subsection.

(3) If a justice of the peace (or in Scotland a justice of the peace, a magistrate or a sheriff) is satisfied by information on oath that there is reasonable ground for suspecting—

(a) that any controlled drugs are, in contravention of this Act or of any regulations made thereunder, in the possession of a person on any premises; or

(b) that a document directly or indirectly relating to, or connected with, a transaction or dealing which was, or an intended transaction or dealing which would if carried out be, an offence under this Act, or in the case of a transaction or dealing carried out or intended to be carried out in a place outside the United Kingdom, an offence against the provision of a corresponding law in force in that place, is in the possession of a person on any premises,

he may grant a warrant authorising any constable acting for the police area in which the premises are situated at any time or times within one month from the date of the warrant, to enter, if need be by force, the premises named in the warrant, and to search the premises and any person found therein and, if there is reasonable ground for suspecting that an offence under this Act has been committed in relation to any controlled drugs found on the premises or in the possession of any such persons, or that a document so found is such a document as is mentioned in paragraph (b) above, to seize and detain those drugs or that document, as the case may be.

(3A) ★ ★ ★ ★ ★

(4) A person commits an offence if he—

(a) intentionally obstructs a person in the exercise of his powers under this section; or

(b) conceals from a person acting in the exercise of his powers under subsection (1) above any such books, documents, stocks or drugs as are mentioned in that subsection; or

(c) without reasonable excuse (proof of which shall lie on him) fails to produce any such books or documents as are so mentioned where their production is demanded by a person in the exercise of his powers under that subsection.

★ ★ ★ ★ ★

European Communities Act 1972
(1972, c. 68)

An Act to make provision in connection with the enlargement of the European Communities to include the United Kingdom, together with (for certain purposes) the Channel Islands, the Isle of Man and Gibraltar [17 October 1972]

Territorial extent: United Kingdom

Note: In section 2, references to a statutory power or duty include a power or duty conferred by an Act of the Scottish Parliament or an instrument made thereunder, and section 2(2) is to be read as applying to regulations made by Scottish Ministers: see the Scotland Act 1998, Sch. 8, para. 5.

PART I   GENERAL PROVISIONS

1 Short title and interpretation

(1) This Act may be cited as the European Communities Act 1972.

(2) In this Act . . .

"the Communities" means the European Economic Community, the European Coal and Steel Community and the European Atomic Energy Community;

"the Treaties" or "the Community Treaties" means, subject to subsection (3) below, the pre-accession treaties, that is to say, those described in Part I of Schedule 1 to this Act, taken with–

★ ★ ★ ★ ★ [full list omitted]

and any expression defined in Schedule 1 to this Act has the meaning there given to it.

(3) If Her Majesty by Order in Council declares that a treaty specified in the Order is to be regarded as one of the Community Treaties as herein defined, the Order shall be conclusive that it is to be so regarded; but a treaty entered into by the United Kingdom after the 22nd January 1972, other than a pre-accession treaty to which the United Kingdom accedes on terms settled on or before that date, shall not be so regarded unless it is so specified, nor be so specified unless a draft of the Order in Council has been approved by resolution of each House of Parliament.

(4) For purposes of subsections (2) and (3) above, "treaty" includes any international agreement, and any protocol or annex to a treaty or international agreement.

Note: The full list of Treaties in s. 1(2) includes those adopted and ratified by the UK since 1972 as well as the original treaties, so that major constitutional changes such as the incorporation of the Single European Act of 1986 and the Maastricht Treaty, 1992 are achieved by amendments to the subsection. Most recently, the European Communities (Amendment) Act 2002 adds the Nice Treaty to the list in s. 1(2).

2 General implementation of Treaties

(1) All such rights, powers, liabilities, obligations and restrictions from time to time created or arising by or under the Treaties, and all such remedies and procedures from time to time provided for by or under the Treaties, as in accordance with the Treaties are without further enactment to be given legal effect or used in the United Kingdom shall be recognised and available in law, and be enforced, allowed and followed accordingly; and the expression "enforceable Community right" and similar expressions shall be read as referring to one to which this subsection applies.

(2) Subject to Schedule 2 to this Act, at any time after its passing Her Majesty may by Order in Council, and any designated Minister or department may by regulations, make provision—

(a) for the purpose of implementing any Community obligation of the United Kingdom, or enabling any such obligation to be implemented, or of enabling any rights enjoyed or to be enjoyed by the United Kingdom under or by virtue of the Treaties to be exercised; or

(b) for the purpose of dealing with matters arising out of or related to any such obligation or rights or the coming into force, or the operation from time to time, of subsection (1) above;

and in the exercise of any statutory power or duty, including any power to give directions or to legislate by means of orders, rules, regulations or other subordinate instrument, the person entrusted with the power or duty may have regard to the objects of the Communities and to any such obligation or rights as aforesaid.

In this subsection "designated Minister or Department" means such Minister of the Crown or government department as may from time to time be designated by Order in Council in relation to any matter or for any purpose, but subject to such restrictions or conditions (if any) as may be specified by the Order in Council.

(3) There shall be charged on and issued out of the Consolidated Fund or, if so determined by the Treasury, the National Loans Fund the amounts required to meet any Community obligation to make payments to any of the Communities or member States, or any Community obligation in respect of contributions to the capital or reserves of the European Investment Bank or in respect of loans to the Bank, or to redeem any notes or obligations issued or created in respect of any such Community obligation; and, except as otherwise provided by or under any enactment,—

(a) any other expenses incurred under or by virtue of the Treaties or this Act by any Minister of the Crown or government department may be paid out of moneys provided by Parliament; and

(b) any sums received under or by virtue of the Treaties or this Act by any Minister of the Crown or government department, save for such sums as may be required for disbursements permitted by any other enactment, shall be paid into the Consolidated Fund or, if so determined by the Treasury, the National Loans Fund.

(4) The provision that may be made under subsection (2) above includes, subject to Schedule 2 to this Act, any such provision (of any such extent) as might be made by Act of Parliament, and any enactment passed or to be passed, other than one contained in this Part of this Act, shall be construed and have effect subject to the foregoing provisions of this section; but, except as may be provided by any Act passed after this Act, Schedule 2 shall have effect in connection with the powers conferred by this and the following sections of this Act to make Orders in Council and regulations.

(5), (6) ★ ★ ★ ★ ★

3   Decisions on, and proof of, Treaties and Community instruments, etc.

(1) For the purposes of all legal proceedings any question as to the meaning or effect of any of the Treaties, or as to the validity, meaning or effect of any Community instrument, shall be treated as a question of law (and, if not referred to the European Court, be for determination as such in accordance with the principles laid down by and any relevant decision of the European Court).

(2) Judicial notice shall be taken of the Treaties, of the Official Journal of the Communities and of any decision of, or expression of opinion by, the European Court on any such question as aforesaid; and the Official Journal shall be admissible as evidence of any instrument or other act thereby communicated of any of the Communities or of any Community institution.

(3), (4), (5) ★ ★ ★ ★ ★

★ ★ ★ ★ ★

Section 2   SCHEDULE 2
              PROVISIONS AS TO SUBORDINATE LEGISLATION

1.—(1) The powers conferred by section 2(2) of this Act to make provision for the purposes mentioned in section 2(2)(a) and (b) shall not include power—

(a) to make any provision imposing or increasing taxation; or

(b) to make any provision taking effect from a date earlier than that of the making of the instrument containing the provision; or

(c) to confer any power to legislate by means of orders, rules regulations or other subordinate instrument, other than rules of procedure for any court or tribunal; or

(d) to create any new criminal offence punishable with imprisonment for more than two years or punishable on summary conviction with imprisonment for more than three months or with a fine of more than [level 5 on the standard scale] (if not calculated on a daily basis) or with a fine of more than [£100 a day].

(2) Sub-paragraph (1)(c) above shall not be taken to preclude the modification of a power to legislate conferred otherwise than under section 2(2), or the extension of any such power to purposes of the like nature as those for which it was conferred; and a power to give directions as to matters of administration is not to be regarded as a power to legislate within the meaning of sub-paragraph (1)(c).

2.—(1) Subject to paragraph 3 below, where a provision contained in any section of this Act confers power to make regulations (otherwise than by modification or extension of an existing power), the power shall be exercisable by statutory instrument.

(2) Any statutory instrument containing an Order in Council or regulations made in the exercise of a power so conferred, if made without a draft having been approved by resolution of each House of Parliament, shall be subject to annulment in pursuance of a resolution of either House.

Local Government Act 1972
(1972, c. 70)

An Act to make provision with respect to local government and the functions of local authorities in England and Wales; to amend Part II of the Transport Act 1968; to confer rights of appeal in respect of decisions relating to licences under the Home Counties (Music and Dancing) Licensing Act 1926; to make further provision with respect to magistrates' courts committees; to abolish certain inferior courts of record; and for connected purposes   [26 October 1972]

Territorial extent: England and Wales

★ ★ ★ ★ ★

[PART VA   ACCESS TO MEETINGS AND DOCUMENTS OF CERTAIN AUTHORITIES, COMMITTEES AND SUB-COMMITTEES

Note: This Part was added by the Local Government (Access to Information) Act 1985. It now also applies to Community Health Councils: Community Health Councils (Access to Information) Act 1988.

100A   Admission to meetings of principal councils

(1) A meeting of a principal council shall be open to the public except to the extent that they are excluded (whether during the whole or part of the proceedings) under subsection (2) below or by resolution under subsection (4) below.

(2) The public shall be excluded from a meeting of a principal council during an item of business whenever it is likely, in view of the nature of the business to be transacted or the nature of the proceedings, that, if members of the public were present during that item, confidential information would be disclosed to them in breach of the obligation of confidence; and nothing in this Part shall be taken to authorise or require the disclosure of confidential information in breach of the obligation of confidence.

(3) For the purposes of subsection (2) above, "confidential information" means—

(a) information furnished to the council by a Government department upon terms (however expressed) which forbid the disclosure of the information to the public; and

(b) information the disclosure of which to the public is prohibited by or under any enactment or by the order of a court;

and, in either case, the reference to the obligation of confidence is to be construed accordingly.

(4) A principal council may by resolution exclude the public from a meeting during an item of business whenever it is likely, in view of the nature of the business to be transacted or the nature of the proceedings, that if members of the public were present during that item there would be disclosure to them of exempt information, as defined in section 100I below.

(5), (6) ★ ★ ★ ★ ★

(7) Nothing in this section shall require a principal council to permit the taking of photographs of any proceedings, or the use of any means to enable persons not present to see or hear any proceedings (whether at the time or later), or the making of any oral report on any proceedings as they take place.

(8) This section is without prejudice to any power of exclusion to suppress or prevent disorderly conduct or other misbehaviour at a meeting.

100B Access to agenda and connected reports

(1) Copies of the agenda for a meeting of a principal council and, subject to subsection (2) below, copies of any report for the meeting shall be open to inspection by members of the public at the offices of the council in accordance with subsection (3) below.

(2) If the proper officer thinks fit, there may be excluded from the copies of reports provided in pursuance of subsection (1) above the whole of any report which, or any part which, relates only to items during which, in his opinion, the meeting is likely not to be open to the public.

(3) Any document which is required by subsection (1) above to be open to inspection shall be so open at least [five] clear days before the meeting, except that—

    (a) where the meeting is convened at shorter notice, the copies of the agenda and reports shall be open to inspection from the time the meeting is convened, and

    (b) where an item is added to an agenda copies of which are open to inspection by the public, copies of the item (or of the revised agenda), and the copies of any report for the meeting relating to the item, shall be open to inspection from the time the item is added to the agenda;

but nothing in this subsection requires copies of any agenda, item or report to be open to inspection by the public until copies are available to members of the council.

(4) An item of business may not be considered at a meeting of a principal council unless either–

    (a) a copy of the agenda including the item (or a copy of the item) is open to inspection by members of the public in pursuance of subsection (1) above for at least [five] clear days before the meeting or, where the meeting is convened at shorter notice, from the time the meeting is convened; or

    (b) by reason of special circumstances, which shall be specified in the minutes, the chairman of the meeting is of the opinion that the item should be considered at the meeting as a matter of urgency.

(5)–(8) ★ ★ ★ ★ ★

100C Inspection of minutes and other documents after meetings

(1) After a meeting of a principal council the following documents shall be open to inspection by members of the public at the offices of the council until the expiration of the period of six years beginning with the date of the meeting, namely—

    (a) the minutes, or a copy of the minutes, of the meeting, excluding so much of the minutes of proceedings during which the meeting was not open to the public as discloses exempt information;

    (b) where applicable, a summary under subsection (2) below;

    (c) a copy of the agenda for the meeting; and

    (d) a copy of so much of any report for the meeting as relates to any item during which the meeting was open to the public.

(2) ★ ★ ★ ★ ★

100D   Inspection of background papers
[(1) Subject, in the case of section 100C(1), to subsection (2) below, if and so long as copies of the whole or part of a report for a meeting of a principal council are required by section 100B(1) or 100C(1) above to be open to inspection by members of the public—
   (a) those copies shall each include a copy of a list compiled by the proper officer, of the background papers for the report or the part of the report; and
   (b) at least one copy of each of the documents included in that list shall also be open to inspection at the offices of the council.]
(2) Subsection (1) above does not require a copy . . . of any document included in the list, to be open to inspection after the expiration of the period of four years beginning with the date of the meeting.
(3)–(5) ★ ★ ★ ★ ★

100E   Application to committees and sub-committees
(1) Sections 100A to 100D above shall apply in relation to a committee or sub-committee of a principal council as they apply in relation to a principal council.
(2)–(4) ★ ★ ★ ★ ★

100F   ★ ★ ★ ★ ★

100G   Principal councils to publish additional information
(1) A principal council shall maintain a register stating–
   (a) the name and address of every member of the council for the time being and the ward or division which he represents; and
   [(b) in respect of every committee or sub-committee of the council—
     (i) the members of the council who are members of the committee or sub-committee or who are entitled, in accordance with any standing orders relating to the committee or sub-committee, to speak at its meetings or any of them;
     (ii) the name and address of every other person who is a member of the committee or sub-committee or who is entitled, in accordance with any standing orders relating to the committee or sub-committee, to speak at its meetings or any of them otherwise than in the capacity of an officer of the council; and
     (iii) the functions in relation to the committee or sub-committee of every person falling within sub-paragraph (i) above who is not a member of the committee or sub-committee and of every person falling within sub-paragraph (ii) above.
(2) A principal council shall maintain a list—
   (a) specifying those powers of the council which, for the time being, are exercisable from time to time by officers of the council in pursuance of arrangements made under this Act or any other enactment for their discharge by those officers; and
   (b) stating the title of the officer by whom each of the powers so specified is for the time being so exercisable;
but this subsection does not require a power to be specified in the list if the arrangements for its discharge by the officer are made for a specified period not exceeding six months.
(3), (4) ★ ★ ★ ★ ★]

★ ★ ★ ★ ★

PART VI   DISCHARGE OF FUNCTIONS

101   Arrangements for discharge of functions by local authorities
(1) Subject to any express provision contained in this Act or any Act passed after this Act, a local authority may arrange for the discharge of any of their functions—

    (a) by a committee, a sub-committee or an officer of the authority; or

    (b) by any other local authority.

(1A), (1B), (1C) ★ ★ ★ ★ ★

(2) Where by virtue of this section any functions of a local authority may be discharged by a committee of theirs, then, unless the local authority otherwise direct, the committee may arrange for the discharge of any of those functions by a sub-committee or an officer of the authority and where by virtue of this section any functions of a local authority may be discharged by a sub-committee of the authority, then, unless the local authority or the committee otherwise direct, the sub-committee may arrange for the discharge of any of those functions by an officer of the authority.

(3) Where arrangements are in force under this section for the discharge of any functions of a local authority by another local authority, then, subject to the terms of the arrangements, that other authority may arrange for the discharge of those functions by a committee, sub-committee or officer of theirs and subsection (2) above shall apply in relation to those functions as it applies in relation to the functions of that other authority.

(4) Any arrangements made by a local authority or committee under this section for the discharge of any functions by a committee, sub-committee, officer or local authority shall not prevent the authority or committee by whom the arrangements are made from exercising those functions.

(5) Two or more local authorities may discharge any of their functions jointly and, where arrangements are in force for them to do so,–

    (a) they may also arrange for the discharge of those functions by a joint committee of theirs or by an officer of one of them and subsection (2) above shall apply in relation to those functions as it applies in relation to the functions of the individual authorities; and

    (b) any enactment relating to those functions or the authorities by whom or the areas in respect of which they are to be discharged shall have effect subject to all necessary modifications in its application in relation to those functions and the authorities by whom and the areas in respect of which (whether in pursuance of the arrangements or otherwise) they are to be discharged.

(5A), (5B) ★ ★ ★ ★ ★

(6) A local authority's functions with respect to levying, or issuing a precept for, a rate . . . shall be discharged only by the authority.

★ ★ ★ ★ ★

111 Subsidiary powers of local authorities

(1) Without prejudice to any powers exercisable apart from this section but subject to the provisions of this Act and any other enactment passed before or after this Act, a local authority shall have power to do anything (whether or not involving the expenditure, borrowing or lending of money or the acquisition or disposal of any property or rights) which is calculated to facilitate, or is conducive or incidental to, the discharge of any of their functions.

(2) For the purposes of this section, transacting the business of a parish or community meeting or any other parish or community business shall be treated as a function of the parish or community council.

(3) A local authority shall not by virtue of this section raise money, whether by means of rates, precepts or borrowing, or lend money except in accordance with the enactments relating to those matters respectively.

(4) In this section "local authority" includes the Common Council.

112 Appointment of staff

(1) Without prejudice to section 111 above but subject to the provisions of this Act, a local authority shall appoint such officers as they think necessary for the proper discharge by

the authority of such of their or another authority's functions as fall to be discharged by them and the carrying out of any obligations incurred by them in connection with an agreement made by them in pursuance of section 113 below.

(2) An officer appointed under subsection (1) above shall hold office on such reasonable terms and conditions, including conditions as to remuneration, as the authority appointing him think fit.

(3) Subject to subsection (4) below, any enactment or instrument made under an enactment which requires or empowers all local authorities or local authorities of any description or committees of local authorities to appoint a specified officer shall, to the extent that it makes any such provision, cease to have effect.

The reference in this section to committees of local authorities does not include a reference to any committee of which some members are required to be appointed by a body or person other than a local authority.

(4)–(6) ★ ★ ★ ★ ★

★ ★ ★ ★ ★

PART XI   GENERAL PROVISIONS AS TO LOCAL AUTHORITIES

Legal proceedings

222   Power of local authorities to prosecute or defend legal proceedings

(1) Where a local authority consider it expedient for the promotion or protection of the interests of the inhabitants of their area—

(a) they may prosecute or defend or appear in any legal proceedings and, in the case of civil proceedings, may institute them in their own name, and

(b) they may, in their own name, make representations in the interests of the inhabitants at any public inquiry held by or on behalf of any Minister or public body under any enactment.

(2) In this section "local authority" includes the Common Council [and the London Fire and Emergency Planning Authority.]

★ ★ ★ ★ ★

Byelaws

235   Power of councils to make byelaws for good rule and government and suppression of nuisances

(1) The council of a district [, the council of a principal area in Wales] and the council of a London borough may make byelaws for the good rule and government of the whole or any part of the district [principal area] or borough, as the case may be, and for the prevention and suppression of nuisances therein.

(2) The confirming authority in relation to byelaws made under this section shall be the Secretary of State.

(3) Byelaws shall not be made under this section for any purpose as respects any area if provision for that purpose as respects that area is made by, or is or may be made under, any other enactment.

★ ★ ★ ★ ★

[SCHEDULE 12A   ACCESS TO INFORMATION: EXEMPT INFORMATION

PART I   DESCRIPTIONS OF EXEMPT INFORMATION

1. Information relating to a particular employee, former employee or applicant to become an employee of, or a particular office-holder, former office-holder or applicant to become an office-holder under, the authority.

2. Information relating to a particular employee, former employee or applicant to become an employee of, or a particular officer, former officer or applicant to become an officer appointed by—

    (a) a magistrates' court committee, [. . .]

    (b) a probation committee [within the meaning of the Probation Service Act 1993] [;or

    (c) a local probation board within the meaning of the Criminal Justice and Court Services Act 2000.]

[2A. Information relating to a particular chief officer, former chief officer or application to become a chief officer of a local probation board within the meaning of the Criminal Justice and Court Services Act 2000.]

3. Information relating to any particular occupier or former occupier of, or applicant for accommodation provided by or at the expense of the authority.

4. Information relating to any particular applicant for, or recipient or former recipient of, any service provided by the authority.

5. Information relating to any particular applicant for, or recipient or former recipient of, any financial assistance provided by the authority.

6. Information relating to the adoption, care, fostering or education of any particular child.

7. Information relating to the financial or business affairs of any particular person (other than the authority).

8. The amount of any expenditure proposed to be incurred by the authority under any particular contract for the acquisition of property or the supply of goods or services.

9. Any terms proposed or to be proposed by or to the authority in the course of negotiations for a contract for the acquisition or disposal of property or the supply of goods or services.

10. The identity of the authority (as well as of any other person, by virtue of paragraph 7 above) as the person offering any particular tender for a contract for the supply of goods or services.

11. Information relating to any consultations or negotiations, or contemplated consultations or negotiations, in connection with any labour relations matter arising between the authority or a Minister of the Crown and employees of, or office-holders under, the authority.

12. Any instructions to counsel and any opinion of counsel (whether or not in connection with any proceedings) and any advice received, information obtained or action to be taken in connection with—

    (a) any legal proceedings by or against the authority, or

    (b) the determination of any matter affecting the authority, (whether, in either case, proceedings have been commenced or are in contemplation).

13. Information which, if disclosed to the public, would reveal that the authority proposes—

    (a) to give under any enactment a notice under or by virtue of which requirements are imposed on a person; or

    (b) to make an order or direction under any enactment.

14. Any action taken or to be taken in connection with the prevention, investigation or prosecution of crime.

15. The identity of a protected informant.]

★ ★ ★ ★ ★

Local Government Act 1974
(1974, c. 7)

An Act to make further provision, in relation to England and Wales, with respect to the payment of grants to local authorities, rating and valuation, borrowing and lending by local authorities and the classification of highways; to extend the powers of the Countryside Commission to give financial assistance; to provide for the establishment of Commissions for the investigation of administrative action taken by or on behalf of local and other authorities; to restrict certain grants under the Transport Act 1968; to provide for the removal or relaxation of certain statutory controls affecting local government activities; to make provision in relation to the collection of sums by local author- ities on behalf of water authorities; to amend section 259(3) of the Local Government Act 1972 and to make certain minor amendments of or consequential on that Act; and for connected purposes   [8 February 1974]

Territorial extent: England and Wales

PART III   LOCAL GOVERNMENT ADMINISTRATION

23   The Commissions for Local Administration

(1) For the purpose of conducting investigations in accordance with this Part of this Act, there shall be—

   (a) a body of commissioners to be known as the Commission for Local Administra- tion in England, and

   (b) a body consisting of two or more commissioners to be known as the Commission for Local Administration in Wales.

[but each of the Commissions may include persons appointed to act as advisers, not exceeding the number appointed to conduct investigations.]

(2) The Parliamentary Commissioner shall be a member of each of the Commissions.

[(2A) The Welsh Administration Ombudsman shall be a member of the Commission for Local Administration in Wales (so that where the offices of Parliamentary Commissioners and Welsh Administration Ombudsman are held by different persons, the Commission for Local Administration in Wales shall consist of at least three Commissioners.]

(3) In the following provisions of this Part of this Act the expression "Local Commis- sioner" means a person, other than the Parliamentary Commissioner, [the Welsh Administra- tion Ombudsman,] [or an advisory member] who is a member of one of the Commissions.

(4) Appointments to the office of . . . Commissioner shall be made by Her Majesty on the recommendation of the Secretary of State after consultation with the appropriate representa- tive body, and a person so appointed shall, subject to subsection (6) below, hold office during good behaviour.

(5) . . . Commissioners may be appointed to serve either as full-time commissioners or as part-time commissioners.

(6) A Commissioner may be relieved of office by Her Majesty at his own request or may be removed from office by Her Majesty on grounds of incapacity or misbehaviour, and shall in any case vacate office on completing the year of service in which he attains the age of sixty-five years.

(7) The Secretary of State shall designate two of the Local Commissioners for England as

chairman and vice-chairman respectively of the Commission for Local Administration in England and, in the event of there being more than one Local Commissioner for Wales, shall designate one of them as chairman of the Commission for Local Administration in Wales.

(8) The Commission for Local Administration in England shall divide England into areas and shall provide, in relation to each area, for one or more of the Local Commissioners to be responsible for the area; and where the Commission for Local Administration in Wales consist of more than one Local Commissioner they may, if they think fit, act in a similar way in Wales.

A Local Commissioner may, by virtue of this Subsection, be made responsible for more than one area.

(9), (10), (11), (12), (12A), (12B) and (13) ★ ★ ★ ★ ★

24   . . .

25   Authorities subject to investigation
(1) This Part of this Act applies to [the following authorities]—
- (a)   any local authority,

    . . .
- [(ab)   a National Park Authority;]
- (b)   any joint board the constituent authorities of which are all local authorities,
- [(ba)   the Commission for the New Towns;
- (bb)   any development corporation established for the purposes of a new town;

    . . .
- (bd)   any urban development corporation established by an order under section 135 of the Local Government, Planning and Land Act 1980;]
- [(be)   any housing action trust established under Part III of the Housing Act 1988,]
- [(bf)   the Urban Regeneration Agency;]
- [(bg)   a fire authority constituted by a Combination Scheme under the Fire Services Act 1947;]
- [(c)   any joint authority established by Part IV of the Local Government Act 1985;
- [(cza)   the London Fire and Emergency Planning Authority;]
- (ca)   [any police authority established under section 3 of the Police Act 1996]; . . .
- (d)   [in relation to the flood defence functions of the Environment Agency, within the meaning of the Water Resources Act 1991, the Environment Agency and any regional flood defence committee] [; and
- (e)   The London Transport Users' Committee.]

(2) Her Majesty may by Order in Council provide that this Part of this Act shall also apply, subject to any modifications or exceptions specified in the Order, to any authority specified in the Order, being an authority which is established by or under an Act of Parliament, and which has power to levy a rate, or to issue a precept.

(3)–(5) ★ ★ ★ ★ ★

26   Matters subject to investigation
(1) Subject to the provisions of this Part of this Act where a written complaint is made by or on behalf of a member of the public who claims to have sustained injustice in consequence of maladministration in connection with action taken by or on behalf of an authority to which this Part of this Act applies, being action taken in the exercise of administrative functions of that authority, a Local Commissioner may investigate that complaint.

(2) A complaint shall not be entertained under this Part of this Act unless [it is made in writing to the Local Commissioner, specifying the action alleged to constitute maladministration, or]
- (a)   it is made inviting to a member of the authority, or of any other authority concerned, specifying the action alleged to constitute maladministration, and

(b) it is referred to the Local Commissioner, with the consent of the person aggrieved, or of a person acting on his behalf, by that member, or by any other person who is a member of any authority concerned, with a request to investigate the complaint.

(3) If the Local Commissioner is satisfied that any member of any authority concerned has been requested to refer the complaint to a Local Commissioner, and has not done so, the Local Commissioner may, if he thinks fit, dispense with the requirements in subsection (2)(b) above.

(4) A complaint shall not be entertained unless it was made to [the Local Commissioner or] a member of any authority concerned within twelve months from the day on which the person aggrieved first had notice of the matters alleged in the complaint, but a Local Commissioner may conduct an investigation pursuant to a complaint not made within that period if he considers that [it is reasonable] to do so.

(5) Before proceeding to investigate a complaint, a Local Commissioner shall satisfy himself that the complaint has been brought, by or on behalf of the person aggrieved, to the notice of the authority to which the complaint relates and that that authority has been afforded a reasonable opportunity to investigate, and reply to, the complaint.

(6) A Local Commissioner shall not conduct an investigation under this Part of this Act in respect of any of the following matters, that is to say, —

(a) any action in respect of which the person aggrieved has or had a right of appeal, reference or review to or before a tribunal constituted by or under any enactment;

(b) any action in respect of which in the person aggrieved has or had a right of appeal to a Minister of the Crown or the National Assembly for Wales; or

(c) any action in respect of which the person aggrieved has or had a remedy by way of proceedings in any court of law:

Provided that a Local Commissioner may conduct an investigation notwithstanding the existence of such a right or remedy if satisfied that in the particular circumstances it is not reasonable to expect the person aggrieved to resort or have resorted to it.

(7) A Local Commissioner shall not conduct an investigation in respect of any action which in his opinion affects all or most of the inhabitants of the [following area:

[(aa)where the complaint relates to a National Park Authority, the area of the Park for which it is such an authority;]

(a) where the complaint relates to the Commission for the New Towns, the area of the new town or towns to which the complaint relates;

(b) . . .;

[(ba)where the complaint relates to the Urban Regeneration Agency, any designated area within the meaning of Part III of the Leasehold Reform, Housing and Urban Development Act 1993;]

(c) in any other case, the area of the authority concerned.]

(8) Without prejudice to the preceding provisions of this section, a Local Commissioner shall not conduct an investigation under this Part of this Act in respect of any such action or matter as is described in Schedule 5 to this Act.

(9) Her Majesty may by Order in Council amend the said Schedule 5 so as [to add to or to exclude from the provisions of that Schedule (as it has effect for the time being)] such actions or matters as may be described in the Order; and any Order made by virtue of this subsection shall be subject to annulment in pursuance of a resolution of either House of Parliament.

(10) In determining whether to initiate, continue or discontinue an investigation, a Local Commissioner shall, subject to the proceeding provisions of this section, act at discretion; and any question whether a complaint is duly made under this Part of this Act shall be determined by the Local Commissioner.

(11), (12), (13) ★ ★ ★ ★ ★

27   Provisions relating to complaints

(1) A complaint under this Part of this Act may be made by any individual, or by any body of persons whether incorporated or not, not being—

(a) a local authority or other authority or body constituted for purposes of the public service or of local government, [including the National Assembly for Wales,] or for the purposes of carrying on under national ownership any industry or undertaking or part of an industry or undertaking;

(b) any other authority or body whose members are appointed by Her Majesty or any Minister of the Crown or government department [or by the National Assembly for Wales], or whose revenues consist wholly or mainly of moneys provided by Parliament [or the National Assembly for Wales].

(2) ★ ★ ★ ★ ★

28   Procedure in respect of investigations

(1) Where a Local Commissioner proposes to conduct an investigation pursuant to a complaint, he shall afford to the authority concerned, and to any person who is alleged in the complaint to have taken or authorised the action complained of, an opportunity to comment on any allegations contained in the complaint.

(2) Every such investigation shall be conducted in private, but except as aforesaid the procedure for conducting an investigation shall be such as the Local Commissioner considers appropriate in the circumstances of the case; and without prejudice to the generality of the preceding provision the Local Commissioner may obtain information from such persons and in such manner, and make such inquiries as he thinks fit, and may determine whether any person may be represented (by counsel or solicitor or otherwise) in the investigation.

(3) ★ ★ ★ ★ ★

(4) The conduct of an investigation under this Part of this Act shall not affect any action taken by the authority concerned, or any power or duty of that authority to take further action with respect to any matters subject to the investigation.

29   Investigations: further provisions

(1) For the purposes of an investigation under this Part of this Act a Local Commissioner may require any member or officer of the authority concerned, or any other person who in his opinion is able to furnish information or produce documents relevant to the investigation, to furnish any such information or produce any such documents.

(2) For the purposes of any such investigation a Local Commissioner shall have the same powers as the High Court in respect of the attendance and examination of witnesses, and in respect of the production of documents.

(3) A Local Commissioner may, under subsection (1) above, require any person to furnish information concerning communications between the authority concerned and any Government department [or the National Assembly for Wales], or to produce any correspondence or other documents forming part of any such written communications.

(4) No obligation to maintain secrecy or other restriction upon the disclosure of information obtained by or furnished to persons in Her Majesty's service, whether imposed by any enactment or by any rule of law, shall apply to the disclosure of information in accordance with subsection (3) above; and where that subsection applies the Crown shall not be entitled to any such privilege in respect of the production of documents or the giving of evidence as is allowed by law in legal proceedings.

(5)–(10) ★ ★ ★ ★ ★

30   Reports on investigations

(1) In any case where a Local Commissioner conducts an investigation, or decides not to conduct an investigation, he shall send a report of the results of the investigation, or as the case may be a statement of his reasons for not conducting an investigation—

(a) to the person, if any, who referred the complaint to the Local Commissioner in accordance with section 26(2) above, and

(b) to the complainant, and

(c) to the authority concerned, and to any other authority or person who is alleged in the complaint to have taken or authorised the action complained of.

(2) ★ ★ ★ ★ ★

(2A), (2AA) . . .

(3) Apart from identifying the authority or authorities concerned the report shall not . . .

(a) mention the name of any person, or

(b) contain any particulars which, in the opinion of the Local Commissioner, are likely to identify any person and can be omitted without impairing the effectiveness of the report,

unless, after taking into account the public interest as well as the interests of the complainant and of persons other than the complainant, the Local Commissioner considers it necessary to mention the name of that person or to include in the report any such particulars.

(3A) . . .

[(3AA) Nothing in subsection (3) above prevents a report—

(a) mentioning the name of, or

(b) containing particulars likely to identify, the Mayor of London or any member of the London Assembly.]

(4) Subject to the provisions of subsection (7) below, the authority concerned shall for a period of three weeks make copies of the report available for inspection by the public without charge at all reasonable hours at one or more of their offices; and any person shall be entitled to take copies of, or extracts from, the report when so made available.

[(4A) Subject to subsection (7) below, the authority concerned shall supply a copy of the report to any person on request if he pays such charge as the authority may reasonably require.

(5) Not later than [two weeks] after the report is received by the authority concerned, the proper officer of the authority shall give public notice, by advertisement in the newspapers and such other ways as appear to him appropriate, that [copies of the report will be available as provided by subsections (4) and (4A)] above, and shall specify the date, being a date [not more than one week after the public notice is first given] from which the period of three weeks will begin.

(6) ★ ★ ★ ★ ★

(7) The Local Commissioner may, if he thinks fit after taking into account the public interest as well as the interests of the complainant and of persons other than the complainant, direct that a report specified in the direction shall not be subject to the provisions of subsections (4) [,(4A) and (5) above.]

31 Reports on investigations: further provisions

(1) If in the opinion of the Local Commissioner, as set out in the report, injustice has been caused to the person aggrieved in consequence of maladministration, the report shall be laid before the authority concerned, and it shall be the duty of that authority to consider the report, and to notify the Local Commissioner of the action which the authority have taken, or propose to take.

(2) If the Local Commissioner—

(a) does not receive any such notification within a reasonable time; or

(b) is not satisfied with the action which the authority concerned have taken; or

(c) does not within a reasonable time receive confirmation from the authority concerned that they have taken action, as proposed, to the satisfaction of the Local Commissioner, he shall make a further report setting out those facts; and section 30 above shall apply, with any necessary modifications, to that further report.

[(2A) A report under subsection (2) above shall be laid before the authority concerned as it shall be the duty of the authority to consider the report and to notify the Local Commissioner of the action which the authority have taken, or propose to take.]

[(3) In any case where—

(a) a report is laid before an authority under subsection (1) [or (2A)] above, and

(b) on consideration of the report, it appears to the authority that a payment should be made to, or some other benefit should be provided for, a person who has suffered injustice in consequence of maladministration [to which the report relates,]

the authority may incur such expenditure as appears to them to be appropriate in making such a payment or providing such a benefit.]

31A, 32, 33   ★ ★ ★ ★ ★

34   Interpretation of Part III

(1), (2) ★ ★ ★ ★ ★

(3) It is hereby declared that nothing in this Part of this Act authorises or requires a Local Commissioner to question the merits of a decision taken without maladministration by an authority in the exercise of a discretion vested in that authority.

Section 26   SCHEDULE 5
                MATTERS NOT SUBJECT TO INVESTIGATION

1. The commencement or conduct of civil or criminal proceedings before any court of law.

2. Action taken by any authority in connection with the investigation or prevention of crime.

3.–(1) Action taken in matters relating to contractual or other commercial transactions of any authority to which Part III of this Act applies, including transactions falling within sub-paragraph (2) below but excluding transactions falling within sub-paragraph (3) below.

(2) The transactions mentioned in sub-paragraph (1) above as included in the matters which, by virtue of that sub-paragraph, are not subject to investigation are all transactions of an authority to which Part III of this Act applies relating to the operation of public passenger transport, the carrying on of a dock or harbour undertaking, the provision of entertainment, or the provision and operation of industrial establishments and of markets, [other than transactions relating to the grant, renewal or revocation of a licence to occupy a pitch or stall in a fair or market, or the attachment of any condition to such a licence.]

(3) The transactions mentioned in sub-paragraph (1) above as not included in those matters are—

(a) transactions for or relating to the acquisition or disposal of land [or the provision of moorings (not being moorings provided in connection with a dock or harbour undertaking)]; and

(b) all transactions (not being transactions falling within sub-paragraph (2) above) in the discharge of functions exercisable under any public general Act, other than those required for the procurement of the goods and services necessary to discharge those functions.

4. Action taken in respect of appointments or removals, pay, discipline, superannuation or other personnel matters.

5.—(1) . . .

(2) Any action concerning—

   (a) the giving of instruction, whether secular or religious, or

   (b) conduct, curriculum, internal organisation, management or discipline, whether—

      (i) in any school maintained by the authority, or

      (ii) in any college of education or establishment of further education maintained by the authority.

[6. Any action taken by an authority mentioned in section 25(1)(ba) or (bb) or this Act which is not action in connection with functions in relation to housing.

7. Action taken by an authority mentioned in section 25(1)(bd) of this Act which is not action in connection with functions in relation to town and country planning.]

[8. Action taken by the Urban Regeneration Agency which is not action in connection with functions in relation to town and country planning.]

House of Commons Disqualification Act 1975
(1975, c. 24)

An Act to consolidate certain enactments relating to disqualification for membership of the House of Commons   [8 May 1975]

Territorial extent: United Kingdom

1 Disqualification of holders of certain offices and places

(1) Subject to the provisions of this Act, a person is disqualified for membership of the House of Commons who for the time being—

   [(za)is a Lord Spiritual;]

   (a) holds any of the judicial offices specified in Part I of Schedule 1 to this Act;

   (b) is employed in the civil service of the Crown, whether in an established capacity or not, and whether for the whole or part of his time;

   (c) is a member of any of the regular armed forces of the Crown or the Ulster Defence Regiment;

   (d) is a member of any police force maintained by a police authority; [(da) is a member of the National Criminal Intelligence Service or the National Crime Squad;]

   (e) is a member of the legislature of any country or territory outside the Commonwealth [other than Ireland]; or

   (f) holds any office described in Part II or Part III of Schedule 1.

(2), (3) ★ ★ ★ ★ ★

(4) Except as provided by this Act, a person shall not be disqualified for membership of the House of Commons by reason of his holding an office or place of profit under the Crown or any other office or place; and a person shall not be disqualified for appointment to or for holding any office or place by reason of his being a member of that House.

2 Ministerial offices

(1) Not more than ninety-five persons being the holders of offices specified in Schedule 2 to this Act (in this section referred to as Ministerial offices) shall be entitled to sit and vote in the House of Commons at any one time.

(2) If at any time the number of members of the House of Commons who are holders of Ministerial offices exceeds the number entitled to sit and vote in that House under subsection (1) above, none except any who were both members of that House and holders of Ministerial offices before the excess occurred shall sit or vote therein until the number has been reduced, by death, resignation or otherwise, to the number entitled to sit and vote as aforesaid.

(3) A person holding a Ministerial office is not disqualified by this Act by reason of any office held by him ex officio as the holder of that Ministerial office.

3   Reserve and Auxiliary Forces etc. ★ ★ ★ ★ ★

4   Stewardship of Chiltern Hundreds, etc.

For the purposes of the provisions of this Act relating to the vacation of the seat of a member of the House of Commons who becomes disqualified by this Act for membership of that House, the office of steward or bailiff of Her Majesty's three Chiltern Hundreds of Stoke, Desborough and Burnham, or of the Manor of Northstead, shall be treated as included among the offices described in Part III of Schedule 1 to this Act.

5   Power to amend Schedule 1

(1) If at any time it is resolved by the House of Commons that Schedule 1 to this Act be amended, whether by the addition or omission of any office or the removal of any office from one Part of the Schedule to another, or by altering the description of any office specified therein, Her Majesty may by Order in Council amend that Schedule accordingly.

(2) ★ ★ ★ ★ ★

6   Effects of disqualification and provision for relief

(1) Subject to any order made by the House of Commons under this section,—

  (a) if any person disqualified by this Act for membership of that House, or for membership for a particular constituency, is elected as a member of that House, or as a member for that constituency, as the case may be, his election shall be void; and

  (b) if any person being a member of that House becomes disqualified by this Act for membership for the constituency for which he is sitting, his seat shall be vacated.

(2) If, in a case falling or alleged to fall within subsection (1) above, it appears to the House of Commons that the grounds of disqualification or alleged disqualification under this Act which subsisted or arose at the material time have been removed, and that it is otherwise proper so to do, that House may by order direct that any such disqualification incurred on those grounds at that time shall be disregarded for the purposes of this section.

(3), (4) ★ ★ ★ ★ ★

7   Jurisdiction of Privy Council as to disqualification

(1) Any person who claims that a person purporting to be a member of the House of Commons is disqualified by this Act, or has been so disqualified at any time since his (election, may apply to Her Majesty in Council, in accordance with such rules as Her Majesty in Council may prescribe, for a declaration to that effect.

(2) Section 3 of the Judicial Committee Act 1833 (reference to the Judicial Committee of the Privy Council of appeals to Her Majesty in Council) shall apply to any application under this section as it applies to an appeal to Her Majesty in Council from a court.

(3)–(5) ★ ★ ★ ★ ★

8, 9 ★ ★ ★ ★ ★

10 ...

★ ★ ★ ★ ★

Section 2   SCHEDULE 2
                              MINISTERIAL OFFICE

Prime Minister and First Lord of the Treasury.
Lord President of the Council.
Lord Privy Seal.
Chancellor of the Duchy of Lancaster.
Paymaster General.

President of the Board of Trade.
Secretary of State.
Chancellor of the Exchequer.
Minister of Agriculture, Fisheries and Food.
Minister of State.
Chief Secretary to the Treasury.
Minister in charge of a public department of Her Majesty's Government in the United
    Kingdom (if not within the other provisions of this Schedule).
Attorney General.
. . .
Solicitor General.
[Advocate General for Scotland.]
. . .
Parliamentary Secretary to the Treasury.
Financial Secretary to the Treasury.
Parliamentary Secretary in a Government Department other than the Treasury, or not in a
department.
Junior Lord of the Treasury.
Treasurer of Her Majesty's Household.
Comptroller of Her Majesty's Household.
Vice-Chamberlain of Her Majesty's Household.
Assistant Government Whip.

Ministerial and Other Salaries Act 1975
(1975, c. 27)

*An Act to consolidate the enactments relating to the salaries of Ministers and Opposition Leaders
and Chief Whips and to other matters connected therewith*   [8 May 1975]

Territorial extent: United Kingdom

1   Salaries
    (1) Subject to the provisions of this Act—
        (a) there shall be paid to the holder of any Ministerial office specified in Schedule 1 to
           this Act such salary as is provided for by that Schedule; and
        (b) there shall be paid to the Leaders and Whips of the Opposition such salaries as are
           provided for by Schedule 2 to this Act.
    (2) There shall be paid to the Lord Chancellor a salary (which shall be charged on and
paid out of the Consolidated Fund of the United Kingdom) at such rate as together with the
salary payable to him as Speaker of the House of Lords will amount to [[£2,500] a year more
than the salary payable to the Lord Chief Justice], . . .
    (3) There shall be paid to the Speaker of the House of Commons a salary (which shall be
charged on and paid out of the Consolidated Fund of the United Kingdom) of [£60,000] a
year; and on a dissolution of Parliament the Speaker of the House of Commons at the time of
the dissolution shall for this purpose be deemed to remain Speaker until a Speaker is chosen by
the New Parliament.
    (4) . . .
    (5) ★ ★ ★ ★ ★

1A, 1B ★ ★ ★ ★ ★

2   Opposition Leaders and Whips

(1) In this Act "Leader of the Opposition" means, in relation to either House of Parliament, that Member of that House who is for the time being the Leader in that House of the party in opposition to Her Majesty's Government having the greatest numerical strength in the House of Commons; and "Chief Opposition Whip" means, in relation to either House of Parliament, the person for the time being nominated as such by the Leader of the Opposition in that House; and "Assistant Opposition Whip", in relation to the House of Commons, means a person for the time being nominated as such, and to be paid as such, by the Leader of the Opposition in the House of Commons.

(2) If any doubt arises as to which is or was at any material time the party in opposition to Her Majesty's Government having the greatest numerical strength in the House of Commons, or as to who is or was at any material time the leader in that House of such a party, the question shall be decided for the purposes of this Act by the Speaker of the House of Commons, and his decision, certified in writing under his hand, shall be final and conclusive.

(3) If any doubt arises as to who is or was at any material time the Leader in the House of Lords of the said party, the question shall be decided for the purposes of this Act by the Lord Chancellor, and his decision, certified in writing under his hand, shall be final and conclusive.

3   ★ ★ ★ ★ ★

4   Interpretation

(1) In this Act—

"Junior Lord of the Treasury" means any Lord Commissioner of the Treasury other than the First Lord and the Chancellor of the Exchequer;

"Minister of State" and "Parliamentary Secretary" have the same meanings as in the House of Commons Disqualification Act 1975.

(2) ★ ★ ★ ★ ★

European Parliament Elections Act 1978
(1978, c. 10)

An Act to make provision for and in connection with the election of representatives to the Parliament of the European Communities, and to prevent any treaty providing for any increase in the powers of the Parliament from being ratified by the United Kingdom unless approved by Act of Parliament   [5 May 1978]

Territorial extent: United Kingdom

Note: This Act was originally entitled the European Assembly Elections Act. References to the Assembly should now be read as references to the Parliament: European Communities (Amendment) Act 1986, s. 3(1). The Act has been extensively amended also by the European Parliamentary Elections Act 1999.

1   Election of MEPs

This Act makes provision for the election in the United Kingdom of Members of the European Parliament ("MEPs").

2   Electoral regions and number of MEPs

(1) The United Kingdom shall be divided into electoral regions.

(2) England shall be divided into nine electoral regions.

(3) Scotland, Wales and Northern Ireland shall each constitute a single electoral region.

(4) The number of MEPs elected in the United Kingdom shall be 87, of whom–

    (a) 71 shall be elected for electoral regions in England,

    (b) 8 shall be elected for Scotland,

    (c) 5 shall be elected for Wales, and

    (d) 3 shall be elected for Northern Ireland.

(5) Schedule 2 (which sets out the electoral regions in England and makes provision for the number of MEPs to be elected for each region) shall have effect.

[3   Electoral system in Great Britain

(1) The system of election in an electoral region in Great Britain shall be a regional list system complying with the following conditions.

(2) A vote may be cast for a registered party, or an individual candidate, named on the ballot paper.

(3) The first seat shall be allocated to the party or individual candidate with the greatest number of votes.

(4) The second and subsequent seats shall be allocated in the same way, except that the number of votes given to a party to which one or more seats have already been allocated shall be divided by the number of seats allocated plus one.

(5) In allocating the second or any subsequent seat there shall be disregarded any votes given to—

    (a) a party to which there has already been allocated a number of seats equal to the number of names on the party's list of candidates, and

    (b) an individual candidate to whom a seat has already been allocated.

(6) Seats allocated to a party shall be filled by the persons named on the party's list of candidates in the order in which they appear on that list.

(7) For the purposes of subsections (3) and (4) fractions shall be taken into account.

(8) In this section—

    (a) "registered party" means a party registered under any enactment providing for the registration of political parties;

    (b) A reference to a party's "list of candidates" is a reference to the list submitted in accordance with regulations made as required by paragraph 2(3B) of Schedule 1.

3A   Electoral system in Northern Ireland

The system of election in Northern Ireland shall be a single transferable vote system under which–

    (a) a vote is capable of being given so as to indicate the voter's order of preference for the candidates, and

    (b) a vote is capable of being transferred to the next choice—

        (i)   when the vote is not required to give a prior choice the necessary quota of votes, or

        (ii) when, owing to the deficiency in the number of votes given for a prior choice, that choice is eliminated from the list of candidates.]

3B, 3C, 4, 5   ★ ★ ★ ★ ★

6   Parliamentary approval of treaties increasing Parliament's powers

(1) No treaty which provides for any increase in the powers of the Parliament shall be ratified by the United Kingdom unless it has been approved by an Act of Parliament.

(2) In this section "treaty" includes any international agreement, and any protocol or annex to a treaty or international agreement.

Note: Section 3(4) of the European Communities (Amendment) Act 1986 provides that for the purposes of this section the Single European Act is approved. Equivalent provisions are made by section 1 of the European Communities (Amendment) Act 1993, section 2 of the European Union (Accessions) Act 1994 and s. 2 of the European Communities (Amendment) Act 1998.

★ ★ ★ ★ ★

Highways Act 1980
(1980, c. 66)

An Act to consolidate the Highways Acts 1959 to 1971 and related enactments with amendments to give effect to recommendations of the Law Commission   [13 November 1980]

Territorial extent: England and Wales

Obstruction of highways and streets

137   Penalty for wilful obstruction
    (1) If a person, without lawful authority or excuse, in any way wilfully obstructs the free passage along a highway he is guilty of an offence and liable to a fine not exceeding [level 3 on the standard scale].
    (2) . . .

Magistrates' Courts Act 1980
(1980, c. 43)

An Act to consolidate certain enactments relating to the jurisdiction of, and the practice and procedure before, magistrates' courts and the functions of justices' clerks, and to matters connected therewith, with amendments to give effect to recommendations of the Law Commission
                                                                              [1 August 1980]

Territorial extent: England and Wales

PART I   CRIMINAL JURISDICTION AND PROCEDURE

Jurisdiction to issue process and deal with charges

1   Issue of summons to accused or warrant for his arrest
    (1) Upon an information being laid before a justice of the peace for an area to which this section applies that any person has, or is suspected of having, committed an offence, the justice may, in any of the events mentioned in subsection (2) below, but subject to subsections (3) to (5) below,—
        (a) issue a summons directed to that person requiring him to appear before a magistrates' court for the area to answer to the information, or
        (b) issue a warrant to arrest that person and bring him before a magistrates' court for the area or such magistrates' court as is provided in subsection (5) below.
    (2) ★ ★ ★ ★ ★
    (3) No warrant shall be issued under this section unless the information is in writing and substantiated on oath.
    (4) No warrant shall be issued under this section for the arrest of any person who has attained the age of 18 years unless—
        (a) the offence to which the warrant relates is an indictable offence or is punishable with imprisonment, or
        (b) the person's address is not sufficiently established for a summons to be served on him.
    (5)–(7) ★ ★ ★ ★ ★

(8) The areas to which this section applies are [any commission area in England, or preserved county in Wales].

★ ★ ★ ★ ★

[6   Application for dismissal

(1) Where a notice of the prosecution case has been given in respect of proceedings before a magistrates' court, the accused, or any of them, may, within the prescribed period, or within such further period as the court may on application allow, make an application in writing to the court ("an application for dismissal") for the charge or, as the case may be, any of the charges to be dismissed.]

(2)–(14) ★ ★ ★ ★ ★

★ ★ ★ ★ ★

[8A   Reporting restrictions

(1) Except as provided in this section, it shall not be lawful—

    (a) to publish in Great Britain a written report of an application for dismissal to a magistrates' court under section 6 above; or

    (b) to include in a relevant programme for reception in Great Britain a report of such an application,

if (in either case) the report contains any matter other than matter permitted by this section.

(2) A magistrates' court may, on an application for the purpose made with reference to proceedings on an application for dismissal, order that subsection (1) above shall not apply to reports of those proceedings.

(3) Where in the case of two or more accused one of them objects to the making of an order under subsection (2) above, the magistrates' court shall make the order if, and only if, the court is satisfied, after hearing the representations of the accused, that it is in the interests of justice to do so.

(4) An order under subsection (2) above shall not apply to reports of proceedings under subsection (3) above, but any decision of the court to make or not to make such an order may be contained in reports published or included in a relevant programme before the time authorised by subsection (5) below.

(5) It shall not be unlawful under this section to publish or include in a relevant programme a report of an application for dismissal containing any matter other than matter permitted by subsection (9) below where the application is successful.

(6) Where—

    (a) two or more persons are charged in the same proceedings; and

    (b) applications for dismissal are made by more than one of them, subsection (5) above shall have effect as if for the words "the application is" there were substituted the words "all the applications are".

(7) It shall not be unlawful under this section to publish or include in a relevant programme a report of an unsuccessful application for dismissal at the conclusion of the trial of the person charged, or of the last of the persons charged to be tried.

(8) Where, at any time during its consideration of an application for dismissal, the court proceeds to try summarily the case of one or more of the accused under section 25(3) or (7) below, while dismissing the application for dismissal of the other accused or one or more of the other accused, it shall not be unlawful under this section to publish or include in a relevant programme as part of a report of the summary trial, after the court determines to proceed as aforesaid, a report of so much of the application for dismissal containing any matter other than matter permitted by subsection (9) below as takes place before the determination.

(9) The following matters may be published or included in a relevant programme without

an order under subsection (2) above before the time authorised by subsection (5) or (7) above, that is to say—

    (a) the identity of the magistrates' court and the names of the justices composing it;

    (b) the names, age, home address and occupation of the accused;

    (c) the offence, or offences, or a summary of them, with which the accused is or are charged;

    (d) the names of legal representatives engaged in the proceedings;

    (e) where the proceedings are adjourned, the date and place to which they are adjourned;

    (f) the arrangements as to bail;

    (g) whether legal aid was granted to the accused or any of the accused.

(10) The addresses that may be published or included in a relevant programme under subsection (9) are addresses—

    (a) at any relevant time; and

    (b) at the time of their publication or inclusion in a relevant programme.

(11) If a report is published or included in a relevant programme in contravention of this section, the following persons, that is to say–

    (a) in the case of a publication of a written report as part of a newspaper or periodical, any proprietor, editor or publisher of the newspaper or periodical;

    (b) in the case of a publication of a written report otherwise than as part of a newspaper or periodical, the person who publishes it;

    (c) in the case of the inclusion of a report in a relevant programme, any body corporate which is engaged in providing the service in which the programme is included and any person having functions in relation to the programme corresponding to those of the editor of a newspaper,

shall be liable on summary conviction to a fine not exceeding level 5 on the standard scale.

(12) Proceedings for an offence under this section shall not, in England and Wales, be instituted otherwise than by or with the consent of the Attorney General.

(13) Subsection (1) above shall be in addition to, and not in derogation from, the provisions of any other enactment with respect to the publication of reports of court proceedings.

(14) In this section—

"publish", in relation to a report, means publish the report, either by itself or as part of a newspaper or periodical, for distribution to the public;

"relevant programme" means a programme included in a programme service (within the meaning of the Broadcasting Act 1990); and

"relevant time" means a time when events giving rise to the charges to which the proceedings relate occurred.]

★ ★ ★ ★ ★

PART VI   RECOGNIZANCES

Recognizances to keep the peace or be of good behaviour

115   Binding over to keep the peace or be of good behaviour

(1) The power of a magistrates' court on the complaint of any person to adjudge any other person to enter into a recognizance, with or without sureties, to keep the peace or to be of good behaviour towards the complaint shall be exercised by order on complaint.

(2) ★ ★ ★ ★ ★

(3) If any person ordered by a magistrates' court under subsection (1) above to enter into a recognizance, with or without sureties, to keep the peace or to be of good behaviour fails to

comply with the order, the court may commit him to custody for a period not exceeding 6 months or until he sooner complies with the order.

★ ★ ★ ★ ★

British Nationality Act 1981
(1981, c. 61)

An Act to make fresh provision about citizenship and nationality, and to amend the Immigration Act 1971 as regards the right of abode in the United Kingdom   [30 October 1981]

Territorial extent: United Kingdom

Note: A new form of British Nationality, British National (Overseas), has been created by the Hong Kong (British Nationality) Order 1986 (SI 1986 No. 948) with effect from 1 July 1987. See the text of the Order for details. Amendments to this Act made by the Order consequent on this new category are incorporated in the text.

PART I   BRITISH CITIZENSHIP

Acquisition after commencement

1   Acquisition by birth or adoption
(1) A person born in the United Kingdom after commencement [, or in a qualifying territory on or after the appointed day] shall be a British citizen if at the time of the birth his father or mother is—
  (a) a British citizen; or
  (b) settled in the United Kingdom [or that territory].
(2) A new-born infant who, after commencement, is found abandoned in the United Kingdom [, or on or after the appointed day is found abandoned in a qualifying territory] shall, unless the contrary is shown, be deemed for the purposes of subsection (1)—
  (a) to have been born in the United Kingdom after commencement [or in that territory on or after the appointed day]; and
  (b) to have been born to a parent who at the time of the birth was a British citizen or settled in the United Kingdom [or that territory].
(3) A person born in the United Kingdom after commencement who is not a British citizen by virtue of subsection (1) or (2) shall be entitled to be registered as a British citizen if, while he is a minor—
  (a) his father or mother becomes a British citizen or becomes settled in the United Kingdom; and
  (b) an application is made for his registration as a British citizen.
(4) A person born in the United Kingdom after commencement who is not a British citizen by virtue of subsection (1) or (2) shall be entitled, on an application for his registration as a British citizen made at any time after he has attained the age of ten years, to be registered as such a citizen if, as regards each of the first ten years of that person's life, the number of days on which he was absent from the United Kingdom in that year does not exceed 90.
  [(5) Where—
  (a) any court in the United Kingdom [or, on or after the appointed day, any court in a qualifying territory] makes an order authorising the adoption of a minor who is not a British citizen; or
  (b) a minor who is not a British citizen is adopted under a Convention adoption,

that minor shall, if the requirements of subsection (5A) are met, be a British citizen as from the date on which the order is made or the Convention adoption is effected, as the case may be.

(5A) Those requirements are that on the date on which the order is made or the Convention adoption is effected (as the case may be)—

(a) the adopter or, in the case of a joint adoption, one of the adopters is a British citizen; and

(b) in a case within subsection (5)(b), the adopter or, in the case of a joint adoption, both of the adopters are habitually resident in the United Kingdom.]

(6) Where an order [or a Convention adoption] in consequence of which any person became a British citizen by virtue of subsection (5) ceases to have effect, whether on annulment or otherwise, the cesser shall not affect the status of that person as a British citizen.

(7) If in the special circumstances of any particular case the Secretary of State thinks fit, he may for the purposes of subsection (4) treat the person to whom the application relates as fulfilling the requirement specified in that subsection although, as regards any one or more of the first ten years of that person's life, the number of days on which he was absent from the United Kingdom in that year or each of the years in question exceeds 90.

(8) In this section and elsewhere in this Act "settled" has the meaning given by section 50 [and in this section "Convention adoption" has the same meaning as in the Adoption Act 1976 and the Adoption (Scotland) Act 1978].

2   Acquisition by descent

(1) A person born outside the United Kingdom [and the qualifying territories] after commencement shall be a British citizen if at the time of the birth his father or mother—

(a) is a British citizen otherwise than by descent; or

(b) is a British citizen and is serving outside the United Kingdom [and the qualifying territories] in service to which this paragraph applies, his or her recruitment for that service having taken place in the United Kingdom [or a qualifying territory]; or

(c) is a British citizen and is serving outside the United Kingdom [and the qualifying territories] in service under a Community institution, his or her recruitment for that service having taken place in a country which at the time of the recruitment was a member of the Communities.

(2) Paragraph (b) of subsection (1) applies to—

(a) Crown service under the government of the United Kingdom [or of a qualifying territory]; and

(b) service of any description for the time being designated under subsection (3).

(3) For the purposes of this section the Secretary of State may by order made by statutory instrument designate any description of service which he considers to be closely associated with the activities outside the United Kingdom [and the qualifying territories] of Her Majesty's government in the United Kingdom [or in a qualifying territory].

(4) Any order made under subsection (3) shall be subject to annulment in pursuance of a resolution of either House of Parliament.

3   Acquisition by registration: minors

(1) If while a person is a minor an application is made for his registration as a British citizen, the Secretary of State may, if he thinks fit, cause him to be registered as such a citizen.

(2) A person born outside the United Kingdom [and the qualifying territories] shall be entitled, on an application for his registration as a British citizen made within the period of twelve months from the date of the birth, to be registered as such a citizen if the requirements specified in subsection (3) or, in the case of a person born stateless, the requirements specified in paragraphs (a) and (b) of that subsection, are fulfilled in the case of either that person's father or his mother ("the parent in question").

(3) The requirements referred to in subsection (2) are—

(a) that the parent in question was a British citizen by descent at the time of the birth; and

(b) that the father or mother of the parent in question—

(i) was a British citizen otherwise than by descent at the time of the birth of the parent in question; or

(ii) became a British citizen otherwise than by descent at commencement, or would have become such a citizen otherwise than by descent at commencement but for his or her death; and

(c) that, as regards some period of three years ending with a date not later than that date of the birth—

(i) the parent in question was in the United Kingdom [or a qualifying territory] at the beginning of that period; and

(ii) the number of days on which the parent in question was absent from the United Kingdom [and the qualifying territories] in the period does not exceed 270.

(4) If in the special circumstances of any particular case the Secretary of State thinks fit, he may treat subsection (2) as if the reference to twelve months were a reference to six years.

(5) A person born outside the United Kingdom [and the qualifying territories] shall be entitled, on an application for his registration as a British citizen made while he is a minor, to be registered as such a citizen if the following requirements are satisfied, namely—

(a) that at the time of that person's birth his father or mother was a British citizen by descent; and

(b) subject to subsection (6), that that person and his father and mother were in the United Kingdom [or a qualifying territory] at the beginning of the period of three years ending with the date of the application and that, in the case of each of them, the number of days on which the person in question was absent from the United Kingdom [and the qualifying territories] in that period does not exceed 270; and

(c) subject to subsection (6), that the consent of his father and mother to the registration has been signified in the prescribed manner.

(6) In the case of an application under subsection (5) of the registration of a person as a British citizen—

(a) if his father or mother died, or their marriage was terminated, on or before the date of the application, or his father and mother were legally separated on that date, the references to his father and mother in paragraph (b) of that subsection shall be read either as references to his father or as references to his mother;

(b) if his father or mother died on or before that date, the reference to his father and mother in paragraph (c) of that subsection shall be read as a reference to either of them; and

(c) if he was born illegitimate, all those references shall be read as references to his mother.

4   Acquisition by registration: British [overseas territories] citizens etc.

(1) This section applies to any person who is a British [overseas territories] citizen, [a British National [(Overseas),] a British Overseas citizen, a British subject under this Act or a British protected person.

(2) A person to whom this section applies shall be entitled, on an application for his registration as a British citizen, to be registered as such a citizen if the following requirements are satisfied in the case of that person, namely—

(a) subject to subsection (3), that he was in the United Kingdom at the beginning of the period of five years ending with the date of the application and that the numberof days on which he was absent from the United Kingdom in that period does not exceed 450; and

(b) that the number of days on which he was absent from the United Kingdom in the period of twelve months so ending does not exceed 90; and

(c) that he was not at any time in the period of twelve months so ending subject under the immigration laws to any restriction on the period for which he might remain in the United Kingdom; and

(d) that he was not at any time in the period of five years so ending in the United Kingdom in breach of the immigration laws.

(3) So much of subsection (2)(a) as requires the person in question to have been in the United Kingdom at the beginning of the period there mentioned shall not apply in relation to a person who was settled in the United Kingdom immediately before commencement.

(4) If in the special circumstances of any particular case the Secretary of State thinks fit, he may for the purposes of subsection (2) do all or any of the following things, namely—

(a) treat the person to whom the application relates as fulfilling the requirement specified in subsection (2)(a) or subsection (2)(b), or both, although the number of days on which he was absent from the United Kingdom in the period there mentioned exceeds the number there mentioned;

(b) disregard any such restriction as is mentioned in subsection (2)(c), not being a restriction to which that person was subject on the date of the application;

(c) treat that person as fulfilling the requirement specified in subsection (2)(d) although he was in the United Kingdom in breach of the immigration laws in the period there mentioned.

(5) If, on an application for registration as a British citizen made by a person to whom this section applies, the Secretary of State is satisfied that the applicant has at any time served in service to which this subsection applies, he may, if he thinks fit in the special circumstances of the applicant's case, cause him to be registered as such a citizen.

(6) Subsection (5) applies to—

(a) Crown service under the government of [a British overseas territory]; and

(b) paid or unpaid service (not falling within paragraph (a)) as a member of any body established by law in [a British overseas territory] members of which are appointed by or on behalf of the Crown.

[4A   Acquisition by registration: further provision for British overseas territories citizens

(1) If an application is made to register as a British citizen a person who is a British overseas territories citizen, the Secretary of State may if he thinks fit cause the person to be so registered.

(2) Subsection (1) does not apply in the case of a British overseas territories citizen who—

(a) is such a citizen by virtue only of a connection with the Sovereign Base Areas of Akrotiri and Dhekelia; or

(b) has ceased to be a British citizen as a result of a declaration of renunciation.]

5   Acquisition by registration: nationals for purposes of the Community treaties

A [British overseas territories citizen] who falls to be treated as a national of the United Kingdom for the purposes of the Community Treaties shall be entitled to be registered as a British citizen if an application is made for his registration as such a citizen.

6   Acquisition by naturalisation

(1) If, on an application for naturalisation as a British citizen made by a person of full age and capacity, the Secretary of State is satisfied that the applicant fulfils the requirements of Schedule 1 for naturalisation as such a citizen under this subsection, he may, if he thinks fit, grant to him a certificate of naturalisation as such a citizen.

(2) If, on an application for naturalisation as a British citizen made by a person of full age and capacity who on the date of the application is married to a British citizen, the Secretary of

State is satisfied that the applicant fulfils the requirements of Schedule 1 for naturalisation as such a citizen under this subsection, he may, if he thinks fit, grant to him a certificate of naturalisation as such a citizen.

7–10 ★ ★ ★ ★ ★

Acquisition at commencement

11 Citizens of UK and Colonies who are to become British citizens at commencement

(1) Subject to subsection (2), a person who immediately before commencement—

(a) was a citizen of the United Kingdom and Colonies; and

(b) had the right of abode in the United Kingdom under the Immigration Act 1971 as then in force,

shall at commencement become a British citizen.

(2) A person who was registered as a citizen of the United Kingdom and Colonies under section 1 of the British Nationality (No 2) Act 1964 (stateless persons) on the ground mentioned in subsection (1)(a) of that section (namely that his mother was a citizen of the United Kingdom and Colonies at the time when he was born) shall not become a British citizen under subsection (1) unless—

(a) his mother becomes a British citizen under subsection (1) or would have done so but for her death; or

(b) immediately before commencement he had the right of abode in the United Kingdom by virtue of section 2(1)(c) of the Immigration Act 1971 as then in force (settlement in United Kingdom, combined with five or more years' ordinary residence there as a citizen of the United Kingdom and Colonies).

(3) ★ ★ ★ ★ ★

Renunciation and resumption

12 Renunciation

(1) If any British citizen of full age and capacity makes in the prescribed manner a declaration of renunciation of British citizenship, then, subject to subsection (3) and (4), the Secretary of State shall cause the declaration to be registered.

(2) On the registration of a declaration made in pursuance of this section the person who made it shall cease to be a British citizen.

(3) A declaration made by a person in pursuance of this section shall not be registered unless the Secretary of State is satisfied that the person who made it will after the registration have or acquire some citizenship or nationality other than British citizenship; and if that person does not have any such citizenship or nationality on the date of registration and does not acquire some such citizenship or nationality within six months from that date, he shall be, and be deemed to have remained, a British citizen notwithstanding the registration.

(4) The Secretary of State may withhold registration of any declaration made in pursuance of this section if it is made during any war in which Her Majesty may be engaged in right of Her Majesty's government in the United Kingdom.

(5) For the purposes of this section any person who has been married shall be deemed to be of full age.

13, 14 ★ ★ ★ ★ ★

PART II   BRITISH [OVERSEAS TERRITORIES] CITIZENSHIP

Acquisition after commencement

15   Acquisition by birth or adoption

(1) A person born in a [British overseas territory] after commencement shall be a [British overseas territories citizen] if at the time of the birth his father or mother is—

    (a) a [British overseas territories citizen]; or

    (b) settled in a [British overseas territory].

(2) A new-born infant who, after commencement, is found abandoned in a British overseas territory shall, unless the contrary is shown, be deemed for the purposes of subsection (1)—

    (a) to have been born in that territory after commencement; and

    (b) to have been born to a parent who at the time of the birth was a [British overseas territories citizen] or settled in a [British overseas territory].

(3) A person born in a [British overseas territory] after commencement who is not a [British overseas territories citizen] by virtue of subsection (1) or (2) shall be entitled to be registered as such a citizen if, while he is a minor—

    (a) his father or mother becomes such a citizen or becomes settled in a [British overseas territory]; and

    (b) an application is made for his registration as such a citizen.

(4) A person born in a [British overseas territory] after commencement who is not a [British overseas territories citizen] by virtue of subsection (1) or (2) shall be entitled, on an application for registration as a [British overseas territories citizen] made at any time after he has attained the age of ten years, to be registered as such a citizen if, as regards each of the first ten years of that person's life, the number of days on which he was absent from the territory in that year does not exceed 90.

(5), (6) ★ ★ ★ ★ ★

(7) If in the special circumstances of any particular case the Secretary of State thinks fit, he may for the purposes of subsection (4) treat the person to whom the application relates as fulfilling the requirements specified in that subsection although, as regards any one or more of the first ten years of that person's life, the number of days on which he was absent from the [British overseas territory] there mentioned in that year or each of the years in question exceeds 90.

16   Acquisition by descent

(1) A person born outside the dependent territories after commencment shall be a [British overseas territories citizen] if at the time of the birth his father or mother—

    (a) is such a citizen otherwise than by descent; or

    (b) is such a citizen and is serving outside the [British overseas territories] in service to which this paragraph applies, his or her recruitment for that service having taken place in a [British overseas territory].

(2) Paragraph (b) of subsection (1) applies to—

    (a) Crown service under the government of a [British overseas territory]; and

    (b) service of any description for the time being designated under subsection (3).

(3) For the purposes of this section the Secretary of State may by order made by statutory instrument designate any description of service which he considers to be closely associated with the activities outside the [British overseas territories] of the government of any [British overseas territory].

(4) Any order made under subsection (3) shall be subject to annulment in pursuance of a resolution of either House of Parliament.

17–25 ★ ★ ★ ★ ★

PART III   BRITISH OVERSEAS CITIZENSHIP

26   Citizens of UK and Colonies who are to become British Overseas citizens at commencement

Any person who was a citizen of the United Kingdom and Colonies immediately before commencement and who does not at commencement become either a British citizen or a [British overseas territories citizen] shall at commencement become a British Overseas citizen.

27-35   ★ ★ ★ ★ ★

PART V   MISCELLANEOUS AND SUPPLEMENTARY

36   ★ ★ ★ ★ ★

37   Commonwealth citizenship

(1) Every person who—

    (a) under [the British Nationality Acts 1981 and 1983] [or the British Overseas Territories Act 2002] is a British citizen, a [British overseas territories citizen], [a British National (Overseas),] a British Overseas citizen or a British subject; or

    (b) under any enactment for the time being in force in any country mentioned in Schedule 3 is a citizen of that country,

shall have the status of a Commonwealth citizen.

(2) Her Majesty may by Order in Council amend Schedule 3 by the alteration of any entry, the removal of any entry, or the insertion of any additional entry.

(3) Any Order in Council made under this section shall be subject to annulment in pursuance of a resolution of either House of Parliament.

(4) After commencement no person shall have the status of a Commonwealth citizen or the status of a British subject otherwise than under this Act.

Note: Schedule 3 (not printed) lists those countries currently members of the Commonwealth.

38-39   ★ ★ ★ ★ ★

40   Deprivation of citizenship

(1) Subject to the provisions of this section, the Secretary of State may by order deprive any British citizen to whom the subsection applies of his British citizenship if the Secretary of State is satisfied that the registration or certificate of naturalisation by virtue of which he is such a citizen was obtained by means of fraud, false representation or the concealment of any material fact.

(2) Subsection (1) applies to any British citizen who—

    (a) became a British citizen after commencement by virtue of—

        (i) his registration as a British citizen under any provision of [the British Nationality Acts 1981 and 1983]; or

        (ii) a certificate of naturalisation granted to him under section 6; or

    (b) being immediately before commencement a citizen of the United Kingdom and Colonies by virtue of registration as such a citizen under any provision of the British Nationality Acts 1948 to 1964, became at commencement a British citizen; or

    (c) at any time before commencement became a British subject (within the meaning of that expression at that time), or a citizen of Eire or of the Republic of Ireland, by virtue of a certificate of naturalisation granted to him or in which his name was included.

(3) Subject to the provisions of this section, the Secretary of State may by order deprive any British citizen to whom this subsection applies of his British citizenship if the Secretary of State is satisfied that that citizen—

(a) has shown himself by act or speech to be disloyal or disaffected towards Her Majesty; or

(b) has, during any war in which Her Majesty was engaged, unlawfully traded or communicated with an enemy or been engaged in or associated with any business that was to his knowledge carried on in such a manner as to assist an enemy in that war; or

(c) has, within the period of five years from the relevant date, been sentenced in any country to imprisonment for a term of not less than twelve months.

(4) Subsection (3) applies to any British citizen who falls within paragraph (a) or (c) of subsection (2); and in subsection (3) "the relevant date", in relation to a British citizen to whom subsection (3) applies, means the date of the registration by virtue of which he is such a citizen or, as the case may be, the date of the grant of the certificate of naturalisation by virtue of which he is such a citizen.

(5) The Secretary of State—

(a) shall not deprive a person of British citizenship under this section unless he is satisfied that it is not conducive to the public good that that person should continue to be a British citizen; and

(b) shall not deprive a person of British citizenship under subsection (3) on the ground mentioned in paragraph (c) of that subsection if it appears to him that that person would thereupon become stateless.

(6) Before making an order under this section the Secretary of State shall give the person against whom the order is proposed to be made notice in writing informing him of the ground or grounds on which it is proposed to be made and of his right to an inquiry under this section.

(7) If the person against whom the order is proposed to be made applies in the prescribed manner for an inquiry, the Secretary of State shall, and in any other case the Secretary of State may, refer the case to a committee of inquiry consisting of a chairman, being a person possessing judicial experience, appointed by the Secretary of State and of such other members appointed by the Secrtetary of State as he thinks proper.

(8)–(10) ★ ★ ★ ★ ★

41 ★ ★ ★ ★ ★

42 Registration and naturalisation: general provisions

(1) Subject to subsection (2)—

(a) a person shall not be registered under any provision of this Act as a citizen of any description or as a British subject; and

(b) a certificate of naturalisation shall not be granted to a person under any provision of this Act,

unless—

(i) any fee payable by virtue of this Act in connection with the registration or as the case may be, the grant of the certificate has been paid; and

(ii) the person concerned has within the prescribed time taken an oath of allegiance in the form indicated in Schedule 5.

(2) So much of subsection (1) as requires the taking of an oath of allegiance shall not apply to a person who—

(a) is not of full age; or

(b) is already a British citizen, a [British overseas territories citizen], [a British National (Overseas),] a British Overseas citizen, a British subject, or a citizen of any country of which Her Majesty is Queen.

(3) Any provision of this Act which provides for a person to be entitled to registration as a citizen of any description or as a British subject shall have effect subject to the preceding provisions of this section.

(4) A person registered under any provision of this Act as a British citizen, or as a [British overseas territories citizen], [or as a British National (Overseas),] or as a British Overseas citizen, or as a British subject, shall be a citizen of that description or, as the case may be, [a British National (Overseas) or] a British subject as from the date on which he is so registered.

(5) A person to whom a certificate of naturalisation as a British citizen or as a [British overseas territories citizen] is granted under any provision of this Act shall be a citizen of that description as from the date on which the certificate is granted.

43 ★ ★ ★ ★ ★

44 Decisions involving exercise of discretion

(1) Any discretion vested by or under this Act in the Secretary of State, a Governor or a Lieutenant-Governor shall be exercised without regard to the race, colour or religion of any person who may be affected by its exercise.

(2) The Secretary of State, a Governor or a Lieutenant-Governor, as the case may be, shall not be required to assign any reason for the grant or refusal of any application under this Act the decision on which is at his discretion; and the decision of the Secretary of State or a Governor or Lieutenant-Governor on any such application shall not be subject to appeal to, or review in, any court.

(3) Nothing in this section affects the jurisdiction of any court to entertain proceedings of any derscription concerning the rights of any person under any provision of this Act.

45-46 ★ ★ ★ ★ ★

47 Legitimated children

(1) A person born out of wedlock and legitimated by the subsequent marriage of his parents shall, as from the date of the marriage, be treated for the purposes of this Act as if he had been born legitimate.

(2) A person shall be deemed for the purposes of this section to have been legitimated by the subsequent marriage of his parents if by the law of the place in which his father was domiciled at the time of the marriage the marriage operated immediately or subsequently to legitimate him, and not otherwise.

48 Posthumous children

Any reference in this Act to the status or descriptions of the father or mother of a person at the time of that person's birth shall, in relation to a person born after the death of his father or mother, be construed as a reference to the status or description of the parent in question at the time of that parent's death; and where that death occurred before, and the birth occurs after, commencement, the status or description which would have been applicable to the father or mother had he or she died after commencement shall be deemed to be the status or description applicable to him or her at the time of his or her death.

49 . . .

50 Interpretation

(1) In this Act, unless the context otherwise requires–

"the 1948 Act" means the British Nationality Act 1948:

"alien" means a person who is neither a Commonwealth citizen nor a British protected person nor a citizen of the Republic of Ireland;

★ ★ ★ ★ ★

"association" means an unincorporated body of persons;

["British National (Overseas)" means a person who is a British National (Overseas) under the Hong Kong (British Nationality) Order 1986, and "status of a British National (Overseas)" shall be construed accordingly;

"British Overseas citizen" includes a person who is a British Overseas citizen under the Hong Kong (British Nationality) Order 1986;]

["British overseas territory" means a territory mentioned in Schedule 6;]

"British protected person" means a person who is a member of any class of person declared to be British protected persons by an Order in Council for the time being in force under section 38 or is a British protected person by virtue of the Solomon Islands Act 1978;

★ ★ ★ ★ ★

"Crown service" means the service of the Crown, whether within Her Majesty's dominions or elsewhere;

"Crown service under the government of the United Kingdom" means Crown service under Her Majesty's government in the United Kingdom or under Her Majesty's government in Northern Ireland or under the Scottish Administration;

. . .

"enactment" includes an enactment comprised in Northern Ireland legislation;

"foreign country" means a country other than the United Kingdom, a [British overseas territory], a country mentioned in Schedule 3 and the Republic of Ireland;

★ ★ ★ ★ ★

"immigration laws"—

    (a) in relation to the United Kingdom, means the Immigration Act 1971 and any law for purposes similar to that Act which is for the time being or has at any time been in force in any part of the United Kingdom;

    (b) in relation to a [British overseas territory], means any law for purposes similar to the Immigration Act 1971 which is for the time being or has at any time been in force in that territory;

"the Islands" means the Channel Islands and the Isle of Man;

"minor" means a person who has not attained the age of eighteen years;

"prescribed" means prescribed by regulations made under section 41;

["qualifying territory" means a British Overseas Territory other than the Sovereign Base Areas of Akrotiri and Dhekelia.]

"settled" shall be construed in accordance with subsections (2) to (4);

"ship" includes a hovercraft;

★ ★ ★ ★ ★

"United Kingdom consulate" means the office of a consular officer of Her Majesty's government in the United Kingdom where a register of births is kept or, where there is no such office, such office as may be prescribed.

(2) Subject to subsection (3), references in this Act to a person being settled in the United Kingdom or in a [British overseas territory] are references to his being ordinarily resident in the United Kingdom or, as the case may be, in that territory without being subject under the immigration laws to any restriction on the period for which he may remain.

(3), (4) ★ ★ ★ ★ ★

(5) It is hereby declared that a person is not to be treated for the purpose of any provision of this Act as ordinarily resident in the United Kingdom or in a [British overseas territory] at a time when he is in the United Kingdom or, as the case may be, in that territory in breach of the immigration laws.

(6)–(8) ★ ★ ★ ★ ★

(9) For the purposes of this Act—

    (a) the relationship of mother and child shall be taken to exist between a woman and any child (legitimate or illegitimate) born to her; but

    (b) subject to section 47, the relationship of father and child shall be taken to exist only between a man and any legitimate child born to him;

and the expressions "mother", "father", "parent", "child" and "descended" shall be construed accordingly.

(10)–(13) ★ ★ ★ ★ ★

51–53 ★ ★ ★ ★ ★

Sections 6, 18 | SCHEDULE 1
REQUIREMENTS FOR NATURALISATION

Naturalisation as a British citizen under section 6(1)

1.—(1) Subject to paragraph 2, the requirements for naturalisation as a British citizen under section 6(1) are, in the case of any person who applies for it—

- (a) the requirements specified in sub-paragraph (2) of this paragraph, or the alternative requirement specified in sub-paragraph (3) of this paragraph; and
- (b) that he is of good character; and
- (c) that he has a sufficient knowledge of the English, Welsh or Scottish Gaelic language; and
- (d) that either–
  - (i) his intentions are such that, in the event of a certificate of naturalisation as a British citizen being granted to him, his home or (if he has more than one) his principal home will be in the United Kingdom; or
  - (ii) he intends, in the event of such a certificate being granted to him, to enter into, or continue in, Crown service under the government of the United Kingdom, or service under an international organisation of which the United Kingdom or Her Majesty's government therein is a member, or service in the employment of a company or association established in the United Kingdom.

(2) The requirements referred to in sub-paragraph (1)(a) of this paragraph are—

- (a) that the applicant was in the United Kingdom at the beginning of the period of five years ending with the date of the application, and that the number of days on which he was absent from the United Kingdom in that period does not exceed 450; and
- (b) that the number of days on which he was absent from the United Kingdom in the period of twelve months so ending does not exceed 90; and
- (c) that he was not at any time in the period of twelve months so ending subject under the immigration laws to any restriction on the period for which he might remain in the United Kingdom; and
- (d) that he was not at any time in the period of five years so ending in the United Kingdom in breach of the immigration laws.

(3) The alternative requirement referred to in sub-paragraph (1)(a) of this paragraph is that on the date of the application he is serving outside the United Kingdom in Crown service under the government of the United Kingdom.

2. ★ ★ ★ ★ ★

Naturalisation as a British citizen under section 6(2)

3. Subject to paragraph 4, the requirements for naturalisation as a British citizen under section 6(2) are, in the case of any person who applies for it—

- (a) that he was in the United Kingdom at the beginning of the period of three years ending with the date of the application, and that the number of days on which he was absent from the United Kingdom in that period does not exceed 270; and
- (b) that the number of days on which he was absent from the United Kingdom in the period of twelve months so ending does not exceed 90; and
- (c) that on the date of the application he was not subject under the immigration laws

to any restriction on the period for which he might remain in the United Kingdom; and

(d) that he was not at any time in the period of three years ending with the date of the application in the United Kingdom in breach of the immigration laws; and

(e) the requirement specified in paragraph 1(1)(b).

★ ★ ★ ★ ★

Contempt of Court Act 1981
(1981, c. 49)

An Act to amend the law relating to contempt of court and related matters   [27 July 1981]

Territorial extent: United Kingdom (ss. 1 – 6, 8 – 11, Sch. 1); England and Wales (ss. 12 – 14); Scotland (s. 15); England, Wales and Northern Ireland (s. 7). For additional provisions applying to Northern Ireland see Sch. 4.

Strict liability

1   The strict liability rule
In this Act "the strict liability rule" means the rule of law whereby conduct may be treated as a contempt of court as tending to interfere with the course of justice in particular legal proceedings regardless of intent to do so.

2   Limitation of scope of strict liability
(1) The strict liability rule applies only in relation to publications, and for this purpose "publication" includes any speech, writing, [programme included in a programme service] or other communication in whatever form, which is addressed to the public at large or any section of the public.

(2) The strict liability rule applies only to a publication which creates a substantial risk that the course of justice in the proceedings in question will be seriously impeded or prejudiced.

(3) The strict liability rule applies to a publication only if the proceedings in question are active within the meaning of this section at the time of the publication.

(4) Schedule 1 applies for determining the times at which proceedings are to be treated as active within the meaning of this section.

[(5) In this section, "programme service" has the same meaning as in the Broadcasting Act 1990.]

3   Defence of innocent publication or distribution
(1) A person is not guilty of contempt of court under the strict liability rule as the publisher of any matter to which that rule applies if at the time of publication (having taken all reasonable care) he does not know and has no reason to suspect that relevant proceedings are active.

(2) A person is not guilty of contempt of court under the strict liability rule as the distributor of a publication containing any such matter if at the time of distribution (having taken all reasonable care) he does not know that it contains such matter and has no reason to suspect that it is likely to do so.

(3) The burden of proof of any fact tending to establish a defence afforded by this section to any person lies upon that person.

(4) . . .

4   Contemporary reports of proceedings

(1) Subject to this section a person is not guilty of contempt of court under the strict liability rule in respect of a fair and accurate report of legal proceedings held in public, published contemporaneously and in good faith.

(2) In any such proceedings the court may, where it appears to be necessary for avoiding a substantial risk of prejudice to the administration of justice in those proceedings, or in any other proceedings pending or imminent, order that the publication of any report of the proceedings, or any part of the proceedings, be postponed for such period as the court thinks necessary for that purpose.

[(2A) Where in proceedings for any offence which is an administration of justice offence for the purposes of section 54 of the Criminal Procedure and Investigations Act 1996 (acquittal tainted by administration of justice offence) it appears to the court that there is a possibility that (by virtue of that section) proceedings may be taken against a person for an offence of which he has been acquitted, subsection (2) of this section shall apply as if those proceedings were pending or imminent.]

(3) ★ ★ ★ ★ ★

(4) . . .

5   Discussion of public affairs

A publication made as or as part of a discussion in good faith of public affairs or other matters of general public interest is not to be treated as a contempt of court under the strict liability rule if the risk of impediment or prejudice to particular legal proceedings is merely incidental to the discussion.

6   Savings

Nothing in the foregoing provisions of this Act—

    (a) prejudices any defence available at common law to a charge of contempt of court under the strict liability rule;

    (b) implies that any publication is punishable as contempt of court under that rule which would not be so punishable apart from those provisions;

    (c) restricts liability for contempt of court in respect of conduct intended to impede or prejudice the administration of justice.

7   Consent required for institution of proceedings

Proceedings for a contempt of court under the strict liability rule (other than Scottish proceedings) shall not be instituted except by or with the consent of the Attorney General or on the motion of a court having jurisdiction to deal with it.

Other aspects of law and procedure

8   Confidentiality of jury's deliberations

(1) Subject to subsection (2) below, it is a contempt of court to obtain, disclose or solicit any particulars of statements made, opinions expressed, arguments advanced or votes cast by members of a jury in the course of their deliberations in any legal proceedings.

(2) This section does not apply to any disclosure of any particulars—

    (a) in the proceedings in question for the purpose of enabling the jury to arrive at their verdict, or in connection with the delivery of that verdict, or

    (b) in evidence in any subsequent proceedings for an offence alleged to have been committed in relation to the jury in the first mentioned proceedings,

or to the publication of any particulars so disclosed.

(3) Proceedings for a contempt of court under this section (other than Scottish proceedings) shall not be instituted except by or with the consent of the attorney general or on the motion of a court having jurisdiction to deal with it.

9   Use of tape recorders

(1) Subject to subsection (4) below, it is a contempt of court–

   (a)   to use in court, or bring into court for use, any tape recorder or other instrument for recording sound, except with the leave of the court;

   (b)   to publish a recording of legal proceedings made by means of any such instrument, or any recording derived directly or indirectly from it, by playing it in the hearing of the public or any section of the public, or to dispose of it or any recording so derived, with a view to such publication;

   (c)   to use any such recording in contravention of any conditions of leave granted under paragraph (a).

(2) Leave under paragraph (a) of subsection (1) may be granted or refused at the discretion of the court, and if granted may be granted subject to such conditions as the court thinks proper with respect to the use of any recording made pursuant to the leave; and where leave has been granted the court may at the like discretion withdraw or amend it either generally or in relation to any particular part of the proceedings.

(3) Without prejudice to any other power to deal with an act of contempt under paragraph (a) of subsection (1), the court may order the instrument, or any recording made with it, or both, to be forfeited; and any object so forfeited shall (unless the court otherwise determines on application by a person appearing to be the owner) be sold or otherwise disposed of in such manner as the court may direct.

(4) This section does not apply to the making or use of sound recordings for purposes of official transcripts of proceedings.

10   Sources of information

No court may require a person to disclose, nor is any person guilty of contempt of court for refusing to disclose, the source of information contained in a publication for which he is responsible, unless it be established to the satisfaction of the court that disclosure is necessary in the interests of justice or national security or for the prevention of disorder or crime.

11   Publication of matters exempted from disclosure in court

In any case where a court (having power to do so) allows a name or other matter to be withheld from the public in proceedings before the court, the court may give such directions prohibiting the publication of that name or matter in connection with the proceedings as appear to the court to be necessary for the purpose of which it was so withheld.

12   Offences of contempt of magistrates' courts

(1) A magistrates' court has jurisdiction under this section to deal with any person who—

   (a)   wilfully insults the justice or justices, any witness before or officer of the court or any solicitor or counsel having business in the court, during his or their sitting or attendance in court or in going to or returning from the court; or

   (b)   wilfully interrupts the proceedings of the court or otherwise misbehaves in court.

(2) In any such case the court may order any officer of the court, or any constable, to take the offender into custody and detain him until the rising of the court; and the court may, if it thinks fit, commit the offender to custody for a specified period not exceeding one month or impose on him a fine not exceeding [£2,500], or both.

(2A) ★ ★ ★ ★ ★

(3) . . .

(4), (5) ★ ★ ★ ★ ★

13   . . .

Penalties for contempt and kindred offences

14   Proceedings in England and Wales

(1) In any case where a court has power to commit a person to prison for contempt of

court and (apart from this provision) no limitation applies to the period of committal, the committal shall (without prejudice to the power of the court to order his earlier discharge) be for a fixed term, and that term shall not on any occasion exceed two years in the case of committal by a superior court, or one month in the case of committal by an inferior court.

(2) In any case where an inferior court has power to fine a person for contempt of court and (apart from the provision) no limit applies to the amount of the fine, the fine shall not on any occasion exceed [£2,500].

(2A), (3), (4) ★ ★ ★ ★ ★

[(4A) For the purposes of the preceding provisions of this section a county court shall be treated as a superior court and not as an inferior court.]

(5) ★ ★ ★ ★ ★

15 Penalties for contempt of court in Scottish proceedings

(1) In Scottish proceedings, when a person is committed to prison for contempt of court the committal shall (without prejudice to the power of the court to order his earlier discharge) be for a fixed term.

(2) The maximum penalty which may be imposed by way of imprisonment or fine for contempt of court in Scottish proceedings shall be two years' imprisonment or a fine or both, except that—

    (a) where the contempt is dealt with by the sheriff in the course of or in connection with proceedings other than criminal proceedings on indictment, such penalty shall not exceed three months' imprisonment or a fine [of level 4 on the standard scale] or both; and

    (b) where the contempt is dealt with by the district court, such penalty shall not exceed sixty days' imprisonment or a fine of [level 4 on the standard scale] or both.

(3)–(5) ★ ★ ★ ★ ★

(6) . . .

16–21 ★ ★ ★ ★ ★

Section 2

SCHEDULE 1
TIMES WHEN PROCEEDINGS ARE ACTIVE FOR PURPOSES OF SECTION 2

Preliminary

1. In this Schedule "criminal proceedings" means proceedings against a person in respect of an offence, not being appellate proceedings or proceedings commenced by motion for committal or attachment in England and Wales or Northern Ireland; and "appellate proceedings" means proceedings on appeal from or for the review of the decision of a court in any proceedings.

2. Criminal, appellate and other proceedings are active within the meaning of section 2 at the times respectively prescribed by the following paragraphs of this Schedule; and in relation to proceedings in which more than one of the steps described in any of those paragraphs is taken, the reference in that paragraph is a reference to the first of those steps.

Criminal proceedings

3. Subject to the following provisions of this Schedule, criminal proceedings are active from the relevant initial step specified in paragraph 4 [or 4A] until concluded as described in paragraph 5.

4. The initial steps of criminal proceedings are:–

    (a) arrest without warrant;

    (b) the issue, or in Scotland the grant, of a warrant for arrest;

    (c) the issue of a summons to appear, or in Scotland the grant of a warrant to cite;

    (d) the service of an indictment or other document specifying the charge;

    (e) except in Scotland, oral charge.

[4A. Where as a result of an order under section 54 of the Criminal Procedure and Investigations Act 1996 (acquittal tainted by administration of justice offence) proceedings are brought against a person for an offence of which he has previously been acquitted, the initial step of the proceedings is a certification under subsection (2) of that section; and paragraph 4 has effect subject to this.]

    5. Criminal proceedings are concluded—

    (a) by acquittal or, as the case may be, by sentence;

    (b) by any other verdict, finding, order or decision which puts an end to the proceedings;

    (c) by discontinuance or by operation of law.

    6. The reference in paragraph 5(a) to sentence includes any order or decision consequent on conviction or finding of guilt which disposes of the case, either absolutely or subject to future events, and a deferment of sentence under [section 1 of the Powers of Criminal Courts (Sentencing) Act 2000], section 219 or 432 of the Criminal Procedure (Scotland) Act 1975 or Article 14 of the Treatment of Offenders (Northern Ireland) Order 1976.

    7. Proceedings are discontinued within the meaning of paragraph 5(c)—

    (a) in England and Wales or Northern Ireland, if the charge or summons is withdrawn or a *nolle prosequi* entered; .

    (b) in Scotland, if the proceedings are expressly abandoned by the prosecutor or are deserted *simpliciter*;

    (c) in the case of proceedings in England and Wales or Northern Ireland commenced by arrest without warrant, if the person arrested is released, otherwise than on bail, without having been charged.

    8.—10. ★ ★ ★ ★ ★

    11. Criminal proceedings against a person which become active on the issue or the grant of a warrant for his arrest cease to be active at the end of the period of twelve months beginning with the date of the warrant unless he has been arrested within that period, but become active again if he is subsequently arrested.

Other proceedings at first instance

    12. Proceedings other than criminal proceedings and appellate proceedings are active from the time when arrangements for the hearing are made or, if no such arrangements are previously made, from the time the hearing begins, until the proceedings are disposed of or discontinued or withdrawn; and for the purposes of this paragraph any motion or application made in or for the purposes of any proceedings, and any pre-trial review in the county court, is to be treated as a distinct proceeding.

    13. In England and Wales or Northern Ireland arrangements for the hearing of proceedings to which paragraph 12 applies are made within the meaning of that paragraph—

    (a) in the case of proceedings in the High Court for which provision is made by rules of court for setting down for trial, when the case is set down;

    (b) in the case of any proceedings, when a date for the trial or hearing is fixed.

    14. In Scotland arrangements for the hearing of proceedings to which paragraph 12 applies are made within the meaning of that paragraph—

    (a) in the case of an ordinary action in the Court of Session or in the sheriff court, when the record is closed;

    (b) in the case of a motion or application, when it is enrolled or made;

    (c) in any other case, when the date for a hearing is fixed or a hearing is allowed.

Appellate proceedings

15. Appellate proceedings are active from the time when they are commenced—
   (a) by application for leave to appeal or apply for review, or by notice of such an application;
   (b) by notice of appeal or of application for review;
   (c) by other originating process,
until disposed of or abandoned, discontinued or withdrawn.

16. Where, in appellate proceedings relating to criminal proceedings, the court—
   (a) remits the case to the court below; or
   (b) orders a new trial or a *venire de novo*, or in Scotland grants authority to bring a new prosecution,
any further or new proceedings which result shall be treated as active from the conclusion of the appellate proceedings.

★ ★ ★ ★ ★

Indecent Displays (Control) Act 1981
(1981, c. 42)

An Act to make fresh provision with respect to the public display of indecent matter; and for purposes connected therewith   [27 July 1981]

Territorial extent: England and Wales, Scotland

1 Indecent displays

(1) If any indecent matter is publicly displayed the person making the display and any person causing or permitting the display to be made shall be guilty of an offence.

(2) Any matter which is displayed in or so as to be visible from any public place shall, for the purposes of this section, be deemed to be publicly displayed.

(3) In subsection (2) above, "public place", in relation to the display of any matter, means any place to which the public have or are permitted to have access (whether on payment or otherwise) while that matter is displayed except—
   (a) a place to which the public are permitted to have access only on payment which is or includes payment for that display; or
   (b) a shop or any part of a shop to which the public can only gain access by passing beyond an adequate warning notice;
but the exclusions contained in paragraphs (a) and (b) above shall only apply where persons under the age of 18 years are not permitted to enter while the display in question is continuing.

(4) Nothing in this section applies in relation to any matter—
   [(a) included by any person in a television broadcasting service or other television programme service (within the meaning of Part I of the Broadcasting Act 1990);] or
   (b) included in the display of an art gallery or museum and visible only from within the gallery or museum; or
   (c) displayed by or with the authority of, and visible only from within a building occupied by, the Crown or any local authority; or
   (d) included in a performance of a play (within the meaning of the Theatres Act 1968); or
   [(e) included in a film exhibition as defined in the Cinemas Act 1985—

    (i) given in a place which as regards that exhibition is required to be licensed under section 1 of the Act or by virtue only of section 5, 7 or 8 of that Act is not required to be so licensed; or

    (ii) which is an exhibition to which section 6 of that Act applies given by an exempted organisation as defined by subsection (6) of that section.]

(5) In this section "matter" includes anything capable of being displayed, except that it does not include an actual human body or any part thereof; and in determining for the purpose of this section whether any displayed matter is indecent—

    (a) there shall be disregarded any part of that matter which is not exposed to view; and

    (b) account may be taken of the effect of juxtaposing one thing with another.

(6) A warning notice shall not be adequate for the purposes of this section unless it complies with the following requirements—

    (a) The warning notice must contain the following words, and no others—

"WARNING

Persons passing beyond this notice will find material on display which they may consider indecent. No admittance to persons under 18 years of age."

    (b) The word "WARNING" must appear as a heading.

    (c) No pictures or other matter shall appear on the notice.

    (d) The notice must be so situated that no one could reasonably gain access to the shop or part of the shop in question without being aware of the notice and it must be easily legible by any person gaining such access.

★ ★ ★ ★ ★

Supreme Court Act 1981
(1981, c. 54)

An Act to consolidate with amendments the Supreme Court of Judicature (Consolidation) Act 1925 and other enactments relating to the Supreme Court in England and Wales and the administration of justice therein; to repeal certain obsolete or unnecessary enactments so relating; to amend Part VIII of the Mental Health Act 1959, the Courts-Martial (Appeals) Act 1968, the Arbitration Act 1979 and the law relating to county courts; and for connected purposes   [28 July 1981]

Territorial extent: England and Wales

PART I   CONSTITUTION OF SUPREME COURT

The Supreme Court

1   The Supreme Court

(1) The Supreme Court of England and Wales shall consist of the Court of Appeal, the High Court of Justice and the Crown Court, each having such jurisdiction as is conferred on it by or under this or any other Act.

(2) The Lord Chancellor shall be president of the Supreme Court.

2, 3   ★ ★ ★ ★ ★

The High Court

4   The High Court

(1) The High Court shall consist of—

(a) the Lord Chancellor;

(b) the Lord Chief Justice;

(c) the President of the Family Division;

(d) the Vice-Chancellor;

[(dd) the Senior Presiding Judge;]

[(ddd) the vice-president of the Queen's Bench Division;] and

(e) not more than [98] puisne judges of that court.

(2) The puisne judges of the High Court shall be styled "Justices of the High Court".

(3) All the judges of the High Court shall, except where this Act expressly provides otherwise, have in all respects equal power, authority and jurisdiction.

(4)–(6) ★ ★ ★ ★ ★

5–9 ★ ★ ★ ★ ★

10 Appointment of judges of Supreme Court

(1) Whenever the office of Lord Chief Justice, Master of the Rolls, President of the Family Division or Vice-Chancellor is vacant, Her Majesty may by letters patent appoint a qualified person to that office.

(2) Subject to the limits on numbers for the time being imposed by sections 2(1) and 4(1), Her Majesty may from time to time by letters patent appoint qualified persons as Lords Justices of Appeal or as puisne judges of the High Court.

(3) No person shall be qualified for appointment—

(a) as Lord Chief Justice, Master of the Rolls, President of the Family Division or Vice-Chancellor, unless he is qualified for appointment as a Lord Justice of Appeal or is a judge of the Court of Appeal;

(b) as a Lord Justice of Appeal, [unless—

(i) he has a 10 year High Court qualification within the meaning of section 71 of the Courts and Legal Services Act 1990; or

(ii) he is a judge of the High Court;] or

(c) as a puisne judge of the High Court, [unless—

(i) he has a 10 year High Court qualification within the meaning of section 71of the Courts and Legal Services Act 1990; or

(ii) he is a Circuit Judge who has held that office for at least 2 years.]

(4) Every person appointed to an office mentioned in subsection (1) or as a Lord Justice of Appeal or puisne judge of the High Court shall, as soon as may be after his acceptance of office, take the oath of allegiance and the judicial oath, as set out in the Promissory Oaths Act 1868, in the presence of the Lord Chancellor.

11 Tenure of office of judges of Supreme Court

(1) This section applies to the office of any judge of the Supreme Court except the Lord Chancellor.

(2) A person appointed to an office to which this section applies shall vacate it on the day on which he attains the age of [seventy] years unless by virtue of this section he has ceased to hold it before then.

(3) A person appointed to an office to which this section applies shall hold that office during good behaviour, subject to a power of removal by Her Majesty on an address presented to Her by both Houses of Parliament.

(4)–(6) ★ ★ ★ ★ ★

(7) A person who holds an office to which this section applies may at any time resign it by giving the Lord Chancellor notice in writing to that effect.

(8) The Lord Chancellor, if satisfied by means of a medical certificate that a person holding an office to which this section applies—

(a) is disabled by permanent infirmity from the performance of the duties of his office; and

(b) is for the time being incapacitated from resigning his office, may, subject to sub-section (9), by instrument under his hand declare that person's office to have been vacated; and the instrument shall have the like effect for all purposes as if that person had on the date of the instrument resigned his office.

(9) A declaration under subsection (8) with respect to a person shall be of no effect unless it is made—

(a) in the case of any of the Lord Chief Justice, the Master of the Rolls, the President of the Family Division and the Vice-Chancellor, with the concurrence of two others of them;

(b) in the case of a Lord Justice of Appeal, with the concurrence of the Master of the Rolls;

(c) in the case of a puisne judge of any Division of the High Court, with the concurrence of the senior judge of that Division.

(10) ★ ★ ★ ★ ★

12   Salaries etc of judges of Supreme Court

(1) Subject to subsections (2) and (3), there shall be paid to judges of the Supreme Court, other than the Lord Chancellor, such salaries as may be determined by the Lord Chancellor with the concurrence of the Minister for the Civil Service.

(2) Until otherwise determined under this section, there shall be paid to the judges mentioned in subsection (1) the same salaries as at the commencement of this Act.

(3) Any salary payable under this section may be increased, but not reduced, by a determination or further determination under this section.

(4) . . .

(5)–(7) ★ ★ ★ ★ ★

13–18   ★ ★ ★ ★ ★

PART II   JURISDICTION THE HIGH COURT

General jurisdiction

19   General jurisdiction

(1) The High Court shall be a superior court of record.

(2) Subject to the provisions of this Act, there shall be exercisable by the High Court—

(a) all such jurisdiction (whether civil or criminal) as is conferred on it by this or any other Act; and

(b) all such other jurisdiction (whether civil or criminal) as was exercisable by it immediately before the commencment of this Act (including jurisdiction conferred on a judge of the High Court by any statutory provision).

(3), (4) ★ ★ ★ ★ ★

★ ★ ★ ★ ★

Other particular fields of jurisdiction

29   Orders of mandamus, prohibition and certiorari

(1) The High Court shall have jurisdiction to make orders of mandamus, prohibition and certiorari in those classes of cases in which it had power to do so immediately before the commencement of this Act.

(2) Every such order shall be final, subject to any right of appeal therefrom.

(3) In relation to the jurisdiction of the Crown Court, other than its jurisdiction in

matters relating to trial on indictment, the High Court shall have all such jurisdiction to make orders of mandamus, prohibition or certiorari as the High Court possesses in relation to the jurisdiction of an inferior court.

(4) The power of the High Court under any enactment to require justices of the peace or a judge or officer of a county court to do any act relating to the duties of their respective offices, or to require a magistrates' court to state a case for the opinion of the High Court, in any case where the High Court formerly had by virtue of any enactment jurisdiction to make a rule absolute, or an order, for any of those purposes, shall be exercisable by order of mandamus.

(5) In any enactment—

(a) references to a writ of mandamus, of prohibition or of certiorari shall be read as references to the corresponding order; and

(b) references to the issue or award of any such writ shall be read as references to the making of the corresponding order.

[(6) In subsection (3) the reference to the Crown Court's jurisdiction in matters relating to trial on indictment does not include its jurisdiction relating to orders under section 17 of the Access to Justice Act 1999.]

30 ★ ★ ★ ★ ★

31 **Application for judicial review**

(1) [Subject to subsection (3A)] application to the High Court for one or more of the following forms of relief, namely—

(a) an order of mandamus, prohibition or certiorari;

(b) a declaration or injunction under subsection (2); or

(c) an injunction under section 30 restraining a person not entitled to do so from acting in an office to which that section applies,

shall be made in accordance with rules of court by a procedure to be known as an application for judicial review.

(2) A declaration may be made or an injunction granted under this subsection in any case where an application for judicial review, seeking that relief, has been made and the High Court considers that, having regard to—

(a) the nature of the matters in respect of which relief may be granted by orders of mandamus, prohibition or certiorari;

(b) the nature of the persons and bodies against whom relief may be granted by such orders; and

(c) all the circumstances of the case, it would be just and convenient for the declaration to be made or for the injunction to be granted, as the case may be.

(3) No application for judicial review shall be made unless the leave of the High Court has been obtained in accordance with rules of court; and the court shall not grant leave to make such an application unless it considers that the applicant has a sufficient interest in the matter to which the application relates.

(3A) ★ ★ ★ ★ ★

(4) On an application for judicial review the High Court may award damages to the applicant if—

(a) he has joined with his application a claim for damages arising from any matter to which the application relates; and

(b) the court is satisfied that, if the claim had been made in an action begun by the applicant at the time of making his application, he would have been awarded damages.

(5) If, on an application for judicial review seeking an order of certiorari, the High Court quashes the decision to which the application relates, the High Court may remit the matter to the court, tribunal or authority concerned, with a direction to reconsider it and reach a decision in accordance with the findings of the High Court.

(6) Where the High Court considers that there has been undue delay in making an application for judicial review, the court may refuse to grant—
  (a) leave for the making of the application; or
  (b) any relief sought on the application, if it considers that the granting of the relief sought would be likely to cause substantial hardship to, or substantially prejudice the rights of, any person or would be detrimental to good administration.

(7) Subsection (6) is without prejudice to any enactment or rule of court which has the effect of limiting the time within which an application for judicial review may be made.

Note: The provisions of s. 31 are implemented by Part 54 of the Civil Procedure Rules 1998 (replacing Order 53 of the Rules of the Supreme Court), printed below.

★ ★ ★ ★ ★

Canada Act 1982
(1982, c. 11)

An Act to give effect to a request by the Senate and House of Commons of Canada
[29 March 1982]

Territorial extent: Canada

Whereas Canada has requested and consented to the enactment of an Act of the Parliament of the United Kingdom to give effect to the provisions hereinafter set forth and the Senate and the House of Commons of Canada in Parliament assembled have submitted an address to Her Majesty requesting that Her Majesty may graciously be pleased to cause a Bill to be laid before the Parliament of the United Kingdom for that purpose:

Be it therefore enacted by the Queen's Most Excellent Majesty, by and with the advice and consent of the Lords Spiritual and Temporal, and Commons, in this present Parliament assembled, and by the authority of the same, as follows:

1   Constitution Act, 1982 enacted
The Constitution Act, 1982 set out in Schedule B to this Act is hereby enacted for and shall have the force of law in Canada and shall come into force as provided in that Act.

2   Termination of power to legislate for Canada
No Act of the Parliament of the United Kingdom passed after the Constitution Act, 1982 comes into force shall extend to Canada as part of its law.

3   French version
So far as it is not contained in Schedule B, the French version of this Act is set out in Schedule A to this Act and has the same authority in Canada as the English version thereof.

4   Short title
This Act may be cited as the Canada Act 1982.

★ ★ ★ ★ ★

SCHEDULE B   CONSTITUTION ACT, 1982
PART I   CANADIAN CHARTER OF RIGHTS AND FREEDOMS

Whereas Canada is founded upon principles that recognize the supremacy of God and the rule of law:

Guarantee of Rights and Freedoms

1   Rights and freedoms in Canada

The *Canadian Charter of Rights and Freedoms* guarantees the rights and freedoms set out in it subject only to such reasonable limits prescribed by law as can be demonstrably justified in a free and democratic society.

Fundamental Freedoms

2   Fundamental freedoms

Everyone has the following fundamental freedoms:

    (a) freedom of conscience and religion;

    (b) freedom of thought, belief, opinion and expression, including freedom of the press and other media of communication;

    (c) freedom of peaceful assembly; and

    (d) freedom of association.

Democratic Rights

3   Democratic rights of citizens

Every citizen of Canada has the right to vote in an election of members of the House of Commons or of a legislative assembly and to be qualified for membership therein.

4   Maximum duration of legislative bodies

(1) No House of Commons and no legislative assembly shall continue for longer than five years from the date fixed for the return of the writs at a general election of its members.

Continuation in special circumstances

(2) In time of real or apprehended war, invasion or insurrection, a House of Commons may be continued by Parliament and a legislative assembly may be continued by the legislature beyond five years if such continuation is not opposed by the votes of more than one-third of the members of the House of Commons or the legislative assembly, as the case may be.

5   Annual sitting of legislative bodies

There shall be a sitting of Parliament and of each legislature at least once every twelve months.

Mobility Rights

6   Mobility of citizens

(1) Every citizen of Canada has the right to enter, remain in and leave Canada.

Rights to move and gain livelihood

(2) Every citizen of Canada and every person who has the status of a permanent resident of Canada has the right

    (a) to move to and take up residence in any province; and

    (b) to pursue the gaining of a livelihood in any province.

Limitation

(3) The rights specified in subsection (2) are subject to

    (a) any laws or practices of general application in force in a province other than those that discriminate among persons primarily on the basis of province of present or previous residence; and

    (b) any laws providing for reasonable residency requirements as a qualification for the receipt of publicly provided social services.

Affirmative action programs

(4) Subsections (2) and (3) do not preclude any law, program or activity that has as its object the amelioration in a province of conditions of individuals in that province who are socially or economically disadvantaged if the rate of employment in that province is below the rate of employment in Canada.

Legal Rights

7 Life, liberty and security of person

Everyone has the right to life, liberty and security of the person and the right not to be deprived thereof except in accordance with the principles of fundamental justice.

8 Search or seizure

Everyone has the right to be secure against unreasonable search or seizure.

9 Detention or imprisonment

Everyone has the right not to be arbitrarily detained or imprisoned.

10 Arrest or detention

Everyone has the right on arrest or detention

    (a) to be informed promptly of the reasons therefor;

    (b) to retain and instruct counsel without delay and to be informed of that right;

and

    (c) to have the validity of the detention determined by way of *habeas corpus* and to be released if the detention is not lawful.

11 Proceedings in criminal and penal matters

Any person charged with an offence has the right

    (a) to be informed without unreasonable delay of the specific offence;

    (b) to be tried within a reasonable time;

    (c) not to be compelled to be a witness in proceedings against that person in respect of the offence;

    (d) to be presumed innocent until proven guilty according to law in a fair and public hearing by an independent and impartial tribunal;

    (e) not to be denied reasonable bail without just cause;

    (f) except in the case of an offence under military law tried before a military tribunal, to the benefit of trial by jury where the maximum punishment for the offence is imprisonment for five years or a more severe punishment;

    (g) not to be found guilty on account of any act or omission unless, at the time of the act or omission, it constituted an offence under Canadian or international law or was criminal according to the general principles of law recognized by the community of nations;

    (h) if finally acquitted of the offence, not to be tried for it again and, if finally found guilty and punished for the offence, not to be tried or punished for it again; and

    (i) if found guilty of the offence and if the punishment for the offence has been varied between the time of commission and the time of sentencing, to the benefit of the lesser punishment.

12 Treatment or punishment

Everyone has the right not to be subjected to any cruel and unusual treatment or punishment.

13 Self-crimination

A witness who testifies in any proceedings has the right not to have any incriminating evidence so given used to incriminate that witness in any other proceedings, except in a prosecution for perjury or for the giving of contradictory evidence.

14 Interpreter

A party or witness in any proceedings who does not understand or speak the language in which the proceedings are conducted or who is deaf has the right to the assistance of an interpreter.

Equality Rights

15 Equality before and under law and equal protection and benefit of law

(1) Every individual is equal before and under the law and has the right to the equal protection and equal benefit of the law without discrimination and, in particular, without discrimination based on race, national or ethnic origin, colour, religion, sex, age or mental or physical disability.

Affirmative action programs

(2) Subsection (1) does not preclude any law, program or activity that has as its object the amelioration of conditions of disadvantaged individuals or groups including those that are disadvantaged because of race, national or ethnic origin, colour, religion, sex, age or mental or physical disability.

Official Languages of Canada

16 Official languages of Canada

(1) English and French are the official languages of Canada and have equality of status and equal rights and privileges as to their use in all institutions of the Parliament and government of Canada.

(2), (3) ★ ★ ★ ★ ★

17–23 ★ ★ ★ ★ ★

Enforcement

24 Enforcement of guaranteed rights and freedoms

(1) Anyone whose rights or freedoms, as guaranteed by this Charter, have been infringed or denied may apply to a court of competent jurisdiction to obtain such remedy as the court considers appropriate and just in the circumstances.

Exclusion of evidence bringing administration of justice into disrepute

(2) Where, in proceedings under subsection (1), a court concludes that evidence was obtained in a manner that infringed or denied any rights or freedoms guaranteed by this Charter, the evidence shall be excluded if it is established that, having regard to all the circumstances, the admission of it in the proceedings would bring the administration of justice into disrepute.

General

25 Aboriginal rights and freedoms not affected by Charter

The guarantee in this Charter of certain rights and freedoms shall not be construed so as to abrogate or derogate from any aboriginal, treaty or other rights or freedoms that pertain to the aboriginal peoples of Canada including

(a) any rights or freedoms that have been recognised by the Royal Proclamation of October 7, 1763; and

(b) any rights or freedoms that may be acquired by the aboriginal peoples of Canada by way of land claims settlement.

26 Other rights and freedoms not affected by Charter

The guarantee in this Charter of certain rights and freedoms shall not be construed as denying the existence of any other rights or freedoms that exist in Canada.

27   Multicultural heritage
This Charter shall be interpreted in a manner consistent with the preservation and enhancement of the multicultural heritage of Canadians.

28   Rights guaranteed equally to both sexes
Notwithstanding anything in this Charter, the rights and freedoms referred to in it are guaranteed equally to male and female persons.

29   Rights respecting certain schools preserved
Nothing in this Charter abrogates or derogates from any rights or privileges guaranteed by or under the Constitution of Canada in respect of denominational, separate or dissentient schools.

30   ★ ★ ★ ★ ★

31   Legislative powers not extended
Nothing in this Charter extends the legislative powers of any body or authority.

Application of Charter

32   Application of Charter
 (1) This Charter applies
  (a) to the Parliament and government of Canada in respect of all matters within the authority of Parliament including all matters relating to the Yukon Territory and Northwest Territories; and
  (b) to the legislature and government of each province in respect of all matters within the authority of the legislature of each province.

Exception
 (2) Notwithstanding subsection (1), section 15 shall not have effect until three years after this section comes into force.

33   Exceptions where express declaration
 (1) Parliament or the legislature of a province may expressly declare in an Act of Parliament or of the legislature, as the case may be, that the Act or a provision thereof shall operate notwithstanding a provision included in section 2 or sections 7 to 15 of this Charter.

Operation of exception
 (2) An Act or a provision of an Act in respect of which a declaration made under this section is in effect shall have such operation as it would have but for the provision of this Charter referred to in the declaration.

Five year limitation
 (3) A declaration made under subsection (1) shall cease to have effect five years after it comes into force or on such earlier date as may be specified in the declaration.

Re-enactment
 (4) Parliament or the legislature of a province may re-enact a declaration made under subsection (1).

Five year limitation
 (5) Subsection (3) applies in respect of a re-enactment made under subsection (4).

Citation

34   Citation
This Part may be cited as the *Canadian Charter of Rights and Freedoms*.

★ ★ ★ ★ ★

Note: Schedule A to this Act is a French language version of the Act, and Schedule B is also printed in English and French. Both texts have equal status.

Civic Government (Scotland) Act 1982
(1982, c. 45)

An Act to make provision as regards Scotland for the licensing and regulation of certain activities; for the preservation of public order and safety and the prevention of crime; for prohibiting the taking of and dealing with indecent photographs of children; as to certain powers of constables and others;
★ ★ ★ ★ ★   [28 October 1982]

Territorial extent: Scotland

PART V   PUBLIC PROCESSIONS

62   Notification of processions

(1) A person proposing to hold a procession in public shall give written notice of that proposal in accordance with subsections (2) and (3) below

    (a) to the [local authority] in whose area the procession is to be held, or if it is to be held in the areas of more than one such [authority], to each such [authority] [and

    [(aa) if the procession is to be held to any extent in a National Park, to the national park authority for the National Park;]

    (b) to the chief constable].

(2) Notice shall be given for the purposes of subsection (1) above by—

    (a) its being posted to the main office of the [local authority] [and (where subsection (1)(aa) above applies) of the national park authority,] [and to the chief constable] so that in the normal course of post it might be expected to arrive not later than 7 days before the date when the procession is to be held; or

    (b) its being delivered by hand to [those offices] not later than 7 days before that date.

(3) The notice to be given under subsection (1) above shall specify—

    (a) the date and time when the procession is to be held;

    (b) its route;

    (c) the number of persons likely to take part in it;

    (d) the arrangements for its control being made by the person proposing to hold it; and

    (e) the name and address of that person.

(4) A [local authority] may, on application in accordance with subsection (5) below by a person proposing to hold a procession in public in their area

    (a) made to them [and

    [(aa) if the procession is to be held to any extent in a National Park, intimated to the national park authority for the National Park,]

    (b) intimated to the chief constable,]

within the period of 7 days before the date when the procession is to be held, make an order dispensing with the requirements of subsection (2) above in relation to the time limits for the giving of notice of that proposal.

(5) An application under subsection (4) above shall specify the matters mentioned in subsection (3) above and, where an order has been made under the said subsection (4), the application for it shall be treated as notice duly given for the purposes of subsection (1) above.

(6)–(11) ★ ★ ★ ★ ★

(12) In this section and in sections 63 to 65 of this Act—

"procession in public" means a procession in a public place;

"chief constable" means, in relation to a [local authority], the chief constable of the police force for the area which comprises or includes the area of the [authority]; and

"public place" has the same meaning as in [Part II of the Public Order Act 1986].

63 Functions of [local authorities] in relation to processions

(1) The [local authority] may, after consulting the chief constable [and (where section 62(1)(aa) of this Act applies) the national park authority] in respect of a procession notice of which has been given or falls to be treated as having been given in accordance with section 62(1) of this Act, make an order—

    (i) prohibiting the holding of the procession; or

    (ii) imposing conditions on the holding of it.

(1A) ★ ★ ★ ★ ★

(2) The conditions which may be imposed under subsection (1) [or (1A)] above on the holding of a procession may include conditions—

    (a) as to the date, time and duration of the procession;

    (b) as to the route to be taken by it;

    (c) prohibiting its entry into any public place specified in the order.

(3) A [local authority] shall—

    (a) where notice of a proposal to hold a procession has been given or falls to be treated as having been given in accordance with section 62(1) [or (1A) above] of this Act, deliver at least 2 days before the date when, in terms of the notice, the procession is to be held, to the person who gave the notice—

        (i) where they have made an order under subsection (1) above, a copy of it and a written statement of the reasons for it; . . .

        (ii) where they decide not to make [an order under subsection (1) above or to revoke an order already made under subsection (1) or (1A) above], notification of that fact;

        [(iii) where they have under subsection (1A) above varied such an order, a copy of the order as varied and a written statement of the reasons for the variation; and]

    (b) where they have made an order under subsection (1) [or (1A)] above in relation to a proposal to hold a procession, make such arrangements as will ensure that persons who might take or are taking part in that procession are made aware of the fact that the order has been made [and, if the order has been varied under subsection (1A) above, that it has been so varied] and of its effect; [and

    (c) where they have revoked an order made under subsection (1) or (1A) above in relation to a proposal to hold a procession, make such arrangements as will ensure that persons who might take or are taking part in that procession are made aware of the fact that the order has been revoked.]

(4) The [local authority] shall comply with subsection (3) above—

    (a) as early as possible;

    (b) only in so far as it is reasonably practicable for them to do so.

64 Appeals against orders under section 63

(1) An appeal to the sheriff shall lie at the instance of a person who, in accordance with section 62 of this Act, has or falls to be treated as having given notice of a proposal to hold a procession in public [against—

    (a) an order made under section 63(1) or (1A) of this Act; or

    (b) a variation under section 63(1A) of this Act of an order made under section 63(1) or (1A), in relation to the procession.

(2) An appeal under this section shall be made by way of summary application and shall be lodged with the sheriff clerk within 14 days from the date on which the copy of the order and statement of reasons were received by the appellant.

(3) On good cause being shown, the sheriff may hear an appeal under this section notwithstanding that it was not lodged within the time mentioned in subsection (2) above.

(4) The sheriff may uphold an appeal under this section only if he considers that the [local authority] in arriving at their decision to make [or, as the case may be, to vary] the order—

(a) erred in law;
(b) based their decision on any incorrect material fact;
(c) exercised their discretion in an unreasonable manner; or
(d) otherwise acted beyond their powers.

(5)–(9) ★ ★ ★ ★ ★

65   Offences and enforcement

(1) Subject to subsection (3) below, a person who holds a procession in public—

(a) without—
(i) having given or being a person who is treated as having given notice in accordance with section 62 of this Act of his proposal to do so; and
(ii) there being in force in relation to the procession an exempting order under section 62(6) of this Act;
(b) in contravention of an order under section 63(1) [or (1A)] or 64(6)(a)(ii) of this Act prohibiting the holding of it;
(c) otherwise than in accordance with a condition imposed by an order under section 63(1) [or (1A)] or 64(6)(a)(ii) of this Act in relation to the procession; or
(d) otherwise than in accordance with the particulars of its date, time and route specified—
(i) in the notice given under section 62(1) to (3) of this Act; or
(ii) where an order has been made under subsection (4) of that section, in the application for the order,

except to the extent that a condition referred to in paragraph (c) above relates to its date, time or route, shall be guilty of an offence and liable, on summary conviction, to a fine not exceeding £500 or to imprisonment for a period not exceeding 3 months or to both.

(2) Subject to subsection (3) below, a person who takes part in a procession in public—

(a) in respect of which—
(i) notice has not been or is not treated as having been given in accordance with section 62 of this Act; and
(ii) there is not in force an exempting order under section 62(6) of this Act in relation to the procession;
(b) in relation to which an order has been made under section 63(1) [or (1A)] or 64(6)(a)(ii) of this Act prohibiting the holding of it;
(c) which is held otherwise than in accordance with a condition imposed by an order under section 63(1) [or (1A)] or 64(6)(a)(ii) of this Act in relation to the procession; or
(d) which is held otherwise than in accordance with the particulars of its date, time and route specified—
(i) in the notice given under section 62(1) to (3) of this Act; or
(ii) where an order has been made under subsection (4) of that section, in the application for the order

except to the extent that a condition referred to in paragraph (c) above relates to its date, time or route,

and refuses to desist when required to do so by a constable in uniform shall be guilty of an offence and liable, on summary conviction, to a fine not exceeding £200.

★ ★ ★ ★ ★

(4) Subject to subsection (5) below, a constable may arrest without warrant a person

whom he reasonably suspects of committing or having committed an offence under this section.

(5) A constable who is not in uniform shall produce his identification if required to do so by any person whom he is arresting under subsection (4) above.

66   Relationship of sections 62 to 65 with Public Order Act 1936
Sections 62 to 65 of this Act are subject to [Part II of the Public Order Act 1986]; and, without prejudice to that generality—

(a) an order under those sections, so far as relating to the same matters as those to which any directions given under section 12 of that Act relate, shall be subject to those directions . . . ; and

(b) anything done in conformity with any such directions . . . or omitted, in conformity therewith, to be done shall not be an offence under section 65 of this Act.

★ ★ ★ ★ ★

Representation of the People Act 1983
(1983, c. 2)

An Act to consolidate the Representation of the People Acts of 1949, 1969, 1977, 1978 and 1980, The Electoral Registers Acts of 1949 and 1953, the Elections (Welsh Forms) Act 1964, Part III of the Local Government Act 1972, sections 6 to 10 of the Local Government (Scotland) Act 1973, the Representation of the People (Armed Forces) Act 1976, the Returning Officers (Scotland) Act 1977, section 3 of the Representation of the People Act 1981, section 62 of and Schedule 2 to the Mental Health (Amendment) Act 1982, and connected provisions; and to repeal as obsolete the Representation of the People Act 1979 and other enactments related to the Representation of the People Acts [8 February 1983]

Territorial extent: United Kingdom

PART I   PARLIAMENTARY AND LOCAL GOVERNMENT FRANCHISE AND ITS EXERCISE

Parliamentary and local government franchise

[1   Parliamentary electors
(1) A person is entitled to vote as an elector at a parliamentary election in any constituency if on the date of the poll he—

(a) is registered in the register of parliamentary electors for that constituency;

(b) is not subject to any legal incapacity to vote (age apart);

(c) is either a Commonwealth citizen or a citizen of the Republic of Ireland; and

(d) is of voting age (that is, 18 years or over).

(2) A person is not entitled to vote as an elector—

(a) more than once in the same constituency at any parliamentary election; or

(b) in more than one constituency at a general election.]

★ ★ ★ ★ ★

75   Prohibition of expenses not authorised by election agent
[(1) No expenses shall, with a view to promoting or procuring the election of a candidate (or, in the case of an election of the London members of the London Assembly at an ordinary

election, a registered political party or candidates of that party) at an election, be incurred by any person other than the candidate. his election agent and persons authorised in writing by the election agent on account—

    (a) of holding public meetings or organising any public display; or

    (b) of issuing advertisements, circulars or publications; or

    (c) of otherwise presenting to the electors the candidate or his views or the extent or nature of his backing or disparaging another candidate, or

    (d) in the case of an election of the London members of the London Assembly at an ordinary election, of otherwise presenting to the electors the candidate's registered political party (if any) or the views of that party or the extent or nature of that party's backing or disparaging any other registered political party

but paragraph (c) or (d) of this subsection shall not—

    (i) restrict the publication of any matter relating to the election in a newspaper or other periodical or in a broadcast made by the British Broadcasting Corporation or or by Sianel Pedwar Cymru or in a programme included in any service licensed under Part I or III of the Broadcasting Act 1990 or Part I or II of the Broadcasting Act 1996;

    (ii) apply to any expenses incurred by any person which do not exceed in the aggregate the permitted sum (and are not incurred by that person as part of a concerted plan of action), or to expenses incurred by any person in travelling or in living away from home or similar personal expenses.]

[(1ZA) For the purposes of subsection (1)(ii) above, "the permitted sum" means—

    (a) in respect of a candidate at a parliamentary election, £500;

    (b) in respect of a candidate at a local government election, £50 together with an additional 0.5p for every entry in the register of local government electors for the electoral area in question as it has effect on the last day for publication of notice of the election;

and expenses shall be regarded as incurred by a person "as part of a concerted plan of action" if they are incurred by that person in pursuance of any plan or other arrangement whereby that person and one or more other persons are to incur, with a view to promoting or procuring the election of the same candidate, expenses which (disregarding subsection (1)(ii)) fall within subsection (1) above.]

[(1A) In the application of subsection (1) above in relation to an election of the London members of the London Assembly at an ordinary election, any reference to the candidate includes a reference to all or any of the candidates of a registered political party; and in the application of subsection (1ZA) above in relation to such an election the reference to the same candidate includes a reference to all or any of the candidates of the same registered political party.]

(2) Where a person incurs any expenses required by this section to be authorised by the election agent—

    (a) that person shall within 21 days after the day on which the result of the election is declared deliver to the appropriate officer a return of the amount of those expenses, stating the election at which and the candidate in whose support they were incurred, and

    (b) the return shall be accompanied by a declaration made by that person (or in the case of an association or body of persons, by a director, general manager, secretary or other similar officer of the association or body) verifying the return and giving particulars of the matters for which the expenses were incurred,

but this subsection does not apply to any person engaged or employed for payment or promise of payment by the candidate or his election agent.

(3), (4) ★ ★ ★ ★ ★

(5) If a person—

(a) incurs, or aids, abets, counsels or procures any other person to incur. any expenses in contravention of this section, or

(b) knowingly makes the declaration required by subsection (2) falsely, he shall be guilty of a corrupt practice; and if a person fails to deliver or send any declaration or return or a copy of it as required by this section he shall be guilty of an illegal practice, but—

(i) the court before whom a person is convicted under this subsection may, if they think it just in the special circumstances of the case, mitigate or entirely remit any incapacity imposed by virtue of section 173 below; and

(ii) a candidate shall not be liable, nor shall his election be avoided, for a corrupt or illegal practice under this subsection committed by an agent without his consent or connivance.

(6) ★ ★ ★ ★ ★

92 Broadcasting from outside United Kingdom

[(1) No person shall, with intent to influence persons to give or refrain from giving their votes at a parliamentary or local government election, include, or aid, abet, counsel or procure the inclusion of, any matter relating to the election in any programme service (within the meaning of the Broadcasting Act 1990) provided from a place outside the United Kingdom otherwise than in pursuance of arrangements made with—

(a) the British Broadcasting Corporation;

(b) Sianel Pedwar Cymru; or

(c) the holder of any licence granted by the Independent Television Commission or the Radio Authority,

for the reception and re-transmission of that matter by that body or the holder of that licence.]

(2) An offence under this section shall be an illegal practice, but the court before whom a person is convicted of an offence under this section may, if they think it just in the special circumstances of the case, mitigate or entirely remit any incapacity imposed by virtue of section [160(5)] below.

(3) ★ ★ ★ ★ ★

93 Broadcasting during elections

(1) In relation to a parliamentary or local government election [other than an Authority election]—

(a) pending such an election it shall not be lawful for any item about the constituency or electoral area to be

[(i) broadcast by the British Broadcasting Corporation or Sianel Pedwar Cymru; or

(ii) included in any service licensed under Part I or III of the Broadcasting Act 1990 or Part I or II of the Broadcasting Act 1996]

if any of the persons who are for the time being candidates at the election takes part in the item and the broadcast is not made with his consent; and

(b) where an item about a constituency or electoral area is so broadcast pending such an election there, then if the broadcast either is made before the latest time for delivery of nomination papers, or is made after that time but without the consent of any candidate remaining validly nominated, any person taking part in the item for the purpose of promoting or procuring his election shall be guilty of an illegal practice, unless the broadcast is so made without his consent.

(2) For the purposes of subsection (1) above—

(a) a parliamentary election shall be deemed to be pending during the period ending with the close of the poll and beginning—

(i) at a general election, with the date of the dissolution of Parliament or any earlier time at which Her Majesty's intention to dissolve Parliament is announced; or

(ii) at a by-election, with the date of the issue of the writ for the election or any earlier date on which a certificate of the vacancy is notified in the London Gazette in accordance with the Recess Elections Act 1975; and

(b) a local government election shall be deemed to be pending during the period ending with the close of the poll and beginning [with the last date on which notice of the election may be published in accordance with rules made under section 36 or, in Scotland, section 42 above].

(3) ...

94–96 ★ ★ ★ ★ ★

97 Disturbances at election meetings

(1) A person who at a lawful public meeting to which this section applies acts, or incites others to act, in a disorderly manner for the purpose of preventing the transaction of the business for which the meeting was called together shall be guilty of an illegal practice.

[(2) This section applies to a political meeting held in an electoral region in connection with a European parliamentary election between the last date on which notice of election may be published in accordance with the elections rules and the date of the poll.]

(3) If a constable reasonably suspects any person of committing an offence under subsection (1) above, he may if requested so to do by the chairman of the meeting require that person to declare to him immediately his name and address and, if that person refuses or fails so to declare his name and address or gives a false name and address, he shall be liable on summary conviction to a fine not exceeding [level 1 on the standard scale,] ...

This subsection does not apply in Northern Ireland.

98, 99 ★ ★ ★ ★ ★

100 Illegal canvassing by police officers

(1) No member of a police force shall by word, message, writing or in any other manner, endeavour to persuade any person to give, or dissuade any person from giving, his vote, whether as an elector or as proxy—

(a) at any parliamentary election for a constituency, or

(b) at any local government election for any electoral area, wholly or partly within the police area.

(2) A person acting in contravention of subsection (1) above shall be liable [on summary conviction to a fine not exceeding level 3 on the standard scale, but] nothing in that subsection shall subject a member of a police force to any penalty for anything done in the discharge of his duty as a member of the force.

(3) In this section references to a member of a police force and to a police area are to be taken in relation to Northern Ireland as references to a member of the Royal Ulster Constabulary and to Northern Ireland.

★ ★ ★ ★ ★

Police and Criminal Evidence Act 1984
(1984, c. 60)

An Act to make further provision in relation to the powers and duties of the police, persons in police detention, criminal evidence, police discipline and complaints against the police; to provide for arrangements for obtaining the views of the community on policing and for a rank of deputy chief constable; to amend the law relating to the Police Federations and Police Forces and Police Cadets in Scotland; and for connected purposes [31 October 1984]

Territorial extent: England and Wales

Note: For the application of this Act to investigating officers of the Customs and Excise see the Police and Criminal Evidence Act 1984 (Application to Customs and Excise) Order 1985 (SI 1985 No 1800) and for its application to the investigation of offences conducted by officers of the armed services police see the Police and Criminal Evidence (Application to the Armed Forces) Order 1997 (SI 1997 No 15).

PART I   POWERS TO STOP AND SEARCH

1   Power of constable to stop and search persons, vehicles etc

(1) A constable may exercise any power conferred by this section—

(a) in any place to which at the time when he proposes to exercise the power the public or any section of the public has access, on payment or otherwise, as of right or by virtue of express or implied permission; or

(b) in any other place to which people have ready access at the time when he proposes to exercise the power but which is not a dwelling.

(2) Subject to subsection (3) to (5) below, a constable—

(a) may search—

(i) any person or vehicle;

(ii) anything which is in or on a vehicle, for stolen or prohibited articles [or any article to which subsection (8A) belowapplies]; and

(b) may detain a person or vehicle for the purpose of such a search.

(3) This section does not give a constable power to search a person or vehicle or anything in or on a vehicle unless he has reasonable grounds for suspecting that he will find stolen or prohibited articles [or any article to which subsection (8A) below applies].

(4) If a person is in a garden or yard occupied with and used for the purposes of a dwelling or on other land so occupied and used, a constable may not search him in the exercise of the power conferred by this section unless the constable has reasonable grounds for believing—

(a) that he does not reside in the dwelling; and

(b) that he is not in the place in question with the express or implied permission of a person who resides in the dwelling.

(5) If a vehicle is in a garden or yard occupied with and used for the purposes of a dwelling or on other land so occupied and used, a constable may not search the vehicle or anything in or on it in the exercise of the power conferred by this section unless he has reasonable grounds for believing—

(a) that the person in charge of the vehicle does not reside in the dwelling; and

(b) that the vehicle is not in the place in question with the express or implied permission of a person who resides in the dwelling.

(6) If in the course of such a search a constable discovers an article which he has reasonable grounds for suspecting to be a stolen or prohibited article [or an article to which subsection (8A) applies], he may seize it.

(7) An article is prohibited for the purposes of this Part of this Act if it is—

(a) an offensive weapon; or

(b) an article—

(i) made or adapted for use in the course of or in connection with an offence to which this sub-paragraph applies; or

(ii) intended by the person having it with him for such use by him or by some other person.

(8) The offences to which subsection (7)(b)(i) above applies are—

    (a) burglary;

    (b) theft;

    (c) offences under section 12 of the Theft Act 1968 (taking motor vehicle or other conveyance without authority); and

    (d) offences under section 15 of that Act (obtaining property by deception).

[(8A) This subsection applies to any article in relation to which a person has committed, or is committing or is going to commit an offence under section 139 of the Criminal Justice Act 1988.]

(9) In this Part of this Act "offensive weapon" means any article—

    (a) made or adapted for use for causing injury to persons; or

    (b) intended by the person having it with him for such use by him or by some other person.

2   Provisions relating to search under section 1 and other powers

(1) A constable who detains a person or vehicle in the exercise—

    (a) of the power conferred by section 1 above; or

    (b) of any other power—

        (i) to search a person without first arresting him; or

        (ii) to search a vehicle without making an arrest, need not conduct a search if it appears to him subsequently—

        (i) that no search is required; or

        (ii) that a search is impracticable.

(2) If a constable contemplates a search, other than a search of an unattended vehicle, in the exercise—

    (a) of the power conferred by section 1 above; or

    (b) of any other power, except the power conferred by section 6 below and the power conferred by section 27(2) of the Aviation Security Act 1982—

        (i) to search a person without first arresting him; or

        (ii) to search a vehicle without making an arrest, it shall be his duty, subject to subsection (4) below, to take reasonable steps before he commences the search to bring to the attention of the appropriate person–

        (i) if the constable is not in uniform, documentary evidence that he is a constable; and

        (ii) whether he is in uniform or not, the matters specified in subsection (3) below; and the constable shall not commence the search until he has performed that duty.

(3) The matters referred to in subsection (2)(ii) above are—

    (a) the constable's name and the name of the police station to which he is attached;

    (b) the object of the proposed search;

    (c) the constable's grounds for proposing to make it; and

    (d) the effect of section 3(7) or (8) below, as may be appropriate.

(4) A constable need not bring the effect of section 3(7) or (8) below to the attention of the appropriate person if it appears to the constable that it will not be practicable to make the record in section 3(1) below.

(5) In this section "the appropriate person" means—

    (a) if the constable proposes to search a person, that person; and

    (b) if he proposes to search a vehicle, or anything in or on a vehicle, the person in charge of the vehicle.

(6) On completing a search of an unattended vehicle or anything in or on such a vehicle in the exercise of any such power as is mentioned in subsection (2) above a constable shall leave a notice—

    (a) stating that he has searched it;

(b) giving the name of the police station to which he is attached;

(c) stating that an application for compensation for any damage caused by the search may be made to that police station; and

(d) stating the effect of section 3(8) below.

(7) ★ ★ ★ ★ ★

(8) The time for which a person or vehicle may be detained for the purposes of such a search is such time as is reasonably required to permit a search to be carried out either at the place where the person or vehicle was first detained or nearby.

(9) Neither the power conferred by section 1 above nor any other power to detain and search a person without first arresting him or to detain and search a vehicle without making an arrest is to be construed—

(a) as authorising a constable to require a person to remove any of his clothing in public other than an outer coat, jacket or gloves; or

(b) as authorising a constable not in uniform to stop a vehicle.

(10) ★ ★ ★ ★ ★

3 Duty to make records concerning searches

(1) Where a constable has carried out a search in the exercise of any such power as is mentioned in section 2(1) above, other than a search—

(a) under section 6 below; or

(b) under section 27(2) of the Aviation Security Act 1982, he shall make a record of it in writing unless it is not practicable to do so.

(2) If—

(a) a constable is required by subsection (1) above to make a record of a search; but

(b) it is not practicable to make the record on the spot, he shall make it as soon as practicable after the completion of the search.

(3) The record of a search of a person shall include a note of his name, if the constable knows it, but a constable may not detain a person to find out his name.

(4) If a constable does not know the name of the person whom he has searched, the record of the search shall include a note otherwise describing that person.

(5) The record of a search of a vehicle shall include a note describing the vehicle.

(6) The record of a search of a person or a vehicle—

(a) shall state—

(i) the object of the search;

(ii) the grounds for making it;

(iii) the date and time when it was made;

(iv) the place where it was made;

(v) whether anything, and if so what, was found;

(vi) whether any, and if so what, injury to a person or damage to property appears to the constable to have resulted from the search; and

(b) shall identify the constable making it.

(7) If a constable who conducted a search of a person made a record of it, the person who was searched shall be entitled to a copy of the record if he asks for one before the end of the period specified in subsection (9) below.

(8) If—

(a) the owner of a vehicle which has been searched or the person who was in charge of the vehicle at the time when it was searched asks for a copy of the record of the search before the end of the period specified in subsection (9) below; and

(b) the constable who conducted the search made a record of it, the person who made the request shall be entitled to a copy.

(9) The period mentioned in subsections (7) and (8) above is the period of 12 months beginning with the date on which the search was made.

(10) ★ ★ ★ ★ ★

4   Road checks

(1) This section shall have effect in relation to the conduct of road checks by police officers for the purpose of ascertaining whether a vehicle is carrying—

(a) a person who has committed an offence other than a road traffic offence or a [vehicle] excise offence;

(b) a person who is a witness to such an offence;

(c) a person intending to commit such an offence; or

(d) a person who is unlawfully at large.

(2) For the purposes of this section a road check consists of the exercise in a locality of the power conferred by section [163 of the Road Traffic Act 1988] in such a way as to stop during the period for which its exercise in that way in that locality continues all vehicles or vehicles selected by any criterion.

(3) Subject to subsection (5) below, there may only be such a road check if a police officer of the rank of superintendent or above authorises it in writing.

(4) An officer may only authorise a road check under subsection (3) above—

(a) for the purpose specified in subsection (1)(a) above, if he has reasonable grounds—

(i) for believing that the offence is a serious arrestable offence; and

(ii) for suspecting that the person is, or is about to be, in the locality in which vehicles would be stopped if the road check were authorised;

(b) for the purpose specified in subsection (1)(b) above, if he has reasonable grounds for believing that the offence is a serious arrestable offence;

(c) for the purpose specified in subsection (1)(c) above, if he has reasonable grounds—

(i) for believing that the offence would be a serious arrestable offence; and

(ii) for suspecting that the person is, or is about to be, in the locality in which vehicles would be stopped if the road check were authorised;

(d) for the purpose specified in subsection (1)(d) above, if he has reasonable grounds for suspecting that the person is, or is about to be, in that locality.

(5) An officer below the rank of superintendent may authorise such a road check if it appears to him that it is required as a matter of urgency for one of the purposes specified in subsection (1) above.

(6) If an authorisation is given under subsection (5) above, it shall be the duty of the officer who gives it—

(a) to make a written record of the time at which he gives it; and

(b) to cause an officer of the rank of superintendent or above to be informed that it has been given.

(7)–(14) ★ ★ ★ ★ ★

(15) Where a vehicle is stopped in a road check, the person in charge of the vehicle at the time when it is stopped shall be entitled to obtain a written statement of the purpose of the road check if he applies for such a statement not later than the end of the period of twelve months from the day on which the vehicle was stopped.

(16) Nothing in this section affects the exercise by police officers of any power to stop vehicles for purposes other than those specified in subsection (1) above.

5-7 ★ ★ ★ ★ ★

PART II   POWERS OF ENTRY, SEARCH AND SEIZURE

Search warrants

8   Power of justice of the peace to authorise entry and search of premises

(1) If on an application made by a constable a justice of the peace is satisfied that there are reasonable grounds for believing—

- (a) that a serious arrestable offence has been committed; and
- (b) that there is material on premises specified in the application which is likely to be of substantial value (whether by itself or together with other material) to the investigation of the offence; and
- (c) that the material is likely to be relevant evidence; and
- (d) that it does not consist of or include items subject to legal privilege, excluded material or special procedure material; and
- (e) that any of the conditions specified in subsection (3) below applies, he may issue a warrant authorising a constable to enter and search the premises.

(2) A constable may seize and retain anything for which a search has been authorised under subsection (1) above.

(3) The conditions mentioned in subsection (1)(e) above are—

- (a) that it is not practicable to communicate with any person entitled to grant entry to the premises;
- (b) that it is practicable to communicate with a person entitled to grant entry to the premises but it is not practicable to communicate with any person entitled to grant access to the evidence;
- (c) that entry to the premises will not be granted unless a warrant is produced;
- (d) that the purpose of a search may be frustrated or seriously prejudiced unless a constable arriving at the premises can secure immediate entry to them.

(4) In this Act "relevant evidence", in relation to an offence, means anything that would be admissible in evidence at a trial for the offence.

(5) The power to issue a warrant conferred by this section is in addition to any such power otherwise conferred.

[(6) This section applies in relation to a relevant offence (as defined in section 28D(4) of the Immigration Act 1971) as it applies in relation to a serious arrestable offence.]

Note: 'Serious arrestable offence' is extended to include an offence under s. 17 of the Crime (Sentences) Act 1997 by s. 18 of that Act.

9   Special provisions as to access

(1) A constable may obtain access to excluded material or special procedure material for the purposes of a criminal investigation by making an application under Schedule 1 below and in accordance with that Schedule.

(2) Any Act (including a local Act) passed before this Act under which a search of premises for the purposes of a criminal investigation could be authorised by the issue of a warrant to a constable shall cease to have effect so far as it relates to the authorisation of searches—

- (a) for items subject to legal privilege; or
- (b) for excluded material; or
- (c) for special procedure material consisting of documents or records other than documents.

(2A) ★ ★ ★ ★ ★

10   Meaning of "items subject to legal privilege"

(1) Subject to subsection (2) below, in this Act "items subject to legal privilege" means—

- (a) communications between a professional legal adviser and his client or any person representing his client made in connection with the giving of legal advice to the client;

(b) communications between a professional legal adviser and his client or any person representing his client or between such an adviser or his client or any such representative and any other person made in connection with or in contemplation of legal proceedings and for the purposes of such proceedings; and

(c) items enclosed with or referred to in such communications and made—

   (i) in connection with the giving of legal advice; or

   (ii) in connection with or in contemplation of legal proceedings and for the purposes of such proceedings,

when they are in the possession of a person who is entitled to possession of them.

(2) Items held with the intention of furthering a criminal purpose are not items subject to legal privilege.

11 Meaning of "excluded material"

(1) Subject to the following provisions of this section, in this Act "excluded material" means—

(a) personal records which a person has acquired or created in the course of any trade, business, profession or other occupation or for the purposes of any paid or unpaid office and which he holds in confidence;

(b) human tissue or tissue fluid which has been taken for the purposes of diagnosis or medical treatment and which a person holds in confidence;

(c) journalistic material which a person holds in confidence and which consists—

   (i) of documents; or

   (ii) of records other than documents.

(2) A person holds material other than journalistic material in confidence for the purposes of this section if he holds it subject—

(a) to an express or implied undertaking to hold it in confidence; or

(b) to a restriction on disclosure or an obligation of secrecy contained in any enactment, including an enactment contained in an Act passed after this Act.

(3) A person holds journalistic material in confidence for the purposes of this section if—

(a) he holds it subject to such an undertaking, restriction or obligation; and

(b) it has been continuously held (by one or more persons) subject to such an undertaking, restriction or obligation since it was first acquired or created for the purposes of journalism.

12 Meaning of "personal records"

In this Part of this Act "personal records" means documentary and other records concerning an individual (whether living or dead) who can be identified from them and relating—

(a) to his physical or mental health;

(b) to spiritual counselling or assistance given or to be given to him; or

(c) to counselling or assistance given or to be given to him, for the purposes of his personal welfare, by any voluntary organisation or by any individual who—

   (i) by reason of his office or occupation has responsibilities for his personal welfare; or

   (ii) by reason of an order of a court has responsibilities for his supervision.

13 Meaning of "journalistic material"

(1) Subject to subsection (2) below, in this Act "journalistic material" means material acquired or created for the purposes of journalism.

(2) Material is only journalistic material for the purposes of this Act if it is in the possession of a person who acquired or created it for the purposes of journalism.

(3) A person who receives material from someone who intends that the recipient shall use it for the purposes of journalism is to be taken to have acquired it for those purposes.

14   Meaning of "special procedure material"

(1) In this Act "special procedure material" means—

(a) material to which subsection (2) below applies; and

(b) journalistic material, other than excluded material.

(2) Subject to the following provisions of this section, this subsection applies to material, other than items subject to legal privilege and excluded material, in the possession of a person who—

(a) acquired or created it in the course of any trade, business, profession or other occupation or for the purposes of any paid or unpaid office; and

(b) holds it subject—

(i) to an express or implied undertaking to hold it in confidence; or

(ii) to a restriction or obligation such as is mentioned in section 11(2)(b) above

(3)–(6) ★ ★ ★ ★ ★

15   Search warrants—safeguards

(1) This section and section 16 below have effect in relation to the issue to constables under any enactment, including an enactment contained in an Act passed after this Act, of warrants to enter and search premises; and an entry on or search of premises under a warrant is unlawful unless it complies with this section and section 16 below.

(2) Where a constable applies for any such warrant, it shall be his duty—

(a) to state—

(i) the ground on which he makes the application; and

(ii) the enactment under which the warrant would be issued;

(b) to specify the premises which it is desired to enter and search; and

(c) to identify, so far as is practicable, the articles or persons to be sought.

(3) An application for such a warrant shall be made ex parte and supported by an information in writing.

(4) The constable shall answer on oath any question that the justice of the peace or judge hearing the application asks him.

(5) A warrant shall authorise an entry on one occasion only.

(6) A warrant—

(a) shall specify—

(i) the name of the person who applies for it;

(ii) the date on which it is issued;

(iii) the enactment under which it is issued; and

(iv) the premises to be searched; and

(b) shall identify, so far as is practicable, the articles or persons to be sought.

(7), (8) ★ ★ ★ ★ ★

16   Execution of warrants

(1) A warrant to enter and search premises may be executed by any constable.

(2) Such a warrant may authorise persons to accompany any constable who is executing it.

(3) Entry and search under a warrant must be within one month from the date of its issue.

(4) Entry and search under a warrant must be at a reasonable hour unless it appears to the constable executing it that the purpose of a search may be frustrated on an entry at a reasonable hour.

(5) Where the occupier of premises which are to be entered and searched is present at the time when a constable seeks to execute a warrant to enter and search them, the constable—

(a) shall identify himself to the occupier and, if not in uniform, shall produce to him documentary evidence that he is a constable;

(b) shall produce the warrant to him; and

(c) shall supply him with a copy of it.

(6) Where—

    (a) the occupier of such premises is not present at the time when a constable seeks to execute such a warrant; but

    (b) some other person who appears to the constable to be in charge of the premises is present,

subsection (5) above shall have effect as if any reference to the occupier were a reference to that other person.

(7) If there is no person present who appears to the constable to be in charge of the premises, he shall leave a copy of the warrant in a prominent place on the premises.

(8) A search under a warrant may only be a search to the extent required for the purpose for which the warrant was issued.

(9) A constable executing a warrant shall make an endorsement on it stating–

    (a) whether the articles or persons sought were found; and

    (b) whether any articles were seized, other than articles which were sought.

(10)–(12) ★ ★ ★ ★ ★

Entry and search without search warrant

17 Entry for purpose of arrest etc.

(1) Subject to the following provisions of this section, and without prejudice to any other enactment, a constable may enter and search any premises for the purpose—

    (a) of executing—

        (i) a warrant of arrest issued in connection with or arising out of criminal proceedings; or

        (ii) a warrant of commitment issued under section 76 of the Magistrates' Courts Act 1980;

    (b) of arresting a person for an arrestable offence;

    (c) of arresting a person for an offence under—

        (i) section 1 (prohibition of uniforms in connection with political objects) . . . of the Public Order Act 1936;

        (ii) any enactment contained in sections 6 to 8 or 10 of the Criminal Law Act 1977 (offences relating to entering and remaining on property);

        [(iii) section 4 of the Public Order Act 1986 (fear or provocation of violence)] [; or

        (iv) section 76 of the Criminal Justice and Public Order Act 1994 (failure to comply with an interim possession order);]

    [(ca) of arresting, in pursuance of section 32(1A) of the Children and Young Persons Act 1969, any child or young person who has been remanded or committed to local authority accommodation under section 23(1) of that Act;

    (cb) of recapturing any person who is, or is deemed for any purpose to be, unlawfully at large while liable to be detained—

        (i) in a prison, remand centre, young offender institution or secure training centre, or

        (ii) in pursuance of [section 92 of the Powers of Criminal Courts (Sentencing) Act 2000] (dealing with children and young persons guilty of grave crimes), in any other place;]

    (d) of recapturing [any person whatever] who is unlawfully at large and whom he is pursuing; or

    (e) of saving life or limb or preventing serious damage to property.

(2) Except for the purpose specified in paragraph (e) of subsection (1) above, the powers of entry and search conferred by this section—

    (a) are only exercisable if the constable has reasonable grounds for believing that the person whom he is seeking is on the premises; and

    (b) are limited, in relation to premises consisting of two or more separate dwellings, to powers to enter and search—

        (i) any parts of the premises which the occupiers of any dwelling comprised in the premises use in common with the occupiers of any other such dwelling; and

        (ii) any such dwelling in which the constable has reasonable grounds for believing that the person whom he is seeking may be.

    (3) The powers of entry and search conferred by this section are only exercisable for the purposes specified in subsection (1)(c)(ii) [or (iv)] above by a constable in uniform.

    (4) The power of search conferred by this section is only a power to search to the extent that is reasonably required for the purpose for which the power of entry is exercised.

    (5) Subject to subsection (6) below, all the rules of common law under which a constable has power to enter premises without a warrant are hereby abolished.

    (6) Nothing in subsection (5) above affects any power of entry to deal with or prevent a breach of the peace.

18   Entry and search after arrest

    (1) Subject to the following provisions of this section, a constable may enter and search any premises occupied or controlled by a person who is under arrest for an arrestable offence, if he has reasonable grounds for suspecting that there is on the premises evidence, other than items subject to legal privilege, that relates—

        (a) to that offence; or

        (b) to some other arrestable offence which is connected with or similar to that offence.

    (2) A constable may seize and retain anything for which he may search under subsection (1) above.

    (3) The power to search conferred by subsection (1) above is only a power to search to the extent that is reasonably required for the purpose of discovering such evidence.

    (4) Subject to subsection (5) below, the powers conferred by this section may not be exercised unless an officer of the rank of inspector or above has authorised them in writing.

    (5) A constable may conduct a search under subsection (1) above—

        (a) before taking the person to a police station; and

        (b) without obtaining an authorisation under subsection (4) above, if the presence of that person at a place other than a police station is necessary for the effective investigation of the offence.

    (6) If a constable conducts a search by virtue of subsection (5) above, he shall inform an officer of the rank of inspector or above that he has made the search as soon as practicable after he has made it.

    (7) An officer who—

        (a) authorises a search; or

        (b) is informed of a search under subsection (6) above, shall make a record in writing—

        (i) of the ground for the search; and

        (ii) of the nature of the evidence that was sought.

    (8) If the person who was in occupation or control of the premises at the time of the search is in police detention at the time the record is to be made, the officer shall make the record as part of his custody record.

Seizure etc.

19   General power of seizure etc.

    (1) The powers conferred by subsections (2), (3) and (4) below are exercisable by a constable who is lawfully on any premises.

    (2) The constable may seize anything which is on the premises if he has reasonable grounds for believing—

(a) that it has been obtained in consequence of the commission of an offence; and

(b) that it is necessary to seize it in order to prevent it being concealed, lost, damaged, altered or destroyed.

(3) The constable may seize anything which is on the premises if he has reasonable grounds for believing—

(a) that it is evidence in relation to an offence which he is investigating or any other offence; and

(b) that it is necessary to seize it in order to prevent the evidence being concealed, lost, altered or destroyed.

(4) The constable may require any information which is [stored in any electronic form] and is accessible from the premises to be produced in a form in which it can be taken away [or from which it can readily be produced in a visible and legible form] if he has reasonable grounds for believing—

(a) that—

(i) it is evidence in relation to an offence which he is investigating or any other offence; or

(ii) it has been obtained in consequence of the commission of an offence; and

(b) that it is necessary to do so in order to prevent it being concealed, lost, tampered with or destroyed.

(5) The powers conferred by this section are in addition to any power otherwise conferred.

(6) No power of seizure conferred on a constable under any enactment (including an enactment contained in an Act passed after this Act) is to be taken to authorise the seizure of an item which the constable exercising the power has reasonable grounds for believing to be subject to legal privilege.

20 Extension of powers of seizure to computerised information

(1) Every power of seizure which is conferred by an enactment to which this section applies on a constable who has entered premises in the exercise of a power conferred by an enactment shall be construed as including a power to require any information [stored in any electronic form] and accessible from the premises to be produced in a form in which it can be taken away [or from which it can readily be produced in a visible and legible form].

(2) This section applies—

(a) to any enactment contained in an Act passed before this Act;

(b) to sections 8 and 18 above;

(c) to paragraph 13 of Schedule 1 to this Act; and

(d) to any enactment contained in an Act passed after this Act.

21 Access and copying

(1) A constable who seizes anything in the exercise of a power conferred by any enactment, including an enactment contained in an Act passed after this Act, shall, if so requested by a person showing himself—

(a) to be the occupier of premises on which it was seized; or

(b) to have had custody or control of it immediately before the seizure, provide that person with a record of what he seized.

(2) The officer shall provide the record within a reasonable time from the making of the request for it.

(3) Subject to subsection (8) below, if a request for permission to be granted access to anything which—

(a) has been seized by a constable; and

(b) is retained by the police for the purpose of investigating an offence, is made to the officer in charge of the investigation by a person who had custody or control of the thing immediately before it was so seized or by someone acting on behalf of such a person the officer shall allow the person who made the request access to it under the supervision of a constable.

(4) Subject to subsection (8) below, if a request for a photograph or copy of any such thing is made to the officer in charge of the investigation by a person who had custody or control of the thing immediately before it was so seized, or by someone acting on behalf of such a person, the officer shall—

    (a) allow the person who made the rquest access to it under the supervision of a constable for the purpose of photographing or copying it; or

    (b) photograph or copy it, or cause it to be photographed or copied.

(5) A constable may also photograph or copy, or have photographed or copied, anything which he has power to seize, without a request being made under subsection (4) above.

(6) Where anything is photographed or copied under subsection (4)(b) above, the photograph or copy shall be supplied to the person who made the request.

(7) The photograph or copy shall be so supplied within a reasonable time from the making of the request.

(8) There is no duty under this section to grant access to, or to supply a photograph or copy of, anything if the officer in charge of the investigation for the purposes of which it was seized has reasonable grounds for believing that to do so would prejudice—

    (a) that investigation;

    (b) the investigation of an offence other than the offence for the purposes of investigating which the thing was seized; or

    (c) any criminal proceedings which may be brought as a result of—

        (i) the investigation of which he is in charge; or

        (ii) any such investigation as is mentioned in paragraph (b) above.

22 Retention

(1) Subject to subsection (4) below, anything which has been seized by a constable or taken away by a constable following a requirement made by virtue of section 19 or 20 above may be retained so long as is necessary in all the circumstances.

(2) Without prejudice to the generality of subsection (1) above—

    (a) anything seized for the purposes of a criminal investigation may be retained, except as provided by subsection (4) below—

        (i) for use as evidence at a trial for an offence; or

        (ii) for forensic examination or for investigation in connection with an offence;

        and

    (b) anything may be retained in order to establish its lawful owner, where there are reasonable grounds for believing that it has been obtained in consequence of the commission of an offence.

(3) Nothing seized on the ground that it may be used—

    (a) to cause physical injury to any person;

    (b) to damage property;

    (c) to interfere with evidence; or

    (d) to assist in escape from police detention or lawful custody,

may be retained when the person from whom it was seized is no longer in police detention or the custody of a court or is in the custody of a court but has been released on bail.

(4) Nothing may be retained for either of the purposes mentioned in subsection (2)(a) above if a photograph or copy would be sufficient for that purpose.

(5) Nothing in this section affects any power of a court to make an order under section 1 of the Police (Property) Act 1897

[(6) This section also applies to anything retained by the police under section 28H(5) of the Immigration Act 1971.]

23, 23A ★ ★ ★ ★ ★

PART III   ARREST

24   Arrest without warrant for arrestable offences

(1) The powers of summary arrest conferred by the following subsections shall apply—

(a) to offences for which the sentence is fixed by law;

(b) to offences for which a person of [18] years of age or over (not previously convicted) may be sentenced to imprisonment for a term of five years (or might be so sentenced but for the restrictions imposed by section 33 of the Magistrates' Courts Act 1980); and

(c) to the offences to which subsection (2) below applies, and in this Act "arrestable offence" means any such offence.

(2) The offences to which this subsection applies are—

(a) offences for which a person may be arrested under the customs and excise Acts, as defined in section 1(1) of the Customs and Excise Management Act 1979;

(b) offences under [the Official Secrets Act 1920] that are not arrestable offences by virtue of the term of imprisonment for which a person may be sentenced in respect of them;

[(bb) offences under any provision of the Official Secrets Act 1989 except section 8(1), (4) or (5);]

(c) offences under section . . . 22 (causing prostitution of women) or 23 (procuration of girl under 21) of the Sexual Offences Act 1956;

[(ca) an offence under section 46 of the Criminal Justice and Police Act 2001;]

(d) offences under section 12(1) (taking motor vehicle or other conveyance without authority etc.) or 25(1) (going equipped for stealing, etc.) of the Theft Act 1968;. . . .

[(e) any offence under the Football (Offences) Act 1991];

[(f) an offence under section 2 of the Obscene Publications Act 1959 (publication of obscene matter);

(g) an offence under section 1 of the Protection of Children Act 1978 (indecent photographs and pseudo-photographs of children);]

[(ga) an offence under section 1 of the Sexual Offences Act 1985 (kerb-crawling);

(gb) an offence under subsection (4) of section 170 of the Road Traffic Act 1988 (failure to stop and report an accident) in respect of an accident to which that section applies by virtue of subsection (1)(a) of that section (accidents causing personal injury);]

[(h) an offence under section 166 of the Criminal Justice and Public Order Act 1994 (sale of tickets by unauthorised persons);]

[(i) an offence under section 19 of the Public Order Act 1986 (publishing etc., material intended or likely to stir up racial hatred);]

[(j) an offence under section 167 of the Criminal Justice and Public Order Act 1994 (touting for hire car services)];

[(k) an offence under section 1(1) of the Prevention of Crime Act 1953 (prohibition of the carrying of offensive weapons without lawful authority or reasonable excuse);

(l) an offence under section 139(1) of the Criminal Justice Act 1988 (offence of having article with blade or point in public place);

(m) an offence under section 139A(1) or (2) of the Criminal Justice Act 1988 (offence of having article with blade or point (or offensive weapon) on school premises);]

[(n) an offence under the Protection from Harassment Act 1997 (harassment);]

[(o) an offence under section [60AA(7)] of the Criminal Justice and Public Order Act 1994 (failing to comply with requirement to remove mask etc.);]

[(p) an offence falling within section 32(1)(a) of the Crime and Disorder Act 1998 ([racially or religiously aggravated] harassment);]

[(q) an offence under section 14J or 21C of the Football Spectators Act 1989 (failure to comply with requirements imposed by or under a banning order or a notice under section 21B);]

[(qa) an offence under section 12(4) of the Criminal Justice and Police Act 2001.]

[(r) ...]

[(s) an offence under section 1(1) or (2) or 6 of the Wildlife and Countryside Act 1981 (taking, possessing, selling etc of wild birds) in respect of a bird included in Schedule 1 to that Act or any part of, or anything derived from, such a bird;

(t) an offence under any of the following provisions of the Wildlife and Countryside Act 1981—
    (i) section 1(5) (disturbance of wild birds),
    (ii) section 9 or 13(1)(a) or (2) (taking, possessing, selling etc of wild animals or plants),
    (iii) section 14 (introduction of new species etc)];

[(u) an offence under section 21C(1) or 21D(1) of the Aviation Security Act 1982 (unauthorised presence in restricted zone or on aircraft);

(v) an offence under section 39(1) of the Civil Aviation Act 1982 (trespass on aerodrome)].

(3) Without prejudice to section 2 of the Criminal Attempts Act 1981, the powers of summary arrest conferred by the following subsections shall also apply to the offences of—
    (a) conspiring to commit any of the offences mentioned in subsection (2) above;
    (b) attempting to commit any such offence [other than an offence under section 12(1) of the Theft Act 1968];
    (c) inciting, aiding, abetting, counselling or procuring the commission of any such offence;

and such offences are also arrestable offences for the purposes of this Act.

(4) Any person may arrest without a warrant—
    (a) anyone who is in the act of committing an arrestable offence;
    (b) anyone whom he has reasonable grounds for suspecting to be committing such an offence.

(5) Where an arrestable offence has been committed, any person may arrest without a warrant—
    (a) anyone who is guilty of the offence;
    (b) anyone whom he has reasonable grounds for suspecting to be guilty of it.

(6) Where a constable has reasonable grounds for suspecting that an arrestable offence has been committed, he may arrest without a warrant anyone whom he has reasonable grounds for suspecting to be guilty of the offence.

(7) A constable may arrest without a warrant—
    (a) anyone who is about to commit an arrestable offence;
    (b) anyone whom he has reasonable grounds for suspecting to be about to commit an arrestable offence.

25 General arrest conditions

(1) Where a constable has reasonable grounds for suspecting that any offence which is not an arrestable offence has been committed or attempted, or is being committed or attempted, he may arrest the relevant person if it appears to him that service of a summons is impracticable or inappropriate because any of the general arrest conditions is satisfied.

(2) In this section "the relevant person" means any person whom the constable has reasonable grounds to suspect of having committed or having attempted to commit the offence or of being in the course of committing or attempting to commit it.

(3) The general arrest conditions are—

(a) that the name of the relevant person is unknown to, and cannot be readily ascertained by, the constable;

(b) that the constable has reasonable grounds for doubting whether a name furnished by the relevant person as his name is his real name;

(c) that—

  (i) the relevant person has failed to furnish a satisfactory address for service; or

  (ii) the constable has reasonable grounds for doubting whether an address furnished by the relevant person is a satisfactory address for service;

(d) that the constable has reasonable grounds for believing that arrest is necessary to prevent the relevant person—

  (i) causing physical injury to himself or any other person;

  (ii) suffering physical injury;

  (iii) causing loss of or damage to property;

  (iv) committing an offence against public decency; or

  (v) causing an unlawful obstruction of the highway;

(e) that the constable has reasonable grounds for believing that arrest is necessary to protect a child or other vulnerable person from the relevant person.

(4) For the purposes of subsection (3) above an address is a satisfactory address for service if it appears to the constable—

(a) that the relevant person will be at it for a sufficiently long period for it to be possible to serve him with a summons; or

(b) that some other person specified by the relevant person will accept service of a summons for the relevant person at it.

(5) Nothing in subsection (3)(d) above authorises the arrest of a person under sub-paragraph (iv) of that paragraph except where members of the public going about their normal business cannot reasonably be expected to avoid the person to be arrested.

(6) This section shall not prejudice any power of arrest conferred apart from this section.

26   Repeal of statutory powers of arrest without warrant or order

(1) Subject to subsection (2) below, so much of any Act (including a local Act) passed before this Act as enables a constable—

(a) to arrest a person for an offence without a warrant; or

(b) to arrest a person otherwise than for an offence without a warrant or an order of a court,

shall cease to have effect.

(2) Nothing in subsection (1) above affects the enactments specified in Schedule 2 to this Act.

27   ★ ★ ★ ★ ★

28   Information to be given on arrest

(1) Subject to subsection (5) below, where a person is arrested, otherwise than by being informed that he is under arrest, the arrest is not lawful unless the person arrested is informed that he is under arrest as soon as is practicable after his arrest.

(2) Where a person is arrested by a constable, subsection (1) above applies regardless of whether the fact of the arrest is obvious.

(3) Subject to subsection (5) below, no arrest is lawful unless the person arrested is informed of the ground for the arrest at the time of, or as soon as is practicable after, the arrest.

(4) Where a person is arrested by a constable, subsection (3) above applies regardless of whether the ground for the arrest is obvious.

(5) Nothing in this section is to be taken to require a person to be informed—
  (a) that he is under arrest; or
  (b) of the ground for the arrest, if it was not reasonably practicable for him to be so informed by reason of his having escaped from arrest before the information could be given.

29   Voluntary attendance at police station etc.

Where for the purpose of assisting with an investigation a person attends voluntarily at a police station or at any other place where a constable is present or accompanies a constable to a police station or any such other place without having been arrested—
  (a) he shall be entitled to leave at will unless he is placed under arrest;
  (b) he shall be informed at once that he is under arrest if a decision is taken by a constable to prevent him from leaving at will.

30   Arrest elsewhere than at police station

(1) Subject to the following provisions of this section, where a person—
  (a) is arrested by a constable for an offence; or
  (b) is taken into custody by a constable after being arrested for an offence by a person other than a constable,
at any place other than a police station, he shall be taken to a police station by a constable as soon as practicable after the arrest.

(2) Subject to subsections (3) and (5) below, the police station to which an arrested person is taken under subsection (1) above shall be a designated police station.

(3)–(5) ★ ★ ★ ★ ★

(6) If the first police station to which an arrested person is taken after his arrest is not a designated police station, he shall be taken to a designated police station not more than six hours after his arrival at the first police station unless he is released previously.

(7) A person arrested by a constable at a place other than a police station shall be released if a constable is satisfied, before the person arrested reaches a police station, that there are no grounds for keeping him under arrest.

(8), (9) ★ ★ ★ ★ ★

(10) Nothing in subsection (1) above shall prevent a constable delaying taking a person who has been arrested to a police station if the presence of that person elsewhere is necessary in order to carry out such investigations as it is reasonable to carry out immediately.

(11)–(13) ★ ★ ★ ★ ★

31   Arrest for further offence

Where—
  (a) a person—
    (i) has been arrested for an offence; and
    (ii) is at a police station in consequence of that arrest; and
  (b) it appears to a constable that, if he were released from that arrest, he would be liable to arrest for some other offence,
he shall be arrested for that other offence.

32   Search upon arrest

(1) A constable may search an arrested person, in any case where the person to be searched has been arrested at a place other than a police station, if the constable has reasonable grounds for believing that the arrested person may present a danger to himself or others.

(2) Subject to subsections (3) to (5) below, a constable shall also have power in any such case—
  (a) to search the arrested person for anything—
    (i) which he might use to assist him to escape from lawful custody; or
    (ii) which might be evidence relating to an offence; and

(b) to enter and search any premises in which he was when arrested or immediately before he was arrested for evidence relating to the offence for which he has been arrested.

(3) The power to search conferred by subsection (2) above is only a power to search to the extent that is reasonably required for the purpose of discovering any such thing or any such evidence.

(4) The powers conferred by this section to search a person are not to be construed as authorising a constable to require a person to remove any of his clothing in public other than an outer coat, jacket or gloves [but they do authorise a search of a person's mouth].

(5) A constable may not search a person in the exercise of the power conferred by subsection (2)(a) above unless he has reasonable grounds for believing that the person to be searched may have concealed on him anything for which a search is permitted under that paragraph.

(6) A constable may not search premises in the exercise of the power conferred by subsection (2)(b) above unless he has reasonable grounds for believing that there is evidence for which a search is permitted under that paragraph on the premises.

(7) In so far as the power of search conferred by subsection (2)(b) above relates to premises consisting of two or more separate dwellings, it is limited to a power to search–

(a) any dwelling in which the arrest took place or in which the person arrested was immediately before his arrest; and

(b) any parts of the premises which the occupier of any such dwelling uses in common with the occupiers of any other dwellings comprised in the premises.

(8) A constable searching a person in the exercise of the power conferred by subsection (1) above may seize and retain anything he finds, if he has reasonable grounds for believing that the person searched might use it to cause physical injury to himself or to any other person.

(9) A constable searching a person in the exercise of the power conferred by subsection (2)(a) above may seize and retain anything he finds, other than an item subject to legal privilege, if he has reasonable grounds for believing—

(a) that he might use it to assist him to escape from lawful custody; or

(b) that it is evidence of an offence or has been obtained in consequence of the commission of an offence.

(10) Nothing in this section shall be taken to affect the power conferred by [section 43 of the Terrorism Act 2000.]

33 ★ ★ ★ ★ ★

PART IV   DETENTION

Detention—conditions and duration

34   Limitations on police detention

(1) A person arrested for an offence shall not be kept in police detention except in accordance with the provisions of this Part of this Act.

(2) Subject to subsection (3) below, if at any time a custody officer—

(a) becomes aware, in relation to any person in police detention, that the grounds for the detention of that person have ceased to apply; and

(b) is not aware of any other grounds on which the continued detention of that person could be justified under the provisions of this Part of this Act,

it shall be the duty of the custody officer, subject to subsection (4) below, to order his immediate release from custody.

(3) No person in police detention shall be released except on the authority of a custody officer at the police station where his detention was authorised or, if it was authorised at more than one station, a custody officer at the station where it was last authorised.

(4) A person who appears to the custody officer to have been unlawfully at large when he was arrested is not to be released under subsection (2) above.

(5)–(7) ★ ★ ★ ★ ★

35 Designated police stations

(1) The chief officer of police for each police area shall designate the police stations in his area which, subject to sections 30(3) and (5) above, are to be the stations in that area to be used for the purpose of detention arrested persons.

(2) A chief officer's duty under subsection (1) above is to designate police stations appearing to him to provide enough accommodation for that purpose.

[(2A)] (3), (4) ★ ★ ★ ★ ★

36 Custody officers at police stations

(1) One or more custody officers shall be appointed for each designated police station.

(2) A custody officer for [a police station designated under s 35(1) above] shall be appointed—

- (a) by the chief officer of police for the area in which the designated police station is situated; or
- (b) by such other police officer as the chief officer of police for that area may direct.

[(2A)] ★ ★ ★ ★ ★

(3) No officer may be appointed a custody officer unless he is of at least the rank of sergeant.

(4) An officer of any rank may perform the functions of a custody officer at a designated police station if a custody officer is not readily available to perform them.

(5) Subject to the following provisions of this section and to section 39(2) below, none of the functions of a custody officer in relation to a person shall be performed by an officer who at the time when the function falls to be performed is involved in the investigation of an offence for which that person is in police detention at that time.

(6)–(10) ★ ★ ★ ★ ★

37 Duties of custody officer before charge

(1) Where—

- (a) a person is arrested for an offence—
    - (i)   without a warrant; or
    - (ii) under a warrant not endorsed for bail, the custody officer at each police station where he is detained after his arrest shall determine whether he has before him sufficient evidence to charge that person with the offence for which he was arrested and may detain him at the police station for such period as is necessary to enable him to do so.

(2) If the custody officer determines that he does not have such evidence before him, the person arrested shall be released either on bail or without bail, unless the custody officer has reasonable grounds for believing that his detention without being charged is necessary to secure or preserve evidence relating to an offence for which he is under arrest or to obtain such evidence by questioning him.

(3) If the custody officer has reasonable grounds for so believing, he may authorise the person arrested to be kept in police detention.

(4) Where a custody officer authorises a person who has not been charged to be kept in police detention, he shall, as soon as is practicable, make a written record of the grounds for the detention.

(5) Subject to subsection (6) below, the written record shall be made in the presence of the person arrested who shall at that time be informed by the custody officer of the grounds for his detention.

(6) Subsection (5) above shall not apply where the person arrested is, at the time when the written record is made—

  (a) incapable of understanding what is said to him;

  (b) violent or likely to become violent; or

  (c) in urgent need of medical attention.

(7) Subject to section 41(7) below, if the custody officer determines that he has before him sufficient evidence to charge the person arrested with the offence for which he was arrested, the person arrested—

  (a) shall be charged; or

  (b) shall be released without charge, either on bail or without bail.

(8) ★ ★ ★ ★ ★

(9) If the person arrested is not in a fit state to be dealt with under subsection (7) above, he may be kept in police detention until he is.

(10) The duty imposed on the custody officer under subsection (1) above shall be carried out by him as soon as practicable after the person arrested arrives at the police station or, in the case of a person arrested at the police station, as soon as practicable after the arrest.

(11)–(14) . . .

(15) ★ ★ ★ ★ ★

38 Duties of custody officer after charge

(1) Where a person arrested for an offence otherwise than under a warrant endorsed for bail is charged with an offence, the custody officer shall order his release from police detention, either on bail or without bail, unless—

  (a) if the person arrested is not an arrested juvenile—

    (i) his name or address cannot be ascertained or the custody officer has reasonable grounds for doubting whether a name or address furnished by him as his name or address is his real name or address;

    [(ii) the custody officer has reasonable grounds for believing that the person arrested will fail to appear in court to answer to bail;

    (iii) in the case of a person arrested for an imprisonable offence, the custody officer has reasonable grounds for believing that the detention of the person arrested is necessary to prevent him from committing an offence;

    [(iiia) in a case of a person who has attained the age of 18, the custody officer has reasonable grounds for believing that the detention of the person is necessary to enable a sample to be taken from him under section 63B below;]

    (iv) in the case of a person arrested for an offence which is not an imprisonable offence, the custody officer has reasonable grounds for believing that the detention of the person arrested is necessary to prevent him from causing physical injury to any other person or from causing loss of or damage to property;

    (v) the custody officer has reasonable grounds for believing that the detention of the person arrested is necessary to prevent him from interfering with the administration of justice or with the investigation of offences or of a particular offence; or

    (vi) the custody officer has reasonable grounds for believing that the detention of the person arrested is necessary for his own protection;]

  (b) if he is an arrested juvenile—

    (i) any of the requirements of paragraph (a) above is satisfied; or

    (ii) the custody officer has reasonable grounds for believing that he ought to be detained in his own interests.

(2) If the release of a person arrested is not required by subsection (1) above, the custody officer may authorise him to be kept in police detention [but may not authorise a person to be

kept in police detention by virtue of subsection (1)(a)(iiia) after the end of the period of six hours beginning when he was charged with the offence.].

(2A) ★ ★ ★ ★ ★

(3) Where a custody officer authorises a person who has been charged to be kept in police detention, he shall, as soon as practicable, make a written record of the grounds for the detention.

(4) Subject to subsection (5) below, the written record shall be made in the presence of the person charged who shall at that time be informed by the custody officer of the grounds for his detention.

(5) Subsection (4) above shall not apply where the person charged is, at the time when the written record is made—

    (a) incapable of understanding what is said to him;

    (b) violent or likely to become violent; or

    (c) in urgent need of medical attention.

[(6) Where a custody officer authorises an arrested juvenile to be kept in police detention under subsection (1) above, the custody officer shall, unless he certifies—

    (a) that by reason of such circumstances as are specified in the certificate, it is impracticable for him to do so; or

    (b) in the case of an arrested juvenile who has attained the [age of 12 years], that no secure accommodation is available and that keeping him in other local authority accommodation would not be adequate to protect the public from serious harm from him,

secure that the arrested juvenile is moved to local authority accommodation.]

(6A) ★ ★ ★ ★ ★

[(6B) Where an arrested juvenile is moved to local authority accommodation under subsection 6 above, it shall be lawful for any person acting on behalf of the authority to detain him.]

(7), (7A), (8) ★ ★ ★ ★ ★

39 Responsibilities in relation to persons detained

(1) Subject to subsection (2) and (4) below, it shall be the duty of the custody officer at a police station to ensure—

    (a) that all persons in police detention at that station are treated in accordance with this Act and any code of practice issued under it and relating to the treatment of persons in police detention; and

    (b) that all matters relating to such persons which are required by this Act or by such codes of practice to be recorded are recorded in the custody records relating to such persons.

(2)–(5) ★ ★ ★ ★ ★

(6) Where—

    (a) an officer of higher rank than the custody officer gives directions relating to a person in police detention; and

    (b) the directions are at variance—

        (i) with any decision made or action taken by the custody officer in the performance of a duty imposed on him under this Part of this Act; or

        (ii) with any decision or action which would be for the directions have been made or taken by him in the performance of such a duty,

the custody officer shall refer the matter at once to an officer of the rank of superintendent or above who is responsible for the police station for which the custody officer is acting as custody officer.

40 Review of police detention

(1) Reviews of the detention of each person in police detention in connection with the

investigation of an offence shall be carried out periodically in accordance with the following provisions of this section—

    (a) in the case of a person who has been arrested and charged, by the custody officer; and

    (b) in the case of a person who has been arrested but not charged, by an officer of at least the rank of inspector who has not been directly involved in the investigation.

  (2) The officer to whom it falls to carry out a review is referred to in this section as a "review officer".

  (3) Subject to subsection (4) below—

    (a) the first review shall be not later than six hours after the detention was first authorised;

    (b) the second review shall be not later than nine hours after the first;

    (c) subsequent reviews shall be at intervals of not more than nine hours.

  (4) A review may be postponed—

    (a) if, having regard to all the circumstances prevailing at the latest time for it specified in subsection (3) above, it is not practicable to carry out the review at that time;

    (b) without prejudice to the generality of paragraph (a) above—

      (i) if at that time the person in detention is being questioned by a police officer and the review officer is satisfied that an interruption of the questioning for the purpose of carrying out the review would prejudice the investigation in connection with which he is being questioned; or

      (ii) if at that time no review officer is readily available.

  (5) If a review is postponed under subsection (4) above it shall be carried out as soon as practicable after the latest time specified for it in subsection (3) above.

  (6) If a review is carried out after postponement under subsection (4) above, the fact that it was so carried out shall not affect any requirement of this section as to the time at which any subsequent review is to be carried out.

  (7) The review officer shall record the reasons for any postponement of a review in the custody record.

  (8) Subject to subsection (9) below, where the person whose detention is under review has not been charged before the time of the review, section 37(1) to (6) above shall have effect in relation to him, but with the substitution—

    (a) of references to the person whose detention is under review for references to the person arrested; and

    (b) of references to the review officer for references to the custody officer.

  (9) Where a person has been kept in police detention by virtue of section 37(9) above, section 37(1) to (6) shall not have effect in relation to him but it shall be the duty of the review officer to determine whether he is yet in a fit state.

  (10) Where the person whose detention is under review has been charged before the time of the review, section 38(1) to (6) above shall have effect in relation to him, with the substitution of references to the person whose detention is under review for references to the person arrested.

  (11) Where—

    (a) an officer of higher rank than the review officer gives directions relating to a person in police detention; and

    (b) the directions are at variance—

      (i) with any decision made or action taken by the review officer in the performance of a duty imposed on him under this Part of this Act; or

      (ii) with any decision or action which would but for the directions have been made or taken by him in the performance of such a duty, the review officer shall refer the matter at once to an officer of the rank of superintendent or above who is responsible for the police station for which the review officer is acting as review officer in connection with the detention.

(12) Before determining whether to authorise a person's continued detention the review officer shall give—

(a) that person (unless he is asleep); or

(b) any solicitor representing him who is available at the time of the review, an opportunity to make representations to him about the detention.

(13), (14) ★ ★ ★ ★ ★

40A ★ ★ ★ ★ ★

41   Limits on period of detention without charge

(1) Subject to the following provisions of this section and to sections 42 and 43 below, a person shall not be kept in police detention for more than 24 hours without being charged.

(2) The time from which the period of detention of a person is to be calculated (in this Act referred to as "the relevant time")—

(a) in the case of a person to whom this paragraph applies, shall be—

(i) the time at which that person arrives at the relevant police station; or

(ii) the time 24 hours after the time of that person's arrest, whichever is the earlier;

(b) in the case of a person arrested outside England and Wales, shall be—

(i) the time at which that person arrives at the first police station to which he is taken in the police area in England or Wales in which the offence for which he was arrested is being investigated; or

(ii) the time 24 hours after the time of that person's entry into England and Wales,

whichever is the earlier;

(c) in the case of a person who—

(i) attends voluntarily at a police station; or

(ii) accompanies a constable to a police station without having been arrested, and is arrested at the police station, the time of his arrest;

(d) in any other case, except where subsection (5) below applies, shall be the time at which the person arrested arrives at the first police station to which he is taken after his arrest.

(3)–(6) ★ ★ ★ ★ ★

(7) Subject to subsection (8) below, a person who at the expiry of 24 hours after the relevant time is in police detention and has not been charged shall be released at that time either on bail or without bail.

(8) Subsection (7) above does not apply to a person whose detention for more than 24 hours after the relevant time has been authorised or is otherwise permitted in accordance with section 42 or 43 below.

(9) ★ ★ ★ ★ ★

42   Authorisation of continued detention

(1) Where a police officer of the rank of superintendent or above who is responsible for the police station at which a person is detained has reasonable grounds for believing that—

(a) the detention of that person without charge is necessary to secure or preserve evidence relating to an offence for which he is under arrest or to obtain such evidence by questioning him;

(b) an offence for which he is under arrest is a serious arrestable offence; and

(c) the investigation is being conducted diligently and expeditiously, he may authorise the keeping of that person in police detention for a period expiring at or before 36 hours after the relevant time.

(2) Where an officer such as is mentioned in subsection (1) above has authorised the keeping of a person in police detention for a period expiring less than 36 hours after the relevant time, such an officer may authorise the keeping of that person in police detention for a further period expiring not more than 36 hours after that time if the conditions specified in subsection (1) above are still satisfied when he gives the authorisation.

(3) If it is proposed to transfer a person in police detention to another police area, the officer determining whether or not to authorise keeping him in detention under subsection (1) above shall have regard to the distance and the time the journey would take.

(4) No authorisation under subsection (1) above shall be given in respect of any person—
  (a) more than 24 hours after the relevant time; or
  (b) before the second review of his detention under section 40 above has been carried out.

(5) Where an officer authorises the keeping of a person in police detention under subsection (1) above, it shall be his duty—
  (a) to inform that person of the grounds for his continued detention; and
  (b) to record the grounds in that person's custody record.

(6) Before determining whether to authorise the keeping of a person in detention under subsection (1) or (2) above, an officer shall give—
  (a) that person; or
  (b) any solicitor representing him who is available at the time when it falls to the officer to determine whether to give the authorisation,
an opportunity to make representations to him about the detention.

(7), (8) ★ ★ ★ ★ ★

(9) Where—
  (a) an officer authorises the keeping of a person in detention under subsection (1) above; and
  (b) at the time of the authorisation he has not yet exercised a right conferred on him by section 56 or 58 below,
the officer—
  (i) shall inform him of that right;
  (ii) shall decide whether he should be permitted to exercise it;
  (iii) shall record the decision in his custody record; and
  (iv) if the decision is to refuse to permit the exercise of the right, shall also record the grounds for the decision in that record.

(10) Where an officer has authorised the keeping of a person who has not been charged in detention under subsection (1) or (2) above, he shall be released from detention, either on bail or without bail, not later than 36 hours after the relevant time, unless—
  (a) he has been charged with an offence; or
  (b) his continued detention is authorised or otherwise permitted in accordance with section 43 below.

(11) A person released under subsection (10) above shall not be re-arrested without a warrant for the offence for which he was previously arrested unless new evidence justifying a further arrest has come to light since his release [; but this subsection does not prevent an arrest under section 46A below].

43 Warrants of further detention

(1) Where, on an application on oath made by a constable and supported by an information, a magistrate's court is satisfied that there are reasonable grounds for believing that the further detention of the person to whom the application relates is justified, it may issue a warrant of further detention authorising the keeping of that person in police detention.

(2) A court may not hear an application for a warrant of further detention unless the person to whom the application relates—

(a) has been furnished with a copy of the information; and

(b) has been brought before the court for the hearing.

(3) The person to whom the application relates shall be entitled to be legally represented at the hearing and, if he is not so represented but wishes to be so represented—

(a) the court shall adjourn the hearing to enable him to obtain representation; and

(b) he may be kept in police detention during the adjournment.

(4) A person's further detention is only justified for the purposes of this section or section 44 below if—

(a) his detention without charge is necessary to secure or preserve evidence relating to an offence for which he is under arrest or to obtain such evidence by questioning him;

(b) an offence for which he is under arrest is a serious arrestable offence; and

(c) the investigation is being conducted diligently and expeditiously.

(5) Subject to subsection (7) below, an application for a warrant of further detention may be made—

(a) at any time before the expiry of 36 hours after the relevant time; or

(b) in a case where—

(i) it is not practicable for the magistrates' court to which the application will be made to sit at the expiry of 36 hours after the relevant time; but

(ii) the court will sit during the 6 hours following the end of that period, at any time before the expiry of the said 6 hours.

(6) In a case to which subsection (5)(b) above applies—

(a) the person to whom the application relates may be kept in police detention until the application is heard; and

(b) the custody officer shall make a note in that person's custody record—

(i) of the fact that he was kept in police detention for more than 36 hours after the relevant time; and

(ii) of the reason why he was so kept.

(7) If—

(a) an application for a warrant of further detention is made after the expiry of 36 hours after the relevant time; and

(b) it appears to the magistrates' court that it would have been reasonable for the police to make it before the expiry of that period,

the court shall dismiss the application.

(8) Where on an application such as is mentioned in subsection (1) above a magistrates' court is not satisfied that there are reasonable grounds for believing that the further detention of the person to whom the application relates is justified, it shall be its duty—

(a) to refuse the application; or

(b) to adjourn the hearing of it until a time not later than 36 hours after the relevant time.

(9) The person to whom the application relates may be kept in police detention during the adjournment.

(10) A warrant of further detention shall—

(a) state the time at which it is issued;

(b) authorise the keeping in police detention of the person to whom it relates for the period stated in it.

(11) Subject to subsection (12) below, the period stated in a warrant of further detention shall be such period as the magistrates' court thinks fit, having regard to the evidence before it.

(12) The period shall not be longer than 36 hours.

(13) ★ ★ ★ ★ ★

(14) Any information submitted in support of an application under this section shall state—

(a) the nature of the offence for which the person to whom the application relates has been arrested;

(b) the general nature of the evidence on which that person was arrested;

(c) what inquiries relating to the offence have been made by the police and what further inquiries are proposed by them;

(d) the reasons for believing the continued detention of that person to be necessary for the purposes of such further inquiries.

(15) Where an application under this section is refused, the person to whom the application relates shall forthwith be charged or, subject to subsection (16) below, released, either on bail or without bail.

(16) A person need not be released under subsection (15) above—

(a) before the expiry of 24 hours after the relevant time; or

(b) before the expiry of any longer period for which his continued detention is or has been authorised under section 42 above.

(17) Where an application under this section is refused, no further application shall be made under this section in repect of the person to whom the refusal relates, unless supported by evidence which has come to light since the refusal.

(18) Where a warrant of further detention is issued, the person to whom it relates shall be released from police detention, either on bail or without bail, upon or before the expiry of the warrant unless he is charged.

(19) A person released under subsection (18) above shall not be re-arrested without a warrant for the offence for which he was previously arrested unless new evidence justifying a further arrest has come to light since his release [; but this subsection does not prevent an arrest under section 46A below].

44   Extension of warrants of further detention

(1) On an application on oath made by a constable and supported by an information a magistrates' court may extend a warrant of further detention issued under section 43 above if it is satisfied that there are reasonable grounds for believing that the further detention of the person to whom the application relates is justified.

(2) Subject to subsection (3) below, the period for which a warrant of further detention may be extended shall be such period as the court thinks fit, having regard to the evidence before it.

(3) The period shall not—

(a) be longer than 36 hours; or

(b) end later than 96 hours after the relevant time.

(4) Where a warrant of further detention has been extended under subsection (1) above, or further extended under this subsection, for a period ending before 96 hours after the relevant time, on an application such as is mentioned in that subsection a magistrates' court may further extend the warrant if it is satisfied as there mentioned; and subsections (2) and (3) above apply to such further extensions as they apply to extensions under subsection (1) above.

(5) A warrant of further detention shall, if extended or further extended under this section, be endorsed with a note of the period of the extension.

(6) Subsections (2), (3), and (14) of section 43 above shall apply to an application made under this section as they apply to an application made under that section.

(7), (8) ★ ★ ★ ★ ★

45   Detention before charge—supplementary

(1) In sections 43 and 44 of this Act "magistrates' court" means a court consisting of two or more justices of the peace sitting otherwise than in open court.

(2) Any reference in this Part of this Act to a period of time or a time of day is to be treated as approximate only.

45A ★ ★ ★ ★ ★

Detention—miscellaneous

46   Detention after charge

(1) Where a person—

(a) is charged with an offence; and

(b) after being charged—

(i)   is kept in police detention; or

(ii) is detained by a local authority in pursuance of arrangements made under section 38(6) above,

he shall be brought before a magistrates' court in accordance with the provisions of this section.

(2) If he is to be brought before a magistrates' court for the petty sessions area in which the police station at which he was charged is situated, he shall be brought before such a court as soon as is practicable and in any event not later than the first sitting after he is charged with the offence.

(3) If no magistrates' court for that area is due to sit either on the day on which he is charged or on the next day, the custody officer for the police station at which he was charged shall inform the [justices' chief executive] for the area that there is a person in the area to whom subsection (2) above applies.

(4) If the person charged is to be brought before a magistrates' court for a petty sessions area other than that in which the police station at which he was charged is situated, he shall be removed to that area as soon as is practicable and brought before such a court as soon as is practicable after this arrival in the area and in any event not later than the first sitting of a magistrates' court for that area after this arrival in the area.

(5) If no magistrates' court for that area is due to sit either on the day on which he arrives in the area or on the next day—

(a) he shall be taken to a police station in the area; and

(b) the custody officer at that station shall inform the [justices' chief executive] for the area that there is a person in the area to whom subsection (4) applies.

(6) Subject to subsection (8) below, where [the justices' chief executive] for a petty sessions area has been informed—

(a) under subsection (3) above that there is a person in the area to whom subsection (2) above applies; or

(b) under subsection (5) above that there is a person in the area to whom subsection (4) above applies,

[the justices' chief executive] shall arrange for a magistrates' court to sit not later than the day next following the relevant day.

(7) In this section "the relevant day"—

(a) in relation to a person who is to be brought before a magistrates' court for the petty sessions area in which the police station at which he was charged is situated, means the day on which he was charged; and

(b) in relation to a person who is to be brought before a magistrates' court for any other petty sessions area, means the day on which he arrives in the area.

(8) Where the day next following the relevant day is Christmas Day, Good Friday or a Sunday, the duty of the [justices' chief executive] under subsection (6) above is a duty to arrange for a magistrates' court to sit not later than the first day after the relevant day which is not one of those days.

(9) ★ ★ ★ ★ ★

[46A   Power of arrest for failure to answer to police bail

(1) A constable may arrest without a warrant any person who, having been released on

bail under this Part of this Act subject to a duty to attend at a police station, fails to attend at that police station at the time appointed for him to do so.

(2) A person who is arrested under this section shall be taken to the police station appointed as the place at which he is to surrender to custody as soon as practicable after the arrest.

(3) For the purpose of—

(a) section 30 above (subject to the obligation in subsection (2) above), and

(b) section 31 above,

an arrest under the section shall be treated as an arrest for an offence.]

47 Bail after arrest

(1) Subject to subsection (2) below, a release on bail of a person under this Part of this Act shall be a release on bail granted in accordance with [sections 3, 3A, 5 and 5A of the Bail Act 1976 as they apply to bail granted by a constable].

[(1A) The normal powers to impose conditions of bail shall be available to him where a custody officer releases a person on bail under section 38(1) above (including that subsection as applied by section 40(10) above) but not in any other cases.

In this subsection "the normal powers to impose conditions of bail" has the meaning given in section 3(6) of the Bail Act 1976.]

(2) Nothing in the Bail Act 1976 shall prevent the re-arrest without warrant of a person released on bail subject to a duty to attend at a police station if new evidence justifying a further arrest has come to light since his release.

(3), (3A), (4) ★ ★ ★ ★ ★

(5) . . .

(6)–(8) ★ ★ ★ ★ ★

47A–52 ★ ★ ★ ★ ★

PART V   QUESTIONING AND TREATMENT OF PERSONS BY POLICE

53 Abolition of certain powers of constables to search persons

(1) Subject to subsection (2) below, there shall cease to have effect any Act (including a local Act) passed before this Act in so far as it authorises—

(a) any search by a constable of a person in police detention at a police station; or

(b) an intimate search of a person by a constable; and any rule of common law which authorises a search such as is mentioned in paragraph (a) or (b) above is abolished.

(2) Nothing in subsection (1)(a) above shall affect paragraph 6(2) of Schedule 3 to the Prevention of Terrorism (Temporary Provisions) Act 1984.

54 Search of detained persons

(1) The custody officer at a police station shall ascertain and record or cause to be recorded everything which a person has with him when he is—

(a) brought to the station after being arrested elsewhere or after being committed to custody by an order or sentence of a court; or

(b) [arrested at the station or detained there [as a person falling within section 34(7), under section 37 above].]

(2) In the case of an arrested person the record shall be made as part of his custody record.

(3) Subject to subsection (4) below, a custody officer may seize and retain any such thing or cause any such thing to be seized and retained.

(4) Clothes and personal effects may only be seized if the custody officer—

(a) believes that the person from whom they are seized may use them—

(i) to cause physical injury to himself or any other person;

    (ii) to damage property;

    (iii) to interfere with evidence; or

    (iv) to assist him to escape; or

  (b) has reasonable grounds for believing that they may be evidence relating to an offence.

(5) Where anything is seized, the person from whom it is seized shall be told the reason for the seizure unless he is—

  (a) violent or likely to become violent; or

  (b) incapable of understanding what is said to him.

(6) Subject to subsection (7) below, a person may be searched if the custody officer considers it necessary to enable him to carry out his duty under subsection (1) above and to the extent that the custody officer considers necessary for that purpose.

[(6A) A person who is in custody at a police station or is in police detention otherwise than at a police station may at any time be searched in order to ascertain whether he has with him anything which he could use for any of the purposes specified in subsection (4)(a) above.

(6B) Subject to subsection (6C) below, a constable may seize and retain, or cause to be seized and retained, anything found on such a search.

(6C) A constable may only seize clothes and personal effects in the circumstances specified in subsection (4) above.]

(7) An intimate search may not be conducted under this section.

(8) A search under this section shall be carried out by a constable.

(9) The constable carrying out a search shall be of the same sex as the person searched.

[54A   Searches and examination to ascertain identity

(1) If an officer of at least the rank of inspector authorises it, a person who is detained in a police station may be searched or examined, or both—

  (a) for the purpose of ascertaining whether he has any mark that would tend to identify him as a person involved in the commission of an offence; or

  (b) for the purpose of facilitating the ascertainment of his identity.

(2) An officer may only give an authorisation under subsection (1) for the purpose mentioned in paragraph (a) of that subsection if—

  (a) the appropriate consent to a search or examination that would reveal whether the mark in question exists has been withheld; or

  (b) it is not practicable to obtain such consent.

(3) An officer may only give an authorisation under subsection (1) in a case in which subsection (2) does not apply if—

  (a) the person in question has refused to identify himself; or

  (b) the officer has reasonable grounds for suspecting that that person is not who he claims to be.

(4) An officer may give an authorisation under subsection (1) orally or in writing but, if he gives it orally, he shall confirm it in writing as soon as is practicable.

(5) Any identifying mark found on a search or examination under this section may be photographed—

  (a) with the appropriate consent; or

  (b) if the appropriate consent is withheld or it is not practicable to obtain it, without it.

(6) Where a search or examination may be carried out under this section, or a photograph may be taken under this section, the only persons entitled to carry out the search or examination, or to take the photograph, are—

  (a) constables; and

  (b) persons who (without being constables) are designated for the purposes of this section by the chief officer of police for the police area in which the police station in question is situated;

and section 117 (use of force) applies to the exercise by a person falling within paragraph (b) of the powers conferred by the preceding provisions of this section as it applies to the exercise of those powers by a constable.

(7) A person may not under this section carry out a search or examination of a person of the opposite sex or take a photograph of any part of the body of a person of the opposite sex.

(8) An intimate search may not be carried out under this section.

(9) A photograph taken under this section—

(a) may be used by, or disclosed to, any person for any purpose related to the prevention or detection of crime, the investigation of an offence or the conduct of a prosecution; and

(b) after being so used or disclosed, may be retained but may not be used or disclosed except for a purpose so related.]

(10)–(12) ★ ★ ★ ★ ★

55 Intimate searches

(1) Subject to the following provisions of this section, if an officer of at least the rank of [inspector] has reasonable grounds for believing—

(a) that a person who has been arrested and is in police detention may have concealed on him anything which—

(i) he could use to cause physical injury to himself or others; and

(ii) he might so use while he is in police detention or in the custody of a court; or

(b) that such a person—

(i) may have a Class A drug concealed on him; and

(ii) was in possession of it with the appropriate criminal intention before his arrest,

he may authorise [an intimate] search of that person.

(3) ★ ★ ★ ★ ★

(4) An intimate search which is only a drug offence search shall be by way of examination by a suitably qualified person.

(5) Except as provided by subsection (4) above, an intimate search shall be by way of examination by a suitably qualified person unless an officer of at least the rank of [inspector] considers that this is not practicable.

(6) An intimate search which is not carried out as mentioned in subsection (5) above shall be carried out by a constable.

(7) A constable may not carry out an intimate search of a person of the opposite sex.

(8) No intimate search may be carried out except—

(a) at a police station;

(b) at a hospital;

(c) at a registered medical practitioner's surgery; or

(d) at some other place used for medical purposes.

(9) An intimate search which is only a drug offence search may not be carried out at a police station.

(10) If an intimate search of a person is carried out, the custody record relating to him shall state—

(a) which parts of his body were searched; and

(b) why they were searched.

(11) ★ ★ ★ ★ ★

(12) This custody officer at a police station may seize and retain anything which is found on an intimate search of a person, or cause any such thing to be seized and retained—

(a) if he believes that the person from whom it is seized may use it—
    (i) to cause physical injury to himself or any other person;
    (ii) to damage property;
    (iii) to interfere with evidence; or
    (iv) to assist him to escape; or
(b) if he has reasonable grounds for believing that it may be evidence relating to an offence.

(13) Where anything is seized under this section, the person from whom it is seized shall be told the reason for the seizure unless he is—
(a) violent or likely to become violent; or
(b) incapable of understanding what is said to him.

(14)–(16) ★ ★ ★ ★ ★

(17) In this section—

★ ★ ★ ★ ★

"Class A drug" has the meaning assigned to it by section 2(1)(b) of the Misuse of Drugs Act 1971;

"drug offence search" means an intimate search for a Class A drug which an officer has authorised by virtue of subsection (1)(b) above; and

"suitably qualified person" means—
(a) a registered medical practitioner; or
(b) a registered nurse.

56 Right to have someone informed when arrested

(1) Where a person has been arrested and is being held in custody in a police station or other premises, he shall be entitled, if he so requests, to have one friend or relative or other person who is known to him or who is likely to take an interest in his welfare told, as soon as is practicable except to the extent that delay is permitted by this section, that he has been arrested and is being detained there.

(2) Delay is only permitted—
(a) in the case of a person who is in police detention for a serious arrestable offence; and
(b) if an officer of at least the rank of [inspector] authorises it.

(3) In any case the person in custody must be permitted to exercise the right conferred by subsection (1) above within 36 hours from the relevant time as defined in section 41(2) above.

(4) ★ ★ ★ ★ ★

(5) [Subject to subsection (5A) below] an officer may only authorise delay where he has reasonable grounds for believing that telling the named person of the arrest—
(a) will lead to interference with or harm to evidence connected with a serious arrestable offence or interference with or physical injury to other persons; or
(b) will lead to the alerting of other persons suspected of having committed such an offence but not yet arrested for it; or
(c) will hinder the recovery of any property obtained as a result of such an offence.

[(5A) An officer may also authorise delay where the serious arrestable offence is a drug trafficking offence and the officer has reasonable grounds for believing—
(a) that the detained person has benefited from drug trafficking, and
(b) that the recovery of the value of that person's proceeds of drug trafficking will be hindered by telling the named person of the arrest.]

(6) If a delay is authorised—
(a) the detained person shall be told the reason for it; and
(b) the reason shall be noted on his custody record.

(7) The duties imposed by subsection (6) above shall be performed as soon as is practicable.

(8) The rights conferred by this section on a person detained at a police station or other

premises are exercisable whenever he is transferred from one place to another; and this section applies to each subsequent occasion on which they are exercisable as it applies to the first such occasion.

(9) There may be no further delay in permitting the exercise of the right conferred by subsection (1) above once the reason for authorising delay ceases to subsist.

[(10) Nothing in this section applies to a person arrested or detained under the terrorism provisions.]

57 ★ ★ ★ ★ ★

58 Access to legal advice

(1) A person arrested and held in custody in a police station or other premises shall be entitled, if he so requests, to consult a solicitor privately at any time.

(2) Subject to subsection (3) below, a request under subsection (1) above and the time at which it was made shall be recorded in the custody record.

(3) Such a request need not be recorded in the custody record of a person who makes it at a time while he is at a court after being charged with an offence.

(4) If a person makes such a request, he must be permitted to consult a solicitor as soon as is practicable except to the extent that delay is permitted by this section.

(5) In any case he must be permitted to consult a solicitor within 36 hours from the relevant time, as defined in section 41(2) above.

(6) Delay in compliance with a request is only permitted—

    (a) in the case of a person who is in police detention for a serious arrestable offence; and

    (b) if an officer of at least the rank of superintendent authorises it.

(7) An officer may give an authorisation under subsection (6) above orally or in writing but, if he gives it orally, he shall confirm it in writing as soon as is practicable.

(8) [Subject to subsection (8A) below] an officer may only authorise delay where he has reasonable grounds for believing that the exercise of the right conferred by subsection (1) above at the time when the person detained desires to exercise it—

    (a) will lead to interference with or harm to evidence connected with a serious arrestable offence or interference with or physical injury to other persons; or

    (b) will lead to the alerting of other persons suspected of having committed such an offence but not yet arrested for it; or

    (c) will hinder the recovery of any property obtained as a result of such an offence.

[(8A) An officer may also authorise delay where the serious arrestable offence is a drug trafficking offence and the officer has reasonable grounds for believing—

    (a) that the detained person has benefited from drug trafficking, and

    (b) that the recovery of the value of that person's proceeds of drug trafficking will be hindered by the exercise of the right conferred by subsection (1) above.]

(9) If delay is authorised—

    (a) the detained person shall be told the reason for it; and

    (b) the reason shall be noted on his custody record.

(10) The duties imposed by subsection (9) above shall be performed as soon as is practicable.

(11) There may be no further delay in permitting the exercise of the right conferred by subsection (1) above once the reason for authorising delay ceases to subsist.

[(12) Nothing in this section applies to a person arrested or detained under the terrorism provisions.]

59 . . .

60 Tape-recording of interviews

(1) It shall be the duty of the Secretary of State—

(a) to issue a code of practice in connection with the tape-recording of interviews of persons suspected of the commission of criminal offences which are held by police officers at police stations; and

(b) to make an order requiring the tape-recording of interviews of persons suspected of the commission of criminal offences, or of such descriptions of criminal offences as may be specified in the order, which are so held, in accordance with the code as it has effect for the time being.

(2) An order under subsection (1) above shall be made by statutory instrument and shall be subject to annulment in pursuance of a resolution of either House of Parliament.

[60A Visual recording of interviews

(1) The Secretary of State shall have power—

(a) to issue a code of practice for the visual recording of interviews held by police officers at police stations; and

(b) to make an order requiring the visual recording of interviews so held, and requiring the visual recording to be in accordance with the code for the time being in force under this section.

(2) A requirement imposed by an order under this section may be imposed in relation to such cases or police stations in such areas, or both, as may be specified or described in the order.

(3) An order under subsection (1) above shall be made by statutory instrument and shall be subject to annulment in pursuance of a resolution of either House of Parliament.

(4) In this section—

(a) references to any interview are references to an interview of a person suspected of a criminal offence; and

(b) references to a visual recording include references to a visual recording in which an audio recording is comprised.]

61 Fingerprinting

(1) Except as provided by this section no person's fingerprints may be taken without the appropriate consent.

(2) Consent to the taking of a person's fingerprints must be in writing if it is given at a time when he is at a police station.

(3) The fingerprints of a person detained at a police station may be taken without the appropriate consent—

(a) if an officer of at least the rank of [inspector] authorises them to be taken; or

(b) if—

(i) he has been charged with a recordable offence or informed that he will be reported for such an offence; and

(ii) he has not had his fingerprints taken in the course of the investigation of the offence by the police.

[(3A) Where a person charged with a recordable offence or informed that he will be reported for such an offence has already had his fingerprints taken as mentioned in paragraph (b)(ii) of subsection (3) above, that fact shall be disregarded for the purposes of that subsection if—

(a) the fingerprints taken on the previous occasion do not constitute a complete set of his fingerprints; or

(b) some or all of the fingerprints taken on the previous occasion are not of sufficient quality to allow satisfactory analysis, comparison or matching (whether in the case in question or generally).]

(4) An officer may only give an authorisation under subsection (3)(a) above if he has reasonable grounds—

(a) for suspecting the involvement of the person whose fingerprints are to be taken in a criminal offence; and

(b) for believing that his fingerprints will tend to confirm or disprove his involvement [or will facilitate the ascertainment of his identity (within the meaning of s 54A) or both;]

[but an authorisation shall not be given for the purpose only of facilitating the ascertainment of that person's identity except where he has refused to identify himself or the officer has reasonable grounds for suspecting that he is not who he claims to be.]

[(4A) The fingerprints of a person who has answered to bail at a court or police station may be taken without the appropriate consent at the court or station if–

(a) the court, or

(b) an officer of at least the rank of inspector, authorises them to be taken.

(4B) A court or officer may only give an authorisation under subsection (4A) if–

(a) the person who has answered to bail has answered to it for a person whose fingerprints were taken on a previous occasion and there are reasonable grounds for believing that he is not the same person; or

(b) the person who has answered to bail claims to be a different person from a person whose fingerprints were taken on a previous occasion.]

(5) An officer may give an authorisation under subsection (3)(a) [or (4A)] above orally or in writing but, if he gives it orally, he will confirm it in writing as soon as is practicable.

(6) Any person's fingerprints may be taken without the appropriate consent if—

[(a) he has been convicted of a recordable offence;

(b) he has been given a caution in respect of a recordable offence which, at the time of the caution, he has admitted; or

(c) he has been warned or reprimanded under section 65 of the Crime and Disorder Act 1998 for a recordable offence.]

(7) In a case where by virtue of subsection (3) or (6) above a person's fingerprints are taken without the appropriate consent—

(a) he shall be told the reason before his fingerprints are taken; and

(b) the reason shall be recorded as soon as is practicable after the fingerprints are taken.

[(7A) If a person's fingerprints are taken at a police station, whether with or without the appropriate consent—

(a) before the fingerprints are taken, an officer shall inform him that they may be the subject of a speculative search; and

(b) the fact that the person has been informed of this possibility shall be recorded as soon as is practicable after the fingerprints have been taken.]

(8) If he is detained at a police station when the fingerprints are taken, the reason for taking them shall be recorded on his custody record [and, in the case falling within subsection (7A) above, the fact referred to in paragraph (b) of that subsection.]

(8A) ★ ★ ★ ★ ★

(9) Nothing in this section—

(a) affects any power conferred by paragraph 18(2) of Schedule 2 to the Immigration Act 1971, [section 141 of the Immigration and Asylum Act 1999 or regulations made under section 144 of that Act]; or

(b) [applies to a person arrested or detained under the terrorism provisions.]

62   Intimate samples

(1) [Subject to section 63B below,] an intimate sample may be taken from a person in police detention only—

(a) if a police officer of at least the rank of [inspector] authorises it to be taken; and

(b) if the appropriate consent is given.

[(1A) An intimate sample may be taken from a person who is not in police detention but from whom, in the course of the investigation of an offence, two or more non-intimate samples suitable for the same means of analysis have been taken which have proved insufficient—

    (a) if a police officer of at least the rank of [inspector] authorises it to be taken; and

    (b) if the appropriate consent is given.]

(2) An officer may only give an authorisation [under subsection (1) or (1A) above] if he has reasonable grounds—

    (a) for suspecting the involvement of the person from whom the sample is to be taken in a [recordable offence]; and

    (b) for believing that the sample will tend to confirm or disprove his involvement.

(3) An officer may give an authorisation under subsection (1) above orally or in writing but, if he gives it orally, he shall confirm it in writing as soon as is practicable.

(4) The appropriate consent must be given in writing.

(5) Where—

    (a) an authorisation has been given; and

    (b) it is proposed that an intimate sample shall be taken in pursuance of the authorisation,

an officer shall inform the person from whom the sample is to be taken—

    (i) of the giving of the authorisation; and

    (ii) of the grounds for giving it.

(6) The duty imposed by subsection (5)(ii) above includes a duty to state the nature of the offence in which it is suspected that the person from whom the sample is to be taken has been involved.

(7) If an intimate sample is taken from a person—

    (a) the authorisation by virtue of which it was taken;

    (b) the grounds for giving the authorisation; and

    (c) the fact that the appropriate consent was given, shall be recorded as soon as is practicable after the sample is taken.

[(7A) If an intimate sample is taken from a person at a police station—

    (a) before the sample is taken, an officer shall inform him that it may be the subject of a speculative search; and

    (b) the fact that the person has been informed of this possibility shall be recorded as soon as practicable after the sample has been taken.]

(8) If an intimate sample is taken from a person detained at a police station, the matters required to be recorded by subsection (7) [or (7A)] above shall be recorded in his custody record.

(9) An intimate sample, other than a sample of urine [or a dental impression] may only be taken from a person by a registered medical practitioner [or a registered nurse] [and a dental impression may only be taken by a registered dentist.]

(10) Wherethe appropriate consent to the taking of an intimate sample from a person was refused without good cause, in any proceedings against that person for an offence—

    (a) the court, in determining—

        (i) [whether to grant an application for dismissal made by that person under section 6 of the Magistrates' Courts Act 1980 (application for dismissal of charge in course of proceedings with a view to transfer for trial);] or

        (ii) whether there is a case to answer;

            (aa) ★ ★ ★ ★ ★ ; and

    (b) the court or jury, in determining whether that person is guilty of the offence charged,

may draw such inferences from the refusal as appear proper; and the refusal may, on the basis of such inferences, be treated as, or as capable of amounting to corroboration of any evidence against the person in relation to which the refusal is material.

(11) Nothing in this section affects sections [4 to 11 of the Road Traffic Act 1988].

(12) ★ ★ ★ ★ ★

63 Other samples

(1) Except as provided by this section, a non-intimate sample may not be taken from a person without the appropriate consent.

(2) Consent to the taking of a non-intimate sample must be given in writing.

(3) A non-intimate sample may be taken from a person without the appropriate consent if—

(a) he is in police detention or is being held in custody by the police on the authority of a court; and

(b) an officer of at least the rank of [inspector] authorises it to be taken without the appropriate consent.

[(3A) A non-intimate sample may be taken from a person (whether or not he falls within subsection (3)(a) above) without the appropriate consent if—

(a) he has been charged with a recordable offence or informed that he will be reported for such an offence; and

(b) either he has not had a non-intimate sample taken from him in the course of the investigation of the offence by the police or he has had a non-intimate sample taken from him but either it was not suitable for the same means of analysis or, though so suitable, the sample proved insufficient.

(3B) A non-intimate sample may be taken from a person without the appropriate consent if he has been convicted of a recordable offence.]

[(3C) A non-intimate sample may also be taken without the appropriate consent if he is a person to whom section 2 of the Criminal Evidence (Amendment) Act 1997 applies (persons detained following acquittal on grounds of insanity or finding of unfitness to plead).]

(4) An officer may only give an authorisation under subsection (3) above if he has reasonable grounds–

(a) for suspecting the involvement of the person from whom the sample is to be taken in a serious arrestable offence; and

(b) for believing that the sample will tend to confirm or disprove his involvement.

(5) An officer may give an authorisation under subsection (3) above orally or in writing but, if he gives it orally, he shall confirm it in writing as soon as is practicable.

(5A) ★ ★ ★ ★ ★

(6) Where—

(a) an authorisation has been given; and

(b) it is proposed that a non-intimate sample shall be taken in pursuance of the authorisation,

an officer shall inform the person from whom the sample is to be taken—

(i) of the giving of the authorisation; and

(ii) of the grounds for giving it.

(7) the duty imposed by subsection (6)(ii) above includes a duty to state the nature of the offence in which it is suspected that the person from whom the sample is to be taken has been involved.

(8) If a non-intimate sample is taken from a person by virtue of subsection (3) above—

(a) the authorisation by virtue of which it was taken; and

(b) the grounds for giving the authorisation, shall be recorded as soon as is practicable after the sample is taken.

[(8A) In a case where by virtue of subsection (3A), [(3B) or (3C) above] a sample is taken from a person without the appropriate consent—

(a) he shall be told the reason before the sample is taken; and

(b) the reason shall be recorded as soon as practicable after the sample is taken.]

[(8B) If a non-intimate sample is taken from a person at a police station, whether with or without the appropriate consent–

(a) before the sample is taken, an officer shall inform him that it may be the subject of a speculative search; and

(b) the fact that the person has been informed of this possibility shall be recorded as soon as practicable after the sample has been taken.]

(9) If a non-intimate sample is taken from a person detained at a police station, the matters required to be recorded by subsection (8) [or (8A) or (8B)] above shall be recorded in his custody record.

(9A), (10) ★ ★ ★ ★ ★

63A ★ ★ ★ ★ ★

[63B   Testing for presence of Class A drugs

(1) A sample of urine or a non-intimate sample may be taken from a person in police detention for the purpose of ascertaining whether he has any specified Class A drug in his body if the following conditions are met.

(2) The first condition is—

(a) that the person concerned has been charged with a trigger offence; or

(b) that the person concerned has been charged with an offence and a police officer of at least the rank of inspector, who has reasonable grounds for suspecting that the misuse by that person of any specified Class A drug caused or contributed to the offence, has authorised the sample to be taken.

(3) The second condition is that the person concerned has attained the age of 18.

(4) The third condition is that a police officer has requested the person concerned to give the sample.

(5) Before requesting the person concerned to give a sample, an officer must—

(a) warn him that if, when so requested, he fails without good cause to do so he may be liable to prosecution, and

(b) in a case within subsection (2)(b) above, inform him of the giving of the authorisation and of the grounds in question.]

(6)–(8) ★ ★ ★ ★ ★

63C ★ ★ ★ ★ ★

64   Destruction of fingerprints and samples

[(1A) Where—

(a) fingerprints or samples are taken from a person in connection with the investigation of an offence, and

(b) subsection (3) below does not require them to be destroyed, the fingerprints or samples may be retained after they have fulfilled the purposes for which they were taken but shall not be used by any person except for purposes related to the prevention or detection of crime, the investigation of an offence or the conduct of a prosecution.]

(1B) ★ ★ ★ ★ ★

(2) . . .

(3) If—

(a) fingerprints or samples are taken from a person in connection with the investigation of an offence; and

(b) that person is not suspected of having committed the offence, they must [except as provided in [the following subsections of this section]] be destroyed as soon as they have fulfilled the purpose for which they were taken.

[(3AA) Samples and fingerprints are not required to be destroyed under subsection (3) above if—

  (a) they were taken for the purposes of the investigation of an offence of which a person has been convicted; and

  (b) a sample or, as the case may be, fingerprint was also taken from the convicted person for the purposes of that investigation.

(3AB) Subject to subsection (3AC) below, where a person is entitled under subsection (3) above to the destruction of any fingerprint or sample taken from him (or would be but for subsection (3AA) above), neither the fingerprint nor the sample, nor any information derived from the sample, shall be used—

  (a) in evidence against the person who is or would be entitled to the destruction of that fingerprint or sample; or

  (b) for the purposes of the investigation of any offence; and subsection (1B) above applies for the purposes of this subsection as it applies for the purposes of subsection (1A) above.

(3AC) Where a person from whom a fingerprint or sample has been taken consents in writing to its retention—

  (a) that sample need not be destroyed under subsection (3) above;

  (b) subsection (3AB) above shall not restrict the use that may be made of the fingerprint or sample or, in the case of a sample, of any information derived from it; and

  (c) that consent shall be treated as comprising a consent for the purposes of section 63A(1C) above;

and a consent given for the purpose of this subsection shall not be capable of being withdrawn.

(3AD) For the purposes of subsection (3AC) above it shall be immaterial whether the consent is given at, before or after the time when the entitlement to the destruction, of the fingerprint or sample arises.]

(4) . . .

(5)–(7) ★ ★ ★ ★ ★

[64A Photographing of suspects etc.

(1) A person who is detained at a police station may be photographed—

  (a) with the appropriate consent; or

  (b) if the appropriate consent is withheld or it is not practicable to obtain it, without it.

(2) A person proposing to take a photograph of any person under this section—

  (a) may, for the purpose of doing so, require the removal of any item or substance worn on or over the whole or any part of the head or face of the person to be photographed; and

  (b) if the requirement is not complied with, may remove the item or substance himself.

(3) Where a photograph may be taken under this section, the only persons entitled to take the photograph are—

  (a) constables; and

  (b) persons who (without being constables) are designated for the purposes of this section by the chief officer of police for the police area in which the police station in question is situated;

and section 117 (use of force) applies to the exercise by a person falling within paragraph (b) of the powers conferred by the preceding provisions of this section as it applies to the exercise of those powers by a constable.

(4) A photograph taken under this section—

  (a) may be used by, or disclosed to, any person for any purpose related to the prevention or detection of crime, the investigation of an offence or the conduct of a prosecution; and

(b) after being so used or disclosed, may be retained but may not be used or disclosed except for a purpose so related.

(5) In subsection (4)—

(a) the reference to crime includes a reference to any conduct which—

(i) constitutes one or more criminal offences (whether under the law of a part of the United Kingdom or of a country or territory outside the United Kingdom); or

(ii) is, or corresponds to, any conduct which, if it all took place in any one part of the United Kingdom, would constitute one or more criminal offences; and

(b) the references to an investigation and to a prosecution include references, respectively, to any investigation outside the United Kingdom of any crime or suspected crime and to a prosecution brought in respect of any crime in a country or territory outside the United Kingdom.

(6) References in this section to taking a photograph include references to using any process by means of which a visual image may be produced; and references to photographing a person shall be construed accordingly.]

65 Part V—supplementary

(1) In this Part of this Act—

["analysis", in relation to a skin impression, includes comparison and matching;]

"appropriate consent" means—

(a) in relation to a person who has attained the age of 17 years, the consent of that person;

(b) in relation to a person who has not attained that age but has attained the age of 14 years, the consent of that person and his parent or guardian; and

(c) in relation to a person who has not attained the age of 14 years, the consent of his parent or guardian;

["drug trafficking" and "drug trafficking offence" have the same meaning as in the [Drug Trafficking Act 1994];]

["fingerprints", in relation to any person, means a record (in any form and produced by any method) of the skin pattern and other physical characteristics or features of—

(a) any of that person's fingers; or

(b) either of his palms;];

["intimate sample" means—

(a) a sample of blood, semen or any other tissue fluid, urine or pubic hair;

(b) a dental impression;

(c) a swab taken from a person's body orifice other than the mouth;

"intimate search" means a search which consists of the physical examination of a person's body orifices other than the mouth;

"non-intimate sample" means—

(a) a sample of hair other than pubic hair;

(b) a sample taken from a nail or from under a nail;

(c) a swab taken from any part of a person's body including the mouth but not any other body orifice;

(d) saliva;

[(e) a skin impression;]

"registered dentist" has the same meaning as in the Dentists Act 1984;

["skin impression", in relation to any person, means any record (other than a fingerprint) which is a record (in any form and produced by any method) of the skin pattern and other physical characteristics or features of the whole or any part of his foot or of any other part of his body;]

"speculative search", in relation to a person's fingerprints or samples, means such a check against other fingerprints or samples or against information derived from other samples as is referred to in section 63A(1) above;

"sufficient" and "insufficient" in relation to a sample, means [(subject to subsection (2) below)] sufficient or insufficient (in point of quantity or quality) for the purpose of enabling information to be produced by the means of analysis used or to be used in relation to the sample;]

["the terrorism provisions" means section 41 of the Terrorism Act 2000 and any provision of Schedule 7 to that Act conferring a power of detention; and

"terrorism" has the meaning given in section 1 of that Act;]

[and references in this Part to any person's proceeds of drug trafficking are to be construed in accordance with the [Drug Trafficking Act 1994].]

(2) ★ ★ ★ ★ ★

PART VI   CODES OF PRACTICE—GENERAL

66   Codes of practice

(1) The Secretary of State shall issue codes of practice in connection with—

(a) the exercise by police officers of statutory powers—

(i)   to search a person without first arresting him; or

(ii) to search a vehicle without making an arrest;

(b) the detention, treatment, questioning and indication of persons by police officers;

(c) searches of premises by police officers; and

(d) the seizure of property found by police officers on persons or premises.

[(2) Codes shall (in particular) include provisions in connection with the exercise by police officers of powers under section 63B, above.]

67   Codes of practice—supplementary

(1) When the Secretary of State proposes to issue a code of practice to which this section applies, he shall prepare and publish a draft of that code, shall consider any representations made to him about the draft and may modify the draft accordingly.

(2) This section applies to a code of practice under section 60, [60A] or 66 above.

(3) The Secretary of State shall lay before both Houses of Parliament a draft of any code of practice prepared by him under this section.

(4) When the Secretary of State has laid the draft of a code before Parliament, he may bring the code into operation by order made by statutory instrument.

(5) No order under subsection (4) above shall have effect until approved by a resolution of each House of Parliament.

(6) An order bringing a code of practice into operation may contain such transitional provisions or savings as appear to the Secretary of State to be necessary or expedient in connection with the code of practice thereby brought into operation.

(7) The Secretary of State may from time to time revise the whole or any part of a code of practice to which this section applies and issue that revised code; and the foregoing provisions of this section shall apply (with appropriate modifications) to such a revised code as they apply to the first issue of a code.

(7A)–(7C) ★ ★ ★ ★ ★

(8) . . .

(9) Persons other than police officers who are charged with the duty of investigating

offences or charging offenders shall in the discharge of that duty have regard to any relevant provision of such a code.

(10) A failure on the part—

    (a) of a police officer to comply with any provision of such a code; or

    (b) of any person other than a police officer who is charged with the duty of investigating offences or charging offenders to have regard to any relevant provision of such a code in the discharge of the duty,

shall not of itself render him liable to any criminal or civil proceedings.

(11) In all criminal and civil proceedings any such code shall be admissible in evidence; and if any provision of such a code appears to the court or tribunal conducting the proceedings to be relevant to any question arising in the proceedings it shall be taken into account in determining that question.

(12) ★ ★ ★ ★ ★

Note: Extracts from the Codes of Practice issued under this section (as revised) are printed at the end of this book.

PART VIII   EVIDENCE IN CRIMINAL PROCEEDINGS—GENERAL

68-75 ★ ★ ★ ★ ★

Confessions

76 Confessions

(1) In any proceedings a confession made by an accused person may be given in evidence against him in so far as it is relevant to any matter in issue in the proceedings and is not excluded by the court in pursuance of this section.

(2) If, in any proceedings where the prosecution proposes to give in evidence a confession made by an accused person, it is represented to the court that the confession was or may have been obtained—

    (a) by oppression of the person who made it; or

    (b) in consequence of anything said or done which was likely, in the circumstances existing at the time, to render unreliable any confession which might be made by him in consequence thereof,

the court shall not allow the confession to be given in evidence against him except in so far as the prosecution proves to the court beyond reasonable doubt that the confession (notwithstanding that it may be true) was not obtained as aforesaid.

(3) In any proceedings where the prosecution proposes to give in evidence a confession made by an accused person, the court may of its own motion require the prosecution, as a condition of allowing it to do so, to prove that the confession was not obtained as mentioned in subsection (2) above.

(4) The fact that a confession is wholly or partly excluded in pursuance of this section shall not affect the admissibility in evidence—

    (a) of any facts discovered as a result of the confession; or

    (b) where the confession is relevant as showing that the accused speaks, writes or expresses himself in a particular way, of so much of the confession as is necessary to show that he does so.

(5) Evidence that a fact to which this subsection applies was discovered as a result of a statement made by an accused person shall not be admissible unless evidence of how it was discovered is given by him or on his behalf.

(6) Subsection (5) above applies—

    (a) to any fact discovered as a result of a confession which is wholly excluded in pursuance of this section; and

(b) to any fact discovered as a result of a confession which is partly so excluded, if that fact is discovered as a result of the excluded part of the confession.

(7) Nothing in Part VII of this Act shall prejudice the admissibility of a confession made by an accused person.

(8) In this section "oppression" includes torture, inhuman or degrading treatment, and the use or threat of violence (whether or not amounting to torture).

(9) ★ ★ ★ ★ ★

77 Confessions by mentally handicapped persons

(1) Without prejudice to the general duty of the court at a trial on indictment to direct the jury on any matter on which it appears to the court appropriate to do so, where at such a trial—

(a) the case against the accused depends wholly or substantially on a confession by him; and

(b) the court is satisfied—

(i) that he is mentally handicapped; and

(ii) that the confession was not made in the presence of an independent person, the court shall warn the jury that there is special need for caution before convicting the accused in reliance on the confession, and shall explain that the need arises because of the circumstances mentioned in paragraphs (a) and (b) above, but in doing so shall not be required to use any particular form of words.

(2) In any case where at the summary trial of a person for an offence it appears to the court that a warning under subsection (1) above would be required if the trial were on indictment, the court shall treat the case as one in which there is a special need for caution before convicting the accused on his confession.

(3) In this section—

"independent person" does not include a police officer or a person employed for, or engaged on police purposes;

"mentally handicapped", in relation to a person, means that he is in a state of arrested or incomplete development of mind which includes significant impairment of intelligence and social functioning; and

"police purposes" has the meaning assigned to it by [section 101(2) of the Police Act 1996.]

Note: The Police and Criminal Evidence Act 1984 (Application to Customs and Excise) Order 1985 (SI 1985 No. 1800), Art. 10, provides that subsection (3) above "shall be modified to the extent that the definition of 'independent person' shall, in addition to the persons mentioned therein, also include an officer or any other person acting under the authority of the Commissioners of Customs and Excise".

Miscellaneous

78 Exclusion of unfair evidence

(1) In any proceedings the court may refuse to allow evidence on which the prosecution proposes to rely to be given if it appears to the court that, having regard to all the circumstances, including the circumstances in which the evidence was obtained, the admission of the evidence would have such an adverse effect on the fairness of the proceedings that the court ought not to admit it.

(2) Nothing in this section shall prejudice any rule of law requiring a court to exclude evidence.

(3) ★ ★ ★ ★ ★

79–81 ★ ★ ★ ★ ★

PART VIII—SUPPLEMENTARY

82   Part VIII—interpretation

(1) In this Part of this Act—

"confession" includes any statement wholly or partly adverse to the person who made it, whether made to a person in authority or not and whether made in words or otherwise;

★ ★ ★ ★ ★

(2) ★ ★ ★ ★ ★

(3) Nothing in this Part of this Act shall prejudice any power of a court to exclude evidence (whether by preventing questions from being put or otherwise) at its discretion.

83–106   (Repealed and re-enacted by the Police Act 1996, see below.) . . .

PART XI   MISCELLANEOUS AND SUPPLEMENTARY

107–8, 110–1, 113–5 ★ ★ ★ ★ ★

109, 112 . . .

116   Meaning of "serious arrestable offence"

(1) This section has effect for determining whether an offence is a serious arrestable offence for the purposes of this Act.

(2) The following arrestable offences are always serious—

    (a) an offence (whether at common law or under any enactment) specified in Part I of Schedule 5 to this Act; and

    (b) an offence under an enactment specified in Part II of that Schedule [;and

    (c) any of the offences mentioned in paragraphs (a) to (f) of section 1(3) of the Drug Trafficking Act 1994.]

(3) Subject to [subsection (4)] below, any other arrestable offence is serious only if its commission—

    (a) has led to any of the consequences specified in subsection (6) below; or

    (b) is intended or is likely to lead to any of those consequences.

(4) An arrestable offence which consists of making a threat is serious if carrying out the threat would be likely to lead to any of the consequences specified in subsection (6) below.

(5) . . .

(6) The consequences mentioned in subsections (3) and (4) above are

    (a) serious harm to the security of the State or to public order;

    (b) serious interference with the administration of justice or with the investigation of offences or of a particular offence;

    (c) the death of any person;

    (d) serious injury to any person;

    (e) substantial financial gain to any person; and

    (f) serious financial loss to any person.

(7) Loss is serious for the purposes of this section if, having regard to all the circumstances, it is serious for the person who suffers it.

(8) In this section "injury" includes any disease and any impairment of a person's physical or mental condition.

117   Power of constable to use reasonable force

Where any provision of this Act—

    (a) confers a power on a constable; and

    (b) does not provide that the power may only be exercised with the consent of some person, other than a police officer,

the officer may use reasonable force, if necessary, in the exercise of the power.

118 General interpretation

(1) ★ ★ ★ ★ ★

(2) A person is in police detention for the purposes of this Act if—

[(a) he has been taken to a police station after being arrested for an offence or after being arrested under section 41 of the Terrorism Act 2000]]; or

(b) he is arrested at a police station after attending voluntarily at the station or accompanying a constable to it,

and is detained there or is detained elsewhere in the charge of a constable, except that a person who is at a court after being charged is not in police detention for those purposes.

★ ★ ★ ★ ★

Section 9 SCHEDULE 1
SPECIAL PROCEDURE

Making of orders by circuit judge

1. If on an application made by a constable a circuit judge is satisfied that one or other of the sets of access conditions is fulfilled, he may make an order under paragraph 4 below.

2. The first set of access conditions is fulfilled if—

(a) there are reasonable grounds for believing—

(i) that a serious arrestable offence has been committed;

(ii) that there is material which consists of special procedure material or includes special procedure material and does not also include excluded material on premises specified in the application;

(iii) that the material is likely to be of substantial value (whether by itself or together with other material) to the investigation in connection with which the application is made; and

(iv) that the material is likely to be relevant evidence;

(b) other methods of obtaining the material—

(i) have been tried without success; or

(ii) have not been tried because it appeared that they were bound to fail; and

(c) it is in the public interest, having regard—

(i) to the benefit likely to accrue to the investigation if the material is obtained; and

(ii) to the circumstances under which the person in possession of the material holds it,

that the material should be produced or that access to it should be given.

3. The second set of access conditions is fulfilled if—

(a) there are reasonable grounds for believing that there is material which consists of or includes excluded material or special procedure material on premises specified in the application;

(b) but for section 9(2) above a search of the premises for that material could have been authorised by the issue of a warrant to a constable under an enactment other than this Schedule; and

(c) the issue of such a warrant would have been appropriate.

4. An order under this paragraph is an order that the person who appears to the circuit judge to be in possession of the material to which the application relates shall—

(a) produce it to a constable for him to take away; or

(b) give a constable access to it, not later than the end of the period of seven days from the date of the order or the end of such longer period as the order may specify.

5. Where the material consists of information [stored in any electronic form]–

    (a) an order under paragraph 4(a) above shall have effect as an order to produce the material in a form in which it can be taken away and in which it is visible and legible [or from which it can readily be produced in a visible and legible form]; and

    (b) an order under paragraph 4(b) above shall have effect as an order to give a constable access to the material in a form in which it is visible and legible.

6. For the purposes of sections 21 and 22 above material produced in pursuance of an order under paragraph 4(a) above shall be treated as if it were material seized by a constable.

Notices of applications for orders

7. An application for an order under paragraph 4 above shall be made inter partes.

8. Notice of an application for such an order may be served on a person either by delivering it to him or by leaving it at his proper address or by sending it by post to him in a registered letter or by the recorded delivery service.

9. Such a notice may be served—

    (a) on a body corporate, by serving it on the body's secretary or clerk or other similar officer; and

    (b) on a partnership, by serving it on one of the partners.

10. For the purposes of this Schedule, and of section 7 of the Interpretation Act 1978 in its application to this Schedule, the proper address of a person, in the case of secretary or clerk or other similar officer of a body corporate, shall be that of the registered or principal office of that body, in the case of a partner of a firm shall be that of the principal office of the firm, and in any other case shall be the last known address of the person to be served.

11. Where notice of an application for an order under paragraph 4 above has been served on a person, he shall not conceal, destroy, alter or dispose of the material to which the application relates except—

    (a) with the leave of a judge; or

    (b) with the written permission of a constable, until—

        (i) the application is dismissed or abandoned; or

        (ii) he has complied with an order under paragraph 4 above made on the application.

Issue of warrants by circuit judge

12. If on an application made by a constable a circuit judge—

    (a) is satisfied—

        (i) that either set of access conditions is fulfilled; and

        (ii) that any of the further conditions set out in paragraph 14 below is also fulfilled; or

    (b) is satisfied—

        (i) that the second set of access conditions is fufilled; and

        (ii) that an order under paragraph 4 above relating to the material has not been complied with,

he may issue a warrant authorising a constable to enter and search the premises.

13. A constable may seize and retain anything for which a search has been authorised under paragraph 12 above.

14. The further conditions mentioned in paragraph 12(a)(ii) above are—

    (a) that it is not practicable to communicate with any person entitled to grant entry to the premises to which the application relates;

    (b) that it is practicable to communicate with a person entitled to grant entry to the premises but it is not practicable to communicate with any person entitled to grant access to the material;

(c) that the material contains information which–
   (i) is subject to a restriction or obligation such as is mentioned in section 11(2)(b) above; and
   (ii) is likely to be disclosed in breach of it if a warrant is not issued;
(d) that service of notice of an application for an order under paragraph 4 above may seriously prejudice the investigation.

15.—(1) If a person fails to comply with an order under paragraph 4 above, a circuit judge may deal with him as if he had committed a contempt of the Crown Court.

(2) Any enactment relating to contempt of the Crown Court shall have effect in relation to such a failure as if it were such a contempt.

16. ★ ★ ★ ★ ★

★ ★ ★ ★ ★

Section 116

SCHEDULE 5
SERIOUS ARRESTABLE OFFENCES
PART I   OFFENCES MENTIONED IN SECTION 116(2)(a)

1. Treason.
2. Murder.
3. Manslaughter.
4. Rape.
5. Kidnapping.
6. Incest with a girl under the age of 13.
[7. Buggery with a person under the age of 16.]
8. Indecent assault which constitutes an act of gross indecency.
[9. An offence under section 170 of the Customs and Excise Management Act 1979 of being knowingly concerned, in relation to any goods, in any fraudulent evasion or attempt at evasion of a prohibition in force with respect to the goods under section 42 of the Customs Consolidation Act 1876 (prohibition on importing indecent or obscene articles).]

PART II   OFFENCES MENTIONED IN SECTION 116(2)(b)

Explosive Substances Act 1883 (c. 3)

1. Section 2 (causing explosion likely to endanger life or property).

Sexual Offences Act 1956 (c. 69)

2. Section 5 (intercourse with a girl under the age of 13).

Firearms Act 1968 (c. 27)

3. Section 16 (possession of firearms with intent to injure).
4. Section 17(1) (use of firearms and imitation firearms to resist arrest).
5. Section 18 (carrying firearms with criminal intent).
6. . . .

Taking of Hostages Act 1982 (c. 28)

7. Section 1 (hostage-taking).

Aviation Security Act 1982 (c. 36)

8. Section 1 (hi-jacking).

[*Criminal Justice Act 1988 (c. 33)*

   9. Section 134 (torture).]

[*The Road Traffic Act 1988 (c. 52)*

   10. Section 1 (causing death by reckless driving).]

[*Aviation and Maritime Security Act 1990 (c. 31)*

   11. Section 1 (endangering safety at aerodromes).
   12. Section 9 (hijacking of ships).
   13. Section 10 (seizing or exercising control of fixed platforms).]

[*Protection of Children Act 1978 (c. 37)*

   14. Section 1 (indecent photographs and pseudo-photographs of children).]

Obscene Publications Act 1959 (c. 66)

   15. Section 2 (publication of obscene matter).

★ ★ ★ ★ ★

Video Recordings Act 1984
(1984, c. 39)

An Act to make provision for regulating the distribution of video recordings and for connected purposes   [12 July 1984]

Territorial extent: United Kingdom

Preliminary

1   Interpretation of terms
(1) The provisions of this section shall have effect for the interpretation of terms used in this Act.

(2) "Video work" means any series of visual images (with or without sound)—
    (a) produced electronically by the use of information contained on any disc . . . magnetic tape [or any other device capable of storing data electronically], and
    (b) shown as a moving picture.

(3) "Video recording" means any disc . . . magnetic tape [or any other device capable of storing data electronically] containing information by the use of which the whole or a part of a video work may be produced.

(4) "Supply" means supply in any manner, whether or not for reward, and, therefore, includes supply by way of sale, letting on hire, exchange or loan; and references to a supply are to be interpreted accordingly.

2   Exempted works
(1) Subject to subsection (2) [or (3)] below, a video work is for the purposes of this Act an exempted work if, taken as a whole—
    (a) it is designed to inform, educate or instruct;
    (b) it is concerned with sport, religion or music; or
    (c) it is a video game.

(2) A video work is not an exempted work for those purposes if, to any significant extent, it depicts—

(a) human sexual activity or acts of force or restraint associated with such activity;

(b) mutilation or torture of, or other acts of gross violence towards, humans or animals;

(c) human genital organs or human urinary or excretory functions;

[(d) techniques likely to be useful in the commission of offences;] or is [likely] to any significant extent to stimulate or encourage anything falling within paragraph (a) or, in the case of anything falling within paragraph (b), is [likely] to any extent to do so.

[(3) A video work is not an exempted work for those purposes if, to any significant extent, it depicts criminal activity which is likely to any significant extent to stimulate or encourage the commission of offences.]

3 Exempted supplies

(1) The provisions of this section apply to determine whether or not a supply of a video recording is an exempted supply for the purposes of this Act.

(2) The supply of a video recording by any person is an exempted supply if it is neither—

(a) a supply for reward, nor

(b) a supply in the course or furtherance of a business.

(3) Where on any premises facilities are provided in the course or furtherance of a business for supplying video recordings, the supply by any person of a video recording on those premises is to be treated for the purposes of subsection (2) above as a supply in the course or furtherance of a business.

(4) Where a person (in this subsection referred to as the "original supplier") supplies a video recording to a person who, in the course of a business, makes video works or supplies video recordings, the supply is an exempted supply—

(a) if it is not made with a view to any further supply of that recording, or

(b) if it is so made, but is not made with a view to the eventual supply of that recording to the original supplier.

(5)–(12) ★ ★ ★ ★ ★

Designated authority

4 Authority to determine suitability of video works for classification

(1) The Secretary of State may by notice under this section designate any person as the authority responsible for making arrangements—

(a) for determining for the purposes of this Act whether or not video works are suitable for classification certificates to be issued in respect of them, having special regard to the likelihood of video works in respect of which such certificates have been issued being viewed in the home,

(b) in the case of works which are determined in accordance with the arrangements to be so suitable—

[(ia) for assigning a unique title to each video work in respect of which a classification certificate is to be issued,]

(i) for making such other determinations as are required for the issue of classification certificates, and

(ii) for issuing such certificates, and

(c) for maintaining a record of such determinations (whether determinations made in pursuance of arrangements made by that person or by any person previously designated under this section), . . .

(1A), (1B) ★ ★ ★ ★ ★

(2) The power to designate any person by notice under this section includes power—

(a) to designate two or more persons jointly as the authority responsible for making those arrangements, and

(b) to provide that any person holding an office or employment specified in the notice is to be treated as designated while holding that office or employment.

(3) The Secretary of State shall not make any designation under this section unless he is satisfied that adequate arrangements will be made for an appeal by any person against a determination that a video work submitted by him for the issue of a classification certificate—

(a) is not suitable for a classification certificate to be issued in respect of it, or

(b) is not suitable for viewing by persons who have not attained a particular age, or against a determination that no video recording containing the work is to be supplied other than in a licensed sex shop.

(4) The Secretary of State may at any time designate another person in place of any person designated under this section and, if he does so, may give directions as to the transfer of any record kept in pursuance of the arrangements referred to in subsection (1) above; and it shall be the duty of any person having control of any such record or any part of it to comply with the directions.

(5)–(8) ★ ★ ★ ★ ★

4A Criteria for suitability to which special regard to be had

(1) The designated authority shall, in making any determination as to the suitability of a video work, have special regard (among the other relevant factors) to any harm that may be caused to potential viewers or, through their behaviour, to society by the manner in which the work deals with—

(a) criminal behaviour;

(b) illegal drugs;

(c) violent behaviour or incidents;

(d) horrific behaviour or incidents; or

(e) human sexual activity.

(2) For the purposes of this section—

"potential viewer" means any person (including a child or young person) who is likely to view the video work in question if a classification certificate or a classification certificate of a particular description were issued;

"suitability" means suitability for the issue of a classification certificate or suitability for the issue of a certificate of a particular description;

"violent behaviour" includes any act inflicting or likely to result in the infliction of injury; and any behaviour or activity referred to in subsection (1)(a) to (e) above shall be taken to include behaviour or activity likely to stimulate or encourage it.

4B Review of determinations as to suitability

(1) The Secretary of State may by order make provision enabling the designated authority to review any determination made by them, before the coming into force of section 4A of this Act, as to the suitability of a video work.

(2) The order may in particular provide—

(a) for the authority's power of review to be exercisable in relation to such determinations as the authority think fit;

(b) for the authority to determine, on any review, whether, if they were then determining the suitability of the video work to which the determination under review relates, they—

(i) would issue a classification certificate, or

(ii) would issue a different classification certificate;

(c) for the cancellation of a classification certificate, where they determine that they would not issue a classification certificate;

(d) for the cancellation of a classification certificate and issue of a new classification certificate, where they determine that they would issue a different classification certificate;

(e) for any such cancellation or issue not to take effect until the end of such period as may be determined in accordance with the order;

(f) for such persons as may appear to the authority to fall within a specified category of person to be notified of any such cancellation or issue in such manner as may be specified;

(g) for treating a classification certificate, in relation to any act or omission occurring after its cancellation, as if it had not been issued;

(h) for specified provisions of this Act to apply to determinations made on a review subject to such modifications (if any) as may be specified;

(i) for specified regulations made under section 8 of this Act to apply to a video work in respect of which a new classification certificate has been issued subject to such modifications (if any) as may be specified.]

(3)–(6) ★ ★ ★ ★ ★

5   Parliamentary procedure for designation

(1) Where the Secretary of State proposes to make a designation under section 4 of this Act, he shall lay particulars of his proposal before both Houses of Parliament and shall not make the proposed designation until after the end of the period of forty days beginning with the day on which the particulars of his proposal were so laid.

(2), (3) ★ ★ ★ ★ ★

6   Annual report

(1) The designated authority shall, as soon as it is reasonably practicable to do so after 31st December, make a report to the Secretary of State on the carrying out in the year ending with that date of the arrangements referred to in section 4(1) and (3) of this Act (together with a statement of accounts) and on such other matters (if any) as the designated authority consider appropriate or the Secretary of State may require.

(2) The Secretary of State shall lay a copy of any report made to him under this section before each House of Parliament.

Classification and labelling

7   Classification certificates

(1) In this Act "classification certificate" means a certificate—

(a) issued in respect of a video work in pursuance of arrangements made by the designated authority; and

(b) satisfying the requirements of subsection (2) below.

(2) Those requirements are that the certificate must contain [the title assigned to the video work in accordance with section 4(1)(b)(ia) of this Act and]—

(a) a statement that the video work concerned is suitable for general viewing and unrestricted supply (with or without any advice as to the desirability of parental guidance with regard to the viewing of the work by young children or as to the particular suitability of the work for viewing by children [or young children]); or

(b) a statement that the video work concerned is suitable for viewing only by persons who have attained the age (not being more than eighteen years) specified in the certificate and that no video recording containing that work is to be supplied to any person who has not attained the age so specified; or

(c) the statement mentioned in paragraph (b) above together with a statement that no video recording containing that work is to be supplied other than in a licensed sex shop.

8   Requirements as to labelling, etc.

(1) The Secretary of State may, in relation to video works in respect of which classification certificates have been issued, by regulations require such indication as may be specified by the regulations of any of the contents of any classification certificate to be shown in such a manner as may be so specified on any video recording containing the video work in respect of which the certificate was issued or any spool, case or other thing on or in which such a video recording is kept.

(2), (3) ★ ★ ★ ★ ★

★ ★ ★ ★ ★

Cinemas Act 1985
(1985, c. 13)

An Act to consolidate the Cinematograph Acts 1909 to 1982 and certain related enactments, with an amendment to give effect to a recommendation of the Law Commission   [27 March 1985]

Territorial extent: England and Wales, Scotland

Control of exhibitions

1   Licence required for exhibitions

(1) Subject to sections 5 to 8 below, no premises shall be used for a film exhibition unless they are licensed for the purpose under this section.

(2) A licensing authority may [grant to an applicant and from time to time renew or transfer a licence] to use any premises specified in the licence for the purpose of film exhibitions on such terms and conditions and subject to such restrictions as, subject to regulations under section 4 below, they may [so specify.]

(3) Without prejudice to the generality of subsection (2) above, it shall be the duty of a licensing authority, in granting a licence under this section as respects any premises, —

(a) to impose conditions or restrictions prohibiting the admission of children to film exhibitions involving the showing of works designated, by the authority or by such other body as may be specified in the licence, as works unsuitable for children; and

(b) to consider what (if any) conditions or restrictions should be imposed as to the admission of children to other film exhibitions involving the showing of works designated, by the authority or by such other body as may be specified in the licence, as works of such other description as may be so specified.

2   Consent required for exhibitions for children

(1) Subject to sections 5 and 6 below, no premises shall be used, except with the consent of the licensing authority, for a film exhibition organised wholly or mainly as an exhibition for children.

(2) ★ ★ ★ ★ ★

3, 3A, 4 ★ ★ ★ ★ ★

Exempted exhibitions

5   Exhibitions in private dwelling-houses

(1) This section applies to any film exhibition which—

(a) is given in a private dwelling-house,

(b) is one to which the public are not admitted, and

(c) satisfies the condition mentioned in subsection (2) below.

(2) The condition referred to in subsection (1)(c) above is that either—

    (a) the exhibition is not promoted for private gain, or

    (b) the sole or main purpose of the exhibition is to demonstrate any product, to advertise any goods or services or to provide information, education or instruction.

(3) The following exemptions have effect in relation to any film exhibition to which this section applies, that is to say—

    (a) a licence shall not be required by reason only of the giving of the exhibition;

    (b) where the exhibition is given in premises in respect of which a licence is in force, no condition or restriction on or subject to which the licence was granted shall apply to the exhibition;

    (c) regulations under section 4 above shall not apply to the exhibition.

6   Other non-commercial exhibitions

(1) Subject to subsections (4) and (5) below, this section applies to any film exhibition (other than one to which section 5 above applies) which—

    (a) is one to which the public are not admitted or are admitted without payment, or

    (b) does not fall within paragraph (a) above but is given by an exempted organisation,

and (in either case) satisfies the condition mentioned in subsection (2) below.

(2) The condition referred to in subsection (1) above is that either—

    (a) the exhibition is not promoted for private gain, or

    (b) the sole or main purpose of the exhibition is to demonstrate any product, to advertise any goods or services or to provide information, education or instruction.

(3) The following exemptions have effect in relation to any film exhibition to which this section applies, that is to say—

    (a) a licence under section 1 above shall not be required by reason only of the giving of the exhibition unless the pictures are produced by means specified in regulations under section 4 above as means involving such risk that it is inexpedient that this paragraph should have effect;

    (b) where the exhibition is given in premises in respect of which a licence under section 1 above is in force, no condition or restriction on or subject to which the licence was granted shall apply to the exhibition except so far as it relates to the matters specified in section 4(2)(a) above;

    (c) a consent under section 2 above shall not be required by reason only of the giving of the exhibition;

    (d) where the exhibition is given in premises in respect of which a consent under section 2 above is in force, no condition or restriction on or subject to which the consent was granted shall apply to the exhibition;

    (e) regulations under section 4 above making such provision as is mentioned in subsection (2)(b) of that section shall not apply to the exhibition and regulations under that section making such provision as is mentioned in subsection (2)(a) of that section shall not apply to the exhibition unless it is given in premises in respect of which a licence under section 1 above is in force.

(4) A film exhibition is excluded from being one to which this section applies if it is organised solely or mainly as an exhibition for children who are members of a club, society or association the principal object of which is attendance at film exhibitions, unless the exhibition is given in a private dwelling-house or as part of the activities of an educational or religious institution.

(5) A film exhibition is excluded from being one to which this section applies by virtue of paragraph (b) of subsection (1) above if on more than three out of the last preceding seven

days the premises in question were used for the giving of a film exhibition to which this section applied by virtue of that paragraph.

(6) In this section "exempted organisation" means a society, institution, committee or other organisation with respect to which there is in force at the time of the exhibition in question a certificate given by the Secretary of State certifying that he is satisfied that the organisation is not conducted or established for profit; and there shall be paid to the Secretary of State in respect of the giving of such a certificate such reasonable fee as he may determine.

(7), (8) ★ ★ ★ ★ ★

7   Exhibitions in premises used occasionally

(1) Where the premises in which it is proposed to give a film exhibition are premises used occasionally and exceptionally only, and not on more than six days in any one calendar year, for the purposes of such an exhibition, it shall not be necessary to obtain a licence under section 1 above if—

(a) the occupier of the premises has given to the licensing authority, to the fire authority and to the chief officer of police, not less than seven days' notice in writing of his intention so to use the premises; and

(b) he complies with any regulations under section 4 above and, subject to any such regulations, with any conditions imposed by the licensing authority and notified to him in writing.

(2) For the purposes of subsection (1) above, the giving in any premises of an exhibition to which section 5 or 6 above applies shall be disregarded.

8-20   ★ ★ ★ ★ ★

21   Interpretation

(1) In this Act, except where the contrary intention appears,—

★ ★ ★ ★ ★

"child" means a person under the age of sixteen;

"film exhibition" means any exhibition of moving pictures which is produced otherwise than by the simultaneous reception and exhibition of [programmes included in a programme service (within the meaning of the Broadcasting Act 1990];

★ ★ ★ ★ ★

(2) Any reference in this Act to an exhibition which requires a licence under section 1 above is a reference to an exhibition to which that section applies; and any reference in this Act to an exhibition which requires a consent under section 2 above is a reference to an exhibition to which that section applies.

★ ★ ★ ★ ★

Prosecution of Offences Act 1985
(1985, c. 23)

An Act to provide for the establishment of a Crown Prosecution Service for England and Wales; to make provision as to costs in criminal cases; to provide for the imposition of time limits in relation to preliminary stages of criminal proceedings; to amend section 42 of the Supreme Court Act 1981 and section 3 of the Children and Young Persons Act 1969; to make provision with respect to consents to prosecutions; to repeal section 9 of the Perjury Act 1911; and for connected purposes
[23 May 1985]

Territorial extent: England and Wales

PART I   THE CROWN PROSECUTION SERVICE

Constitution and functions of Service

1   The Crown Prosecution Service

(1) There shall be a prosecuting service for England and Wales (to be known as the "Crown Prosecution Service") consisting of—

    (a) the Director of Public Prosecutions, who shall be head of the Service;

    (b) the Chief Crown Prosecutors, designated under subsection (4) below, each of whom shall be the member of the Service responsible to the Director for supervising the operation of the service in his area; and

    (c) the other staff appointed by the Director under this section.

(2) The Director shall appoint such staff for the Service as, with the approval of the Treasury as to numbers, remuneration and other terms and conditions of service, he considers necessary for the discharge of his functions.

(3) The Director may designate any member of the Service who is a barrister or solicitor for the purposes of this subsection, and any person so designated shall be known as a Crown Prosecutor.

(4) The Director shall divide England and Wales into areas and, for each of those areas, designate a Crown Prosecutor for the purposes of this subsection and any person so designated shall be known as a Chief Crown Prosecutor.

(5) The Director may, from time to time, vary the division of England and Wales made for the purpose of subsection (4) above.

(6) Without prejudice to any functions which may have been assigned to him in his capacity as a member of the Service, every Crown Prosecutor shall have all the powers of the Director as to the institution and conduct of proceedings but shall exercise those powers under the direction of the Director.

(7) Where any enactment (whenever passed)—

    (a) prevents any step from being taken without the consent of the Director or without his consent or the consent of another; or

    (b) requires any step to be taken by or in relation to the Director; any consent given by or, as the case may be, step taken by or in relation to, a Crown Prosecutor shall be treated, for the purposes of that enactment, as given by or, as the case may be, taken by or in relation to the Director.

2   The Director of Public Prosecutions

(1) The Director of Public Prosecutions shall be appointed by the Attorney General.

(2) The Director must be a [person who has a 10 year general qualification, within the meaning of section 71 of the Courts and Legal Services Act 1990.]

(3) ★ ★ ★ ★ ★

3   Functions of the Director

(1) The Director shall discharge his functions under this or any other enactment under the superintendence of the Attorney General.

(2) It shall be the duty of the Director—

    (a) to take over the conduct of all criminal proceedings, other than specified proceedings, instituted on behalf of a police force (whether by a member of that force or by any other person);

    (b) to institute and have the conduct of criminal proceedings in any case where it appears to him that—

        (i) the importance or difficulty of the case makes it appropriate that proceedings should be instituted by him; or

        (ii) it is otherwise appropriate for proceedings to be instituted by him;

(c) to take over the conduct of all binding over proceedings instituted on behalf of a police force (whether by a member of that force or by any other person); ★ ★ ★ ★ ★ and

(g) to discharge such other functions as may from time to time be assigned to him by the Attorney General in pursuance of this paragraph.

(3), (4) ★ ★ ★ ★ ★

4, 5 ★ ★ ★ ★ ★

6   Prosecutions instituted and conducted otherwise than by the Service

(1) Subject to subsection (2) below, nothing in this Part shall preclude any person from instituting any criminal proceedings or conducting any criminal proceedings to which the Director's duty to take over the conduct of proceedings does not apply.

(2) Where criminal proceedings are instituted in circumstances in which the Director is not under a duty to take over their conduct, he may nevertheless do so at any stage.

7–9 ★ ★ ★ ★ ★

Guidelines

10   Guidelines for Crown Prosecutors

(1) The Director shall issue a Code for Crown Prosecutors giving guidance on general principles to be applied by them—

(a) in determining, in any case—

(i) whether proceedings for an offence should be instituted or, where proceedings have been instituted, whether they should be discontinued; or

(ii) what charges should be preferred; and

(b) in considering, in any case, representations to be made by them to any magistrates' court about the mode of trial suitable for that case.

(2) The Director may from time to time make alterations in the Code.

(3) The provisions of the Code shall be set out in the Director's report under section 9 of this Act for the year in which the Code is issued; and any alteration in the Code shall be set out in his report under that section for the year in which the alteration is made.

★ ★ ★ ★ ★

Local Government Act 1986
(1986, c. 10)

An Act to require rating authorities to set a rate on or before 1st April; to prohibit political publicity and otherwise restrain local authority publicity; to require the mortgagor's consent and make other provision in connection with the disposal of local authority mortgages; to amend the law as to the effect of retirement and re-election of, and the allowances payable to, members of certain authorities; and for connected purposes   [26 March 1986]

Territorial extent: England and Wales; Scotland [Though note that s. 2A no longer applies to Scotland by virtue of the Ethical Standards in Public Life etc. (Scotland) Act 2000]

★ ★ ★ ★ ★

PART II   LOCAL AUTHORITY PUBLICITY

2   Prohibition of political publicity

(1) A local authority shall not publish any material which, in whole or in part, appears to be designed to affect public support for a political party.

[(2) In determining whether material falls within the prohibition regard shall be had to the content and style of the material, the time and other circumstances of publication and the likely effect on those to whom it is directed and, in particular, to the following matters–

   (a) whether the material refers to a political party or to persons identified with a political party or promotes or opposes a point of view on a question of political controversy which is identifiable as the view of one political party and not of another;

   (b) where the material is part of a campaign, the effect which the campaign appears to be designed to achieve.]

(3) A local authority shall not give financial or other assistance to a person for the publication of material which the authority are prohibited by this section from publishing themselves.

[2A   Prohibition on promoting homosexuality by teaching or by publishing material

(1) A local authority shall not—

   (a) intentionally promote homosexuality or publish material with the intention of promoting homosexuality;

   (b) promote the teaching in any maintained school of the acceptability of homosexuality as a pretended family relationship.

(2) Nothing in subsection (1) above shall be taken to—

   (a) prohibit the doing of anything for the purpose of treating or preventing the spread of disease;

   [(b) prevent the headteacher or governing body of a maintained school, or a teacher employed by a maintained school from taking steps to prevent any form of bullying.]

(3) In any proceedings in connection with the application of this section a court shall draw such inferences as to the intention of the local authority as may reasonably be drawn from the evidence before it.

(4) In subsection (1)(b) above "maintained school" means,—

   (a) in England and Wales, a [maintained school or maintained nursery school within the meaning of the School Standards and Framework Act 1998]; and

   (b) in Scotland, a public school, nursery school or special school, within the meaning of the Education (Scotland) Act 1980.]

Parliamentary Constituencies Act 1986

(1986, c. 56)

An Act to consolidate the House of Commons (Redistribution of Seats) Acts 1949 to 1979 and certain related enactments   [7 November 1986]

Territorial extent: United Kingdom

1   Parliamentary constituencies

(1) There shall for the purpose of parliamentary elections be the county and borough constituencies (or in Scotland the county and burgh constituencies), each returning a single member, which are described in Orders in Council made under this Act.

(2) In this Act and, except where the context otherwise requires, in any Act passed after the Representation of the People Act 1948, "constituency" means an area having separate representation in the House of Commons.

2   The Boundary Commissions

(1) For the purposes of the continuous review of the distribution of seats at parliamentary elections, there shall continue to be four permanent Boundary Commissions, namely a Boundary Commission for England, a Boundary Commission for Scotland, a Boundary Commission for Wales and a Boundary Commission for Northern Ireland.

(2) Schedule 1 to this Act shall have effect with respect to the constitution of, and other matters relating to, the Boundary Commissions.

3   Reports of the Commissions

(1) Each Boundary Commission shall keep under review the representation in the House of Commons of the part of the United Kingdom with which they are concerned and shall, in accordance with subsection (2) below, submit to the Secretary of State reports with respect to the whole of that part of the United Kingdom, either—

(a) showing the constituencies into which they recommend that it should be divided in order to give effect to the rules set out in paragraphs 1 to 6 of Schedule 2 to this Act (read with paragraph 7 of that Schedule), or

(b) stating that, in the opinion of the Commission, no alteration is required to be made in respect of that part of the United Kingdom in order to give effect to the said rules (read with paragraph 7).

(2) Reports under subsection (1) above shall be submitted by a Boundary Commission [not less than eight or more than twelve years] from the date of the submission of their last report under that subsection.

[(2A) A failure by a Boundary Commission to submit a report within the time limit which is appropriate to that report shall not be regarded as invalidating the report for the purpose of any enactment.]

(3) Any Boundary Commission may also from time to time submit to the Secretary of State reports with respect to the area comprised in any particular constituency or constituencies in the part of the United Kingdom with which they are concerned, showing the constituencies into which they recommend that that area should be divided in order to give effect to the rules set out in paragraphs 1 to 6 of Schedule 2 to this Act (read with paragraph 7 of that Schedule).

(4) A report of a Boundary Commission under this Act showing the constituencies into which they recommend that any area should be divided shall state, as respects each constituency, the name by which they recommend that it should be known, and whether they recommend that it should be a county constituency or a borough constituency (or in Scotland a county constituency or a burgh constituency).

(5) As soon as may be after a Boundary Commission have submitted a report to the Secretary of State under this Act, he shall lay the report before Parliament together, except in a case where the report states that no alteration is required to be made in respect of the part of the United Kingdom with which the Commission are concerned, with the draft of an Order in Council for giving effect, whether with or without modifications, to the recommendations contained in the report.

(6) Schedule 2 to this Act which contains the rules referred to above and related provisions shall have effect.

(7), (8) ★ ★ ★ ★ ★

★ ★ ★ ★ ★

Section 2   SCHEDULE 1
                          THE BOUNDARY COMMISSIONS

Constitution

1. The Speaker of the House of Commons shall be the chairman of each of the four Commissions.

2. Each of the four Commissions shall consist of the chairman, a deputy chairman and two other members appointed by the Secretary of State.

3. The deputy chairman—

(a) in the case of the Commission for England shall be a judge of the High Court appointed by the Lord Chancellor,

(b) in the case of the Commission for Scotland shall be a judge of the Court of Session appointed by the Lord President of the Court of Session,

(c) in the case of the Commission for Wales shall be a judge of the High Court appointed by the Lord Chancellor,

(d) in the case of the Commission for Northern Ireland shall be a judge of the High Court in Northern Ireland appointed by the Lord Chief Justice of Northern Ireland.

4. A member of any Commission (other than the chairman) shall hold his appointment for such term and on such conditions as may be determined before his appointment by the person appointing him.

4A.–12. ★ ★ ★ ★ ★

Section 3   SCHEDULE 2
                          RULES FOR REDISTRIBUTION OF SEATS

The rules

1.—(1) The number of constituencies in Great Britain shall not be substantially greater or less than 613.

(2) . . .

(3) The number of constituencies in Wales shall not be less than 35.

(4) The number of constituencies in Northern Ireland shall not be greater than 18 or less than 16, and shall be 17 unless it appears to the Boundary Commission for Northern Ireland that Northern Ireland should for the time being be divided into 16 or (as the case may be) into 18 constituencies.

2. Every constituency shall return a single member.

3. There shall continue to be a constituency which shall include the whole of the City of London and the name of which shall refer to the City of London.

3A. ★ ★ ★ ★ ★

4.—(1) So far as is practicable having regard to rules 1 to [3A]—

(a) in England and Wales,—

(i) no county or part of a county shall be included in a constituency which includes the whole or part of any other county or the whole or part of a London borough,

(ii) no London borough or any part of a London borough shall be included in a constituency which includes the whole or part of any other London borough,

(b) in Scotland, regard shall be had to the boundaries of local authority areas,

(c) in Northern Ireland, no ward shall be included partly in one constituency and partly in another.

[(1A) In sub-paragraph (1)(a) above "county" means in relation to Wales, a preserved county (as defined by section 64 of the Local Government (Wales) Act 1994).]

(2) In sub-paragraph (1)(b) above "area" and "local authority" have the same meanings as in the Local Government (Scotland) Act 1973.

5. The electorate of any constituency shall be as near the electoral quota as is practicable having regard to rules 1 to 4; and a Boundary Commission may depart from the strict application of rule 4 if it appears to them that a departure is desirable to avoid an excessive disparity between the electorate of any constituency and the electoral quota, or between the electorate of any constituency and that of neighbouring constituencies in the part of the United Kingdom with which they are concerned.

6. A Boundary Commission may depart from the strict application of rules 4 and 5 if special geographical considerations, including in particular the size, shape and accessibility of a constituency, appear to them to render a departure desirable.

General and supplementary

7. It shall not be the duty of a Boundary Commission to aim at giving full effect in all circumstances to the above rules [(except rule 3A)], but they shall take account, so far as they reasonably can—

      (a) of the inconveniences attendant on alterations of constituencies other than alterations made for the purposes of rule 4, and

      (b) of any local ties which would be broken by such alterations.

8., 9. ★ ★ ★ ★ ★

Public Order Act 1986
(1986, c. 64)

An Act to abolish the common law offences of riot, rout, unlawful assembly and affray and certain statutory offences relating to public order; to create new offences relating to public order; to control public processions and assemblies; to control the stirring up of racial hatred; to provide for the exclusion of certain offenders from sporting events; to create a new offence relating to the contamination of or interference with goods; to confer power to direct certain trespassers to leave land; to amend section 7 of the Conspiracy and Protection of Property Act 1875, section 1 of the Prevention of Crime Act 1953, Part V of the Criminal Justice (Scotland) Act 1980 and the Sporting Events (Control of Alcohol etc.) Act 1985; to repeal certain obsolete or unnecessary enactments; and for connected purposes   [7 November 1986]

Territorial extent: England and Wales (ss. 1 – 9, 13, 39, 40(4)); England and Wales, Scotland (remainder)

PART I   NEW OFFENCES

1 Riot

    (1) Where 12 or more persons who are present together use or threaten unlawful violence for a common purpose and the conduct of them (taken together) is such as would cause a person of reasonable firmness present at the scene to fear for his personal safety, each of the persons using unlawful violence for the common purpose is guilty of riot.

    (2) It is immaterial whether or not the 12 or more use or threaten unlawful violence simultaneously.

    (3) The common purpose may be inferred from conduct.

    (4) No person of reasonable firmness need actually be, or be likely to be, present at the scene.

    (5) Riot may be committed in private as well as in public places.

(6) A person guilty of riot is liable on conviction on indictment to imprisonment for a term not exceeding ten years or a fine or both.

2   Violent disorder

(1) Where 3 or more persons who are present together use or threaten unlawful violence and the conduct of them (taken together) is such as would cause a person of reasonable firmness present at the scene to fear for his personal safety, each of the persons using or threatening unlawful violence is guilty of violent disorder.

(2) It is immaterial whether or not the 3 or more use or threaten unlawful violence simultaneously.

(3) No person of reasonable firmness need actually be, or be likely to be, present at the scene.

(4) Violent disorder may be committed in private as well as in public places.

(5) A person guilty of violent disorder is liable on conviction on indictment to imprisonment for a term not exceeding 5 years or a fine or both, or on summary conviction to imprisonment for a term not exceeding 6 months or a fine not exceeding the statutory maximum or both.

3   Affray

(1) A person is guilty of affray if he uses or threatens unlawful violence towards another and his conduct is such as would cause a person of reasonable firmness present at the scene to fear for his personal safety.

(2) Where 2 or more persons use or threaten the unlawful violence, it is the conduct of them taken together that must be considered for the purposes of subsection (1).

(3) For the purposes of this section a threat cannot be made by the use of words alone.

(4) No person of reasonable firmness need actually be, or be likely to be, present at the scene.

(5) Affray may be committed in private as well as in public places.

(6) A constable may arrest without warrant anyone he reasonably suspects is committing affray.

(7) A person guilty of affray is liable on conviction on indictment to imprisonment for a term not exceeding 3 years or a fine or both, or on summary conviction to imprisonment for a term not exceeding 6 months or a fine not exceeding the statutory maximum or both.

4   Fear or provocation of violence

(1) A person is guilty of an offence if he—
   (a) uses towards another person threatening, abusive or insulting words or behaviour, or
   (b) distributes or displays to another person any writing, sign or other visible representation which is threatening, abusive or insulting,

with intent to cause that person to believe that immediate unlawful violence will be used against him or another by any person, or to provoke the immediate use of unlawful violence by that person or another, or whereby that person is likely to believe that such violence will be used or it is likely that such violence will be provoked.

(2) An offence under this section may be committed in a public or a private place, except that no offence is committed where the words or behaviour are used, or the writing, sign or other visible representation is distributed or displayed, by a person inside a dwelling and the other person is also inside that or another dwelling.

(3) A constable may arrest without warrant anyone he reasonably suspects is committing an offence under this section.

(4) A person guilty of an offence under this section is liable on summary conviction to imprisonment for a term not exceeding 6 months or a fine not exceeding level 5 on the standard scale or both.

[4A   Intentional harassment, alarm or distress

(1) A person is guilty of an offence if, with intent to cause a person harassment, alarm or distress, he—

  (a) uses threatening, abusive or insulting words or behaviour, or disorderly behaviour, or

  (b) displays any writing, sign or other visible representation which is threatening, abusive or insulting,

thereby causing that or another person harassment, alarm or distress.

(2) An offence under this section may be committed in a public or a private place, except that no offence is committed where the words or behaviour are used, or the writing, sign or other visible representation is displayed, by a person inside a dwelling and the person who is harassed, alarmed or distressed is also inside that or another dwelling.

(3) It is a defence for the accused to prove—

  (a) that he was inside a dwelling and had no reason to believe that the words or behaviour used, or the writing, sign or other visible representation displayed, would be heard or seen by a person outside that or any other dwelling, or

  (b) that his conduct was reasonable.

(4) A constable may arrest without warrant anyone he reasonably suspects is committing an offence under this section.

(5) A person guilty of an offence under this section is liable on summary conviction to imprisonment for a term not exceeding 6 months or a fine not exceeding level 5 on the standard scale or both.]

5   Harassment, alarm or distress

(1) A person is guilty of an offence if he—

  (a) uses threatening, abusive or insulting words or behaviour, or disorderly behaviour, or

  (b) displays any writing, sign or other visible representation which is threatening, abusive or insulting,

within the hearing or sight of a person likely to be caused harassment, alarm or distress thereby.

(2) An offence under this section may be committed in a public or a private place, except that no offence is committed where the words or behaviour are used, or the writing, sign or other visible representation is displayed, by a person inside a dwelling and the other person is also inside that or another dwelling.

(3) It is a defence for the accused to prove—

  (a) that he had no reason to believe that there was any person within hearing or sight who was likely to be caused harassment, alarm or distress, or

  (b) that he was inside a dwelling and had no reason to believe that the words or behaviour used, or the writing, sign or other visible representation displayed, would be heard or seen by a person outside that or any other dwelling, or

  (c) that his conduct was reasonable.

(4) A constable may arrest a person without warrant if—

  (a) he engages in offensive conduct which [a] constable warns him to stop, and

  (b) he engages in further offensive conduct immediately or shortly after the warning.

(5) In subsection (4) "offensive conduct" means conduct the constable reasonably suspects to constitute an offence under this section, and the conduct mentioned in paragraph (a) and the further conduct need not be of the same nature.

(6) A person guilty of an offence under this section is liable on summary conviction to a fine not exceeding level 3 on the standard scale.

6   Mental element: miscellaneous

(1) A person is guilty of riot only if he intends to use violence or is aware that his conduct may be violent.

(2) A person is guilty of violent disorder or affray only if he intends to use or threaten violence or is aware that his conduct may be violent or threaten violence.

(3) A person is guilty of an offence under section 4 only if he intends his words or behaviour, or the writing, sign or other visible representation, to be threatening, abusive or insulting, or is aware that it may be threatening, abusive or insulting.

(4) A person is guilty of an offence under section 5 only if he intends his words or behaviour, or the writing, sign or other visible representation, to be threatening, abusive or insulting, or is aware that it may be threatening, abusive or insulting or (as the case may be) he intends his behaviour to be or is aware that it may be disorderly.

(5) For the purposes of this section a person whose awareness is impaired by intoxication shall be taken to be aware of that of which he would be aware if not intoxicated, unless he shows either that his intoxication was not self-induced or that it was caused solely by the taking or administration of a substance in the course of medical treatment.

(6) In subsection (5) "intoxication" means any intoxication, whether caused by drink, drugs or other means, or by a combination of means.

(7) Subsections (1) and (2) do not affect the determination for the purposes of riot or violent disorder of the number of persons who use or threaten violence.

7 Procedure: miscellaneous

(1) No prosecution for an offence of riot or incitement to riot may be instituted except by or with the consent of the Director of Public Prosecutions.

(2)–(4) ★ ★ ★ ★ ★

8 Interpretation

In this Part—

"dwelling" means any structure or part of a structure occupied as a person's home or as other living accommodation (whether the occupation is separate or shared with others) but does not include any part not so occupied, and for this purpose "structure" includes a tent, caravan, vehicle, vessel or other temporary or movable structure;

"violence" means any violent conduct, so that–

(a) except in the context of affray, it includes violent conduct towards property as well as violent conduct towards persons, and

(b) it is not restricted to conduct causing or intended to cause injury or damage but includes any other violent conduct (for example, throwing at or towards a person a missile of a kind capable of causing injury which does not hit or falls short).

9 Offences abolished

(1) The Common Law offences of riot, rout, unlawful assembly and affray are abolished.

(2) ★ ★ ★ ★ ★

10 ★ ★ ★ ★ ★

PART II   PROCESSIONS AND ASSEMBLIES

11 Advance notice of public processions

(1) Written notice shall be given in accordance with this section of any proposal to hold a public procession intended—

(a) to demonstrate support for or opposition to the views or actions of any person or body of persons,

(b) to publicise a cause or campaign, or

(c) to mark or commemorate an event, unless it is not reasonably practicable to give any advance notice of the procession.

(2) Subsection (1) does not apply where the procession is one commonly or customarily held in the police area (or areas) in which it is proposed to be held or is a funeral procession organised by a funeral director acting in the normal course of his business.

(3) The notice must specify the date when it is intended to hold the procession, the time when it is intended to start it, its proposed route, and the name and address of the person (or of one of the persons) proposing to organise it.

(4) Notice must be delivered to a police station—

    (a) in the police area in which it is proposed the procession will start, or

    (b) where it is proposed the procession will start in Scotland and cross into England, in the first police area in England on the proposed route.

(5) If delivered not less than 6 clear days before the date when the procession is intended to be held, the notice may be delivered by post by the recorded delivery service; but section 7 of the Interpretation Act 1978 (under which a document sent by post is deemed to have been served when posted and to have been delivered in the ordinary course of post) does not apply.

(6) If not delivered in accordance with subsection (5), the notice must be delivered by hand not less than 6 clear days before the date when the procession is intended to be held or, if that is not reasonably practicable, as soon as delivery is reasonably practicable.

(7) Where a public procession is held, each of the persons organising it is guilty of an offence if—

    (a) the requirements of this section as to notice have not been satisfied, or

    (b) the date when it is held, the time when it starts, or its route, differs from the date, time or route specified in the notice.

(8) It is a defence for the accused to prove that he did not know of, and neither suspected nor had reason to suspect, the failure to satisfy the requirements or (as the case may be) the difference of date, time or route.

(9) To the extent that an alleged offence turns on a difference of date, time or route, it is a defence for the accused to prove that the difference arose from circumstances beyond his control or from something done with the agreement of a police officer or by his direction.

(10) A person guilty of an offence under subsection (7) is liable on summary conviction to a fine not exceeding level 3 on the standard scale.

12 Imposing conditions on public processions

(1) If the senior police officer, having regard to the time or place at which and the circumstances in which any public procession is being held or is intended to be held and to its route or proposed route, reasonably believes that—

    (a) it may result in serious public disorder, serious damage to property or serious disruption to the life of the community, or

    (b) the purpose of the persons organising it is the intimidation of others with a view to compelling them not to do an act they have a right to do, or to do an act they have a right not to do,

he may give directions imposing on the persons organising or taking part in the procession such conditions as appear to him necessary to prevent such disorder, damage, disruption or intimidation, including conditions as to the route of the procession or prohibiting it from entering any public place specified in the directions.

(2) In subsection (1) "the senior police officer" means—

    (a) in relation to a procession being held, or to a procession intended to be held in a case where persons are assembling with a view to taking part in it, the most senior in rank of the police officers present at the scene, and

    (b) in relation to a procession intended to be held in a case where paragraph (a) does not apply, the chief officer of police.

(3) A direction given by a chief officer of police by virtue of subsection (2)(b) shall be given in writing.

(4) A person who organises a public procession and knowingly fails to comply with a condition imposed under this section is guilty of an offence, but it is a defence for him to prove that the failure arose from circumstances beyond his control.

(5) A person who takes part in a public procession and knowingly fails to comply with a condition imposed under this section is guilty of an offence, but it is a defence for him to prove that the failure arose from circumstances beyond his control.

(6) A person who incites another to commit an offence under subsection (5) is guilty of an offence.

(7) A constable in uniform may arrest without warrant anyone he reasonably suspects is committing an offence under subsection (4), (5) or (6).

(8) A person guilty of an offence under subsection (4) is liable on summary conviction to imprisonment for a term not exceeding 3 months or a fine not exceeding level 4 on the standard scale or both.

(9) A person guilty of an offence under subsection (5) is liable on summary conviction to a fine not exceeding level 3 on the standard scale.

(10) A person guilty of an offence under subsection (6) is liable on summary conviction to imprisonment for a term not exceeding 3 months or a fine not exceeding level 4 on the standard scale or both, notwithstanding section 45(3) of the Magistrates' Courts Act 1980 (inciter liable to same penalty as incited).

(11) In Scotland this section applies only in relation to a procession being held, and to a procession intended to be held in a case where persons are assembling with a view to taking part in it.

13   Prohibiting public processions

(1) If at any time the chief officer of police reasonably believes that, because of particular circumstances existing in any district or part of a district, the powers under section 12 will not be sufficient to prevent the holding of public processions in that district or part from resulting in serious public disorder, he shall apply to the council of the district for an order prohibiting for such period not exceeding 3 months as may be specified in the application the holding of all public processions (or of any class of public procession so specified) in the district or part concerned.

(2) On receiving such an application, a council may with the consent of the Secretary of State make an order either in the terms of the application or with such modifications as may be approved by the Secretary of State.

(3) Subsection (1) does not apply in the City of London or the metropolitan police district.

(4) If at any time the Commissioner of Police for the City of London or the Commissioner of Police of the Metropolis reasonably believes that, because of particular circumstances existing in his police area or part of it, the powers under section 12 will not be sufficient to prevent the holding of public processions in that area or part from resulting in serious public disorder, he may with the consent of the Secretary of State make an order prohibiting for such period not exceeding 3 months as may be specified in the order the holding of all public processions (or of any class of public procession so specified) in the area or part concerned.

(5) An order made under this section may be revoked or varied by a subsequent order made in the same way, that is, in accordance with subsections (1) and (2) or subsection (4), as the case may be.

(6) An order under this section shall, if not made in writing, be recorded in writing as soon as practicable after being made.

(7) A person who organises a public procession the holding of which he knows is prohibited by virtue of an order under this section is guilty of an offence.

(8) A person who takes part in a public procession the holding of which he knows is prohibited by virtue of an order under this section is guilty of an offence.

(9) A person who incites another to commit an offence under subsection (8) is guilty of an offence.

(10) A constable in uniform may arrest without warrant anyone he reasonably suspects is committing an offence under subsection (7), (8) or (9).

(11) A person guilty of an offence under subsection (7) is liable on summary conviction to imprisonment for a term not exceeding 3 months or a fine not exceeding level 4 on the standard scale or both.

(12) A person guilty of an offence under subsection (8) is liable on summary conviction to a fine not exceeding level 3 on the standard scale.

(13) A person guilty of an offence under subsection (9) is liable on summary conviction to imprisonment for a term not exceeding 3 months or a fine not exceeding level 4 on the standard scale or both, notwithstanding section 45(3) of the Magistrates' Courts Act 1980.

14   Imposing conditions on public assemblies

(1) If the senior police officer, having regard to the time or place at which and the circumstances in which any public assembly is being held or is intended to be held, reasonably believes that—

(a) it may result in serious public disorder, serious damage to property or serious disruption to the life of the community, or

(b) the purpose of the persons organising it is the intimidation of others with a view to compelling them not to do an act they have a right to do, or to do an act they have a right not to do,

he may give directions imposing on the persons organising or taking part in the assembly such conditions as to the place at which the assembly may be (or continue to be) held, its maximum duration, or the maximum number of persons who may constitute it, as appear to him necessary to prevent such disorder, damage, disruption or intimidation.

(2) In subsection (1) "the senior police officer" means—

(a) in relation to an assembly being held, the most senior in rank of the police officers present at the scene, and

(b) in relation to an assembly intended to be held, the chief officer of police.

(3) A direction given by a chief officer of police by virtue of subsection (2)(b) shall be given in writing.

(4) A person who organises a public assembly and knowingly fails to comply with a condition imposed under this section is guilty of an offence, but it is a defence for him to prove that the failure arose from circumstances beyond his control.

(5) A person who takes part in a public assembly and knowingly fails to comply with a condition imposed under this section is guilty of an offence, but it is a defence for him to prove that the failure arose from circumstances beyond his control.

(6) A person who incites another to commit an offence under subsection (5) is guilty of an offence.

(7) A constable in uniform may arrest without warrant anyone he reasonably suspects is committing an offence under subsection (4), (5) or (6).

(8) A person guilty of an offence under subsection (4) is liable on summary conviction to imprisonment for a term not exceeding 3 months or a fine not exceeding level 4 on the standard scale or both.

(9) A person guilty of an offence under subsection (5) is liable on summary conviction to a fine not exceeding level 3 on the standard scale.

(10) A person guilty of an offence under subsection (6) is liable on summary conviction to imprisonment for a term not exceeding 3 months or a fine not exceeding level 4 on the standard scale or both, notwithstanding section 45(3) of the Magistrates' Courts Act 1980.

[14A   Prohibiting trespassory assemblies

(1) If at any time the chief officer of police reasonably believes that an assembly is intended to be held in any district at a place on land to which the public has no right of access or only a limited right of access and that the assembly—

(a) is likely to be held without the permission of the occupier of the land or to conduct itself in such a way as to exceed the limits of any permission of his or the
limits of the public's right of access, and

(b) may result—
(i) in serious disruption to the life of the community, or
(ii) where the land, or a building or monument on it, is of historical, architectural,
archaeological or scientific importance, in significant damage to the land,
building or monument,

he may apply to the council of the district for an order prohibiting for a specified period the
holding of all trespassory assemblies in the district or a part of it, as specified.

(2) On receiving such an application, a council may—

(a) in England and Wales, with the consent of the Secretary of State make an order
either in the terms of the application or with such modifications as may be
approved by the Secretary of State; or

(b) in Scotland, make an order in the terms of the application.

(3) Subsection (1) does not apply in the City of London or the metropolitan police
district.

(4) If at any time the Commissioner of Police for the City of London or the Commissioner
of Police of the Metropolis reasonably believes that an assembly is intended to be held at a
place on land to which the public has no right of access or only a limited right of access in his
police area and that the assembly—

(a) is likely to be held without the permission of the occupier of the land or to conduct itself in such a way as to exceed the limits of any permission of his or the
limits of the public's right of access, and

(b) may result—
(i) in serious disruption to the life of the community, or
(ii) where the land, or a building or monument on it, is of historical, architectural,
archaeological or scientific importance, in significant damage to the land,
building or monument,

he may with the consent of the Secretary of State make an order prohibiting for a specified
period the holding of all trespassory assemblies in this area or a part of it, as specified.

(5) An order prohibiting the holding of trespassory assemblies operates to prohibit any
assembly which—

(a) is held on land to which the public has no right of access or only a limited right of
access, and

(b) takes place in the prohibited circumstances, that is to say, without the permission
of the occupier of the land or so as to exceed the limits of any permission of his or
the limits of the public as right of access.

(6) No order under this section shall prohibit the holding of assemblies for a period
exceeding 4 days or in an area exceeding an area represented by a circle with a radius of 5 miles
from a specified centre.

(7) An order made under this section may be revoked or varied by a subsequent order
made in the same way, that is, in accordance with subsection (1) and (2) or subsection (4), as
the case may be.

(8) Any order under this section shall, if not made in writing, be recorded in writing as
soon as practicable after being made.

(9) In this section and sections 14B and 14C—

"assembly" means an assembly of 20 or more persons;

"land", means land in the open air;

"limited", in relation to a right of access by the public to land, means that their use of it is
restricted to use for a particular purpose (as in the case of a highway or road) or is subject to
other restrictions;

"occupier" means—

    (a) in England and Wales, the person entitled to possession of the land by virtue of an estate or interest held by him; or

    (b) in Scotland, the person lawfully entitled to natural possession of the land, and in subsection (1) and (4) includes the person reasonably believed by the authority applying for or making the order to be the occupier;

"public" includes a section of the public; and

"specified" means specified in an order under this section.

(10), (11) ★ ★ ★ ★ ★

14B   Offences in connection with trespassory assemblies and arrest therefor

(1) A person who organises an assembly the holding of which he knows is prohibited by an order under section 14A is guilty of an offence.

(2) A person who takes part in an assembly which he knows is prohibited by an order under section 14A is guilty of an offence.

(3) In England and Wales, a person who incites another to commit an offence under subsection (2) is guilty of an offence.

(4) A constable in uniform may arrest without a warrant anyone he reasonably suspects to be committing an offence under this section.

(5)–(8) ★ ★ ★ ★ ★

14C   Stopping persons from proceeding to trespassory assemblies

(1) If a constable in uniform reasonably believes that a person is on his way to an assembly within the area to which an order under section 14A applies which the constable reasonably believes is likely to be an assembly which is prohibited by that order, he may, subject to subsection (2) below—

    (a) stop that person, and

    (b) direct him not to proceed in the direction of the assembly.

(2) The power conferred by subsection (1) may only be exercised within the area to which the order applies.

(3) A person who fails to comply with a direction under subsection (1) which he knows has been given to him is guilty of an offence.

(4) A constable in uniform may arrest without a warrant anyone he reasonably suspects to be committing an offence under this section.

(5) A person guilty of an offence under subsection (3) is liable on summary conviction to a fine not exceeding level 3 on the standard scale.]

15   Delegation

(1) The chief officer of police may delegate, to such extent and subject to such conditions as he may specify, any of his functions under sections 12 to [14A] to [an] assistant chief constable; and references in those subsections to the person delegating shall be construed accordingly.

(2) Subsection (1) shall have effect in the City of London and the metropolitan police district as if "[an] assistant chief constable" read "an assistant commissioner of police".

16   Interpretation

In this Part—

★ ★ ★ ★ ★

"public assembly" means an assembly of 20 or more persons in a public place which is wholly or partly open to the air;

"public place" means—

(a) any highway, or in Scotland any road within the meaning of the Roads (Scotland) Act 1984, and

(b) any place to which at the material time the public or any section of the public has access, on payment or otherwise, as of right or by virtue of express or implied permission;

"public procession" means a procession in a public place.

PART III   RACIAL HATRED

Meaning of "racial hatred"

17   Meaning of "racial hatred"

In this Part "racial hatred" means hatred against a group of persons . . . defined by reference to colour, race, nationality (including citizenship) or ethnic or national origins.

Acts intended or likely to stir up racial hatred

18   Use of words or behaviour or display of written material

(1) A person who uses threatening, abusive or insulting words or behaviour, or displays any written material which is threatening, abusive or insulting, is guilty of an offence if—

(a) he intends thereby to stir up racial hatred, or

(b) having regard to all the circumstances racial hatred is likely to be stirred up thereby.

(2) An offence under this section may be committed in a public or a private place, except that no offence is committed where the words or behaviour are used, or the written material is displayed, by a person inside a dwelling and are not heard or seen except by other persons in that or another dwelling.

(3) A constable may arrest without warrant anyone he reasonably suspects is committing an offence under this section.

(4) In proceedings for an offence under this section it is a defence for the accused to prove that he was inside a dwelling and had no reason to believe that the words or behaviour used, or the written material displayed, would be heard or seen by a person outside that or any other dwelling.

(5) A person who is not shown to have intended to stir up racial hatred is not guilty of an offence under this section if he did not intend his words or behaviour, or the written material, to be, and was not aware that it might be, threatening, abusive or insulting.

(6) This section does not apply to words or behaviour used, or written material displayed, solely for the purpose of being [included in a programme service].

19   Publishing or distributing written material

(1) A person who publishes or distributes written material which is threatening, abusive or insulting is guilty of an offence if—

(a) he intends thereby to stir up racial hatred, or

(b) having regard to all the circumstances racial hatred is likely to be stirred up thereby.

(2) In proceedings for an offence under this section it is a defence for an accused who is not shown to have intended to stir up racial hatred to prove that he was not aware of the content of the material and did not suspect, and had no reason to suspect, that it was threatening, abusive or insulting.

(3) References in this Part to the publication or distribution of written material are to its publication or distribution to the public or a section of the public.

20 Public performance of play

(1) If a public performance of a play is given which involves the use of threatening, abusive or insulting words or behaviour, any person who presents or directs the performance is guilty of an offence if—

(a) he intends thereby to stir up racial hatred, or

(b) having regard to all the circumstances (and, in particular, taking the performance as a whole) racial hatred is likely to be stirred up thereby.

(2)–(6) ★ ★ ★ ★ ★

21 Distributing, showing or playing a recording

(1) A person who distributes, or shows or plays, a recording of visual images or sounds which are threatening, abusive or insulting is guilty of an offence if—

(a) he intends thereby to stir up racial hatred, or

(b) having regard to all the circumstances racial hatred is likely to be stirred up thereby.

(2) In this Part "recording" means any record from which visual images or sounds may, by any means, be reproduced; and references to the distribution, showing or playing of a recording are to its distribution, showing or playing to the public or a section of the public.

(3) In proceedings for an offence under this section it is a defence for an accused who is not shown to have intended to stir up racial hatred to prove that he was not aware of the content of the recording and did not suspect, and had no reason to suspect, that it was threatening, abusive or insulting.

(4) This section does not apply to the showing or playing of a recording solely for the purpose of enabling the recording to be [included in a programme service.]

22 Broadcasting or including programme in cable programme service

(1) If a programme involving threatening, abusive or insulting visual images or sounds is [included in a programme service], each of the persons mentioned in subsection (2) is guilty of an offence if—

(a) he intends thereby to stir up racial hatred, or

(b) having regard to all the circumstances racial hatred is likely to be stirred up thereby.

(2) The persons are—

(a) the person providing the . . . programme service,

(a) any person by whom the programme is produced or directed, and

(c) any person by whom offending words or behaviour are used.

(3)–(6) ★ ★ ★ ★ ★

(7), (8) . . .

Racially inflammatory material

23 Possession of racially inflammatory material

(1) A person who has in his possession written material which is threatening, abusive or insulting, or a recording of visual images or sounds which are threatening, abusive or insulting, with a view to—

(a) in the case of written material, its being displayed, published, distributed, broadcast or included in a cable programme service, whether by himself or another, or

(b) in the case of a recording, its being distributed, shown, played, [or included in a programme service], whether by himself or another,

is guilty of an offence if he intends racial hatred to be stirred up thereby or, having regard to all the circumstances, racial hatred is likely to be stirred up thereby.

(2) For this purpose regard shall be had to such display, publication, distribution, showing, playing, [or inclusion in a programme service] as he has, or it may reasonably be inferred that he has, in view.

(3) In proceedings for an offence under this section it is a defence for an accused who is not shown to have intended to stir up racial hatred to prove that he was not aware of the content of the written material or recording and did not suspect, and had no reason to suspect, that it was threatening, abusive or insulting.

(4) ...

24 Powers of entry and search

(1) If in England and Wales a justice of the peace is satisfied by information on oath laid by a constable that there are reasonable grounds for suspecting that a person has possession of written material or a recording in contravention of section 23, the justice may issue a warrant under his hand authorising any constable to enter and search the premises where it is suspected the material or recording is situated.

(2) If in Scotland a sheriff or justice of the peace is satisfied by evidence on oath that there are reasonable grounds for suspecting that a person has possession of written material or a recording in contravention of section 23, the sheriff or justice may issue a warrant authorising any constable to enter and search the premises where it is suspected the material or recording is situated.

(3) A constable entering or searching premises in pursuance of a warrant issued under this section may use reasonable force if necessary.

(4) ★ ★ ★ ★ ★

25 ★ ★ ★ ★ ★

Supplementary provisions

26 Savings for reports of parliamentary or judicial proceedings

(1) Nothing in this Part applies to a fair and accurate report of proceedings in Parliament [or the Scottish Parliament].

(2) Nothing in this Part applies to a fair and accurate report of proceedings publicly heard before a court or tribunal exercising judicial authority where the report is published contemporaneously with the proceedings or, if it is not reasonably practicable or would be unlawful to publish a report of them contemporaneously, as soon as publication is reasonably practicable and lawful.

27 Procedure and punishment

(1) No proceedings for an offence under this Part may be instituted in England and Wales except by or with the consent of the Attorney General.

(2) For the purposes of the rules in England and Wales against charging more than one offence in the same count or information, each of sections 18 to 23 creates one offence.

(3) A person guilty of an offence under this Part is liable—

    (a) on conviction on indictment to imprisonment for a term not exceeding [seven] years or a fine or both;

    (b) on summary conviction to imprisonment for a term not exceeding six months or a fine not exceeding the statutory maximum or both.

28–29 ★ ★ ★ ★ ★

Note: Section 29 provides that "programme service" has the same meaning as in the Broadcasting Act 1990.

30–34, 36, 39 ...

35, 37, 38 ★ ★ ★ ★ ★

40 Amendments repeals and savings

(1)–(3) ★ ★ ★ ★ ★

(4) Nothing in this Act affects the common law powers in England and Wales to deal with or prevent a breach of the peace.

(5) As respects Scotland, nothing in this Act affects any power of a constable under any rule of law.

★ ★ ★ ★ ★

Copyright, Designs and Patents Act 1988
(1988, c. 48)

An Act to restate the law of copyright, with amendments; to make fresh provision as to the rights of performers and others in performances; to confer a design right in original designs; to amend the Registered Designs Act 1949; to make provision with respect to patent agents and trade mark agents; to confer patents and designs jurisdiction on certain county courts; to amend the law of patents; to make provision with respect to devices designed to circumvent copy-protection of works in electronic form; to make fresh provision penalising the fraudulent reception of transmissions; to make the fraudulent application or use of a trade mark an offence; to make provision for the benefit of the Hospital for Sick Children, Great Ormond Street, London; to enable financial assistance to be given to certain international bodies; and for connected purposes   [15 November 1988]

Territorial extent: United Kingdom

Note: Sections 166A and 166B make provision equivalent to section 166 for the Scottish Parliament and the Northern Ireland Assembly.

CHAPTER III   ACTS PERMITTED IN RELATION TO COPYRIGHT WORKS

Public administration

45   Parliamentary and judicial proceedings
(1) Copyright is not infringed by anything done for the purposes of parliamentary or judicial proceedings.

(2) Copyright is not infringed by anything done for the purposes of reporting such proceedings; but this shall not be construed as authorising the copying of a work which is itself a published report of the proceedings.

★ ★ ★ ★ ★

49   Public records
Material which is comprised in public records within the meaning of the Public Records Act 1958, the Public Records (Scotland) Act 1937 or the Public Records Act (Northern Ireland) 1923 [, or in Welsh public records (as defined in the Government of Wales Act 1998)] which are open to public inspection in pursuance of that Act, may be copied, and a copy may be supplied to any person, by or with the authority of any officer appointed under that Act, without infringement of copyright.

CHAPTER X   MISCELLANEOUS AND GENERAL

Crown and Parliamentary copyright

163   Crown copyright
(1) Where a work is made by Her Majesty or by an officer or servant of the Crown in the course of his duties—

(a) the work qualifies for copyright protection notwithstanding section 153(1) (ordinary requirement as to qualification for copyright protection), and

(b) Her Majesty is the first owner of any copyright in the work.

(1A) ★ ★ ★ ★ ★

(2) Copyright in such a work is referred to in this Part as "Crown copyright", notwithstanding that it may be, or have been, assigned to another person.

(3) Crown copyright in a literary, dramatic, musical or artistic work continues to subsist—

(a) until the end of the period of 125 years from the end of the calendar year in which the work was made, or

(b) if the work is published commercially before the end of the period of 75 years from the end of the calendar year in which it was made, until the end of the period of 50 years from the end of the calendar year in which it was first so published.

(4) In the case of a work of joint authorship where one or more but not all of the authors are persons falling within subsection (1), this section applies only in relation to those authors and the copyright subsisting by virtue of their contribution to the work.

(5) Except as mentioned above, and subject to any express exclusion elsewhere in this Part, the provisions of this Part apply in relation to Crown copyright as to other copyright.

(6) This section does not apply to a work if, or to the extent that, Parliamentary copyright subsists in the work (see sections 165[– 166B]).

164 Copyright in Acts and Measures

(1) Her Majesty is entitled to copyright in every Act of Parliament [, Act of the Scottish Parliament, Act of the Northern Ireland Assembly] or Measure of the General Synod of the Church of England.

(2) The copyright subsists from Royal Assent until the end of the period of 50 years from the end of the calendar year in which Royal Assent was given.

(3) References in this Part to Crown copyright (except in section 163) include copyright under this section; and, except as mentioned above, the provisions of this Part apply in relation to copyright under this section as to other Crown copyright.

(4) No other copyright, or right in the nature of copyright, subsists in an Act or Measure.

165 Parliamentary copyright

(1) Where a work is made by or under the direction or control of the House of Commons or the House of Lords—

(a) the work qualifies for copyright protection notwithstanding section 153(1) (ordinary requirement as to qualification for copyright protection), and

(b) the House by whom, or under whose direction or control, the work is made is the first owner of any copyright in the work, and if the work is made by or under the direction or control of both Houses, the two Houses are joint first owners of copyright.

(2) Copyright in such a work is referred to in this Part as "Parliamentary copyright", notwithstanding that it may be, or have been, assigned to another person.

(3) Parliamentary copyright in a literary, dramatic, musical or artistic work continues to subsist until the end of the period of 50 years from the end of the calendar year in which the work was made.

(4) For the purposes of this section, works made by or under the direction or control of the House of Commons or the House of Lords include—

(a) any work made by an officer or employee of that House in the course of his duties, and

(b) any sound recording, film, live broadcast or live cable programme of the proceedings of that House;

but a work shall not be regarded as made by or under the direction or control of either House by reason only of its being commissioned by or on behalf of that House.

(5)–(8) ★ ★ ★ ★ ★

166   Copyright in Parliamentary Bills

(1) Copyright in every Bill introduced into Parliament belongs, in accordance with the following provisions, to one or both of the Houses of Parliament.

(2) Copyright in a public Bill belongs in the first instance to the House into which the Bill is introduced, and after the Bill has been carried to the second House to both Houses jointly, and subsists from the time when the text of the Bill is handed in to the House in which it is introduced.

(3) Copyright in a private Bill belongs to both Houses jointly and subsists from the time when a copy of the Bill is first deposited in either House.

(4) Copyright in a personal Bill belongs in the first instance to the House of Lords, and after the Bill has been carried to the House of Commons to both Houses jointly, and subsists from the time when it is given a First Reading in the House of Lords.

(5) Copyright under this section ceases—

(a) on Royal Assent, or

(b) if the Bill does not receive Royal Assent, on the withdrawal or rejection of the Bill or the end of the Session:

Provided that, copyright in a Bill continues to subsist notwithstanding its rejection in any Session by the House of Lords if, by virtue of the Parliament Acts 1911 and 1949, it remains possible for it to be presented for Royal Assent in that Session.

(6) References in this Part to Parliamentary copyright (except in section 165) include copyright under this section; and, except as mentioned above, the provisions of this Part apply in relation to copyright under this section as to other Parliamentary copyright.

(7) No other copyright, or right in the nature of copyright, subsists in a Bill after copyright has once subsisted under this section; but without prejudice to the subsequent operation of this section in relation to a Bill which, not having passed in one Session, is reintroduced in a subsequent Session.

166A–166B ★ ★ ★ ★ ★

Criminal Justice Act 1988
(1988, c. 33)

An Act to make fresh provision for extradition; to amend the rules of evidence in criminal proceedings; to provide for the reference by the Attorney General of certain questions relating to sentencing to the Court of Appeal; to amend the law with regard to the jurisdiction and powers of criminal courts, the collection, enforcement and remission of fines imposed by coroners, juries, supervision orders, the detention of children and young persons, probation and the probation service, criminal appeals, anonymity in cases of rape and similar cases, orders under sections 4 and 11 of the Contempt of Court Act 1981 relating to trials on indictment, orders restricting the access of the public to the whole or any part of a trial on indictment or to any proceedings ancillary to such a trial and orders restricting the publication of any report of the whole or any part of a trial on indictment or any such ancillary proceedings, the alteration of names of petty sessions areas, officers of inner London magistrates' courts and the costs and expenses of prosecution witnesses and certain other persons; to make fresh provision for the payment of compensation by the Criminal Injuries Compensation Board; to make provision for the payment of compensation for a miscarriage of justice which has resulted in a wrongful conviction; to create an offence of torture and an offence of having an article with a blade or point in a public place; to create further offences relating to weapons; to create a summary offence of possession of an indecent photograph of a child; to amend the Police and Criminal Evidence Act 1984 in relation to searches, computer data about fingerprints and bail for persons in customs detention; to make provision in relation to the taking of body samples by the police in Northern Ireland; to amend the Bail Act 1976; to give a justice of the peace power to authorise entry and search of premises for offensive weapons; to provide for the enforcement of the Video Recordings Act 1984 by officers of a weights and measures authority and in Northern Ireland by Officers of the Department of Economic Development; to extend to the purchase of easements and other rights over land the power to purchase land conferred on the Secretary of State by section 36 of the Prison Act 1952; and for connected purposes   [29 July 1988]

Territorial extent: England and Wales; Northern Ireland (except section 160)

PART XI   MISCELLANEOUS

Miscarriages of justice

133   Compensation for miscarriages of justice

(1) Subject to subsection (2) below, when a person has been convicted of a criminal offence and when subsequently his conviction has been reversed or he has been pardoned on the ground that a new or newly discovered fact shows beyond reasonable doubt that there has been a miscarriage of justice, the Secretary of State shall pay compensation for the miscarriage of justice to the person who has suffered punishment as a result of such conviction or, if he is dead, to his personal representatives, unless the non-disclosure of the unknown fact was wholly or partly attributable to the person convicted.

(2) No payment of compensation under this section shall be made unless an application for such compensation has been made to the Secretary of State.

(3) The question whether there is a right to compensation under this section shall be determined by the Secretary of State.

(4) If the Secretary of State determines that there is a right to such compensation, the amount of the compensation shall be assessed by an assessor appointed by the Secretary of State.

[(4A) In assessing so much of any compensation payable under this section to or in respect of a person as is attributable to suffering, harm to reputation or similar damage, the assessor shall have regard in particular to–

(a) the seriousness of the offence of which the person was convicted and the severity of the punishment resulting from the conviction;

(b) the conduct of the investigation and prosecution of the offence; and

(c) any other convictions of the person and any punishment resulting from them.]

(5)–(7)   ★ ★ ★ ★ ★

Torture

134   Torture

(1) A public official or person acting in an official capacity, whatever his nationality, commits the offence of torture if in the United Kingdom or elsewhere he intentionally inflicts severe pain or suffering on another in the performance or purported performance of his official duties.

(2) A person not falling within subsection (1) above commits the offence of torture, whatever his nationality, if—

(a) in the United Kingdom or elsewhere he intentionally inflicts severe pain or suffering on another at the instigation or with the consent or acquiescence—
(i) of a public official; or
(ii) of a person acting in an official capacity; and

(b) the official or other person is performing or purporting to perform his official duties when he instigates the commission of the offence or consents to or acquiesces in it.

(3) It is immaterial whether the pain or suffering is physical or mental and whether it is caused by an act or an omission.

(4) It shall be a defence for a person charged with an offence under this section in respect of any conduct of his to prove that he had lawful authority, justification or excuse for that conduct.

(5), (6) ★ ★ ★ ★ ★

135   Requirement of Attorney General's consent for prosecutions

Proceedings for an offence under section 134 above shall not be begun—

    (a) in England and Wales, except by, or with the consent of, the Attorney General; or

    (b) in Northern Ireland, except by, or with the consent of, the Attorney General for Northern Ireland.

136-141   ★ ★ ★ ★ ★

142   Power of justice of the peace to authorise entry and search of premises for offensive weapons

(1) If on an application made by a constable a justice of the peace (including, in Scotland, the sheriff) is satisfied that there are reasonable grounds for believing—

    (a) that there are on premises specified in the application—

        (i) knives such as are mentioned in section 1(1) of the Restriction of Offensive Weapons Act 1959; or

        (ii) weapons to which section 141 above applies; and

    (b) that an offence under section 1 of the Restriction of Offensive Weapons Act 1959 or section 141 above has been or is being committed in relation to them; and

    (c) that any of the conditions specified in subsection (3) below applies, he may issue a warrant authorising a constable to enter and search the premises.

(2) A constable may seize and retain anything for which a search has been authorised under subsection (1) above.

(3) The conditions mentioned in subsection (1)(b) above are—

    (a) that it is not practicable to communicate with any person entitled to grant entry to the premises;

    (b) that it is practicable to communicate with a person entitled to grant entry to the premises but it is not practicable to communicate with any person entitled to grant access to the knives or weapons to which the application relates;

    (c) that entry to the premises will not be granted unless a warrant is produced;

    (d) that the purpose of a search may be frustrated or seriously prejudiced unless a constable arriving at the premises can secure immediate entry to them.

143-158   ★ ★ ★ ★ ★

159   Crown Court proceedings—orders restricting or preventing reports or restricting public access

(1) A person aggrieved may appeal to the Court of Appeal, if that court grants leave, against—

    (a) an order under section 4 or 11 of the Contempt of Court Act 1981 made in relation to a trial on indictment;

    [(aa) An order made by the Crown Court under section 58(7) or (8) of the Criminal Procedure and Investigation 1996 in a case where the court has convicted a person on a trial on indictment;]

    (b) any order restricting the access of the public to the whole or any part of a trial on indictment or to any proceedings ancillary to such a trial; and

    (c) any order restricting the publication of any report of the whole or any part of a trial on indictment or any such ancillary proceedings;

and the decision of the Court of Appeal shall be final.

(2) Subject to Rules of Court, the jurisdiction of the Court of Appeal under this section shall be exercised by the criminal division of the Court, and references to the Court of Appeal in this section shall be construed as references to that division.

(3)–(7) ★ ★ ★ ★ ★

★ ★ ★ ★ ★

Elected Authorities (Northern Ireland) Act 1989
(1989, c. 3)

An Act to amend the law relating to the franchise at elections to district councils in Northern Ireland, to make provision in relation to a declaration against terrorism to be made by candidates at such elections and at elections to the Northern Ireland Assembly and by persons co-opted as members of district councils, to amend sections 3 and 4 of the Local Government Act (Northern Ireland) 1972, and for connected purposes [15 March 1989]

Territorial extent: Northern Ireland

1, 2 ★ ★ ★ ★ ★

Disqualification for breach of declaration against terrorism or in consequence of imprisonment or detention

3   Declaration against terrorism: local elections
(1) A person is not validly nominated as a candidate at a local election unless his consent to nomination includes a declaration in the form set out in Part I of Schedule 2 to this Act.

(2) ★ ★ ★ ★ ★

4   Declaration against terrorism: councillors co-opted to fill casual vacancies
(1) A person is not eligible to be chosen by a district council to fill a casual vacancy in the council unless he has made, and served on the clerk of the council, a declaration in the form set out in Part II of Schedule 2 to this Act.

(2) ★ ★ ★ ★ ★

5   Declaration against terrorism: Assembly elections
A person is not validly nominated as a candidate at an election to the Northern Ireland Assembly unless his consent to nomination includes a declaration in the form set out in Part I of Schedule 2 to this Act.

6   Breach of terms of declaration
(1) A person who has made a declaration required for the purposes of section 3, 4 or 5 of this Act in connection with a local election, an election to the Northern Ireland Assembly or the filling of a casual vacancy in a district council acts in breach of the terms of the declaration if at any time after he is declared to be elected at that election or is chosen to fill that vacancy and while he remains a member of the district council or of the Assembly—

   (a) he expresses support for or approval of—
      (i) a proscribed organisation, or
      (ii) acts of terrorism (that is to say, violence for political ends) connected with the affairs of Northern Ireland, and
   (b) he does so—
      (i) at a public meeting, or
      (ii) knowing, or in such circumstances that he can reasonably be expected to

know, that the fact that he has made that expression of support or approval is likely to become known to the public.

(2) For the purposes of subsection (1) above a person shall be taken to express support for, or approval of, any matter if his words or actions could reasonably be understood as expressing support for, or approval of, it.

(3) It is immaterial for the purposes of subsection (1) above—

(a) whether the expression of support or approval is made by spoken or written words, by the display of written matter or by other behaviour, and

(b) whether it is made in the United Kingdom or elsewhere.

(4) This section has effect notwithstanding section 26(1) of the Northern Ireland Constitution Act 1973 (privileges of the Northern Ireland Assembly).

(5) In this section—

"proscribed organisation" has the same meaning as in [section 3 of the Terrorism Act 2000.]

"public meeting" includes—

(a) any meeting in a public place,

(b) any meeting which the public or any section of the public is permitted to attend, whether on payment or otherwise, and

(c) any meeting of the Northern Ireland Assembly, a district council or any committee or sub-committee of the Assembly or such a council (whether or not a meeting which the public is permitted to attend), and

"public place" means—

(a) any highway, and

(b) any place to which at the material time the public or any section of the public has access, on payment or otherwise, as of right or by virtue of express or implied permission.

7 ★ ★ ★ ★ ★

8 ★ ★ ★ ★ ★ (allows disqualification for breach of declaration)

9–13 ★ ★ ★ ★ ★

SCHEDULE 1

★ ★ ★ ★ ★

SCHEDULE 2   DECLARATION AGAINST TERRORISM
PART I   FORM FOR INCLUSION IN CONSENT TO NOMINATION

I declare that, if elected, I will not by word or deed express support for or approval of—

(a) any organisation that is for the time being a proscribed organisation specified in [Schedule 2 to the [Terrorism Act 2000]; or

(b) acts of terrorism (that is to say, violence for political ends) connected with the affairs of Northern Ireland.

★ ★ ★ ★ ★

Extradition Act 1989

(1989, c. 33)

An Act to consolidate enactments relating to extradition under the Criminal Justice Act 1988, the Fugitive Offenders Act 1967 and the Extradition Acts 1870 to 1935, with amendments to give effect to recommendations of the Law Commission and the Scottish Law Commission   [27 July 1989]

Territorial extent: United Kingdom

PART I   INTRODUCTORY

General

1   Liability to extradition

(1) Where extradition procedures under Part III of this Act are available as between the United Kingdom and a foreign state, a person in the United Kingdom who—

    (a) is accused in that state of the commission of an extradition crime; or

    (b) is alleged to be unlawfully at large after conviction of an extradition crime by a court in that state,

may be arrested and returned to that state in accordance with those procedures.

(2) Subject to the provisions of this Act, a person in the United Kingdom who is accused of an extradition crime—

    (a) in a Commonwealth country designated for the purposes of this subsection under section 5(1) below; or

    (b) in a colony, or who is alleged to be unlawfully at large after conviction of such an offence in any such country or in a colony, may be arrested and returned to that country or colony in accordance with extradition procedures under Part III of this Act.

[(2A) Subject to the provisions of this Act, a person in the United Kingdom who–

    (a) is accused in the Hong Kong Special Administrative Region of an extradition crime, or

    (b) is alleged to be unlawfully at large after conviction for such an offence in that Region,

may be arrested and returned to that Region in accordance with extradition procedures under Part III of this Act.]

(3) Where an Order in Council under section 2 of the Extradition Act 1870 is in force in relation to a foreign state, Schedule 1 to this Act (the provisions of which derive from that Act and certain associated enactments) shall have effect in relation to that state, but subject to the limitations, restrictions, conditions, exceptions and qualifications, if any, contained in the Order.

Extradition crime

2   Meaning of "extradition crime"

(1) In this Act, except in Schedule 1, "extradition crime" means—

    (a) conduct in the territory of a foreign state, a designated Commonwealth country, [a colony or the Hong Kong Special Administrative Region] which, if it occurred in the United Kingdom, would constitute an offence punishable with imprisonment for a term of 12 months, or any greater punishment, and which, however described in the law of the foreign state, Commonwealth country or colony [or of the Hong Kong Special Administrative Region], is so punishable under that law;

(b) an extra-territorial offence against the law of a foreign state, designated Commonwealth country or colony which is punishable under that law with imprisonment for a term of 12 months, or any greater punishment, and which satisfies—

    (i)   the condition specified in subsection (2) below; or

    (ii) all the conditions specified in subsection (3) below [; or

    (iii) the condition specified in subsection (3A) below.]

(2) The condition mentioned in subsection (1)(b)(i) above is that in corresponding circumstances equivalent conduct would constitute an extra-territorial offence against the law of the United Kingdom punishable with imprisonment for a term of 12 months, or any greater punishment.

(3) The conditions mentioned in subsection (1)(b)(ii) above are—

    (a) that the foreign state, Commonwealth country or colony [or the Hong Kong Special Administrative Region] bases its jurisdiction on the nationality of the offender;

    (b) that the conduct constituting the offence occurred outside the United Kingdom; . . .

    (c) that, if it occurred in the United Kingdom, it would constitute an offence under the law of the United Kingdom punishable with imprisonment for a term of 12 months, or any greater punishment [; and

    (d) conduct in a vessel, aircraft or hovercraft of the Hong Kong Special Administrative Region shall be treated as if it were conduct in that Region.]

[(3A) The condition mentioned in subsection (1)(b)(iii) above is that the conduct constituting the offence constitutes or, if committed in the United Kingdom would constitute—

    (a) an offence under section 51 or 58 of the International Criminal Court Act 2001 (genocide, crimes against humanity and war crimes),

    (b) an offence under section 52 or 59 of that Act (conduct ancillary to genocide etc. committed outside the jurisdiction), or

    (c) an ancillary offence, as defined in section 55 or 62 of that Act, in relation to any such offence.]

(4) For the purposes of [this Act except Schedule 1]—

    (a) the law of a foreign state, designated Commonwealth country or colony includes the law of any part of it and the law of the United Kingdom includes the law of any part of the United Kingdom;

    (b) conduct in a colony or dependency of a foreign state or of a designated Commonwealth country, or a vessel, aircraft or hovercraft of a foreign state or of such a country, shall be treated as if it were conduct in the territory of that state or country;

    (c) conduct in a vessel, aircraft or hovercraft of a colony of the United Kingdom shall be treated as if it were conduct in that colony; and

    (d) reference shall be made to the law of the colony or dependency of a foreign state or of a designated Commonwealth country, and not (where different) to the law of the foreign state or Commonwealth country, to determine the level of punishment applicable to conduct in that colony or dependency].

[(5) References in this section to an offence under any provision of the International Criminal Court Act 2001, or to an offence ancillary to such an offence, include any corresponding offence under the law of Scotland.]

Return to foreign states

3 Arrangements for availability of Part III procedure

(1) In this Act "extradition arrangements" means arrangements made with a foreign state

under which extradition procedures under Part III of this Act will be available as between the United Kingdom and that state.

(2) For this purpose "foreign state" means any state other than—

    (i) the United Kingdom;

    (ii) a country mentioned in Schedule 3 to the British Nationality Act 1981 (countries whose citizens are Commonwealth citizens);

    (iii) a colony; . . .

    (iv) the Republic of Ireland [; or

    (v) the Hong Kong Special Administrative Region.] but a state which is a party to the European Convention on Extradition done at Paris on 13th December 1957 may be treated as a foreign state.

(3) Extradition arrangements may be—

    (a) arrangements of a general nature made with one or more states and relating to the operation of extradition procedures under Part III of this Act (in this Act referred to as "general extradition arrangements"); or

    (b) arrangements relating to the operation of those procedures in particular cases (in this Act referred to as "special extradition arrangements") made with a state with which there are no general extradition arrangements.

4 Orders in Council as to extradition

(1) Where general extradition arrangements have been made, Her Majesty may, by Order in Council reciting or embodying their terms, direct that this Act, so far as it relates to extradition procedures under Part III of this Act, shall apply as between the United Kingdom and the foreign state, or any foreign state, with which they have been made, subject to the limitations, restrictions, exceptions and qualifications, if any, contained in the Order.

(2) An Order in Council under this section shall not be made unless the general extradition arrangements to which it relates—

    (a) provide for their determination after the expiration of a notice given by a party to them and not exceeding one year or for their denunciation by means of such a notice; and

    (b) are in conformity with the provisions of this Act, and in particular with the restrictions on return contained in Part II of this Act.

(3) An Order in Council under this section shall be conclusive evidence that the arrangements therein referred to comply with this Act and that this Act, so far as it relates to extradition procedures under Part III of this Act, applies in the case of the foreign state, or any foreign state, mentioned in the Order.

(4) An Order in Council under this section shall be laid before Parliament after being made.

(5) An Order in Council under this section which does not provide that a person may only be returned to the foreign state requesting his return if the court of committal is satisfied that the evidence would be sufficient to [make a case requiring an answer by that person if the proceedings were a summary trial of any information against him, and] the extradition crime had taken place within the jurisdiction of the court shall be subject to annulment in pursuance of a resolution of either House of Parliament.

Return to Commonwealth countries and colonies

5 Procedure for designation etc.

(1) Her Majesty may by Order in Council designate for the purposes of section 1(2) above any country for the time being mentioned in Schedule 3 to the British Nationality Act 1981 (countries whose citizens are Commonwealth citizens); and any country so designated is in this Act referred to as a "designated Commonwealth country".

(2) This Act has effect in relation to all colonies.

(3) Her Majesty may by Order in Council direct that this Act shall have effect in relation to the return of persons to, or in relation to persons returned from, any designated Commonwealth country or any colony subject to such exceptions, adaptations or modifications as may be specified in the Order.

(4) Any Order under this section may contain such transitional or other incidental and supplementary provisions as may appear to Her Majesty to be necessary or expedient.

(5) For the purposes of any Order in Council under subsection (1) above, any territory for the external relations of which a Commonwealth country is responsible may be treated as part of that country or, if the Government of that country so requests, as a separate country.

(6) Any Order in Council under this section, other than an Order to which subsection (7) below applies, shall be subject to annulment in pursuance of a resolution of either House of Parliament.

(7) No recommendation shall be made to Her Majesty in Council to make an Order containing any such direction as is authorised by subsection (3) above unless a draft of the Order has been laid before Parliament and approved by resolution of each House of Parliament.

PART II   RESTRICTIONS ON RETURN

6   General restrictions on return

(1) A person shall not be returned under Part III of this Act, or committed or kept in custody for the purposes of return, if it appears to an appropriate authority—
- (a) that the offence of which that person is accused or was convicted is an offence of a political character;
- (b) that it is an offence under military law which is not also an offence under the general criminal law;
- (c) that the request for his return (though purporting to be made on account of an extradition crime) is in fact made for the purpose of prosecuting or punishing him on account of his race, religion, nationality or political opinions; or
- (d) that he might, if returned, be prejudiced at his trial or punished, detained or restricted in his personal liberty by reason of his race, religion, nationality or political opinions.

(2) A person who is alleged to be unlawfully at large after conviction of an extradition crime shall not be returned to a foreign state [or to the Hong Kong Special Administrative Region], or committed or kept in custody for the purposes of return to a foreign state [or to that Region], if it appears to an appropriate authority—
- (a) that the conviction was obtained in his absence; and
- (b) that it would not be in the interest of justice to return him on the grounds of that conviction.

(3) A person accused of an offence shall not be returned, or committed or kept in custody for the purposes of return, if it appears to an appropriate authority that if charged with that offence in the United Kingdom he would be entitled to be discharged under any rule of law relating to previous acquittal or conviction.

(4) A person shall not be returned, or committed or kept in custody for the purposes of such return, unless provision is made by the relevant law, or by an arrangement made with the relevant foreign state, Commonwealth country or colony [or with the Hong Kong Special Administrative Region], for securing that he will not, unless he has first had an opportunity to leave it, be dealt with there for or in respect of any offence committed before his return to it other than—
- (a) the offence in respect of which his return is ordered;
- (b) an offence, other than an offence excluded by subsection (5) below, which is disclosed by the facts in respect of which his return was ordered; or

(c) subject to subsection (6) below, any other offence being an extradition crime in respect of which the Secretary of State [or the Scottish Ministers] may consent to his being dealt with.

(5) The offences excluded from paragraph (b) of subsection (4) above are offences in relation to which an order for the return of the person concerned could not lawfully be made.

(6) The Secretary of State [or the Scottish Ministers] may not give consent under paragraph (c) of that subsection in respect of an offence in relation to which it appears to him [or them] that an order for the return of the person concerned could not lawfully be made, or would not in fact be made.

(7) Any such arrangement as is mentioned in subsection (4) above which is made with a designated Commonwealth country or a colony may be an arrangement made for the particular case or an arrangement of a more general nature; and for the purposes of that subsection a certificate issued by or under the authority of the Secretary of State [or the Scottish Ministers] confirming the existence of an arrangement with a Commonwealth country or a colony and stating its terms shall be conclusive evidence of the matters contained in the certificate.

(8) In relation to a Commonwealth country or a colony the reference in subsection (1) above to an offence of a political character does not include an offence against the life or person of the Head of the Commonwealth or attempting or conspiring to commit, or assisting, counselling or procuring the commission of or being accessory before or after the fact to such an offence, or of impeding the apprehension or prosecution of persons guilty of such an offence.

(9) In this Act "appropriate authority" means—
   (a) the Secretary of State [or, except in section 25(1), in the case of a function that is exercisable in or as regards Scotland, the Scottish Ministers];
   (b) the court of committal;
   (c) the High Court or High Court of Justiciary on an application for habeas corpus or for review of the order of committal.

(10) In this section, in relation to Commonwealth countries and colonies, "race" includes tribe.

PART III   PROCEDURE

General

7   Extradition request and authority to proceed

(1) Subject to the provisions of this Act relating to provisional warrants, a person shall not be dealt with under this Part of this Act except in pursuance of an order of the Secretary of State [or the Scottish Ministers] (in this Act referred to as an "authority to proceed") issued in pursuance of a request (in this Act referred to as an "extradition request") for the surrender of a person under this Act made [to the Secretary of State]—
   [(a) by—
      (i) an authority in a foreign state which appears to the Secretary of State to have the function of making extradition requests in that foreign state, or
      (ii) some person recognised by the Secretary of State as a diplomatic or consular representative of a foreign state; or]
   (b) by or on behalf of the Government of a designated Commonwealth country, or the Governor of a Colony [and an extradition request may be made by facsimile transmission and an authority to proceed issued without waiting to receive the original] [; or
   (c) by or on behalf of the Government of the Hong Kong Special Administrative Region].

(2) There shall be furnished with any such request—
  (a) particulars of the person whose return is requested;
  (b) particulars of the offence of which he is accused or was convicted (including evidence [or, in a case falling within subsection (2A) below, information] sufficient to justify the issue of a warrant for his arrest under this Act);
  (c) in the case of a person accused of an offence, a warrant [or a duly authenticated copy of a warrant] for his arrest issued in the foreign state, Commonwealth country or colony [or in the Hong Kong Special Administrative Region]; and
  (d) in the case of a person unlawfully at large after conviction of an offence, a certificate [or a duly authenticated copy of a certificate] of the conviction and sentence, and copies of them shall be served on the person whose return is requested before he is brought before the court of committal.
[(2A) Where—
  (a) the extradition request is made by a foreign state; and
  (b) an Order in Council falling within section 4(5) above is in force in relation to that state,
it shall be a sufficient compliance with subsection (2)(b) above to furnish information sufficient to justify the issue of a warrant for his arrest under this Act.]

(3) Rules under section 144 of the Magistrates' Courts Act 1980 may make provision as to the procedure for service under subsection (2) above in England and Wales and the High Court of Justiciary may, by Act of Adjournal, make rules as to such procedure in Scotland.

(4) On receipt of any such request the Secretary of State [or the Scottish Ministers] may issue an authority to proceed unless it appears to him [or them] that an order for the return of the person concerned could not lawfully be made, or would not in fact be made, in accordance with the provisons of this Act.

(5) An authority to proceed shall specify the offence or offences under the law of the United Kingdom which it appears to the Secretary of State [or the Scottish Ministers] would be constituted by equivalent conduct in the United Kingdom.

(6) In this section "warrant", in the case of any foreign state, includes any judicial document authorising the arrest of a person accused of a crime.

(7) ★ ★ ★ ★ ★

8   Arrest for purposes of committal

(1) For the purposes of this Part of this Act a warrant for the arrest of a person may be issued—
  (a) on receipt of an authority to proceed—
    (i) by the [Senior District Judge (Chief Magistrate) or another District Judge (Magistrates' Courts) designated by him];
    (ii) by the sheriff of Lothian and Borders;
  (b) without such an authority—
    (i) by a metropolitan magistrate;
    (ii) by a justice of the peace in any part of the United Kingdom; and
    (iii) in Scotland, by a sheriff,
upon information that the said person is or is believed to be in or on his way to the United Kingdom;
and any warrant issued by virtue of paragraph (b) above is in this Act referred to as a "provisional warrant".

(2) In this Act—
  "designated metropolitan magistrate" means a metropolitan stipendiary magistrate designated for the purposes of this Act by the Lord Chancellor; and
  "metropolitan magistrate" means the chief metropolitan stipendiary magistrate or a designated metropolitan magistrate.

(3) A person empowered to issue warrants of arrest under this section may issue such a warrant if he is supplied with such evidence [or, in a case falling within subsection (3A) below, information] as would in his opinion justify the issue of a warrant for the arrest of a person accused or, as the case may be, convicted within his jurisdiction and it appears to him that the conduct alleged would constitute an extradition crime.

[(3A) Where—
(a) the extradition request or, where a provisional warrant is applied for, the request for the person's arrest is made by a foreign state; and
(b) an Order in Council falling within section 4(5) above is in force in relation to that state,

it shall be sufficient for the purposes of subsection (3) above to supply such information as would, in the opinion of the person so empowered, justify the issue of a warrant of arrest.]

(4) Where a provisional warrant is issued under this section, the authority by whom it is issued shall forthwith give notice to the Secretary of State [or the Scottish Ministers], and transmit to him [or them] the information and evidence, or certified copies of the information and evidence, upon which it was issued; and the Secretary of State [or the Scottish Ministers] may in any case, and shall if he decides [or they decide] not to issue an authority to proceed in respect of the person to whom the warrant relates, by order cancel the warrant and, if that person has been arrested under it, discharge him from custody.

(5) A warrant of arrest issued under this section may, without being backed, be executed in any part of the United Kingdom and may be so executed by any person to whom it is directed or by any constable.

(6) Where a warrant is issued under this section for the arrest of a person accused of an offence of stealing or receiving stolen property in a designated Commonwealth country or colony or any other offence committed in such a country or in a colony in respect of property, a justice of the peace in any part of the United Kingdom and in Scotland a sheriff shall have the like power to issue a warrant to search for the property as if the offence had been committed within his jurisdiction.

9   Proceedings for committal

(1) A person arrested in pursuance of a warrant under section 8 above shall (unless previously discharged under subsection (4) of that section) be brought as soon as practicable before a court (in this Act referred to as "the court of committal") . . .

(2)–(11) ★ ★ ★ ★ ★

10   Statement of case by court

(1) If the court of committal refuses to make an order in relation to a person under section 9 above in respect of the offence or, as the case may be, any of the offences to which the authority to proceed relates, the foreign state, Commonwealth country or colony seeking the surrender of that person to it may question the proceeding on the ground that it is wrong in law by applying to the court to state a case for the opinion of the High Court or, in Scotland, the High Court of Justiciary on the question of law involved.

(2)–(14) ★ ★ ★ ★ ★

11   Application for habeas corpus etc.

(1) Where a person is committed under section 9 above, the court shall inform him in ordinary language of his right to make an application for habeas corpus, and shall forthwith give notice of the committal to the Secretary of State [or the Scottish Ministers].

(2) A person committed shall not be returned—
(a) in any case, until the expiration of the period of 15 days beginning with the day on which the order for his committal is made;
(b) if an application for habeas corpus is made in his case, so long as proceedings on that application are pending.

(3) Without prejudice to any jurisdiction of the High Court apart from this section, the court shall order the applicant's discharge if it appears to the court in relation to the offence, or each of the offences, in respect of which the applicant's return is sought, that—

    (a) by reason of the trivial nature of the offence; or

    (b) by reason of the passage of time since he is alleged to have committed it or to have become unlawfully at large, as the case may be; or

    (c) because the accusation against him is not made in good faith in the interests of justice,

it would, having regard to all the circumstances, be unjust or oppressive to return him.

(4) On any such application the court may receive additional evidence relevant to the exercise of its jurisdiction under section 6 above or subsection (3) above.

(5) Proceedings on an application for habeas corpus shall be treated for the purposes of this section as pending (unless they are discontinued) until (disregarding any power of a court to grant leave to appeal out of time) there is no further possibility of an appeal.

(6) In the application of this section to Scotland references to an application for habeas corpus shall be construed as references to an application for review of the order of committal and references to the High Court shall be construed as references to the High Court of Justiciary.

12   Order for return

(1) Where a person is committed under section 9 above and is not discharged by order of the High Court or the High Court of Justiciary, the Secretary of State [or the Scottish Ministers] may by warrant order him to be returned unless his return is prohibited, or prohibited for the time being, by this Act, or the Secretary of State decides [or the Scottish Ministers decide] under this section to make no such order in his case.

(2) Without prejudice to his general discretion as to the making of an order for the return of a person to a foreign state, Commonwealth country or colony [or to the Hong Kong Special Administrative Region]—

    (a) the Secretary of State [or the Scottish Ministers] shall not make an order in the case of any person if it appears to the Secretary of State [or the Scottish Ministers] in relation to the offence, or each of the offences, in respect of which his return is sought, that—

        (i) by reason of its trivial nature; or

        (ii) by reason of the passage of time since he is alleged to have committed it or to have become unlawfully at large, as the case may be; or

        (iii) because the accusation against him is not made in good faith in the interests of justice,

it would, having regard to all the circumstances, be unjust or oppressive to return him; and

    (b) the Secretary of State may decide to make no order for the return of a person accused or convicted of an offence not punishable with death in Great Britain if that person could be or has been sentenced to death for that offence in the country by which the request for his return is made.

(3) An order for return shall not be made in the case of a person who is serving a sentence of imprisonment or detention, or is charged with an offence, in the United Kingdom—

    (a) in the case of a person serving such a sentence, until the sentence has been served;

    (b) in the case of a person charged with an offence, until the charge is disposed of or withdrawn or unless an order is made for it to lie on the file and, if it results in his serving a term of imprisonment or detention, until the sentence has been served.

(4) In the application of this section to Scotland, the reference in subsection (3) above to an order being made for the charge to lie on the file shall be construed as a reference to the diet being deserted pro loco et tempore.

(5) The Secretary of State [or the Scottish Ministers] may decide to make no order under this section for the return of a person committed in consequence of an extradition request if

another extradition request or a requisition under Schedule 1 to this Act has been made in respect of him and it appears to the Secretary of State [or the Scottish Ministers], having regard to all the circumstances of the case and in particular—

    (a) the relative seriousness of the offences in question;

    (b) the date on which each such request was made; and

    (c) the nationality or citizenship of the person concerned and his ordinary residence,

that preference should be given to that other request or requisition.

(6) Notice of the issue of a warrant under this section for the return of a person to a Commonwealth country or colony shall forthwith be given to the person to be returned.

13 ★ ★ ★ ★ ★

14 Simplified procedure

(1) A person may give notice that he waives the rights conferred on him by section 11 above.

(2)–(4) ★ ★ ★ ★ ★

Special extradition arrangements

15 Special extradition arrangements

(1) Where special extradition arrangements have been made in respect of a person, extradition procedures shall be available in the case of that person, as between the United Kingdom and the foreign state with which the arrangements have been made, subject to the limitations, restrictions, exceptions and qualifications, if any, contained in the arrangements.

(2) If the Secretary of State issues a certificate of special extradition arrangements, it shall be conclusive evidence of all matters stated in it.

(3) In subsection (2) above "certificate of special extradition arrangements" means a certificate—

    (a) that special extradition arrangements have been made in respect of a person as between the United Kingdom and a foreign state specified in the certificte; and

    (b) that extradition procedures are available in the case of that person as between the United Kingdom and the foreign state to the extent specified in the certificate.

16 ★ ★ ★ ★ ★

17 Custody

(1) Any person remanded or committed to custody under this Part of this Act shall be committed to the like institution as a person charged with an offence before the court of committal.

(2) If any person who is in custody by virtue of a warrant under this Act escapes out of custody, he may be retaken in any part of the United Kingdom in like manner as a person escaping from custody under a warrant for his arrest issued in that part in respect of an offence committed in that part.

(3) Where a person, being in custody in any part of the United Kingdom whether under this Part of this Act or otherwise, is required to be removed in custody under this Act to another part of the United Kingdom and is so removed by sea or by air, he shall be deemed to continue in legal custody until he reaches the place to which he is required to be removed.

(4) A warrant for the return of any person shall be sufficient authority for all persons to whom it is directed and all constables to receive that person, keep him in custody and convey him into the jurisdiction to which he is to be returned.

18–22 ★ ★ ★ ★ ★

[23. Genocide, crimes against humanity and war crimes

(1) This section applies to—

    (a) any offence that if committed in the United Kingdom would be punishable as—

      (i) an offence under section 51 or 58 of the International Criminal Court Act 2001 (genocide, crimes against humanity and war crimes).

      (ii) an offence under section 52 or 59 of that Act (conduct ancillary to genocide, etc. committed outside the jurisdiction), or

      (iii) an ancillary offence, as defined in section 55 or 62 of that Act, in relation to any such offence as is mentioned in sub-paragraph (i) or (ii); and

    (b) any offence punishable in the United Kingdom under section 1 of the Geneva Conventions Act 1957 (grave breach of schedule conventions).

  (2) For the purposes of this Act—

    (a) an offence to which this section applies shall not be regarded as an offence of a political character, and

    (b) no proceedings in respect of such an offence shall be regarded as a criminal matter of a political character.

  (3) It is not an objection to proceedings against a person in respect of an offence to which this section applies that under the law in force at the time when and in the place where he is alleged to have committed the act of which he is accused, or of which he was convicted, he could not have been punished for it.

  (4) References in this section to an offence under any provision of the International Criminal Court Act 2001, or to an offence ancillary to such an offence, include any corresponding offence under the law of Scotland.]

Official Secrets Act 1989
(1989, c. 6)

An Act to replace section 2 of the Official Secrets Act 1911 by provisions protecting more limited classes of official information   [11 May 1989]

Territorial extent: United Kingdom

1 Security and intelligence

  (1) A person who is or has been—

    (a) a member of the security and intelligence services; or

    (b) a person notified that he is subject to the provisions of this subsection, is guilty of an offence if without lawful authority he discloses any information, document or other article relating to security or intelligence which is or has been in his possession by virtue of his position as a member of any of those services or in the course of his work while the notification is or was in force.

  (2) The reference in subsection (1) above to disclosing information relating to security or intelligence includes a reference to making any statement which purports to be a disclosure of such information or is intended to be taken by those to whom it is addressed as being such a disclosure.

  (3) A person who is or has been a Crown Servant or government contractor is guilty of an offence if without lawful authority he makes a damaging disclosure of any information, document or other article relating to security or intelligence which is or has been in his possession by virtue of his position as such but otherwise than as mentioned in subsection (1) above.

  (4) For the purposes of subsection (3) above a disclosure is damaging if—

    (a) it causes damage to the work of, or of any part of, the security and intelligence service; or

    (b) it is of information or a document or other article which is such that its unauthorised disclosure would be likely to cause such damage or which falls within a class or description of information, documents or articles the unauthorised disclosure of which would be likely to have that effect.

(5) It is a defence for a person charged with an offence under this section to prove that at the time of the alleged offence he did not know, and had no reasonable cause to believe, that the information, document or article in question related to security or intelligence or, in the case of an offence under subsection (3), that the disclosure would be damaging within the meaning of that subsection.

(6)–(8) ★ ★ ★ ★ ★

(9) In this section "security or intelligence" means the work of, or in support of, the security and intelligence services or any part of them, and references to information relating to security or intelligence include references to information held or transmitted by those services or by persons in support of, or of any part of, them.

2 Defence

(1) A person who is or has been a Crown servant or government contractor is guilty of an offence if without lawful authority he makes a damaging disclosure of any information, document or other article relating to defence which is or has been in his possession by virtue of his position as such.

(2) For the purposes of subsection (1) above a disclosure is damaging if—

   (a) it damages the capability of, or of any part of, the armed forces of the Crown to carry out their tasks or leads to loss of life or injury to members of those forces or serious damage to the equipment or installations of those forces; or

   (b) otherwise than as mentioned in paragraph (a) above, it endangers the interests of the United Kingdom abroad, seriously obstructs the promotion or protection by the United Kingdom of those interests or endangers the safety of British citizens abroad; or

   (c) it is of information or of a document or article which is such that its unauthorised disclosure would be likely to have any of those effects.

(3) It is a defence for a person charged with an offence under this section to prove that at the time of the alleged offence he did not know, and had no reasonable cause to believe, that the information, document or article in question related to defence or that its disclosure would be damaging within the meaning of subsection (1) above.

(4) In this section "defence" means—

   (a) the size, shape, organisation, logistics, order of battle, deployment, operations, state of readiness and training of the armed forces of the Crown;

   (b) the weapons, stores or other equipment of those forces and the invention, development, production and operation of such equipment and research relating to it;

   (c) defence policy and strategy and military planning and intelligence;

   (d) plans and measures for the maintenance of essential supplies and services that are or would be needed in time of war.

3 International relations

(1) A person who is or has been a Crown servant or government contractor is guilty of an offence if without lawful authority he makes a damaging disclosure of–

   (a) any information, document or other article relating to international relations; or

   (b) any confidential information, document or other article which was obtained from a State other than the United Kingdom or an international organisation,

being information or a document or article which is or has been in his possession by virtue of his position as a Crown servant or government contractor.

(2) For the purposes of subsection (1) above a disclosure is damaging if—

   (a) it endangers the interests of the United Kingdom abroad, seriously obstructs the promotion or protection by the United Kingdom of those interests or endangers the safety of British citizens abroad; or

(b) it is of information or of a document or article which is such that its unauthorised disclosure would be likely to have any of those effects.

(3) In the case of information or a document or article within subsection (1)(b) above—

(a) the fact that it is confidential, or

(b) its nature or contents, may be sufficient to establish for the purposes of subsection (2)(b) above that the information, document or article is such that its unauthorised disclosure would be likely to have any of the effects there mentioned.

(4) It is a defence for a person charged with an offence under this section to prove that at the time of the alleged offence he did not know, and had no reasonable cause to believe, that the information, document or article in question was such as is mentioned in subsection (1) above or that its disclosure would be damaging within the meaning of that subsection.

(5) In this section "international relations" means the relations between States, between international organisations or between one or more States and one or more such organisations and includes any matter relating to a State other than the United Kingdom or to an international organisation which is capable of affecting the relations of the United Kingdom with another State or with an international organisation.

(6) For the purposes of this section any information, document or article obtained from a State or organisation is confidential at any time while the terms on which it was obtained require it to be held in confidence or while the circumstances in which it was obtained make it reasonable for the State or organisation to expect that it would be so held.

4 Crime and special investigation powers

(1) A person who is or has been a Crown servant or government contractor is guilty of an offence if without lawful authority he discloses any information, document or other article to which this section applies and which is or has been in his possession by virtue of his position as such.

(2) This section applies to any information, document or other article—

(a) the disclosure of which—

(i) results in the commission of an offence; or

(ii) facilitates an escape from legal custody or the doing of any other act prejudicial to the safekeeping of persons in legal custody; or

(iii) impedes the prevention or detection of offences or the apprehension or prosecution of suspected offenders; or

(b) which is such that its unauthorised disclosure would be likely to have any of those effects.

(3) This section also applies to—

(a) any information obtained by reason of the interception of any communication in obedience to a warrant issued under section 2 of the Interception of Communications Act 1985 [or under the authority of an interception warrant under section 5 of the Regulation of Investigatory Powers Act 2000], any information relating to the obtaining of information by reason of any such interception and any document or other article which is or has been used or held for use in, or has been obtained by reason of, any such interception; and

(b) any information obtained by reason of action authorised by a warrant issued under section 3 of the Security Services Act 1989 [or under section 5 of the Intelligence Services Act 1994 or by an authorisation given under section 7 of that Act,] any information relating to the obtaining of information by reason of any such action and any document or other article which is or has been used or held for use in, or has been obtained by reason of, any such action.

(4) It is a defence for a person charged with an offence under this section in respect of a disclosure falling within subsection (2)(a) above to prove that at the time of the alleged offence he did not know, and had no reasonable cause to believe, that the disclosure would have any of the effects there mentioned.

(5) It is a defence for a person charged with an offence under this section in respect of any other disclosure to prove that at the time of the alleged offence he did not know, and had no reasonable cause to believe, that the information, document or article in question was information or a document or article to which this section applies.

(6) In this section "legal custody" includes detention in pursuance of any enactment or any instrument made under an enactment.

5   Information resulting from unauthorised disclosures or entrusted in confidence

(1) Subsection (2) below applies where—

    (a) any information, document or other article protected against disclosure by the foregoing provisions of this Act has come into a person's possession as a result of having been—

        (i) disclosed (whether to him or another) by a Crown servant or government contractor without lawful authority; or

        (ii) entrusted to him by a Crown servant or government contractor on terms requiring it to be held in confidence or in circumstances in which the Crown servant or government contractor could reasonably expect that it would be so held; or

        (iii) disclosed (whether to him or another) without lawful authority by a person to whom it was entrusted as mentioned in sub-paragraph (ii) above; and

    (b) the disclosure without lawful authority of the information, document or article by the person into whose possession it has come is not an offence under any of those provisions.

(2) Subject to subsections (3) and (4) below, the person into whose possession the information, document or article has come is guilty of an offence if he discloses it without lawful authority knowing, or having reasonable cause to believe, that it is protected against disclosure by the foregoing provisions of this Act and that it has come into his possession as mentioned in subsection (1) above.

(3) In the case of information or a document or article protected against disclosure by sections 1 to 3 above, a person does not commit an offence under subsection (2) above unless—

    (a) the disclosure by him is damaging; and

    (b) he makes it knowing, or having reasonable cause to believe, that it would be damaging;

and the question whether a disclosure is damaging shall be determined for the purposes of this subsection as it would be in relation to a disclosure of that information, document or article by a Crown servant in contravention of section 1(3), 2(1) or 3(1) above.

(4) A person does not commit an offence under subsection (2) above in respect of information or a document or other article which has come into his possession as a result of having been disclosed—

    (a) as mentioned in subsection (1)(a)(i) above by a government contractor; or

    (b) as mentioned in subsection (1)(a)(ii) above, unless that disclosure was by a British citizen or took place in the United Kingdom, in any of the Channel Islands or in the Isle of Man or a colony.

(5) For the purposes of this section information or a document or article is protected against disclosure by the foregoing provisions of this Act if–

    (a) it relates to security or intelligence, defence or international relations within the meaning of section 1, 2 or 3 above or is such as is mentioned in section 3(1)(b) above; or

(b) it is information or a document or article to which section 4 above applies; and information or a document or article is protected against disclosure by sections 1 to 3 above if it falls within paragraph (a) above.

(6) A person is guilty of an offence if without lawful authority he discloses any information, document or other article which he knows, or has reasonable cause to believe, to have come into his possession as a result of a contravention of section 1 of the Official Secrets Act 1911.

6 ★ ★ ★ ★ ★

7 Authorised disclosures

(1) For the purposes of this Act a disclosure by—

(a) a Crown servant; or

(b) a person, not being a Crown servant or government contractor, in whose case a notification for the purposes of section 1(1) above is in force,

is madewith lawful authority if, and only if, it is made in accordance with his official duty.

(2) For the purposes of this Act a disclosure by a government contractor is made with lawful authority if, and only if, it is made—

(a) in accordance with an official authorisation; or

(b) for the purposes of the functions by virtue of which he is a government contractor and without contravening an official restriction.

(3) For the purposes of this Act a disclosure made by any other person is made with lawful authority if, and only if, it is made—

(a) to a Crown servant for the purposes of his functions as such; or

(b) in accordance with an official authorisation.

(4) It is a defence for a person charged with an offence under any of the foregoing provisions of this Act to prove that at the time of the alleged offence he believed that he had lawful authority to make the disclosure in question and had no reasonable cause to believe otherwise.

(5) In this section "official authorisation" and "official restriction" mean, subject to subsection (6) below, an authorisation or restriction duly given or imposed by a Crown servant or government contractor or by or on behalf of a prescribed body or a body of a prescribed class.

(6) In relation to section 6 above "official authorisation" includes an authorisation duly given by or on behalf of the State or organisation concerned or, in the case of an organisation, a member of it.

8 Safeguarding of information

(1) Where a Crown servant or government contractor, by virtue of his position as such, has in his possession or under his control any document or other article which it would be an offence under any of the foregoing provisions of this Act for him to disclose without lawful authority he is guilty of an offence if—

(a) being a Crown servant, he retains the document or article contrary to his official duty; or

(b) being a government contractor, he fails to comply with an official direction for the return or disposal of the document or article,

or if he fails to take such care to prevent the unauthorised disclosure of the document or article as a person in his position may reasonably be expected to take.

(2) It is a defence for a Crown servant charged with an offence under subsection (1)(a) above to prove that at the time of the alleged offence he believed that he was acting in accordance with his official duty and had no reasonable cause to believe otherwise.

(3) In subsections (1) and (2) above references to a Crown servant include any person, not

being a Crown servant or government contractor, in whose case a notification for the purposes of section 1(1) above is in force.

(4) Where a person has in his possession or under his control any document or other article which it would be an offence under section 5 above for him to disclose without lawful authority, he is guilty of an offence if—

(a) he fails to comply with an official direction for its return or disposal; or

(b) where he obtained it from a Crown servant or government contractor on terms requiring it to be held in confidence or in circumstances in which that servant or contractor could reasonably expect that it would be so held, he fails to take such care to prevent its unauthorised disclosure as a person in his position may reasonably be expected to take.

(5) Where a person has in his possession or under his control any document or other article which it would be an offence under section 6 above for him to disclose without lawful authority, he is guilty of an offence if he fails to comply with an official direction for its return or disposal.

(6) A person is guilty of an offence if he discloses any official information, document or other article which can be used for the purpose of obtaining access to any information, document or other article protected against disclosure by the foregoing provisions of this Act and the circumstances in which it is disclosed are such that it would be reasonable to expect that it might be used for that purpose without authority.

(7) For the purposes of subsection (6) above a person discloses information or a document or article which is official if—

(a) he has or has had it in his possession by virtue of his position as a Crown servant or government contractor; or

(b) he knows or has reasonable cause to believe that a Crown servant or government contractor has or has had it in his possession by virtue of his position as such.

(8) Subsection (5) of section 5 above applies for the purposes of subsection (6) above as it applies for the purposes of that section.

(9) In this section "official direction" means a direction duly given by a Crown servant or government contractor or by or on behalf of a prescribed body or a body of a prescribed class.

9 Prosecutions

(1) Subject to subsection (2) below, no prosecution for an offence under this Act shall be instituted in England and Wales or in Northern Ireland except by or with the consent of the Attorney General or, as the case may be, the Attorney General for Northern Ireland.

(2) Subsection (1) above does not apply to an offence in respect of any such information, document or article as is mentioned in section 4(2) above but no prosecution for such an offence shall be instituted in England and Wales or in Northern Ireland except by or with the consent of the Director of Public Prosecutions or, as the case may be, the Director of Public Prosecutions for Northern Ireland.

10 Penalties

(1) A person guilty of an offence under any provision of this Act other than section 8(1), (4) or (5) shall be liable—

(a) on conviction on indictment, to imprisonment for a term not exceeding two years or a fine or both;

(b) on summary conviction, to imprisonment for a term not exceeding six months or a fine not exceeding the statutory maximum or both.

(2) A person guilty of an offence under section 8(1), (4) or (5) above shall be liable on summary conviction to imprisonment for a term not exceeding three months or a fine not exceeding level 5 on the standard scale or both.

11 Arrest, search and trial

(1), (2) ★ ★ ★ ★ ★

(3) Section 9(1) of the Official Secrets Act 1911 (search warrants) shall have effect as if references to offences under that Act included references to offences under any provision of this Act other than section 8(1), (4) or (5); and the following provisions of the Police and Criminal Evidence Act 1984, that is to say—

(a) section 9(2) (which excludes items subject to legal privilege and certain other material from powers of search conferred by previous enactments); and

(b) paragraph 3(b) of Schedule 1 (which prescribes access conditions for the special procedure laid down in that Schedule),

shall apply to section 9(1) of the said Act of 1911 as extended by this subsection as they apply to that section as originally enacted.

(4) Section 8(4) of the Official Secrets Act 1920 (exclusion of public from hearing on grounds of national safety) shall have effect as if references to offences under that Act included references to offences under any provision of this Act other than section 8(1), (4) or (5).

(5) Proceedings for an offence under this Act may be taken in any place in the United Kingdom.

12   "Crown servant" and "government contractor"

(1) In this Act "Crown servant" means—

(a) a Minister of the Crown;

[(aa) a member of the Scottish Executive or a Junior Scottish Minister;]

. . .

(c) any person employed in the civil service of the Crown, including Her Majesty's Diplomatic Service, Her Majesty's Overseas Civil Service, the civil service of Northern Ireland and the Northern Ireland Court Service;

(d) any member of the naval, military or air forces of the Crown, including any person employed by an association established for the purposes of [Part XI the Reserve Forces Act 1996];

(e) any constable and any other person employed or appointed in or for the purposes of any police force [including the Police Service of Northern Ireland and the Police Service of Northern Ireland Reserve;]

(f) any person who is member or employee of a prescribed body or a body of a prescribed class and either is prescribed for the purposes of this paragraph or belongs to a prescribed class of members or employees of any such body;

(g) any person who is the holder of a prescribed office or who is an employee of such a holder and either is prescribed for the purposes of this paragraph or belongs to a prescribed class of such employees.

(2) In this Act "government contractor" means, subject to subsection (3) below, any person who is not a Crown servant but who provides, or is employed in the provision of, goods or services—

(a) for the purposes of any Minister or person mentioned in paragraph (a) or (b) of subsection (1) above [, of any office-holder in the Scottish Administration], of any of the services, forces or bodies mentioned in that subsection or of the holder of any office prescribed under that subsection;

[(aa) for the purposes of the National Assembly for Wales; or]

(b) under an agreement or arrangement certified by the Secretary of State as being one to which the government of a State other than the United Kingdom or an international organisation is a party or which is subordinate to, or made for the purposes of implementing, any such agreement or arrangement.

(3) Where an employee or class of employees of any body, or of any holder of an office, is prescribed by an order made for the purposes of subsection (1) above—

(a) any employee of that body, or of the holder of that office, who is not prescribed or is not within the prescribed class; and

(b) any person who does not provide, or is not employed in the provision of, goods or services for the purposes of the performance of those functions of the body or the holder of the office in connection with which the employee or prescribed class of employees is engaged,

shall not be a government contractor for the purposes of this Act.

[(4) In this section "office holder in the Scottish Administration" has the same meaning as in section 126(7)(a) of the Scotland Act 1998.]

[(5) This Act shall apply to the following as it applies to persons falling within the definition of Crown servant–

(a) the First Minister and the Deputy First Minister in Northern Ireland,

(b) Northern Ireland Minister and Junior Ministers.]

13   Other interpretation provisions

(1) In this Act—

"disclose" and "disclosure", in relation to a document or other article, include parting with possession of it;

"international organisation" means, subject to subsections (2) and (3) below, an organisation of which only States are members and includes a reference to any organ of such an organisation;

"prescribed" means prescribed by an order made by the Secretary of State;

"State" includes the government of a State and any organ of its government and references to a State other than the United Kingdom include references to any territory outside the United Kingdom.

(2) In section 12(2)(b) above the reference to an international organisation includes a reference to any such organisation whether or not one of which only States are members and includes a commercial organisation.

(3) In determining for the purposes of subsection (1) above whether only States are members of an organisation, any member which is itself an organisation of which only States are members, or which is an organ of such an organisation, shall be treated as a State.

★ ★ ★ ★ ★

Security Service Act 1989
(1989, c. 5)

An Act to place the Security Service on a statutory basis; to enable certain actions to be taken on the authority of warrants issued by the Secretary of State, with provision for the issue of such warrants to be kept under review by a Commissioner; to establish a procedure for the investigation by a Tribunal or, in some cases, by the Commissioner of complaints about the Service; and for connected purposes   [27 April 1989]

Territorial extent: United Kingdom

1   The Security Service

(1) There shall continue to be a Security Service (in this Act referred to as "the Service") under the authority of the Secretary of State.

(2) The function of the Service shall be the protection of national security and, in particular, its protection against threats from espionage, terrorism and sabotage, from the activities of agents of foreign powers and from actions intended to overthrow or undermine parliamentary democracy by political, industrial or violent means.

(3) It shall also be the function of the Service to safeguard the economic well-being of the United Kingdom against threats posed by the actions or intentions of persons outside the British Islands.

[(4) It shall also be the function of the Service to act in support of the activities of police forces [, the National Criminal Intelligence Service, the National Crime Squad,] and other law enforcement agencies in the prevention and detection of serious crime.]

[(5) Section 81(5) of the Regulation of Investigatory Powers Act 2000 (meaning of "prevention" and "detection"), so far as it relates to serious crime, shall apply for the purposes of this Act as it applies for the purposes of the provisions of that Act not contained in Chapter I of Part I.]

2   The Director-General

(1) The operations of the Service shall continue to be under the control of a Director-General appointed by the Secretary of State.

(2) The Director-General shall be responsible for the efficiency of the Service and it shall be his duty to ensure—

- (a) that there are arrangements for securing that no information is obtained by the Service except so far as necessary for the proper discharge of its functions or disclosed by it except so far as necessary for that purpose or for the purpose of [the prevention or detection of] serious crime [or for the purpose of any criminal proceedings]; and
- (b) that the Service does not take any action to further the interests of any political party]; and
- (c) that there are arrangements, agreed with a person designated by the Secretary of State, for co-ordinating the activities of the Service in pursuance of section 1(4) of this Act with the activities of police forces [, the National Criminal Intelligence Service, the National Crime Squad,] and other law enforcement agencies.]

(3) The arrangements mentioned in subsection (2)(a) above shall be such as to ensure that information in the possession of the Service is not disclosed for use in determining whether a person should be employed, or continue to be employed, by any person, or in any office or capacity, except in accordance with provisions in that behalf approved by the Secretary of State.

(3A), (3B) ★ ★ ★ ★ ★

(4) The Director-General shall make an annual report on the work of the Service to the Prime Minister and the Secretary of State and may at any time report to either of them on any matter relating to its work.

3   ★ ★ ★ ★ ★

4, 5   . . .

★ ★ ★ ★ ★

Broadcasting Act 1990
(1990, c. 42)

An Act to make new provision with respect to the provision and regulation of independent television and sound programme services and of other services provided on television or radio frequencies; to make provision with respect to the provision and regulation of local delivery services; to amend in other respects the law relating to broadcasting and the provision of television and sound programme services and to make provision with respect to the supply and use of information about programmes; to make provision with respect to the transfer of the property, rights and liabilities of the Independent Broadcasting Authority and the Cable Authority and the dissolution of those bodies; to make new provision relating to the Broadcasting Complaints Commission; to provide for the establishment and functions of a Broadcasting Standards Council; to amend the Wireless Teleg-raphy Acts 1949 to 1967 and the Marine, &c., Broadcasting (Offences) Act 1967; to revoke a class licence granted under the Telecommunications Act 1984 to run broadcast relay systems; and for connected purposes. [1 November 1990]

Territorial extent: United Kingdom (in the case of materials reproduced here).

PART I   INDEPENDENT TELEVISION SERVICES

CHAPTER I   REGULATION BY COMMISSION OF TELEVISION SERVICES GENERALLY

Establishment of Independent Television Commission

1   The Independent Television Commission
(1) There shall be a commission to be called the Independent Television Commission (in this Part referred to as "the Commission").
(2) The Commission shall consist of—
    (a) a chairman and a deputy chairman appointed by the Secretary of State; and
    (b) such number of other members appointed by the Secretary of State, not being less than eight nor more than ten, as he may from time to time determine.
(3) ★ ★ ★ ★ ★

Function of Commission

2   Regulation by Commission of provision of television services
(1) It shall be the function of the Commission to regulate, in accordance with this Part [and Part I of the Broadcasting Act 1996], the provision of the following services, namely–
    (a) television programme services [other than satellite services and digital programme services] which are provided from places in the United Kingdom by persons other than the BBC and the Welsh Authority, . . .
    [(aa) satellite television services (as defined by section 43(1)) provided by persons other than the BBC or the Welsh Authority,]
    (b) additional services which are provided from places in the United Kingdom, and to regulate, in accordance with Part II, the provision of local delivery services (within the meaning of that Part) which are so provided,
    [(c) multiplex services (as defined by section 1(1) of the Broadcasting Act 1996) which are provided from places in the United Kingdom by persons other than the BBC, and
    [(cc) digital programme services (as defined by s. 1(4) of the Broadcasting Act 1996) provided by persons who for the purposes of Council Directive 89/552/EEC are under the jurisdiction of the United Kingdom, other than the BBC and the Welsh Authority,
    (d) digital additional services (as defined by section 24(1) of the Broadcasting Act 1996) provided by persons who for the purposes of Council Directive 89/552/EEC are under the jurisdiction of the United Kingdom other than the BBC.]
(2) It shall be the duty of the Commission—
    (a) to discharge their functions under this Part and Part II [and under Part I of the Broadcasting Act 1996] as respects the licensing of the services referred to in subsection (1) in the manner in which they consider is best calculated–
        (i) to ensure that a wide range of such services is available throughout the United Kingdom, and
        (ii) to ensure fair and effective competition in the provision of such services and services connected with them; and
    (b) to discharge their functions under this Part [and Part I of the Broadcasting Act

1996] as respects the licensing of television programmeservices [and multiplex services (as defined by section 1(1) of that Act)] in the manner in which they consider is best calculated to ensure the provision of such services which (taken as a whole) are of high quality and offer a wide range of programmes calculated to appeal to a variety of tastes and interests.

(3)–(6) ★ ★ ★ ★ ★

3-5 ★ ★ ★ ★ ★

General provisions about licensed services

6   General requirements as to licensed services

(1) The Commission shall do all that they can to secure that every licensed service complies with the following requirements, namely—

(a) that nothing is included in its programmes which offends against good taste or decency or is likely to encourage or incite to crime or to lead to disorder or to be offensive to public feeling;

(b) that any news given (in whatever form) in its programmes is presented with due accuracy and impartiality;

(c) that due impartiality is preserved on the part of the person providing the service as respects matters of political or industrial controversy or relating to current public policy;

(d) that due responsibility is exercised with respect to the content of any of its pro-grammes which are religious programmes, and that in particular any such programmes do not involve–

(i) any improper exploitation of any susceptibilities of those watching the programmes, or

(ii) any abusive treatment of the religious views and beliefs of those belonging to a particular religion or religious denomination; and

(e) that its programmes do not include any technical device which, by using images of very brief duration or by any other means, exploits the possibility of conveying a message to, or otherwise influencing the minds of, persons watching the programmes without their being aware, or fully aware, of what has occurred.

(2)–(8) ★ ★ ★ ★ ★

7   General code for programmes

(1) The Commission shall draw up, and from time to time review, a code giving guidance—

(a) as to the rules to be observed with respect to the showing of violence, or the inclusion of sounds suggestive of violence, in programmes included in licensed services, particularly when large numbers of children and young persons may be expected to be watching the programmes;

(b) as to the rules to be observed with respect to the inclusion in such programmes of appeals for donations; and

(c) as to such other matters concerning standards and practice for such programmes as the Commission may consider suitable for inclusion in the code;

and the Commission shall do all that they can to secure that the provisions of the code are observed in the provision of licensed services.

(2) In considering what other matters ought to be included in the code in pursuance of subsection (1)(c), the Commission shall have special regard to programmes included in licensed services in circumstances such that large numbers of children and young persons may be expected to be watching the programmes.

(3) The Commission shall, in drawing up or revising the code under this section, take

account of such of the international obligations of the United Kingdom as the Secretary of State may notify to them for the purposes of this subsection.

(4) The Commission shall publish the code drawn up under this section, and every revision of it, in such manner as they consider appropriate.

8 General provisions as to advertisements

(1) The Commission shall do all that they can to secure that the rules specified in subsection (2) are complied with in relation to licensed services.

(2) Those rules are as follows—

    (a) a licensed service must not include—

        (i) any advertisement which is inserted by or on behalf of any body whose objects are wholly or mainly of a political nature,

        (ii) any advertisement which is directed towards any political end, or

        (iii) any advertisement which has any relation to any industrial dispute (other than an advertisement of a public service nature inserted by, or on behalf of, a government department);

    (b) in the acceptance of advertisements for inclusion in a licensed service there must be no unreasonable discrimination either against or in favour of any particular advertiser; and

    (c) a licensed service must not, without the previous approval of the Commission, include a programme which is sponsored by any person whose business consists, wholly or mainly, in the manufacture or supply of a product, or in the provision of a service, which the licence holder is prohibited from advertising by virtue of any provision of section 9.

(3) Nothing in subsection (2) shall be construed as prohibiting the inclusion in a licensed service of any party political broadcast which complies with the rules (so far as applicable) made by the Commission for the purposes of section 36.

(4) After consultation with the Commission the Secretary of State may make regulations amending, repealing, or adding to the rules specified in subsection (2); but no such regulations shall be made unless a draft of the regulations has been laid before and approved by a resolution of each House of Parliament.

(5) The Commission shall not act as an advertising agent.

9 Control of advertisements

(1) It shall be the duty of the Commission—

    (a) after the appropriate consultation, to draw up, and from time to time review, a code—

        (i) governing standards and practice in advertising and in the sponsoring of programmes, and

        (ii) prescribing the advertisements and methods of advertising or sponsorship to be prohibited, or to be prohibited in particular circumstances; and

    (b) to do all that they can to secure that the provisions of the code are observed in the provision of licensed services;

and the Commission may make different provision in the code for different kinds of licensed services.

(2)–(6) ★ ★ ★ ★ ★

(7) The Commission may give directions to persons holding any class of licences with respect to the times when advertisements are to be allowed.

(8) Directions under this section may be, to any degree, either general or specific and qualified or unqualified; and directions under subsection (7) may, in particular, relate to—

    (a) the maximum amount of time to be given to advertisements in any hour or other period,

    (b) the minimum interval which must elapse between any two periods given over to advertisements and the number of such periods to be allowed in any programme or in any hour or day,

(c) the exclusion of advertisements from a specified part of a licensed service, and may make different provision for different parts of the day, different days of the week, different types of programmes or for other differing circumstances.

(9) The Commission shall—

(a) in drawing up or revising the code, or

(b) in giving any directions under subsection (7),

take account of such of the international obligations of the United Kingdom as the Secretary of State may notify to them for the purposes of this subsection.

10 Government control over licensed services

(1) If it appears to him to be necessary or expedient to do so in connection with his functions as such, the Secretary of State or any other Minister of the Crown may at any time by notice require the Commission to direct the holders of any licences specified in the notice to publish in their licensed services, at such times as may be specified in the notice, such announcement as is so specified, with or without visual images of any picture, scene or object mentioned in the announcement; and it shall be the duty of the Commission to comply with the notice.

(2) Where the holder of a licence publishes any announcement in pursuance of a direction under subsection (1), he may announce that he is doing so in pursuance of such a direction.

(3) The Secretary of State may at any time by notice require the Commission to direct the holders of any licences specified in the notice to refrain from including in the programmes included in their licensed services any matter or classes of matter specified in the notice; and it shall be the duty of the Commission to comply with the notice.

(4) Where the Commission—

(a) have given the holder of any licence a direction in accordance with a notice under subsection (3), or

(b) in consequence of the revocation by the Secretary of State of such a notice, have revoked such a direction,

or where such a notice has expired, the holder of the licence in question may publish in the licensed service an announcement of the giving or revocation of the direction or of the expiration of the notice, as the case may be.

(5), (6) ★ ★ ★ ★ ★

11, 12 ★ ★ ★ ★ ★

Prohibition on providing unlicensed television services

13 Prohibition on providing television services without a licence

(1) Subject to subsection (2), any person who provides any service falling within section 2(1)(a) [, (aa)] [(b), (c) or (cc) or (d)] without being authorised to do so by or under a licence under this Part shall be guilty of an offence.

(2) The Secretary of State may, after consultation with the Commission, by order provide that subsection (1) shall not apply to such services or descriptions of services as are specified in the order.

(3) A person guilty of an offence under this section shall be liable—

(a) on summary conviction, to a fine not exceeding the statutory maximum;

(b) on conviction on indictment, to a fine.

(4) No proceedings in respect of an offence under this section shall be instituted—

(a) in England and Wales, except by or with the consent of the Director of Public Prosecutions;

(b) in Northern Ireland, except by or with the consent of the Director of Public Prosecutions for Northern Ireland.

(5) Without prejudice to subsection (3), compliance with this section shall be enforceable by civil proceedings by the Crown for an injunction or interdict or for any other appropriate relief.

(6) Any order under this section shall be subject to annulment in pursuance of a resolution of either House of Parliament.

14–35 ★ ★ ★ ★ ★

36 Party political broadcasts

(1) Subject to subsection (2), any regional Channel 3 licence or licence to provide Channel 4 or 5 shall include–
- (a) conditions requiring the licence holder to include party political broadcasts in the licensed service; and
- (b) conditions requiring the licence holder to observe such rules with respect to party political broadcasts as the Commission may determine.

(2) Where any determination under section 28(3), is in force, a licence to provide Channel 5 may (but need not) include any such conditions as are mentioned in subsection (1)(a) and (b).

(3) Without prejudice to the generality of paragraph (b) of subsection (1) [but subject to section 14 of the Registration of Political Parties Act 1998], the Commission may determine for the purposes of that subsection—
- (a) the political parties on whose behalf party political broadcasts may be made; and
- (b) in relation to any political party on whose behalf such broadcasts may be made, the length and frequency of such broadcasts.

(4) Any rules made by the Commission for the purposes of this section may make different provision for different cases or circumstances.

37–141 ★ ★ ★ ★ ★

142–161 . . .

162–165 ★ ★ ★ ★ ★

Trade Union and Labour Relations (Consolidation) Act 1992
(1992, c. 52)

An Act to consolidate the enactments relating to collective labour relations, that is to say, to trade unions, employers' associations, industrial relations and industrial action.   [16 July 1992]

Territorial extent: Great Britain (but see section 242 below)

CHAPTER III   CODES OF PRACTICE

Codes of Practice issued by the Secretary of State

203 Issue of Codes of Practice by the Secretary of State

(1) The Secretary of State may issue Codes of Practice containing such practical guidance as he thinks fit for the purpose—
- (a) of promoting the improvement of industrial relations, or
- (b) of promoting what appear to him to be desirable practices in relation to the conduct by trade unions of ballots and elections.

(2) The Secretary of State may from time to time revise the whole or any part of a Code of Practice issued by him and issue that revised Code.

204   Procedure for issue of Code by Secretary of State

(1) When the Secretary of State proposes to issue a Code of Practice, or a revised Code, he shall after consultation with ACAS prepare and publish a draft of the Code, shall consider any representations made to him about the draft and may modify the draft accordingly.

(2) If he determines to proceed with the draft, he shall lay it before both Houses of Parliament and, if it is approved by resolution of each House, shall issue the Code in the form of the draft.

(3) A Code issued under this section shall come into effect on such day as the Secretary of State may by order appoint.

The order may contain such transitional provisions or savings as appear to him to be necessary or expedient.

(4) An order under subsection (3) shall be made by statutory instrument, which shall be subject to annulment in pursuance of a resolution of either House of Parliament.

205   ★ ★ ★ ★ ★

206   Revocation of Code issued by Secretary of State

(1) A Code of Practice issued by the Secretary of State may be revoked by him by order made by statutory instrument.

The order may contain such transitional provisions and savings as appear to him to be appropriate.

(2) An order shall not be made under this section unless a draft of it has been laid before and approved by resolution of each House of Parliament.

Supplementary provisions

207   Effect of failure to comply with Code

(1) A failure on the part of any person to observe any provision of a Code of Practice issued under this Chapter shall not of itself render him liable to any proceedings.

(2) In any proceedings before an industrial tribunal or the Central Arbitration Committee any Code of Practice issued under this Chapter by ACAS shall be admissible in evidence, and any provision of the Code which appears to the tribunal or Committee to be relevant to any question arising in the proceedings shall be taken into account in determining that question.

(3) In any proceedings before a court or industrial tribunal or the Central Arbitration Committee any Code of Practice issued under this Chapter by the Secretary of State shall be admissible in evidence, and any provision of the Code which appears to the court, tribunal or Committee to be relevant to any question arising in the proceedings shall be taken into account in determining that question.

208–219   ★ ★ ★ ★ ★

PART V   INDUSTRIAL ACTION

220   Peaceful picketing

(1) It is lawful for a person in contemplation or furtherance of a trade dispute to attend—
  (a) at or near his own place of work, or
  (b) if he is an official of a trade union, at or near the place of work of a member of the union whom he is accompanying and whom he represents,
for the purpose only of peacefully obtaining or communicating information, or peacefully persuading any person to work or abstain from working.

(2) If a person works or normally works—

(a) otherwise than at any one place, or

(b) at a place the location of which is such that attendance there for a purpose mentioned in subsection (1) is impracticable,

his place of work for the purposes of that subsection shall be any premises of his employer from which he works or from which his work is administered.

(3) In the case of a worker not in employment where—

(a) his last employment was terminated in connection with a trade dispute, or

(b) the termination of his employment was one of the circumstances giving rise to a trade dispute,

in relation to that dispute his former place of work shall be treated for the purposes of subsection (1) as being his place of work.

(4) A person who is an official of a trade union by virtue only of having been elected or appointed to be a representative of some of the members of the union shall be regarded for the purposes of subsection (1) as representing only those members; but otherwise an official of a union shall be regarded for those purposes as representing all its members.

221–239   ★ ★ ★ ★ ★

Criminal offences

240   Breach of contract involving injury to persons or property

(1) A person commits an offence who wilfully and maliciously breaks a contract of service or hiring, knowing or having reasonable cause to believe that the probable consequences of his so doing, either alone or in combination with others, will be—

(a) to endanger human life or cause serious bodily injury, or

(b) to expose valuable property, whether real or personal, to destruction or serious injury.

(2) Subsection (1) applies equally whether the offence is committed from malice conceived against the person endangered or injured or, as the case may be, the owner of the property destroyed or injured, or otherwise.

(3) A person guilty of an offence under this section is liable on summary conviction to imprisonment for a term not exceeding three months or to a fine not exceeding level 2 on the standard scale or both.

(4) This section does not apply to seamen.

241   Intimidation or annoyance by violence or otherwise

(1) A person commits an offence who, with a view to compelling another person to abstain from doing or to do any act which that person has a legal right to do or abstain from doing, wrongfully and without legal authority—

(a) uses violence to or intimidates that person or his wife or children, or injures his property,

(b) persistently follows that person about from place to place,

(c) hides any tools, clothes or other property owned or used by that person, or deprives him of or hinders him in the use thereof,

(d) watch or besets the house or other place where the person resides, works, carries on business or happens to be, or the approach to any such house or place, or

(e) follows that person with two or more other persons in a disorderly manner in or through any street or road.

(2) A person guilty of an offence under this section is liable on summary conviction to imprisonment for a term not exceeding six months or a fine not exceeding level 5 on the standard scale, or both.

(3) A constable may arrest without warrant anyone he reasonably suspects is committing an offence under this section.

242   Restriction of offence of conspiracy: England and Wales

(1) Where in pursuance of any such agreement as is mentioned in section 1(1) of the Criminal Law Act 1977 (which provides for the offence of conspiracy) the acts in question in relation to an offence are to be done in contemplation or furtherance of a trade dispute, the offence shall be disregarded for the purposes of that subsection if it is a summary offence which is not punishable with imprisonment.

(2) This section extends to England and Wales only.

★ ★ ★ ★ ★

Tribunals and Inquiries Act 1992
(1992, c. 53)

An Act to consolidate the Tribunals and Inquiries Act 1971 and certain other enactments relating to tribunals and inquiries.   [16 July 1992]

Territorial extent: United Kingdom

The Council on Tribunals and their functions

1   The Council on Tribunals

(1) There shall continue to be a council entitled the Council on Tribunals (in this Act referred to as "the Council")—

    (a) to keep under review the constitution and working of the tribunals specified in Schedule 1 (being the tribunals constituted under or for the purposes of the statutory provisions specified in that Schedule) and, from time to time, to report on their constitution and working;

    (b) to consider and report on such particular matters as may be referred to the Council under this Act with respect to tribunals other than the ordinary courts of law, whether or not specified in Schedule 1, or any such tribunal; and

    (c) to consider and report on such matters as may be referred to the Council under this Act, or as the council may determine to be of special importance, with respect to administrative procedures involving, or which may involve, the holding by or on behalf of a Minister of a statutory inquiry, or any such procedure.

(2) Nothing in this section authorises or requires the Council to deal with any matter with respect to which the Parliament of Northern Ireland had power to make laws.

2   Composition of the Council and the Scottish Committee

(1) Subject to subsection (3), the Council shall consist of not more than fifteen nor less than ten members appointed by the Lord Chancellor and the [Scottish Ministers], and one of the members shall be so appointed to be chairman of the Council.

(2) There shall be a Scottish Committee of the Council (in this Act referred to as "the Scottish Committee") which, subject to subsection (3), shall consist of–

    (a) either two or three members of the Council designated by the [Scottish Ministers], and

    (b) either three or four persons, not being members of the Council, appointed by the Lord Advocate;

and the Lord Advocate shall appoint one of the members of the Scottish Committee (being a member of the Council) to be chairman of the Scottish Committee.

(3) In addition to the persons appointed or designated under subsection (1) or (2), the Parliamentary Commissioner for Administration shall, by virtue of his office, be a member of the Council and of the Scottish Committee.

(4) In appointing members of the Council regard shall be had to the need for representation of the interests of persons in Wales.

3, 4 ★ ★ ★ ★ ★

Composition and procedure of tribunals and inquiries

5   Recommendations of Council as to appointment of members of tribunals

(1) Subject to section 6 but without prejudice to the generality of section 1(1)(a), the Council may make to the appropriate Minister general recommendations as to the making of appointments to membership of any tribunals mentioned in Schedule 1 or of panels constituted for the purposes of any such tribunals; and (without prejudice to any statutory provisions having effect with respect to such appointments) the appropriate Minister shall have regard to recommendations under this section.

(2) In this section "the appropriate Minister", in relation to appointments of any description, means the Minister making the appointments or, if they are not made by a Minister, the Minister in charge of the government department concerned with the tribunals in question.

(3) ★ ★ ★ ★ ★

6   Appointment of chairmen of certain tribunals

(1) The chairman, or any person appointed to act as chairman, of any of the tribunals to which this subsection applies shall (without prejudice to any statutory provisions as to qualifications) be selected by the appropriate authority from a panel of persons appointed by the Lord Chancellor.

(2) Members of panels constituted under this section shall hold and vacate office under the terms of the instruments under which they are appointed, but may resign office by notice in writing to the Lord Chancellor; and any such member who ceases to hold office shall be eligible for re-appointment.

(3)–(9) ★ ★ ★ ★ ★

7   Concurrence required for removal of members of certain tribunals

(1) Subject to subsection (2), the power of a Minister, other than the Lord Chancellor, to terminate a person's membership of any tribunal specified in Schedule 1, or of a panel constituted for the purposes of any such tribunal, shall be exercisable only with the consent of—

   (a) the Lord Chancellor, the Lord President of the Court of Session and the Lord Chief Justice of Northern Ireland, if the tribunal sits in all parts of the United Kingdom;

   (b) the Lord Chancellor and the Lord President of the Court of Session, if the tribunal sits in all parts of Great Britain;

   (c) the Lord Chancellor and the Lord Chief Justice of Northern Ireland, if the tribunal sits both in England and Wales and in Northern Ireland;

   (d) the Lord Chancellor, if the tribunal does not sit outside England and Wales;

   (e) the Lord President of the Court of Session, if the tribunal sits only in Scotland;

   (f) the Lord Chief Justice of Northern Ireland, if the tribunal sits only in Northern Ireland.

(2), (3) ★ ★ ★ ★ ★

8   Procedural rules for tribunals

(1) The power of a Minister, the Lord President of the Court of Session, the Commissioners of Inland Revenue or the Foreign Compensation Commission to make, approve, confirm or concur in procedural rules for any tribunal specified in Schedule 1 shall be exercisable only after consultation with the Council.

(2)–(4) ★ ★ ★ ★ ★

9   Procedure in connection with statutory inquiries

(1) The Lord Chancellor, after consultation with the Council, may make rules regulating

the procedure to be followed in connection with statutory inquiries held by or on behalf of Ministers; and different provision may be made by any such rules in relation to different classes of such inquiries.

(2), (3) ★ ★ ★ ★ ★

(4) In the application of this section to inquiries held in Scotland–

(a) for any reference to the Lord Chancellor there shall be substituted a reference to the Lord Advocate, and

(b) the Council, in exercising their functions under this section in relation to rules to be made by the Lord Advocate, shall consult with the Scottish Committee.

Judicial control of tribunals etc.

10 Reasons to be given for decisions of tribunals and Ministers

(1) Subject to the provisions of this section and of section 14, where—

(a) any tribunal specified in Schedule 1 gives any decision, or

(b) any Minister notifies any decision taken by him—

(i) after a statutory inquiry has been held by him or on his behalf, or

(ii) in a case in which a person concerned could (whether by objecting or otherwise) have required a statutory inquiry to be so held,

it shall be the duty of the tribunal or Minister to furnish a statement, either written or oral, of the reasons for the decision if requested, on or before the giving or notification of the decision, to state the reasons.

(2) The statement referred to in subsection (1) may be refused, or the specification of the reasons restricted, on grounds of national security.

(3), (4) ★ ★ ★ ★ ★

(5) Subsection (1) does not apply—

(a) to decisions in respect of which any statutory provision has effect, apart from this section, as to the giving of reasons,

(b) to decisions of a Minister in connection with the preparation, making, approval, confirmation, or concurrence in regulations, rules or bye-laws, or orders or schemes of a legislative and not executive character . . .

(6) Any statement of the reasons for a decision referred to in paragraph (a) or (b) of subsection (1), whether given in pursuance of that subsection or of any other statutory provision, shall be taken to form part of the decision and accordingly to be incorporated in the record.

(7), (8) ★ ★ ★ ★ ★

11 ★ ★ ★ ★ ★

12 Supervisory functions of superior courts not excluded by Acts passed before 1st August 1958

(1) As respects England and Wales—

(a) any provision in an Act passed before 1st August 1958 that any order or determination shall not be called into question in any court, or

(b) any provision in such an Act which by similar words excludes any of the powers of the High Court,

shall not have effect so as to prevent the removal of the proceedings into the High Court by order of certiorari or to prejudice the powers of the High Court to make orders of mandamus.

(2) As respects Scotland—

(a) any provision in an Act passed before 1st August 1958 that any order or determination shall not be called into question in any court, or

(b) any provision in such an Act which by similar words excludes any jurisdiction which the Court of Session would otherwise have to entertain an application for reduction or suspension of any order or determination, or otherwise to consider the validity of any order or determination,

shall not have effect so as to prevent the exercise of any such jurisdiction.

(3) Nothing in this section shall apply—

(a) to any order or determination of a court of law, or

(b) where an Act makes special provision for application to the High Court or the Court of Session within a time limited by the Act.

13–19, Schedules ★ ★ ★ ★ ★

European Communities (Amendment) Act 1993
(1993, c. 32)

An Act to make provision consequential on the Treaty on European Union signed at Maastricht on 7th February 1992. [20 July 1993]

Territorial extent: United Kingdom

1 Treaty on European Union

(1) In section 1(2) of the European Communities Act 1972, in the definition of "the Treaties" and "the Community Treaties", after paragraph (j) (inserted by the European Communities (Amendment) Act 1986) there shall be inserted the words

"and

(k) Titles II, III and IV of the Treaty on European Union signed at Maastricht on 7th February 1992, together with the other provisions of the Treaty so far as they relate to those Titles, and the Protocols adopted at Maastricht on that date and annexed to the Treaty establishing the European Community with the exception of the Protocol on Social Policy on page 117 of Cm 1934".

(2) For the purpose of section 6 of the European Parliamentary Elections Act 1978 (approval of treaties increasing the Parliament's powers) the Treaty on European Union signed at Maastricht on 7th February 1992 is approved.

2 Economic and monetary union

No notification shall be given to the Council of the European Communities that the United Kingdom intends to move to the third stage of economic and monetary union (in accordance with the Protocol on certain provisions relating to the United Kingdom adopted at Maastricht on 7th February 1992) unless a draft of the notification has first been approved by Act of Parliament and unless Her Majesty's Government has reported to Parliament on its proposals for the co-ordination of economic policies, its role in the European Council of Finance Ministers (ECOFIN) in pursuit of the objectives of Article 2 of the Treaty establishing the European Community as provided for in Articles 103 and 102a, and the work of the European Monetary Institute in preparation for economic and monetary union.

★ ★ ★ ★ ★

Criminal Justice and Public Order Act 1994
(1994, c. 33)

An Act to make further provision in relation to criminal justice (including employment in the prison service); to amend or extend the criminal law and powers for preventing crime and enforcing that law; to amend the Video Recordings Act 1984; and for purposes connected with those purposes.
[3 November 1994]

Territorial extent: England and Wales, Scotland (ss. 61–66, 163), United Kingdom (ss. 68, 69), England and Wales (remaining provisions printed here). Sections 34–38 (below) have been applied, with modifications, to the armed forces by the Criminal Justice and Public Order Act 1994 (Application to the Armed Forces) Order 1997 (SI 1997/16).

Inferences from accused's silence

34   Effect of accused's failure to mention facts when questioned or charged

(1) Where, in any proceedings against a person for an offence, evidence is given that the accused—

(a) at any time before he was charged with the offence, on being questioned under caution by a constable trying to discover whether or by whom the offence had been committed, failed to mention any fact relied on in his defence in those proceedings; or

(b) on being charged with the offence or officially informed that he might be prosecuted for it, failed to mention any such fact,

being a fact which in the circumstances existing at the time the accused could reasonably have been expected to mention when so questioned, charged or informed, as the case may be, subsection (2) below applies.

(2) Where this subsection applies—

[(a) a magistrates' court inquiring into the case as examining justices;]

(b) a judge, in deciding whether to grant an application made by the accused under—

(i) section 6 of the Criminal Justice Act 1987 (application for dismissal of charge of serious fraud in respect of which notice of transfer has been given under section 4 of that Act); or

(ii) paragraph 5 of Schedule 6 to the Criminal Justice Act 1991 (application for dismissal of charge of violent or sexual offence involving child in respect of which notice of transfer has been given under section 53 of that Act);

(c) the court, in determining whether there is a case to answer; and

(d) the court or jury, in determining whether the accused is guilty of the offence charged,

may draw such inferences from the failure as appear proper.

[(2A) Where the accused was at an authorised place of detention at the time of the failure, subsections (1) and (2) above do not apply if he had not been allowed an opportunity to consult a solicitor prior to being questioned, charged or informed as mentioned in subsection (1) above.]

(3) Subject to any directions by the court, evidence tending to establish the failure may be given before or after evidence tending to establish the fact which the accused is alleged to have failed to mention.

(4) This section applies in relation to questioning by persons (other than constables) charged with the duty of investigating offences or charging offenders as it applies in relation to questioning by constables; and in subsection (1) above "officially informed" means informed by a constable or any such person.

(5) This section does not—

(a) prejudice the admissibility in evidence of the silence or other reaction of the accused in the face of anything said in his presence relating to the conduct in respect of which he is charged, in so far as evidence thereof would be admissible apart from this section; or

(b) preclude the drawing of any inference from any such silence or other reaction of the accused which could properly be drawn apart from this section.

(6) ★ ★ ★ ★ ★

(7) . . .

35 Effect of accused's silence at trial

(1) At the trial of any person . . . for an offence, subsections (2) and (3) below apply unless—

(a) the accused's guilt is not in issue; or

(b) it appears to the court that the physical or mental condition of the accused makes it undesirable for him to give evidence;

but subsection (2) below does not apply if, at the conclusion of the evidence for the prosecution, his legal representative informs the court that the accused will give evidence or, where he is unrepresented, the court ascertains from him that he will give evidence.

(2) Where this subsection applies, the court shall, at the conclusion of the evidence for the prosecution, satisfy itself (in the case of proceedings on indictment, in the presence of the jury) that the accused is aware that the stage has been reached at which evidence can be given for the defence and that he can, if he wishes, give evidence and that, if he chooses not to give evidence, or having been sworn, without good cause refuses to answer any question, it will be permissible for the court or jury to draw such inferences as appear proper from his failure to give evidence or his refusal, without good cause, to answer any question.

(3) Where this subsection applies, the court or jury, in determining whether the accused is guilty of the offence charged, may draw such inferences as appear proper from the failure of the accused to give evidence or his refusal, without good cause, to answer any question.

(4) This section does not render the accused compellable to give evidence on his own behalf, and he shall accordingly not be guilty of contempt of court by reason of a failure to do so.

(5) For the purposes of this section a person who, having been sworn, refuses to answer any question shall be taken to do so without good cause unless—

(a) he is entitled to refuse to answer the question by virtue of any enactment, whenever passed or made, or on the ground of privilege; or

(b) the court in the exercise of its general discretion excuses him from answering it.

(6) . . .

36 Effect of accused's failure or refusal to account for objects, substances or marks

(1) Where—

(a) a person is arrested by a constable, and there is—

   (i)   on is person; or

   (ii) in or on his clothing or footwear; or

   (iii) otherwise in his possession; or

   (iv) in any place in which he is at the time of his arrest, any object, substance or mark, or there is any mark on any such object; and

(b) that or another constable investigating the case reasonably believes that the presence of the object, substance or mark may be attributable to the participation of the person arrested in the commission of an offence specified by the constable; and

(c) the constable informs the person arrested that he so believes, and requests him to account for the presence of the object, substance or mark; and

(d) the person fails or refuses to do so, then if, in any proceedings against the person for the offence so specified, evidence of those matters is given, subsection (2) below applies.

(2) Where this subsection applies–

[(a) a magistrates' court inquiring into the offence as examining justices;]

(b) a judge, in deciding whether to grant an application made by the accused under—

   (i) section 6 of the Criminal Justice Act 1987 (application for dismissal of charge of serious fraud in respect of which notice of transfer has been given under section 4 of that Act); or
   (ii) paragraph 5 of Schedule 6 to the Criminal Justice Act 1991 (application for dismissal of charge of violent or sexual offence involving child in respect of which notice of transfer has been given under section 53 of that Act);
   (c) the court or jury, in determining whether the accused is guilty of the offence charged,
may draw such inferences from the failure or refusal as appear proper.

   (3) Subsections (1) and (2) above apply to the condition of clothing or footwear as they apply to a substance or mark thereon.

   (4) Subsections (1) and (2) above do not apply unless the accused was told in ordinary language by the constable when making the request mentioned in subsection (1)(c) above what the effect of this section would be if he failed or refused to comply with the request.

   [(4A) Where the accused was at an authorised place of detention at the time of the failure or refusal, subsections (1) and (2) above do not apply if he had not been allowed an opportunity to consult a solicitor prior to the request being made.]

   (5) ★ ★ ★ ★ ★

   (6) This section does not preclude the drawing of any inference from a failure or refusal of the accused to account for the presence of an object, substance or mark or from the condition of clothing or footwear which could properly be drawn apart from this section.

   (7) ★ ★ ★ ★ ★

   (8) . . .

37   Effect of accused's failure or refusal to account for presence at a particular place

   (1) Where—
   (a) a person arrested by a constable was found by him at a place at or about the time the offence for which he was arrested is alleged to have been committed; and
   (b) that or another constable investigating the offence reasonably believes that the presence of the person at that place and at that time may be attributable to his participation in the commission of the offence; and
   (c) the constable informs the person that he so believes, and requests him to account for that presence; and
   (d) the person fails or refuses to do so, then if, in any proceedings against the person for the offence, evidence of those matters is given, subsection (2) below applies.

   (2) Where this subsection applies—
   [(a) a magistrates' court inquiring into the offence as examining justices;]
   (b) a judge, in deciding whether to grant an application made by the accused under—
      (i) section 6 of the Criminal Justice Act 1987 (application for dismissal of charge of serious fraud in respect of which notice of transfer has been given under section 4 of that Act); or
      (ii) paragraph 5 of Schedule 6 to the Criminal Justice Act 1991 (application for dismissal of charge of violent or sexual offence involving child in respect of which notice of transfer has been given under section 53 of that Act);
   (c) the court, in determining whether there is a case to answer; and
   (d) the court or jury, in determining whether the accused is guilty of the offence charged,
may draw such inferences from the failure or refusal as appear proper.

   (3) Subsections (1) and (2) do not apply unless the accused was told in ordinary language by the constable when making the request mentioned in subsection (1)(c) above what the effect of this section would be if he failed or refused to comply with the request.

[(3A) Where the accused was at an authorised place of detention at the time of the failure or refusal, subsections (1) and (2) do not apply if he had not been allowed an opportunity to consult a solicitor prior to the request being made.]

(4) ★ ★ ★ ★ ★

(5) This section does not preclude the drawing of any inference from a failure or refusal of the accused to account for his presence at a place which could properly be drawn apart from this section.

(6) ★ ★ ★ ★ ★

(7) . . .

38   Interpretation and savings for sections 34, 35, 36 and 37

(1) In sections 34, 35, 36 and 37 of this Act—

"legal representative" means an authorised advocate or authorised litigator, as defined by section 119(1) of the Courts and Legal Services Act 1990; and

"place" includes any building or part of a building, any vehicle, vessel, aircraft or hover-craft and any other place whatsoever.

(2)–(4) ★ ★ ★ ★ ★

(5) Nothing in sections 34, 35, 36 or 37 prejudices the operation of a provision of any enactment which provides (in whatever words) that any answer or evidence given by a person in specified circumstances shall not be admissible in evidence against him or some other person in any proceedings or class of proceedings (however described, and whether civil or criminal).

In this subsection, the reference to giving evidence is a reference to giving evidence in any manner, whether by furnishing information, making discovery, producing documents or otherwise.

(6) Nothing in sections 34, 35, 36 or 37 prejudices any power of a court, in any proceed-ings, to exclude evidence (whether by preventing questions being put or otherwise) at its discretion.

39   ★ ★ ★ ★ ★

Juries

40   Disqualification for jury service of persons on bail in criminal proceedings

(1) A person who is on bail in criminal proceedings shall not be qualified to serve as a juror in the Crown Court.

(2) In this section "bail in criminal proceedings" has the same meaning as in the Bail Act 1976.

41–47 ★ ★ ★ ★ ★

Sentencing: guilty pleas

48   . . .

49–59 ★ ★ ★ ★ ★

Powers of police to stop and search

60   Powers to stop and search in anticipation of violence

[(1) If a police officer of or above the rank of inspector reasonably believes—

(a) that incidents involving serious violence may take place in any locality in his police area, and that it is expedient to give an authorisation under this section to prevent their occurrence, or

(b) that persons are carrying dangerous instruments or offensive weapons in any locality in his police area without good reason, he may give an authorisation that the powers conferred by this section are to be exercisable at any place within that locality for a specified period not exceeding 24 hours.]

(2) ...

(3) If it appears to [an officer of or above the rank of] superintendent that it is expedient to do so, having regard to offences which have, or are reasonably suspected to have, been committed in connection with any [activity] falling within the authorisation, he may direct that the authorisation shall continue in being for a further [24] hours.

(3A) ★ ★ ★ ★ ★

(4) This section confers on any constable in uniform power—

  (a) to stop any pedestrian and search him or anything carried by him for offensive weapons or dangerous instruments.

  (b) to stop any vehicle and search the vehicle, its driver and any passenger for offensive weapons or dangerous instruments.

  . . .

(5) A constable may, in the exercise of [the powers conferred by subsection (4) above], stop any person or vehicle and make any search he thinks fit whether or not he has any grounds for suspecting that the person or vehicle is carrying weapons or articles of that kind.

(6) If in the course of a search under this section a constable discovers a dangerous instrument or an article which he has reasonable grounds for suspecting to be an offensive weapon, he may seize it.

(7), (8) ★ ★ ★ ★ ★

(9) Any authorisation under this section shall be in writing signed by the officer giving it and shall specify [the grounds on which it is given and] the locality in which and the period during which the powers conferred by this section are exercisable and a direction under subsection (3) above shall also be given in writing or, where that is not practicable, recorded in writing as soon as it is practicable to do so.

[9A] ★ ★ ★ ★ ★

(10) Where a vehicle is stopped by a constable under this section, the driver shall be entitled to obtain a written statement that the vehicle was stopped under the powers conferred by this section if he applies for such a statement not later than the end of the period of twelve months from the day on which the vehicle was stopped . . .

[(10A) A person who is searched by a constable under this section shall be entitled to obtain a written statement that he was searched under the powers conferred by this section if he applies for such a statement not later than the end of the period of twelve months from the day on which he was searched.]

(11) In this section—

★ ★ ★ ★ ★

"dangerous instruments" means instruments which have a blade or are sharply pointed;

"offensive weapon" has the meaning given by section 1(9) of the Police and Criminal Evidence Act 1984 [or, in relation to Scotland, section 47(4) of the Criminal Law (Consolidation) (Scotland) Act 1995]; and

★ ★ ★ ★ ★

"vehicle" includes a caravan as defined in section 29(1) of the Caravan Sites and Control of Development Act 1960.

[(11A) For the purposes of this section, a person carries a dangerous instrument or an offensive weapon if he has it in his possession.]

(12) ★ ★ ★ ★ ★

[60AA Powers to require removal of disguises

(1) Where—

  (a) an authorisation under section 60 is for the time being in force in relation to any locality for any period, or

(b) an authorisation under subsection (3) that the powers conferred by subsection (2) shall be exercisable at any place in a locality is in force for any period,

those powers shall be exercisable at any place in that locality at any time in that period.

(2) This subsection confers power on any constable in uniform—

(a) to require any person to remove any item which the constable reasonably believes that person is wearing wholly or mainly for the purpose of concealing his identity;

(b) to seize any item which the constable reasonably believes any person intends to wear wholly or mainly for that purpose.

(3) If a police officer of or above the rank of inspector reasonably believes—

(a) that activities may take place in any locality in his police area that are likely (if they take place) to involve the commission of offences, and

(b) that it is expedient, in order to prevent or control the activities, to give an authorisation under this subsection, he may give an authorisation that the powers conferred by this section shall be exercisable at any place within that locality for a specified period not exceeding twenty-four hours.

(4) If it appears to an officer of or above the rank of superintendent that it is expedient to do so, having regard to offences which—

(a) have been committed in connection with the activities in respect of which the authorisation was given, or

(b) are reasonably suspected to have been so committed, he may direct that the authorisation shall continue in force for a further twenty-four hours.

(5) If an inspector gives an authorisation under subsection (3), he must, as soon as it is practicable to do so, cause an officer of or above the rank of superintendent to be informed.

(6) Any authorisation under this section—

(a) shall be in writing and signed by the officer giving it; and

(b) shall specify—

(i) the grounds on which it is given;

(ii) the locality in which the powers conferred by this section are exercisable;

(iii) the period during which those powers are exercisable;

and a direction under subsection (4) shall also be given in writing or, where that is not practicable, recorded in writing as soon as it is practicable to do so.

(7) A person who fails to remove an item worn by him when required to do so by a constable in the exercise of his power under this section shall be liable, on summary conviction, to imprisonment for a term not exceeding one month or to a fine not exceeding level 3 on the standard scale or both.

(8) The preceding provisions of this section, so far as they relate to an authorisation by a member of the British Transport Police Force (including one who for the time being has the same powers and privileges as a member of a police force for a police area), shall have effect as if references to a locality or to a locality in his police area were references to any locality in or in the vicinity of any policed premises, or to the whole or any part of any such premises.

(9) In this section 'British Transport Police Force' and 'policed premises' each has the same meaning as in section 60.

(10) The powers conferred by this section are in addition to, and not in derogation of, any power otherwise conferred.

(11) This section does not extend to Scotland.]

60A ★ ★ ★ ★ ★

PART V   PUBLIC ORDER: COLLECTIVE TRESPASS OR NUISANCE ON LAND

Powers to remove trespassers on land

61   Power to remove trespassers on land

(1) If the senior police officer present at the scene reasonably believes that two or more persons are trespassing on land and are present there with the common purpose of residing there for any period, that reasonable steps have been taken by or on behalf of the occupier to ask them to leave and—

(a) that any of those persons has caused damage to the land or to property on the land or used threatening, abusive or insulting words or behaviour towards the occupier, a member of his family or an employee or agent of his, or

(b) that those persons have between them six or more vehicles on the land, he may direct those persons, or any of them, to leave the land and to remove any vehicles or other property they have with them on the land.

(2) Where the persons in question are reasonably believed by the senior police officer to be persons who were not originally trespassers but have become trespassers on the land, the officer must reasonably believe that the other conditions specified in subsection (1) are satisfied after those persons become trespassers before he can exercise the power conferred by that subsection.

(3) A direction under subsection (1) above, if not communicated to the persons referred to in subsection (1) by the police officer giving the direction, may be communicated to them by any constable at the scene.

(4) If a person knowing that a direction under subsection (1) above has been given which applies to him—

(a) fails to leave the land as soon as reasonably practicable, or

(b) having left again enters the land as a trespasser within the period of three months beginning with the day on which the direction was given, he commits an offence and is liable on summary conviction to imprisonment for a term not exceeding three months or a fine not exceeding level 4 on the standard scale, or both.

(5) A constable in uniform who reasonably suspects that a person is committing an offence under this section may arrest him without a warrant.

(6) In proceedings for an offence under this section it is a defence for the accused to show—

(a) that he was not trespassing on the land, or

(b) that he had a reasonable excuse for failing to leave the land as soon as reasonably practicable or, as the case may be, for again entering the land as a trespasser.

(7)–(9) ★ ★ ★ ★ ★

62   Supplementary powers of seizure

(1) If a direction has been given under section 61 and a constable reasonably suspects that any person to whom the direction applies has, without reasonable excuse—

(a) failed to remove any vehicle on the land which appears to the constable to belong to him or to be in his possession or under his control; or

(b) entered the land as a trespasser with a vehicle within the period of three months beginning with the day on which the direction was given, the constable may seize and remove that vehicle.

(2) ★ ★ ★ ★ ★

63–67 ★ ★ ★ ★ ★

68   Offence of aggravated trespass

(1) A person commits the offence of aggravated trespass if he trespasses on land in the

open air and, in relation to any lawful activity which persons are engaging in or are about to engage in on that or adjoining land in the open air, does there anything which is intended by him to have the effect—

(a) of intimidating those persons or any of them so as to deter them or any of them from engaging in that activity,

(b) of obstructing that activity, or

(c) of disrupting that activity.

(2) Activity on any occasion on the part of a person or persons on land is "lawful" for the purposes of this section if he or they may engage in the activity on the land on that occasion without committing an offence or trespassing on the land.

(3) A person guilty of an offence under this section is liable on summary conviction to imprisonment for a term not exceeding three months or a fine not exceeding level 4 on the standard scale, or both.

(4) A constable in uniform who reasonably suspects that a person is committing an offence under this section may arrest him without a warrant.

(5) In this section "land" does not include—

(a) the highways and roads excluded from the application of section 61 by paragraph (b) of the definition of "land" in subsection (9) of that section; or

(b) a road within the meaning of the Roads (Northern Ireland) Order 1993.

69 Powers to remove persons committing or participating in aggravated trespass

(1) If the senior police officer present at the scene reasonably believes—

(a) that a person is committing, has committed or intends to commit the offence of aggravated trespass on land in the open air; or

(b) that two or more persons are trespassing on land in the open air and are present there with the common purpose of intimidating persons so as to deter them from engaging in a lawful activity or of obstructing or disrupting a lawful activity, he may direct that person or (as the case may be) those persons (or any of them) to leave the land.

(2) A direction under subsection (1) above, if not communicated to the persons referred to in subsection (1) by the police officer giving the direction, may be communicated to them by any constable at the scene.

(3) If a person knowing that a direction under subsection (1) above has been given which applies to him—

(a) fails to leave the land as soon as practicable, or

(b) having left again enters the land as a trespasser within the period of three months beginning with the day on which the direction was given, he commits an offence and is liable on summary conviction to imprisonment for a term not exceeding three months or a fine not exceeding level 4 on the standard scale, or both.

(4) In proceedings for an offence under subsection (3) it is a defence for the accused to show—

(a) that he was not trespassing on the land, or

(b) that he had a reasonable excuse for failing to leave the land as soon as practicable or, as the case may be, for again entering the land as a trespasser.

(5) A constable in uniform who reasonably suspects that a person is committing an offence under this section may arrest him without a warrant.

(6) In this section "lawful activity" and "land" have the same meaning as in section 68.

70–76 ★ ★ ★ ★ ★

Powers to remove unauthorised campers

77 Power of local authority to direct unauthorised campers to leave land

(1) If it appears to a local authority that persons are for the time being residing in a vehicle or vehicles within that authority's area—

    (a) on any land forming part of a highway;

    (b) on any other unoccupied land; or

    (c) on any occupied land without the consent of the occupier, the authority may give a direction that those persons and any others with them are to leave the land and remove the vehicle or vehicles and any other property they have with them on the land.

(2) Notice of a direction under subsection (1) must be served on the persons to whom the direction applies, but it shall be sufficient for this purpose for the direction to specify the land and (except where the direction applies to only one person) to be addressed to all occupants of the vehicles on the land, without naming them.

(3) If a person knowing that a direction under subsection (1) above has been given which applies to him—

    (a) fails, as soon as practicable, to leave the land or remove from the land any vehicle or other property which is the subject of the direction, or

    (b) having removed any such vehicle or property again enters the land with a vehicle within the period of three months beginning with the day on which the direction was given, he commits an offence and is liable on summary conviction to a fine not exceeding level 3 on the standard scale.

(4) A direction under subsection (1) operates to require persons who re-enter the land within the said period with vehicles or other property to leave and remove the vehicles or other property as it operates in relation to the persons and vehicles or other property on the land when the direction was given.

(5) In proceedings for an offence under this section it is a defence for the accused to show that his failure to leave or to remove the vehicle or other property as soon as practicable or his re-entry with a vehicle was due to illness, mechanical breakdown or other immediate emergency.

(6), (7) ★ ★ ★ ★ ★

78 Orders for removal of persons and their vehicles unlawfully on land

(1) A magistrates' court may, on a complaint made by a local authority, if satisfied that persons and vehicles in which they are residing are present on land within that authority's area in contravention of a direction given under section 77, make an order requiring the removal of any vehicle or other property which is so present on the land and any person residing in it.

(2) An order under this section may authorise the local authority to take such steps as are reasonably necessary to ensure that the order is complied with and, in particular, may authorise the authority, by its officers and servants—

    (a) to enter upon the land specified in the order; and

    (b) to take, in relation to any vehicle or property to be removed in pursuance of the order, such steps for securing entry and rendering it suitable for removal as may be so specified.

(3) The local authority shall not enter upon any occupied land unless they have given to the owner and occupier at least 24 hours notice of their intention to do so, or unless after reasonable inquiries they are unable to ascertain their names and addresses.

(4) A person who wilfully obstructs any person in the exercise of any power conferred on him by an order under this section commits an offence and is liable on summary conviction to a fine not exceeding level 3 on the standard scale.

(5)–(7) ★ ★ ★ ★ ★

79–162 ★ ★ ★ ★ ★

Closed-circuit television by local authorities

163   Local authority powers to provide closed-circuit television
(1) Without prejudice to any power which they may exercise for those purposes under any other enactment, a local authority may take such of the following steps as they consider will, in relation to their area, promote the prevention of crime or the welfare of the victims of crime—
    (a) providing apparatus for recording visual images of events occurring on any land in their area;
    (b) providing within their area a telecommunications system which, under Part II of the Telecommunictions Act 1984, may be run without a licence;
    (c) arranging for the provision of any other description of telecommunications system within their area or between any land in their area and any building occupied by a public authority.
(2) Any power to provide, or to arrange for the provision of, any apparatus includes power to maintain, or operate, or, as the case may be, to arrange for the maintenance or operation of, that apparatus.
(3) Before taking such a step under this section, a local authority shall consult the chief officer of police for the police area in which the step is to be taken.
    (4), (5) ★ ★ ★ ★ ★

★ ★ ★ ★ ★

Intelligence Services Act 1994
(1994, c. 13)

An Act to make provision about the Secret Intelligence Service and the Government Communications Headquarters, including provision for the issue of warrants and authorisations enabling certain actions to be taken and for the issue of such warrants and authorisations to be kept under review; to make further provision about warrants issued on applications by the Security Service; to establish a procedure for the investigation of complaints about the Secret Intelligence Service and the Government Communications Headquarters; to make provision for the establishment of an Intelligence and Security Committee to scrutinise all three of those bodies; and for connected purposes.
[26 May 1994]

Territorial extent: United Kingdom. Sections 5(1) and 11(1) also apply to the Colonies listed in the Intelligence Services Act 1994 (Dependent Territories) Order 1995 (SI 1995/752).

The Secret Intelligence Service

1   The Secret Intelligence Service
(1) There shall continue to be a Secret Intelligence Service (in this Act referred to as "the Intelligence Service") under the authority of the Secretary of State; and, subject to subsection (2) below, its functions shall be—
    (a) to obtain and provide information relating to the actions or intentions of persons outside the British Islands; and
    (b) to perform other tasks relating to the actions or intentions of such persons.
(2) The functions of the Intelligence Service shall be exercisable only—
    (a) in the interests of national security, with particular reference to the defence and foreign policies of Her Majesty's Government in the United Kingdom; or

(b) in the interests of the economic well-being of the United Kingdom; or

(c) in support of the prevention or detection of serious crime.

2   The Chief of the Intelligence Service

(1) The operations of the Intelligence Service shall continue to be under the control of a Chief of that Service appointed by the Secretary of State.

(2) The Chief of the Intelligence Service shall be responsible for the efficiency of that Service and it shall be his duty to ensure—

(a) that there are arrangements for securing that no information is obtained by the Intelligence Service except so far as necessary for the proper discharge of its functions and that no information is disclosed by it except so far as necessary—

(i)   for that purpose;

(ii) in the interests of national security;

(iii) for the purpose of the prevention or detection of serious crime; or

(iv) for the purpose of any criminal proceedings; and

(b) that the Intelligence Service does not take any action to further the interests of any United Kingdom political party.

(3) Without prejudice to the generality of subsection (2)(a) above, the disclosure of information shall be regarded as necessary for the proper discharge of the functions of the Intelligence Service if it consists of—

(a) the disclosure of records subject to and in accordance with the Public Records Act 1958; or

(b) the disclosure, subject to and in accordance with arrangements approved by the Secretary of State, of information to the Comptroller and Auditor General for the purposes of his functions.

(4) The Chief of the Intelligence Service shall make an annual report on the work of the Intelligence Service to the Prime Minister and the Secretary of State and may at any time report to either of them on any matter relating to its work.

GCHQ

3   The Government Communications Headquarters

(1) There shall continue to be a Government Communications Headquarters under the authority of the Secretary of State; and, subject to subsection (2) below, its functions shall be—

(a) to monitor or interfere with electromagnetic, acoustic and other emissions and any equipment producing such emissions and to obtain and provide information derived from or related to such emissions or equipment and from encrypted material; and

(b) to provide advice and assistance about—

(i)   languages, including terminology used for technical matters, and

(ii) cryptography and other matters relating to the protection of information and other material,

to the armed forces of the Crown, to Her Majesty's Government in the United Kingdom or to a Northern Ireland Department or to any other organisation which is determined for the purposes of this section in such manner as may be specified by the Prime Minister.

(2) The functions referred to in subsection (1)(a) above shall be exercisable only—

(a) in the interests of national security, with particular reference to the defence and foreign policies of Her Majesty's Government in the United Kingdom; or

(b) in the interests of the economic well-being of the United Kingdom in relation to the actions or intentions of persons outside the British Islands; or

(c) in support of the prevention or detection of serious crime.

(3) In this Act the expression "GCHQ" refers to the Government Communications Head-quarters and to any unit or part of a unit of the armed forces of the Crown which is for the

time being required by the Secretary of State to assist the Government Communications Headquarters in carrying out its functions.

4   The Director of GCHQ

(1) The operations of GCHQ shall continue to be under the control of a Director appointed by the Secretary of State.

(2) The Director shall be responsible for the efficiency of GCHQ and it shall be his duty to ensure—

(a) that there are arrangements for securing that no information is obtained by GCHQ except so far as necessary for the proper discharge of its functions and that no information is disclosed by it except so far as necessary for that purpose or for the purpose of any criminal proceedings; and

(b) that GCHQ does not take any action to further the interests of any United Kingdom political party.

(3) Without prejudice to the generality of subsection (2)(a) above, the disclosure of information shall be regarded as necessary for the proper discharge of the functions of GCHQ if it consists of—

(a) the disclosure of records subject to and in accordance with the Public Records Act 1958; or

(b) the disclosure, subject to and in accordance with arrangements approved by the Secretary of State, of information to the Comptroller and Auditor General for the purposes of his functions.

(4) The Director shall make an annual report on the work of GCHQ to the Prime Minister and the Secretary of State and may at any time report to either of them on any matter relating to its work.

Authorisation of certain actions

5   Warrants: general

(1) No entry on or interference with property or with wireless telegraphy shall be unlawful if it is authorised by a warrant issued by the Secretary of State under this section.

(2) The Secretary of State may, on an application made by the Security Service, the Intelligence Service or GCHQ, issue a warrant under this section authorising the taking, subject to subsection (3) below, of such action as is specified in the warrant in respect of any property so specified or in respect of wireless telegraphy so specified if the Secretary of State—

(a) thinks it necessary for the action to be taken [for the purpose of] assisting, as the case may be,—

(i) the Security Service in carrying out any of its functions under the 1989 Act; or

(ii) the Intelligence Service in carrying out any of its functions under section 1 above; or

(iii) GCHQ in carrying out any function which falls within section 3(1)(a) above; and

[(b) is satisfied that the taking of the action is proportionate to what the action seeks to achieve;] and

(c) is satisfied that satisfactory arrangements are in force under section 2(2)(a) of the 1989 Act (duties of the Director-General of the Security Service), section 2(2)(a) above or section 4(2)(a) above with respect to the disclosure of information obtained by virtue of this section and that any information obtained under the warrant will be subject to those arrangements.

[(2A) The matters to be taken into account in considering whether the requirements of subsection (2)(a) and (b) and satisfied in the case of any warrant shall include whether what it is thought necessary to achieve by the conduct authorised by the warrant could reasonably be achieved by other means.]

[(3) A warrant issued on the application of the Intelligence Service or GCHQ for the purposes of the exercise of their functions by virtue of section 1(2)(c) or 3(2)(c) above may not relate to property in the British Islands.

(3A) A warrant issued on the application of the Security Service for the purposes of the exercise of their function under section 1(4) of the Security Service Act 1989 may not relate to property in the British Islands unless it authorises the taking of action in relation to conduct within subsection (3B) below.

(3B) Conduct is within this subsection if it constitutes (or, if it took place in the United Kingdom, would constitute) one or more offences, and either—

    (a) it involves the use of violence, results in substantial financial gain or is conduct by a large number of persons in pursuit of a common purpose; or

    (b) the offence or one of the offences is an offence for which a person who has attained the age of twenty-one [(eighteen in relation to England and Wales)] and has no previous convictions could reasonably be expected to be sentenced to imprisonment for a term of three years or more.]

(4) Subject to subsection (5) below, the Security Service may make an application under subsection (2) above for a warrant to be issued authorising that Service (or a person acting on its behalf) to take such action as is specified in the warrant on behalf of the Intelligence Service or GCHQ and, where such a warrant is issued, the functions of the Security Service shall include the carrying out of the action so specified, whether or not it would otherwise be within its functions.

(5) The Security Service may not make an application for a warrant by virtue of subsection (4) above except where the action proposed to be authorised by the warrant—

    (a) is action in respect of which the Intelligence Service or, as the case may be, GCHQ could make such an application; and

    (b) is to be taken otherwise than in support of the prevention or detection of serious crime.

6   Warrants: procedure and duration, etc.

(1) A warrant shall not be issued except—

    (a) under the hand of the Secretary of State [or, in the case of a warrant by the Scottish Ministers (by virtue of provision made under section 63 of the Scotland Act 1998), a member of the Scottish Executive]; or

    (b) in an urgent case where the Secretary of State has expressly authorised its issue and a statement of the fact is endorsed on it, under the hand of a senior official . . . [; or

    (c) in an urgent case where, the Scottish Ministers have (by virtue of provision made under section 63 of the Scotland Act 1998) expressly authorised its issue and a statement of that fact is endorsed thereon, under the hand of a member of the staff of the Scottish Administration who is in the Senior Civil Service and is designated by the Scottish Ministers as a person under whose hand a warrant may be issued in such a case.]

(2) A warrant shall, unless renewed under subsection (3) below, cease to have effect—

    (a) if the warrant was under the hand of the Secretary of State [or, in the case of a warrant issued by the Scottish Ministers (by virtue of provision made under section 63 of the Scotland Act 1998) a member of the Scottish Executive], at the end of the period of six months beginning with the day on which it was issued; and

    (b) in any other case, at the end of the period ending with the second working day following that day.

(3) If at any time before the day on which a warrant would cease to have effect the Secretary of State considers it necessary for the warrant to continue to have effect for

the purpose for which it was issued, he may by an instrument under his hand renew it for a period of six months beginning with that day.

(4) The Secretary of State shall cancel a warrant if he is satisfied that the action authorised by it is no longer necessary.

(5), (6) ★ ★ ★ ★ ★

7   Authorisation of acts outside the British Islands

(1) If, apart from this section, a person would be liable in the United Kingdom for any act done outside the British Islands, he shall not be so liable if the act is one which is authorised to be done by virtue of an authorisation given by the Secretary of State under this section.

(2) In subsection (1) above "liable in the United Kingdom" means liable under the criminal or civil law of any part of the United Kingdom.

(3) The Secretary of State shall not give an authorisation under this section unless he is satisfied—

(a) that any acts which may be done in reliance on the authorisation or, as the case may be, the operation in the course of which the acts may be done will be necessary for the proper discharge of a function of the Intelligence Service [or GCHQ]; and

(b) that there are satisfactory arrangements in force to secure—
   (i) that nothing will be done in reliance on the authorisation beyond what is necessary for the proper discharge of a function of the Intelligence Service [or GCHQ]; and
   (ii) that, in so far as any act may be done in reliance on the authorisation, their nature and likely consequences will be reasonable, having regard to the purposes for which they are carried out; and

(c) that there are satisfactory arrangements in force under section 2(2)(a) above with respect to the disclosure of information obtained by virtue of this section and that any information obtained by virtue of anything done in reliance on the authorisation will be subject to those arrangements.

(4) Without prejudice to the generality of the power of the Secretary of State to give an authorisation under this section, such an authorisation—

(a) may relate to a particular act or acts, to acts of a description specified in the authorisation or to acts undertaken in the course of an operation so specified;

(b) may be limited to a particular person or persons of a description so specified; and

(c) may be subject to conditions so specified.

(5) An authorisation shall not be given under this section except—

(a) under the hand of the Secretary of State; or

(b) in an urgent case where the Secretary of State has expressly authorised it to be given and a statement of that fact is endorsed on it, under the hand of a senior official . . . ;

(6) An authorisation shall, unless renewed under subsection (7) below, cease to have effect—

(a) if the authorisation was given under the hand of the Secretary of State, at the end of the period of six months beginning with the day on which it was given;

(b) in any other case, at the end of the period ending with the second working day following the day on which it was given.

(7) If at any time before the day on which an authorisation would cease to have effect the Secretary of State considers it necessary for the authorisation to continue to have effect for the purpose for which it was given, he may by an instrument under his hand renew it for a period of six months beginning with that day.

(8) The Secretary of State shall cancel an authorisation if he is satisfied that any act authorised by it is no longer necessary.

(9) ★ ★ ★ ★ ★

8, 9 ...

10   The Intelligence and Security Committee

(1) There shall be a Committee, to be known as the Intelligence and Security Committee and in this section referred to as "the Committee", to examine the expenditure, administration and policy of—

(a) the Security Service;

(b) the Intelligence Service; and

(c) GCHQ.

(2) The Committee shall consist of nine members—

(a) who shall be drawn both from the members of the House of Commons and from the members of the House of Lords; and

(b) none of whom shall be a Minister of the Crown.

(3) The members of the Committee shall be appointed by the Prime Minister after consultation with the Leader of the Opposition, within the meaning of the Ministerial and other Salaries Act 1975; and one of those members shall be so appointed as Chairman of the Committee.

(4) Schedule 3 to this Act shall have effect with respect to the tenure of office of members of, the procedure of and other matters relating to, the Committee; and in that Schedule "the Committee" has the same meaning as in this section.

(5) The Committee shall make an annual report on the discharge of their functions to the Prime Minister and may at any time report to him on any matter relating to the discharge of those functions.

(6) The Prime Minsiter shall lay before each House of Parliament a copy of each annual report made by the Committee under subsection (5) above together with a statement as to whether any matter has been excluded from that copy in pursuance of subsection (7) below.

(7) If it appears to the Prime Minister, after consultation with the Committee, that the publication of any matter in a report would be prejudicial to the continued discharge of the functions of either of the Services or, as the case may be, GCHQ, the Prime Minister may exclude that matter from the copy of the report as laid before each House of Parliament.

11, 12   ★ ★ ★ ★ ★

Trade Marks Act 1994
(1994, c. 26)

An Act to make new provision for registered trade marks, implementing Council Directive No. 89/ 104/EEC of 21st December 1988 to approximate the laws of the Member States relating to trade marks; to make provision in connection with Council Regulation (EC) No. 40/94 of 20th December 1993 of the Community trade mark; to give effect to the Madrid Protocol Relating to the International Registration of Marks of 27th June 1989, and to certain provisions of the Paris Convention for the Protection of Industrial Property of 20th March 1883, as revised and amended; and for connected purposes.   [21 July 1994]

Territorial extent: United Kingdom and (subject to s. 108(2)) the Isle of Man.

★ ★ ★ ★ ★

4   Specially protected emblems

(1) A trade mark which consists of or contains—

(a) the Royal arms, or any of the principal armorial bearings of the Royal arms, or any insignia or device so nearly resembling the Royal arms or any such armorial bearing as to be likely to be mistaken for them or it,

(b) a representation of the Royal crown or any of the Royal flags,

(c) a representation of Her Majesty or any member of the Royal family, or any colourable imitation thereof, or

(d) words, letters or devices likely to lead persons to think that the applicant either has or recently has had Royal patronage or authorisation,

shall not be registered unless it appears to the registrar that consent has been given by or on behalf of Her Majesty or, as the case may be, the relevant member of the Royal family.

(2) A trade mark which consists of or contains a representation of—

(a) the national flag of the United Kingdom (commonly known as the Union Jack), or

(b) the flag of England, Wales, Scotland, Northern Ireland or the Isle of Man, shall not be registered if it appears to the registrar that the use of the trade mark would be misleading or grossly offensive.

Provision may be made by rules identifying the flags to which paragraph (b) applies.

(3), (4), (5) ★ ★ ★ ★ ★

★ ★ ★ ★ ★

99   Unauthorised use of Royal arms, &c.

(1) A person shall not without the authority of Her Majesty use in connection with any business the Royal arms (or arms so closely resembling the Royal arms as to be calculated to deceive) in such manner as to be calculated to lead to the belief that he is duly authorised to use the Royal arms.

(2) A person shall not without the authority of Her Majesty or of a member of the Royal family use in connection with any business any device, emblem or title in such a manner as to be calculated to lead to the belief that he is employed by, or supplies goods or services to, Her Majesty or that member of the Royal family.

(3) A person who contravenes subsection (1) commits an offence and is liable on summary conviction to a fine not exceeding level 2 on the standard scale.

(4) Contravention of subsection (1) or (2) may be restrained by injunction in proceedings brought by—

(a) any person who is authorised to use the arms, device, emblem or title in question, or

(b) any person authorised by the Lord Chamberlain to take such proceedings.

(5) Nothing in this section affects any right of the proprietor of a trade mark containing any such arms, device, emblem or title to use that trade mark.

Criminal Appeal Act 1995
(1995, c. 35)

An Act to amend provisions relating to appeals and references to the Court of Appeal in criminal cases; to establish a Criminal Cases Review Commission and confer functions on, and make other provision in relation to, the Commission; to amend section 142 of the Magistrates' Courts Act 1980 and introduce in Northern Ireland provision similar to those of that section; to amend section 133 of the Criminal Justice Act 1988; and for connected purposes.   [19th July 1995]

Territorial extent: England and Wales, Northern Ireland (except ss. 9, 11)

Note: The "1968 Act" refers to the Criminal Appeal Act 1968 and the "1980 Act" refers to the Criminal Appeal (Northern Ireland) Act 1980.

PART II   THE CRIMINAL CASES REVIEW COMMISSION

The Commission

8   The Commission

(1) There shall be a body corporate to be known as the Criminal Cases Review Commission.

(2) The Commission shall not be regarded as the servant or agent of the Crown or as enjoying any status, immunity or privilege of the Crown; and the Commission's property shall not be regarded as property of, or held on behalf of, the Crown.

(3) The Commission shall consist of not fewer than eleven members.

(4) The members of the Commission shall be appointed by Her Majesty on the recommendation of the Prime Minister.

(5) At least one third of the members of the Commission shall be persons who are legally qualified; and for this purpose a person is legally qualified if—

    (a) he has a ten year general qualification, within the meaning of section 71 of the Courts and Legal Services Act 1990, or

    (b) he is a member of the Bar of Northern Ireland, or solicitor of the Supreme Court of Northern Ireland, of at least ten years' standing.

(6) At least two thirds of the members of the Commission shall be persons who appear to the Prime Minister to have knowledge or experience of any aspect of the criminal justice system and of them at least one shall be a person who appears to him to have knowledge or experience of any aspect of the criminal justice system in Northern Ireland; and for the purposes of this subsection the criminal justice system includes, in particular, the investigation of offences and the treatment of offenders.

(7) ★ ★ ★ ★ ★

References to court

9   Cases dealt with on indictment in England and Wales

(1) Where a person has been convicted of an offence on indictment in England and Wales, the Commission—

    (a) may at any time refer the conviction to the Court of Appeal, and

    (b) (whether or not they refer the conviction) may at any time refer to the Court of Appeal any sentence (not being a sentence fixed by law) imposed on, or in subsequent proceedings relating to, the conviction.

(2) A reference under subsection (1) of a person's conviction shall be treated for all purposes as an appeal by the person under section 1 of the 1968 Act against the conviction.

(3) A reference under subsection (1) of a sentence imposed on, or in subsequent proceedings relating to, a person's conviction on an indictment shall be treated for all purposes as an appeal by the person under section 9 of the 1968 Act against—

    (a) the sentence, and

    (b) any other sentence (not being a sentence fixed by law) imposed on, or in subsequent proceedings relating to, the conviction or any other conviction on the indictment.

(4) On a reference under subsection (1) of a person's conviction on an indictment the Commission may give notice to the Court of Appeal that any other conviction on the indictment which is specified in the notice is to be treated as referred to the Court of Appeal under subsection (1).

(5), (6) ★ ★ ★ ★ ★

10 ★ ★ ★ ★ ★

11 Cases dealt with summarily in England and Wales

(1) Where a person has been convicted of an offence by a magistrates' court in England and Wales, the Commission—

    (a) may at any time refer the conviction to the Crown Court, and

    (b) (whether or not they refer the conviction) may at any time refer to the Crown Court any sentence imposed on, or in subsequent proceedings relating to, the conviction.

(2) A reference under subsection (1) of a person's conviction shall be treated for all purposes as an appeal by the person under section 108(1) of the Magistrates' Courts Act 1980 against the conviction (whether or not he pleaded guilty).

(3) A reference under subsection (1) of a sentence imposed on, or in subsequent proceedings relating to, a person's conviction shall be treated for all purposes as an appeal by the person under section 108(1) of the Magistrates' Courts Act 1980 against—

    (a) the sentence, and

    (b) any other sentence imposed on, or in subsequent proceedings relating to, the conviction or any related conviction.

(4) On a reference under subsection (1) of a person's conviction the Commission may give notice to the Crown Court that any related conviction which is specified in the notice is to be treated as referred to the Crown Court under subsection (1).

(5) For the purposes of this section convictions are related if they are convictions of the same person by the same court on the same day.

(6) On a reference under this section the Crown Court may not award any punishment more severe than that awarded by the court whose decision is referred.

(7) The Crown Court may grant bail to a person whose conviction or sentence has been referred under this section; and any time during which he is released on bail shall not count as part of any term of imprisonment or detention under his sentence.

13 Conditions for making of references

(1) A reference of a conviction, verdict, finding or sentence shall not be made under any of sections 9 to 12 unless—

    (a) the Commission consider that there is a real possibility that the conviction, verdict, finding or sentence would not be upheld were the reference to be made,

    (b) the Commission so consider—

        (i) in the case of a conviction, verdict or finding, because of an argument, or evidence, not raised in the proceedings which led to it or on any appeal or application for leave to appeal against it, or

        (ii) in the case of a sentence, because of an argument on a point of law, or information, not so raised, and

    (c) an appeal against the conviction, verdict, finding or sentence has been determined or leave to appeal against it has been refused.

(2) Nothing in subsection (1)(b)(i) or (c) shall prevent the making of a reference if it appears to the Commission that there are exceptional circumstances which justify making it.

14 Further provisions about references

(1) A reference of a conviction, verdict, finding or sentence may be made under any of sections 9 to 12 either after an application has been made by or on behalf of the person to whom it relates or without an application having been so made.

(2) In considering whether to make a reference of a conviction, verdict, finding or sentence under any of sections 9 to 12 the Commission shall have regard to—

(a) any application or representations made to the Commission by or on behalf of the person to whom it relates,

(b) any other representations made to the Commission in relation to it, and

(c) any other matters which appear to the Commission to be relevant.

(3) In considering whether to make a reference under section 9 or 10 the Commission may at any time refer any point on which they desire the assistance of the Court of Appeal to that Court for the Court's opinion on it; and on a reference under this subsection the Court of Appeal shall consider the point referred and furnish the Commission with the Court's opinion on the point.

(4) Where the Commission make a reference under any of sections 9 to 12 the Commission shall—

(a) give to the court to which the reference is made a statement of the Commission's reasons for making the reference, and

(b) send a copy of the statement to every person who appears to the Commission to be likely to be a party to any proceedings on the appeal arising from the reference.

(5) Where a reference under any of sections 9 to 12 is treated as an appeal against any conviction, verdict, finding or sentence, the appeal may be on any ground relating to the conviction, verdict, finding or sentence (whether or not the ground is related to any reason given by the Commission for making the reference).

(6) In every case in which—

(a) an application has been made to the Commission by or on behalf of any person for the reference under any of sections 9 to 12 of any conviction, verdict, finding or sentence, but

(b) the Commission decide not to make a reference of the conviction, verdict, finding or sentence,

the Commission shall give a statement of the reasons for their decision to the person who made the application.

15 ★ ★ ★ ★ ★

16 Assistance in connection with prerogative of mercy

(1) Where the Secretary of State refers to the Commission any matter which arises in the consideration of whether to recommend the exercise of Her Majesty's prerogative of mercy in relation to a conviction and on which he desires their assistance, the Commission shall—

(a) consider the matter referred, and

(b) give to the Secretary of State a statement of their conclusions on it; and the Secretary of State shall, in considering whether so to recommend, treat the Commission's statement as conclusive of the matter referred.

(2) Where in any case the Commission are of the opinion that the Secretary of State should consider whether to recommend the exercise of Her Majesty's prerogative of mercy in relation to the case they shall give him the reasons for their opinion.

Supplementary powers

17 Power to obtain documents etc.

(1) This section applies where the Commission believe that a person serving in a public body has possession or control of a document or other material which may assist the Commission in the exercise of any of their functions.

(2) Where it is reasonable to do so, the Commission may require the person who is the appropriate person in relation to the public body—

(a) to produce the document or other material to the Commission or to give the Commission access to it, and

(b) to allow the Commission to take away the document or other material or to make and take away a copy of it in such form as they think appropriate, and may direct that person that the document or other material must not be destroyed, damaged or altered before the direction is withdrawn by the Commission.

(3) The documents and other material covered by this section include, in particular, any document or other material obtained or created during any investigation or proceedings relating to—

(a) the case in relation to which the Commission's function is being or may be exercised, or

(b) any other case which may be in any way connected with that case (whether or not any function of the Commission could be exercised in relation to that other case).

(4) The duty to comply with a requirement under this section is not affected by any obligation of secrecy or other limitation on disclosure (including any such obligation or limitation imposed by or by virtue of an enactment) which would otherwise prevent the production of the document or other material to the Commission or the giving of access to it to the Commission.

★ ★ ★ ★ ★

Criminal Procedure (Scotland) Act 1995
(1995, c. 46)

An Act to consolidate certain enactments relating to criminal procedure in Scotland.

[8 November 1995]

Territorial extent: Scotland

★ ★ ★ ★ ★

PART II   POLICE FUNCTIONS

Lord Advocate's instructions

12   Instructions by Lord Advocate as to reporting of offences

The Lord Advocate may, from time to time, issue instructions to a chief constable with regard to the reporting, for consideration of the question of prosecution, of offences alleged to have been committed within the area of such chief constable, and it shall be the duty of a chief constable to whom any such instruction is issued to secure compliance therewith.

13   Powers relating to suspects and potential witnesses

(1) Where a constable has reasonable grounds for suspecting that a person has committed or is committing an offence at any place, he may require—

(a) that person, if the constable finds him at that place or at any place where the constable is entitled to be, to give his name and address and may ask him for an explanation of the circumstances which have given rise to the constable's suspicion;

(b) any other person whom the constable finds at that place or at any place where the constable is entitled to be and who the constable believes has information relating to the offence, to give his name and address.

(2) The constable may require the person mentioned in paragraph (a) of subsection (1) above to remain with him while he (either or both)—

(a) subject to subsection (3) below, verifies any name and address given by the person;

(b) notes any explanation proffered by the person.

(3) The constable shall exercise his power under paragraph (a) of subsection (2) above only where it appears to him that such verification can be obtained quickly.

(4) A constable may use reasonable force to ensure that the person mentioned in paragraph (a) of subsection (1) above remains with him.

(5) A constable shall inform a person, when making a requirement of that person under—

(a) paragraph (a) of subsection (1) above, of his suspicion and of the general nature of the offence which he suspects that the person has committed or is committing;

(b) paragraph (b) of subsection (1) above, of his suspicion, of the general nature of the offence which he suspects has been or is being committed and that the reason for the requirement is that he believes the person has information relating to the offence;

(c) subsection (2) above, why the person is being required to remain with him;

(d) either of the said subsections, that failure to comply with the requirement may constitute an offence.

(6) A person mentioned in—

(a) paragraph (a) of subsection (1) above who having been required—

(i) under that subsection to give his name and address; or

(ii) under subsection (2) above to remain with a constable,

fails, without reasonable excuse, to do so, shall be guilty of an offence and liable on summary conviction to a fine not exceeding level 3 on the standard scale;

(b) paragraph (b) of the said subsection (1) who having been required under that subsection to give his name and address fails, without reasonable excuse, to do so shall be guilty of an offence and liable on summary conviction to a fine not exceeding level 2 on the standard scale.

(7) A constable may arrest without warrant any person who he has reasonable grounds for suspecting has committed an offence under subsection (6) above.

14   Detention and questioning at police station

(1) Where a constable has reasonable grounds for suspecting that a person has committed or is committing an offence punishable by imprisonment, the constable may, for the purpose of facilitating the carrying out of investigations—

(a) into the offence; and

(b) as to whether criminal proceedings should be instigated against the person, detain that person and take him as quickly as is reasonably practicable to a police station or other premises and may thereafter for that purpose take him to any other place and, subject to the following provisions of this section, the detention may continue at the police station or, as the case may be, the other premises or place.

(2) Detention under subsection (1) above shall be terminated not more than six hours after it begins or (if earlier)—

(a) when the person is arrested;

(b) when he is detained in pursuance of any other enactment; or

(c) where there are no longer such grounds as are mentioned in the said subsection (1),

and when a person has been detained under subsection (1) above, he shall be informed immediately upon the termination of his detention in accordance with this subsection that his detention has been terminated.

(3) Where a person has been released at the termination of a period of detention under subsection (1) above he shall not thereafter be detained, under that subsection, on the same grounds or on any grounds arising out of the same circumstances.

(4) Subject to subsection (5) below, where a person has previously been detained in pursuance of any other enactment, and is detained under subsection (1) above on the same grounds or on grounds arising from the same circumstances as those which led to his earlier

detention, the period of six hours mentioned in subsection (2) above shall be reduced by the length of that earlier detention.

(5) Subsection (4) above shall not apply in relation to detention under section 41(3) of the Prisons (Scotland) Act 1989 (detention in relation to introduction etc. into prison of prohibited article), but where a person was detained under section 41(3) immediately prior to his detention under subsection (1) above the period of six hours mentioned in subsection (2) above shall be reduced by the length of that earlier detention.

(6) At the time when a constable detains a person under subsection (1) above, he shall inform the person of his suspicion, of the general nature of the offence which he suspects has been or is being committed and of the reason for the detention; and there shall be recorded—

    (a) the place where detention begins and the police station or other premises to which the person is taken;

    (b) any other place to which the person is, during the detention, thereafter taken;

    (c) the general nature of the suspected offence;

    (d) the time when detention under subsection (1) above begins and the time of the person's arrival at the police station or other premises;

    (e) the time when the person is informed of his rights in terms of subsection (9) below and of subsection (1)(b) of section 15 of this Act and the identity of the constable so informing him;

    (f) where the person requests such intimation to be sent as is specified in section 15(1)(b) of this Act, the time when such request is—

        (i) made;

        (ii) complied with; and

    (g) the time of the person's release from detention or, where instead of being released he is arrested in respect of the alleged offence, the time of such arrest.

(7) Where a person is detained under subsection (1) above, a constable may—

    (a) without prejudice to any relevant rule of law as regards the admissibility in evidence of any answer given, put questions to him in relation to the suspected offence;

    (b) exercise the same powers of search as are available following an arrest.

(8) A constable may use reasonable force in exercising any power conferred by subsection (1), or by paragraph (b) of subsection (7), above.

(9) A person detained under subsection (1) above shall be under no obligation to answer any question other than to give his name and address, and a constable shall so inform him both on so detaining him and on arrival at the police station or other premises.

15 Rights of person arrested or detained

(1) Without prejudice to section 17 of this Act, a person who, not being a person in respect of whose custody or detention subsection (4) below applies—

    (a) has been arrested and is in custody in a police station or other premises, shall be entitled to have intimation of his custody and of the place where he is being held sent to a person reasonably named by him;

    (b) is being detained under section 14 of this Act and has been taken to a police station or other premises or place, shall be entitled to have intimation of his detention and of the police station or other premises or place sent to a solicitor and to one other person reasonably named by him,

without delay or, where some delay is necessary in the interest of the investigation or the prevention of crime or the apprehension of offenders, with no more delay than is so necessary.

(2) A person shall be informed of his entitlement under subsection (1) above—

    (a) on arrival at the police station or other premises; or

(b) where he is not arrested, or as the case may be detained, until after such arrival, on such arrest or detention.

(3) Where the person mentioned in paragraph (a) of subsection (1) above requests such intimation to be sent as is specified in that paragraph there shall be recorded the time when such request is—

(a) made;

(b) complied with.

(4) Without prejudice to the said section 17, a constable shall, where a person who has been arrested and is in such custody as is mentioned in paragraph (a) of subsection (1) above or who is being detained as is mentioned in paragraph (b) of that subsection appears to him to be a child, send without delay such intimation as is mentioned in the said paragraph (a), or as the case may be paragraph (b), to that person's parent if known; and the parent—

(a) in a case where there is reasonable cause to suspect that he has been involved in the alleged offence in respect of which the person has been arrested or detained, may; and

(b) in any other case shall, be permitted access to the person.

(5) The nature and extent of any access permitted under subsection (4) above shall be subject to any restriction essential for the furtherance of the investigation or the well-being of the person.

(6) In subsection (4) above—

(a) "child" means a person under 16 years of age; and

(b) "parent" includes guardian and any person who has the [care] of a child.

16   Drunken persons: power to take to designated place

(1) Where a constable has power to arrest a person without a warrant for any offence and the constable has reasonable grounds for suspecting that that person is drunk, the constable may, if he thinks fit, take him to any place designated by the Secretary of State for the purposes of this section as a place suitable for the care of drunken persons.

(2) A person shall not by virtue of this section be liable to be detained in any such place as is mentioned in subsection (1) above, but the exercise in his case of the power conferred by this section shall not preclude his being charged with any offence.

17   Right of accused to have access to solicitor

(1) Where an accused has been arrested on any criminal charge, he shall be entitled immediately upon such arrest—

(a) to have intimation sent to a solicitor that his professional assistance is required by the accused, and informing the solicitor—

(i) of the place where the person is being detained;

(ii) whether the person is to be liberated; and

(iii) if the person is not to be liberated, the court to which he is to be taken and the date when he is to be so taken; and

(b) to be told what rights there are under—

(i) paragraph (a)above;

(ii) subsection (2) below; and

(iii) section 35(1) and (2) of this Act.

(2) The accused and the solicitor shall be entitled to have a private interview before the examination or, as the case may be, first appearance.

18   Prints, samples etc. in criminal investigations

(1) This section applies where a person has been arrested and is in custody or is detained under section 14(1) of this Act.

(2) A constable may take from the person [, or require the person to provide him with, such relevant physical data] as the constable may, having regard to the circumstances of the suspected offence in respect of which the person has been arrested or detained, reasonably

consider it appropriate to take [from him or require him to provide, and the person so required shall comply with that requirement.].

[(3) Subject to subsection (4) below, all record of any relevant physical data taken from or provided by a person under subsection (2) above, all samples taken under subsection (6) below and all information derived from such samples shall be destroyed as soon as possible following a decision not to institute criminal proceedings against the person or on the conclusion of such proceedings otherwise than with a conviction or an order under section 246(3) of this Act.]

(4) The duty under subsection (3) above to destroy samples taken under subsection (6) below and information derived from such samples shall not apply—

    (a) where the destruction of the sample or the information could have the effect of destroying any sample, or any information derived therefrom, lawfully held in relation to a person other than the person from whom the sample was taken; or

    (b) where the record, sample or information in question is of the same kind as a record, a sample or, as the case may be, information lawfully held by or on behalf of any police force in relation to the person.

(5) No sample, or information derived from a sample, retained by virtue of subsection (4) above shall be used—

    (a) in evidence against the person from whom the sample was taken; or

    (b) for the purposes of the investigation of any offence.

(6) A constable may, with the authority of an officer of a rank no lower than inspector, take from the person—

    (a) from the hair of an external part of the body other than pubic hair, by means of cutting, combing or plucking, a sample of hair or other material;

    (b) from a fingernail or toenail or from under any such nail, a sample of nail or other material;

    (c) from an external part of the body, by means of swabbing or rubbing, a sample of blood or other body fluid, of body tissue or of other material;

    (d) from the inside of the mouth, by means of swabbing, a sample of saliva or other material.

(7) . . .

[(7A) For the purposes of this section and sections 19 and 20 of this Act "relevant physical data" means any—

    (a) fingerprint;

    (b) palm print;

    (c) print or impression other than those mentioned in paragraph (a) and (b) above, of an external part of the body;

    (d) record of a person's skin on an external part of the body created by a device approved by the Secretary of State.

(7B) The Secretary of State by order made by Statutory Instrument may approve a device for the purpose of creating such records as are mentioned in paragraph (d) of subsection (7A) above.]

(8) Nothing in this section shall prejudice—

    (a) any power of search;

    (b) any power to take possession of evidence where there is imminent danger of its being lost or destroyed; or

    (c) any power to take prints, impressions or samples under the authority of a warrant.

Note: This section applies with modifications to a person detained under s. 41 of or Schedule 7 to the Terrorism Act 2000 at a police station is Scotland: *ibid.*, Sch. 8, para. 20 (which see for details of the modifications).

19   Prints, samples etc. in criminal investigations: supplementary provisions

(1) [Without prejudice to any power exercisable under section 19A of this Act, this] section applies where a person convicted of an offence—

(a) has not, since the conviction, had [taken from him, or been required to provide, any relevant physical data or had any impression or sample] taken from him; or

(b) has [at any time had—

    (i) taken from him or been required (whether under paragraph (a) above or under section 18 or 19A of this Act or otherwise) to provide any physical data; or

    (ii) any impression or sample taken from him, which was not suitable for the means of analysis for which the data were taken or required or the impression or sample was taken] from him but it was not suitable for the means of analysis for which it was taken or, though suitable, was insufficient (either in quantity or in quality) to enable information to be obtained by that means of analysis.

(2) Where this section applies, a constable may, within the permitted period—

[(a) take from or require the convicted person to provide him with such relevant physical data as he reasonably considers it appropriate to take or, as the case may be, require the provision of;] and

(b) with the authority of an officer of a rank no lower than inspector, take from the person any sample mentioned in any of paragraphs (a) to (d) of subsection (6) of section 18 of this Act by the means specified in that paragraph in relation to that sample.

(3) A constable—

(a) may require the convicted person to attend a police station for the purposes of subsection (2) above;

(b) may, where the convicted person is in legal custody by virtue of section 295 of this Act, exercise the powers conferred by subsection (2) above in relation to the person in the place where he is for the time being.

(4) In subsection (2) above, "the permitted period" means—

(a) in a case to which paragraph (a) of subsection (1) above applies, the period of one month beginning with the date of the conviction;

(b) in a case to which paragraph (b) of that subsection applies, the period of one month beginning with the date on which a constable of the police force which instructed the analysis receives written intimation that [the relevant physical data were or] the sample . . . was unsuitable or, as the case may be, insufficient as mentioned in that paragraph.

(5) A requirement under subsection (3)(a) above—

(a) shall give the person at least seven days' notice of the date on which he is required to attend;

(b) may direct him to attend at a specified time of day or between specified times of day.

(6) Any constable may arrest without warrant a person who fails to comply with a requirement under subsection (3)(a) above.

19A, 19B   ★ ★ ★ ★ ★

20   Use of prints, samples etc.

Without prejudice to any power to do so apart from this section, [relevant physical data,] impressions and samples lawfully held by or on behalf of any police force or in connection with or as a result of an investigation of an offence and information derived therefrom may be checked against other such [data], impressions, samples and information.

21   ★ ★ ★ ★ ★

22 Liberation by police

(1) Where a person has been arrested and charged with an offence which may be tried summarily, the officer in charge of a police station may—

(a) liberate him upon a written undertaking, signed by him and certified by the officer, in terms of which the person undertakes to appear at a specified court at a specified time; or

(b) liberate him without any such undertaking; or

(c) refuse to liberate him;

(2) A person in breach of an undertaking given by him under subsection (1) above without reasonable excuse shall be guilty of an offence and liable on summary conviction to the following penalties—

(a) a fine not exceeding level 3 on the standard scale; and

(b) imprisonment for a period—

(i) where conviction is in the district court, not exceeding 60 days; or

(ii) where conviction is in the sheriff court, not exceeding 3 months.

(3) The refusal of the officer in charge to liberate a person under subsection (1)(c) above and the detention of that person until his case is tried in the usual form shall not subject the officer to any claim whatsoever.

(4) The penalties provided for in subsection (2) above may be imposed in addition to any other penalty which it is competent for the court to impose, notwithstanding that the total of penalties imposed may exceed the maximum penalty which it is competent to impose in respect of the original offence.

(5) In any proceedings relating to an offence under this section, a writing, purporting to be such an undertaking as is mentioned in subsection (1)(a) above and bearing to be signed and certified, shall be sufficient evidence of the terms of the undertaking given by the arrested person.

22A–34 ★ ★ ★ ★ ★

35 Judicial examination

(1) The accused's solicitor shall be entitled to be present at the examination.

(2) The sheriff may delay the examination for a period not exceeding 48 hours from and after the time of the accused's arrest, in order to allow time for the attendance of the solicitor.

(3) Where the accused is brought before the sheriff for examination on any charge and he or his solicitor intimates that he does not desire to emit a declaration in regard to such a charge, it shall be unnecessary to take a declaration, and, subject to section 36 of this Act, the accused may be committed for further examination or until liberated in due course of law without a declaration being taken.

(4) Nothing in subsection (3) above shall prejudice the right of the accused subsequently to emit a declaration on intimating to the prosecutor his desire to do so; and that declaration shall be taken in further examination.

(5) Where, subsequent to examination or further examination on any charge, the prosecutor desires to question the accused as regards an extrajudicial confession, whether or not a full admission, allegedly made by him to or in the hearing of a constable, which is relevant to the charge and as regards which he has not previously been examined, the accused may be brought before the sheriff for further examination.

(6) Where the accused is brought before the sheriff for further examination the sheriff may delay that examination for a period not exceeding 24 hours in order to allow time for the attendance of the accused's' solicitor.

(7) Any proceedings before the sheriff in examination or further examination shall be conducted in chambers and outwith the presence of any co-accused.

(8) This section applies to procedure on petition, without prejudice to the accused being tried summarily by the sheriff for any offence in respect of which he has been committed until liberated in due course of law.

36 Judicial examination: questioning by prosecutor

(1) Subject to the following provisions of this section, an accused on being brought before the sheriff for examination on any charge (whether the first or a further examination) may be questioned by the prosecutor in so far as such questioning is directed towards eliciting any admission, denial, explanation, justification or comment which the accused may have as regards anything to which subsections (2) to (4) below apply.

(2) This subsection applies to matters averred in the charge, and the particular aims of a line of questions under this subsection shall be to determine—

(a) whether any account which the accused can give ostensibly discloses a defence; and

(b) the nature and particulars of that defence.

(3) This subsection applies to the alleged making by the accused, to or in the hearing of a constable, of an extrajudicial confession (whether or not a full admission) relevant to the charge, and questions under this subsection may only be put if the accused has, before the examination, received from the prosecutor or from a constable a written record of the confession allegedly made.

(4) This subsection applies to what is said in any declaration emitted in regard to the charge by the accused at examination.

(5) The prosecutor shall, in framing questions in exercise of his power under subsection (1) above, have regard to the following principles—

(a) the question should not be designed to challenge the truth of anything said by the accused;

(b) there should be no reiteration of a question which the accused has refused to answer at the examination; and

(c) there should be no leading questions, and the sheriff shall ensure that all questions are fairly put to, and understood by, the accused.

(6) The accused shall be told by the sheriff—

(a) where he is represented by a solicitor at the judicial examination, that he may consult that solicitor before answering any question; and

(b) that if he answers any question put to him at the examination under this section in such a way as to disclose an ostensible defence, the prosecutor shall be under the duty imposed by subsection (10) below.

(7) With the permission of the sheriff, the solicitor for the accused may ask the accused any question the purpose of which is to clarify any ambiguity in an answer given by the accused to the prosecutor at the examination or to give the accused an opportunity to answer any question which he has previously refused to answer.

(8) An accused may decline to answer a question under subsection (1) above; and, where he is subsequently tried on the charge mentioned in that subsection or on any other charge arising out of the circumstances which gave rise to the charge so mentioned, his having so declined may be commented upon by the prosecutor, the judge presiding at the trial, or any co-accused, only where and in so far as the accused (or any witness called on his behalf) in evidence avers something which could have been stated appropriately in answer to that question.

(9) The procedure in relation to examination under this section shall be prescribed by Act of Adjournal.

(10) Without prejudice to any rule of law, on the conclusion of an examination under this section the prosecutor shall secure the investigation, to such extent as is reasonably practicable, of any ostensible defence disclosed in the course of the examination.

(11) The duty imposed by subsection (10) above shall not apply as respects any ostensible defence which is not reasonably capable of being investigated.

37 Judicial examination: record of proceedings

(1) The prosecutor shall provide for a verbatim record to be made by means of shorthand

notes or by mechanical means of all questions to and answers and declarations by the accused in examination, or further examination, under sections 35 and 36 of this Act.

(2) A shorthand writer shall—

   (a) sign the shorthand notes taken by him of the questions, answers and declarations mentioned in subsection (1) above and certify the notes as being complete and correct; and

   (b) retain the notes.

(3) A person recording the questions, answers and declarations mentioned in subsection (1) above by mechanical means shall—

   (a) certify that the record is true and complete;

   (b) specify in the certificate the proceedings to which the record relates; and

   (c) retain the record.

(4) The prosecutor shall require the person who made the record mentioned in subsection (1) above, or such other competent person as he may specify, to make a transcript of the record in legible form; and that person shall—

   (a) comply with the requirement;

   (b) certify the transcript as being a complete and correct transcript of the record purporting to have been made and certified, and in the case of shorthand notes signed, by the person who made the record; and

   (c) send the transcript to the prosecutor.

(5) A transcript certified under subsection (4)(b) above shall, subject to section 38(1) of this Act, be deemed for all purposes to be a complete and correct record of the questions, answers and declarations mentioned in subsection (1) above.

(6) Subject to subsections (7) to (9) below, within 14 days of the date of examination or further examination, the prosecutor shall—

   (a) serve a copy of the transcript on the accused examined; and

   (b) serve a further such copy on the solicitor (if any) for that accused.

(7) Where at the time of further examination a trial diet is already fixed and the interval between the further examination and that diet is not sufficient to allow of the time limits specified in subsection (6) above and subsection (1) of section 38 of this Act, the sheriff shall (either or both)—

   (a) direct that those subsections shall apply in the case with such modifications as to time limits as he shall specify;

   (b) subject to subsection (8) below, postpone the trial diet.

(8) Postponement under paragraph (b) of subsection (7) above alone shall only be competent where the sheriff considers that to proceed under paragraph (a) of that subsection alone, or paragraphs (a) and (b) together, would not be practicable.

(9) Any time limit mentioned in subsection (6) above and subsection (1) of section 38 of this Act (including any such time limit as modified by a direction under subsection (7) above) may be extended, in respect of the case, by the High Court [and an application to the High Court for any such extension shall be disposed of by the High Court or any Lord Commissioner of Justiciary in Court or in Chambers].

(10) A copy of—

   (a) a transcript required by paragraph (a) of subsection (6) above to be served on an accused or by paragraph (b) of that subsection to be served on his solicitor; or

   (b) a notice required by paragraph (a) of section 38(1) of this Act to be served on an accused or on the prosecutor,

shall be served in such manner as may be prescribed by Act of Adjournal; and a written execution purporting to be signed by the person who served such transcript or notice, together with, where appropriate, the relevant post office receipt shall be sufficient evidence of service of such a copy.

38, 39 ★ ★ ★ ★ ★

40   Committal until liberated in due course of law

(1) Every petition shall be signed and no accused shall be committed until liberated in due course of law for any crime or offence without a warrant in writing expressing the particular charge in respect of which he is committed.

(2) Any such warrant for imprisonment which either proceeds on an unsigned petition or does not express the particular charge shall be null and void.

(3) The accused shall immediately be given a true copy of the warrant for imprisonment signed by the constable or person executing the warrant before imprisonment or by the prison officer receiving the warrant.

41–286 ★ ★ ★ ★ ★

PART XIII   MISCELLANEOUS

Lord Advocate

287   Demission of office by Lord Advocate

(1) All indictments which have been raised by a Lord Advocate shall remain effective notwithstanding his subsequently having died or demitted office and may be taken up and proceeded with by his successor.

(2) During any period when the office of Lord Advocate is vacant it shall be lawful to indict accused persons in name of the Solicitor General then in office.

(3) The advocates depute shall not demit office when a Lord Advocate dies or demits office but shall continue in office until their successors receive commissions.

(4) The advocates depute and procurators fiscal shall have power, notwithstanding any vacancy in the office of Lord Advocate, to take up and proceed with any indictment which—

(a) by virtue of subsection (1) above, remains effective; or

(b) by virtue of subsection (2) above, is in the name of the Solicitor General.

(5) For the purposes of this Act, where, but for this subsection, demission of office by one Law Officer would result in the offices of both being vacant, he or, where both demit office on the same day, the person demitting the office of Lord Advocate shall be deemed to continue in office until the warrant of appointment of the person succeeding to the office of Lord Advocate is granted.

(6) The Lord Advocate shall enter upon the duties of his office immediately upon the grant of his warrant of appointment; and he shall as soon as is practicable thereafter take the oaths of office before the Secretary of State or any Lord Commissioner of Justiciary.

288   Intimation of proceedings in High Court to Lord Advocate

(1) In any proceeding in the High Court (other than a proceeding to which the Lord Advocate or a procurator fiscal is a party) it shall be competent for the court to order intimation of such proceeding to the Lord Advocate.

(2) On intimation being made to the Lord Advocate under subsection (1) above, the Lord Advocate shall be entitled to appear and be heard in such proceeding.

[Devolution issues

288A   Rights of appeal for Advocate General: devolution issues

(1) This section applies where—

(a) a person is acquitted or convicted of a charge (whether on indictment or in summary proceedings), and

(b) the Advocate General for Scotland was a party to the proceedings in pursuance of paragraph 6 of Schedule 6 to the Scotland Act 1998 (devolution issues).

(2) The Advocate General for Scotland may refer any devolution issue which has arisen in the proceedings to the High Court for their opinion; and the Clerk of Justiciary shall send to the person acquitted or convicted and to any solicitor who acted for the person at the trial, a copy of the reference and intimation of the date fixed by the Court for a hearing.

(3) The person may, not later than seven days before the date so fixed, intimate in writing to the Clerk of Justiciary and to the Advocate General for Scotland either—

    (a) that he elects to appear personally at the hearing, or

    (b) that he elects to be represented by counsel at the hearing, but, except by leave of the Court on cause shown, and without prejudice to his right to attend, he shall not appear or be represented at the hearing other than by and in conformity with an election under this subsection.

(4) Where there is no intimation under subsection (3)(b), the High Court shall appoint counsel to act at the hearing as amicus curiae.

(5) The costs of representation elected under subsection (3)(b) or of an appointment under subsection (4) shall, after being taxed by the Auditor of the Court of Session, be paid by the Advocate General for Scotland out of money provided by Parliament.

(6) The opinion on the point referred under subsection (2) shall not affect the acquittal or (as the case may be) conviction in the trial.

288B   Appeals to Judicial Committee of the Privy Council

(1) This section applies where the Judicial Committee of the Privy Council determines an appeal under paragraph 13(a) of Schedule 6 to the Scotland Act 1998 against a determination of a devolution issue by the High Court in the ordinary course of proceedings.

(2) The determination of the appeal shall not affect any earlier acquittal or earlier quashing of any conviction in the proceedings.

(3) Subject to subsection (2) above, the High Court shall have the same powers in relation to the proceedings when remitted to it by the Judicial Committee as it would have if it were considering the proceedings otherwise than as a trial court.]

289 ★ ★ ★ ★ ★

290   Accused's right to request identification parade

(1) Subject to subsection (2) below, the sheriff may, on an application by an accused at any time after the accused has been charged with an offence, order that, in relation to the alleged offence, the prosecutor shall hold an identification parade in which the accused shall be one of those constituting the parade.

(2) The sheriff shall make an order in accordance with subsection (1) above only after giving the prosecutor an opportunity to be heard and only if—

    (a) an identification parade, such as is mentioned in subsesction (1) above, has not been held at the instance of the prosecutor;

    (b) after a request by the accused, the prosecutor has refused to hold, or has unreasonably delayed holding, such an identification parade; and

    (c) the sheriff considers the application under subsection (1) above to be reasonable.

★ ★ ★ ★ ★

Asylum and Immigration Act 1996
(1996, c. 49)

An Act to amend and supplement the Immigration Act 1971 and the Asylum and Immigration Appeals Act 1993; to make further provision with respect to persons subject to immigration control and the employment of such persons; and for connected purposes.   [24 July 1996]

Territorial extent: United Kingdom. The Act extends, with modifications, to Jersey and Guernsey: see SI 1998 Nos 1070 and 1264.

Note: "The 1993 Act": Asylum and Immigration Appeals Act 1993.

5–7 ★ ★ ★ ★ ★

Persons subject to immigration control

8   Restrictions on employment

(1) Subject to subsection (2) below, if any person ("the employer") employs a person subject to immigration control ("the employee") who has attained the age of 16, the employer shall be guilty of an offence if—

    (a) the employee has not been granted leave to enter or remain in the United Kingdom; or

    (b) the employee's leave is not valid and subsisting, or is subject to a condition precluding him from taking up employment,

and (in either case) the employee does not satisfy such conditions as may be specified in an order made by the Secretary of State.

(2) Subject to subsection (3) below, in proceedings under this section, it shall be a defence to prove that–

    (a) before the employment began, there was produced to the employer a document which appeared to him to relate to the employee and to be of a description specified in an order made by the Secretary of State; and

    (b) either the document was retained by the employer, or a copy or other record of it was made by the employer in a manner specified in the order in relation to documents of that description.

(3) The defence afforded by subsection (2) above shall not be available in any case where the employer knew that his employment of the employee would constitute an offence under this section.

(4) A person guilty of an offence under this section shall be liable on summary conviction to a fine not exceeding level 5 on the standard scale.

(5) Where an offence under this section committed by a body corporate is proved to have been committed with the consent or connivance of, or to be attributable to any neglect on the part of—

    (a) any director, manager, secretary or other similar officer of the body corporate; or

    (b) any person who was purporting to act in any such capacity, he as well as the body corporate shall be guilty of the offence and shall be liable to be proceeded against and punished accordingly.

(6)–(8) ★ ★ ★ ★ ★

[8A   Code of practice

(1) The Secretary of State must issue a code of practice as to the measures which an employer is to be expected to take, or not to take, with a view to securing that, while avoiding the commission of an offence under section 8, he also avoids unlawful discrimination.

(2) "Unlawful discrimination" means—

    (a) discrimination in contravention of section 4(1) of the Race Relations Act 1976 ("the 1976 Act"); or

    (b) in relation to Northern Ireland, discrimination in contravention of Article 6(1) of the Race Relations (Northern Ireland) Order 1997 ("the 1997 Order").

(3) Before issuing the code, the Secretary of State must–

    (a) prepare and publish a draft of the proposed code; and

    (b) consider any representations about it which are made to him.

(4) In preparing the draft, the Secretary of State must consult—
  (a) the Commission for Racial Equality;
  (b) the Equality Commission for Northern Ireland; and
  (c) such organisations and bodies (including organisations or associations or organisations representative of employers or of workers) as he considers appropriate.

(5) If the Secretary of State decides to proceed with the code, he must lay a draft of the code before both Houses of Parliament.

(6) The draft code may contain modifications to the original proposals made in the light of representations to the Secretary of State.

(7) After laying the draft code before Parliament, the Secretary of State may bring the code into operation by an order made by statutory instrument.

(8) An order under subsection (7)—
  (a) shall be subject to annulment in pursuance of a resolution of either House of Parliament;
  (b) may contain such transitional provisions or savings as appear to the Secretary of State to be necessary or expedient in connection with the code.

(9) A failure on the part of any person to observe a provision of the code does not of itself make him liable to any proceedings.

(10) But the code is admissible in evidence—
  (a) in proceedings under the 1976 Act before an employment tribunal;
  (b) in proceedings under the 1997 Order before an industrial tribunal.

(11) If any provision of the code appears to the tribunal to be relevant to any question arising in such proceedings, that provision is to be taken into account in determining the question.

(12), (13) ★ ★ ★ ★ ★]

Broadcasting Act 1996
(1996, c. 55)

An Act to make new provision about the broadcasting in digital form of television and sound programme services and the broadcasting in that form on television or radio frequencies of other services; to amend the Broadcasting Act 1990; to make provision about rights to televise sporting or other events of national interest; to amend in other respects the law relating to the provision of television and sound programme services; to provide for the establishment and functions of a Broadcasting Standards Commission and for the dissolution of the Broadcasting Complaints Commission and the Broadcasting Standards Council; to make provision for the transfer to other persons of property, rights and liabilities of the British Broadcasting Corporation relating to their transmission network; and for connected purposes. [24 July 1996]

Territorial extent: United Kingdom

PART I   DIGITAL TERRESTRIAL TELEVISION BROADCASTING

Introductory

1   Multiplex services and digital programme services

(1) In this Part "multiplex service" means a service provided by any person which consists in the broadcasting for general reception of two or more services specified in subsection (3) by combining the relevant information in digital form, together with any broadcasting in digital form of digital additional services (as defined by section 24(1)).

[(1A) In subsection (1) "for general reception" means for general reception in, or in any area in, the United Kingdom.]

(2) A service in respect of which a licence under section 7 is in force is not prevented from being a multiplex service at a particular time merely because only one service specified in subsection (3) is being broadcast in digital form at that time.

(3) The services referred to in subsections (1) and (2) are—

(a) a digital programme service (as defined by subsection (4)), or

(b) a qualifying service (as defined by section 2(2)).

(4) In this Part "digital programme service" means a service consisting in the provision by any person of television programmes (together with any ancillary services, as defined by section 24(2)) with a view to their being broadcast in digital form for general reception, whether by him or by some other person, but does not include—

(a) a qualifying service,

(b) a teletext service, or

(c) any service in the case of which the visual images to be broadcast do not consist wholly or mainly of images capable of being seen as moving pictures,

except, in the case of a service falling within paragraph (b) or (c), to the extent that it is an ancillary service.

[(4A) In subsection (4) "for general reception" means for general reception in, or in any area in, the United Kingdom.]

(5) The Secretary of State may, if having regard to developments in broadcasting technology he considers it appropriate to do so, by order amend the definition of "digital programme service" in subsection (4).

(6) No order under subsection (5) shall be made unless a draft of the order has been laid before and approved by a resolution of each House of Parliament.

(7) In this section–

"broadcast" means broadcast otherwise than—

(a) by satellite, or

(b) in the provision of a local delivery service (as defined by section 72(1) of the 1990 Act), and

. . .

2 ★ ★ ★ ★ ★

General provisions about licences

3 Licences under Part I

(1) Any licence granted by the Independent Television Commission (in this Part referred to as "the Commission") under this Part shall be in writing and (subject to the provisions of this Part) shall continue in force for such period as is provided, in relation to a licence of the kind in question, by the relevant provision of this Part.

(2) A licence may be so granted for the provision of such a service as is specified in the licence or for the provision of a service of such a description as is so specified.

(3) The Commission—

(a) shall not grant a licence to any person unless they are satisfied that he is a fit and proper person to hold it, and

(b) shall do all that they can to secure that, if they cease to be so satisfied in the case of any person holding a licence, that person does not remain the holder of the licence; and nothing in this Part shall be construed as affecting the operation of this subsection or of section 5(1) or (2)(b) or (c).

(4) The Commission may vary a licence by a notice served on the licence holder if—

(a) in the case of a variation of the period for which a licence having effect for a specified period is to continue in force, the licence holder consents, or

(b) in the case of any other variation, the licence holder has been given a reasonable opportunity of making representations to the Commission about the variation.

(5) Paragraph (a) of subsection (4) does not affect the operation of section 17(1)(b); and that subsection shall not authorise the variation of any conditions included in a licence in pursuance of section 13(1).

(6) A licence granted to any person under this Part shall not be transferable to any other person without the previous consent in writing of the Commission.

(7) Without prejudice to the generality of subsection (6), the Commission shall not give their consent for the purposes of that subsection unless they are satisfied that any such other person would be in a position to comply with all of the conditions included in the licence which would have effect during the periods for which it is to be in force.

(8) The holding by any person of a licence to provide any service shall not relieve him of any requirement to hold a licence under section 1 of the Wireless Telegraphy Act 1949 or section 7 of the Telecommunications Act 1984 in connection with the provision of that service.

4-17 ★ ★ ★ ★ ★

Digital programme services

18 Licensing of digital programme services

(1) An application for a licence to provide digital programme services (in this Part referred to as a "digital programme licence") shall—
(a) be made in such manner as the Commission may determine, and
(b) be accompanied by such fee (if any) as they may determine.

(2) At any time after receiving such an application and before determining it, the Commission may require the applicant to furnish such additional information as they may consider necessary for the purpose of considering the application.

(3) Any information to be furnished to the Commission under this section shall, if they so require, be in such form or verified in such manner as they may specify.

(4) Where an application for a digital programme licence is made to the Commission in accordance with the provisions of this section, they shall grant the licence unless precluded from doing so by section 3(3)(a) or 5(1).

(5) Subject to subsection (6), sections 6 to 12 of the 1990 Act (general provisions relating to services licensed under Part I of that Act) shall apply in relation to a digital programme service licensed under this Part as they apply in relation to a service licensed under that Part of that Act.

(6) In its application in relation to a digital programme service—
(a) section 6 of the 1990 Act shall have effect with the omission of subsection (8), and
(b) section 12(1)(b) of that Act shall have effect as if the reference to the Commission's functions under Chaper II of Part I of that Act included a reference to their functions under this Part.

19-33 ★ ★ ★ ★ ★

34 Promotion of equal opportunities and fair treatment

(1) Any multiplex licence or digital programme licence shall include conditions requiring the licence holder—
(a) to make arrangements for promoting, in relation to employment by him, equality of opportunity between men and women and between persons of different racial groups,
(b) to make arrangements for promoting, in relation to employment by him, the fair treatment of disabled persons, and

(c) to review those arrangements from time to time.

(2) In subsection (1) "racial group" has the same meaning as in the Race Relations Act 1976, and "disabled person" has the same meaning as in the Disability Discrimination Act 1995.

35–39 ★ ★ ★ ★ ★

PART II   DIGITAL TERRESTRIAL SOUND BROADCASTING

Introductory

40–96 ★ ★ ★ ★ ★

PART IV   SPORTING AND OTHER EVENTS OF NATIONAL INTEREST

97   Listed events

(1) For the purposes of this Part, a listed event is a sporting or other event of national interest which is for the time being included in a list drawn up by the Secretary of State for the purposes of this Part.

(2) The Secretary of State shall not at any time draw up, revise or cease to maintain such a list as is mentioned in subsection (1) unless he has first consulted—

(a) the BBC,

(b) the Welsh Authority,

(c) the Commission, and

(d) in relation to a relevant event, the person from whom the rights to televise that event may be acquired;

and for the purposes of this subsection a relevant event is a sporting or other event of national interest which the Secretary of State proposes to include in, or omit from, the list.

(3) As soon as he has drawn up or revised such a list as is mentioned in subsection (1), the Secretary of State shall publish the list in such manner as he considers appropriate for bringing it to the attention of—

(a) the persons mentioned in subsection (2), and

(b) every person who is the holder of a licence granted by the Commission under Part I of the 1990 Act or a digital programme licence granted by them under Part I of this Act.

(4) In this section "national interest" includes interest within England, Scotland, Wales or Northern Ireland.

(5) The addition of any relevant event to such a list as is mentioned in subsection (1) shall not affect—

(a) the validity of any contract entered into before the date on which the Secretary of State consulted the persons mentioned in subsection (2) in relation to the proposed addition, or

(b) the exercise of any rights acquired under such a contract.

(6) The list drawn up by the Secretary of State for the purposes of section 182 of the 1990 Act, as that list is in force immediately before the commencement of this section, shall be taken to have been drawn up for the purposes of this Part.

★ ★ ★ ★ ★

Criminal Procedure and Investigations Act 1996
(1996, c. 25)

An Act to make provision about criminal procedure and criminal investigations.   [4 July 1996]

Territorial extent: England and Wales, Northern Ireland (ss. 22 – 24, 26, 41, 58); England and Wales, Scotland (ss. 37, 38, 40); England and Wales (s. 39); United Kingdom (ss. 59, 60). In its application to Northern Ireland the Act is subject to modifications as set out in Sch. 4 (not reprinted).

PART II   CRIMINAL INVESTIGATIONS

22   Introduction

(1) For the purposes of this Part a criminal investigation is an investigation conducted by police officers with a view to it being ascertained—

(a) whether a person should be charged with an offence, or

(b) whether a person charged with an offence is guilty of it.

(2) In this Part references to material are to material of all kinds, and in particular include references to—

(a) information, and

(b) objects of all descriptions.

(3) In this Part references to recording information are to putting it in a durable or retrievable form (such as writing or tape).

23   Code of practice

(1) The Secretary of State shall prepare a code of practice containing provisions designed to secure—

(a) that where a criminal investigation is conducted all reasonable steps are taken for the purposes of the investigation and, in particular, all reasonable lines of inquiry are pursued;

(b) that information which is obtained in the course of a criminal investigation and may be relevant to the investigation is recorded;

(c) that any record of such information is retained;

(d) that any other material which is obtained in the course of a criminal investigation and may be relevant to the investigation is retained;

(e) that information falling within paragraph (b) and material falling within paragraph (d) is revealed to a person who is involved in the prosecution of criminal proceedings arising out of or relating to the investigation and who is identified in accordance with prescribed provisions;

(f) that where such a person inspects information or other material in pursuance of a requirement that it be revealed to him, and he requests that it be disclosed to the accused, the accused is allowed to inspect it or is given a copy of it;

(g) that where such a person is given a document indicating the nature of information or other material in pursuance of a requirement that it be revealed to him, and he requests that it be disclosed to the accused, the accused is allowed to inspect it or is given a copy of it;

(h) that the person who is to allow the accused to inspect information or other material or to give him a copy of it shall decide which of those (inspecting or giving a copy) is appropriate;

(i) that where the accused is allowed to inspect material as mentioned in paragraph (f) or (g) and he requests a copy, he is given one unless the person allowing the inspection is of opinion that it is not practicable or not desirable to give him one;

    (j) that a person mentioned in paragraph (e) is given a written statement that prescribed activities which the code requires have been carried out.

(2)–(8) ★ ★ ★ ★ ★

24, 25 ★ ★ ★ ★ ★

26 Effect of code

(1) A person other than a police officer who is charged with the duty of conducting an investigation with a view to it being ascertained—

    (a) whether a person should be charged with an offence, or

    (b) whether a person charged with an offence is guilty of it, shall in discharging that duty have regard to any relevant provision of a code which would apply if the investigation were conducted by police officers.

(2) A failure—

    (a) by a police officer to comply with any provision of a code for the time being in operation by virtue of an order under section 25, or

    (b) by a person to comply with subsection (1), shall not in itself render him liable to any criminal or civil proceedings.

(3) In all criminal and civil proceedings a code in operation at any time by virtue of an order under section 25 shall be admissible in evidence.

(4) If it appears to a court or tribunal conducting criminal or civil proceedings that—

    (a) any provision of a code in operation at any time by virtue of an order under section 25, or

    (b) any failure mentioned in subsection (2)(a) or (b), is relevant to any question arising in the proceedings, the provision or failure shall be taken into account in deciding the question.

27–36 ★ ★ ★ ★ ★

Reporting restrictions

37 Restrictions on reporting

(1) Except as provided by this section—

    (a) no written report of proceedings falling within subsection (2) shall be published in Great Britain;

    (b) no report of proceedings falling within subsection (2) shall be included in a relevant programme for reception in Great Britain.

(2) The following proceedings fall within this subsection—

    (a) a preparatory hearing;

    (b) an application for leave to appeal in relation to such a hearing;

    (c) an appeal in relation to such a hearing.

(3) The judge dealing with a preparatory hearing may order that subsection (1) shall not apply, or shall not apply to a specified extent, to a report of—

    (a) the preparatory hearing, or

    (b) an application to the judge for leave to appeal to the Court of Appeal under section 35(1) in relation to the preparatory hearing.

(4)–(8) ★ ★ ★ ★ ★

(9) Subsection (1) does not apply to a report which contains only one or more of the following matters–

    (a) the identity of the court and the name of the judge;

    (b) the names, ages, home addresses and occupations of the accused and witnesses;

    (c) the offence or offences, or a summary of them, with which the accused is or are charged;

    (d) the names of counsel and solicitors in the proceedings;

(e) where the proceedings are adjourned, the date and place to which they are adjourned;

(f) any arrangements as to bail;

(g) [whether a right to representation funded by the Legal Services Commission as part of the Criminal Defence Services was granted to the accused or any of the accused.]

(10) The addresses that may be published or included in a relevant programme under subsection (9) are addresses—

(a) at any relevant time, and

(b) at the time of their publication or inclusion in a relevant programme; and "relevant time" here means a time when events giving rise to the charges to which the proceedings relate occurred.

(11) Nothing in this section affects any prohibition or restriction imposed by virtue of any other enactment on a publication or on matter included in a programme.

(12) In this section—

(a) "publish", in relation to a report, means publish the report, either by itself or as part of a newspaper or periodical, for distribution to the public;

(b) expressions cognate with "publish" shall be construed accordingly;

(c) "relevant programme" means a programme included in a programme service, within the meaning of the Broadcasting Act 1996.

38 Offences in connection with reporting

(1) If a report is published or included in a relevant programme in contravention of section 37 each of the following persons in guilty of an offence—

(a) in the case of a publication of a written report as part of a newspaper or periodical, any proprietor, editor or publisher of the newspaper or periodical;

(b) in the case of a publication of a written report otherwise than as part of a newspaper or periodical, the person who publishes it;

(c) in the case of the inclusion of a report in a relevant programme, any body corporate which is engaged in providing the service in which the programme is included and any person having functions in relation to the programme corresponding to those of an editor of a newspaper.

(2) A person guilty of an offence under this section is liable on summary conviction to a fine of an amount not exceeding level 5 on the standard scale.

(3) Proceedings for an offence under this section shall not be instituted in England and Wales otherwise than by or with the consent of the Attorney General.

(4) Subsection (12) of section 37 applies for the purposes of this section as it applies for the purposes of that.

PART IV   RULINGS

39 Meaning of pre-trial hearing

(1) For the purposes of this Part a hearing is a pre-trial hearing if it relates to a trial on indictment and it takes place—

(a) after the accused has been committed for trial for the offence concerned [or sent for trial under section 51 of the Crime and Disorder Act 1998] or after the proceedings for the trial have been transferred to the Crown Court, and

(b) before the start of the trial.

(2), (3) ★ ★ ★ ★ ★

40 Power to make rulings

(1) A judge may make at a pre-trial hearing a ruling as to—

(a) any question as to the admissibility of evidence;

(b) any other question of law relating to the case concerned.

(2) A ruling may be made under this section—

(a) on an application by a party to the case, or

(b) of the judge's own motion.

(3) Subject to subsection (4), a ruling made under this section has binding effect from the time it is made until the case against the accused or, if there is more than one, against each of them is disposed of; and the case against an accused is disposed of if—

(a) he is acquitted or convicted, or

(b) the prosecutor decides not to proceed with the case against him.

(4)–(7) ★ ★ ★ ★ ★

41 Restrictions on reporting

(1) Except as provided by this section—

(a) no written report of matters falling within subsection (2) shall be published in Great Britain;

(b) no report of matters falling within subsection (2) shall be included in a relevant programme for reception in Great Britain.

(2) The following matters fall within this subsection—

(a) a ruling made under section 40;

(b) proceedings on an application for a ruling to be made under section 40;

(c) an order that a ruling made under section 40 be discharged or varied or further varied;

(d) proceedings on an application for a ruling made under section 40 to be discharged or varied or further varied.

(3) The judge dealing with any matter falling within subsection (2) may order that subsection (1) shall not apply, or shall not apply to a specified extent, to a report of the matter.

(4) Where there is only one accused and he objects to the making of an order under subsection (3) the judge shall make the order if (and only if) satisfied after hearing the representations of the accused that it is in the interests of justice to do so; and if the order is made it shall not apply to the extent that a report deals with any such objection or representations.

(5) Where there are two or more accused and one or more of them objects to the making of an order under subsection (3) the judge shall make the order if (and only if) satisfied after hearing the representations of each of the accused that it is in the interests of justice to do so; and if the order is made it shall not apply to the extent that a report deals with any such objection or representations.

(6) Subsection (1) does not apply to—

(a) the publication of a report of matters, or

(b) the inclusion in a relevant programme of a report of matters, at the conclusion of the trial of the accused or of the last of the accused to be tried.

(7), (8) ★ ★ ★ ★ ★

42–57 ★ ★ ★ ★ ★

Derogatory assertions

58 Orders in respect of certain assertions

(1) This section applies where a person has been convicted of an offence and a speech in mitigation is made by him or on his behalf before—

(a) a court determining what sentence should be passed on him in respect of the offence, or

(b) a magistrates' court determining whether he should be committed to the Crown Court for sentence.

(2) This section also applies where a sentence has been passed on a person in respect of an offence and a submission relating to the sentence is made by him or on his behalf before—

(a) a court hearing an appeal against or reviewing the sentence, or

(b) a court determining whether to grant leave to appeal against the sentence.

(3) Where it appears to the court that there is a real possibility that an order under subsection (8) will be made in relation to the assertion, the court may make an order under subsection (7) in relation to the assertion.

(4) Where there are substantial grounds for believing—

(a) that an assertion forming part of the speech or submission is derogatory to a person's character (for instance, because it suggests that his conduct is or has been criminal, immoral or improper), and

(b) that the assertion is false or that the facts asserted are irrelevant to the sentence, the court may make an order under subsection (8) in relation to the assertion.

(5) An order under subsection (7) or (8) must not be made in relation to an assertion if it appears to the court that the assertion was previously made—

(a) at the trial at which the person was convicted of the offence, or

(b) during any other proceedings relating to the offence.

(6) Section 59 has effect where a court makes an order under subsection (7) or (8).

(7) An order under this subsection—

(a) may be made at any time before the court has made a determination with regard to sentencing;

(b) may be revoked at any time by the court;

(c) subject to paragraph (b), shall cease to have effect when the court makes a determination with regard to sentencing.

(8) An order under this subsection—

(a) may be made after the court has made a determination with regard to sentencing, but only if it is made as soon as is reasonably practicable after the making of the determination;

(b) may be revoked at any time by the court;

(c) subject to paragraph (b), shall cease to have effect at the end of the period of 12 months beginning with the day on which it is made;

(d) may be made whether or not an order has been made under subsection (7) with regard to the case concerned.

59   Restriction on reporting of assertions

(1) Where a court makes an order under section 58(7) or (8) in relation to any assertion, at any time when the order has effect the assertion must not—

(a) be published in Great Britain in a written publication available to the public, or

(b) be included in a relevant programme for reception in Great Britain.

(2) In this section—

"relevant programme" means a programme included in a programme service, within the meaning of the Broadcasting Act 1990;

"written publication" includes a film, a soundtrack and any other record in permanent form but does not include an indictment or other document prepared for use in particular legal proceedings.

(3) For the purposes of this section an assertion is published or included in a programme if the material published or included—

(a) names the person about whom the assertion is made or, without naming him, contains enough to make it likely that members of the public will identify him as the person about whom it is made, and

(b) reproduces the actual wording of the matter asserted or contains its substance.

60   Reporting of assertions: offences

(1) If an assertion is published or included in a relevant programme in contravention of section 59, each of the following persons is guilty of an offence—

(a) in the case of publication in a newspaper or periodical, any proprietor, any editor and any publisher of the newspaper or periodical;

(b) in the case of publication in any other form, the person publishing the assertion;

(c) in the case of an assertion included in a relevant programme, any body corporate engaged in providing the service in which the programme is included and any person having functions in relation to the programme corresponding to those of an editor of a newspaper.

(2) A person guilty of an offence under this section is liable on summary conviction to a fine of an amount not exceeding level 5 on the standard scale.

(3) Where a person is charged with an offence under this section it is a defence to prove that at the time of the alleged offence—

(a) he was not aware, and neither suspected nor had reason to suspect, that an order under section 58(7) or (8) had effect at that time, or

(b) he was not aware, and neither suspected nor had reason to suspect, that the publication or programme in question was of, or (as the case may be) included, the assertion in question.

(4)–(6) ★ ★ ★ ★ ★

★ ★ ★ ★ ★

Defamation Act 1996

(1996, c. 31)

An Act to amend the law of defamation and to amend the law of limitation with respect to actions for defamation or malicious falsehood.   [4 July 1996]

Territorial extent: United Kingdom

★ ★ ★ ★ ★

Evidence concerning proceedings in Parliament

13   Evidence concerning proceedings in Parliament

(1) Where the conduct of a person in or in relation to proceedings in Parliament is in issue in defamation proceedings, he may waive for the purposes of those proceedings, so far as concerns him, the protection of any enactment or rule of law which prevents proceedings in Parliament being impeached or questioned in any court or place out of Parliament.

(2) Where a person waives that protection—

(a) any such enactment or rule of law shall not apply to prevent evidence being given, questions being asked or statements, submissions, comments or findings being made about his conduct, and

(b) none of those things shall be regarded as infringing the privilege of either House of Parliament.

(3) The waiver by one person of that protection does not affect its operation in relation to another person who has not waived it.

(4) Nothing in this section affects any enactment or rule of law so far as it protects a person (including a person who has waived the protection referred to above) from legal liability for words spoken or things done in the course of, or for the purposes of or incidental to, any proceedings in Parliament.

(5) Without prejudice to the generality of subsection (4), that subsection applies to—

(a) the giving of evidence before either House or a committee;

(b) the presentation or submission of a document to either House or a committee;

(c) the preparation of a document for the purposes of or incidental to the transacting of any such business;

(d) the formulation, making or publication of a document, including a report, by or pursuant to an order of either House or a committee; and

(e) any communication with the Parliamentary Commissioner for Standards or any person having functions in connection with the registration of Members' interests.

In this subsection "a committee" means a committee of either House or a joint committee of both Houses of Parliament.

Statutory privilege

14   Reports of court proceedings absolutely privileged

(1) A fair and accurate report of proceedings in public before a court to which this section applies, if published contemporaneously with the proceedings, is absolutely privileged.

(2) A report of proceedings which by an order of the court, or as a consequence of any statutory provision, is required to be postponed shall be treated as published contemporaneously if it is published as soon as practicable after publication is permitted.

(3) This section applies to—

(a) any court in the United Kingdom,

(b) the European Court of Justice or any court attached to that court,

(c) the European Court of Human Rights, and

(d) any international criminal tribunal established by the Security Council of the United Nations or by an international agreement to which the United Kingdom is a party.

In paragraph (a) "court" includes any tribunal or body exercising the judicial power of the State.

(4) ★ ★ ★ ★ ★

15   Reports, &c. protected by qualified privilege

(1) The publication of any report or other statement mentioned in Schedule 1 to this Act is privileged unless the publication is shown to be made with malice, subject as follows.

(2) In defamation proceedings in respect of the publication of a report or other statement mentioned in Part II of that Schedule, there is no defence under this section if the plaintiff shows that the defendant—

(a) was requested by him to publish in a suitable manner a reasonable letter or statement by way of explanation or contradiction, and

(b) refused or neglected to do so. For this purpose "in a suitable manner" means in the same manner as the publication complained of or in a manner that is adequate and reasonable in the circumstances.

(3) This section does not apply to the publication to the public, or a section of the public, of matter which is not of public concern and the publication of which is not for the public benefit.

(4) Nothing in this section shall be construed—

(a) as protecting the publication of matter the publication of which is prohibited by law, or

(b) as limiting or abridging any privilege subsisting apart from this section.

16–19   ★ ★ ★ ★ ★

20   Short title and saving

(1) This Act may be cited as the Defamation Act 1996.

(2) Nothing in this Act affects the law relating to criminal libel.

SCHEDULES

SCHEDULE 1
QUALIFIED PRIVILEGE

PART I   STATEMENTS HAVING QUALIFIED PRIVILEGE WITHOUT EXPLANATION OR CONTRADICTION

1.   A fair and accurate report of proceedings in public of a legislature anywhere in the world.

2.   A fair and accurate report of proceedings in public before a court anywhere in the world.

3.   A fair and accurate report of proceedings in public of a person appointed to hold a public inquiry by a government or legislature anywhere in the world.

4.   A fair and accurate report of proceedings in public anywhere in the world of an international organisation or an international conference.

5.   A fair and accurate copy of or extract from any register or other document required by law to be open to public inspection.

6.   A notice or advertisement published by or on the authority of a court, or of a judge or officer of a court, anywhere in the world.

7.   A fair and accurate copy of or extract from matter published by or on the authority of a government or legislature anywhere in the world.

8.   A fair and accurate copy of or extract from matter published anywhere in the world by an international organisation or an international conference.

PART II   STATEMENTS PRIVILEGED SUBJECT TO EXPLANATION OR CONTRADICTION

9.—(1) A fair and accurate copy of or extract from a notice or other matter issued for the information of the public by or on behalf of—

 (a) a legislature in any member State or the European parliament;

 (b) the government of any member State, or any authority performing governmental functions in any member State or part of a member State, or the European Commission;

 (c) an international organisation or international conference.

(2) In this paragraph "governmental functions" includes police functions.

10.   A fair and accurate copy of or extract from a document made available by a court in any member State or the European Court of Justice (or any court attached to that court), or by a judge or officer of any such court.

11.—(1) A fair and accurate report of proceedings at any public meeting or sitting in the United Kingdom of—

 (a) a local authority [, local authority committee or in the case of a local authority which are operating executive arrangement, the executive of that authority or a committee of that executive];

 (b) a justice or justices of the peace acting otherwise than as a court exercising judicial authority;

 (c) a commission, tribunal, committee or person appointed for the purposes of any inquiry by any statutory provision, by Her Majesty or by a Minister of the Crown [a minister of the Scottish Executive] or a Northern Ireland Department;

 (d) a person appointed by a local authority to hold a local inquiry in pursuance of any statutory provision;

 (e) any other tribunal, board, committee or body constituted by or under, and exercising functions under, any statutory provision.

(1A), (2) ★ ★ ★ ★ ★

★ ★ ★ ★ ★

Education Act 1996

(1996, c. 56)

An Act to consolidate the Education Act 1944 and certain other enactments relating to education, with amendments to give effect to a recommendation of the Law Commission.   [24 July 1996]

Territorial extent: England and Wales

★ ★ ★ ★ ★

Sex education

403   Sex education: manner of provision

(1) The ... governing body and head teacher shall take such steps as are reasonably practicable to secure that where sex education is given to any registered pupils at a maintained school, it is given in such a manner as to encourage those pupils to have due regard to moral considerations and the value of family life.

[(1A) The Secretary of State must issue guidance designed to secure that when sex education is given to registered pupils at maintained schools—

(a) they learn the nature of marriage and its importance for family life and the bringing up of children, and

(b) they are protected from teaching and materials which are inappropriate having regard to the age and the religious and cultural background of the pupils concerned.

(1B) In discharging their functions under subsection (1) governing bodies and head teachers must have regard to the Secretary of State's guidance.

(1C) Guidance under subsection (1A) must include guidance about any material which may be producedby NHSbodies for use for the purposes of sex education in schools.

(1D) The Secretary of State may at any time revise his guidance under subsection (1A).]

(2) In [this section] "maintained school" includes a [community or foundation special school] established in a hospital, and "NHS Body" has the same meaning as in section 22 of the National Health Service Act 1977.

404   Sex education: statements of policy

(1) The governing body of a maintained school shall—

(a) make, and keep up to date, a separate written statement of their policy with regard to the provision of sex education, and

(b) make copies of the statement available for inspection (at all reasonable times) by parents of registered pupils at the school and provide a copy of the statement free of charge to any such parent who asks for one.

[(1A) A statement under subsection (1) must include a statement of the effect of section 405.]

(2) In subsection (1) "maintained school" includes, in relation to pupils who are provided with secondary education, a community or foundation special school established in a hospital.

(3) ...

405   Exemption from sex education

If the parent of any pupil in attendance at a maintained school requests that he may be wholly or partly excused from receiving sex education at the school, the pupil shall, except so far as such education is comprised in the National Curriculum, be so excused accordingly until the request is withdrawn.

Politics

406   Political indoctrination

(1) The local education authority, governing body and head teacher shall forbid—

(a) the pursuit of partisan political activities by any of those registered pupils at a maintained school who are junior pupils, and

(b) the promotion of partisan political views in the teaching of any subject in the school.

(2) In the case of activities which take place otherwise than on the school premises, subsection (1)(a) applies only where arrangements for junior pupils to take part in the activities are made by—

(a) any member of the school's staff (in his capacity as such), or

(b) anyone acting on behalf of the school or of a member of the school's staff (in his capacity as such).

(3) In this section "maintained school" includes a [community or foundation special school] established in a hospital.

407   Duty to secure balanced treatment of political issues

(1) The local education authority, governing body and head teacher shall take such steps as are reasonably practicable to secure that where political issues are brought to the attention of pupils while they are—

(a) in attendance at a maintained school, or

(b) taking part in extra-curricular activities which are provided or organised for registered pupils at the school by or on behalf of the school, they are offered a balanced presentation of opposing views.

(2) In this section "maintained school" includes a [community or foundation special school] established in a hospital.

★ ★ ★ ★ ★

Employment Rights Act 1996
(1996, c. 18)

An Act to consolidate enactments relating to employment rights.   [22 May 1996]

Territorial extent: England and Wales, Scotland

Note: The sections in Part XIII which are printed here apply to the civil service, the armed forces and parliamentary staff the major provisions of the Act, relating to contracts of employment, time off and maternity rights. The earlier sections (Part IVA) are added by the Public Interest Disclosure Act 1998.

★ ★ ★ ★ ★

[PART IVA   PROTECTED DISCLOSURES

43A   Meaning of "protected disclosure"

In this Act a "protected disclosure" means a qualifying disclosure (as defined by section 43B) which is made by a worker in accordance with any of sections 43C to 43H.

43B   Disclosures qualifying for protection

(1) In this Part a "qualifying disclosure" means any disclosure of information which, in

the reasonable belief of the worker making the disclosure, tends to show one or more of the following–

(a) that a criminal offence has been committed, is being committed or is likely to be committed,

(b) that a person has failed, is failing or is likely to fail to comply with any legal obligation to which he is subject,

(c) that a miscarriage of justice has occurred, is occurring or is likely to occur,

(d) that the health or safety of any individual has been, is being or is likely to be endangered,

(e) that the environment has been, is being or is likely to be damaged, or

(f) that information tending to show any matter falling within any one of the preceding paragraphs has been, is being or is likely to be deliberately concealed.

(2) For the purposes of subsection (1), it is immaterial whether the relevant failure occurred, occurs or would occur in the United Kingdom or elsewhere, and whether the law applying to it is that of the United Kingdom or of any other country or territory.

(3) A disclosure of information is not a qualifying disclosure if the person making the disclosure commits an offence by making it.

(4) A disclosure of information in respect of which a claim to legal professional privilege (or, in Scotland, to confidentiality as between client and professional legal adviser) could be maintained in legal proceedings is not a qualifying disclosure if it is made by a person to whom the information had been disclosed in the course of obtaining legal advice.

(5) In this Part "the relevant failure", in relation to a qualifying disclosure, means the matter falling within paragraphs (a) to (f) of subsection (1).

43C   Disclosure to employer or other responsible person

(1) A qualifying disclosure is made in accordance with this section if the worker makes the disclosure in good faith—

(a) to his employer, or

(b) where the worker reasonably believes that the relevant failure relates solely or mainly to—

(i) the conduct of a person other than his employer, or

(ii) any other matter for which a person other than his employer has legal responsibility,

to that other person.

(2) A worker who, in accordance with a procedure whose use by him is authorised by his employer, makes a qualifying disclosure to a person other than his employer, is to be treated for the purposes of this Part as making the qualifying disclosure to his employer.

43D   Disclosure to legal adviser

A qualifying disclosure is made in accordance with this section if it is made in the course of obtaining legal advice.

43E   Disclosure to Minister of the Crown

A qualifying disclosure is made in accordance with this section if—

(a) the worker's employer is—

(i) an individual appointed under any enactment [including any enactment comprised in or in an instrument made under an Act of the Scottish Parliament] by a Minister of the Crown, or

(ii) a body any of whose members are so appointed, and

(b) the disclosure is made in good faith to a Minister of the Crown.

43F   Disclosure to prescribed person

(1) A qualifying disclosure is made in accordance with this section if the worker—

(a) makes the disclosure in good faith to a person prescribed by an order made by the Secretary of State for the purposes of this section, and

(b) reasonably believes—

(i) that the relevant failure falls within any description of matters in respect of which that person is so prescribed, and

(ii) that the information disclosed, and any allegation contained in it, are substantially true.

(2) An order prescribing persons for the purposes of this section may specify persons or descriptions of persons, and shall specify the descriptions of matters in respect of which each person, or persons of each description, is or are prescribed.

43G Disclosure in other cases

(1) A qualifying disclosure is made in accordance with this section if—

(a) the worker makes the disclosure in good faith,

(b) he reasonably believes that the information disclosed, and any allegation contained in it, are substantially true,

(c) he does not make the disclosure for purposes of personal gain,

(d) any of the conditions in subsection (2) is met, and

(e) in all the circumstances of the case, it is reasonable for him to make the disclosure.

(2) The conditions referred to in subsection (1)(d) are—

(a) that, at the time he makes the disclosure, the worker reasonably believes that he will be subjected to a detriment by his employer if he makes a disclosure to his employer or in accordance with section 43F,

(b) that, in a case where no person is prescribed for the purposes of section 43F in relation to the relevant failure, the worker reasonably believes that it is likely that evidence relating to the relevant failure will be concealed or destroyed if he makes a disclosure to his employer, or

(c) that the worker has previously made a disclosure of substantially the same information—

(i) to his employer, or

(ii) in accordance with section 43F.

(3) In determining for the purposes of subsection (1)(c) whether it is reasonable for the worker to make the disclosure, regard shall be had, in particular, to—

(a) the identity of the person to whom the disclosure is made,

(b) the seriousness of the relevant failure,

(c) whether the relevant failure is continuing or is likely to occur in the future,

(d) whether the disclosure is made in breach of a duty of confidentiality owed by the employer to any other person,

(e) in a case falling within subsection (2)(c)(i) or (ii), any action which the employer or the person to whom the previous disclosure in accordance with section 43F was made has taken or might reasonably be expected to have taken as a result of the previous disclosure, and

(f) in a case falling within subsection (2)(c)(i), whether in making the disclosure to the employer the worker complied with any procedure whose use by him was authorised by the employer.

(4) For the purposes of this section a subsequent disclosure may be regarded as a disclosure of substantially the same information as that disclosed by a previous disclosure as mentioned in subsection (2)(c) even though the subsequent disclosure extends to information about action taken or not taken by any person as a result of the previous disclosure.

43H Disclosure of exceptionally serious failure

(1) A qualifying disclosure is made in accordance with this section if—

(a) the worker makes the disclosure in good faith,

(b) he reasonably believes that the information disclosed, and any allegation contained in it, are substantially true,

(c) he does not make the disclosure for purposes of personal gain,

(d) the relevant failure is of an exceptionally serious nature, and

(e) in all the circumstances of the case, it is reasonable for him to make the disclosure.

(2) In determining for the purposes of subsection (1)(e) whether it is reasonable for the worker to make the disclosure, regard shall be had, in particular, to the identity of the person to whom the disclosure is made.

43J   Contractual duties of confidentiality

(1) Any provision in an agreement to which this section applies is void in so far as it purports to preclude the worker from making a protected disclosure.

(2) This section applies to any agreement between a worker and his employer (whether a worker's contract or not), including an agreement to refrain from instituting or continuing any proceedings under this Act or any proceedings for breach of contract.

43K   Extension of meaning of "worker" etc. for Part IVA

(1) For the purposes of this Part "worker" includes an individual who is not a worker as defined by section 230(3) but who—

(a) works or worked for a person in circumstances in which—

(i) he is or was introduced or supplied to do that work by a third person, and

(ii) the terms on which he is or was engaged to do the work are or were in practice substantially determined not by him but by the person for whom he works or worked, by the third person or by both of them,

(b) contracts or contracted with a person, for the purposes of that person's business, for the execution of work to be done in a place not under the control or management of that person and would fall within section 230(3)(b) if for "personally" in that provision there were substituted "(whether personally or otherwise)",

(c) works or worked as a person providing general medical services, general dental services, general ophthalmic services or pharmaceutical services in accordance with arrangements made—

(i) by a Health Authority under section 29, 35, 38 or 41 of the National Health Service Act 1977, or

(ii) by a Health Board under section 19, 25, 26 or 27 of the National Health Service (Scotland) Act 1978, or

(d) is or was provided with work experience provided pursuant to a training course or programme or with training for employment (or with both) otherwise than—

(i) under a contract of employment, or

(ii) by an educational establishment on a course run by that establishment; and any reference to a worker's contract, to employment or to a worker being "employed" shall be construed accordingly.

(2) For the purposes of this Part "employer" includes—

(a) in relation to a worker falling within paragraph (a) of subsection (1), the person who substantially determines or determined the terms on which he is or was engaged,

(b) in relation to a worker falling within paragraph (c) of that subsection, the authority or board referred to in that paragraph, and

(c) in relation to a worker falling within paragraph (d) of that subsection, the person providing the work experience or training.

(3) In this section "educational establishment" includes any university, college, school or other educational establishment.]

43L–47A ★ ★ ★ ★ ★

[47B   Protected disclosures

(1) A worker has the right not to be subjected to any detriment by any act, or any deliberate failure to act, by his employer done on the ground that the worker has made a protected disclosure.]

(2), (3) ★ ★ ★ ★ ★

48–103 ★ ★ ★ ★ ★

[103A   Protected Disclosure

An employee who is dismissed shall be regarded for the purposes of this Part as unfairly dismissed if the reason (or, if more than one, the principal reason) for the dismissal is that the employee made a protected disclosure.]

104–190 ★ ★ ★ ★ ★

PART XIII   MISCELLANEOUS

CHAPTER I   PARTICULAR TYPES OF EMPLOYMENT

Crown employment etc.

191   Crown Employment

(1) Subject to sections 192 and 193, the provisions of this Act to which this section applies have effect in relation to Crown employment and persons in Crown employment as they have effect in relation to other employment and other employees or workers.

(2) This section applies to—

(a) Parts I to III,

[(aa) Part IVA,]

(b) Part V, apart from section 45,

(c) Parts VI to VIII,

(d) in Part IX, sections 92 and 93,

(e) Part X, apart from section 101, and

(f) this Part and Parts XIV and XV.

(3) In this Act "Crown employment" means employment under or for the purposes of a government department or any officer or body exercising on behalf of the Crown functions conferred by a statutory provision.

(4) For the purposes of the application of provisions of this Act in relation to Crown employment in accordance with subsection (1)—

(a) references to an employee or a worker shall be construed as references to a person in Crown employment,

(b) references to a contract of employment, or a worker's contract, shall be construed as references to the terms of employment of a person in Crown employment,

(c) references to dismissal, or to the termination of a worker's contract, shall be construed as references to the termination of Crown employment,

(d) references to redundancy shall be construed as references to the existence of such circumstances as are treated, in accordance with any arrangements falling within section 177(3) for the time being in force, as equivalent to redundancy in relation to Crown employment, and

(e) references to an undertaking shall be construed—

(i) in relation to a Minister of the Crown, as references to his functions or (as the context may require) to the department of which he is in charge, and

(ii) in relation to a government department, officer or body, as references to the functions of the department, officer or body or (as the context may require) to the department, officer or body.

(5) Where the terms of employment of a person in Crown employment restrict his right to take part in—

    (a) certain political activities, or

    (b) activities which may conflict with his official functions, nothing in section 50 requires him to be allowed time off work for public duties connected with any such activities.

  (6) ★ ★ ★ ★ ★

192 Armed forces

  (1) Section 191—

    (a) applies to service as a member of the naval, military or air forces of the Crown but subject to the following provisions of this section, and

    (b) applies to employment by an association established for the purposes of Part XI of the Reserve Forces Act 1996.

  (2) The provisions of this Act which have effect by virtue of section 191 in relation to service as a member of the naval, military or air forces of the Crown are—

    (a) Part I,

    [(aa) in Part V, section 45A, and sections 48 and 49 so far as relating to that section,]

    (b) in Part VI, sections 55 to 57,

    (c) Parts VII and VIII,

    (d) in Part IX, sections 92 and 93,

    (e) Part X, apart from sections 100 to 103 and 134, and

    (f) this Part and Parts XIV and XV.

  (3) Her Majesty may by Order in Council—

    (a) amend subsection (2) by making additions to, or omissions from, the provisions for the time being specified in that subsection, and

    (b) make any provision for the time being so specified apply to service as a member of the naval, military or air forces of the Crown subject to such exceptions and modifications as may be specified in the Order in Council,

but no provision contained in Part II may be added to the provisions for the time being specified in subsection (2).

  (4)–(8) ★ ★ ★ ★ ★

193 National security

  (1) The provisions of this Act to which this section applies do not have effect in relation to any Crown employment in respect of which there is in force a certificate issued by or on behalf of a Minister of the Crown certifying that employment of a description specified in the certificate, or the employment of a particular person so specified, is (or, at a time specified in the certificate, was) required to be excepted from those provisions for the purpose of safeguarding national security.

  (2) This section applies to—

    (a) Part I, so far as it relates to itemised pay statements,

    (b) Part III,

    [(bb) Part IVA,]

    [(bc) in Part V, section 47B,]

    (c) in Part VI, sections 50 to 54,

    (d) in Part VII, sections 64 and 65, and sections 69 and 70 so far as relating to those sections,

    (e) in Part IX, sections 92 and 93, except where they apply by virtue of section 92(4),

    (f) Part X, except so far as relating to a dismissal which is treated as unfair—

        (i) by section 99(1) to (3), 100 or 103, or

        (ii) by subsection (1) of section 105 by reason of the application or subsection (2), (3) or (6) of that section, and

(g) this Part and Parts XIV and XV (so far as relating to any of the provisions specified in paragraphs (a) to (f)).

(3) Any document purporting to be a certificate issued as mentioned in subsection (1)—

(a) shall be received in evidence, and

(b) unless the contrary is proved, shall be deemed to be such a certificate.

[(4) Part IVA and sections 47B and 103A do not have effect in relation to employment for the purposes of the Security Service, the Secret Intelligence Service or the Government Communication Headquarters.]

★ ★ ★ ★ ★

Police Act 1996
(1996, c. 16)

An Act to consolidate the Police Act 1964, Part IX of the Police and Criminal Evidence Act 1984, Chapter I of Part I of the Police and Magistrates' Courts Act 1994 and certain other enactments relating to the police.   [22 May 1996]

Territorial extent: England and Wales (and in the case of Part III (ss. 59–64) Scotland).

PART I   ORGANISATION OF POLICE FORCES

Police areas

1   Police areas

(1) England and Wales shall be divided into police areas.

(2) The police areas referred to in subsection (1) shall be—

(a) those listed in Schedule 1 (subject to any amendment made to that Schedule by an order under section 32 below, section 58 of the Local Government Act 1972, or section 17 of the Local Government Act 1992),

(b) the metropolitan police district, and

(c) the City of London police area.

(3) References in Schedule 1 to any local government area are to that area as it is for the time being . . .

Forces outside London

2   Maintenance of police forces

A police force shall be maintained for every police area for the time being listed in Schedule 1.

3   Establishment of police authorities

(1) There shall be a police authority for every police area for the time being listed in Schedule 1.

(2) A police authority established under this section for any area shall be a body corporate to be known by the name of the area with the adddition of the words "Police Authority".

4   Membership of police authorities etc.

(1) Subject to subsection (2), each police authority established under section 3 shall consist of seventeen members.

(2) The Secretary of State may by order provide in relation to a police authority specified in the order that the number of its members shall be a specified odd number greater than seventeen.

(3) A statutory instrument containing an order under subsection (2) shall be laid before Parliament after being made.

(4) Schedules 2 and 3 shall have effect in relation to police authorities established under section 3 and the appointment of their members.

5   Reduction in size of police authorities etc.

(1) This section applies to any order under section 4(2) which varies or revokes an earlier order so as to reduce the number of a police authority's members.

(2) Before making an order to which this section applies, the Secretary of State shall consult—

    (a) the authority,

    (b) the councils which are relevant councils in relation to the authority for the purposes of Schedule 2, and

    (c) any selection panel, constituted under regulations made in accordance with [section 29(2) of the Justices of the Peace Act 1997], which is responsible, or is represented on a joint committee which is responsible, for the appointment of members of the authority.

(3) An order to which this section applies may include provision as to the termination of the appointment of the existing members of the authority and the making of new appointments or re-appointments.

[The metropolitan police force

5A   Maintenance of the metropolitan police force
A police force shall be maintained for the metropolitan police district.

5B   Establishment of the Metropolitan Police Authority
(1) There shall be a police authority for the metropolitan police district.

(2) The police authority established under this section shall be a body corporate to be known as the Metropolitan Police Authority.

5C   Membership etc. of the Metropolitan Police Authority
(1) The Metropolitan Police Authority shall consist of twenty three members (subject to subsection (2)).

(2) The Secretary of State may by order provide that the number of members of the Metropolitan Police Authority shall be a specified odd number not less than seventeen.

(3) Before making an order under subsection (2) which reduces the number of members of the Metropolitan Police Authority, the Secretary of State shall consult—

    (a) the Greater London Authority;

    (b) the Metropolitan Police Authority; and

    (c) the person or body responsible for the appointment of members of the Greater London Magistrates' Courts authority under regulations made under section 30B of the Justices of the Peace Act 1997 (which, by virtue of paragraph 5(b) of Schedule 2A to this Act, appoints magistrates to be members of the Metropolitan Police Authority).

(4) An order under subsection (2) which reduces the number of members of the Metropolitan Police Authority may include provision as to the termination of the appointment of the existing members of the Metropolitan Police Authority and the making of new appointments or re-appointments.

(5) A statutory instrument containing an order under subsection (2) shall be laid before Parliament after being made.

(6) Schedules 2A and 3 shall have effect in relation to the Metropolitan Police Authority and the appointment of its members.

The metropolitan police and forces outside London]

6   General functions of police authorities

(1) Every police authority established under section 3 shall secure the maintenance of an efficient and effective police force for its area.

(2) In discharging its functions, every police authority established under section 3 shall have regard to—

(a) any objectives determined by the Secretary of State under section 37,

(b) any objectives determined by the authority under section 7,

(c) any performance targets established by the authority, whether in compliance with a direction under section 38 or otherwise, and

(d) any local policing plan issued by the authority under section 8.

(3) In discharging any function to which a code of practice issued under section 39 relates, a police authority established under section 3 shall have regard to the code.

(4) A police authority shall comply with any direction given to it by the Secretary of State under section 38 or 40.

[(5) This section shall apply in relation to the Metropolitan Police Authority as it applies in relation to a police authority established under section 3.]

7   Local policing objectives

(1) Every police authority established under section 3 shall, before the beginning of each financial year, determine objectives for the policing of the authority's area during that year.

(2) Objectives determined under this section may relate to matters to which objectives determined under section 37 also relate, or to other matters, but in any event shall be so framed as to be consistent with the objectives determined under that section.

(3) Before determining objectives under this section, a police authority shall—

(a) consult the chief constable for the area, and

(b) consider any views obtained by the authority in accordance with arrangements made under section 96.

8   Local policing plan

(1) Every police authority established under section 3 shall, before the beginning of each financial year, issue a plan setting out the proposed arrangements for the policing of the authority's area during the year ("the local policing plan").

(2) The local policing plan shall include a statement of the authority's priorities for the year, of the financial resources expected to be available and of the proposed allocation of those resources, and shall give particulars of—

(a) any objectives determined by the Secretary of State under section 37,

(b) any objectives determined by the authority under section 7, . . .

(c) any performance targets established by the authority, whether in compliance with a direction under section 38 or otherwise [; and

(d) any action proposed for the purpose of complying with the requirements of Part I of the Local Government Act 1999 (best value)].

(3) A draft of the local policing plan shall be prepared by the chief constable for the area and submitted by him to the police authority for it to consider.

(4) Before issuing a local policing plan which differs from the draft submitted by the chief constable under subsection (3), a police authority shall consult the chief constable.

(5) A police authority shall arrange for every local policing plan issued by it under this section to be published in such manner as appears to it to be appropriate, and shall send a copy of the plan to the Secretary of State.

9   Annual reports by police authorities

(1) As soon as possible after the end of each financial year every police authority

established under section 3 shall issue a report relating to the policing of the authority's area for the year.

(2) A report issued by a police authority under this section for any year shall include an assessment of the extent to which the local policing plan for that year issued under section 8 has been carried out.

(3) A police authority shall arrange for every report issued by it under this section to be published in such manner as appears to it to be appropriate, and shall send a copy of the report to the Secretary of State.

[9A General functions of the Commissioner of Police of the Metropolis

(1) The metropolitan police force shall be under the direction and control of the Commissioner of Police of the Metropolis appointed under section 9B.

(2) In discharging his functions, the Commissioner of Police of the Metropolis shall have regard to the local policing plan issued by the Metropolitan Police Authority under section 8.

9B Appointment of Commissioner of Police of the Metropolis

(1) There shall be a Commissioner of Police of the Metropolis.

(2) Any appointment of a Commissioner of Police of the Metropolis shall be made by Her Majesty by warrant under Her sign manual.

(3) A person appointed as Commissioner of Police of the Metropolis shall hold office at Her Majesty's pleasure.

(4) Any appointment of a Commissioner of Police of the Metropolis shall be subject to regulations under section 50.

(5) Before recommending to Her Majesty that She appoint a person as the Commissioner of Police of the Metropolis, the Secretary of State shall have regard to—

(a) any recommendations made to him by the Metropolitan Police Authority; and

(b) any representations made to him by the Mayor of London.

(6) Any functions exercisable by the Mayor of London under subsection (5) may only be exercised by him personally.

9C Functions of Deputy Commissioner of Police of the Metropolis

(1) The Deputy Commissioner of Police of the Metropolis may exercise any or all of the powers and duties of the Commissioner of Police of the Metropolis—

(a) during any absence, incapacity or suspension from duty of the Commissioner,

(b) during any vacancy in the office of the Commissioner, or

(c) at any other time, with the consent of the Commissioner.

(2) The Deputy Commissioner of Police of the Metropolis shall not have power to act by virtue of subsection (1)(a) or (b) for a continuous period exceeding three months, except with the consent of the Secretary of State.

(3) The Deputy Commissioner of Police of the Metropolis shall also have all the powers and duties of an Assistant Commissioner of Police of the Metropolis.

9D Appointment of Deputy Commissioner of Police of the Metropolis

(1) There shall be a Deputy Commissioner of Police of the Metropolis.

(2) Any appointment of a Deputy Commissioner shall be made by Her Majesty by warrant under Her sign manual.

(3) A person appointed as the Deputy Commissioner shall hold office at Her Majesty's pleasure.

(4) Any appointment of a Deputy Commissioner shall be subject to regulations under section 50.

(5) Before recommending to Her Majesty that She appoint a person as the Deputy Commissioner, the Secretary of State shall have regard to—

(a) any recommendations made to him by the Metropolitan Police Authority; and

(b) any representations made to him by the Commissioner.

(6) In this section—

"the Commissioner" means the Commissioner of Police of the Metropolis;

"Deputy Commissioner" means Deputy Commissioner of Police of the Metropolis.

9E   Removal of Commissioner or Deputy Commissioner

(1) The Metropolitan Police Authority, acting with the approval of the Secretary of State, may call upon the Commissioner of Police of the Metropolis to retire in the interests of efficiency or effectiveness.

(2) Before seeking the approval of the Secretary of State under subsection (1), the Metropolitan Police Authority shall give the Commissioner of Police of the Metropolis an opportunity to make representations and shall consider any representations that he makes.

(3) Where the Commissioner of Police of the Metropolis is called upon to retire under subsection (1), he shall retire on such date as the Metropolitan Police Authority may specify or on such earlier date as may be agreed upon between him and the Authority.

(4) This section shall apply in relation to the Deputy Commissioner of Police of the Metropolis as it applies to the Commissioner of Police of the Metropolis.

(5) This section is without prejudice to—

    (a) section 9B(3),

    (b) section 9D(3),

    (c) any regulations under section 50, or

    (d) any regulations under the Police Pensions Act 1976.

9F   Assistant Commissioners of Police of the Metropolis

(1) The ranks that may be held in the metropolitan police force shall include that of Assistant Commissioner of Police of the Metropolis ("Assistant Commissioner").

(2) Any appointment of an Assistant Commissioner shall be made by the Metropolitan Police Authority, but subject to the approval of the Secretary of State and to regulations under section 50.

(3) Subsections (1) to (3) of section 9E shall apply in relation to an Assistant Commissioner as they apply to the Commissioner of Police of the Metropolis.

(4) Subsection (3) is without prejudice to—

    (a) any regulations under section 50, or

    (b) any regulations under the Police Pensions Act 1976.

(5) An Assistant Commissioner may exercise any of the powers and duties of the Commissioner of Police of the Metropolis with the consent of the Commissioner.

(6) Subsection (5) is without prejudice to any regulations under section 50.

9FA   ★ ★ ★ ★ ★

9G   Commanders

(1) The ranks that may be held in the metropolitan police force shall include that of Commander.

(2) Any appointment of a Commander in the metropolitan police force shall be made by the Metropolitan Police Authority, but subject to the approval of the Secretary of State and to regulations under section 50.

(3) Subsections (1) to (3) of section 9E shall apply in relation to a Commander in the metropolitan police force as they apply to the Commissioner of Police of the Metropolis.

(4) Subsection (3) is without prejudice to—

    (a) any regulations under section 50, or

    (b) any regulations under the Police Pensions Act 1976.

9H   Other members of the metropolitan police force

(1) The ranks that may be held in the metropolitan police force shall be such as may be prescribed by regulations under section 50.

(2) The ranks so prescribed in the case of the metropolitan police force shall include, in addition to the ranks of—

   (a) Commissioner of Police of the Metropolis,
   (b) Deputy Commissioner of Police of the Metropolis,
   (c) Assistant Commissioner of Police of the Metropolis,
   [(ca) Deputy Assistant Commissioner of Police of the Metropolis, and]
   (d) Commander,

those of [chief superintendent,] superintendent, chief inspector, inspector, sergeant and constable.

(3) In the metropolitan police force, appointments and promotions to any rank below that of Commander shall be made in accordance with regulations under section 50 by the Commissioner of Police of the Metropolis.]

10 General functions of chief constables

(1) A police force maintained under section 2 shall be under the direction and control of the chief constable appointed under section 11.

(2) In discharging his functions, every chief constable shall have regard to the local policing plan issued by the police authority for his area under section 8.

11 Appointment and removal of chief constables

(1) The chief constable of a police force maintained under section 2 shall be appointed by the police authority responsible for maintaining the force, but subject to the approval of the Secretary of State and to regulations under section 50.

(2) Without prejudice to any regulations under section 50 or under the Police Pensions Act 1976, the police authority, acting with the approval of the Secretary of State, may call upon the chief constable to retire in the interests of efficiency or effectiveness.

(3) Before seeking the approval of the Secretary of State under subsection (2), the police authority shall give the chief constable an opportunity to make representations and shall consider any representations that he makes.

(4) A chief constable who is called upon to retire under subsection (2) shall retire on such date as the police authority may specify or on such earlier date as may be agreed upon between him and the authority.

[11A Appointment and removal of deputy chief constables

(1) Every police force maintained under section 2 shall have a deputy chief constable.

(2) The appointment of a person to be the deputy chief constable of a police force shall be made, in accordance with regulations under section 50, by the police authority responsible for maintaining that force. but only after consultation with the chief constable and subject to the approval of the Secretary of State.

(3) Subsections (2) to (4) of section 11 shall apply in relation to a deputy chief constable as they apply in relation to a chief constable.]

12 Assistant chief constables

(1) The ranks that may be held in a police force maintained under section 2 shall include that of assistant chief constable; and in every such police force there shall be at least one person holding that rank.

(2) Appointments and promotions to the rank of assistant chief constable shall be made, in accordance with regulations under section 50, by the police authority after consultation with the chief constable and subject to the approval of the Secretary of State.

(3) Subsections (2), (3) and (4) of section 11 shall apply to an assistant chief constable as they apply to a chief constable.

   (4)–(6) ...

[12A Power of deputy to exercise functions of chief constable

(1) A deputy chief constable of a police force may exercise or perform any or all of the powers or duties of the chief constable of that force—

(a) during any absence, incapacity or suspension from duty of the chief constable,

(b) during any vacancy in the office of the chief constable, or

(c) at any other time, with the consent of the chief constable.

(2) A police authority responsible for maintaining a police force may designate a person holding the rank of assistant chief constable in that force to exercise or perform any or all of the powers or duties of the chief constable of that force—

(a) during any absence, incapacity or suspension from duty of both the chief constable and the deputy chief constable, or

(b) during any vacancy in the offices of both the chief constable and the deputy chief constable.

(3) Only one person shall be authorised to act at any one time by virtue of a designation under subsection (2).

(4) The power to act by virtue of subsection (1)(a) or (b) or subsection (2) shall not be exercisable for a continuous period exceeding three months except with the consent of the Secretary of State.

(5) The provisions of subsections (1) and (2) shall be without prejudice to any other enactment that makes provision for the exercise by any other person of powers conferred on a chief constable.]

13   Other members of police forces

(1) The ranks that may be held in a police force maintained under section 2 shall be such as may be prescribed by regulations under section 50 and the ranks so prescribed shall include, in addition to chief constable [, deputy chief constable] and assistant chief constable, the ranks of [chief superintendent], superintendent, chief inspector, inspector, sergeant and constable.

(2) ...

(3) Appointments and promotions to any rank below that of assistant chief constable in any police force maintained under section 2 shall be made, in accordance with regulations under section 50, by the chief constable.

14   Police fund

(1) Each police authority established under section 3 shall keep a fund to be known as the police fund.

(2) Subject to any regulations under the Police Pensions Act 1976, all receipts of the police authority shall be paid into the police fund and all expenditure of the authority shall be paid out of that fund.

(3) Accounts shall be kept by each police authority of payments made into or out of the police fund.

15-19   ★ ★ ★ ★ ★

20   Questions on police matters at council meetings

(1) Every relevant council shall make arrangements (whether by standing orders or otherwise) for enabling questions on the discharge of the functions of a police authority to be put by members of the council at a meeting of the council for answer by a person nominated by the authority for that purpose.

(2) On being given reasonable notice by a relevant council of a meeting of that council at which questions on the discharge of the police authority's functions are to be put, the police authority shall nominate one or more of its members to attend the meeting to answer those questions.

(3) In this section "relevant council" has the same meaning as in Schedule 2.

21   ★ ★ ★ ★ ★

General provisions

22   Reports by chief constables to police authorities

(1) Every chief constable shall, as soon as possible after the end of each financial year, submit to the police authority a general report on the policing during that year of the area for which his force is maintained.

(2) A chief constable shall arrange for a report submitted by him under subsection (1) to be published in such manner as appears to him to be appropriate.

(3) The chief constable of a police force shall, whenever so required by the police authority, submit to that authority a report on such matters as may be specified in the requirement, being matters connected with the policing of the area for which the force is maintained.

(4) A report submitted under subsection (3) shall be in such form as the police authority may specify.

(5) If it appears to the chief constable that a report in compliance with subsection (3) would contain information which in the public interest ought not to be disclosed, or is not needed for the discharge of the functions of the police authority, he may request that authority to refer the requirement to submit the report to the Secretary of State; and in any such case the requirement shall be of no effect unless it is confirmed by the Secretary of State.

(6) The police authority may arrange, or require the chief constable to arrange, for a report submitted under subsection (3) to be published in such manner as appears to the authority to be appropriate.

. . .

23–24   ★ ★ ★ ★ ★

25   Provision of special services

(1) The chief officer of police of a police force may provide, at the request of any person, special police services at any premises or in any locality in the police area for which the force is maintained, subject to the payment to the police authority of charges on such scales as may be determined by the authority.

(1A) ★ ★ ★ ★ ★

26–28   ★ ★ ★ ★ ★

29   Attestation of constables

Every member of a police force maintained for a police area and every special constable appointed for a police area shall, on appointment, be attested as a constable by making a declaration in the form set out in Schedule 4—

(a) in the case of a member of the metropolitan police force or a special constable appointed for the metropolitan police district, before the Commissioner or an Assistant Commissioner of Police of the Metropolis, and

(b) . . . before a justice of the peace having jurisdiction within the police area.

30   Jurisdiction of constables

(1) A member of a police force shall have all the powers and privileges of a constable throughout England and Wales and the adjacent United Kingdom waters.

(2) A special constable shall have all the powers and privileges of a constable in the police area for which he is appointed and, where the boundary of that area includes the coast, in the adjacent United Kingdom waters.

(3), (3A)–(6) ★ ★ ★ ★ ★

31   . . .

Alteration of police areas

32   Power to alter police areas by order

(1) The Secretary of State may by order make alterations in police areas in England and Wales other than the City of London police area.

(2) The alterations that may be made by an order under this section include alterations that result in a reduction or an increase in the number of police areas, but not alterations that result in the abolition of the metropolitan police district.

(3) The Secretary of State shall not exercise his power under this section to make alterations unless either—

(a) he has received a request to make the alterations from the police authority for each of the areas . . . affected by them, or

(b) it appears to him to be expedient to make the alterations in the interests of efficiency or effectiveness.

(4), (5) ★ ★ ★ ★ ★

33–35 ★ ★ ★ ★ ★

PART II   CENTRAL SUPERVISION, DIRECTION AND FACILITIES

Functions of Secretary of State

36   General duty of Secretary of State

(1) The Secretary of State shall exercise his powers under the provisions of this Act referred to in subsection (2) in such manner and to such extent as appears to him to be best calculated to promote the efficiency and effectiveness of the police.

(2) The provisions of this Act mentioned in subsection (1) are—

(a) Part I;

(b) this Part;

(c) Part III (other than sections 61 and 62);

(d) in Chapter II of Part IV, section 85 and Schedule 6; and

(e) in Part V, section 95.

37   Setting of objectives for police authorities

(1) The Secretary of State may by order determine objectives for the policing of the areas of all police authorities established under section 3.

(2) Before making an order under this section the Secretary of State shall consult—

(a) persons whom he considers to represent the interests of police authorities established under section 3, and

(b) persons whom he considers to represent the interests of chief constables of forces maintained by those authorities.

(3) A statutory instrument containing an order under this section shall be laid before Parliament after being made.

38   Setting of performance targets

(1) Where an objective has been determined under section 37, the Secretary of State may direct police authorities to establish levels of performance ("performance targets") to be aimed at in seeking to achieve the objective.

(2) A direction under this section may be given to all police authorities established under section 3 or to one or more particular authorities.

(3) A direction given under this section may impose conditions with which the performance targets must conform, and different conditions may be imposed for different authorities.

(4) The Secretary of State shall arrange for any direction given under this section to be published in such manner as appears to him to be appropriate.

39   Codes of practice

(1) The Secretary of State may issue codes of practice relating to the discharge by police authorities established under section 3 of any of their functions.

(2) The Secretary of State may from time to time revise the whole or part of any code of practice issued under this section.

(3) The Secretary of State shall lay before Parliament a copy of any code of practice, and of any revision of a code of practice, issued by him under this section.

40 Power to give directions to police authorities after adverse reports

(1) The Secretary of State may at any time require the inspectors of constabulary to carry out, for the purposes of this section, an inspection under section 54 of any police force maintained under section 2.

(2) Where a report made to the Secretary of State under section 54 on an inspection carried out for the purposes of this section states—

(a) that, in the opinion of the person making the report, the force inspected is not efficient or not effective, or

(b) that in his opinion, unless remedial measures are taken, the force will cease to be efficient or will cease to be effective,

the Secretary of State may direct the police authority responsible for maintaining the force to take such measures as may be specified in the direction.

41 Directions as to minimum budget

(1) The power of the Secretary of State to give directions under section 40 to a police authority established under section 3 shall include power to direct the authority that the amount of its budget requirement for any financial year (under section 43 of the Local Government Finance Act 1992) shall not be less than an amount specified in the direction.

(2) The power exercisable by virtue of subsection (1), and any direction given under that power, are subject to any limitation imposed under Chapter V of Part I of the Local Government Finance Act 1992.

(3) A direction shall not be given by virtue of subsection (1) in relation to a financial year at any time after the end of the preceding December.

(4) Where the Secretary of State gives a direction to a police authority by virtue of subsection (1), any precept issued or calculation made by the authority under Part I of the Local Government Finance Act 1992 which is inconsistent with the direction shall be void.

42 Removal of chief constables, etc.

(1) The Secretary of State may require a police authority to exercise its power under section 11 to call upon the chief constable to retire in the interests of efficiency or effectiveness.

(2) Before requiring the exercise of that power or approving the exercise of that or the similar power exercisable with respect to [a deputy chief constable or] an assistant chief constable, the Secretary of State shall give the chief constable [, the deputy chief constable or, as the case may be, the assistant chief constable] an opportunity to make representations to him and shall consider any representations so made.

(3) Where representations are made under this section the Secretary of State may, and in a case where he proposes to require the exercise of the power mentioned in subsection (1) shall, appoint one or more persons (one at least of whom shall be a person who is not an officer of police or of a Government department) to hold an inquiry and report to him and shall consider any report made under this subsection.

(4) The costs incurred by a chief constable [, deputy chief constable] or assistant chief constable in respect of an inquiry under this section, taxed in such manner as the Secretary of State may direct, shall be defrayed out of the police fund.

(5) ★ ★ ★ ★ ★

43 Reports from police authorities

(1) A police authority shall, whenever so required by the Secretary of State, submit to the Secretary of State a report on such matters connected with the discharge of the authority's functions, or otherwise with the policing of its area, as may be specified in the requirement.

(2) A requirement under subsection (1) may specify the form in which a report is to be given.

(3) The Secretary of State may arrange, or require the police authority to arrange, for a report under this section to be published in such manner as appears to him to be appropriate.

44 Reports from chief constables

(1) The Secretary of State may require a chief constable to submit to him a report on such matters as may be specified in the requirement, being matters connected with the policing of the chief constable's police area.

(2) A requirement under subsection (1) may specify the form in which a report is to be given.

(3) The Secretary of State may arrange, or require the chief constable to arrange, for a report under this section to be published in such manner as appears to the Secretary of State to be appropriate.

(4) Every chief constable shall, as soon as possible after the end of each financial year, submit to the Secretary of State the like report as is required by section 22(1) to be submitted to the police authority.

. . .

45 ★ ★ ★ ★ ★

46 Police grant

(1) Subject to the following provisions of this section, the Secretary of State shall for each financial year make grants for police purposes to—
(a) police authorities for areas other than the metropolitan police district, and
(b) the Receiver for the Metropolitan Police District; and in those provisions references to police authorities shall be taken as including references to the Receiver.

(2) For each financial year the Secretary of State shall with the approval of the Treasury determine—
(a) the aggregate amount of grants to be made under this section, and
(b) the amount of the grant to be made to each authority; and any determination may be varied by further determinations under this subsection.

(3) The Secretary of State shall prepare a report setting out any determination under subsection (2), and stating the considerations which he took into account in making the determination.

(4) In determining the allocation among police authorities of the whole or any part of the aggregate amount of grants, the Secretary of State may exercise his discretion by applying such formulae or other rules as he considers appropriate.

(5) The considerations which the Secretary of State takes into account in making a determination under subsection (2), and the formulae and other rules referred to in subsection (4), may be different for different authorities or different classes of authority.

(6)–(8) ★ ★ ★ ★ ★

47–49 ★ ★ ★ ★ ★

50 Regulations for police forces

(1) Subject to the provisions of this section, the Secretary of State may make regulations as to the government, administration and conditions or service of police forces.

(2) Without prejudice to the generality of subsection (1), regulations under this section may make provision with respect to—
(a) the ranks to be held by members of police forces;
(b) the qualifications for appointment and promotion of members of police forces;
(c) periods of service on probation;
(d) voluntary retirement of members of police forces;

(e) the conduct, efficiency and effectiveness of members of police forces and the maintenance of discipline;

(f) the suspension of members of a police force from membership of that force and from their office as constable;

(g) the maintenance of personal records of members of police forces;

(h) the duties which are or are not to be performed by members of police forces;

(i) the treatment as occasions of police duty of attendance at meetings of the Police Federations and of any body recognised by the Secretary of State for the purposes of section 64;

(j) the hours of duty, leave, pay and allowances of members of police forces; and

(k) the issue, use and return of police clothing, personal equipment and accoutrements.

(3) Without prejudice to the powers conferred by this section, regulations under this section shall—

(a) establish, or make provision for the establishment of, procedures for cases in which a member of a police force may be dealt with by dismissal, requirement to resign, reduction in rank, reduction in rate of pay, fine, reprimand or caution, and

(b) make provision for securing that any case in which a senior officer may be dismissed or dealt with in any of the other ways mentioned in paragraph (a) is decided—

(i) where he is a member of the metropolitan police force, by the Commissioner of Police of the Metropolis, and

(ii) where he is a member of any other force, by the police authority which maintains the force or by a committee of that authority.

For the purposes of this subsection "senior officer" means a member of a police force holding a rank above that of [chief] superintendent.

(4) In relation to any matter as to which provision may be made by regulations under this section, the regulations may, subject to subsection (3)(b),—

(a) authorise or require provision to be made by, or confer discretionary powers on, the Secretary of State, police authorities, chief officers of police or other persons, or

(b) authorise or require the delegation by any person of functions conferred on that person by or under the regulations.

(5) Regulations under this section for regulating pay and allowances may be made with retrospective effect to any date specified in the regulations, but nothing in this subsection shall be construed as authorising pay or allowances payable to any person to be reduced retrospectively.

(6) Regulations under this section as to conditions of service shall secure that appointments for fixed terms are not made except where the person appointed holds the rank of superintendent or a higher rank.

(7), (8) ★ ★ ★ ★ ★

51–53 ★ ★ ★ ★ ★

Inspectors of constabulary

54 Appointment and functions of inspectors of constabulary

(1) Her Majesty may appoint such number of inspectors (to be known as "Her Majesty's Inspectors of Constabulary") as the Secretary of State may with the consent of the Treasury determine, and of the persons so appointed one may be appointed as chief inspector of constabulary.

(2) The inspectors of constabulary shall inspect, and report to the Secretary of State on

the efficiency and effectiveness of, every police force maintained for a police area [and the National Criminal Intelligence Service . . . the National Crime Squad] [and the Central Police Training and Development Authority].

[(2A) The inspectors of constabulary may inspect, and report to the Secretary of State on, a police authority's compliance with the requirements of Part I of the Local Government Act 1999 (best value).]

(3) The inspectors of constabulary shall carry out such other duties for the purpose of furthering police efficiency and effectiveness as the Secretary of State may from time to time direct.

(4) The chief inspector of constabulary shall in each year submit to the Secretary of State a report in such form as the Secretary of State may direct, and the Secretary of State shall lay a copy of that report before Parliament.

(5) The inspectors of constabulary shall be paid such salary and allowances as the Secretary of State may with the consent of the Treasury determine.

55   Publication of reports

(1) Subject to subsection (2), the Secretary of State shall arrange for any report received by him under section 54(2) [or (2A)] to be published in such manner as appears to him to be appropriate.

(2) The Secretary of State may exclude from publication under subsection (1) any part of a report if, in his opinion, the publication of that part—

(a) would be against the interests of national security, or

(b) might jeopardise the safety of any person.

(3) The Secretary of State shall send a copy of the published report—

(a) . . . to the police authority maintaining the police force to which the report relates, and

(b) to the chief officer of police of that police force.

(4) The police authority shall invite the chief officer of police to submit comments on the published report to the authority before such date as it may specify.

(5) The police authority shall prepare comments on the published report and shall arrange for–

(a) its comments,

(b) any comments submitted by the chief officer of police in accordance with subsection (4), and

(c) any response which the authority has to the comments submitted by the chief officer of police,

to be published in such manner as appears to the authority to be appropriate.

(6) The police authority (except where it is the Secretary of State) shall send a copy of any document published under subsection (5) to the Secretary of State.

(7), (8) ★ ★ ★ ★ ★

56–58 ★ ★ ★ ★ ★

PART III   POLICE REPRESENTATIVE INSTITUTIONS

59   Police Federation

(1) There shall continue to be a Police Federation for England and Wales and a Police Federation of Scotland for the purpose of representing members of the police forces in those countries respectively in all matters affecting their welfare and efficiency, except for—

(a) questions of promotion affecting individuals, and

(b) (subject to subsection (2)) questions of discipline affecting individuals.

(2) A Police Federation may represent a member of a police force at any proceedings

brought under regulations made in accordance with section 50(3) above or section 26(2A) of the Police (Scotland) Act 1967 or on an appeal from any such proceedings.

(3) Except on an appeal to a police appeals tribunal or as provided by section 84, a member of a police force may only be represented under subsection (2) by another member of a police force.

(4) The Police Federations shall act through local and central representative bodies.

(5) The Police Federations and every branch of a Federation shall be entirely independent of, and subject to subsection (6) unassociated with, any body or person outside the police service, but may employ persons outside the police service in an administrative or advisory capacity.

(6) The Secretary of State–

(a) may authorise a Police Federation or a branch of a Federation to be associated with a person or body outside the police service in such cases and manner, and subject to such conditions and restrictions, as he may specify, and

(b) may vary or withdraw an authorisation previously given; and anything for the time being so authorised shall not be precluded by subsection (5).

(7) This section applies to police cadets as it applies to members of police forces, and references to the police service shall be construed accordingly.

(8) ★ ★ ★ ★ ★

60   Regulations for Police Federation

(1) The Secretary of State may by regulations–

(a) prescribe the constitution and proceedings of the Police Federations, or

(b) authorise the Federations to make rules concerning such matters relating to their constitution and proceedings as may be specified in the regulations.

(2) Without prejudice to the generality of subsection (1), regulations under this section may make provision–

(a) with respect to the membership of the Federations;

(b) with respect to the raising of funds by the Federations by voluntary subscription and the use and management of funds derived from such subscriptions;

(c) with respect to the manner in which representations may be made by committees or bodies of the Federations to police authorities, chief officers of police and the Secretary of State;

(d) for the payment by the Secretary of State of expenses incurred in connection with the Federations and for the use by the Federations of premises provided by police authorities for police purposes; and

(e) for modifying any regulations under the Police Pensions Act 1976, section 50 above or section 26 of the Police (Scotland) Act 1967 in relation to any member of a police force who is the secretary or an officer of a Police Federation and for requiring the appropriate Federation to make contributions in respect of the pay, pension or allowances payable to or in respect of any such person.

(2A), (3)–(6) ★ ★ ★ ★ ★

61   The Police Negotiating Board for the United Kingdom

(1) There shall continue to be a Police Negotiation Board for the United Kingdom for the consideration by persons representing the interests of—

(a) the authorities who between them maintain the police forces in Great Britain and the [Police Service of Northern Ireland,]

[(aa) the Service Authority for the National Criminal Intelligence Service and the National Crime Squad];

(b) the persons who are members of those police forces or [the police service] or are police cadets, [(ba) the persons who are members of the National Criminal Intelligence Service within section 9(1)(a) or (b) of the Police Act 1997 or members of the National Crime Squad within section 55(1)(a) or (b) of that Act];

(c) the Commissioner of Police of the Metropolis, and

(d) the Secretary of State, of questions relating to hours of duty, leave, pay and allowances, pensions or the issue, use and return of police clothing, personal equipment and accoutrements.

(2) The Chairman and any deputy chairman or chairmen of the Board shall be appointed by the Prime Minister.

(3) Subject to subsection (2), the Board shall continue to be constituted in accordance with such arrangements, made after consultations between the Secretary of State and organisations representing the interests of the persons referred to in paragraphs (a), (b) and (c) of subsection (1), as appear to the Secretary of State to be satisfactory.

(4) The Secretary of State may—

(a) pay to the Chairman and to any deputy chairman or chairmen of the Board such fees as the Secretary of State may, with the approval of the Treasury, determine, and

(b) defray any expenses incurred by the Board.

62, 63 ★ ★ ★ ★ ★

64 Membership of trade unions

(1) Subject to the following provisions of this section, a member of a police force shall not be a member of any trade union, or of any association having for its objects, or one of its objects, to control or influence the pay, pensions or conditions of service of any police force.

(2) Where a person was a member of a trade union before becoming a member of a police force, he may, with the consent of the chief officer of police, continue to be a member of that union during the time of his service in the police force.

(3) If any question arises whether any body is a trade union or an association to which this section applies, the question shall be determined by the chief registrar of friendly societies.

(4) This section applies to police cadets as it applies to members of a police force, and references to a police force or to service in a police force shall be construed accordingly.

(4A), (4B) ★ ★ ★ ★ ★

(5) Nothing in this section applies to membership of the Police Federations, or of any body recognised by the Secretary of State for the purposes of this section as representing members of police forces who are not members of those Federations.

PART IV   COMPLAINTS, DISCIPLINARY PROCEEDINGS ETC.

CHAPTER I   COMPLAINTS

Interpretation

65 Interpretation of Chapter I

In this Chapter—

"the appropriate authority" means—

. . .

(b) in relation to a member of any police force—

(i) if he is a senior officer, the police authority for the force's area, and

(ii) if he is not a senior officer, the chief officer of police of the force;

"the Authority" means the Police Complaints Authority;

"complaint" means a complaint about the conduct of a member of a police force which is submitted—

    (a) by a member of the public, or

    (b) on behalf of a member of the public and with his written consent;

"disciplinary proceedings" means proceedings identified as such by regulations under section 50;

"investigating officer" means a member of a police force appointed under section 68(3) or, as the case may be, section 69(5) or (6) to investigate a complaint;

"senior officer" means a member of a police force holding a rank above that of [chief] superintendent;

"serious injury" means a fracture, damage to an internal organ, impairment of bodily function, a deep cut or a deep laceration.

The Police Complaints Authority

66 The Police Complaints Authority

(1) The authority known as "the Police Complaints Authority" shall continue in existence as a body corporate.

(2) Schedule 5 shall have effect in relation to the Authority.

Handling of Complaints etc.

67 Preliminary

(1) Where a complaint is submitted to the chief officer of police for a police area, he shall take any steps that appear to him to be desirable for the purpose of obtaining or preserving evidence relating to the conduct complained of.

(2) After complying with subsection (1), the chief officer shall determine whether he is the appropriate authority in relation to the member of a police force whose conduct is the subject of the complaint.

(3) If the chief officer determines that he is not the appropriate authority, he shall—

    (a) send the complaint or, if it was submitted orally, particulars of it, to the appropriate authority, and

    (b) give notice that he has done so to the person by whom or on whose behalf the complaint was submitted.

(4) Nothing in this Chapter shall have effect in relation to a complaint in so far as it relates to the direction or control of a police force by the chief officer of police or the person performing the functions of the chief officer of police.

(5) If any conduct to which a complaint wholly or partly relates is or has been the subject of criminal or disciplinary proceedings, none of the provisions of this Chapter which relate to the recording and investigation of complaints shall have effect in relation to the complaint in so far as it relates to that conduct.

68 Investigation of complaints: senior officers

(1) Where a complaint about the conduct of a senior officer—

    (a) is submitted to the appropriate authority, or

    (b) is sent to the appropriate authority under section 67(3), the appropriate authority shall record and, subject to subsection (2), investigate it.

(2) If satisfied that the conduct complained of, even if proved, would not justify criminal or disciplinary proceedings, the appropriate authority may deal with the complaint according to the appropriate authority's discretion.

(3) In any other case, the appropriate authority shall appoint a member of the appropriate authority's force or of some other force to investigate the complaint.

(4) If the appropriate authority requests the chief officer of police of a police force to

provide a member of his force for appointment under subsection (3), the chief officer shall comply with the request.

(5) No member of a police force of a rank lower than that of the member whose conduct is the subject of the complaint may be appointed under subsection (3).

(6) Unless an investigation under this section is supervised by the Authority under section 72, the investigating officer shall submit his report on it to the appropriate authority.

69   Investigation of complaints: standard procedure

(1) If a chief officer of police determines that he is the appropriate authority in relation to a member of a police force—

(a)   whose conduct is the subject of a complaint, and

(b)   who is not a senior officer, he shall record the complaint.

(2) After recording a complaint under subsection (1), the chief officer of police shall consider whether the complaint is suitable for informal resolution and may appoint a member of his force to assist him.

(3) A complaint is not suitable for informal resolution unless—

(a)   the member of the public concerned gives his consent, and

(b)   the chief officer of police is satisfied that the conduct complained of, even if proved, would not justify criminal or disciplinary proceedings.

(4) If it appears to the chief officer of police that the complaint is suitable for informal resolution, he shall seek to resolve it informally and may appoint a member of his force to do so on his behalf.

(5) If it appears to the chief officer of police that the complaint is not suitable for informal resolution, he shall appoint a member of his own or some other force to investigate it formally.

(6) If, after attempts have been made to resolve a complaint informally, it appears to the chief officer of police—

(a)   that informal resolution of the complaint is impossible, or

(b)   that the complaint is for any other reason not suitable for informal resolution, he shall appoint a member of his own or some other force to investigate it formally.

(7) A member of a police force may not be appointed to investigate a complaint formally if he has previously been appointed to act in relation to it under subsection (4).

(8) If a chief officer of police requests the chief officer of police of some other force to provide a member of that other force for appointment under subsection (5) or (6), that chief officer shall comply with the request.

(9) Unless the investigation is supervised by the Authority under section 72, the investigating officer shall submit his report on it to the chief officer of police who appointed him.

70   References of complaints to Authority

(1) The appropriate authority—

(a)   shall refer to the Authority—

(i)   any complaint alleging that the conduct complained of resulted in the death of, or serious injury to, some other person, and

(ii)   any complaint of a description specified for the purposes of this section in regulations made by the Secretary of State, and

(b)   may refer to the Authority any complaint which is not required to be referred to them.

(2) The Authority may require the submission to them for consideration of any complaint not referred to them by the appropriate authority; and the appropriate authority shall comply with any such requirement not later than the end of the period specified for the purposes of this subsection in regulations made by the Secretary of State.

(3) Where a complaint falls to be referred to the Authority under subsection (1)(a), the appropriate authority shall refer it to them not later than the end of the period specified for the purposes of sub-paragraph (i) or, as the case may be, (ii) of that subsection in regulations made by the Secretary of State.

71 References of other matters to Authority

(1) The appropriate authority may refer to the Authority any matter to which this section applies, if it appears to the appropriate authority that the matter ought to be referred by reason—

(a) of its gravity, or

(b) of exceptional circumstances.

(2) This section applies to any matter which—

(a) appears to the appropriate authority to indicate that a member of a police force may have committed a criminal offence or behaved in a manner which would justify disciplinary proceedings, and

(b) is not the subject of a complaint.

72 Supervision of investigations by Authority

(1) The Authority shall supervise the investigation of—

(a) any complaint alleging that the conduct of a member of a police force resulted in the death of, or serious injury to, some other person,

(b) any other description of complaint specified for the purposes of this section in regulations made by the Secretary of State, and

(c) any complaint which is not within paragraph (a) or (b), and any matter referred to the Authority under section 71, if the Authority determine that it is desirable in the public interest that they should do so.

(2) Where the Authority have made a determination under subsection (1)(c), they shall notify it to the appropriate authority.

(3) Where an investigation is to be supervised by the Authority, they may require—

(a) that no appointment is made under section 68(3) or 69(5) unless they have given notice to the appropriate authority that they approve the person whom that authority propose to appoint, or

(b) if such an appointment has already been made and the Authority are not satisfied with the person appointed, that—

(i) the appropriate authority, as soon as is reasonably practicable, select another member of a police force and notify the Authority that it proposes to appoint him, and

(ii) the appointment is not made unless the Authority give notice to the appropriate authority that they approve that person.

(4) The Secretary of State shall by regulations authorise the Authority, subject to any restrictions or conditions specified in the regulations, to impose requirements as to a particular investigation additional to any requirements imposed by virtue of subsection (3).

(5) A member of a police force shall comply with any requirement imposed on him by virtue of regulations under subsection (4).

73 Reports on investigations etc.

(1) At the end of an investigation which the Authority have supervised, the investigating officer shall–

(a) submit a report on the investigation to the Authority, and

(b) send a copy of the report to the appropriate authority.

(2) After considering a report submitted to them under subsection (1), the Authority shall submit an appropriate statement to the appropriate authority.

(3) If it is practicable to do so, the Authority, when submitting the appropriate statement

under subsection (2), shall send a copy of it to the member of a police force whose conduct has been investigated.

(4) If—

(a) the investigation related to a complaint, and

(b) it is practicable to do so, the Authority shall also send a copy of the appropriate statement to the person by or on behalf of whom the complaint was submitted.

(5) The power to issue an appropriate statement includes power to issue separate statements in respect of the disciplinary and criminal aspects of an investigation.

(6) No disciplinary proceedings shall be brought before the appropriate statement is submitted to the appropriate authority.

(7) Subject to subsection (8), neither the appropriate authority nor the Director of Public Prosecutions shall bring criminal proceedings before the appropriate statement is submitted to the appropriate authority.

(8) The restriction imposed by subsection (7) does not apply if it appears to the Director that there are exceptional circumstances which make it undesirable to wait for the submission of the appropriate statement.

(9) In this section "appropriate statement" means a statement—

(a) as to whether the investigation was or was not conducted to the Authority's satisfaction,

(b) specifying any respect in which it was not so conducted, and

(c) dealing with any such other matters as the Secretary of State may by regulations provide.

74   Steps to be taken after investigation: senior officers

On receiving—

(a) a report concerning the conduct of a senior officer which is submitted to it under section 68(6), or

(b) a copy of a report concerning the conduct of a senior officer which is sent to it under section 73(1),

the appropriate authority shall send a copy of the report to the Director of Public Prosecutions unless the report satisfies the appropriate authority that no criminal offence has been committed.

75   Steps to be taken after investigation: standard procedure

(1) Nothing in this section or section 76 has effect in relation to senior officers.

(2) On receiving—

(a) a report concerning the conduct of a member of a police force who is not a senior officer which is submitted to him under section 69(9), or

(b) a copy of a report concerning the conduct of such a member which is sent to him under section 73(1),

a chief officer of police shall determine whether the report indicates that a criminal offence may have been committed by a member of the police force for his area.

(3) If the chief officer determines that the report indicates that a criminal offence may have been committed by a member of the police force for his area, he shall send a copy of the report to the Director of Public Prosecutions.

(4) After the Director has dealt with the question of criminal proceedings, the chief officer shall, in such cases as may be prescribed by regulations made by the Secretary of State, send the Authority a memorandum which—

(a) is signed by the chief officer,

(b) states whether he has brought (or proposes to bring) disciplinary proceedings in respect of the conduct which was the subject of the investigation, and

(c) if he has not brought (or does not propose to bring) such proceedings, gives his reasons.

(5) If the chief officer considers that the report does not indicate that a criminal offence may have been committed by a member of the police force for his area, he shall, in such cases as may be prescribed by regulations made by the Secretary of State, send the Authority a memorandum to the effect which—

(a) is signed by the chief officer,

(b) states whether he has brought (or proposes to bring) disciplinary proceedings in respect of the conduct which was the subject of the investigation, and

(c) if he has not brought (or does not propose to bring) such proceedings, gives his reasons.

(6) Where the investigation—

(a) related to conduct which was the subject of a complaint, and

(b) was not supervised by the Authority,

the chief officer shall, if he is required by virtue of regulations under subsection (4) or (5) to send the Authority a memorandum, at the same time send them a copy of the complaint, or of the record of the complaint, and a copy of the report of the investigation.

(7) Where a chief officer has sent the Authority a memorandum under subsection (4) or (5), he shall—

(a) if the memorandum states that he proposes to bring disciplinary proceedings, bring and proceed with them, and

(b) if the memorandum states that he has brought such proceedings, proceed with them.

76 Powers of Authority as to disciplinary proceedings

(1) Where a memorandum under section 75 states that a chief officer of police has not brought disciplinary proceedings or does not propose to bring such proceedings, the Authority may recommend him to bring such proceedings.

(2) Where a chief officer has brought disciplinary proceedings in accordance with a recommendation under subsection (1), he shall proceed with them.

(3) If after the Authority have made a recommendation under this section and consulted the chief officer he is still unwilling to bring disciplinary proceedings, they may direct him to do so.

(4) Where the Authority give a chief officer a direction under this section, they shall supply him with a written statement of their reasons for doing so.

(5) Subject to subsection (6), it shall be the duty of a chief officer to comply with such a direction.

(6) The Authority may withdraw a direction given under this section.

(7) A chief officer shall—

(a) advise the Authority of what action he has taken in response to a recommendation or direction under this section, and

(b) supply the Authority with such other information as they may reasonably require for the purposes of discharging their functions under this section.

77 Information as to the manner of dealing with complaints etc.

Every police authority in carrying out its duty with respect to the maintenance of an efficient and effective police force, and inspectors of constabulary in carrying out their duties with respect to the efficiency and effectiveness of any police force, shall keep themselves informed as to the working of sections 67 to 76 in relation to the force.

78 Constabularies maintained by authorities other than police authorities

(1) An agreement for the establishment in relation to any body of constables maintained by an authority, other than a police authority, of procedures corresponding or similar to any of those established by or by virtue of this Chapter may, with the approval of the Secretary

of State, be made between the Authority and the authority maintaining the body of constables.

(2) Where no such procedures are in force in relation to a body of constables, the Secretary of State may by order establish such procedures.

(3) An agreement under this section may at any time be varied or terminated with the approval of the Secretary of State.

(4)–(7) ★ ★ ★ ★ ★

79 Reports

(1) The Authority shall, at the request of the Secretary of State, report to him on such matters relating generally to their functions as the Secretary of State may specify, and the Authority may for that purpose carry out research into any such matters.

(2) The Authority may make a report to the Secretary of State on any matters coming to their notice under this Chapter to which they consider that his attention should be drawn by reason of their gravity or of other exceptional circumstances.

(3) The Authority shall send a copy of any report under subsection (2)—

    (a) to the police authority and the chief officer of police of any police force which appears to the Authority to be concerned, or

    (b) if the report concerns a body of constables such as is mentioned in section 78, to the authority maintaining it and the officer having the direction and the control of it.

(4) As soon as practicable after the end of each calendar year the Authority shall make to the Secretary of State a report on the discharge of their functions during that year.

(5) The Secretary of State shall lay before Parliament a copy of every report received by him under this section and shall cause every such report to be published.

(6) ★ ★ ★ ★ ★

80 Restriction on disclosure of information

(1) No information received by the Authority in connection with any of their functions under sections 67 to 79 or regulations made by virtue of section 81 shall be disclosed by any person who is or has been a member, officer or servant of the Authority except—

    (a) to the Secretary of State or to a member, officer or servant of the Authority or, so far as may be necessary for the proper discharge of the functions of the Authority to other persons,

    (b) for the purposes of any criminal, civil or disciplinary proceedings, or

    (c) in the form of a summary or other general statement made by the Authority which does not identify the person from whom the information was received or any person to whom it relates.

(2) Any person who discloses information in contravention of this section shall be guilty of an offence and liable on summary conviction to a fine of an amount not exceeding level 5 on the standard scale.

81–83 ★ ★ ★ ★ ★

CHAPTER II   DISCIPLINARY AND OTHER PROCEEDINGS

84 Representation at disciplinary and other proceedings

(1) A member of a police force of the rank of [chief] superintendent or below may not be dismissed, required to resign or reduced in rank by a decision taken in proceedings under regulations made in accordance with section 50(3)(a) unless he has been given an opportunity to elect to be legally represented at any hearing held in the course of those proceedings.

(2) Where a member of a police force makes an election to which subsection (1) refers, he may be represented at the hearing, at his option, either by counsel or by a solicitor.

(3) Except in a case where a member of a police force of the rank of [chief] superintendent

or below has been given an opportunity to elect to be legally represented and has so elected, he may be represented at the hearing only by another member of a police force.

(4) Regulations under section 50 shall specify—

(a) a procedure for notifying a member of a police force of the effect of subsections (1) to (3) above,

(b) when he is to be notified of the effect of those subsections, and

(c) when he is to give notice whether he wishes to be legally represented at the hearing.

(5) If a member of a police force—

(a) fails without reasonable cause to give notice in accordance with the regulations that he wishes to be legally represented, or

(b) gives notice in accordance with the regulations that he does not wish to be legally represented,

he may be dismissed, required to resign or reduced in rank without his being legally represented.

(6) If a member of a police force has given notice in accordance with the regulations that he wishes to be legally represented, the case against him may be presented by counsel or a solicitor whether or not he is actually so represented.

85   Appeals against dismissal etc.

(1) A member of a police force who is dismissed, required to resign or reduced in rank by a decision taken in proceedings under regulations made in accordance with section 50(3) may appeal to a police appeals tribunal against the decision except where he has a right of appeal to some other person; and in that case he may appeal to a police appeals tribunal from any decision of that other person as a result of which he is dismissed, required to resign or reduced in rank.

(2) Where a police appeals tribunal allows an appeal it may, if it considers that it is appropriate to do so, make an order dealing with the appellant in a way—

(a) which appears to the tribunal to be less severe than the way in which he was dealt with by the decision appealed against, and

(b) in which he could have been dealt with by the person who made that decision.

(3) The Secretary of State may make rules as to the procedure on appeals to police appeals tribunals under this section.

(4)–(6) ★ ★ ★ ★ ★

86   Admissibility of statements in subsequent proceedings

(1) Subject to subsection (2), no statement made by a person for the purpose of the informal resolution of a complaint shall be admissible in any subsequent criminal, civil or disciplinary proceedings.

(2) A statement is not rendered inadmissible by subsection (1) if it consists of or includes an admission relating to a matter which does not fall to be resolved informally.

(3) In this section "complaint" and "disciplinary proceedings" have the meanings given in section 65.

87   ★ ★ ★ ★ ★

88   Liability for wrongful acts of constables

(1) The chief officer of police for a police area shall be liable in respect of torts committed by constables under his direction and control in the performance or purported performance of their functions in like manner as a master is liable in respect of torts committed by his servants in the course of their employment, and accordingly shall in respect of any such tort be treated for all purposes as a joint tortfeasor.

(2) There shall be paid out of the police fund—

(a) any damages or costs awarded against the chief officer of police in any proceedings brought against him by virtue of this section and any costs incurred by him in any such proceedings so far as not recovered by him in the proceedings; and

(b) any sum required in connection with the settlement of any claim made against the chief officer of police by virtue of this section, if the settlement is approved by the police authority.

(3) Any proceedings in respect of a claim made by virtue of this section shall be brought against the chief officer of police for the time being or, in the case of a vacancy in that office, against the person for the time being performing the functions of the chief officer of police; and references in subsections (1) and (2) to the chief officer of police shall be construed accordingly.

(4) A police authority may, in such cases and to such extent as appear to it to be appropriate, pay out of the police fund—

(a) any damages or costs awarded against a person to whom this subsection applies in proceedings for a tort committed by that person,

(b) any costs incurred and not recovered by such a person in such proceedings, and

(c) any sum required in connection with the settlement of a claim that has or might have given rise to such proceedings.

(5) Subsection (4) applies to a person who is—

(a) a member of the police force maintained by the police authority,

(b) a constable for the time being required to serve with that force by virtue of section 24 or 98 [of this Act, or section 23 of the Police Act 1997], or

(c) a special constable appointed for the authority's police area.

PART V   MISCELLANEOUS AND GENERAL

Offences

89   Assaults on constables

(1) Any person who assaults a constable in the execution of his duty, or a person assisting a constable in the execution of his duty, shall be guilty of an offence and liable on summary conviction to imprisonment for a term not exceeding six months or to a fine not exceeding level 5 on the standard scale, or to both.

(2) Any person who resists or wilfully obstructs a constable in the execution of his duty, or a person assisting a constable in the execution of his duty, shall be guilty of an offence and liable on summary conviction to imprisonment for a term not exceeding one month or to a fine not exceeding level 3 on the standard scale, or to both.

(3) This section also applies to a constable who is a member of a police force maintained in Scotland or Northern Ireland when he is executing a warrant, or otherwise acting in England and Wales, by virtue of any enactment conferring powers on him in England and Wales.

90   Impersonation, etc.

(1) Any person who with intent to deceive impersonates a member of a police force or special constable, or makes any statement or does any act calculated falsely to suggest that he is such a member or constable, shall be guilty of an offence and liable on summary conviction to imprisonment for a term not exceeding six months or to a fine not exceeding level 5 on the standard scale, or to both.

(2) Any person who, not being a constable, wears any article of police uniform in circumstances where it gives him an appearance so nearly resembling that of a member of a police force as to be calculated to deceive shall be guilty of an offence and liable on summary conviction to a fine not exceeding level 3 on the standard scale.

(3) Any person who, not being a member of a police force or special constable, has in his possession any article of police uniform shall, unless he proves that he obtained possession of

that article lawfully and has possession of it for a lawful purpose, be guilty of an offence and liable on summary conviction to a fine not exceeding level 1 on the standard scale.

(4) In this section—

    (a) "article of police uniform" means any article of uniform or any distinctive badge or mark or document of identification usually issued to members of police forces or special constables, or anything having the appearance of such an article, badge, mark or document, and

    [(aa) "member of a police force" includes a member of the British Transport Police Force.]

    (b) "special constable" means a special constable appointed for a police area.

91   Causing disaffection

(1) Any person who causes, or attempts to cause, or does any act calculated to cause, disaffection amongst the members of any police force, or induces or attempts to induce, or does any act calculated to induce, any member of a police force to withhold his services, shall be guilty of an offence and liable—

    (a) on summary conviction, to imprisonment for a term not exceeding six months or to a fine not exceeding the statutory maximum, or to both;

    (b) on conviction on indictment, to imprisonment for a term not exceeding two years or to a fine, or to both.

(2) This section applies to special constables appointed for a police area as it applies to [members of the British Transport Police Force and] members of a police force.

92   ★ ★ ★ ★ ★

93   Acceptance of gifts and loans

(1) A police authority may, in connection with the discharge of any of its functions, accept gifts of money, and gifts or loans of other property, on such terms as appear to the authority to be appropriate.

(2) The terms on which gifts or loans are accepted under subsection (1) may include terms providing for the commercial sponsorship of any activity of the police authority or of the police force maintained by it.

. . .

94, 95   ★ ★ ★ ★ ★

96   Arrangements for obtaining the views of the community on policing

(1) Arrangements shall be made for each police area for obtaining—

    (a) the views of people in that area about matters concerning the policing of the area, and

    (b) their co-operation with the police in preventing crime in that area.

(2) Except as provided by subsections (3) to (6), arrangements for each police area shall be made by the police authority after consulting the chief constable as to the arrangements that would be appropriate.

. . .

(6) The Common Council of the City of London shall issue guidance to the Commissioner of Police for the City of London concerning arrangements for the City of London police area; and the Commissioner shall make arrangements under this section after taking account of that guidance.

(7)–(10) ★ ★ ★ ★ ★

SCHEDULE 2   POLICE AUTHORITIES ESTABLISHED
UNDER SECTION 3

Membership of police authorities

1.—(1) Where, by virtue of section 4, a police authority is to consist of seventeen members—

    (a) nine of those members shall be members of a relevant council appointed under paragraph 2,

    (b) five shall be persons appointed under paragraph 5, and

    (c) three shall be magistrates appointed under paragraph 8.

(2) Where, by virtue of an order under subsection (2) of that section, a police authority is to consist of more than seventeen members—

    (a) a number which is greater by one than the number of members provided for in paragraphs (b) and (c) below shall be members of a relevant council appointed under paragraph 2,

    (b) such number as may be prescribed by the order, not exceeding one third of the total membership, shall be persons appointed under paragraph 5, and

    (c) the remainder shall be magistrates appointed under paragraph 8.

Appointment of members by relevant councils

2.—(1) In the case of a police authority in relation to which there is only one relevant council, the members of the police authority referred to in paragraph 1(1)(a) or (2)(a) shall be appointed by that council.

(2) In any other case, those members shall be appointed by a joint committee consisting of persons appointed by the relevant councils from among their own members.

3. The number of members of the joint committee, and the number of those members to be appointed by each relevant council, shall be such as the councils may agree or, in the absence of agreement, as may be determined by the Secretary of State.

4.—(1) A council or joint committee shall exercise its power to appoint members of a police authority under paragraph 2 so as to ensure that, so far as practicable, [in the case of the members for whose appointment it is responsible the proportion who are members of any given party—

    (a) where it is a council that is responsible for their appointment, is the same as the proportion of the members of the council who are members of that party; and

    (b) where it is a joint committee that is so responsible, is the same as the proportion of the members of the relevant councils taken as a whole who are members of that party.]

. . .

Appointment of independent members

5. The members of a police authority referred to in paragraph 1(1)(b) or (2)(b) shall be appointed—

    (a) by the members of the police authority appointed under paragraph 2 or 8,

    (b) from among persons on a short-list prepared by the Secretary of State in accordance with Schedule 3.

6.—(1) Every police authority shall arrange for a notice stating—

    (a) the name of each of its members appointed under paragraph 5, and

    (b) such other information relating to him as the authority considers appropriate, to be published in such manner as appears to it to be appropriate.

(2) A police authority shall send to the Secretary of State a copy of any notice which it has arranged to be published under sub-paragraph (1).

Appointment of magistrates

7.   The members of a police authority referred to in paragraph 1(1)(c) or (2)(c)—

(a)   must be magistrates for an area all or part of which constitutes or forms part of the authority's area, and

(b)   shall be appointed in accordance with paragraph 8; and in that paragraph references to a panel are references to a selection panel constituted under regulations made in accordance with [section 29(2) of the Justices of the Peace Act 1997].

8.—(1)   Where there is a panel for an area which constitutes or includes the police authority's area, that panel shall make the appointment.

(2)   Where the area of more than one panel falls wholly or partly within the police authority's area, the appointment shall be made by a joint committee consisting of representatives from the panels concerned.

(3)   The number of members of a joint committee, and the number of those members to be appointed by each panel, shall be such as the panels may agree or, in the absence of agreement, as may be determined by the Lord Chancellor.

[SCHEDULE 2A   THE METROPOLITAN POLICE AUTHORITY

Membership

1.—(1)   Where the Metropolitan Police Authority is to consist of twenty three members—

(a)   twelve of those members shall be members of the London Assembly appointed under paragraph 2,

(b)   seven shall be persons appointed under paragraph 3, and

(c)   four shall be magistrates appointed under paragraph 5.

(2)   Where, by virtue of an order under section 5C(2), the Metropolitan Police Authority is to consist of a number of members other than twenty three—

(a)   a number which is greater by one than the number of members provided for in paragraphs (b) and (c) shall be members of the London Assembly appointed under paragraph 2,

(b)   such number as may be prescribed by the order, not exceeding one third of the total membership, shall be persons appointed under paragraph 3, and

(c)   the remainder shall be magistrates appointed under paragraph 5.

Appointment of members by the Mayor

2.—(1)   The members of the Metropolitan Police Authority referred to in paragraph 1(1)(a) or (2)(a) shall be appointed by the Mayor of London in accordance with this paragraph.

(2)   One of those members must be the Deputy Mayor, except as provided by paragraphs 9(2)(b) and 17(b) of Schedule 4 to the Greater London Authority Act 1999 or unless the Deputy Mayor is disqualified from being appointed as or being a member of the Metropolitan Police Authority under paragraph 7 below.

(3)   The Mayor (or, where paragraph 9(2)(b) or 17(b) of Schedule 4 to that Act applies, the Chair of the London Assembly) shall ensure that, so far as practicable, [in the case of the members of the Authority who are members of the London Assembly appointed under this paragraph, the proportion who are members of any given party is the same as the proportion of the members of the London Assembly who are members of that party.]

Appointment of independent members

3.—(1)   The members of the Metropolitan Police Authority referred to in paragraph 1(1)(b) or (2)(b) shall be appointed in accordance with this paragraph.

(2) One shall be appointed by the Secretary of State.

(3) The remainder shall be appointed—

(a) by the members of the Metropolitan Police Authority appointed under paragraph 2 or 5,

(b) from among persons on a short-list prepared by the Secretary of State in accordance with Schedule 3.

(4)–(6) ★ ★ ★ ★ ★

4. ★ ★ ★ ★ ★

Appointment of magistrates

5. The members of the Metropolitan Police Authority referred to in paragraph 1(1)(c) or (2)(c)—

(a) must be magistrates for commission areas which are wholly or partly within the metropolitan police district, and

(b) shall be appointed by the person or body responsible for the appointment of members of the Greater London Magistrates' Courts Authority under regulations made under section 30B of the Justices of the Peace Act 1997.

6., 6A. ★ ★ ★ ★ ★

Disqualification

7.—(1) Subject to sub-paragraphs (3) and (4), a person shall be disqualified for being appointed as or being a member of the Metropolitan Police Authority if—

(a) he holds any paid office or employment appointments to which are or may be made or confirmed by the Metropolitan Police Authority or any committee or sub-committee of the Metropolitan Police Authority, or by a joint committee on which the Metropolitan Police Authority is represented, or by a person holding any such office or employment;

(b) a bankruptcy order has been made against him, or his estate has been sequestrated or he has made a composition or arrangement with, or granted a trust deed for, his creditors;

(c) he is subject to a disqualification order [or disqualification undertaking] under the Company Directors Disqualification Act 1986, [to a disqualification order under Part II of the Companies (Northern Ireland] Order 1989,] or to an order made under section 429(2)(b) of the Insolvency Act 1986 (failure to pay under county court administration order); or

(d) he has within five years before the date of his appointment or since his appointment been convicted in the United Kingdom, the Channel Islands or the Isle of Man of an offence, and has had passed on him a sentence of imprisonment (whether suspended or not) for a period of not less than three months.

(2)–(5) ★ ★ ★ ★ ★

8.—(1) Without prejudice to paragraph 7, a person shall be disqualified for being appointed as a member of the Metropolitan Police Authority under paragraph 3 if—

(a) he has not yet attained the age of twenty-one years, or

(b) neither his principal or only place of work, nor his principal or only place of residence, has been in the metropolitan police district during the whole of the period of twelve months ending with the day of appointment.

(2) Without prejudice to paragraph 7, a person shall be disqualified for being a member so appointed if, at any time, neither his principal or only place of work, nor his principal or only place of residence, is within the metropolitan police district.

9.—(1) Without prejudice to paragraph 7, a person shall be disqualified for being appointed as a member of the Metropolitan Police Authority under paragraph 3, and for being a member so appointed, if he is–

(a) a member of a London borough council;

(b) the Mayor of London;

(c) a member of the London Assembly;

(d) a magistrate for a commission area which is wholly or partly within the metropolitan police district;

(e) a member of the selection panel for the metropolitan police district established under Schedule 3;

(f) a member of a police force;

(g) an officer or employee of a police authority; or

(h) an officer or employee of the Greater London Authority or of a London borough council.

(2) A person shall not be regarded for the purposes of sub-paragraph (1)(h) as an employee of a London borough council by reason of his holding—

(a) the post of head teacher or principal of a school, college or other educational institution or establishment which is maintained or assisted by a local education authority; or

(b) any other post as a teacher or lecturer in any such school, college, institution or establishment.

10.–20B. ★ ★ ★ ★ ★

Mayor's functions to be exercised by him personally

21. Any functions exercisable by the Mayor of London under this Schedule may only be exercised by him personally.

Interpretation

22. In this Schedule—

["commission area" has the same meaning as in the Justices of the Peace Act 1997; "magistrate" has the same meaning as in the Justices of the Peace Act 1997.]

SCHEDULE 4   FORM OF DECLARATION

I, ... of . . . . do solemnly and sincerely declare and affrirm that I will well and truly serve Our Sovereign Lady the Queen in the office of constable, without favour or affection, malice or ill will; and that I will to the best of my power cause the peace to be kept and preserved, and prevent all offences against the persons and properties of Her Majesty's subjects; and that while I continue to hold the said office I will to the best of my skill and knowledge discharge all the duties thereof faithfully according to law.

SCHEDULE 5   THE POLICE COMPLAINTS AUTHORITY

Constitution of Authority

1.—(1) The Police Complaints Authority shall consist of a chairman and not less than eight other members.

(2) The chairman shall be appointed by Her Majesty.

(3) The other members shall be appointed by the Secretary of State.

(4) The members of the Authority shall not include any person who is or has been a constable in any part of the United Kingdom.

(5) Persons may be appointed as whole-time or part-time members of the Authority.

(6) The Secretary of State may appoint not more than two of the members of the Authority to be deputy chairmen.

Status of Authority

2.   The Authority shall not be regarded as the servant or agent of the Crown or as enjoying any status, privilege or immunity of the Crown; and the Authority's property shall not be regarded as property of or property held on behalf of the Crown.

★ ★ ★ ★ ★

Justices of the Peace Act 1997
(1997, c. 25)

An Act to consolidate the Justices of the Peace Act 1979 and provisions of Part IV of the Police and Magistrates' Courts Act 1994.
[19 March 1997]

Territorial extent: England and Wales

PART V   PROTECTION AND INDEMNIFICATION OF JUSTICES AND JUSTICES' CLERKS

51   Immunity for acts within jurisdiction

(1)   No action shall lie against any justice of the peace or justices' clerk in respect of any act or omission of his–

    (a)   in the execution of his duty—

        (i)   as such a justice; or

        (ii)   as such a clerk exercising, by virtue of any statutory provision, any of the functions of a single justice; and

    (b)   with respect to any matter within his jurisdiction. [(2) In this section references to a justices' clerk include any person appointed by a magistrates' courts committee to assist a justices' clerk.]

52   Immunity for certain acts beyond jurisdiction

(1)   An action shall lie against any justice of the peace or justices' clerk in respect of any act or omission of his—

    (a)   in the purported execution of his duty—

        (i)   as such a justice; or

        (ii)   as such a clerk exercising, by virtue of any statutory provision, any of the functions of a single justice; but

    (b)   with respect to a matter which is not within his jurisdiction, if, but only if, it is proved that he acted in bad faith.

[(2) In this section references to a justices' clerk include any person appointed by a magistrates' courts committee to assist a justices' clerk.]

53   Where action prohibited, proceedings may be set aside

If any action is brought in circumstances in which this Part of this Act provides that no action is to lie, a judge of the court in which the action is brought may, on the application of the defendant and upon an affidavit as to the facts, set aside the proceedings in the action, with or without costs, as the judge thinks fit.

[53A   Costs in legal proceedings

(1)   A court may not order any justice of the peace or justices' clerk to pay costs in any

proceedings in respect of any act or omission of his in the execution (or purported execution) of his duty—

    (a) as such a justice; or

    (b) as such a clerk exercising, by virtue of any statutory provision, any of the functions of a single justice.

  (2) Subsection (1) above does not apply in relation to—

    (a) any proceedings in which a justice or justices' clerk is being tried for an offence or is appealing against a conviction; or

    (b) any proceedings in which it is proved that a justice or justices' clerk acted in bad faith in respect of the matters giving rise to the proceedings.

  (3) Where a court is prevented by subsection (1) above from ordering a justice or justices' clerk to pay costs in any proceedings, the court may instead order the making by the Lord Chancellor of a payment in respect of the costs of a person in the proceedings.]

54 Indemnification of justices and justices' clerks

  (1) For the purposes of subsection (2) below, the following amounts are "relevant amounts" in relation to a justice of the peace or justices' clerk—

    (a) any costs which he reasonably incurs—

       (i) in or in connection with proceedings . . . in respect of anything done or omitted in the exercise (or purported exercise) of his duty as a justice of the peace or justices' clerk; or

      (ii) in taking steps to dispute any claim which might be made in such proceedings;

    (b) any damages awarded against him or costs ordered to be paid by him in any such proceedings; and

    (c) any sums payable by him in connection with a reasonable settlement of any such proceedings or claim,

and relevant amounts relate to criminal matters if the duty mentioned in paragraph (a)(i) above relates to criminal matters.

  (2) Subject to the provisions of this section, a justice of the peace or justices' clerk—

    (a) shall be indemnified [by the appropriate authority] in respect of relevant amounts which relate to criminal matters unless it is proved, in respect of the matters giving rise to the proceedings or claim, that he acted in bad faith; and

    (b) in respect of other relevant amounts—

       (i) may be indemnified out of local funds [unless it is proved in respect of the matters giving rise to the proceedings or claim, that he acted in bad faith]; and

      (ii) shall be so indemnified if, in respect of the matters giving rise to the proceedings or claim, he acted reasonably and in good faith.

  (2A) ★ ★ ★ ★ ★

  (3) Any question whether, or to what extent, a person is to be indemnified under this section shall be determined by the magistrates' courts committee for the area for which he acted at the material time.

  (4) A determination under subsection (3) above with respect to any such costs or sums as are mentioned in subsection (1)(a) or (c) above may, if the person claiming to be indemnified so requests, be made in advance before those costs are incurred or the settlement made, as the case may be.

  (5) Any such determination in advance for indemnity in respect of costs to be incurred shall be subject to such limitations, if any, as the committee think proper and to the subsequent determination of the amount of the costs reasonably incurred and shall not affect any other determination which may fail to be made in connection with the proceedings or claim in question.

  (6) An appeal shall lie to a person appointed for the purpose by the Lord Chancellor—

(a) on the part of the person claiming to be indemnified, from any decision of the magistrates' courts committee under subsection (3) or (4) above, other than a decision to postpone until after the conclusion of the proceedings any determination with respect to his own costs or to impose limitations on making a determination in advance for indemnity in respect of such costs;

(b) on the part of any paying authority, from any determination of the magistrates' courts committee under subsection (3) above other than a determination in advance for indemnity in respect of costs to be incurred by the person claiming to be indemnified.

(7)–(9) ★ ★ ★ ★ ★

★ ★ ★ ★ ★

Law Officers Act 1997
(1997, c. 60)

An Act to enable functions of the Attorney General and of the Attorney General for Northern Ireland to be exercised by the Solicitor General; and for connected purposes.   [31 July 1997]

Territorial extent: United Kingdom

1   The Attorney General and the Solicitor General

(1) Any function of the Attorney General may be exercised by the Solicitor General.

(2) Anything done by or in relation to the Solicitor General in the exercise of or in connection with a function of the Attorney General has effect as if done by or in relation to the Attorney General.

(3) The validity of anything done in relation to the Attorney General, or done by or in relation to the Solicitor General, is not affected by a vacancy in the office of Attorney General.

(4) Nothing in this section—

(a) prevents anything being done by or in relation to the Attorney General in the exercise of or in connection with any function of his; or

(b) requires anything done by the Solicitor General to be done in the name of the Solicitor General instead of the name of the Attorney General.

(5) It is immaterial for the purposes of this section whether a function of the Attorney General arises under an enactment or otherwise.

★ ★ ★ ★ ★

Local Government (Contracts) Act 1997
(1997, c. 65)

An Act to make provision about the powers of local authorities (including probation committees and the Receiver for the Metropolitan Police District) to enter into contracts; to enable expenditure of local authorities making administrative arrangements for magistrates' courts to be treated for some purposes as not being capital expenditure; and for connected purposes.   [27 November 1997]

Territorial extent: England and Wales, Scotland (so far as reproduced here).

Contracts for provision of assets or services

1   Functions to include power to enter into contracts

(1) Every statutory provision conferring or imposing a function on a local authority confers power on the local authority to enter into a contract with another person for the provision or making available of assets or services, or both (whether or not together with goods) for the purposes of, or in connection with, the discharge of the function by the local authority.

(2) Where—
- (a) a local authority enters into a contract such as is mentioned in subsection (1) ("the provision contract") under any statutory provision, and
- (b) in connection with the provision contract, a person ("the financier") makes a loan to, or provides any other form of finance for, a party to the provision contract other than the local authority,

the statutory provision also confers power on the local authority to enter into a contract with the financier, or any insurer of or trustee for the financier, in connection with the provision contract.

(3) The following are local authorities for the purposes of this Act—
- (a) any authority with respect to the finances of which Part IV of the Local Government and Housing Act 1989 has effect at the time in question,
- (b) any probation committee, [and] [(c) the Receiver for the Metropolitan Police District, and]
- (d) any local authority or joint board as defined in section 235(1) of the Local Government (Scotland) Act 1973.

(4) In this Act "assets" means assets of any description (whether tangible or intangible), including (in particular) land, buildings, roads, works, plant, machinery, vehicles, vessels, apparatus, equipment and computer software.

(5) Regulations may be made amending subsection (4).

Certified contracts

(2) Certified contracts to be intra vires

(1) Where a local authority has entered into a contract, the contract shall, if it is a certified contract, have effect (and be deemed always to have had effect) as if the local authority had had power to enter into it (and had exercised that power properly in entering into it).

(2) For the purposes of this Act a contract entered into by a local authority is a certified contract if (and, subject to subsections (3) and (4), only if) the certification requirements have been satisfied by the local authority with respect to the contract and they were so satisfied before the end of the certification period.

(3) A contract entered into by a local authority shall be treated as a certified contract during the certification period if the contract provides that the certification requirements are intended to be satisfied by the local authority with respect to the contract before the end of that period.

(4) Where a local authority has entered into a contract which is a certified contract ("the existing contract") and the existing contract is replaced by a contract entered into by it with a person or persons not identical with the person or persons with whom it entered into the existing contract, the replacement contract is also a certified contract if—
- (a) the period for which it operates or is intended to operate ends at the same time as the period for which the existing contract was to operate, and
- (b) apart from that, its provisions are the same as those of the existing contract.

(5) In this Act "the certification period", in relation to a contract entered into by a local authority, means the period of six weeks beginning with the day on which the local authority entered into the contract.

(6) Subsection (1) is subject to section 5 (special provisions about judicial reviews and audit reviews).

(7) The application of subsection (1) in relation to a contract entered into by a local authority does not affect any claim for damages made by a person who is not (and has never been) a party to the contract in respect of a breach by the local authority of any duty to do, or

not to do, something before entering into the contract (including, in particular, any such duty imposed by a statutory provision for giving effect to any Community obligation relating to public procurement or by section 17(1) of the Local Government Act 1988).

3   The certification requirements

(1) In this Act "the certification requirements", in relation to a contract entered into by a local authority, means the requirements specified in subsections (2) to (4).

(2) The requirement specified in this subsection is that the local authority must have issued a certificate (whether before or after the contract is entered into)—

    (a) including details of the period for which the contract operates or is to operate,

    (b) describing the purpose of the contract,

    (c) containing a statement that the contract is or is to be a contract falling within section 4(3) or (4),

    (d) stating that the local authority had or has power to enter into the contract and specifying the statutory provision, or each of the statutory provisions, conferring the power,

    (e) stating that a copy of the certificate has been or is to be given to each person to whom a copy is required to be given by regulations,

    (f) dealing in a manner prescribed by regulations with any matters required by regulations to be dealt with in certificates under this section, and

    (g) confirming that the local authority has complied with or is to comply with any requirement imposed by regulations with respect to the issue of certificates under this section.

(3) The requirement specified in this subsection is that the local authority must have secured that the certificate is signed by any person who is required by regulations to sign it.

(4) The requirement specified in this subsection is that the local authority must have obtained consent to the issue of a certificate under this section from each of the persons with whom the local authority has entered, or is to enter, into the contract.

4   Certified contracts: supplementary

(1) Where the certification requirements have been satisfied in relation to a contract by a local authority, the certificate which has been issued shall have effect (and be deemed always to have had effect) as if the local authority had had power to issue it (and had exercised that power properly in issuing it); and a certificate which has been so issued is not invalidated by reason that anything in the certificate is inaccurate or untrue.

(2) Where the certification requirements have been satisfied in relation to a contract by a local authority within section 1(3)(a) or (d), the local authority shall secure that throughout the period for which the contract operates—

    (a) a copy of the certificate which has been issued is open to inspection by members of the public at all reasonable times without payment, and

    (b) members of the public are afforded facilities for obtaining copies of that certificate on payment of a reasonable fee.

(3) A contract entered into by a local authority falls within this subsection if—

    (a) it is entered into with another person for the provision or making available of services (whether or not together with assets or goods) for the purposes of, or in connection with, the discharge by the local authority of any of its functions, and

    (b) it operates, or is intended to operate, for a period of at least five years.

(4) A contract entered into by a local authority falls within this subsection if it is entered into, in connection with a contract falling within subsection (3), with—

    (a) a person who, in connection with that contract, makes a loan to, or provides any other form of finance for, a party to that contract other than the local authority, or

    (b) any insurer of or trustee for such a person.

(5) Regulations may be made amending subsection (3) or (4).

5   Special provision for judicial reviews and audit reviews

(1) Section 2(1) does not apply for the purposes of determining any question arising on—

(a) an application for judicial review, or

(b) an audit review, as to whether a local authority had power to enter into a contract (or exercised any power properly in entering into a contract).

(2) Section 2(1) has effect subject to any determination or order made in relation to a certified contract on—

(a) an application for judicial review, or

(b) an audit review.

(3) Where, on an application for judicial review or an audit review relating to a certified contract entered into by a local authority, a court—

(a) is of the opinion that the local authority did not have power to enter into the contract (or exercised any power improperly in entering into it), but

(b) (having regard in particular to the likely consequences for the financial provision of the local authority, and for the provision of services to the public, of a decision that the contract should not have effect) considers that the contract should have effect,

the court may determine that the contract has (and always has had) effect as if the local authority had had power to enter into it (and had exercised that power properly in entering into it).

(4) In this section and sections 6 and 7 references to an application for judicial review include any appeal (or further appeal) against a determination or order made on such an application.

6   Relevant discharge terms

(1) No determination or order made in relation to a certified contract on—

(a) an application for judicial review, or

(b) an audit review, shall affect the enforceability of any relevant discharge terms relating to the contract.

(2) In this section and section 7 "relevant discharge terms", in relation to a contract entered into by a local authority, means terms—

(a) which have been agreed by the local authority and any person with whom the local authority entered into the contract,

(b) which either form part of the contract or constitute or form part of another agreement entered into by them not later than the day on which the contract was entered into, and

(c) which provide for a consequence mentioned in subsection (3) to ensue in the event of the making of a determination or order in relation to the contract on an application for judicial review or an audit review.

(3) Those consequences are—

(a) the payment of compensatory damages (measured by reference to loss incurred or loss of profits or to any other circumstances) by one of the parties to the other,

(b) the adjustment between the parties of rights and liabilities relating to any assets or goods provided or made available under the contract, or

(c) both of those things.

(4) Where a local authority has agreed relevant discharge terms with any person with whom it has entered into a contract and the contract is a certified contract, the relevant discharge terms shall have effect (and be deemed always to have had effect) as if the local authority had had power to agree them (and had exercised that power properly in agreeing them).

7 Absence of relevant discharge terms

(1) Subsection (2) applies where—

(a) the result of determination or order made by a court on an application for judicial review or an audit review is that a certified contract does not have effect, and

(b) there are no relevant discharge terms having effect between the local authority and a person who is a party to the contract.

(2) That person shall be entitled to be paid by the local authority such sums (if any) as he would have been entitled to be paid by the local authority if the contract—

(a) had had effect until the time when the determination or order was made, but

(b) had been terminated at that time by acceptance by him of a repudiatory breach by the local authority.

(3) For the purposes of this section the circumstances in which there are no relevant discharge terms having effect between the local authority and a person who is a party to the contract include (as well as circumstances in which no such terms have been agreed) circumstances in which the result of a determination or order of a court, made (despite section 6(4)) on an application for judicial review or an audit review, is that such terms do not have effect.

★ ★ ★ ★ ★

National Health Service (Private Finance) Act 1997
(1997, c. 56)

An Act to make provision about the powers of National Health Service trusts to enter into agreements. [15 July 1997]

Territorial extent: England and Wales, Scotland, Northern Ireland in accordance with section 2.

1 Powers of NHS trusts to enter into agreements

(1) The powers of a National Health Service trust include power to enter into externally financed development agreements.

(2) For the purposes of this section, an agreement is an externally financed development agreement if it is certified as such in writing by the Secretary of State.

(3) The Secretary of State may give a certificate under this section if—

(a) in his opinion the purpose or main purpose of the agreement is the provision of facilities in connection with the discharge by the trust of any of its functions; and

(b) a person proposes to make a loan to, or provide any other form of finance for, another party in connection with the agreement.

(4) If a National Health Service trust enters into an externally financed development agreement it may also, in connection with that agreement, enter into an agreement with a person who falls within subsection (3)(b) in relation to the externally financed development agreement.

(5) In subsection (3)—

"another party" means any party to the agreement other than the trust; and

"facilities" includes—

(a) works, buildings, plant, equipment or other property; and

(b) services.

(6) The fact that an agreement made by a National Health Service trust has not been certified under this section does not affect its validity.

★ ★ ★ ★ ★

Northern Ireland Arms Decommissioning Act 1997
(1997, c. 7)

An Act to make provision connected with Northern Ireland about the decommissioning of firearms, ammunition and explosives; and for connected purposes.   [27 February 1997]

Territorial extent: United Kingdom

1 Decommissioning scheme

(1) In this Act a "decommissioning scheme" is any scheme which–

(a) is made by the Secretary of State to facilitate the decommissioning of firearms, ammunition and explosives in Northern Ireland, and

(b) includes provisions satisfying the requirements of sections 2 and 3 (whether or not it also includes other provisions).

(2) ★ ★ ★ ★ ★

2 Duration of decommissioning scheme

(1) A decommissioning scheme must identify a period during which firearms, ammunition and explosives may be dealt with in accordance with the scheme ("the amnesty period").

(2) The amnesty period must end before—

(a) [27 February 2003], or

(b) such later day as the Secretary of State may by order from time to time appoint.

(3) A day appointed by an order under subsection (2)(b) must not be–

(a) more than twelve months after the day on which the order is made, or

(b) [later than 27 February 2007].

(4) An order under subsection (2)(b) shall be made by statutory instrument; and no order shall be made unless a draft has been laid before, and approved by resolution of, each House of Parliament.

3 Methods of decommissioning

(1) A decommissioning scheme must make provision for one or more of the following ways of dealing with firearms, ammunition and explosives (and may make provision for others)—

(a) transfer to the Commission mentioned in section 7, or to a designated person, for destruction;

(b) depositing for collection and destruction by the Commission or a designated person;

(c) provision of information for the purpose of collection and destruction by the Commission or a designated person;

(d) destruction by persons in unlawful possession.

(2) In subsection (1) "designated person" means a person designated by the Secretary of State or, in the case of firearms, ammunition or explosives transferred or collected in the Republic of Ireland, a person designated by the Minister for Justice of the Republic.

4 Amnesty

(1) No proceedings shall be brought for an offence listed in the Schedule to this Act in respect of anything done in accordance with a decommissioning scheme.

(2)–(4) ★ ★ ★ ★ ★

5 Evidence

(1) A decommissioned article, or information derived from it, shall not be admissible in evidence in criminal proceedings.

(2) Evidence of anything done, and of any information obtained, in accordance with a decommissioning scheme shall not be admissible in criminal proceedings.

(3) Subsections (1) and (2) shall not apply to the admission of evidence adduced in criminal proceedings on behalf of the accused.

(4) Subsection (1) shall not apply to proceedings for an offence alleged to have been committed by the use of, or in relation to, something which was a decommissioned article at the time when the offence is alleged to have been committed.

6 Testing decommissioned articles

(1) A person who has received a decommissioned article shall not carry out, or cause or permit anyone else to carry out, a test or procedure in relation to the article the purpose of which is—

  (a) to discover information about anything done with or in relation to any decommissioned article,

  (b) to discover who has been in contact with, or near to, any decommissioned article,

  (c) to discover where any decommissioned article was at any time (including the conditions under which it was kept),

  (d) to discover when any decommissioned article was in contact with, or near to, a particular person or when it was in a particular place or kept under particular conditions,

  (e) to discover when or where any decommissioned article was made, or

  (f) to discover the composition of any decommissioned article.

(2), (3) ★ ★ ★ ★ ★

7 The Commission

(1) In this section "the Commission" means an independent organisation established by an agreement, made in connection with the affairs of Northern Ireland between Her Majesty's Government in the United Kingdom and the Government of the Republic of Ireland, to facilitate the decommissioning of firearms, ammunition and explosives.

(2) The Secretary of State may by order—

  (a) confer on the Commission the legal capacities of a body corporate;

  (b) confer on the Commission, in such cases, to such extent and with such modifications as the order may specify, any of the privileges and immunities set out in Part I of Schedule 1 to the International Organisations Act 1968;

  (c) confer on members and servants of the Commission and members of their families who form part of their households, in such cases, to such extent and with such modifications as the order may specify any of the privileges and immunities set out in Parts II, III and V of that Schedule;

  (d) make provision about the waiver of privileges and immunities. In this subsection "servants of the Commission" includes agents of, and persons carrying out work for or giving advice to, the Commission.

(3)–(6) ★ ★ ★ ★ ★

8 Arms in England and Wales and Scotland

(1) This section applies to any scheme which—

  (a) is made by the Secretary of State, for purposes relating to the affairs of Northern Ireland, to facilitate the decommissioning of firearms, ammunition and explosives in England and Wales or in Scotland, and

  (b) includes provisions satisfying the requirement of sections 2 and 3 (whether or not it also includes other provisions).

(2) The Secretary of State may by order provide that a scheme to which this section applies shall be a decommissioning scheme for the purposes of this Act.

(3) In relation to a scheme which is a decommissioning scheme by virtue of subsection (2), the Schedule to this Act shall have effect with the substitution for any offence under the law of Northern Ireland of such similar offence under the law of England and Wales, or as the case may be of Scotland, as the Secretary of State may specify by order.

(4) An order under this section shall be made by statutory instrument; and no order shall be made unless a draft has been laid before, and approved by resolution of, each House of Parliament.

Police Act 1997
(1997, c. 50)

An Act to make provision for the National Criminal Intelligence Service and the National Crime Squad; to make provision about entry on and interference with property and with wireless telegraphy in the course of the prevention or detection of serious crime; to make provision for the Police Information Technology Organisation; to provide for the issue of certificates about criminal records; to make provision about the administration and organisation of the police; to repeal certain enactments about rehabilitation of offenders; and for connected purposes. [21 March 1997]

Territorial extent: United Kingdom (sections printed).

PART III AUTHORISATION OF ACTION IN RESPECT OF PROPERTY

The Commissioners

91 The Commissioners

(1) The Prime Minister [, after consultation with the Scottish Ministers] shall appoint for the purposes of this Part—
(a) a Chief Commissioner, and
(b) such number of other Commissioners as the Prime Minister thinks fit.

(2) The persons appointed under subsection (1) shall be persons who hold or have held high judicial office within the meaning of the Appellate Jurisdiction Act 1876.

(3) Subject to subsections (4) to (7), each Commissioner shall hold and vacate office in accordance with the terms of his appointment.

(4) Each Commissioner shall be appointed for a term of three years.

(5) A person who ceases to be a Commissioner (otherwise than under subsection (7)) may be reappointed under this section.

(6) Subject to subsection (7), a Commissioner shall not be removed from office before the end of the term for which he is appointed unless [–
(a) a resolution approving his removal has been passed by each House of Parliament; and
(b) a resolution approving his removalhas beenpassedby the Scottish Parliament.]

(7) ★ ★ ★ ★ ★

(8) The Secretary of State shall pay to each Commissioner [, other than a Commissioner carrying out functions as mentioned in subsection 8A] such allowances as the Secretary of State considers appropriate.

[(8A) The Scottish Ministers shall pay to any Commissioner who carries out his functions under this part wholly or mainly in Scotland such allowances as the Scottish Ministers consider appropriate.]

(9) The Secretary of State shall, after consultation with the Chief Commissioner, [and subject to the approval of the Treasury as to numbers] provide the Commissioners [and any Assistant Surveillance Commissioners holding office under section 63 of the Regulation of Investigatory Powers Act 2000] [, other than any Commissioner carrying out functions as mentioned in subsection (9A),] with such staff as the Secretary of State considers necessary for the discharge of their functions.

[(9A) The Scottish Ministers shall, after consultation with the Chief Commissioner, provide any Commissioner who carries out his functions under this part wholly or mainly in Scotland with such staff as the Scottish Ministers consider necessary for the discharge of his functions.]

(10) The decisions of the Chief Commissioner or, subject to sections 104 and 106, any other Commissioner (including decisions as to his jurisdiction) shall not be subject to appeal or liable to be questioned in any court.

Authorisations

92   Effect of authorisation under Part III
No entry on or interference with property or with wireless telegraphy shall be unlawful if it is authorised by an authorisation having effect under this Part.

93   Authorisations to interfere with property etc.
(1) Where subsection (2) applies, an authorising officer may authorise—
  (a) the taking of such action, in respect of such property in the relevant area, as he may specify,
  [(ab) the taking of such action falling within subsection (1A) in respect of property outside the relevant area, as he may specify, or]
  (b) the taking of such action in the relevant area as he may specify, in respect of wireless telegraphy.

(1A) The action falling within this subsection is action for maintaining or retrieving any equipment, apparatus or device the placing or use of which in the relevant area has been authorised under this Part or Part II of the Regulation of Investigatory Powers Act 2000 or under any enactment contained in or made under an Act of the Scottish Parliament which makes provision equivalent to that made by Part II of that Act of 2000.

(1B) Subsection (1) applies where the authorising officer is a customs officer with the omission of—
  (a) the words "in the relevant area" in each place where they occur; and
  (b) paragraph (ab).]

(2) This subsection applies where the authorising officer believes—
  (a) that it is necessary for the action specified to be taken [for the purpose of preventing or detecting] serious crime, and
  (b) [that the taking of the action is proportionate to what the action seeks to achieve.]

[(2A) Subsection (2) applies where the authorising officer is the Chief Constable or the Deputy Chief Constable of the Royal Ulster Constabulary as if the reference in subsection (2)(a) to preventing or detecting serious crime included a reference to the interests of national security.

(2B) The matters to be taken into account in considering whether the requirements of subsection (2) are satisfied in the case of any authorisation shall include whether what it is thought necessary to achieve by the authorised action could reasonably be achieved by other means.]

(3) An authorising officer shall not give an authorisation under this section except on an application made—
  (a) if the authorising officer is within subsection (5)(a) to [(ea) or (ee)], by a member of his police force,
  [(aa) if the authorising officer is within subsection (5)(eb) to (ed), by a member, as the case may be, of the Royal Navy Regulating Branch, the Royal Military Police or the Royal Air Force Police,]
  (b) if the authorising officer is within subsection (5)(f), by a member of the National Criminal Intelligence Service,

    (c) if the authorising officer is within subsection (5)(g), by a member of the National Crime Squad, or

    (d) if the authorising officer is within subsection (5)(h), by a customs officer.

(4) For the purposes of subsection (2), conduct which constitutes one or more offences shall be regarded as serious crime if, and only if,—

    (a) it involves the use of violence, results in substantial financial gain or is conduct by a large number of persons in pursuit of a common purpose, or

    (b) the offence or one of the offences is an offence for which a person who has attained the age of twenty-one and has no previous convictions could reasonably be expected to be sentenced to imprisonment for a term of three years or more,

and, where the authorising officer is within subsection (5)(h), it relates to an assigned matter within the meaning of section 1(1) of the Customs and Excise Management Act 1979.

(5) In this section "authorising officer" means—

    (a) the chief constable of a police force maintained under section 2 of the Police Act 1996 (maintenance of police forces for areas in England and Wales except London);

    (b) the Commissioner, or an Assistant Commissioner, of Police of the Metropolis;

    (c) the Commissioner of Police for the City of London;

    (d) the chief constable of a police force maintained under or by virtue of section 1 of the Police (Scotland) Act 1967 (maintenance of police forces for areas in Scotland);

    (e) the Chief Constable or a Deputy Chief Constable of the Royal Ulster Constabulary;

    [(ea) the Chief Constable of the Ministry of Defence Police;

    (eb) the Provost Marshal of the Royal Navy Regulating Branch;

    (ec) the Provost Marshal of the Royal Military Police;

    (ed) the Provost Marshal of the Royal Air Force Police;

    (ee) the Chief Constable of the British Transport Police;]

    (f) the Director General of the National Criminal Intelligence Service;

    (g) the Director General of the National Crime Squad [or any person holding the rank of assistant chief constable in that squad who is designated for the purposes of this paragraph by that Director General]; or

    (h) [any] customs officer designated by the Commissioners of Customs and Excise for the purposes of this paragraph.

(6), (6A), (6B) ★ ★ ★ ★ ★

(7) The powers conferred by, or by virtue of, this section are additional to any other powers which a person has as a constable either at common law or under or by virtue of any other enactment and are not to be taken to affect any of those other powers.

94 ★ ★ ★ ★ ★

95 Authorisations: form and duration etc.

(1) An authorisation shall be in writing, except that in an urgent case an authorisation (other than one given by virtue of section 94) may be given orally.

(2) An authorisation shall, unless renewed under subsection (3), cease to have effect—

    (a) if given orally or by virtue of section 94, at the end of the period of 72 hours beginning with the time when it took effect;

    (b) in any other case, at the end of the period of three months beginning with the day on which it took effect.

(3) If at any time before an authorisation would cease to have effect the authorising officer who gave the authorisation, or in whose absence it was given, considers it necessary for the authorisation to continue to have effect for the purpose for which it was issued, he may, in writing, renew it for a period of three months beginning with the day on which it would cease to have effect.

(4) A person shall cancel an authorisation given by him if satisfied that the [authorisation is one in relation to which the requirement of paragraphs (a) to (b) of section 93(2) are no longer satisfied.]

(5)–(7) ★ ★ ★ ★ ★

96   Notification of authorisations etc.

(1) Where a person gives, renews or cancels an authorisation, he shall, as soon as is reasonably practicable and in accordance with arrangements made by the Chief Commissioner, give notice in writing that he has done so to a Commissioner appointed under section 91(1)(b).

(2) Subject to subsection (3), a notice under this section shall specify such matters as the Secretary of State may by order prescribe.

(3) A notice under this section of the giving or renewal of an authorisation shall specify—

  (a) whether section 97 applies to the authorisation or renewal, and

  (b) where that section does not apply by virtue of subsection (3) of that section, the grounds on which the case is believed to be one of urgency.

(4) Where a notice is given to a Commissioner under this section, he shall, as soon as is reasonably practicable, scrutinise the notice.

(5), (6) ★ ★ ★ ★ ★

Authorisations requiring approval

97   Authorisations requiring approval

(1) An authorisation to which this section applies shall not take effect until—

  (a) it has been approved in accordance with this section by a Commissioner appointed under section 91(1)(b), and

  (b) the person who gave the authorisation has been notified under subsection (4).

(2) Subject to subsection (3), this section applies to an authorisation if, at the time it is given, the person who gives it believes—

  (a) that any of the property specified in the authorisation–

    (i) is used wholly or mainly as a dwelling or as a bedroom in a hotel, or

    (ii) constitutes office premises, or

  (b) that the action authorised by it is likely to result in any person acquiring knowledge of—

    (i) matters subject to legal privilege,

    (ii) confidential personal information, or

    (iii) confidential journalistic material.

(3) This section does not apply to an authorisation where the person who gives it believes that the case is one of urgency.

(4) Where a Commissioner receives a notice under section 96 which specifies that this section applies to the authorisation, he shall as soon as is reasonably practicable–

  (a) decide whether to approve the authorisation or refuse approval, and

  (b) give written notice of his decision to the person who gave the authorisation.

(5) A Commissioner shall approve an authorisation if, and only if, he is satisfied that there are reasonable grounds for believing the matters specified in section 93(2).

(6)–(8) ★ ★ ★ ★ ★

98   Matters subject to legal privilege

(1) Subject to subsection (5) below, in section 97 "matters subject to legal privilege" means matters to which subsection (2), (3) or (4) below applies.

(2) This subsection applies to communications between a professional legal adviser and—

  (a) his client, or

  (b) any person representing his client, which are made in connection with the giving of legal advice to the client.

(3) This subsection applies to communications—

    (a) between a professional legal adviser and his client or any person representing his client, or

    (b) between a professional legal adviser or his client or any such representative and any other person,

which are made in connection with or in contemplation of legal proceedings and for the purposes of such proceedings.

(4) This subsection applies to items enclosed with or referred to in communications of the kind mentioned in subsection (2) or (3) and made—

    (a) in connection with the giving of legal advice, or

    (b) in connection with or in contemplation of legal proceedings and for the purposes of such proceedings.

(5) For the purposes of section 97—

    (a) communications and items are not matters subject to legal privilege when they are in the possession of a person who is not entitled to possession of them, and

    (b) communications and items held, or oral communications made, with the intention of furthering a criminal purpose are not matters subject to legal privilege.

99   Confidential personal information

(1) In section 97 "confidential personal information" means—

    (a) personal information which a person has acquired or created in the course of any trade, business, profession or other occupation or for the purposes of any paid or unpaid office, and which he holds in confidence, and

    (b) communications as a result of which personal information—

        (i) is acquired or created as mentioned in paragraph (a), and

        (ii) is held in confidence.

(2) For the purposes of this section "personal information" means information concerning an individual (whether living or dead) who can be identified from it and relating—

    (a) to his physical or mental health, or

    (b) to spiritual counselling or assistance given or to be given to him.

(3) A person holds information in confidence for the purposes of this section if he holds it subject—

    (a) to an express or implied undertaking to hold it in confidence, or

    (b) to a restriction on disclosure or an obligation of secrecy contained in any enactment (including an enactment contained in an Act passed after this Act).

100   Confidential journalistic material

(1) In section 97 "confidential journalistic material" means—

    (a) material acquired or created for the purposes of journalism which—

        (i) is in the possession of persons who acquired or created it for those purposes,

        (ii) is held subject to an undertaking, restriction or obligation of the kind mentioned in section 99(3), and

        (iii) has been continuously held (by one or more persons) subject to such an undertaking, restriction or obligation since it was first acquired or created for the purposes of journalism, and

    (b) communications as a result of which information is acquired for the purposes of journalism and held as mentioned in paragraph (a)(ii).

(2) For the purposes of subsection (1), a person who receives material, or acquires information, from someone who intends that the recipient shall use it for the purposes of journalism is to be taken to have acquired it for those purposes.

101–102   ...

103 Quashing of authorisations etc.

(1) Where, at any time, a Commissioner appointed under section 91(1)(b) is satisfied that, at the time an authorisation was given or renewed, there were no reasonable grounds for believing the matters specified in section 93(2), he may quash the authorisation or, as the case may be, renewal.

(2) Where, in the case of an authorisation or renewal to which section 97 does not apply, a Commissioner appointed under section 91(1)(b) is at any time satisfied that, at the time the authorisation was given or, as the case may be, renewed, —

(a) there were reasonable grounds for believing any of the matters specified in subsection (2) of section 97, and

(b) there were no reasonable grounds for believing the case to be one of urgency for the purposes of subsection (3) of that section,

he may quash the authorisation or, as the case may be, renewal.

(3) Where a Commissioner quashes an authorisation or renewal under subsection (1) or (2), he may order the destruction of any records relating to information obtained by virtue of the authorisation (or, in the case of a renewal, relating wholly or partly to information so obtained after the renewal) other than records required for pending criminal or civil proceedings.

(4)–(9) ★ ★ ★ ★ ★

Appeals

104 Appeals by authorising officers

(1) An authorising officer who gives an authorisation, or in whose absence it is given, may, within the prescribed period, appeal to the Chief Commissioner against—

(a) any refusal to approve the authorisation or any renewal of it under section 97;

(b) any decision to quash the authorisation, or any renewal of it, under subsection (1) of section 103;

(c) any decision to quash the authorisation, or any renewal of it, under subsection (2) of that section;

(d) any decision to cancel the authorisation under subsection (4) of that section;

(e) any decision to order the destruction of records under subsection (5) of that section;

(f) any refusal to make an order under subsection (6) of that section;

[(g) ★ ★ ★ ★ ★]

(2) In subsection (1), "the prescribed period" means the period of seven days beginning with the day on which the refusal, decision or, as the case may be, determination appealed against is reported to the authorising officer.

(3) In determining an appeal within subsection (1)(a), the Chief Commissioner shall, if he is satisfied that there are reasonable grounds for believing the matters specified in section 93(2), allow the appeal and direct the Commissioner to approve the authorisation or renewal under that section.

(4)–(8) ★ ★ ★ ★ ★

105 ★ ★ ★ ★ ★

General

106 ...

107 Supplementary provisions relating to Commissioners

(1) The Chief Commissioner shall keep under review the performance of functions under this Part.

(2) The Chief Commissioner shall make an annual report on the [matters with which he is concerned] to the Prime Minister [and to the Scottish Ministers] and may at any time report to him [or them (as the case may require)] on [anything relating to any of those matters.]

(3) The Prime Minister shall lay before each House of Parliament a copy of each annual report made by the Chief Commissioner under subsection (2) together with a statement as to whether any matter has been excluded from that copy in pursuance of subsection (4) below.

[(3A) The Scottish Ministers shall lay before the Scottish Parliament a copy of each annual report made by the Chief Commissioner under subsection (2), together with a statement as to whether any matter has been excluded from that copy in pursuance of subsection (4) below.]

(4) The Prime Minister may exclude a matter from the copy of a report as laid before each House of Parliament, if it appears to him, after consultation with the Chief Commissioner [and the Scottish Ministers], that the publication of that matter in the report would be prejudicial to [any of the purposes for which authorisations may be given or granted under this Part of this Act or Part II of the Regulation of Investigatory Powers Act 2000 or under any enactment contained in or made under an act of the Scottish Parliament which makes provision equivalent to that made by Part II of that Act of 2000 or] to the discharge of—

> (a) the functions of any police authority,
> (b) the functions of the Service Authority for the National Criminal Intelligence Service or the Service Authority for the National Crime Squad, or
> (c) the duties of the Commissioners of Customs and Excise,

(5)–(5C) ★ ★ ★ ★ ★

(6) . . .

108 ★ ★ ★ ★ ★

Protection from Harassment Act 1997
(1997, c. 40)

An Act to make provision for protecting persons from harassment and similar conduct.

[21 March 1997]

Territorial extent: England and Wales (sections printed). Sections 8–11 make corresponding provisions for Scotland; s. 13 provides for equivalent legislation by Order for Northern Ireland.

England and Wales

1 Prohibition of harassment

(1) A person must not pursue a course of conduct—

> (a) which amounts to harassment of another, and
> (b) which he knows or ought to know amounts to harassment of the other.

(2) For the purposes of this section, the person whose course of conduct is in question ought to know that it amounts to harassment of another if a reasonable person in possession of the same information would think the course of conduct amounted to harassment of the other.

(3) Subsection (1) does not apply to a course of conduct if the person who pursued it shows—

> (a) that it was pursued for the purpose of preventing or detecting crime,
> (b) that it was pursued under any enactment or rule of law or to comply with any

condition or requirement imposed by any person under any enactment, or

(c) that in the particular circumstances the pursuit of the course of conduct was reasonable.

2   Offence of harassment

(1) A person who pursues a course of conduct in breach of section 1 is guilty of an offence.

(2) A person guilty of an offence under this section is liable on summary conviction to imprisonment for a term not exceeding six months, or a fine not exceeding level 5 on the standard scale, or both.

(3) In section 24(2) of the Police and Criminal Evidence Act 1984 (arrestable offences), after paragraph (m) there is inserted—

"(n) An offence under section 2 of the Protection from Harassment Act 1997 (harassment)."

3   Civil remedy

(1) An actual or apprehended breach of section 1 may be the subject of a claim in civil proceedings by the person who is or may be the victim of the course of conduct in question.

(2) On such a claim, damages may be awarded for (among other things) any anxiety caused by the harassment and any financial loss resulting from the harassment.

(3) Where—

(a) in such proceedings the High Court or a county court grants an injunction for the purpose of restraining the defendant from pursuing any conduct which amounts to harassment, and

(b) the plaintiff considers that the defendant has done anything which he is prohibited from doing by the injunction,

the plaintiff may apply for the issue of a warrant for the arrest of the defendant.

(4) An application under subsection (3) may be made—

(a) where the injunction was granted by the High Court, to a judge of that court, and

(b) where the injunction was granted by a county court, to a judge or district judge of that or any other county court.

(5) The judge or district judge to whom an application under subsection (3) is made may only issue a warrant if—

(a) the application is substantiated on oath, and

(b) the judge or district judge has reasonable grounds for believing that the defendant has done anything which he is prohibited from doing by the injunction.

(6) Where—

(a) the High Court or a county court grants an injunction for the purpose mentioned in subsection (3)(a), and

(b) without reasonable excuse the defendant does anything which he is prohibited from doing by the injunction,

he is guilty of an offence.

(7) Where a person is convicted of an offence under subsection (6) in respect of any conduct, that conduct is not punishable as a contempt of court.

(8) A person cannot be convicted of an offence under subsection (6) in respect of any conduct which has been punished as a contempt of court.

(9) A person guilty of an offence under subsection (6) is liable—

(a) on conviction on indictment, to imprisonment for a term not exceeding five years, or a fine, or both, or

(b) on summary conviction, to imprisonment for a term not exceeding six months, or a fine not exceeding the statutory maximum, or both.

4   Putting people in fear of violence

(1) A person whose course of conduct causes another to fear, on at least two occasions,

that violence will be used against him is guilty of an offence if he knows or ought to know that his course of conduct will cause the other so to fear on each of those occasions.

(2) For the purposes of this section, the person whose course of conduct is in question ought to know that it will cause another to fear that violence will be used against him on any occasion if a reasonable person in possession of the same information would think the course of conduct would cause the other so to fear on that occasion.

(3) It is a defence for a person charged with an offence under this section to show that—

 (a) his course of conduct was pursued for the purpose of preventing or detecting crime,

 (b) his course of conduct was pursued under any enactment or rule of law or to comply with any condition or requirement imposed by any person under any enactment, or

 (c) the pursuit of his course of conduct was reasonable for the protection of himself or another or for the protection of his or another's property.

(4) A person guilty of an offence under this section is liable—

 (a) on conviction on indictment, to imprisonment for a term not exceeding five years, or a fine, or both, or

 (b) on summary conviction, to imprisonment for a term not exceeding six months, or a fine not exceeding the statutory maximum, or both.

(5), (6) ★ ★ ★ ★ ★

5 Restraining orders

(1) A court sentencing or otherwise dealing with a person ("the defendant") convicted of an offence under section 2 or 4 may (as well as sentencing him or dealing with him in any other way) make an order under this section.

(2) The order may, for the purpose of protecting the victim of the offence, or any other person mentioned in the order, from further conduct which—

 (a) amounts to harassment, or

 (b) will cause a fear of violence,

prohibit the defendant from doing anything described in the order.

(4)–(6) ★ ★ ★ ★ ★

6 ★ ★ ★ ★ ★

7 Interpretation of this group of sections

(1) This section applies for the interpretation of sections 1 to 5.

(2) References to harassing a person include alarming the person or causing the person distress.

(3) A "course of conduct" must involve conduct on at least two occasions.

[(3A) A person's conduct on any occasion shall be taken, if aided, abetted, counselled or procured by another—

 (a) to be conduct on that occasion of the other (as well as conduct of the person whose conduct it is); and

 (b) to be conduct in relation to which the other's knowledge and purpose, and what he ought to have known, are the same as they were in relation to what was contemplated or reasonably foreseeable at the time of the aiding, abetting, counselling or procuring.]

(4) "Conduct" includes speech.

8–16 ★ ★ ★ ★ ★

Special Immigration Appeals Commission Act 1997
(1997, c. 68)

An Act to establish the Special Immigration Appeals Commission; to make provision with respect to its jurisdiction; and for connected purposes. [17 December 1997]

Territorial extent: United Kingdom

1 Establishment of the Commission

(1) There shall be a commission, known as the Special Immigration Appeals Commission, for the purpose of exercising the jurisdiction conferred by this Act.

(2) Schedule 1 to this Act shall have effect in relation to the Commission.

[(3) The Commission shall be a superior court of record.

(4) A decision of the Commission shall be questioned in legal proceedings only in accordance with—.

(a) section 7, or

(b) section 30(5)(a) of the Anti-terrorism, Crime and Security Act 2001 (derogation).]

2 Jurisdiction: appeals

[(1) A person may appeal to the Special Immigration Appeals Commission against a decision which he would be entitled to appeal against under Part IV of the Immigration and Asylum Act 1999 ("the 1999 Act") but for a public interest provision.

(1A) Subsection (1) does not apply to an appeal under section 59(2) of the 1999 Act.

(1B) "Public interest provision" means any of sections 60(9), 62(4), 64(1) or (2) or 70(1) to (6) of the 1999 Act.

(1C) A reference in this Act to an appeal under this section includes a reference to an appeal under regulation 29(1) of the Immigration (European Economic Area) Regulations 2000 (other than on the ground mentioned in paragraph (2) of that regulation) which lies to the Commission as a result of regulation 31 of those Regulations.]

(2) A person may appeal to the Special Immigration Appeals Commission against the refusal of an entry clearance if he would be entitled to appeal against the refusal under [section 59(2) of the 1999 Act but for section 60(9) of that Act] (exclusion conducive to public good), and–

(a) he seeks to rely on an enforceable Community right or any provision made under section 2(2) of the European Communities Act 1972, or

(b) he seeks to enter the United Kingdom under immigration rules making provision about entry—

(i) to exercise rights of access to a child resident there,

(ii) as the spouse or fiance of a person present and settled there, or

(iii) as the parent, grandparent or other dependent relative of a person present and settled there.

(3) Schedule 2 to this Act (which makes supplementary provision relating to appeals under this section) shall have effect.

(4) In this section, "immigration rules" has the same meaning as in the Immigration Act 1971.

[2A Jurisdiction: racial discrimination and human rights

(1) A person who alleges that an authority has, in taking an appealable decision, racially discriminated against him or acted in breach of his human rights may appeal to the Commission against that decision.

(2) For the purposes of this section—

(a) an authority racially discriminates against a person if he acts, or fails to act, in relation to that other person in a way which is unlawful by virtue of section 19B of the Race Relations Act 1976; and

    (b) an authority acts in breach of a person's human rights if he acts, or fails to act, in relation to that other person in a way which is made unlawful by section 6(1) of the Human Rights Act 1998.

(3) Subsections (4) and (5) apply if, in any appellate proceedings being heard by the Commission, a question arises as to whether an authority has, in taking a decision which is the subject of the proceedings, racially discriminated against the appellant or acted in breach of the appellant's human rights.

(4) The Commission has jurisdiction to consider the question.

(5) If the Commission decides that the authority concerned—

    (a) racially discriminated against the appellant; or

    (b) acted in breach of the appellant's human rights, the appeal may be allowed on [the ground in question].

(6) "Authority" means—

    (a) the Secretary of State;

    (b) an immigration officer;

    (c) a person responsible for the grant or refusal of entry clearance.

(7) "Appealable decision" means a decision against which a person would be entitled to appeal under Part IV of the 1999 Act but for a public interest provision.

(8) "The 1999 Act" and "public interest provision" have the same meaning as in section 2.

(9) A reference in this Act to an appeal under this section includes a reference to an appeal under regulation 29(1) of the Immigration (European Economic Area) Regulations 2000, on the ground mentioned in paragraph (2) of that regulation, which lies to the Commission as a result of regulation 31 of those Regulations.]

3 ★ ★ ★ ★ ★

4 Determination of appeals

(1) The Special Immigration Appeals Commission on an appeal to it under this Act—

    (a) shall allow the appeal if it considers—

        (i) that the decision or action against which the appeal is brought was not in accordance with the law or with any immigration rules applicable to the case, or

        (ii) where the decision or action involved the exercise of a discretion by the Secretary of State or an officer, that the discretion should have been exercised differently, and

    (b) in any other case, shall dismiss the appeal.

[(1A) If a certificate under section 70(4)(b) of the Immigration and Asylum Act 1999 has been issued, the Commission on an appeal to it under this Act may, instead of determining the appeal, quash the certificate and remit the appeal to an adjudicator.]

(2) Where an appeal is allowed, the Commission shall give such directions for giving effect to the determination as it thinks requisite, and may also make recommendations with respect to any other action which it considers should be taken in the case under the Immigration Act 1971; and it shall be the duty of the Secretary of State and of any officer to whom directions are given under this subsection to comply with them.

(3) In this section, "immigration rules" has the same meaning as in the Immigration Act 1971.

5 Procedure in relation to jurisdiction under sections 2 and 3

(1) The Lord Chancellor may make rules—

    (a) for regulating the exercise of the rights of appeal conferred by section 2 or 2A above,

    (b) for prescribing the practice and procedure to be followed on or in connection with appeals under section 2 or 2A above including the mode and burden of proof and admissibility of evidence on such appeals, and

    (c) for other matters preliminary or incidental to or arising out of such appeals, including proof of the decisions of the Special Immigration Appeals Commission.

(2) Rules under this section shall provide that an appellant has the right to be legally represented in any proceedings before the Commission on an appeal under [section 2 or 2A] above, subject to any power conferred on the Commission by such rules.

(3) Rules under this section may, in particular—

    (a) make provision enabling proceedings before the Commission to take place without the appellant being given full particulars of the reasons for the decision which is the subject of the appeal,

    (b) make provision enabling the Commission to hold proceedings in the absence of any person, including the appellant and any legal representative appointed by him,

    (c) make provision about the functions in proceedings before the Commission of persons appointed under section 6 below, and

    (d) make provision enabling the Commission to give the appellant a summary of any evidence taken in his absence.

(4) Rules under this section may also include provision—

    (a) enabling any functions of the Commission which relate to matters preliminary or incidental to an appeal, or which are conferred by Part II of Schedule 2 to the Immigration Act 1971, to be performed by a single member of the Commission, or

    (b) conferring on the Commission such ancillary powers as the Lord Chancellor thinks necessary for the purposes of the exercise of its functions.

(5) The power to make rules under this section shall include power to make rules with respect to applications to the Commission under paragraphs 22 to 24 of Schedule 2 to the Immigration Act 1971 and matters arising out of such applications.

(6) In making rules under this section the Lord Chancellor shall have regard, in particular, to—

    (a) the need to secure that decisions which are the subject of appeals are properly reviewed, and

    (b) the need to secure that information is not disclosed contrary to the public interest.

(7) . . .

(8) The power to make rules under this section shall be exercisable by statutory instrument.

(9) No rules shall be made under this section unless a draft of them has been laid before and approved by resolution of each House of Parliament.

6 Appointment of person to represent the appellant's interests

(1) The relevant law officer may appoint a person to represent the interests of an appellant in any proceedings before the Special Immigration Appeals Commission from which the appellant and any legal representative of his are excluded.

(2) For the purposes of subsection (1) above, the relevant law officer is–

    (a) in relation to proceedings before the Commission in England and Wales, the Attorney General,

    (b) in relation to proceedings before the Commission in Scotland, the Lord Advocate, and

    (c) in relation to proceedings before the Commission in Northern Ireland, the Attorney General for Northern Ireland.

(3) A person appointed under subsection (1) above—

    (a) if appointed for the purposes of proceedings in England and Wales, shall have a general qualification for the purposes of section 71 of the Courts and Legal Services Act 1990,

(b) if appointed for the purposes of proceedings in Scotland, shall be—
   (i) an advocate, or
   (ii) a solicitor who has by virtue of section 25A of the Solicitors (Scotland) Act 1980 rights of audience in the Court of Session and the High Court of Justiciary, and

(c) if appointed for the purposes of proceedings in Northern Ireland, shall be a member of the Bar of Northern Ireland.

(4) A person appointed under subsection (1) above shall not be responsible to the person whose interests he is appointed to represent.

7   Appeals from the Commission

(1) Where the Special Immigration Appeals Commission has made a final determination of an appeal, any party to the appeal may bring a further appeal to the appropriate appeal court on any question of law material to that determination.

(2) An appeal under this section may be brought only with the leave of the Commission or, if such leave is refused, with the leave of the appropriate appeal court.

(3) In this section "the appropriate appeal court" means—

(a) in relation to a determination made by the Commission in England and Wales, the Court of Appeal,

(b) in relation to a determination made by the Commission in Scotland, the Court of Session, and

(c) in relation to a determination made by the Commission in Northern Ireland, the Court of Appeal in Northern Ireland.

★ ★ ★ ★ ★

Audit Commission Act 1998
(1998, c. 18)

An Act to consolidate Part III of the Local Government Finance Act 1982 and other enactments relating to the Audit Commission for Local Authorities and the National Health Service in England and Wales.   [11 June 1998]

Territorial extent: England and Wales

PART I   THE AUDIT COMMISSION

1   The Audit Commission

(1) There shall continue to be a body known as the Audit Commission for Local Authorities and the National Health Service in England and Wales.

(2) The Commission shall consist of not less than 15 nor more than 20 members appointed by the Secretary of State.

(3) The Secretary of State shall appoint one of the members to be chairman and another to be deputy chairman.

(4) An appointment under subsection (2) or (3) shall be made after consultation with such organisations and other bodies as appear to the Secretary of State to be appropriate.

(5) ★ ★ ★ ★ ★

2   ★ ★ ★ ★ ★

3 Appointment of auditors

(1) An auditor appointed by the Commission to audit the accounts of a body whose accounts are required to be audited in accordance with this Act ("a body subject to audit") may be—

(a) an officer of the Commission,

(b) an individual who is not an officer of the commission, or

(c) a firm of individuals who are not officers of the Commission.

(2) Where two or more auditors are appointed in relation to the accounts of a body, some but not others may be officers of the Commission and they may be appointed—

(a) to act jointly;

(b) to act separately in relation to different parts of the accounts; or

(c) to discharge different functions in relation to the audit.

(3) Before appointing an auditor or auditors to audit the accounts of a body other than a health service body the Commission shall consult that body.

(4)–(11) ★ ★ ★ ★ ★

4 Code of audit practice

(1) The Commission shall prepare, and keep under review, a code of audit practice prescribing the way in which auditors are to carry out their functions under this Act.

(2) A different code may be prepared with respect to the audit of the accounts of health service bodies as compared with the code applicable to the accounts of other bodies.

(3) A code prepared under this section shall embody what appears to the Commission to be the best professional practice with respect to the standards, procedures and techniques to be adopted by auditors.

(4) A code does not come into force until approved by a resolution of each House of Parliament, and its continuation in force is subject to its being so approved at intervals of not more than five years.

(5) Subsection (4) does not preclude alterations to a code being made by the Commission in the intervals between its being approved in accordance with that subsection.

(6) The Commission shall send copies of any code prepared under this section, and of any alterations made to such a code, to the Secretary of State who shall lay them before Parliament; and the Commission shall from time to time publish any such code as for the time being in force.

(7) Before preparing or altering a code applicable to any accounts, the Commission shall consult—

(a) if the accounts are or include those of health service bodies, such organisations connected with the health service as appear to the Commission to be concerned;

(b) if the accounts are or include those of other bodies, such associations of local authorities as appear to the Commission to be concerned; and

(c) in any case, such bodies of accountants as appear to the Commission to be appropriate.

5 General duties of auditors

(1) In auditing accounts required to be audited in accordance with this Act, an auditor shall by examination of the accounts and otherwise satisfy himself—

(a) if they are accounts of a health service body, that they are prepared in accordance with directions under subsection (2), (2A) (NHS trusts) or (2B) (fundholding practices) of section 98 of the National Health Service Act 1997;

(b) in any other case, that they are prepared in accordance with regulations under section 27;

(c) that they comply with the requirements of all other statutory provisions applicable to the accounts;

(d) that proper practices have been observed in the compilation of the accounts;

(e) that the body whose accounts are being audited has made proper arrangements for securing economy, efficiency and effectiveness in its use of resources; and

(f) that that body, if required to publish information in pursuance of a direction under section 44 (performance information), has made such arrangements for collecting and recording the information and for publishing it as are required for the performance of its duties under that section.

(2) The auditor shall comply with the code of audit practice applicable to the accounts being audited as that code is for the time being in force.

(3)–(7) ★ ★ ★ ★ ★

6   Auditors' right to documents and information

(1) An auditor has a right of access at all reasonable times to every document relating to a body subject to audit which appears to him necessary for the purposes of his functions under this Act.

(2) An auditor may—

(a) require a person holding or accountable for any such document to give him such information and explanation as he thinks necessary for the purposes of his functions under this Act; and

(b) if he thinks it necessary, require the person to attend before him in person to give the information or explanation or to produce the document.

(3)–(7) ★ ★ ★ ★ ★

7   ★ ★ ★ ★ ★

8   Immediate and other reports in public interest

In auditing accounts required to be audited in accordance with this Act, the auditor shall consider—

(a) whether, in the public interest, he should make a report on any matter coming to his notice in the course of the audit, in order for it to be considered by the body concerned or brought to the attention of the public, and

(b) whether the public interest requires any such matter to be made the subject of an immediate report rather than of a report to be made at the conclusion of the audit.

9   General report

(1) When an auditor has concluded his audit of the accounts of any body under this Act he shall, subject to subsection (2), enter on the relevant statement of accounts prepared pursuant to regulations under section 27 (or, where no such statement is required to be prepared, on the accounts)—

(a) a certificate that he has completed the audit in accordance with this Act, and

(b) his opinion on the statement (or, as the case may be, on the accounts).

(2) Where an auditor makes a report to the body concerned under section 8 at the conclusion of the audit, he may include the certificate and opinion referred to in subsection (1) in that report instead of making an entry on the statement or accounts.

10–13   ★ ★ ★ ★ ★

Public inspection etc. and action by the auditor

14   Inspection of statements of accounts and auditors' reports

(1) A local government elector for the area of a body subject to audit, other than a health service body, may—

(a) inspect and make copies of any statement of accounts prepared by the body pursuant to regulations under section 27;

(b) inspect and make copies of any report, other than an immediate report, made to the body by an auditor; and

(c) require copies of any such statement or report to be delivered to him on payment of a reasonable sum for each copy.

(2) A document which a person is entitled to inspect under this section may be inspected by him at all reasonable times and without payment.

(3) A person who has the custody of any such document and—

(a) obstructs a person in the exercise of a right under this section to inspect or make copies of the document, or

(b) refuses to give copies of the document to a person entitled under this section to obtain them,

is guilty of an offence and liable on summary conviction to a fine not exceeding level 3 on the standard scale.

(4) References in this section to copies of a document include references to copies of any part of it.

15 Inspection of documents and questions at audit

(1) At each audit under this Act, other than an audit of accounts of a health service body, any persons interested may—

(a) inspect the accounts to be audited and all books, deeds, contracts, bills, vouchers and receipts relating to them, and

(b) make copies of all or any part of the accounts and those other documents.

(2) At the request of a local government elector for any area to which the accounts relate, the auditor shall give the elector, or any representative of his, an opportunity to question the auditor about the accounts.

(3) Nothing in this section entitles a person—

(a) to inspect so much of any accounts or other document as contains personal information about a member of the staff of the body whose accounts are being audited; or

(b) to require any such information to be disclosed in answer to any question.

(4), (5) ★ ★ ★ ★ ★

16 Right to make objections at audit

(1) At each audit of accounts under this Act, other than an audit of accounts of a health service body, a local government elector for an area to which the accounts relate, or any representative of his, may attend before the auditor and (in accordance with subsection (2)) make objections—

(a) as to any matter in respect of which the auditor could take action under section 17 . . .

(b) as to any other matter in respect of which the auditor could make a report under section 8.

(2) No objection may be made under subsection (1) unless the auditor has received written notice of the proposed objection and of the grounds on which it is to be made.

(3) An elector sending a notice to an auditor for the purposes of subsection (2) shall at the same time send a copy of the notice to the body whose accounts are being audited.

17, 19 ★ ★ ★ ★ ★

18, 20-23 . . .

24 Power of auditor to apply for judicial review

(1) Subject to section 31(3) of the Supreme Court Act 1981 (no application for judicial review without leave) the auditor appointed in relation to the accounts of a body other than a health service body may make an application for judicial review with respect to—

(a) any decision of that body, or

(b) any failure by that body to act,

which it is reasonable to believe would have an effect on the accounts of that body.

(2) The existence of the powers conferred on an auditor under this Act is not a ground for refusing an application falling within subsection (1) (or an application for leave to make such an application).

(3) On an application for judicial review made as mentioned in subsection (1), the court may make such order as it thinks fit for the payment, by the body to whose decision the application relates, of expenses incurred by the auditor in connection with the application.

★ ★ ★ ★ ★

Bank of England Act 1998
(1998, c. 11)

An Act to make provision about the constitution, regulation, financial arrangements and functions of the Bank of England, including provision for the transfer of supervisory functions; to amend the Banking Act 1987 in relation to the provision and disclosure of information; to make provision relating to appointments to the governing body of a designated agency under the Financial Services Act 1986; to amend Schedule 5 to that Act; to make provision relating to the registration of Government stocks and bonds; to make provision about the application of section 207 of the Companies Act 1989 to bearer securities; and for connected purposes.   [23 April 1998]

Territorial extent: United Kingdom

1   Court of directors
(1) There shall continue to be a court of directors of the Bank.

(2) The court shall consist of a Governor, 2 Deputy Governors and 16 directors of the Bank, all of whom shall be appointed by Her Majesty.

(3) On the day on which this Act comes into force, all persons who are, immediately before that day, holding office as director of the Bank shall vacate their office.

(4) ★ ★ ★ ★ ★

2   Functions of court of directors
(1) The court of directors of the Bank shall manage the Bank's affairs, other than the formulation of monetary policy.

(2) In particular, the court's functions under subsection (1) shall include determining the Bank's objectives (including objectives for its financial management) and strategy.

(3) In determining the Bank's objectives and strategy, the court's aim shall be to ensure the effective discharge of the Bank's functions.

(4) Subject to that, in determining objectives for the financial management of the Bank, the court's aim shall be to ensure the most efficient use of the Bank's resources.

3–10   ★ ★ ★ ★ ★

11   Objectives
In relation to monetary policy, the objectives of the Bank of England shall be—
   (a) to maintain price stability, and
   (b) subject to that, to support the economic policy of Her Majesty's Government, including its objectives for growth and employment.

12   Specification of matters relevant to objectives
(1) The Treasury may by notice in writing to the Bank specify for the purposes of section 11—
   (a) what price stability is to be taken to consist of, or
   (b) what the economic policy of Her Majesty's Government is to be taken to be.

(2) The Treasury shall specify under subsection (1) both of the matters mentioned there—

    (a) before the end of the period of 7 days beginning with the day on which this Act comes into force, and

    (b) at least once in every period of 12 months beginning on the anniversary of the day on which this Act comes into force.

(3) Where the Treasury give notice under this section they shall—

    (a) publish the notice in such manner as they think fit, and

    (b) lay a copy of it before Parliament.

13–18 ★ ★ ★ ★ ★

19 Reserve powers

(1) The Treasury, after consultation with the Governor of the Bank, may by order give the Bank directions with respect to monetary policy if they are satisfied that the directions are required in the public interest and by extreme economic circumstances.

(2) An order under this section may include such consequential modifications of the provisions of this Part relating to the Monetary Policy Committee as the Treasury think fit.

(3) A statutory instrument containing an order under this section shall be laid before Parliament after being made.

(4) Unless an order under this section is approved by resolution of each House of Parliament before the end of the period of 28 days beginning with the day on which it is made, it shall cease to have effect at the end of that period.

(5) In reckoning the period of 28 days for the purposes of subsection (4), no account shall be taken of any time during which Parliament is dissolved or prorogued or during which either House is adjourned for more than 4 days.

(6) An order under this section which does not cease to have effect before the end of the period of 3 months beginning with the day on which it is made shall cease to have effect at the end of that period.

(7) While an order under this section has effect, section 11 shall not have effect.

★ ★ ★ ★ ★

Crime and Disorder Act 1998
(1998, c. 37)

An Act to make provision for preventing crime and disorder; to create certain racially-aggravated offences; to abolish the rebuttable presumption that a child is doli incapax and to make provision as to the effect of a child's failure to give evidence at his trial; to abolish the death penalty for treason and piracy; to make changes to the criminal justice system; to make further provision for dealing with offenders; to make further provision with respect to remands and committals for trial and the release and recall of prisoners; to amend Chapter I of Part II of the Crime (Sentences) Act 1997 and to repeal Chapter I of Part III of the Crime and Punishment (Scotland) Act 1997; to make amendments designed to facilitate, or otherwise desirable in connection with, the consolidation of certain enactments; and for connected purposes. [31 July 1998]

Territorial extent: England, Wales, Scotland. Certain provisions (not reproduced here) concerning the abolition of the death penalty for treason and piracy apply to Northern Ireland.

Crime and disorder: general

1 Anti-social behaviour orders

(1) An application for an order under this section may be made by a relevant authority if

it appears to the authority that the following conditions are fulfilled with respect to any person aged 10 or over, namely—

> (a) that the person has acted, since the commencement date, in an anti-social manner, that is to say, in a manner that caused or was likely to cause harassment, alarm or distress to one or more persons not of the same household as himself; and
>
> (b) that such an order is necessary to protect persons in the local government area in which the harassment, alarm or distress was caused or was likely to be caused from further anti-social acts by him;

and in this section "relevant authority" means the council for the local government area or any chief officer of police any part of whose police area lies within that area.

(2) A relevant authority shall not make such an application without consulting each other relevant authority.

(3) Such an application shall be made by complaint to the magistrates' court whose commission area includes the place where it is alleged that the harassment, alarm or distress was caused or was likely to be caused.

(4) If, on such an application, it is proved that the conditions mentioned in subsection (1) above are fulfilled, the magistrates' court may make an order under this section (an "anti-social behaviour order") which prohibits the defendant from doing anything described in the order.

(5) For the purpose of determining whether the condition mentioned in subsection (1)(a) above is fulfilled, the court shall disregard any act of the defendant which he shows was reasonable in the circumstances.

(6) The prohibitions that may be imposed by an anti-social behaviour order are those necessary for the purpose of protecting from further anti-social acts by the defendant–

> (a) persons in the local government area; and
>
> (b) persons in any adjoining local government area specified in the application for the order;

and a relevant authority shall not specify an adjoining local government area in the application without consulting the council for that area and each chief officer of police any part of whose police area lies within that area.

(7) An anti-social behaviour order shall have effect for a period (not less than two years) specified in the order or until further order.

(8) Subject to subsection (9) below, the applicant or the defendant may apply by complaint to the court which made an anti-social behaviour order for it to be varied or discharged by a further order.

(9) Except with the consent of both parties, no anti-social behaviour order shall be discharged before the end of the period of two years beginning with the date of service of the order.

(10) If without reasonable excuse a person does anything which he is prohibited from doing by an anti-social behaviour order, he shall be liable–

> (a) on summary conviction, to imprisonment for a term not exceeding six months or to a fine not exceeding the statutory maximum, or to both; or
>
> (b) on conviction on indictment, to imprisonment for a term not exceeding five years or to a fine, or to both.

(11), (12) ★ ★ ★ ★ ★

2 Sex offender orders

(1) If it appears to a chief officer of police that the following conditions are fulfilled with respect to any person in his police area, namely—

> (a) that the person is a sex offender; and
>
> (b) that the person has acted, since the relevant date, in such a way as to give

reasonable cause to believe that an order under this section is necessary to protect the public from serious harm from him,

the chief officer may apply for an order under this section to be made in respect of the person.

(2) Such an application shall be made by complaint to the magistrates' court whose commission area includes any place where it is alleged that the defendant acted in such a way as is mentioned in subsection (1)(b) above.

(3) If, on such an application, it is proved that the conditions mentioned in subsection (1) above are fulfilled, the magistrates' court may make an order under this section (a "sex offender order") which prohibits the defendant from doing anything described in the order.

(4) The prohibitions that may be imposed by a sex offender order are those necessary for the purpose of protecting the public from serious harm from the defendant.

(5) A sex offender order shall have effect from a period (not less than five years) specified in the order or until further order; and while such an order has effect, Part I of the Sex Offenders Act 1997 shall have effect as if—

(a) the defendant were subject to the notification requirements of that Part; and

(b) in relation to the defendant, the relevant date (within the meaning of that Part) were the date of service of the order.

(6) Subject to subsection (7) below, the applicant or the defendant may apply by complaint to the court which made a sex offender order for it to be varied or discharged by a further order.

(7) Except with the consent of both parties, no sex offender order shall be discharged before the end of the period of five years beginning with the date of service of the order.

(8) If without reasonable excuse a person does anything which he is prohibited from doing by a sex offender order, he shall be liable—

(a) on summary conviction, to imprisonment for a term not exceeding six months or to a fine not exceeding the statutory maximum, or to both; or

(b) on conviction on indictment, to imprisonment for a term not exceeding five years or to a fine, or to both.

(9) Where a person is convicted of an offence under subsection (8) above, it shall not be open to the court by or before which he is so convicted to make an order under subsection (1)(b) (conditional discharge) of [section 12 of the Powers of Criminal Courts (Sentencing) Act 2000] in respect of the offence.

3 Sex offender orders: supplemental

(1) In section 2 above and this section "sex offender" means a person who—

(a) has been convicted of a sexual offence to which Part I of the Sex Offenders Act 1997 applies;

(b) has been found not guilty of such an offence by reason of insanity, or found to be under a disability and to have done the act charged against him in respect of such an offence;

(c) has been cautioned by a constable, in England and Wales or Northern Ireland, in respect of such an offence which, at the time when the caution was given, he had admitted; or

(d) has been punished under the law in force in a country or territory outside the United Kingdom for an act which—

(i) constituted an offence under that law; and

(ii) would have constituted a sexual offence to which that Part applies if it had been done in any part of the United Kingdom.

(2) In subsection (1) of section 2 above "the relevant date", in relation to a sex offender, means—

(a) the date or, as the case may be, the latest date on which he has been convicted, found, cautioned or punished as mentioned in subsection (1) above; or

(b) if later, the date of the commencement of that section.

(3)–(7) ★ ★ ★ ★ ★

4   Appeals against orders

(1) An appeal shall lie to the Crown Court against the making by a magistrates' court of an anti-social behaviour order or sex offender order.

(2) On such an appeal the Crown Court—

    (a) may make such orders as may be necessary to give effect to its determination of the appeal; and

    (b) may also make such incidental or consequential orders as appear to it to be just

(3) Any order of the Crown Court made on an appeal under this section (other than one directing that an application be re-heard by a magistrates' court), shall, for the purposes of section 1(8) or 2(6) above, be treated as if it were an order of the magistrates' court from which the appeal was brought and not an order of the Crown Court.

5–11   ★ ★ ★ ★ ★

11   Child safety orders

(1) Subject to subsection (2) below, if a magistrates' court, on the application of a local authority, is satisfied that one or more of the conditions specified in subsection (3) below are fulfilled with respect to a child under the age of 10, it may make an order (a "child safety order") which—

    (a) places the child, for a period (not exceeding the permitted maximum) specified in the order, under the supervision of the responsible officer; and

    (b) requires the child to comply with such requirements as are so specified.

(2) A court shall not make a child safety order unless it has been notified by the Secretary of State that arrangements for implementing such orders are available in the area in which it appears that the child resides or will reside and the notice has not been withdrawn.

(3) The conditions are—

    (a) that the child has committed an act which, if he had been aged 10 or over, would have constituted an offence;

    (b) that a child safety order is necessary for the purpose of preventing the commission by the child of such an act as is mentioned in paragraph (a) above;

    (c) that the child has contravened a ban imposed by a curfew notice; and

    (d) that the child has acted in a manner that caused or was likely to cause harassment, alarm or distress to one or more persons not of the same household as himself.

(4) The maximum period permitted for the purposes of subsection (1)(a) above is three months or, where the court is satisfied that the circumstances of the case are exceptional, 12 months.

(5) The requirements that may be specified under subsection (1)(b) above are those which the court considers desirable in the interests of—

    (a) securing that the child receives appropriate care, protection and support and is subject to proper control; or

    (b) preventing any repetition of the kind of behaviour which led to the child safety order being made.

(6) Proceedings under this section or section 12 below shall be family proceedings for the purposes of the 1989 Act or section 65 of the Magistrates' Courts Act 1980 ("the 1980 Act"); and the standard of proof applicable to such proceedings shall be that applicable to civil proceedings.

(7) In this section "local authority" has the same meaning as in the 1989 Act.

(8) In this section and section 12 below, "responsible officer", in relation to a child safety order, means one of the following who is specified in the order, namely—

    (a) a social worker of a local authority social services department; and

(b) a member of a youth offending team.

12 ★ ★ ★ ★ ★

13 Appeals against child safety orders
(1) An appeal shall lie to the High Court against the making by a magistrates' court of a child safety order; and on such an appeal the High Court—
(a) may make such orders as may be necessary to give effect to its determination of the appeal; and
(b) may also make such incidental or consequential orders as appear to it to be just.
(2) ★ ★ ★ ★ ★

14 Local child curfew schemes
(1) A local authority [or a chief officer of police] may make a scheme (a "local child curfew scheme") for enabling the authority [or (as the case may be) the officer]—
(a) subject to and in accordance with the provisions of the scheme; and
(b) if, after such consultation as is required by the scheme, the authority [or (as the case may be the officer] considers it necessary to do so for the purpose of maintaining order,
to give a notice imposing, for a specified period (not exceeding 90 days), a ban to which subsection (2) below applies.
(2) This subsection applies to a ban on children of specified ages (under 10) being in a public place within a specified area—
(a) during specified hours (between 9 am and 6 am); and
(b) otherwise than under the effective control of a parent or a responsible person aged 18 or over.
(3) Before making a local child curfew scheme, a local authority shall consult—
(a) every chief officer of police any part of whose police area lies within its area; and
(b) such other persons or bodies as it considers appropriate.
[(3A) Before making a local child curfew scheme, a chief officer of police shall consult–
(a) every local authority any part of whose area lies within the area to be specified; and
(b) such other persons as he considers appropriate.]
[(4) A local child curfew scheme shall, if made by a local authority, be made under the common seal of the authority.
(4A) A local child curfew scheme shall not have effect until it is confirmed by the Secretary of State.]
(5) The Secretary of State—
(a) may confirm, or refuse to confirm, a local curfew scheme submitted under this section for confirmation; and
(b) may fix the date on which such a scheme is to come into operation; and if no date is so fixed, the scheme shall come into operation at the end of the period of one month beginning with the date of its confirmation.
(6) A notice given under a local child curfew scheme (a "curfew notice") may specify different hours in relation to children of different ages.
(7), (8) ★ ★ ★ ★ ★

15 Contravention of curfew notices
(1) Subsections (2) and (3) below apply where a constable has reasonable cause to believe that a child is in contravention of a ban imposed by a curfew notice.
(2) The constable shall, as soon as practicable, inform the local authority for the area that the child has contravened the ban.
(3) The constable may remove the child to the child's place of residence unless he has

reasonable cause to believe that the child would, if removed to that place, be likely to suffer significant harm.

(4) ★ ★ ★ ★ ★

16, 17, 18 ★ ★ ★ ★ ★

CHAPTER II SCOTLAND

19 Anti-social behaviour orders

(1) A local authority may make an application for an order under this section if it appears to the authority that the following conditions are fulfilled with respect to any person of or over the age of 16, namely—

  (a) that the person has—

   (i) acted in an anti-social manner, that is to say, in a manner that caused or was likely to cause alarm or distress; or

   (ii) pursued a course of anti-social conduct, that is to say, pursued a course of conduct that caused or was likely to cause alarm or distress,

to one or more persons not of the same household as himself in the authority's area (and in this section "anti-social acts" and "anti-social conduct" shall be construed accordingly); and

  (b) that such an order is necessary to protect persons in the authority's area from further anti-social acts or conduct by him.

(2) An application under subsection (1) above shall be made by summary application to the sheriff within whose sheriffdom the alarm or distress was alleged to have been caused or to have been likely to be caused.

(3) On an application under subsection (1) above, the sheriff may, if he is satisfied that the conditions mentioned in that subsection are fulfilled, make an order under this section (as "anti-social behaviour") which, for the purpose of protecting persons in the area of the local authority from further anti-social acts or conduct by the person against whom the order is sought, prohibits him from doing anything described in the order.

(4) For the purpose of determining whether the condition mentioned in subsection (1)(a) is fulfilled, the sheriff shall disregard any act of the person in respect of whom the application is made which that person shows was reasonable in the circumstances.

(5) This section does not apply in relation to anything done before the commencement of this section.

(6) Nothing in this section shall prevent a local authority from instituting any legal proceedings otherwise than under this section against any person in relation to any anti-social act or conduct.

(7) In this section "conduct" includes speech and a course of conduct must involve conduct on at least two occasions.

(8) In this section and section 21 below "local authority" means a council constituted under section 2 of the Local Government etc. (Scotland) Act 1994 and any reference to the area of such an authority is a reference to the local government area within the meaning of that Act for which it is so constituted.

20 Sex offender orders

(1) An application for an order under this section may be made by a chief constable if it appears to him that the conditions mentioned in subsection (2) below are fulfilled with respect to any person in the area of his police force.

(2) The conditions are—

  (a) that the person in respect of whom the application for the order is made is—

   (i) of or over the age of 16 years; and

   (ii) a sex offender; and

  (b) that the person has acted, since the relevant date, in such a way as to give reasonable cause to believe that an order under this section is necessary to protect the public from serious harm from him.

(3) An application under subsection (1) above shall be made by summary application to the sheriff within whose sheriffdom the person is alleged to have acted as mentioned in subsection (2)(b) above.

(4) On an application under subsection (1) above the sheriff may—

  (a) pending the determination of the application, make any such interim order as he considers appropriate; and

  (b) if he is satisfied that the conditions mentioned in subsection (2) above are fulfilled, make an order under this section ("a sex offender order") which prohibits the person in respect of whom it is made from doing anything described in the order.

(5) The prohibitions that may be imposed by an order made under subsection (4) above are those necessary for the purpose of protecting the public from serious harm from the person in respect of whom the order is made.

(6)–(8) ★ ★ ★ ★ ★

21   Procedural provisions with respect to orders

(1) Before making an application under—

  (a) section 19(1) above;

  (b) subsection (7)(b)(i) below,

the local authority shall consult the relevant chief constable.

(2) Before making an application under section 20(1) above or subsection (7)(b)(i) below, the chief constable shall consult the local authority within whose area the person in respect of whom the order is sought is for the time being.

(3)–(5) ★ ★ ★ ★ ★

(6) Subsections (7) to (9) below apply to anti-social behaviour orders and sex offender orders and subsections (8) and (9) below apply to an order made under section 20(4) above.

(7) An order to which this subsection applies—

  (a) shall have effect for a period specified in the order or indefinitely; and

  (b) may at any time be varied or revoked on a summary application by–

    (i) the local authority or, as the case may be, chief constable who obtained the order; or

    (ii) the person subject to the order.

(8) The clerk of the court by which an order to which this subsection applies is made or varied shall cause a copy of the order are so made or varied to be—

  (a) given to the person named in the order; or

  (b) sent to the person so named by registered post or by the recorded delivery service.

(9), (10) ★ ★ ★ ★ ★

22   Offences in connection with breach of orders

(1) Subject to subsection (3) below, if without reasonable excuse a person breaches an anti-social behaviour order by doing anything which he is prohibited from doing by the order, he shall be guilty of an offence and shall be liable—

  (a) on summary conviction, to a term of imprisonment not exceeding six months or to a fine not exceeding the statutory maximum or to both; or

  (b) on conviction on indictment, to imprisonment for a term not exceeding five years or to a fine or to both.

(2) Subsection (3) applies where—

  (a) the breach of the anti-social behaviour order referred to in subsection (1) above consists in the accused having acted in a manner prohibited by the order which constitutes a separate offence (in this section referred to as the "separate offence"); and

(3) Where this subsection applies, the accused shall not be liable to be proceeded against for an offence under subsection (1) above but, subject to subsection (4) below, the court which sentences him for that separate offence shall, in determining the appropriate sentence or disposal for that offence, have regard to—
  (a) the fact that the offence was committed by him while subject to an anti-social behaviour order;
  (b) the number of such orders to which he was subject at the time of the commission of the offence.
  (c) any previous conviction of the accused of an offence under subsection (1) above; and
  (d) the extent to which the sentence or disposal in respect of any such previous conviction of the accused differed, by virtue of this subsection, from that which the court would have imposed but for this subsection.
(4)–(7) ★ ★ ★ ★ ★

23-27 ★ ★ ★ ★ ★

PART II   CRIMINAL LAW

Racially [or religiously] aggravated offences: England and Wales

28   Meaning of "racially [or religiously] aggravated"
(1) An offence is racially [or religiously] aggravated for the purposes of sections 29 to 32 below if—
  (a) at the time of committing the offence, or immediately before or after doing so, the offender demonstrates towards the victim of the offence hostility based on the victim's membership (or presumed membership) of a racial [or religious] group; or
  (b) the offence is motivated (wholly or partly) by hostility towards members of a racial [or religious] group based on their membership of that group.
(2) In subsection (1)(a) above—
"membership", in relation to a racial [or religious] group, includes association with members of that group;
"presumed" means presumed by the offender.
(3) It is immaterial for the purposes of paragraph (a) or (b) of subsection (1) above whether or not the offender's hostility is also based, to any extent, on [any other factor not mentioned in that paragraph.]
(4) In this section "racial group" means a group of persons defined by reference to race, colour, nationality (including citizenship) or ethnic or national origins.
[(5) In this section "religious group" means a group of persons defined by reference to religious belief or lack of religious belief.]

29   Racially [or religiously] aggravated assaults
(1) A person is guilty of an offence under this section if he commits—
  (a) an offence under section 20 of the Offences Against the Person Act 1861 (malicious wounding or grievous bodily harm);
  (b) an offence under section 47 of that Act (actual bodily harm); or
  (c) common assault,
which is racially [or religiously] aggravated for the purposes of this section.
(2) A person guilty of an offence falling within subsection (1)(a) or (b) above shall be liable—
  (a) on summary conviction, to imprisonment for a term not exceeding six months or to a fine not exceeding the statutory maximum, or to both;

    (b) on conviction on indictment, to imprisonment for a term not exceeding seven years or to a fine, or to both.

  (3) A person guilty of an offence falling within subsection (1)(c) above shall be liable—

    (a) on summary conviction, to imprisonment for a term not exceeding six months or to a fine not exceeding the statutory maximum, or to both;

    (b) on conviction on indictment, to imprisonment for a term not exceeding two years or to a fine, or to both.

30 Racially [or religiously] aggravated criminal damage

  (1) A person is guilty of an offence under this section if he commits an offence under section 1(1) of the Criminal Damage Act 1971 (destroying or damaging property belonging to another) which is racially [or religiously] aggravated for the purposes of this section.

  (2) A person guilty of an offence under this section shall be liable—

    (a) on summary conviction, to imprisonment for a term not exceeding six months or to a fine not exceeding the statutory maximum, or to both;

    (b) on conviction on indictment, to imprisonment for a term not exceeding fourteen years or to a fine, or to both.

  (3) For the purposes of this section, section 28(1)(a) above shall have effect as if the person to whom the property belongs or is treated as belonging for the purposes of that Act were the victim of the offence.

31 Racially [or religiously] aggravated public order offences

  (1) A person is guilty of an offence under this section if he commits—

    (a) an offence under section 4 of the Public Order Act 1986 (fear or provocation of violence);

    (b) an offence under section 4A of that Act (intentional harassment, alarm or distress); or

    (c) an offence under section 5 of that Act (harassment, alarm or distress), which is racially [or religiously] aggravated for the purposes of this section.

  (2) A constable may arrest without warrant anyone whom he reasonably suspects to be committing an offence falling within subsection (1)(a) or (b) above.

  (3) A constable may arrest a person without warrant if—

    (a) he engages in conduct which a constable reasonably suspects to constitute an offence falling within subsection (1)(c) above;

    (b) he is warned by that constable to stop; and

    (c) he engages in further such conduct immediately or shortly after the warning.

The conduct mentioned in paragraph (a) above and the further conduct need not be of the same nature.

  (4) A person guilty of an offence falling within subsection (1)(a) or (b) above shall be liable—

    (a) on summary conviction, to imprisonment for a term not exceeding six months or to a fine not exceeding the statutory maximum, or to both;

    (b) on conviction on indictment, to imprisonment for a term not exceeding two years or to a fine, or to both.

  (5) A person guilty of an offence falling within subsection (1)(c) above shall be liable on summary conviction to a fine not exceeding level 4 on the standard scale.

  (6), (7) ★ ★ ★ ★ ★

32 Racially [or religiously] aggravated harassment etc.

  (1) A person is guilty of an offence under this section if he commits—

    (a) an offence under section 2 of the Protection from Harassment Act 1997 (offence of harassment); or

    (b) an offence under section 4 of that Act (putting people in fear of violence), which is racially [or religiously] aggravated for the purposes of this section.

(2) ★ ★ ★ ★ ★
(3) A person guilty of an offence falling within subsection (1)(a) above shall be liable—
  (a) on summary conviction, to imprisonment for a term not exceeding six months or to a fine not exceeding the statutory maximum, or to both;
  (b) on conviction on indictment, to imprisonment for a term not exceeding two years or to a fine, or to both.
(4) A person guilty of an offence falling within subsection (1)(b) above shall be liable—
  (a) on summary conviction, to imprisonment for a term not exceeding six months or to a fine not exceeding the statutory maximum, or to both;
  (b) on conviction on indictment, to imprisonment for a term not exceeding seven years or to a fine, or to both.
(5)–(7) ★ ★ ★ ★ ★
★ ★ ★ ★ ★

European Communities (Amendment) Act 1998
(1998, c. 21)

An Act to make provision consequential on the Treaty signed at Amsterdam on 2 October 1997 amending the Treaty on European Union, the Treaties establishing the European Communities and certain related Acts.   [11 June 1998]

Territorial extent: United Kingdom

Note: This Act amends s. 1 of the European Communities Act 1972 by adding to the list of Treaties the Treaty of Amsterdam. That treaty is declared by s. 2 of the Act to be approved for the purpose of s. 6 of the European Parliamentary Elections Act 1978.

Finance Act 1998
(1998, c. 36)

An Act to grant certain duties, to alter other duties, and to amend the law relating to National Debt and the Public Revenue, and to make further provision in connection with Finance. [31 July 1998]

Territorial extent: United Kingdom

The European single currency

163   Adoption of single currency by other member States
  (1) The Treasury may, to such extent as appears to them appropriate in connection with any of the matters falling within subsection (2) below, by regulations modify the application and effect as respects—
  (a) transactions in a currency other than sterling,
  (b) instruments denominated in such a currency, and
  (c) the bringing into account of amounts expressed in, or by reference to, such a currency,
of any enactment or subordinate legislation relating to any matter under the care and management of the Commissioners of Inland Revenue.
  (2) The matters falling within this subsection are—
  (a) the adoption or proposed adoption by other member States of the single currency; and
  (b) any transitional measures or other arrangements applying or likely to apply in relation to the adoption of the single currency by other member States.

(3) Without prejudice to the generality of subsection (1) above, the power conferred by that subsection includes power by regulations to provide—

(a) for liabilities to pay amounts to the Commissioners of Inland Revenue under any enactment or subordinate legislation relating to taxation to be capable of being discharged, in accordance with the regulations, by payments in the single currency;

(b) for elections made for the purposes of section 93(1)(b) or 94(2)(b) of the Finance Act 1993 (computation of a company's profits in a foreign currency) to have effect as modified in accordance with the regulations; and

(c) for such persons as may be described in the regulations to be treated as having made elections for any of those purposes in such terms as may be provided for in the regulations.

(4) The power to make regulations under this section includes—

(a) power to impose charges to taxation;

(b) power to amend or repeal any enactment; and

(c) power to make such incidental, supplemental, consequential and transitional provision as appears to the Treasury to be appropriate.

(5) The power to make regulations under this section shall be exercisable by statutory instrument subject to annulment in pursuance of a resolution of the House of Commons.

(6) In this section—

"enactment" includes any enactment contained in this Act (other than this section) and any enactment passed after this Act;

"other member State" means a member State other than the United Kingdom;

"subordinate legislation" has the same meaning as in the Interpretation Act 1978.

(7) References in this section to the adoption of the single currency are references to the adoption of the single currency in accordance with the Treaty establishing the European Community, and the reference in subsection (3)(a) above to that currency shall be construed accordingly.

Government of Wales Act 1998
(1998, c. 38)

An Act to establish and make provision about the National Assembly for Wales and the Offices of Auditor General for Wales and Welsh Administration Ombudsman; to reform certain Welsh public bodies and abolish certain of the Welsh public bodies; and for connected purposes. [31 July 1998]

Territorial extent: United Kingdom (although many of the provisions will apply only in Wales).

PART I   THE NATIONAL ASSEMBLY FOR WALES

The Assembly

1   The Assembly

(1) There shall be an Assembly for Wales to be known as the National Assembly for Wales or Cynulliad Cenedlaethol Cymru (but referred to in this Act as the Assembly).

(2) The Assembly shall be a body corporate.

(3) The exercise by the Assembly of its functions is to be regarded as done on behalf of the Crown.

2   Membership

(1) The Assembly shall consist of—

(a) one member for each Assembly constituency, and

(b) members for each Assembly electoral region.

(2) The Assembly constituencies and Assembly electoral regions, and the number of Assembly seats for each Assembly electoral region, shall be as provided for by or in accordance with Schedule 1.

(3) Members of the Assembly (referred to in this Act as Assembly members) shall be returned in accordance with the provision made by and under this Act for—

(a) the holding of ordinary elections of Assembly members, and

(b) the filling of vacancies in Assembly seats.

(4) An ordinary election involves the holding of elections for the return of the entire Assembly.

(5) The term of office of an Assembly member—

(a) begins when he is declared to be returned as an Assembly member, and

(b) continues until the end of the day before the day of the poll at the next ordinary election.

(6) But an Assembly member may at any time resign his seat by giving notice to—

(a) the presiding officer, or

(b) any person authorised by the standing orders of the Assembly to receive the notice.

(7) The validity of anything done by the Assembly is not affected by any vacancy in its membership.

Ordinary elections

3   Time of ordinary elections

(1) The poll at the first ordinary election shall be held on a day appointed by order made by the Secretary of State.

(2) The poll at each subsequent ordinary election shall be held on the first Thursday in May in the fourth calendar year following that in which the previous ordinary election was held.

(3) But the Secretary of State may by order require the poll at such an ordinary election to be held on a day which is neither—

(a) more than one month earlier, nor

(b) more than one month later,

than the first Thursday in May.

(4)–(6) ★ ★ ★ ★ ★

4   Voting at ordinary elections

(1) Each person entitled to vote at an ordinary election in an Assembly constituency shall have two votes.

(2) One (referred to in this Act as a constituency vote) is to be given for a candidate to be the Assembly member for the Assembly constituency.

(3) The other (referred to in this Act as an electoral region vote) is to be given for—

(a) a registered political party which has submitted a list of candidates to be Assembly members for the Assembly electoral region in which the Assembly constituency is included, or

(b) an individual who is a candidate to be an Assembly member for that Assembly electoral region.

(4) The Assembly member for the Assembly constituency shall be returned under the simple majority system.

(5) The Assembly members for the Assembly electoral region shall be returned under the additional member system of proportional representation in accordance with sections 5 to 7.

(6) The person who is to be returned as the Assembly member for each Assembly

constituency in the Assembly electoral region must be determined before it is determined who are to be returned as the Assembly members for that Assembly electoral region.

(7) At an ordinary election a person may not be a candidate to be the Assembly member for more than one Assembly constituency.

(8) In this Act "registered political party" means a party registered under any enactment providing for the registration of political parties.

5   Party lists and individual candidates

(1) Any registered political party may submit a list of candidates to be Assembly members for the Assembly electoral region.

(2) The list is to be submitted to the regional returning officer.

(3) The list has effect in relation to—

(a) the ordinary election, and

(b) any vacancies in seats of Assembly members returned for Assembly electoral regions which occur after that election and before the next ordinary election.

(4) The list must not include more than twelve persons (but may include only one).

(5) The list must not include a person—

(a) who is included on any other list submitted for the Assembly electoral region or any list submitted for another Assembly electoral region,

(b) who is an individual candidate to be an Assembly member for the Assembly electoral region or another Assembly electoral region,

(c) who is a candidate to be the Assembly member for an Assembly constituency which is not included in the Assembly electoral region, or

(d) who is a candidate to be the Assembly member for an Assembly constituency included in the Assembly electoral region but is not a candidate of the party.

(6) ★ ★ ★ ★ ★

6   Calculation of electoral region figures

(1) For each registered political party by which a list of candidates has been submitted for the Assembly electoral region—

(a) there shall be added together the number of electoral region votes given for the party in the Assembly constituencies included in the Assembly electoral region, and

(b) the number arrived at under paragraph (a) shall then be divided by the aggregate of one and the number of candidates of the party returned as Assembly members for any of those Assembly constituencies.

(2) For each individual candidate to be an Assembly member for the Assembly electoral region there shall be added together the number of electoral region votes given for him in the Assembly constituencies included in the Assembly electoral region.

(3) The number arrived at—

(a) in the case of a registered political party, under subsection (1)(b), or

(b) in the case of an individual candidate, under subsection (2),

is referred to in this Act as the electoral region figure for that party or individual candidate.

7   Return of electoral region members

(1) The first seat for the Assembly electoral region shall be allocated to the party or individual candidate with the highest electoral region figure.

(2) The second and subsequent seats for the Assembly electoral region shall be allocated to the party or individual candidate with the highest electoral region figure after any recalculation required by subsection (3) has been carried out.

(3) This subsection requires a recalculation under section 6(1)(b) in relation to a party—

(a) for the first application of subsection (2), if the application of subsection (1) resulted in the allocation of a seat to the party, or

(b) for any subsequent application of subsection (2), if the previous application of that subsection did so;

and a recalculation shall be carried out after adding one to the aggregate mentioned in section 6(1)(b).

(4) An individual candidate already returned as an Assembly member shall be disregarded.

(5) Seats for the Assembly electoral region which are allocated to a party shall be filled by the persons on the party's list in the order in which they appear on the list.

(6) Once a party's list has been exhausted (by the return of persons included on it as Assembly members for Assembly constituencies or by the previous application of subsection (1) or (2)) the party shall be disregarded.

(7)–(10) ★ ★ ★ ★ ★

Vacancies

8   Constituency seats

(1) This section applies where the seat of an Assembly member returned for an Assembly constituency is vacant.

(2) Subject to subsection (6), an election shall be held in the Assembly constituency to fill the vacancy.

(3) At the election to fill the vacancy, each person entitled to vote at the election shall have only a constituency vote; and the Assembly member for the Assembly constituency shall be returned under the simple majority system.

(4) The date of the poll at the election shall be fixed by the presiding officer in accordance with subsection (5).

(5) The date fixed shall be not later than three months after the occurrence of the vacancy, except that if the vacancy does not come to the presiding officer notice within one month of its occurrence the date fixed shall be not later than three months after the vacancy comes to his notice.

(6) An election shall not be held if it appears to the presiding officer that the latest date which may be fixed for the poll would fall within the period of three months preceding an ordinary election.

(7) A person may not be a candidate in an election to fill a vacancy if he is an Assembly member or a candidate in another such election.

(8), (9) ★ ★ ★ ★ ★

9   Electoral region seats

(1) This section applies where the seat of an Assembly member returned for an Assembly electoral region is vacant.

(2) If the Assembly member was returned (under section 7 or this section) from the list of a registered political party, the regional returning officer shall notify to the presiding officer the name of the person who is to fill the vacancy.

(3) A person's name may only be so notified if he—

(a) is included on that list,

(b) is willing to serve as an Assembly member for the assembly electoral region, and

(c) is not a person to whom subsection (4) applies.

(4) This subsection applies to a person if—

(a) he is not a member of the party, and

(b) the party gives notice to the regional returning officer that his name is not to be notified to the presiding officer as the name of the person who is to fill the vacancy.

(5) But where there is more than one person who satisfies the conditions in subsection

(3), the regional returning officer may only notify the name of whichever of them was the higher, or highest, on the list.

(6) A person whose name is notified under subsection (2) shall be treated as declared to be returned as an Assembly member for the Assembly electoral region on the day on which notification of his name is received by the presiding officer.

(7) If—

(a) the Assembly member whose seat is vacant was returned as an individual candidate, or

(b) he was returned from the list of a registered political party but there is no-one who satisfies the conditions in subsection (3),

the seat shall remain vacant until the next ordinary election.

The franchise and conduct of elections

10   Entitlement to vote

(1) The persons entitled to vote at an election of Assembly members (or of an Assembly member) in an Assembly constituency are those who on the day of the poll—

(a) would be entitled to vote as electors at a local government election in an electoral area wholly or partly included in the Assembly constituency, and

(b) are registered in the register of local government electors at an address within the Assembly constituency.

(2) But a person is not entitled as an elector—

(a) to cast more than one constituency vote, or more than one electoral region vote, in the same Assembly constituency at any ordinary election.

(b) to vote in more than one Assembly constituency at any ordinary election, or

(c) to cast more than one vote in an election held under section 8.

11   ★ ★ ★ ★ ★

Disqualification

12   Disqualification from being Assembly member

(1) A person is disqualified from being an Assembly member if—

(a) he is disqualified from being a member of the House of Commons under paragraphs (a) to (e) of section 1(1) of the House of Commons Disqualification Act 1975 (judges, civil servants, members of the armed forces, members of police forces and members of foreign legislatures),

(b) he holds any of the offices for the time being designated by Order in Council as offices disqualifying persons from being Assembly members.

(c) he holds the office of Auditor General for Wales or the office of Welsh Administration Ombudsman, or

(d) he is disqualified from being a member of a local authority under section 17(2)(b) or 18(7) of the Audit Commission Act 1998 (members of local authorities who are responsible for incurring or authorising unlawful expenditure or whose wilful misconduct has caused a loss or deficiency).

(2) Subject to section 13(1) and (2), a person is also disqualified from being an Assembly member if he is disqualified otherwise than under the House of Commons Disqualification Act 1975 (either generally or in relation to a particular constituency) from being a member of the House of Commons or from sitting and voting in it.

(3)–(6) ★ ★ ★ ★ ★

13   Exceptions and relief from disqualification

(1) A person is not disqualified from being an Assembly member merely because—

(a) he is a peer (whether of the United Kingdom, Great Britain, England or Scotland), or

[(b) he is a Lord Spiritual.]

(2) A citizen of the European Union who is resident in the United Kingdom is not disqualified from being an Assembly member merely because of section 3 of the Act of Settlement (disqualification of persons born outside the United Kingdom other than Commonwealth citizens and citizens of the Republic of Ireland).

(3), (4) ★ ★ ★ ★ ★

14 Effect of disqualification

(1) If a person who is disqualified from being an Assembly member, or from being an Assembly member for a particular Assembly constituency or Assembly electoral region, is returned as an Assembly member or as an Assembly member for that Assembly constituency or Assembly electoral region, his return shall be void and his seat vacant.

(2) If an Assembly member becomes disqualified from being an Assembly member or from being an Assembly member for the Assembly constituency or Assembly electoral region for which he is sitting, he shall cease to be an Assembly member (so that his seat is vacant).

(3), (4) ★ ★ ★ ★ ★

(5) The validity of anything done by the Assembly is not affected by the disqualification of any person from being an Assembly member or from being an Assembly member for the Assembly constituency or Assembly electoral region for which he purports to sit.

15–20 ★ ★ ★ ★ ★

PART II   ASSEMBLY FUNCTIONS

Introduction

21 Introductory

The Assembly shall have the functions which are—
(a) transferred to, or made exercisable by, the Assembly by virtue of this Act, or
(b) conferred or imposed on the Assembly by or under this Act or any other Act.

Transfer of Ministerial functions to Assembly

22 Transfer of Ministerial functions

(1) Her Majesty may by Order in Council—
(a) provide for the transfer to the Assembly of any function so far as exercisable by a Minister of the Crown in Relation to Wales,
(b) direct that any function so far as so exercisable shall be exercisable by the Assembly concurrently with the Minister of the Crown, or
(c) direct that any function so far as exercisable by a Minister of the Crown in relation to Wales shall be exercisable by the Minister only with the agreement of, or after consultation with, the Assembly.

(2) The Secretary of State shall, before the first ordinary election, lay before each House of Parliament the draft of an Order in Council under this section making provision for the transfer of such functions in each of the fields specified in Schedule 2 as the Secretary of State considers appropriate.

(3) An Order in Council under this section may contain any appropriate consequential, incidental, supplementary or transitional provisions or savings (including provisions in the form of amendments or repeals of enactments).

(4), (5) ★ ★ ★ ★ ★

23 General transfer of property, rights and liabilities etc.

(1) There shall be transferred to and vest in the Assembly by virtue of this subsection all

property, rights and liabilities to which a Minister of the Crown is entitled or subject, at the coming into force of an Order in Council under section 22, in connection with any function exercisable by the Minister which is transferred by the Order in Council.

(2) there may be continued by or in relation to the Assembly anything (including legal proceedings) which relates to—

(a) any function exercisable by a Minister of the Crown which is transferred by an Order in Council under section 22, or

(b) any property, rights or liabilities transferred by subsection (1) as the result of the transfer or any such function by such an Order in Council,

and which is in the process of being done by or in relation to the Minister immediately before the coming into force of the Order of the Council.

(3) Anything which was done by a Minister of the Crown for the purpose of or in connection with—

(a) any function exercisable by the Minister which is transferred by an Order in Council under section 22, or

(b) any property, rights or liabilities transferred by subsection (1) as the result of the transfer of any such function by such an Order in Council,

and which effect immediately before the coming into force of the Order in Council shall have effect as if done by the Assembly.

(4) the Assembly shall be substituted for any Minister of the Crown in any instruments, contracts or legal proceedings which relate to–

(a) any function exercisable by the Minister which is transferred by an Order in Council under section 22, or

(b) any property, rights or liabilities transferred by subsection (1) as the result of the transfer of any such function by such an Order in Council,

and which are made or commenced before the coming into force of the Order in Council.

24-28 ★ ★ ★ ★ ★

29   Implementation of Community law

(1) The power to designate a Minister of the Crown or government department under section 2(2) of the European Communities Act 1972 may be exercised to designate the Assembly.

(2) Accordingly, the Assembly may exercise the power to make regulations conferred by section 2(2) of the European Communities Act 1972 in relation to any matter, or for any purpose, if the Assembly has been designated in relation to that matter or for that purpose, but subject to such restrictions or conditions (if any) as may be specified by the Order in Council designating the Assembly.

(3)–(5) ★ ★ ★ ★ ★

30   Consultation about public appointments

(1) Her Majesty may by Order in Council make provision requiring any Minister of the Crown or other person to consult the Assembly before—

(a) appointing a person to a specified public post,

(b) recommending, consenting to or approving the appointment of a person to a specified public post,

(c) nominating a person for appointment to a specified public post, or

(d) selecting persons with a view to the appointment of one or more of them to a specified public post (whether or not by the person subject to the requirement).

(2) In subsection (1) "a specified public post" means—

(a) a public office specified, or of a description specified, in the Order in Council, or

(b) membership, or membership of a description so specified, or a public body so specified or of a description so specified.

(3) An Order in Council under this section may not specify any public office or body, or public offices or bodies of any description, unless the office or body exercises, or all offices or bodies of the description exercise, functions in or in relation to Wales or a part of Wales (whether or not they also exercise functions in or in relation to any other area).

(4)–(9) ★ ★ ★ ★ ★

31   Consultation about government's legislative programme

(1) As soon as is reasonably practicable after the beginning of each session of Parliament, the Secretary of State for Wales shall undertake with the Assembly such consultation about the government's legislative programme for the session as appears to him to be appropriate but including attending and participating in proceedings of the Assembly relating to the programme on at least one occasion.

(2) For this purpose the government's legislative programme for a session of Parliament consists of the bills which (at the beginning of the session) are intended to be introduced into either House of Parliament during the session by a Minister of the Crown.

(3) If at any time after the beginning of a session of Parliament—

    (a) it is decided that a bill should be introduced into either House of Parliament during the session by a Minister of the Crown, and

    (b) no consultation about the bill has been undertaken under subsection (1), the Secretary of State for Wales shall undertake with the Assembly such consultation about the bill as appears to him to be appropriate.

(4) this section does not require the Secretary of State for Wales to undertake consultation with the Assembly about a bill if he considers that there are considerations relating to the bill which make it inappropriate for him to do so.

32   Support of culture etc.

The Assembly may do anything it considers appropriate to support—

    (a) museums, art galleries or libraries in Wales,

    (b) buildings of historical or architectural interest, or other places of historical interest, in Wales,

    (c) the Welsh language, or

    (d) the arts, crafts, sport or other cultural or recreational activities in Wales.

33   Consideration of matters affecting Wales

The Assembly may consider, and make appropriate representations about, any matter affecting Wales.

34   ★ ★ ★ ★ ★

35   Inquiries

(1) The Assembly may cause an inquiry to be held into any matter relevant to the exercise of any of its functions.

(2) Subsections (2) to (5) of section 250 of the Local Government Act 1972 (witnesses and costs at local inquiries) shall apply in relation to an inquiry held under subsection (1) as if it were a local inquiry held under that section and the Assembly were the Minister causing it to be held.

36   Polls for ascertaining views of the public

(1) The Assembly may hold a poll in an area consisting of Wales or any part (or parts) of Wales for the purpose of ascertaining the view of those polled about whether or how any of the Assembly's functions (other than those under section 33) should be exercised.

(2) The persons entitled to vote in poll under this section are those who—

    (a) would be entitled to vote as electors at a local government election in an electoral area wholly or partly included in the area in which the poll is held, and

(b) are registered in the register of local government electors at an address within the area in which the poll is held.

(3)–(7) ★ ★ ★ ★ ★

37 ★ ★ ★ ★ ★

38   Legal proceedings

Where the Assembly considers it appropriate for the promotion or protection of the public interest it may institute in its own name, defend or appear in any legal proceedings relating to matters with respect to which any functions of the Assembly are exercisable.

39   Contracts

The Secretary of State may by order provide that the Local Government (Contracts) Act 1997 shall apply in relation to contracts entered into by the Assembly but subject to any appropriate modifications.

40   Supplementary powers

The Assembly may do anything (including the acquisition or disposal of any property or rights) which is calculated to facilitate, or is conducive or incidental to, the exercise of any of its functions.

41–43 ★ ★ ★ ★ ★

44   Parliamentary procedures for subordinate legislation

(1) This section applies where a function to make subordinate legislation (including a function conferred or imposed by, or after the passing of, this Act) has been transferred to, or made exercisable by, the Assembly by an Order in Council under section 22.

(2) Subject to subsections (4) and (5), any relevant Parliamentary procedural provision relating to the function shall not have effect in relation to the exercise of the function by the Assembly.

(3) For the purposes of this Act "relevant Parliamentary procedural provision" means provision—

(a) requiring any instrument made in the exercise of the function, or a draft of any such instrument, to be laid before Parliament or either House of Parliament.

(b) for the annulment or approval of any such instrument or draft by or in pursuance of a resolution of either House of Parliament or of both Houses,

(c) prohibiting the making of any such instrument without that approval,

(d) for any such instrument to be a provisional order (that is, an order which requires to be confirmed by Act of Parliament), or

(e) requiring any order (within the meaning of the Statutory Orders (Special Procedure) Act 1945) to be subject to special Parliamentary procedure.

(4)–(6) ★ ★ ★ ★ ★

45 ★ ★ ★ ★ ★

PART III   ASSEMBLY PROCEDURE

Introductory

46   Regulation of procedure

(1) The procedure of the Assembly (including that of committees of the Assembly and sub-committees of such committees) shall be regulated by the standing orders of the Assembly.

(2) But subsection (1) is subject to any other provision of this Act or any other enactment which regulates, or provides for the regulation of, the procedure of the Assembly (or of committees of the Assembly or sub-committees of such committees).

(3) The standing orders may make different provision for different circumstances.

(4) Section 50 makes provision for the making of standing orders to have effect when the Assembly first meets; but the Assembly may remake or revise the standing orders at any time.

(5) The Assembly may not delegate the function of remaking or revising the standing orders.

(6) The standing orders shall not be remade or revised unless a motion to approve the standing orders or revisions is passed by the Assembly on a vote in which at least two-thirds of the Assembly members voting support the motion.

47 Equal treatment of English and Welsh languages

(1) The Assembly shall in the conduct of its business give effect, so far as is both appropriate in the circumstances and reasonably practicable, to the principle that the English and Welsh languages should be treated on a basis of equality.

(2) In determining how to comply with subsection (1), the Assembly shall have regard to the spirit of any guidelines under section 9 of the Welsh Language Act 1993.

(3) the standing orders shall be made in both English and Welsh.

48 Equal opportunities in conduct of business

The Assembly shall make appropriate arrangements with a view to securing that its business is conducted with due regard to the principle that there should be equality of opportunity for all people.

49–51 ★ ★ ★ ★ ★

Offices and committees

52 Presiding officer and deputy

(1) The Assembly shall elect from among the Assembly members—
   (a) the presiding officer, and
   (b) the deputy presiding officer.

(2) The offices specified in subsection (1) shall be known by such titles as the standing orders may provide (but are referred to in this Act as the presiding officer and the deputy presiding officer).

(3) the presiding officer and the deputy presiding officer may not be Assembly members who represent the same party.

53 Assembly First Secretary and Assembly Secretaries

(1) The Assembly shall elect one of the Assembly members to be Assembly First Secretary or Prif Ysgrifennydd y Cynulliad.

(2) The Assembly First Secretary shall appoint Assembly Secretaries, or Ys-grifenyddion y Cynulliad, from among the Assembly members (and may at any time remove a person from office as an Assembly Secretary).

(3) The standing orders must specify the maximum number of Assembly Secretaries that may be appointed.

(4) The Assembly First Secretary, and each of the Assembly Secretaries, is a Crown servant for the purposes of the Official Secrets Act 1989.

54 Committees

(1) The Assembly—
   (a) shall establish the committees which it is required to establish by the following provisions of this Part, and
   (b) may establish any other committees which it considers appropriate.

(2) The members of any committee established by the Assembly under subsection (1)(b)—
   (a) shall be elected b the Assembly from among the Assembly members, and
   (b) shall, unless the committee exists solely to provide advice, be elected so as to

secure that, as far as is practicable, the balance of the parties in the Assembly is reflected in the membership of the committee.

55 ★ ★ ★ ★ ★

The statutory committees

56   Executive committee

(1) There shall be a committee of the Assembly whose members shall be—
   (a) the Assembly First Secretary, who shall chair it, and
   (b) the Assembly Secretaries.

(2) The Committee shall be known by such title as the standing orders may provide (but is referred to in this Act as the executive committee).

(3) The Assembly First Secretary shall allocate accountability in the fields in which the Assembly has functions to members of the executive committee so that, in the case of each of those fields, accountability in the field is allocated either to one of the Assembly Secretaries or to him.

(4) The Assembly First Secretary need not make an allocation under subsection (3) to every member of the executive committee; but the number of Assembly Secretaries to whom no such allocation in made shall not exceed such number as may be specified in, or determined in accordance with, the standing orders.

(5) For the purposes of this section and section 57 "accountability", in relation to a member of the executive committee and a field, means that he is the member of the executive committee accountable to the Assembly (in accordance with standing orders under subsection (7)) for the exercise of the Assembly's functions in that field, except the exercise of functions by the executive committee (or by the Assembly itself).

(6) The Assembly First Secretary is accountable to the Assembly (in accordance with standing orders under subsection (7)) for the exercise of functions by the executive committee.

(7) The standing orders must include provision for allowing Assembly members to question (orally or in writing, as Assembly members prefer)—
   (a) each member of the executive committee about the exercise of the Assembly's functions in the field or fields in which he is accountable, except the exercise of functions by the executive committee (or by the Assembly itself), and
   (b) the Assembly First Secretary about the exercise of functions by the executive committee.

(8) In this section—
   (a) references to the exercise of functions by the executive committee include the exercise of functions by a sub-committee of that committee or by members of the Assembly's staff in pursuance of a delegation to the Assembly's staff by either that committee or such a sub-committee, and
   (b) references to the exercise of functions by the Assembly itself include the exercise of functions by members of the Assembly's staff in pursuance of a delegation to the Assembly's staff by the Assembly itself.

57   Subject committees

(1) The Assembly shall establish committees with responsibilities in the fields in which the Assembly has functions.

(2) The committees established under this section shall be known by such titles as the standing orders may provide (but are referred to in this Act as subject committees).

(3) There shall be the same number of—
   (a) subject committees, and
   (b) members of the executive committee to whom the Assembly First Secretary allocates accountability in any of the fields in which the Assembly has functions.

(4) The division between the subject committees of the fields in which those committees have responsibilities and the division between members of the executive committee of the fields in which accountability is allocated to members of that committee shall be the same; and the member of the executive committee who has accountability in the field or fields in which a subject committee has responsibilities shall be a member of that subject committee.

(5)–(8) ★ ★ ★ ★ ★

58 Subordinate legislation scrutiny committee

(1) The Assembly shall establish a committee with responsibilities relating to the scrutiny of relevant Welsh subordinate legislation.

(2) For the purposes of this section "relevant Welsh subordinate legislation" is any subordinate legislation—

(a) which is made or proposed to be made, or

(b) which, or a draft of which, is (or but for paragraph 2(4) of Schedule 7 would be) required to be confirmed or approved,

by the Assembly (whether or not jointly with a Minister of the Crown or government department).

(3) The committee established under this section shall be known by such title as the standing orders may provide (but is referred to in this Act as the subordinate legislation scrutiny committee).

(4) The subordinate legislation scrutiny committee shall—

(a) consider any proposed Assembly general subordinate legislation when the draft statutory instrument containing it has been laid before the Assembly, and

(b) report to the Assembly whether or not the special attention of the Assembly should be drawn to it on any of the grounds specified in the standing orders for the purposes of this subsection.

(5)–(7) ★ ★ ★ ★ ★

59 Members of scrutiny committee etc.

(1) The subordinate legislation scrutiny committee shall have such number of members as the standing orders may provide.

(2) The members of the subordinate legislation scrutiny committee shall be elected by the Assembly from among the Assembly members so as to secure that, as far as is practicable, the balance of the parties in the Assembly is reflected in the membership of the committee.

(3) Neither the Assembly First Secretary nor an Assembly Secretary may be a member of the subordinate legislation scrutiny committee.

(4) The Assembly shall elect one of the members of the subordinate legislation scrutiny committee to chair the committee but it may not be chaired by a member who represents the largest party with an executive role.

(5)–(7) ★ ★ ★ ★ ★

60–63 ★ ★ ★ ★ ★

Procedures relating to subordinate legislation

64 Standing orders to provide procedures

The standing orders must provide procedures (referred to in this Act as the subordinate legislation procedures) for—

(a) the preparation, and

(b) the making, confirmation and approval,

of orders, regulations, rules and other subordinate legislation.

65 Regulatory appraisals

(1) The subordinate legislation procedures must include provision for securing that an appraisal (referred to in this Act as a regulatory appraisal) as to the likely costs and benefits of

complying with any proposed Assembly general subordinate legislation is carried out before a draft of the statutory instrument containing the subordinate legislation is laid before the Assembly.

(2) But the subordinate legislation procedures may provide that a regulatory appraisal need not be carried out in relation to any proposed Assembly general subordinate legislation if in the particular circumstances it is inappropriate or not reasonably practicable for one to be carried out.

(3) The subordinate legislation procedures must also include provision for securing that, if a regulatory appraisal indicates that the costs of complying with any proposed Assembly general subordinate legislation are likely to be significant—

    (a) appropriate consultation (including consultation with representatives of business) is carried out, and

    (b) the regulatory appraisal is published, before a draft of the statutory instrument containing the subordinate legislation is laid before the Assembly.

66 Making of Assembly general subordinate legislation

(1) Assembly general subordinate legislation shall be made by being signed by the presiding officer, the deputy presiding officer, the Assembly First Secretary or such other person as may be authorised by the subordinate legislation procedures.

(2) Assembly general subordinate legislation may not be made until a draft of the statutory instrument containing it has been laid before, and approved by a resolution of, the Assembly.

(3) The subordinate legislation procedures must include provision for securing that Assembly general subordinate legislation may be made by being signed otherwise than by the presiding officer only in the absence of the presiding officer.

(4)–(7) ★ ★ ★ ★ ★

67 ★ ★ ★ ★ ★

68 Financial initiative

(1) The subordinate legislation procedures must include provision requiring the recommendation of the executive committee for the making by the Assembly of any Assembly general subordinate legislation which may give rise to the payment of any sums by the Assembly.

(2) The provision included in the subordinate legislation procedures in pursuance of subsection (1) may contain an exception from the requirement of a recommendation in circumstances in which the sums are unlikely to be significant.

Other provisions about standing orders

69 Preservation of order

(1) The standing orders must include provision for preserving order in proceedings of the Assembly (including proceedings of a committee of the Assembly or of a sub-committee of such a committee).

(2) In particular, standing orders made for preserving order in such proceedings must include provision for—

    (a) preventing conduct which would constitute a criminal offence, and

    (b) a sub judice rule,

and may include provision for excluding Assembly members from the proceedings and for withdrawing their rights and privileges as Assembly members for the period of their exclusion.

70 Openness

(1) The standing orders must include provision—

    (a) for all proceedings of the Assembly itself to be held in public, and

(b) for all proceedings of a committee of the Assembly, or a subcommittee of such a committee, to be held in public except where the standing orders otherwise provide.

(2) But the standing orders may include provision as to conditions to be complied with by any member of the public attending proceedings of the Assembly (including proceedings of a committee of the Assembly or of a sub-committee of such a committee) and, in particular, provision for excluding from the proceedings any member of the public who does not comply with the conditions.

(3) The standing orders must include provision for—

(a) the publication of a report of the proceedings of the Assembly itself, and

(b) the publication of a report of the proceedings of a committee of the Assembly, or a sub-committee of such a committee, unless the proceedings were not held in public, as soon as reasonably practicable after the day on which the proceedings take place.

(4) The standing orders must include provision for any documents in the possession or under the control of the Assembly which contain material relating to any proceedings of the Assembly (including proceedings of a committee of the Assembly or of a sub-committee of such a committee) which have taken place, or are to take place, to be open to inspection by members of the public except where the standing orders otherwise provide.

(5) The standing orders must include provision—

(a) establishing procedures for the investigation of complaints about actions or failures on the part of the Assembly and for dealing with reports by the Welsh Administration Ombudsman and the Health and Service Commissioner for Wales of investigations pursuant to complaints relating to the Assembly, and

(b) for publicising details of those procedures.

71 ★ ★ ★ ★ ★

72 Integrity

(1) The standing orders must include provision for a register of interests of Assembly members and for—

(a) registrable interests (as defined in the standing orders) to be registered in it, and

(b) the publication of the register.

(2) The standing orders must include provision for requiring any Assembly member who has–

(a) a financial interest (as defined in the standing orders) in any matter, or

(b) any other interest, or an interest of any other kind, specified in the standing orders in any matter,

to declare that interest before taking part in any proceedings of the Assembly (including proceedings of a committee of the Assembly or of a sub-committee of such a committee) relating to that matter.

(3) The standing orders may include provision—

(a) for preventing or restricting the participation in any proceedings of the Assembly (including proceedings of a committee of the Assembly or of a sub-committee of such a committee) of an Assembly member if he has a registrable interest, or an interest mentioned in subsection (2), in any matter to which the proceedings relate, and

(b) for preventing or restricting the exercise of a function by a member of the executive committee, or the exercise of a function by an Assembly member by virtue of section 59(6), if he has a registrable interest, or an interest mentioned in subsection (2), in any matter to which the function relates.

(4) The standing orders must include provision prohibiting an Assembly member—

(a) from advocating or initiating any cause or matter on behalf of any person, by any means specified in the standing orders, in consideration of any payment or benefit in kind of a description so specified, or

(b) from urging, in consideration of any such payment or benefit in kind, another Assembly member to advocate or initiate any cause or matter on behalf of any person by any such means.

(5) The standing orders may include provision—

(a) for excluding from proceedings of the Assembly (including proceedings of a committee of the Assembly or of a sub-committee of such a committee) an Assembly member who fails to comply with or contravenes any provision included in the standing orders in pursuance of subsections (1) to (4), and

(b) for withdrawing his rights and privileges as an Assembly member for the period of his exclusion.

(6) An Assembly member who—

(a) takes part in any proceedings of the Assembly (including proceedings of a committee of the Assembly or of a sub-committee of such a committee) without having complied with, or in contravention of, any provision included in the standing orders in pursuance of subsection (1), (2) or (3)(a),

(b) exercises any function in contravention of any provision included in the standing orders in pursuance of subsection (3)(b), or

(c) contravenes any provision included in the standing orders in pursuance of subsection (4),

is guilty of an offence.

(7) A person guilty of an offence under subsection (6) is liable on summary conviction to a fine not exceeding level 5 on the standard scale.

(8) A prosecution for an offence under subsection (6) shall not be instituted except by or with the consent of the Director of Public Prosecutions.

73–75 ★ ★ ★ ★ ★

Miscellaneous

76 Attendance of Secretary of State for Wales

(1) The Secretary of State for Wales shall be entitled to attend and participate in any proceedings of the Assembly.

(2) Subsection (1) does not confer on the Secretary of State for Wales—

(a) any right to vote, or

(b) a right to attend or participate in the proceedings of a committee of the Assembly or any sub-committee of such a committee.

(3) The standing orders must include provision for any documents which—

(a) contain material relating to any proceedings of the Assembly itself which have taken place or are to take place, and

(b) are made available to all Assembly members,

to be made available to the Secretary of State for Wales no later than the time when they are made available to Assembly members who are not members of the executive committee.

77 Defamation

(1) For the purposes of the law of defamation—

(a) any statement made in, for the purposes of or for purposes incidental to proceedings of the Assembly (including proceedings of a committee of the Assembly or of a sub-committee), and

(b) the publication by or under the authority of the Assembly of a report of such proceedings,

is absolutely privileged.

(2) Subsection (1)(a) applies, in particular, to any statement made in—

(a) evidence given before the Assembly, a committee of the Assembly or a sub-committee,

(b) a document laid before the Assembly or such a committee or sub-committee,

(c) a document prepared for the purposes of, or for purposes incidental to, the transaction of business by the Assembly or such a committee or sub-committee,

(d) a document (other than a report to which subsection (1)(b) applies) formulated, made or published by or under the authority of the Assembly or such a committee or sub-committee,

(e) any communication—

(i) between any person and a person having functions in connection with the registration of interests of Assembly members, or

(ii) between any person and an Assembly member,

in connection with such registration, or

(f) any communication—

(i) between any person and a person having functions in connection with the investigation of complaints about actions or failures on the part of the Assembly, or

(ii) between any person and an Assembly member,

in connection with any such complaint.

(3)–(5) ★ ★ ★ ★ ★

78, 79 ★ ★ ★ ★ ★

PART IV   ASSEMBLY FINANCE

Payments to Assembly etc.

80   Grants to Assembly

(1) The Secretary of State shall from time to time make payments to the Assembly out of money provided by Parliament of such amounts as he may determine.

(2) Any Minister of the Crown, and any government department, may make to the Assembly payments of such amounts as the Minister or department may determine.

81–105 ★ ★ ★ ★ ★

106   Community law

(1) A Community obligation of the United Kingdom is also an obligation of the Assembly if, and to the extent that, the obligation could be implemented (or enabled to be implemented) or complied with by the exercise by the Assembly of any of its functions.

(2) Subsection (1) does not apply in the case of a Community obligation of the United Kingdom if—

(a) it is an obligation to achieve a result defined by reference to a quantity (whether expressed as an amount, proportion or ratio or otherwise), and

(b) the quantity relates to the United Kingdom (or to an area including the United Kingdom or to an area consisting of a part of the United Kingdom which includes the whole part of Wales).

(3)–(6) ★ ★ ★ ★ ★

107   Human rights

(1) The Assembly has no power—

(a) to make, confirm or approve any subordinate legislation, or

(b) to do any other act,

so far as the subordinate legislation or act is incompatible with any of the Convention rights.

(2) Subsection (1) does not enable a person—
(a) to bring any proceedings in a court or tribunal, or
(b) to rely on any of the Convention rights in any such proceedings, in respect of an act unless he would be a victim for the purposes of Article 34 of the Convention if proceedings were brought in the European Court of Human Rights in respect of that act.

(3), (4) ★ ★ ★ ★ ★

(5) In this Act "the Convention rights" has the same meaning as in the Human Rights Act 1998 and in subsection (2) "the Convention" has the same meaning as in that Act.

108   International obligations

(1) If a Minister of the Crown considers that any action proposed to be taken by the Assembly would be incompatible with any international obligation, he may by order direct that the proposed action shall not be taken.

(2) If a Minister of the Crown considers that any action capable of being taken by the Assembly is required for the purpose of giving effect to any international obligation, he may by order direct the Assembly to take the action.

(3) If a Minister of the Crown considers that any subordinate legislation made, or which could be revoked, by the Assembly is incompatible with any international obligation, he may by order revoke the legislation.

(4)–(11) ★ ★ ★ ★ ★

Decisions about Assembly functions

109   Resolution of devolution issues
Schedule 8 (which makes provision about devolution issues) has effect.
Note: Schedule 8 is not included for reasons of space; there are broadly equivalent provisions relating to Scotland in Schedule 6 to the Scotland Act 1998 (q.v.).

110   Power to vary retrospective decisions

(1) This section applies where any court or tribunal decides that the Assembly did not have the power to make a provision of subordinate legislation which it has purported to make.

(2) The court or tribunal may make an order—
(a) removing or limiting any retrospective effect of the decision, or
(b) suspending the effect of the decision for any period and on any conditions to allow the defect to be corrected.

(3) In determining whether to make an order under this section, the court or tribunal shall (among other things) have regard to the extent to which persons who are not parties to the proceedings would otherwise be adversely affected by the decision.

(4) Where a court or tribunal is considering whether to make an order under this section, it shall order notice (or intimation) of that fact to be given to the relevant law officer and the Assembly (unless he or it is a party to the proceedings).

(5) Where the relevant law officer or the Assembly is given notice (or intimation) under subsection (4), he or it may take part as a party in the proceedings so far as they relate to the making of the order.

(6)–(8) ★ ★ ★ ★ ★

Investigation of complaints

111   Welsh Administration Ombudsman

(1) There shall be an office of Welsh Administration Ombudsman or Ombwdsmon Gweinyddiaeth Cymru.

(2) Schedule 9 (which makes provision about the Welsh Administration Ombudsman

and, in particular, enables him to investigate administrative action taken by the Assembly and certain other public bodies in Wales in response to complaints claiming maladministration) has effect.

112-114 ★ ★ ★ ★ ★

115 Consultation with business
The Assembly shall carry out consultation with such organisations representative of business and such other organisations as it considers appropriate having regard to the impact of the exercise by the Assembly of its functions on the interests of business.

116-118 ★ ★ ★ ★ ★

Miscellaneous

119 ★ ★ ★ ★ ★

120 Equality of opportunity
(1) The Assembly shall make appropriate arrangements with a view to securing that its functions are exercised with due regard to the principle that there should be equality of opportunity for all people.
(2) After each financial year the Assembly shall publish a report containing—
   (a) a statement of the arrangements made in pursuance of subsection (1) which had effect during that financial year, and
   (b) an assessment of how effective those arrangements were in promoting equality of opportunity.

121 Sustainable development
(1) The Assembly shall make a scheme setting out how it proposes, in the exercise of its functions, to promote sustainable development.
(2) The Assembly shall keep the scheme under review and in the year following each ordinary election (after the first) shall consider whether it should be remade or revised.
(3) The Assembly may not delegate the function of making, or remaking or revising, the scheme.
(4) The Assembly shall publish the scheme when first made and whenever subsequently remade and, if the scheme is revised without being remade, shall publish either the revisions or the scheme as revised (as it considers appropriate).
(5) The Assembly shall consult such persons or bodies as it considers appropriate before making, remaking or revising the scheme.
(6) After each financial year the Assembly shall publish a report of how its proposals as set out in the scheme were implemented in that financial year.
(7) In the year following each ordinary election (after the first) the Assembly shall publish a report containing an assessment of how effective its proposals (as set out in the scheme and implemented) have been in promoting sustainable development.

122 English and Welsh texts of Assembly instruments
(1) The English and Welsh texts of any subordinate legislation made by the Assembly which is in both English and Welsh when made shall be treated for all purposes as being of equal standing.
(2) The Assembly may by order provide in respect of any Welsh word or phrase that, where it appears in the Welsh text of any subordinate legislation made by the Assembly, it is to be taken as having the same meaning as the English word or phrase specified in relation to it in the order.
(3) An order under subsection (2) may, in respect of any Welsh word or phrase, make different provision for different purposes.

(4) Subordinate legislation made by the Assembly shall, subject to any provision to the contrary contained in it, be construed in accordance with any order under subsection (2).

123   Provision of information to Treasury
Where it appears to the Treasury that any information in the possession or under the control of the Assembly is required for the exercise of any function by the Treasury, the Treasury may require the Assembly to provide the information to the Treasury in such form as the Treasury may reasonably specify.

124   Documentary evidence
A document purporting to be—
  (a)   duly executed under the seal of the Assembly, or
  (b)   signed on behalf of the Assembly,
shall be received in evidence and shall, unless the contrary is proved, be taken to be so executed or signed.

★ ★ ★ ★ ★

SCHEDULE 2   FIELDS IN WHICH FUNCTIONS ARE TO BE TRANSFERRED BY FIRST ORDER IN COUNCIL

1. Agriculture, forestry, fisheries and food.
2. Ancient monuments and historic buildings.
3. Culture (including museums, galleries and libraries).
4. Economic development.
5. Education and training.
6. The environment.
7. Health and health services.
8. Highways.
9. Housing.
10. Industry.
11. Local government.
12. Social services.
13. Sport and recreation.
14. Tourism.
15. Town and country planning.
16. Transport.
17. Water and flood defence.
18. The Welsh language.

Human Rights Act 1998
(1998, c. 42)

An Act to give further effect to rights and freedoms guaranteed under the European Convention on Human Rights; to make provision with respect to holders of certain judicial offices who become judges of the European Court of Human Rights; and for connected purposes.   [9 November 1998]

Territorial extent: United Kingdom

Introduction

1   The Convention Rights
   (1) In this Act "the Convention rights" means the rights and fundamental freedoms set out in—
      (a)   Articles 2 to 12 and 14 of the Convention,

(b) Articles 1 to 3 of the First Protocol, and

(c) Articles 1 and 2 of the Sixth Protocol,

as read with Articles 16 to 18 of the Convention.

(2) Those Articles are to have effect for the purposes of this Act subject to any designated derogation or reservation (as to which see sections 14 and 15).

(3) The Articles are set out in Schedule 1.

(4) The Secretary of State may by order make such amendments to this act as he considers appropriate to reflect the effect, in relation to the United Kingdom, of a protocol.

(5) In subsection (4) "protocol" means a protocol to the Convention—

(a) which the United Kingdom has ratified; or

(b) which the United Kingdom has signed with a view to ratification.

(6) No amendment may be made by an order under subsection (4) so as to come into force before the protocol concerned is in force in relation to the United Kingdom.

Note: Schedule 1 is omitted, as the relevant Articles of and Protocols to the Convention are printed as part of the Convention at pp. 521–24. Note that Article 13 of the Convention (effective remedy) is not incorporated by s 1.

2   Interpretation of Convention rights

(1) A court or tribunal determining a question which has arisen in connection with a Convention right must take into account any—

(a) judgment, decision, declaration or advisory opinion of the European Court of Human Rights

(b) opinion of the Commission given in a report adopted under Article 31 of the Convention,

(c) decision of the Commission in connection with Article 26 or 27(2) of the convention, or

(d) decision of the Committee of Ministers taken under Article 46 of the Convention.

whenever made or given, so far as, in the opinion of the court or tribunal, it is relevant to the proceedings in which that question has arisen.

(2), (3) ★ ★ ★ ★ ★

Legislation

3   Interpretation of legislation

(1) So far as it is possible to do so, primary legislation and subordinate legislation must be read and given effect in a way which is compatible with Convention rights.

(2) This section—

(a) applies to primary legislation and subordinate legislation whenever enacted;

(b) does not affect the validity, continuing operation or enforcement of any incompatible primary legislation; and

(c) does not affect the validity, continuing operation or enforcement of any incompatible subordinate legislation if (disregarding any possibility of revocation) primary legislation prevents removal of the incompatibility.

4   Declaration of incompatibility

(1) Subsection (2) applies in any proceedings in which a court determines whether a provision of primary legislation is compatible with a Convention right.

(2) If the court is satisfied that the provision is incompatible with a Convention right, it may make a declaration of that incompatibility.

(3) Subsection (4) applies in any proceedings in which a court determines whether a provision of subordinate legislation, made in the exercise of a power conferred by primary legislation, is compatible with a Convention right.

(4) If the court is satisfied—

(a) that the provision is incompatible with a Convention right, and

(b) that (disregarding any possibility of revocation) the primary legislation concerned prevents removal of the incompatibility,

it may make a declaration of that incompatibility.

(5) In this section "court" means—

(a) the House of Lords;

(b) the Judicial Committee of the Privy Council;

(c) the Courts-Martial Appeal Court;

(d) in Scotland, the High Court of Justiciary sitting otherwise than as a trial court or the Court of Session;

(e) in England and Wales or Northern Ireland, the High Court or the Court of Appeal.

(6) A declaration under this section ("a declaration of incompatibility")—

(a) does not affect the validity, continuing operation or enforcement of the provision in respect of which it is given; and

(b) is not binding on the parties to the proceedings in which it is made.

5 Right of Crown to intervene

(1) Where a court is considering whether to make a declaration of incompatibility, the Crown is entitled to notice in accordance with rules of court.

(2) In any case to which subsection (1) applies—

(a) a Minister of the Crown (or a person nominated by him),

(b) a member of the Scottish Executive,

(c) a Northern Ireland Minister,

(d) a Northern Ireland department,

is entitled, on giving notice in accordance with rules of court, to be joined as a party to the proceedings.

(3) Notice under subsection (2) may be given at any time during the proceedings.

(4) A person who has been made a party to criminal proceedings (other than in Scotland) as the result of a notice under subsection (2) may, with leave, appeal to the House of Lords against any declaration of incompatibility made in the proceedings.

(5) In subsection (4)—

"criminal proceedings" includes all proceedings before the Courts-Martial Appeal Court and

"leave" means leave granted by the court making the declaration of incompatibility or by the House of Lords.

Public authorities

6 Acts of public authorities

(1) It is unlawful for a public authority to act in a way which is incompatible with a Convention right.

(2) Subsection (1) does not apply to an act if—

(a) as the result of one or more provisions of primary legislation, the authority could not have acted differently; or

(b) in the case of one or more provisions of, or made under, primary legislation which cannot be read or given effect in a way which is compatible with the Convention rights, the authority was acting so as to give effect to or enforce those provisions.

(3) In this section "public authority" includes–

(a) a court or tribunal, and

(b) any person certain of whose functions are functions of a public nature, but does not include either House of Parliament or a person exercising functions in connection with proceedings in Parliament.

(4) In subsection (3) "Parliament" does not include the House of Lords in its judicial capacity.

(5) In relation to a particular act, a person is not a public authority by virtue only of subsection (3)(b) if the nature of the act is private.

(6) "An act" includes a failure to act but does not include a failure to—

    (a) introduce in, or lay before, Parliament a proposal for legislation; or

    (b) make any primary legislation or remedial order.

7 Proceedings

(1) A person who claims that a public authority has acted (or proposes to act) in a way which is made unlawful by section 6(1) may—

    (a) bring proceedings against the authority under this Act in the appropriate court or tribunal, or

    (b) rely on the convention right or rights concerned in any legal proceedings, but only if he is (or would be) a victim of the unlawful act.

(2) In subsection (1)(a) "appropriate court or tribunal" means such court or tribunal as may be determined in accordance with rules; and proceedings against an authority include a counterclaim or similar proceedings.

(3) If the proceedings are brought on an application for judicial review, the applicant is to be taken to have a sufficient interest in relation to the unlawful act only if he is, or would be, a victim of that act.

(4) If the proceedings are made by way of a petition for judicial review in Scotland, the applicant shall be taken to have title and interest to sue in relation to the unlawful act only if he is, or would be, a victim of that act.

(5) Proceedings under subsection (1)(a) must be brought before the end of—

    (a) the period of one year beginning with the date on which the act complained of took place; or

    (b) such longer period as the court or tribunal considers equitable having regard to all the circumstances,

but that is subject to any rule imposing a stricter time limit in relation to the procedure in question.

(6) In subsection (1)(b) "legal proceedings" includes—

    (a) proceedings brought by or at the instigation of a public authority; and

    (b) an appeal against the decision of a court or tribunal.

(7) For the purposes of this section, a person is a victim of an unlawful act only if he would be a victim for the purposes of Article 34 of the Convention if proceedings were brought in the European Court of Human Rights in respect of that act.

(8) Nothing in this Act creates a criminal offence.

(9)–(13) ★ ★ ★ ★ ★

8 Judicial remedies

(1) In relation to any act (or proposed act) of a public authority which the court finds is (or would be) unlawful, it may grant such relief or remedy, or make such order, within its powers as it considers just and appropriate.

(2) But damages may be awarded only by a court which has power to award damages, or to order the payment of compensation, in civil proceedings.

(3) No award of damages is to be made unless, taking account of all the circumstances of the case, including—

    (a) any other relief or remedy granted, or order made, in relation to the act in question (by that or any other court), and

    (b) the consequences of any decision (of that or any other court) in respect of that act, the court is satisfied that the award is necessary to afford just satisfaction to the person in whose favour it is made.

(4) In determining—

    (a) whether to award damages, or

(b) the amount of an award,

the court must take into account the principles applied by the European Court of Human Rights in relation to the award of compensation under Article 41 of the Convention.

(5), (6) ★ ★ ★ ★ ★

9   Judicial acts

(1) Proceedings under section 7(1)(a) in respect of a judicial act may be brought only—

    (a) by exercising a right of appeal;

    (b) on an application (in Scotland a petition) for a judicial review; or

    (c) in such other forum as may be prescribed by rules.

(2) That does not affect any rule of law which prevents a court from being the subject of judicial review.

(3) In proceedings under this Act in respect of a judicial act done in good faith, damages may not be awarded otherwise than to compensate a person to the extent required by Article 5(5) of the Convention.

(4) An award of damages permitted by subsection (3) is to be made against the Crown; but no award may be made unless the appropriate person, if not a party to the proceedings, is joined.

(5) In this section—

"appropriate person" means the minister responsible for the court concerned or a person or government department nominated by him;

"court" includes a tribunal;

"judge" includes a member of a tribunal, a justice of the peace and a clerk or other officer entitled to exercise the jurisdiction of a court;

"judicial act" means a judicial act of a court and includes an act done on the instructions, or on behalf, of a judge; and

"rules" has the same meaning as in section 7(9).

Remedial action

10   Power to take remedial action

(1) This section applies if—

    (a) a provision of legislation has been declared under section 4 to be incompatible with a Convention right and, if an appeal lies—

        (i) all persons who may appeal have stated in writing that they do not intend to do so;

        (ii) the time for bringing an appeal has expired and no appeal has been brought within that time; or

        (iii) an appeal brought within that time has been determined or abandoned; or

    (b) it appears to a Minister of the Crown or Her Majesty in Council that, having regard to a finding of the European Court of Human Rights made after the coming into force of this section in proceedings against the United Kingdom, a provision of legislation is incompatible with an obligation of the United Kingdom arising from the Convention.

(2) If a Minister of the Crown considers that there are compelling reasons for proceedings under this section, he may by order make such amendments to the legislation as he considers necessary to remove the incompatibility.

(3) If, in the case of subordinate legislation, a Minister of the Crown considers—

    (a) that it is necessary to amend the primary legislation under which the subordinate legislation in question was made, in order to enable the incompatibility to be removed, and

    (b) that there are compelling reasons for proceeding under this section,

he may by order make such amendments to the primary legislation as he considers necessary.

Other rights and proceedings

11   Safeguard for existing human rights

A person's reliance on a Convention right does not restrict—

    (a) any other right or freedom conferred on him by or under any law having effect in any part of the United Kingdom; or

    (b) his right to make any claim or bring any proceedings which he could make or bring apart from sections 7 to 9.

12   Freedom of expression

(1) This section applies if a court is considering whether to grant any relief which, if granted, might affect the exercise of the Convention right to freedom of expression.

(2) If the person against whom the application for relief is made ("the respondent") is neither present nor represented, no such relief is to be granted unless the court is satisfied—

    (a) that the applicant has taken all practicable steps to notify the respondent; or

    (b) that there are compelling reasons why the respondent should not be notified.

(3) No such relief is to be granted so as to restrain publication before trial unless the court is satisfied that the applicant is likely to establish that publication should not be allowed.

(4) The court must have particular regard to the importance of the Convention right to freedom of expression and, where the proceedings relate to material which the respondent claims, or which appears to the court, to be journalistic, literary or artistic material (or to conduct connected with such material), to—

    (a) the extent to which—

        (i) the material has, or is about to, become available to the public; or

        (ii) it is, or would be, in the public interest for the material to be published;

    (b) any relevant privacy code.

(5) In this section—

"court" includes a tribunal; and

"relief" includes any remedy or order (other than in criminal proceedings).

13   Freedom of thought, conscience and religion

(1) If a court's determination of any question arising under this Act might affect the exercise by a religious organisation (itself or its members collectively) of the Convention right to freedom of thought, conscience and religion, it must have particular regard to the importance of that right.

(2) In this section 'court' includes a tribunal.

14   Derogations

(1) In this Act "designated derogation" means . . . any derogation by the United Kingdom from an Article of the Convention, or of any protocol to the Convention, which is designated for the purposes of this Act in an order made by the Secretary of State.

(2) The derogation referred to in subsection (1)(a) is set out in Part I of Schedule 3.

(3) If a designated derogation is amended or replaced it ceases to be a designated derogation.

(4) But subsection (3) does not prevent the Secretary of State from exercising his power under subsection (1)(b) to make a fresh designation order in respect of the Article concerned.

(5) the Secretary of State must by order make such amendments to Schedule 3 as he considers appropriate to reflect—

    (a) any designation order; or

    (b) the effect of subsection (3).

(6) A designation order may be made in anticipation of the making by the United Kingdom of a proposed derogation.

15   Reservations

(1) In this Act "designated reservation" means—

(a) the United Kingdom's reservation to Article 2 of the First Protocol to the Convention; and

(b) any other reservation by the United Kingdom to an Article of the Convention, or of any protocol to the Convention, which is designated for the purposes of this Act in an order made by the Secretary of State.

(2) The text of the reservation referred to in subsection (1)(a) is set out in Part II of Schedule 3.

(3) If a designated reservation is withdrawn wholly or in part it ceases to be a designated reservation.

(4) But subsection (3) does not prevent the Secretary of State from exercising his power under subsection (1)(b) to make a fresh designation order in respect of the Article concerned.

(5) The Secretary of State must by order make such amendments to this Act as he considers appropriate to reflect–

(a) any designation order; or

(b) the effect of subsection (3).

16–18 ★ ★ ★ ★ ★

Parliamentary procedure

19 Statements of compatibility

(1) A Minister of the Crown in charge of a bill in either House of Parliament must, before Second Reading of the Bill—

(a) make a statement to the effect that in his view the provisions of the Bill are compatible with the Convention rights ("a statement of compatibility"); or

(b) make a statement to the effect that although he is unable to make a statement of compatibility the government nevertheless wishes the House to proceed with the Bill.

(2) The statement must be in writing and be published in such manner as the Minister making it considers appropriate.

★ ★ ★ ★ ★

Note: See note to s 1 for details of the Articles reproduced in Schedule 1.

Northern Ireland Act 1998
(1998, c. 47)

An Act to make provision for the government of Northern Ireland for the purpose of implementing the agreement reached at multi-party talks on Northern Ireland set out in Command Paper 3883.　　　　　　　　　　　　　　　　　　　　　　　　　　[19 November 1998]

Territorial extent: Northern Ireland

Note: Section 4 and Schedules 2 and 3 list the matters excepted, reserved and transferred to the Assembly but are not included in this text.

PART I PRELIMINARY

1 Status of Northern Ireland

(1) It is hereby declared that Northern Ireland in its entirety remains part of the United Kingdom and shall not cease to be so without the consent of a majority of the people of Northern Ireland voting in an poll held for the purposes of this section in accordance with Schedule 1.

(2) But if the wish expressed by a majority in such a poll is that Northern Ireland should cease to be part of the United Kingdom and form part of a united Ireland the Secretary of State shall lay before Parliament such proposals to give effect to that wish as may be agreed between Her Majesty's Government in the United Kingdom and the Government of Ireland.

2–4 ★ ★ ★ ★ ★

PART II   LEGISLATIVE POWERS

General

5   Acts of the Northern Ireland Assembly

(1) Subject to sections 6 to 8, the Assembly may make laws, to be known as Acts.

(2) A Bill shall become an Act when it has been passed by the Assembly and has received Royal Assent.

(3) A Bill receives Royal Assent at the beginning of the day on which Letters Patent under the Great Seal of Northern Ireland signed with Her Majesty's own hand signifying Her Assent are notified to the Presiding Officer.

(4) The date of Royal Assent shall be written on the Act by the Presiding Officer, and shall form part of the Act.

(5) The validity of any proceedings leading to the enactment of an Act of the Assembly shall not be called into question in any legal proceedings.

(6) This section does not affect the power of the Parliament of the United Kingdom to make laws for Northern Ireland, but an Act of the Assembly may modify any provision made by or under an Act of Parliament in so far as it is part of the law of Northern Ireland.

6   Legislative competence

(1) A provision of an Act is not law if it is outside the legislative competence of the Assembly.

(2) A provision is outside that competence if any of the following paragraphs apply—

 (a) it would form part of the law of a country or territory other than Northern Ireland, or confer or remove functions exercisable otherwise than in or as regards Northern Ireland;

 (b) it deals with an excepted matter and is not ancillary to other provisions (whether in the Act or previously enacted) dealing with reserved or transferred matters;

 (c) it is incompatible with any of the Convention rights;

 (d) it is incompatible with Community law;

 (e) it discriminates against any person or class of person on the ground of religious belief or political opinion;

 (f) it modifies an enactment in breach of section 7.

(3) For the purposes of this Act, a provision is ancillary to other provisions if it is a provision—

 (a) which provides for the enforcement of those other provisions or is otherwise necessary or expedient for making those other provisions effective; or

 (b) which is otherwise incidental to, or consequential on, those provisions; and references in this Act to provisions previously enacted are references to provisions contained in, or in any instrument made under, other Northern Ireland legislation or an Act of Parliament

(4) Her Majesty may by Order in Council specify functions which are to be treated, for such purposes of this Act as may be specified, as being, or as not being, functions which are exercisable in or as regards Northern Ireland.

(5) No recommendation shall be made to Her Majesty to make an Order in Council under subsection (4) unless a draft of the Order has been laid before and approved by resolution of each House of Parliament.

7 Entrenched enactments

(1) Subject to subsection (2), the following enactments shall not be modified by an Act of the Assembly or subordinate legislation made, confirmed or approved by a Minister or Northern Ireland department—

    (a) the European Communities Act 1972;

    (b) the Human Rights Act 1998; and

    (c) section 43(1) to (6) and (8), section 67, sections 84 to 86, section 95(3) and (4) and section 98.

(2) Subsection (1) does not prevent an Act of the Assembly or subordinate legislation modifying section 3(3) or (4) or 11(1) of the European Communities Act 1972.

(3) In this Act "Minister", unless the context otherwise requires, means the First Minister, the deputy First Minister or a Northern Ireland Minister.

8 ★ ★ ★ ★ ★

Scrutiny and stages of Bills

9 Scrutiny by Ministers

(1) A Minister in charge of a Bill shall, on or before introduction of it in the Assembly, make a statement to the effect that in his view the Bill would be within the legislative competence of the Assembly.

(2) The statement shall be in writing and shall be published in such manner as the Minister making the statement considers appropriate.

10 Scrutiny by Presiding Officer

(1) Standing orders shall ensure that a Bill is not introduced in the Assembly if the Presiding Officer decides that any provision of it would not be within the legislative competence of the Assembly.

(2) Subject to subsection (3)—

    (a) the Presiding Officer shall consider a Bill both on its introduction and before the Assembly enters on its final stage; and

    (b) if he considers that the Bill contains—

        (i) any provision which deals with an excepted matter and is ancillary to other provisions (whether in the Bill or previously enacted) dealing with reserved or transferred matters; or

        (ii) any provision which deals with a reserved matter,

he shall refer it to the Secretary of State; and

    (c) the Assembly shall not proceed with the Bill or, as the case may be, enter on its final stage unless—

        (i) the Secretary of State's consent to the consideration of the Bill by the Assembly is signified; or

        (ii) the Assembly is informed that in his opinion the Bill does not contain any such provision as is mentioned in paragraph (b)(i) and (ii).

(3) Subsection (2)(b) and (c) shall not apply—

    (a) where, in the opinion of the Presiding Officer, each provision of the Bill which deals with an excepted or reserved matter is ancillary to other provisions (whether in the Bill or previously enacted) dealing with transferred matters only; or

    (b) on the introduction of a Bill, where the Bill has been endorsed with a statement that the Secretary of State has consented to the Assembly considering the Bill.

(4) In this section and section 14 "final stage", in relation to a Bill, means the stage in the Assembly's proceedings at which the Bill falls finally to be passed or rejected.

11 Scrutiny by the Judicial Committee

(1) The Attorney General for Northern Ireland may refer the question of whether a

provision of a Bill would be within the legislative competence of the Assembly to the Judicial Committee for decision.

(2) Subject to subsection (3), he may make a reference in relation to a provision of a Bill at any time during—

(a) the period of four weeks beginning with the passing of the Bill, and

(b) the period of four weeks beginning with any subsequent approval of the Bill in accordance with standing orders made by virtue of section 13(6).

(3) If he notifies the Presiding Officer that he does not intend to make a reference in relation to a provision of a Bill, he shall not make such a reference unless, after the notification, the Bill is approved as mentioned in subsection (2)(b).

(4) If the Judicial Committee decide that any provision of a Bill would be within the legislative competence of the Assembly, their decision shall be taken as applying also to that provision if contained in the Act when enacted.

12 ★ ★ ★ ★ ★

13 Stages of Bills

(1) Standing orders shall include provision—

(a) for general debate on a Bill with an opportunity for members to vote on its general principles;

(b) for the consideration of, and an opportunity for members to vote on, the details of a Bill; and

(c) for a final stage at which a Bill can be passed or rejected but not amended.

(2) Standing orders may, in relation to different types of Bill, modify provisions made in pursuance of subsection (1)(a) or (b).

(3) Standing orders—

(a) shall include provision for establishing such a committee as is mentioned in paragraph 11 of Strand One of the Belfast Agreement;

(b) may include provision for the details of a Bill to be considered by the committee in such circumstances as may be specified in the orders.

(4) Standing orders shall include provision—

(a) requiring the Presiding Officer to send a copy of each Bill, as soon as reasonably practicable after introduction, to the Northern Ireland Human Rights Commission; and

(b) enabling the Assembly to ask the Commission, where the Assembly thinks fit, to advise whether a Bill is compatible with human rights (including the Convention rights).

(5) Standing orders shall provide for an opportunity for the reconsideration of a Bill after its passing if (and only if)—

(a) the Judicial Committee decide that any provision of the Bill would not be within the legislative competence of the Assembly;

(b) a reference made in relation to a provision of the Bill under section 11 has been withdrawn following a request for withdrawal under section 12;

(c) a decision is made in relation to the Bill under section 14(4) or (5); or

(d) a motion under section 15(1) is passed by either House of Parliament.

(6) Standing orders shall, in particular, ensure that any Bill amended on reconsideration is subject to a final stage at which it can be approved or rejected but not amended.

(7) References in subsection (5) and other provisions of this Act to the passing of a Bill shall, in the case of a Bill which has been amended on reconsideration, be read as references to the approval of the Bill.

Royal Assent

14   Submission by Secretary of State

(1) It shall be the Secretary of State who submits Bills for Royal Assent.

(2) The Secretary of State shall not submit a Bill for Royal Assent at any time when—

    (a) the Attorney General for Northern Ireland is entitled to make a reference in relation to a provision of the Bill under section 11; or

    (b) any such reference has been made but has not been decided or otherwise disposed of by the Judicial Committee.

(3) If—

    (a) the Judicial Committee have decided that any provision of a Bill would not be within the legislative competence of the Assembly; or

    (b) a reference made in relation to a provision of the Bill under section 11 has been withdrawn following a request for withdrawal under section 12,

the Secretary of State shall not submit the Bill in its unamended form for Royal Assent.

(4) The Secretary of State may, unless he consents to it, decide not to submit for Royal Assent a Bill containing a provision—

    (a) which the Secretary of State considers deals with an excepted matter and is ancillary to other provisions (whether in the Bill or previously enacted) dealing with reserved or transferred matters; or

    (b) which the Secretary of State considers deals with a reserved matter, if the Bill has not been referred to him under subsection (2) of section 10 (whether by virtue of subsection (3)(a) of that section or otherwise) before the Assembly enters on its final stage.

(5) The Secretary of State may decide not to submit for Royal Assent a Bill which contains a provision which he considers—

    (a) would be incompatible with any international obligations, with the interests of defence or national security or with the protection of public safety or public order; or

    (b) would have an adverse effect on the operation of the single market in goods and services within the United Kingdom.

15   Parliamentary control where consent given

(1) Subject to subsections (2) and (3), a Bill to which the Secretary of State has consented under this Part shall not be submitted by him for Royal Assent unless he has first laid it before Parliament and either—

    (a) the period of 20 days beginning with the date on which it is laid has expired without notice having been given in either House of a motion that the Bill shall not be submitted for Royal Assent; or

    (b) if notice of such a motion is given within that period, the motion has been rejected or withdrawn.

(2) Subsection (1) shall not apply to a Bill if the Secretary of State considers that it contains no provision which deals with an excepted or reserved matter except a provision which is ancillary to other provisions (whether in the Bill or previously enacted) dealing with transferred matters only.

(3)–(6) ★ ★ ★ ★ ★

PART III   EXECUTIVE AUTHORITIES

Authorities

16   First Minister and deputy First Minister

(1) Each Assembly shall, within a period of six weeks beginning with its first meeting, elect from among its members the First Minister and the deputy First Minister.

(2) Each candidate for either office must stand for election jointly with a candidate for the other office.

(3) Two candidates standing jointly shall not be elected to the two offices without the support of a majority of the members voting in the election, a majority of the designated Nationalists voting and a majority of the designated Unionists voting.

(4) The First Minister and the deputy First Minister—

    (a) shall not take up office until each of them has affirmed the terms of the pledge of office; and

    (b) subject to the provisions of this Part, shall hold office until the conclusion of the next election for First Minister and deputy First Minister.

(5) The holder of the office of First Minister or deputy First Minister may by notice in writing to the Presiding Officer designate a Northern Ireland Minister to exercise the functions of that office—

    (a) during any absence or incapacity of the holder; or

    (b) during any vacancy in that office arising otherwise than under subsection (7)(a);

but a person shall not have power to act by virtue of paragraph (a) for a continuous period exceeding 6 weeks.

(6) The First Minister or the deputy First Minister—

    (a) may at any time resign by notice in writing to the Presiding Officer; and

    (b) shall cease to hold office if he ceases to be a member of the Assembly otherwise than by virtue of a dissolution.

(7) If either the First Minister or the deputy First Minister ceases to hold office at any time, whether by resignation or otherwise, the other—

    (a) shall also cease to hold office at that time; but

    (b) may continue to exercise the functions of his office until the election required by subsection (8).

(8) Where the offices of the First Minister and the deputy First Minister become vacant at any time an election shall be held under this section to fill the vacancies within a period of six weeks beginning with that time.

(9) Standing orders may make provision with respect to the holding of elections under this section.

(10) In this Act "the pledge of office" means the pledge of office which, together with the code of conduct to which it refers, is set out in Annex A to Strand One of the Belfast Agreement (the text of which Annex is reproduced in Schedule 4).

Note: See s. 3 of the Northern Ireland Act 2000 for modifications made to this section on the restoration of devolved government (following its suspension under s. 1 of that Act).

17   Ministerial offices

(1) The First Minister and the deputy First Minister acting jointly may at any time, and shall where subsection (2) applies, determine—

    (a) the number of Ministerial offices to be held by Northern Ireland Ministers; and

    (b) the functions to be exercisable by the holder of each such office.

(2) This subsection applies where provision is made by an Act of the Assembly for establishing a new Northern Ireland department or dissolving an existing one.

(3) In making a determination under subsection (1), the First Minister and the deputy First Minister shall ensure that the functions exercisable by those in charge of the different Northern Ireland departments existing at the date of the determination are exercisable by the holders of different Ministerial offices.

(4) The number of Ministerial offices shall not exceed 10 or such greater number as the Secretary of State may by order provide.

(5) A determination under subsection (1) shall not have effect unless it is approved by a resolution of the Assembly passed with cross-community support.

18 Northern Ireland Ministers

(1) Where—

    (a) an Assembly is elected under section 31 or 32;

    (b) a determination under section 17(1) takes effect;

    (c) a resolution which causes one or more Ministerial offices to become vacant is passed under section 30(2);

    (d) the period of exclusion imposed by a resolution under section 30(2) comes to an end; or

    (e) such other circumstances obtain as may be specified in standing orders, all Northern Ireland Ministers shall cease to hold office and the Ministerial offices shall be filled by applying subsections (2) to (6) within a period so specified.

(2) The nominating officer of the political party for which the formula in subsection (5) gives the highest figure may select a Ministerial office and nominate a person to hold it who is a member of the party and of the Assembly.

(3) If—

    (a) the nominating officer does not exercise the power conferred by subsection (2) within a period specified in standing orders; or

    (b) the nominated person does not take up the selected Ministerial office within that period,

that power shall become exercisable by the nominating officer of the political party for which the formula in subsection (5) gives the next highest figure.

(4) Subsections (2) and (3) shall be applied as many times as may be necessary to secure that each of the Ministerial offices is filled.

(5) The formula is—

$$\frac{S}{1 + M}$$

where—

S = the number of seats in the Assembly which were held by members of the party on the day on which the Assembly first met following its election;

M = the number of Ministerial offices (if any) which are held by members of the party.

(6) Where the figures given by the formula for two or more political parties are equal, each of those figures shall be recalculated with S being equal to the number of first preference votes cast for the party at the last general election of members of the Assembly.

(7) The holding of office as First Minister or deputy First Minister shall not prevent a person being nominated to hold a Ministerial office.

(8) A Northern Ireland Minister shall not take up office until he has affirmed the terms of the pledge of office.

(9) A Northern Ireland Minister shall cease to hold office if—

    (a) he resigns by notice in writing to the First Minister and the deputy First Minister;

    (b) he ceases to be a member of the Assembly otherwise than by virtue of a dissolution; or

    (c) he is dismissed by the nominating officer who nominated him (or that officer's successor) and the Presiding Officer is notified of his dismissal.

(10) Where a Ministerial office is vacant otherwise than by virtue of subsection (1), the nominating officer of the party on whose behalf the previous incumbent was nominated may nominate a person to hold the office who is a member of the party and of the Assembly.

(11) If—

    (a) the nominating officer does not exercise the power conferred by subsection (10) within a period specified in standing orders; or

    (b) the nominated person does not take up the office within that period, the vacancy, shall be filled by applying subsections (2) to (6) within a period specified in standing orders.

(12) Where—

(a) the Assembly has resolved under section 30(2) that a political party does not enjoy its confidence; and

(b) the party's period of exclusion has not come to an end,

the party shall be disregarded for the purposes of any application of subsections (2) to (6).

(13) In this section "nominating officer"—

(a) in relation to a party registered under the Registration of Political Parties Act 1998, means the registered nominating officer or a member of the Assembly nominated by him for the purposes of this section;

(b) in relation to any other political party, means the person who appears to the Presiding Officer to be the leader of the party, or a member of the Assembly nominated by that person for the purposes of this section.

19 Junior Ministers

(1) The First Minister and the deputy First Minister acting jointly may at any time determine—

(a) that a number of members of the Assembly specified in the determination shall be appointed as junior Ministers in accordance with such procedures for their appointment as are so specified; and

(b) that the functions exercisable by virtue of each junior Ministerial office shall be those specified in relation to that office in the determination.

(2) Procedures specified in a determination under this section may apply such formulae or other rules as the First Minister and the deputy First Minister consider appropriate.

(3) A determination under this section shall—

(a) make provision as to the circumstances in which a junior Minister shall cease to hold office, and for the filling of vacancies; and

(b) provide that a junior Minister shall not take up office until he has affirmed the terms of the pledge of office.

(4) A determination under this section shall not take effect until it has been approved by a resolution of the Assembly.

(5) Where a determination under this section takes effect—

(a) any junior Ministers previously appointed shall cease to hold office; and

(b) the procedures specified in the determination shall be applied within a period specified in standing orders.

[19A   Disqualification for certain offices

(1) No person may—

(a) stand for election as First Minister or as deputy First Minister, or be elected as such,

(b) be nominated to hold a Ministerial office,

(c) be appointed as a junior Minister, or

(d) be nominated under paragraph 7 of Schedule 1 to the Police (Northern Ireland) Act 2000 (members of the Northern Ireland Policing Board drawn from the Northern Ireland Assembly),

if he is the holder of a disqualifying office.

(2) A Minister or junior Minister ceases to hold that office on becoming the holder of a disqualifying office.

(3) A person holding office as a member of the Northern Ireland Policing Board in accordance with paragraph 7 of Schedule 1 to the Police (Northern Ireland) Act 2000 ceases to hold that office on becoming the holder of a disqualifying office.

(4) In this section "disqualifying office" means—

(a) Minister of the Government of Ireland; or

(b) chairman or deputy chairman of—
    (i) a committee of the Dáil Éireann (House of Representatives of Ireland);
    (ii) a committee of the Seanad Éireann (Senate of Ireland); or
    (iii) a joint committee of the Oireachtas (National Parliament of Ireland).]

20   The Executive Committee

(1) There shall be an Executive Committee of each Assembly consisting of the First Minister, the deputy First Minister and the Northern Ireland Ministers.

(2) The First Minister and the deputy First Minister shall be chairmen of the Committee.

(3) The Committee shall have the functions set out in paragraphs 19 and 20 of Strand One of the Belfast Agreement.

21   ★ ★ ★ ★ ★

22   Statutory functions

(1) An Act of the Assembly or other enactment may confer functions on a Minister (but not a junior Minister) or a Northern Ireland department by name.

(2) Functions conferred on a Northern Ireland department by an enactment passed or made before the appointed day shall, except as provided by an Act of the Assembly or other subsequent enactment, continue to be exercisable by that department.

23   Prerogative and executive powers

(1) The executive power in Northern Ireland shall continue to be vested in Her Majesty.

(2) As respects transferred matters, the prerogative and other executive powers of Her Majesty in relation to Northern Ireland shall, subject to subsection (3), be exercisable on Her Majesty's behalf by any Minister or Northern Ireland department.

(3) As respects the Northern Ireland Civil Service and the Commissioner for Public Appointments for Northern Ireland, the prerogative and other executive powers of Her Majesty in relation to Northern Ireland shall be exercisable on Her Majesty's behalf by the First Minister and the deputy First Minister acting jointly.

(4) The First Minister and deputy First Minister acting jointly may by prerogative order under subsection (3) direct that such of the powers mentioned in that subsection as are specified in the order shall be exercisable on Her Majesty's behalf by a Northern Ireland Minister or Northern Ireland department so specified.

24   Community law, Convention rights etc.

(1) A Minister or Northern Ireland department has no power to make, confirm or approve any subordinate legislation, or to do any act, so far as the legislation or act—
    (a) is incompatible with any of the Convention rights;
    (b) is incompatible with Community law;
    (c) discriminates against a person or class of person on the ground of religious belief or political opinion;
    (d) in the case of an act, aids or incites another person to discriminate against a person or class of person on that ground; or
    (e) in the case of legislation, modifies an enactment in breach of section 7.

(2) Subsection (1)(c) and (d) does not apply in relation to any act which is unlawful by virtue of the Fair Employment (Northern Ireland) Act 1976, or would be unlawful but for some exception made by virtue of Part V of that Act.

25   Excepted and reserved matters

(1) If any subordinate legislation made, confirmed or approved by, a Minister or Northern Ireland department contains a provision dealing with an excepted or reserved matter, the Secretary of State may by order revoke the legislation.

(2) An order made under subsection (1) shall recite the reasons for revoking the legislation and may make provision having retrospective effect.

26   International obligations

(1) If the Secretary of State considers that any action proposed to be taken by a Minister or Northern Ireland department would be incompatible with any international obligations, with the interests of defence or national security or with the protection of public safety or public order, he may by order direct that the proposed action shall not be taken.

(2) If the Secretary of State considers that any action capable of being taken by a Minister or Northern Ireland department is required for the purpose of giving effect to any international obligations, of safeguarding the interests of defence or national security or of protecting public safety or public order, he may by order direct that the action shall be taken.

(3) In subsections (1) and (2), "action" includes making, confirming or approving subordinate legislation and, in subsection (2), includes introducing a Bill in the Assembly.

(4) If any subordinate legislation made, confirmed or approved by a Minister or Northern Ireland department contains a provision which the Secretary of State considers—

(a) would be incompatible with any international obligations, with the interests of defence or national security or with the protection of public safety or public order; or

(b) would have an adverse effect on the operation of the single market in goods and services within the United Kingdom,

the Secretary of State may by order revoke the legislation.

(5) An order under this section shall recite the reasons for making the order and may make provision having retrospective effect.

27-28   ★ ★ ★ ★ ★

PART IV   THE NORTHERN IRELAND ASSEMBLY

Presiding Officer and Commission

39   Presiding Officer

(1) Each Assembly shall as its first business elect from among its members a Presiding Officer and deputies.

(2) A person elected Presiding Officer or deputy shall hold office until the conclusion of the next election for Presiding Officer under subsection (1) unless—

(a) he previously resigns;

(b) he ceases to be a member of the Assembly otherwise than by virtue of a dissolution; or

(c) the Assembly elects from among its members a person to hold office as Presiding Officer or deputy in his place.

(3) If the Presiding Officer or a deputy ceases to hold office (otherwise than under subsection (2)(c)) before the Assembly is dissolved, the Assembly shall elect another from among its members to fill his place.

(4) The Presiding Officer's functions may be exercised by a deputy if the office of Presiding Officer is vacant or the Presiding Officer is for any reason unable to act.

(5) The Presiding Officer may (subject to standing orders) authorise a deputy to exercise functions on his behalf.

(6) Standing orders may include provision as to the participation (including voting) of the Presiding Officer and deputies in the proceedings of the Assembly.

(7) A person shall not be elected under subsections (1) to (3) without cross-community support.

40   Commission

(1) There shall be a body corporate, to be known as the Northern Ireland Assembly Commission ("the Commission"), to perform—

(a) the functions conferred on the Commission by virtue of any enactment; and

(b) any functions conferred on the Commission by resolution of the Assembly.

(2) The members of the Commission shall be—

(a) the Presiding Officer; and

(b) the prescribed number of members of the Assembly appointed in accordance with standing orders.

(3) In subsection (2) "the prescribed number" means 5 or such other number as may be prescribed by standing orders.

[(3A) A member of the Assembly who is—

(a) a minister of the Government of Ireland; or

(b) chairman or deputy chairman of—

(i) a committee of the Dail Éireann (House of Representatives of Ireland),

(ii) a committee of the Seanad Éireann (Senate of Ireland), or

(iii) a joint committee of the Oireachtas (National Parliament of Ireland), may not be appointed as a member of the Commission.]

(4) The Commission shall provide the Assembly, or ensure that the Assembly is provided, with the property, staff and services required for the Assembly's purposes.

(5) The Assembly may give special or general directions to the Commission for the purpose of or in connection with the exercise of the Commission's functions.

(6) Proceedings by or against the Assembly (other than proceedings on the Crown side of the Queen's Bench Division) shall be instituted by or against the Commission on behalf of the Assembly.

(7) Any property or liabilities acquired or incurred in relation to matters within the general responsibility of the Commission to which (apart from this subsection) the Assembly would be entitled or subject shall be treated for all purposes as property or liabilities of the Commission.

(8) Any expenses of the Commission shall be defrayed out of money appropriated by Act of the Assembly.

(9) Any sums received by the Commission shall be paid into the Consolidated Fund of Northern Ireland, subject to any provision made by Act of the Assembly for the disposal of or accounting for such sums.

(10) Schedule 5 (which makes further provision about the Commission) shall have effect.

Proceedings etc.

41 Standing orders

(1) The proceedings of the Assembly shall be regulated by standing orders.

(2), (3) ★ ★ ★ ★ ★

42 Petitions of concern

(1) If 30 members petition the Assembly expressing their concern about a matter which is to be voted on by the Assembly, the vote on that matter shall require cross-community support.

(2) Standing orders shall make provision with respect to the procedure to be followed in petitioning the Assembly under this section, including provision with respect to the period of notice required.

(3) Standing orders shall provide that the matter to which a petition under this section relates may be referred, in accordance with paragraphs 11 and 13 of Strand One of the Belfast Agreement, to the committee established under section 13(3)(a).

43 Members' interests

(1) Standing orders shall include provision for a register of interests of members of the Assembly, and for—

(a) registrable interests (as defined in standing orders) to be registered in it; and

(b) the register to be published and made available for public inspection.

(2)–(8) ★ ★ ★ ★ ★

44–49 ★ ★ ★ ★ ★

50   Privilege

(1) For the purposes of the law of defamation, absolute privilege shall attach to—

(a) the making of a statement in proceedings of the Assembly; and

(b) the publication of a statement under the Assembly's authority.

(2) A person is not guilty of contempt of court under the strict liability rule as the publisher of any matter—

(a) in the course of proceedings of the Assembly which relate to a Bill or subordinate legislation; or

(b) to the extent that it consists of a fair and accurate report of such proceedings which is made in good faith.

(3) In this section—

"statement" has the same meaning as in the Defamation Act 1996;

"the strict liability rule" has the same meaning as in the Contempt of Court Act 1981

51-67 ★ ★ ★ ★ ★

PART VII   HUMAN RIGHTS AND EQUAL OPPORTUNITIES

Human rights

68   The Northern Ireland Human Rights Commission

(1) There shall be a body corporate to be known as the Northern Ireland Human Rights Commission.

(2) The Commission shall consist of a Chief Commissioner and other Commissioners appointed by the Secretary of State.

(3) In making appointments under this section, the Secretary of State shall as far as practicable secure that the Commissioners, as a group, are representative of the community in Northern Ireland.

(4) Schedule 7 (which makes supplementary provision about the Commission) shall have effect.

69   The Commission's functions

(1) The Commission shall keep under review the adequacy and effectiveness in Northern Ireland of law and practice relating to the protection of human rights.

(2) The Commission shall, before the end of the period of two years beginning with the commencement of this section, make to the Secretary of State such recommendations as it thinks fit for improving—

(a) its effectiveness;

(b) the adequacy and effectiveness of the functions conferred on it by this Part;

and

(c) the adequacy and effectiveness of the provisions of this Part relating to it.

(3) The Commission shall advise the Secretary of State and the Executive Committee of the Assembly of legislative and other measures which ought to be taken to protect human rights—

(a) as soon as reasonably practicable after receipt of a general or specific request for advice; and

(b) on such other occasions as the Commission thinks appropriate.

(4) The Commission shall advise the Assembly whether a Bill is compatible with human rights—

(a) as soon as reasonably practicable after receipt of a request for advice; and

(b) on such other occasions as the Commission thinks appropriate.

(5) The Commission may—

(a) give assistance to individuals in accordance with section 70; and

(b) bring proceedings involving law or practice relating to the protection of human rights.

(6) The Commission shall promote understanding and awareness of the importance of human rights in Northern Ireland; and for this purpose it may undertake, commission or provide financial or other assistance for—

(a) research; and

(b) educational activities.

(7) The Secretary of State shall request the Commission to provide advice of the kind referred to in paragraph 4 of the Human Rights section of the Belfast Agreement.

(8) For the purpose of exercising its functions under this section the Commission may conduct such investigations as it considers necessary or expedient.

(9) The Commission may decide to publish its advice and the outcome of its research and investigations.

(10) The Commission shall do all that it can to ensure the establishment of the committee referred to in paragraph 10 of that section of that Agreement.

(11) In this section—

(a) a reference to the Assembly includes a reference to a committee of the Assembly;

(b) "human rights" includes the Convention rights.

70   Assistance by Commission

(1) This section applies to—

(a) proceedings involving law or practice relating to the protection of human rights which a person in Northern Ireland has commenced, or wishes to commence; or

(b) proceedings in the course of which such a person relies, or wishes to rely, on such law or practice.

(2) Where the person applies to the Northern Ireland Human Rights Commission for assistance in relation to proceedings to which this section applies, the Commission may grant the application on any of the following grounds—

(a) that the case raises a question of principle;

(b) that it would be unreasonable to expect the person to deal with the case without assistance because of its complexity, or because of the person's position in relation to another person involved, or for some other reason;

(c) that there are other special circumstances which make it appropriate for the Commission to provide assistance.

(3) Where the Commission grants an application under subsection (2) it may—

(a) provide, or arrange for the provision of, legal advice;

(b) arrange for the provision of legal representation;

(c) provide any other assistance which it thinks appropriate.

(4) Arrangements made by the Commission for the provision of assistance to a person may include provision for recovery of expenses from the person in certain circumstances.

71   Restrictions on application of rights

(1) Nothing in section 6(2)(c), 24(1)(a) or 69(5)(b) shall enable a person—

(a) to bring any proceedings in a court or tribunal on the aground that any legislation or act is incompatible with the Convention rights; or

(b) to rely on any of the Convention rights in any such proceedings, unless he would be a victim for the purposes of article 34 of the Convention if proceedings in respect of the legislation or act were brought in the European Court of Human Rights.

(2) Subsection (1) does not apply to the Attorney General, the Attorney General for Northern Ireland, the Advocate General for Scotland or the Lord Advocate.

(3) Section 6(2)(c)—

(a) does not apply to a provision of an Act of the Assembly if the passing of the Act is, by virtue of subsection (2) of section 6 of the Human Rights Act 1998, not unlawful under subsection (1) of that section; and

(b) does not enable a court or tribunal to award in respect of the passing of an Act of the Assembly any damages which it could not award on finding the passing of the Act unlawful under that subsection.

(4) Section 24(1)(a)—

(a) does not apply to an act which, by virtue of subsection (2) of section 6 of the Human Rights Act 1998, is not unlawful under subsection (1) of that section; and

(b) does not enable a court or tribunal to award in respect of an act any damages which it could not award on finding the act unlawful under that subsection.

(5) In this section "the Convention" has the same meaning as in the Human Rights Act 1998.

72–79 ★ ★ ★ ★ ★

PART VIII   MISCELLANEOUS

80   Legislative power to remedy ultra vires acts

(1) The Secretary of State may by order make such provision as he considers necessary or expedient in consequence of—

(a) any provision of an Act of the Assembly which is not, or may not be, within the legislative competence of the Assembly; or

(b) any purported exercise by a Minister or Northern Ireland department of his or its functions which is not, or may not be, a valid exercise of those functions.

(2) An order under this section may—

(a) make provision having retrospective effect;

(b) make consequential or supplementary provision, including provision amending or repealing any Northern Ireland legislation, or any instrument made under such legislation;

(c) make transitional or saving provision.

81   Powers of courts or tribunals to vary retrospective decisions

(1) This section applies where any court or tribunal decides that—

(a) any provision of an Act of the Assembly is not within the legislative competence of the Assembly; or

(b) a Minister or Northern Ireland department does not have the power to make, confirm or approve a provision of subordinate legislation that he or it has purported to make, confirm or approve.

(2) The court or tribunal may make an order—

(a) removing or limiting any retrospective effect of the decision; or

(b) suspending the effect of the decision for any period and on any conditions to allow the defect to be corrected.

(3) In deciding whether to make an order under this section, the court or tribunal shall (among other things) have regard to the extent to which persons who are not parties to the proceedings would otherwise be adversely affected.

(4) Where a court or tribunal is considering whether to make an order under this section, it shall order notice of that fact to be given to—

(a) the Attorney General for Northern Ireland; and

(b) where the decision mentioned in subsection (1) relates to a devolution issue (within the meaning of Schedule 10), the appropriate authority,

unless the person to whom the notice would be given is a party to the proceedings.

(5) A person to whom notice is given under subsection (4) or, where such notice is given to the First Minister and the deputy First Minister, those Ministers acting jointly may take part as a party in the proceedings so far as they relate to the making of the order.

(6) Paragraphs 37 and 38 of Schedule 10 apply with necessary modifications for the purposes of subsections (4) and (5) as they apply for the purposes of that Schedule.

(7) In this section "the appropriate authority" means—

    (a) in relation to proceedings in Northern Ireland, the First Minister and the deputy First Minister;

    (b) in relation to proceedings in England and Wales, the Attorney General;

    (c) in relation to proceedings in Scotland, the Lord Advocate and the Advocate General for Scotland.

82 The Judicial Committee

(1) Any decision of the Judicial Committee in proceedings under this Act shall stated in open court and shall be binding in all legal proceedings (other than proceedings before the Committee).

(2) No member of the Judicial Committee shall sit and act as a member of the Committee in proceedings under this Act unless he holds or has held—

    (a) the office of a Lord of Appeal in Ordinary; or

    (b) high judicial office as defined in section 25 of the Appellate Jurisdiction Act 1876 (ignoring for this purpose section 5 of the Appellate Jurisdiction Act 1887).

(3) Her Majesty may by Order in Council—

    (a) confer on the Judicial Committee in relation to proceedings under this Act such powers as Her Majesty considers necessary or expedient;

    (b) apply the Judicial Committee Act 1833 in relation to proceedings under this Act with exceptions or modifications;

    (c) make rules for regulating the procedure in relation to proceedings under this Act before the Judicial Committee.

(4) A statutory instrument containing an Order in Council under subsection (3)(a) or (b) shall be subject to annulment in pursuance of a resolution of either House of Parliament.

(5) In this section "proceedings under this Act" means proceedings on a question referred to the Judicial Committee under section 11 or proceedings under Schedule 10.

83 Interpretation of Acts of the Assembly etc.

(1) This section applies where—

    (a) any provision of an Act of the Assembly, or of a Bill for such an Act, could be read either—

        (i) in such a way as to be within the legislative competence of the Assembly; or

        (ii) in such a way as to be outside that competence; or

    (b) any provision of subordinate legislation made, confirmed or approved, or purporting to be made, confirmed or approved, by a Northern Ireland authority could be read either—

        (i) in such a way as not to be invalid by reason of section 24 or, as the case may be, section 76; or

        (ii) in such a way as to be invalid by reason of that section.

(2) The provision shall be read in the way which makes it within that competence or, as the case may be, does not make it invalid by reason of that section, and shall have effect accordingly.

(3) In this section "Northern Ireland authority" means a Minister, a Northern Ireland department or a public authority (within the meaning of section 76) carrying out functions relating, to Northern Ireland.

★ ★ ★ ★ ★

Northern Ireland (Sentences) Act 1998
(1998, c. 35)

An Act to make provision about the release of certain persons serving sentences of imprisonment in Northern Ireland.   [28 July 1998]

Territorial extent: Northern Ireland

Sentence Review commissioners

1 Sentence Review commissioners

(1) The Secretary of State shall appoint Sentence Review Commissioners.

(2) The Secretary of State shall so far as reasonably practicable ensure that at any time—

(a) at least one of the commissioners is a lawyer, and

(b) at least one is a psychiatrist or a psychologist.

(3) In making appointments the Secretary of State shall have regard to the desirability of the Commissioners, as a group, commanding widespread acceptance throughout the community in Northern Ireland.

(4) Schedule 1 (which makes further provision about the Commissioners) shall have effect.

(5) In subsection (2)(a) "lawyer" means a person who holds a legal qualification in the United Kingdom.

2 ★ ★ ★ ★ ★

Eligibility for release

3 Applications

(1) A prisoner may apply to Commissioners for a declaration that he is eligible for release in accordance with the provisions of this Act.

(2) The Commissioners shall grant the application if (and only if)—

(a) the prisoner is serving a sentence of imprisonment for a fixed term in Northern Ireland and the first three of the following four conditions are satisfied, or

(b) the prisoner is serving a sentence of imprisonment for life in Northern Ireland and the following four conditions are satisfied.

(3) The first condition is that the sentence—

(a) was passed in Northern Ireland for a qualifying offence, and

(b) is one of imprisonment for life or for a term of at least five years.

(4) The second condition is that the prisoner is not a supporter of a specified organisation.

(5) The third condition is that, if the prisoner were released immediately, he would not be likely—

(a) to become a supporter of a specified organisation, or

(b) to become concerned in the commission, preparation or instigation of acts of terrorism connected with the affairs of Northern Ireland.

(6) The fourth condition is that, if the prisoner were released immediately, he would not be a danger to the public.

(7) A qualifying offence is an offence which—

(a) was committed before 10 April 1998,

(b) was when committed a scheduled offence within the meaning of the Northern Ireland (Emergency Provisions) Act 1973, 1978, 1991 or 1996, and

(c) was not the subject of a certificate of the Attorney General for Northern Ireland that it was not to be treated as a scheduled offence in the case concerned.

(8) A specified organisation is an organisation specified by order of the Secretary of State; and he shall specify any organisation which he believes—

(a) is concerned in terrorism connected with the affairs of Northern Ireland, or in promoting or encouraging it, and

(b) has not established or is not maintaining a complete and unequivocal ceasefire.

(9) In applying subsection (8)(b) the Secretary of State shall in particular take into account whether an organisation—

(a) is committed to the use now and in the future of only democratic and peaceful means to achieve its objectives;

(b) has ceased to be involved in any acts of violence or of preparation for violence;

(c) is directing or promoting acts of violence or of preparation for violence;

(d) is co-operating fully with any Commission of the kind referred to in section 7 of the Northern Ireland Arms Decommissioning Act 1997 in implementing the Decommissioning section of the agreement reached at multi-party talks on Northern Ireland set out in Command Paper 3883.

(10) The Secretary of State shall from time to time review the list of organisations specified under subsection (8); and if he believes—

(a) that paragraph (a) or (b) of that subsection does not apply to a specified organisation, or

(b) that paragraphs (a) and (b) apply to an organisation which is not specified, he shall make a new order under subsection (8).

★ ★ ★ ★ ★

Nuclear Explosions (Prohibition and Inspections) Act 1998
(1998, c. 7)

An Act to enable effect to be given to certain provisions of the Comprehensive Nuclear-Test-Ban Treaty adopted in New York on 10 September 1996 and the Protocol to that Treaty; and for connected purposes.   [18 March 1998]

Territorial extent: United Kingdom

Nuclear explosions

1   Causing a nuclear explosion

(1) Any person who knowingly causes a nuclear weapon test explosion or any other nuclear explosion is guilty of an offence and liable on conviction on indictment to imprisonment for life.

(2) Nothing in subsection (1) shall apply to a nuclear weapon explosion carried out in the course of an armed conflict.

(3) If in proceedings for an offence under this section any question arises as to whether a nuclear weapon explosion was or was not carried out in the course of an armed conflict, that question shall be determined by the Secretary of State; and a certificate purporting to set out any such determination and to be signed by the Secretary of State shall be received in evidence and be deemed to be so signed without further proof, unless the contrary is shown.

2   Application of section 1

(1) Section 1 shall apply to acts done in the United Kingdom or elsewhere.

(2) So far as it applies to acts done outside the United Kingdom, section 1 applies to—

(a) United Kingdom nationals,

(b) Scottish partnerships, and

(c) bodies incorporated under the law of any part of the United Kingdom.

(3) For the purposes of subsection (2), a United Kingdom national is an individual who is—

(a) a British citizen, a [British overseas territories citizen], a British National (Overseas) or a British Overseas citizen,

(b) a person who under the British Nationality Act 1981 is a British subject, or

(c) a British protected person within the meaning of that Act.

(4) Her Majesty may by Order in Council extend the application of section 1, so far as it applies to acts done outside the United Kingdom, to bodies incorporated under the law of any of the Channel Islands, the Isle of Man or any colony.

(5) Proceedings for an offence committed under section 1 outside the United Kingdom may be taken, and the offence may for incidental purposes be treated as having been committed, in any place in the United Kingdom.

3   Provision supplementary to section 1

(1) Proceedings for an offence under section 1 shall not be instituted—

(a) in England and Wales, except by or with the consent of the Attorney General;

(b) in Northern Ireland, except by or with the consent of the Attorney General for Northern Ireland.

(2) The court by or before which a person is convicted of an offence under section 1 may order that anything shown to the court's satisfaction to relate to the offence shall be forfeited, and either destroyed or otherwise dealt with in such manner as the court may order.

(3) In particular, the court may order the thing to be dealt with as the Secretary of State may see fit; and in such a case the Secretary of State may direct that it be destroyed or otherwise dealt with.

(4) Where—

(a) the court proposes to order anything to be forfeited under this section, and

(b) a person claiming to have an interest in it applies to be heard by the court, the court must not order it to be forfeited unless he has been given an opportunity to show cause why the order should not be made.

★ ★ ★ ★ ★

Public Interest Disclosure Act 1998
(1998, c. 23)

An Act to protect individuals who make certain disclosures of information in the public interest; to allow such individuals to bring action in respect of victimisation; and for connected purposes.
[2 July 1998]

Territorial extent: England and Wales, Scotland

Note: This Act adds new sections to the Employment Rights Act 1996 and consists almost entirely of additions and textual amendments. The most important of the provisions added are printed as part of that Act, above.

Public Processions (Northern Ireland) Act 1998
(1998, c. 2)

An Act to amend the law relating to public procession in Northern Ireland; to provide for the establishment and functions of the Parades Commission for Northern Ireland; and for connected purposes.
[16 February 1998]

Territorial extent: Northern Ireland

1   The Commission
(1) There shall be established a body to be known as the Parades Commission for Northern Ireland (in this Act referred to as "the Commission").
(2) Schedule 1 has effect in relation to the Commission.

2   Functions of the Commission
(1) It shall be the duty of the Commission—
(a) to promote greater understanding by the general public of issues concerning public processions;
(b) to promote and facilitate mediation as a means of resolving disputes concerning public processions;
(c) to keep itself generally informed as to the conduct of public processions and protest meetings;
(d) to keep under review, and make such recommendations as it thinks fit to the Secretary of State concerning, the operation of this Act.
(2) The Commission may in accordance with the following provisions of this Act—
(a) facilitate mediation between parties to particular disputes concerning proposed public processions and take such other steps as appears to the Commission to be appropriate for resolving such disputes;
(b) issue determinations in respect of particular proposed public processions.
(3) For the purposes of its functions under this section, the Commission may, with the approval of the Secretary of State—
(a) provide financial or other assistance to any person or body on such terms and conditions as the Commission may determine;
(b) commission research.

3   Code of Conduct
(1) The Commission shall issue a code (in this Act referred to as "the Code of Conduct")—
(a) providing guidance to persons organising a public procession or protest meeting; and
(b) regulating the conduct of persons organising or taking part in a public procession or protest meeting.
(2) The Commission—
(a) shall keep the Code of Conduct under review; and
(b) may from time to time revise the whole or any part of the Code of Conduct and issue the revised Code of Conduct.
(3) Schedule 2 has effect in relation to the Code of Conduct.

4   Procedural rules
(1) The Commission shall issue a set of rules (in this Act referred to as "the procedural rules") for the purpose of regulating and prescribing the practice and procedure to be followed—
(a) by the Commission in exercising the functions mentioned in section 2(2); and
(b) by other persons or bodies in their dealings with the Commission in connection with the exercise of those functions.
(2) In particular (but without prejudice to the generality of subsection (1)) the procedural rules may—
(a) provide for the determination by the Commission of the particular cases in relation to which the functions mentioned in section 2(2) are to be exercised;
(b) prescribe the manner in which, and the time within which, specified actions may or must be taken (whether by the Commission or by other persons or bodies) for the purposes of the exercise by the Commission of those functions;
(c) require notice of specified determinations of the Commission made in the exercise of those functions to be published in such form and manner as may be specified.
(3) In subsection (2) "specified" means specified in the procedural rules.

(4) The Commission—
   (a) shall keep the procedural rules under review; and
   (b) may from time to time revise the whole or any part of the procedural rules and issue the revised procedural rules.
(5) Schedule 2 has effect in relation to the procedural rules.

5 Guidelines

(1) The Commission shall issue a set of guidelines (in this Act referred to as "guidelines") as to the exercise by the Commission of its functions under section 8.
(2) The Commission—
   (a) shall keep the guidelines under review; and
   (b) may from time to time revise the whole or any part of the guidelines and issue the revised guidelines.
(3) Schedule 2 has effect in relation to the guidelines.

Advance notice of public processions and related protest meetings

6 Advance notice of public processions and related protest meetings

(1) A person proposing to organise a public procession shall give notice of that proposal in accordance with subsections (2) to (4) to a member of the Royal Ulster Constabulary not below the rank of sergeant by leaving the notice with him at the police station nearest to the proposed starting place of that procession.
(2) Notice under this section shall be given—
   (a) not less than 28 days before the date on which the procession is to be held; or
   (b) if that is not reasonably practicable, as soon as it is reasonably practicable to give such notice.
(3) Notice under this section shall—
   (a) be given in writing in such form as may be prescribed by regulations made by the Secretary of State; and
   (b) be signed by the person giving the notice.
(4) The form prescribed under subsection (3)(a) shall require a person giving notice under this section to specify—
   (a) the date and time when the procession is to be held;
   (b) its route;
   (c) the number of persons likely to take part in it;
   (d) the names of any bands which are to take part in it;
   (e) the arrangements for its control being made by the person proposing to organise it;
   (f) the name and address of that person;
   (g) where the notice is given as mentioned in paragraph (b) of subsection (2), the reason why it was not reasonably practicable to give notice in accordance with paragraph (a) of that subsection; and
   (h) such other matters as appear to the Secretary of State to be necessary for, or appropriate for facilitating, the exercise by the Commission, the Secretary of State or members of the Royal Ulster Constabulary of any function in relation to the procession.
(5) This section does not apply where the procession is—
   (a) a funeral procession; or
   (b) a procession of a class or description specified in an order made by the Secretary of State.
(6) The Chief Constable shall ensure that a copy of a notice given under this section is immediately sent to the Commission.
(7) A person who organises or takes part in a public procession—

(a) in respect of which the requirements of this section as to a notice have not been satisfied; or

(b) which is held on a date, at a time or along a route which differs from the date, time or route specified in relation to it in the notice given under this section,

shall be guilty of an offence.

(8) In proceedings for an offence under subsection (7) it is a defence for the accused to prove that he did not know of, and neither suspected nor had reason to suspect, the failure to satisfy the requirements of this section or (as the case may be) the difference of date, time or route.

(9) To the extent that an alleged offence under subsection (7) turns on a difference of date, time or route it is a defence for the accused to prove that the difference arose from—

(a) circumstances beyond his control;

(b) something done in compliance with conditions imposed under section 8; or

(c) something done with the agreement of a member of the Royal Ulster Constabulary not below the rank of inspector or by his direction.

(10) A person guilty of an offence under subsection (7) shall be liable on summary conviction to imprisonment for a term not exceeding 6 months or to a fine not exceeding level 5 on the standard scale, or to both.

7   Advance notice of protest meetings related to public processions

(1) Where notice has been given under section 6 in relation to a public procession, a person proposing to organise a related protest meeting shall give notice of that proposal in accordance with subsections (2) to (4) to a member of the Royal Ulster Constabulary not below the rank of sergeant by leaving the notice with him at the police station nearest to the place at which the meeting is to be held.

(2) Notice under this section shall be given—

(a) not later than 14 days before the date on which the meeting is to be held; or

(b) if that is not reasonably practicable, as soon as it is reasonably practicable to give such notice.

(3) Notice under this section shall—

(a) be given in writing in such form as may be prescribed by regulations made by the Secretary of State; and

(b) be signed by the person giving the notice.

(4) The form prescribed under subsection (3)(a) shall require a person giving notice under this section to specify—

(a) the date and time when the meeting is to be held;

(b) the place at which it is to be held;

(c) the number of persons likely to take part in it;

(d) the arrangements for its control being made by the person proposing to organise it;

(e) the name and address of that person; (f) where the notice is given as mentioned in paragraph (b) of subsection (2), the reason why it was not reasonably practicable to give notice in accordance with paragraph (a) of that subsection; and

(g) such other matters as appear to the Secretary of State to be necessary for, or appropriate for facilitating, the exercise by the Secretry of State or members of the Royal Ulster Constabulary of any function in relation to the meeting.

(5) The Chief Constable shall ensure that a copy of a notice given under this section is immediately sent to the Commission.

(6) A person who organises or takes part in a protest meeting—

(a) in respect of which the requirements of this section as to notice have not been satisfied; or

(b) which is held on a date or at a time or place which differs from the date, time or place specified in relation to it in the notice given under this section,

shall be guilty of an offence.

(7) In proceedings for an offence under subsection (6) it is a defence for the accused to prove that he did not know of, and neither suspected nor had reason to suspect, the failure to satisfy the requirements of this section or (as the case may be) the difference of date, time or place.

(8) To the extent that an alleged offence under subsection (6) turns on a difference of date, time or place it is a defence for the accused to prove that the difference arose from—

(a) circumstances beyond his control;

(b) something done in compliance with conditions imposed under Article 4(2) of the Public Order (Northern Ireland) Order 1987; or

(c) something done with the agreement of a member of the Royal Ulster Constabulary not below the rank of inspector or by his direction.

(9) A person guilty of an offence under subsection (6) shall be liable on summary conviction to imprisonment for a term not exceeding 6 months or to a fine not exceeding level 5 on the standard scale, or to both.

The Commission's power to impose conditions on public processions

8 The Commission's power to impose conditions on public processions

(1) The Commission may issue a determination in respect of a proposed public procession imposing on the persons organising or taking part in it such conditions as the Commission considers necessary.

(2) Without prejudice to the generality of subsection (1), the conditions imposed under that subsection may include conditions as to the route of the procession or prohibiting it from entering any place.

(3) Conditions imposed under subsection (1) may incorporate or be framed by reference to—

(a) the Code of Conduct; or

(b) any other document—

(i) prepared by the person or body organising the procession in question; and

(ii) approved by the Commission for the purposes of this section.

(4) The Commission may, in accordance with the procedural rules, amend or revoke any determination issued under this section.

(5) In considering in any particular case—

(a) whether to issue a determination under this section;

(b) whether to amend or revoke a determination issued under this section; or

(c) what conditions should be imposed by a determination (or amended determination) issued under this section,

the Commission shall have regard to the guidelines.

(6) The guidelines shall in particular (but without prejudice to the generality of section 5(1)) provide for the Commission to have regard to—

(a) any public disorder or damage to property which may result from the procession;

(b) any disruption to the life of the community which the procession may cause;

(c) any impact which the procession may have on relationships within the community;

(d) any failure of a person of a description specified in the guidelines to comply with the Code of Conduct (whether in relation to the procession in question or any related protest meeting or in relation to any previous procession or protest meeting); and

(e) the desirability of allowing a procession customarily held along a particular route to be held along that route.

(7) A person who knowingly fails to comply with a condition imposed under this section shall be guilty of an offence, but it is a defence for him to prove that the failure arose—

(a) from circumstances beyond his control; or

(b) from something done by direction of a member of the Royal Ulster Constabulary not below the rank of inspector.

(8) A person who incites another to commit an offence under subsection (7) shall be guilty of an offence.

(9) A person guilty of an offence under subsection (7) or (8) shall be liable on summary conviction to imprisonment for a term not exceeding 6 months or to a fine not exceeding level 5 on the standard scale, or to both.

9   Review by Secretary of State of determination of Commission under section 8

(1) The Secretary of State shall, on an application made by the Chief Constable, review a determination issued by the Commission under section 8.

(2) On a review of a determination under this section the Secretary of State may—

(a) revoke the determination;

(b) amend the determination by amending or revoking any condition imposed by the determination or by adding any new condition; or

(c) confirm the determination.

(3) In considering in any particular case—

(a) whether to revoke, amend or confirm a determination; or

(b) what amendments should be made to a determination,

the Secretary of State shall have regard to the guidelines.

(4) Wherever practicable the Secretary of State shall before revoking, amending or confirming a determination under this section consult the Commission; but nothing in this subsection shall affect the validity of any revocation, amendment or confirmation under this section.

(5) A determination of the Commission which is amended by the Secretary of State under this section shall be treated for the purposes of this Act (except section 8(4)) as if it had been issued by the Commission as so amended.

(6) Where a determination of the Commission in relation to a public procession has been revoked by the Secretary of State under this section, the Commission shall not issue any further determination under section 8 in relation to that procession.

(7) The Secretary of State shall immediately notify the Commission where any determination of the Commission is revoked, amended or confirmed under this section.

10   Saving for powers of a constable

Nothing in section 8 or 9 or in any determination of the Commission affects the common law powers of a constable to take action to deal with or prevent a breach of the peace.

Secretary of State's powers to prohibit public processions

11   Secretary of State's powers to prohibit public processions

(1) If, in the case of any proposed public procession, the Secretary of State is of the opinion that, having regard to—

(a) any serious public disorder or serious damage to property which may result from the procession;

(b) any serious disruption to the life of the community which the procession may cause;

(c) any serious impact which the procession may have on relationships within the community; and

(d) any undue demands which the procession may cause to be made on the police or military forces,

it is necessary in the public interest to do so, he may by order prohibit the holding of that procession.

(2) If, in relation to any area and any period of time not exceeding 28 days, the Secretary of State is of the opinion that, having regard to—

(a) any serious public disorder or serious damage to property which may result from public processions of a particular class or description in that area in that period;

(b) any serious disruption to the life of the community which such processions may cause;

(c) any serious impact which such processions may have on relationships within the community;

(d) any undue demands which such processions may cause to be made on the police or military forces; and

(e) the extent of the powers exercisable under subsection (1), it is necessary in the public interest to do so, he may by order prohibit the holding of all public processions of that class or description in that area in that period.

(3) If, in relation to any area and any period of time not exceeding 28 days, the Secretary of State is of the opinion that, having regard to—

(a) any serious public disorder or serious damage to property which may result from public processions in that area in that period;

(b) any serious disruption to the life of the community which such processions may cause;

(c) any serious impact which such processions may have on relationships within the community;

(d) any undue demands which such processions may cause to be made on the police or military forces; and

(e) the extent of the powers exercisable under subsections (1) and (2), it is necessary in the public interest to do so, he may by order prohibit the holding of all public processions in that area in that period.

(4) An order under subsection (2) or (3) may exempt any procession, or any procession of any class or description, specified in the order.

(5) Wherever practicable the Secretary of State shall before making an order under this section consult—

(a) the Commission; and

(b) the Chief Constable,

but nothing in this subsection shall affect the validity of any such order.

(6) The power to make an order under this section includes power to revoke or amend any such order.

(7) An order made under subsection (1) in relation to a public procession has effect to revoke any previous determination made by the Commission under section 8 in relation to that procession, and an order made under subsection (2) or (3) has effect to revoke any previous determination made by the Commission under that section in relation to any public procession the holding of which is prohibited by the order.

(8) A person who organises or takes part in a public procession the holding of which he knows is prohibited by an order under this section shall be guilty of an offence.

(9) A person guilty of an offence under subsection (8) shall be liable on summary conviction to imprisonment for a term not exceeding 6 months or to a fine not exceeding level 5 on the standard scale, or to both.

General regulation of public processions

12   Registration of bands taking part in public processions

(1) The Secretary of State may by order provide for the registration of bands.

(2) Without prejudice to the generality of subsection (1), an order under that subsection may provide for—

(a) applications for registration or the renewal of registration to be made to such court or other body or person as may be specified in the order;

(b) the procedure for the making and hearing of such applications (including the making and hearing of objections);

(c) the grounds on which such applications may be refused;

(d) the issue and duration of certificates of registration;

(e) appeals against decisions made in relation to such applications; (f) the cancellation of registration and the procedure in relation thereto;

(g) registration to be subject to such conditions as may be specified in or determined under the order;

(h) the order not to apply to such bands or bands of such descriptions as may be specified in or determined under the order;

(i) such other matters as appear to the Secretary of State to be necessary or expedient for the proper functioning of the system of registration provided for by the order.

(3) Any power to make rules of court regulating the practice or procedure of a court specified as mentioned in subsection (2)(a) includes power to make such provision as may be necessary or expedient for carrying into effect the provisions of an order under subsection (1).

(4) A person who knowingly takes part in a public procession as a member of a band which—

(a) is one to which an order under subsection (1) applies, but is not registered under that order; or

(b) does not comply with any condition subject to which it is registered under such an order,

shall be guilty of an offence.

(5) A person guilty of an offence under subsection (4) shall be liable on summary conviction to imprisonment for a term not exceeding 6 months or to a fine not exceeding level 5 on the standard scale, or to both.

13   Control of alcohol at public processions

(1) Where a constable in uniform reasonably suspects that a person to whom this subsection applies is consuming intoxicating liquor, the constable may require that person—

(a) to surrender anything in his possession which is, or which the constable reasonably believes to be, intoxicating liquor; and

(b) to state his name and address.

(2) Subsection (1) applies to a person—

(a) who is taking part in a public procession; or

(b) who is among those who have assembled with a view to taking part in a public procession; or

(c) who—

(i) is otherwise present at, or is in the vicinity of, a place on the route or proposed route of a public procession; and

(ii) is in a public place, other than licensed premises.

(3) Where a constable in uniform reasonably suspects that a person to whom this subsection applies is in possession of intoxicating liquor, the constable may require that person—

(a) to surrender anything in his possession which is, or which the constable reasonably believes to be, intoxicating liquor; and

(b) to state his name and address.

(4) Subsection (3) applies to a person who is in a passenger vehicle which is being used for the principal purpose of carrying passengers for the whole or any part of a journey to a place in the vicinity of the route or proposed route of a public procession.

(5) A constable may dispose of anything surrendered to him under this section in such manner as he considers appropriate.

(6) A person who fails without reasonable cause to comply with a requirement imposed on him under subsection (1) or (3) shall be guilty of an offence and liable on summary conviction to a fine not exceeding level 2 on the standard scale.

(7) A constable who imposes a requirement on a person under subsection (1) or (3) shall inform that person of his suspicion and that failing without reasonable cause to comply with a requirement imposed under that subsection is an offence.

(8) A constable in uniform may—

(a) stop a passenger vehicle; and

(b) search the vehicle and any person in the vehicle, if he has reasonable grounds to suspect that intoxicating liquor is being carried on the vehicle and that the vehicle is being used for the principal purpose mentioned in subsection (4).

(9) The powers of a constable under this section may only be exercised in relation to a particular public procession in the period—

(a) beginning 6 hours before the proposed starting time of that procession; and

(b) ending at midnight on the day on which the persons taking part in the procession disperse.

(10) Where a proposed public procession does not take place but persons have assembled with a view to taking part in the procession, subsection (9) shall have effect as if for the reference in paragraph (b) to the persons taking part in the procession there were substituted reference to the persons assembled with a view to taking part in the procession.

14 Breaking up public procession

(1) A person who for the purpose of preventing or hindering any lawful public procession or of annoying persons taking part in or endeavouring to take part in any such procession—

(a) hinders, molests or obstructs those persons or any of them;

(b) acts in a disorderly way towards those persons or any of them; or

(c) behaves offensively and abusively towards those persons or any of them, shall be guilty of an offence.

(2) A person guilty of an offence under subsection (1) shall be liable on summary conviction to imprisonment for a term not exceeding 6 months or to a fine not exceeding level 5 on the standard scale, or to both.

★ ★ ★ ★ ★

Registration of Political Parties Act 1998
(1998, c. 48)

An Act to make provision about the registration of political parties.   [19 November 1998]

Territorial extent: United Kingdom

The register of political parties

1 The register

(1) There shall be a register to be known as the register of political parties.

(2) The register shall be maintained by the registrar or other officer who performs the duty of registration of companies in England and Wales under the Companies Act 1985.

Registration

2 Applications for registration

(1) A party may apply for inclusion in the register by sending to the registrar—

(a) an application which complies with the requirements of Schedule 1, and

(b) a declaration that the party intends to have one or more candidates at a relevant election.

(2) the following elections are relevant for this purpose—

(a) parliamentary elections,

(b) elections to the European Parliament,
(c) elections to the Scottish Parliament,
(d) elections to the National Assembly for Wales,
(e) elections to the New Northern Ireland Assembly,
(f) local government elections, and
(g) local elections in Northern Ireland.

3   Grant of applications

(1) The registrar shall grant an application by a party under section 2 unless in his opinion it proposes a registered name which—

(a) would be likely to result in the party's being confused by voters with a party which is already registered,
(b) comprises more than six words,
(c) is obscene or offensive,
(d) includes words the publication of which would be likely to amount to the commission of an offence,
(e) includes any script other than Roman script, or (f) includes any word or expression prohibited by order made by the Secretary of State.

(2) An order under subsection (1)(f) may except the use of a word or expression from the prohibition in specified circumstances.

4   ★ ★ ★ ★ ★

5   Emblems

(1) A party's application under section 2 may include a request for the registration of up to three emblems to be used by the party on ballot papers.

(2) The registrar shall grant a request under this section in relation to an emblem unless in his opinion it—

(a) would be likely to be confused by voters with an emblem which is already registered for another party;
(b) is obscene or offensive;
(c) is of such a character that its publication would be likely to amount to the commission of an offence; or
(d) includes a word or expression prohibited under section 3(1)(f).

(3) ★ ★ ★ ★ ★

6–9   ★ ★ ★ ★ ★

Speaker's Committee

10   Speaker's committee

Before the registrar decides any question arising under section 3, 5, 6 or 18 he may seek advice from a committee of Members of the House of Commons appointed by the Speaker for the purpose.

Access to the register

11   General access

(1) The Secretary of State shall make regulations requiring the registrar—

(a) to allow anyone to inspect the register, or any part of it, in such manner as the regulations may prescribe, and
(b) to provide copies of the register, or any part of it, on request.

(2) Regulations under this section may impose conditions, or enable the registrar to impose conditions, including conditions as to the payment of fees.

12   Request by Secretary of State

On receipt of a request by the Secretary of State the registrar shall send a copy of the register to—

(a) the Secretary of State;

(b) any person specified in the request.

Effects of registration

13 ★ ★ ★ ★ ★

14 Party political broadcasts
(1) A broadcaster shall not include in its broadcasting services any party political broadcast made on behalf of a political party which is not registered under this Act.
(2) In this section "broadcaster" means—
(a) the holder of a licence under the Broadcasting Act 1990 or 1996,
(b) the British Broadcasting Corporation, and
(c) Sianel Pedwar Cymru.

15–18 ★ ★ ★ ★ ★

Miscellaneous and general

19 False statements: offence
(1) It is an offence knowingly or recklessly to make a statement to the registrar which—
(a) is made, or purports to be made, on behalf of a party for any purpose of this Act, and
(b) is false in any material particular.
(2) A person guilty of an offence under subsection (1) shall be liable on summary conviction to a fine not exceeding level 5 on the standard scale.

★ ★ ★ ★ ★

Scotland Act 1998
(1998, c. 46)

An Act to provide for the establishment of a Scottish Parliament and Administration and other changes in the government of Scotland; to provide for changes in the constitution and functions of certain public authorities; to provide for the variation of the basic rate of income tax in relation to income of Scottish taxpayers in accordance with a resolution of the Scottish Parliament; to amend the law about parliamentary constituencies in Scotland; and for connected purposes
[19 November 1998]

Territorial extent: United Kingdom (although many of the provisions will apply only in Scotland) except for s. 25 which extends to Scotland alone.

PART I   THE SCOTTISH PARLIAMENT

The Scottish parliament

1 The Scottish Parliament
(1) There shall be a Scottish Parliament.
(2) One member of the Parliament shall be returned for each constituency (under the simple majority system) at an election held in the constituency.
(3) Members of the Parliament for each region shall be returned at a general election under the additional member system of proportional representation provided for in this part and vacancies among such members shall be filled in accordance with this Part.

(4) The validity of any proceedings of the Parliament is not affected by any vacancy in its membership.

(5) Schedule 1 (which makes provision for the constituencies and regions for the purposes of this Act and the number of regional members) shall have effect.

General elections

2 Ordinary general elections

(1) The day on which the poll at the first ordinary general election for membership of the Parliament shall be held, and the day, time and place for the meeting of the Parliament following that poll, shall be appointed by order made by the Secretary of State.

(2) The poll at subsequent ordinary general elections shall be held on the first Thursday in May in the fourth calendar year following that in which the previous ordinary general election was held, unless the day of the poll is determined by a proclamation under subsection (5).

(3) If the poll is to be held on the first Thursday in May, the Parliament—

  (a) is dissolved by virtue of this section at the beginning of the minimum period which ends with that day, and

  (b) shall meet within the period of seven days beginning immediately after the day of the poll.

(4) In subsection (3), "the minimum period" means the period determined in accordance with an order under section 12(1).

(5) If the Presiding Officer proposes a day for the holding of the poll which is not more than one month earlier, nor more than one month later, than the first Thursday in May, Her Majesty may by proclamation under the Scottish Seal—

  (a) dissolve the Parliament,

  (b) require the poll at the election to be held on the day proposed, and

  (c) require the Parliament to meet within the period of seven days beginning immediately after the day of the poll.

(6) In this Act "the Scottish Seal" means Her Majesty's Seal appointed by the Treaty of Union to be kept and used in Scotland in place of the Great Seal of Scotland.

3 Extraordinary general elections

(1) The Presiding Officer shall propose a day for the holding of a poll if—

  (a) the Parliament resolves that it should be dissolved and, if the resolution is passed on a division, the number of members voting in favour of it is not less than two-thirds of the total number of seats for members of the Parliament, or

  (b) any period during which the Parliament is required under section 46 to nominate one of its members for appointment as First Minister ends without such a nomination being made.

(2) If the Presiding Officer makes such a proposal, Her Majesty may by proclamation under the Scottish Seal—

  (a) dissolve the Parliament and require an extraordinary general election to be held,

  (b) require the poll at the election to be held on the day proposed, and

  (c) require the Parliament to meet within the period of seven days beginning immediately after the day of the poll.

(3) If a poll is held under this section within the period of six months ending with the day on which the poll at the next ordinary general election would be held (disregarding section 2(5)), that ordinary general election shall not be held.

(4) Subsection (3) does not affect the year in which the subsequent ordinary general election is to be held.

4 ★ ★ ★ ★ ★

5   Candidates

(1) At a general election, the candidates may stand for return as constituency members or regional members.

(2) A person may not be a candidate to be a constituency member for more than one constituency.

(3) The candidates to be regional members shall be those included in a list submitted under subsection (4) or individual candidates.

(4) Any registered political party may submit to the regional returning officer a list of candidates to be regional members for a particular region (referred to in this Act, in relation to the region, as the party's "regional list").

(5) A registered political party's regional list has effect in relation to the general election and any vacancy occurring among the regional members after that election and before the next general election.

(6) Not more than twelve persons may be included in the list (but the list may include only one person).

(7) A registered political party's regional list must not include a person—

- (a) who is included in any other list submitted under subsection (4) for the region or any list submitted under that subsection for another region,
- (b) who is an individual candidate to be a regional member for the region or another region,
- (c) who is a candidate to be a constituency member for a constituency not included in the region, or
- (d) who is a candidate to be a constituency member for a constituency included in the region but is not a candidate of that party.

(8) A person may not be an individual candidate to be a regional member for a particular region if he is—

- (a) included in a list submitted under subsection (4) for the region or another region,
- (b) an individual candidate to be a regional member for another region,
- (c) a candidate to be a constituency member for a constituency not included in the region, or
- (d) a candidate of any registered political party to be a constituency member for a constituency included in the region.

(9) In this Act, "registered political party" means a party registered under the Registration of Political Parties Act 1998.

6   Poll for regional members

(1) This section and sections 7 and 8 are about the return of regional members at a general election.

(2) In each of the constituencies for the Parliament, a poll shall be held at which each person entitled to vote as elector may give a vote (referred to in this Act as a "regional vote") for—

- (a) a registered political party which has submitted a regional list, or
- (b) an individual candidate to be a regional member for the region.

(3) The right conferred on a person by subsection (2) is in addition to any right the person may have to vote in any poll for the return of a constituency member.

7   Calculation of regional figures

(1) The persons who are to be returned as constituency members for constituencies included in the region must be determined before the persons who are to be returned as the regional members for the region.

(2) For each registered political party which has submitted a regional list, the regional figure for the purposes of section 8 is—

(a) the total number of regional votes given for the party in all the constituencies included in the region,
divided by

(b) the aggregate of one plus the number of candidates of the party returned as constituency members for any of those constituencies.

(3) Each time a seat is allocated to the party under section 8, that figure shall be recalculated by increasing (or further increasing) the aggregate in subsection (2)(b) by one.

(4) For each individual candidate to be a regional member for the region, the regional figure for the purposes of section 8 is the total number of regional votes given for him in all the constituencies included in the region.

8   Allocation of seats to regional members

(1) The first regional member seat shall be allocated to the registered political party or individual candidate with the highest regional figure.

(2) the second and subsequent regional member seats shall be allocated to the registered political party or individual candidate with the highest regional figure, after any recalculation required by section 7(3) has been carried out.

(3) An individual candidate already returned as a constituency or regional member shall be disregarded.

(4) Seats for the region which are allocated to a registered political party shall be filled by the persons in the party's regional list in the order in which they appear in the list.

(5) For the purposes of this section and section 10, a person in a registered political party's regional list who is returned as a member of the Parliament shall be treated as ceasing to be in the list (even if his return is void).

(6) Once a party's regional list has been exhausted (by the return of persons included in it as constituency members or by the previous application of subsection (1) or (2)) the party shall be disregarded.

(7) If (on the application of subsection (1) or any application of subsection (2)) the highest figure is the regional figure of two or more parties or individual candidates—

(a)   the subsection in question shall apply to each of them; or

(b)   if paragraph (a) would result in more than the correct number of seats for the region being allocated, the subsection in question shall apply as if the regional figure for each of those parties or candidates had been adjusted in accordance with subsection (8).

(8) The regional figure for a party or candidate is adjusted in accordance with this subsection by—

(a)   adding one vote to the total number of regional votes given for the party or candidate in all the constituencies included in the region; and

(b)   (in the case of a party) recalculating the regional figure accordingly.

(9) If, on the application of the subsection in question in accordance with subsection (7)(b), seats would be allocated to two or more parties or individual candidates and that would result in more than the correct number of seats for the region being allocated, the regional returning officer shall decide between them by lot.]

Vacancies

9   Constituency vacancies

(1) Where the seat of a constituency member is vacant, an election shall be held to fill the vacancy (subject to subsection (4)).

(2) The date of the poll shall be fixed by the Presiding Officer.

(3) the date shall fall within the period of three months—

(a)   beginning with the occurrence of the vacancy, or

(b)   if the vacancy does not come to the notice of the Presiding Officer within the period of one month beginning with its occurrence, beginning when it does come to his notice.

(4) the election shall not be held if the latest date for holding the poll would fall within the period of three months ending with the day on which the poll at the next ordinary general election would be held (disregarding section 2(5)).

(5) For the purposes of this section, the date on which a vacancy is to be treated as occurring shall be determined under standing orders.

(6) A person may not be a candidate at such an election if he is a member of the parliament or a candidate in another election to fill a vacancy.

10   Regional vacancies

(1) This section applies where the seat of a regional member is vacant.

(2) If the regional member was returned as an individual candidate, or the vacancy is not filled in accordance with the following provisions, the seat shall remain vacant until the next general election.

(3) If the regional member was returned (under section 8 or this section) from a registered political party's regional list, the regional returning officer shall notify the Presiding Officer of the name of the person who is to fill the vacancy.

(4) He must be a person who—

(a)   is included in that list, and

(b)   is willing to serve as a regional member for the region.

(5) Where more than one person satisfies the conditions in subsection (4), the regional returning officer shall notify the name of whichever of them was higher, or highest, in the list.

(6), (7) ★ ★ ★ ★ ★

Franchise and conduct of elections

11   Electors

(1) The persons entitled to vote as electors at an election for membership of the parliament held in any constituency are those who on the day of the poll—

(a)   would be entitled to vote as electors at a local government election in an electoral area falling wholly or partly within the constituency, and

(b)   are registered in the register of local government electors at an address within the constituency.

(2) A person is not entitled to vote as elector in any constituency—

(a)   more than once at a poll for the return of a constituency member, or

(b)   more than once at a poll for the return of regional members,

or to vote as elector in more than one constituency at a general election.

12   ★ ★ ★ ★ ★

Duration of membership

13   Term of office of members

The term of office of a member of the Parliament begins on the day on which the member is declared to be returned and ends with the dissolution of the Parliament.

14   Resignation of members

A member of the Parliament may at any time resign his seat by giving notice in writing to the Presiding Officer.

Disqualification

15   Disqualification from membership of the Parliament

(1) A person is disqualified from being a member of the Parliament (subject to section 16) if–

(a) he is disqualified from being a member of the House of Commons under paragraphs (a) to (e) of section 1(1) of the House of Commons Disqualification Act 1975 (judges, civil servants, members of the armed forces, members of police forces and members of foreign legislatures),

(b) he is disqualified otherwise than under that Act (either generally or in relation to a particular parliamentary constituency) from being a member of the House of Commons or from sitting and voting in it,

(c) he is a Lord of Appeal in Ordinary, or

(d) he is an office-holder of a description specified in an Order in Council made by Her Majesty under this subsection.

(2) An office-holder of a description specified in an Order in Council made by Her Majesty under this subsection is disqualified from being a member of the Parliament for any constituency or region of a description specified in the Order in relation to the office-holder.

(3) In this section "office-holder" includes employee or other post-holder.

16   Exceptions and relief from disqualification

(1) A person is not disqualified from being a member of the Parliament merely because—

(a) he is a peer (whether of the United Kingdom, Great Britain, England or Scotland), or

[(b) he is a Lord Spiritual.]

(2) A citizen of the European Union who is resident in the United Kingdom is not disqualified from being a member of the Parliament merely because of section 3 of the Act of Settlement (disqualification of persons born outside the United Kingdom other than Commonwealth citizens and citizens of the Republic of Ireland).

(3)–(5) ★ ★ ★ ★ ★

17   Effect of disqualification

(1) If a person who is disqualified from being a member of the Parliament or from being a member for a particular constituency or region is returned as a member of the Parliament or (as the case may be) as a member for the constituency or region, his return shall be void and his seat vacant.

(2) If a member of the Parliament becomes disqualified from being a member of the Parliament or from being a member for the particular constituency or region for which he is sitting, he shall cease to be a member of the Parliament (so that his seat is vacant).

(3), (4) ★ ★ ★ ★ ★

(5) The validity of any proceedings of the Parliament is not affected by the disqualification of any person from being a member of the Parliament or from being a member for the constituency or region for which he purports to sit.

18   ★ ★ ★ ★ ★

Presiding Officer and administration

19   Presiding Officer

(1) The Parliament shall, at its first meeting following a general election, elect from among its members a Presiding Officer and two deputies.

(2) A person elected Presiding Officer or deputy shall hold office until the conclusion of the next election for Presiding Officer under subsection (1) unless he previously resigns, ceases to be a member of the Parliament otherwise than by virtue of a dissolution or is removed from office by resolution of the Parliament.

(3) If the Presiding Officer or a deputy ceases to hold office before the Parliament is dissolved, the Parliament shall elect another from among its members to fill his place.

(4) The Presiding Officer's functions may be exercised by a deputy if the office of Presiding Officer is vacant or the Presiding Officer is for any reason unable to act.

(5) The Presiding Officer may (subject to standing orders) authorise any deputy to exercise functions on his behalf.

(6) Standing orders may include provision as to the participation (including voting) of the Presiding Officer and deputies in the proceedings of the Parliament.

(7) The validity of any act of the Presiding Officer or a deputy is not affected by any defect in his election.

20   Clerk of the Parliament

(1) There shall be a Clerk of the Parliament.

(2) The Clerk shall be appointed by the Scottish Parliamentary Corporate Body (established under section 21).

21   Scottish Parliamentary Corporate Body

(1) There shall be a body corporate to be known as "the Scottish Parliamentary Corporate Body" (referred to in this Act as the Parliamentary corporation) to perform the functions conferred on the corporation by virtue of this Act or any other enactment.

(2) the members of the corporation shall be—
   (a) the Presiding Officer, and
   (b) four membersof the Parliament appointedin Accordancewith standing orders.

(3) The corporation shall provide the Parliament, or ensure that the Parliament is provided, with the property, staff and services required for the Parliament's purposes.

(4) The Parliament may give special or general directions to the corporation for the purpose of or in connection with the exercise of the corporation's functions.

(5)–(8) ★ ★ ★ ★ ★

Proceedings etc.

22   Standing orders

(1) The proceedings of the Parliament shall be regulated by standing orders.

(2) ★ ★ ★ ★ ★

23   Power to call for witnesses and documents

(1) the Parliament may require any person—
   (a) to attend its proceedings for the purpose of giving evidence, or
   (b) to produce documents in his custody or under his control, concerning any subject for which any member of the Scottish Executive has general responsibility.

(2) Subject to subsection (3), the Parliament may impose such a requirement on a person outside Scotland only in connection with the discharge by him of—
   (a) functions of the Scottish Administration, or
   (b) functions of a Scottish public authority or cross-border public authority, or Border rivers functions (within the meaning of section 111(4)), which concern a subject for which any member of the Scottish Executive has general responsibility.

(3)–(9) ★ ★ ★ ★ ★

24–26   ★ ★ ★ ★ ★

27   Participation of the Scottish Law Officers

(1) If the Lord Advocate or the Solicitor General for Scotland is not a member of the Parliament–
   (a) he may participate in the proceedings of the Parliament to the extent permitted by standing orders, but may not vote, and
   (b) standing orders may in other respects provide that they are to apply to him as if he were such a member.

(2) Subsection (1) is without prejudice to section 39.

(3) The Lord Advocate or the Solicitor General for Scotland may, in any proceedings of the Parliament, decline to answer any question or produce any document relating to the operation of the system of criminal prosecution in any particular case if he considers that answering the question or producing the document—

(a) might prejudice criminal proceedings in that case, or

(b) would otherwise be contrary to the public interest.

Legislation

28   Acts of the Scottish Parliament

(1) Subject to section 29, the Parliament may make laws, to be known as Acts of the Scottish Parliament.

(2) Proposed Acts of the Scottish Parliament shall be known as Bills; and a Bill shall become an Act of the Scottish Parliament when it has been passed by the Parliament and has received Royal Assent.

(3) A Bill receives Royal Assent at the beginning of the day on which Letters Patent under the Scottish Seal signed with Her Majesty's own hand signifying Her Assent are recorded in the Register of the Great Seal.

(4) The date of Royal Assent shall be written on the Act of the Scottish Parliament by the Clerk, and shall form part of the Act.

(5) the validity of an Act of the Scottish Parliament is not affected by any invalidity in the proceedings of the Parliament leading to its enactment.

(6) Every Act of the Scottish Parliament shall be judicially noticed.

(7) This section does not affect the power of the Parliament of the United Kingdom to make laws for Scotland.

29   Legislative competence

(1) An Act of the Scottish Parliament is not law so far as any provision of the Act is outside the legislative competence of the Parliament.

(2) A provision is outside the competence so far as any of the following paragraphs apply—

(a) it would form part of the law of a country or territory other than Scotland, or confer or remove functions exercisable otherwise than in or as regards Scotland,

(b) it relates to reserved matters,

(c) it is in breach of the restrictions in Schedule 4,

(d) it is incompatible with any of the Convention rights or with Community law,

(e) it would remove the Lord Advocate from his position as head of the systems of criminal prosecution and investigation of deaths in Scotland.

(3) For the purposes of this section, the question whether a provision of an Act of the Scottish Parliament relates to a reserved matter is to be determined, subject to subsection (4), by reference to the purpose of the provision, having regard (among other things) to its effect in all the circumstances.

(4) A provision which—

(a) would otherwise not relate to reserved matters, but

(b) makes modifications of Scots private law, or Scots criminal law, as it applies to reserved matters,

is to be treated as relating to reserved matters unless the purpose of the provision is to make the law in question apply consistently to reserved matters and otherwise.

30   Legislative competence: supplementary

(1) Schedule 5 (which defines reserved matters) shall have effect.

(2) Her Majesty may by order in Council make any modifications of Schedule 4 or 5 which She considers necessary or expedient.

(3) Her Majesty may by Order in Council specify functions which are to be treated, for such purposes of this Act as may be specified, as being, or as not being, functions which are exercisable in or as regards Scotland.

(4) An Order in Council under this section may also make such modifications of—

- (a) any enactment or prerogative instrument (including any enactment comprised in or made under this Act), or
- (b) any other instrument or document, as Her Majesty considers necessary or expedient in connection with other provision made by the Order.

31   Scrutiny of Bills before introduction

(1) A member of the Scottish Executive in charge of a Bill shall, on or before introduction of the Bill in the Parliament state that in his view the provisions of the Bill would be within the legislative competence of the Parliament.

(2) The Presiding Officer shall, on or before the introduction of a Bill in the Parliament, decide whether or not in his view the provisions of the Bill would be within the legislative competence of the Parliament and state his decision.

(3) The form of any statement, and the manner in which it is to be made, shall be determined under standing orders, and standing orders may provide for any statement to be published.

32   Submission of Bills for Royal Assent

(1) It is for the Presiding Officer to submit Bills for Royal Assent.

(2) The Presiding Officer shall not submit a Bill for Royal Assent at any time when—

- (a) the Advocate General, the Lord Advocate or the Attorney General is entitled to make a reference in relation to the Bill under section 33,
- (b) any such reference has been made but has not been decided or otherwise disposed of by the Judicial Committee, or
- (c) an order may be made in relation to the Bill under section 35.

(3) The Presiding Officer shall not submit a Bill in its unamended form for Royal Assent if—

- (a) the Judicial Committee have decided that the Bill or any provision of it would not be within the legislative competence of the Parliament, or
- (b) a reference made in relation to the Bill under section 33 has been withdrawn following a request for withdrawal of the reference under section 34(2)(b).

(4) In this Act—

"Advocate General" means the Advocate General for Scotland,

"Judicial Committee" means the Judicial Committee of the Privy Council.

33   Scrutiny of bills by the Judicial Committee

(1) The Advocate General, the Lord Advocate or the Attorney General may refer the question of whether a Bill or any provision of a Bill would be within the legislative competence of the Parliament to the Judicial Committee for decision.

(2) Subject to subsection (3), he may make a reference in relation to a Bill at any time during—

- (a) the period of four weeks beginning with the passing of the Bill, and
- (b) any period of four weeks beginning with any subsequent approval of the Bill in accordance with standing orders made by virtue of section 36(5).

(3) He shall not make a reference in relation to a Bill if he has notified the Presiding Officer that he does not intend to make a reference in relation to the Bill, unless the Bill has been approved as mentioned in subsection (2)(b) since the notification.

34   ECJ references

(1) This section applies where—

- (a) a reference has been made in relation to a Bill under section 33,

(b) a reference for a preliminary ruling has been made by the Judicial Committee in connection with that reference, and

(c) neither of those references has been decided or otherwise disposed of.

(2) If the Parliament resolves that it wishes to reconsider the Bill—

(a) the Presiding Officer shall notify the Advocate General, the Lord Advocate and the Attorney General of that fact, and

(b) the person who made the reference in relation to the Bill under section 33 shall request the withdrawal of the reference.

(3) In this section "a reference for a preliminary ruling" means a reference of a question to the European Court under Article 177 of the Treaty establishing the European Community, Article 41 of the Treaty establishing the European Coal and Steel Community or Article 150 of the Treaty establishing the European Atomic Energy Community.

35 Power to intervene in certain cases

(1) If a Bill contains provisions—

(a) which the Secretary of State has reasonable grounds to believe would be incompatible with any international obligations or the interests of defence or national security, or

(b) which make modifications of the law as it applies to reserved matters and which the Secretary of State has reasonable grounds to believe would have an adverse effect on the operation of the law as it applies to reserved matters,

he may make an order prohibiting the Presiding Officer from submitting the Bill for Royal Assent.

(2) the order must identify the Bill and the provisions in question and state the reasons for making the order.

(3) The order may be made at any time during—

(a) the period of four weeks beginning with the passing of the Bill,

(b) any period of four weeks beginning with any subsequent approval of the Bill in accordance with standing orders made by virtue of section 36(5),

(c) if a reference is made in relation to the Bill under section 33, the period of four weeks beginning with the reference being decided or otherwise disposed of by the Judicial Committee.

(4) The Secretary of State shall not make an order in relation to a Bill if he has notified the Presiding Officer that he does not intend to do so unless the Bill has been approved as mentioned in subsection (2)(b) since the notification.

(5) An order in force under this section at a time when such approval is given shall cease to have effect.

36 Stages of Bills

(1) Standing orders shall include provision—

(a) for general debate on a Bill with an opportunity for members to vote on its general principles,

(b) for the consideration of, and an opportunity for members to vote on, the details of a Bill, and

(c) for a final stage at which a Bill can be passed or rejected.

(2) Subsection (1) does not prevent standing orders making provision to enable the Parliament to expedite proceedings in relation to a particular Bill.

(3) Standing orders may make provision different from that required by subsection (1) for the procedure applicable to Bills of any of the following kinds—

(a) Bills which restate the law,

(b) Bills which repeal spent enactments,

(c) private Bills.

(4) Standing orders shall provide for an opportunity for the reconsideration of a Bill after its passing if (and only if)—

    (a) the Judicial Committee decide that a Bill or any provision of it would not be within the legislative competence of the Parliament;

    (b) a reference made in relation to the Bill under section 33 is withdrawn following a request for withdrawal of the reference under section 34(2)(b), or

    (c) an order is made in relation to the bill under section 35.

(5) Standing orders shall, in particular, ensure that any Bill amended on reconsideration is subject to a final stage at which it can be approved or rejected.

(6) References in subsection (4), sections 28(2) and 38(1)(a) and paragraph 7 of Schedule 3 to the passing of a Bill shall, in the case of a Bill which has been amended on reconsideration, be read as references to the approval of the Bill.

Other provisions

37 Acts of Union

The Union with Scotland Act 1706 and the Union with England Act 1707 have effect subject to this Act.

38 ★ ★ ★ ★ ★

39 Members' interests

(1) Provision shall be made for a register of interests of members of the Parliament and for the register to be published and made available for public inspection.

(2) Provision shall be made—

    (a) requiring members of the Parliament to register in that register financial interests (including benefits in kind), as defined for the purposes of this paragraph,

    (b) requiring that any member of the Parliament who has a financial interest (including benefits in kind), as defined for the purposes of this paragraph, in any matter declares that interest before taking part in any proceedings of the Parliament relating to that matter.

(3) Provision made in pursuance of subsection (2) shall include any provision which the Parliament considers appropriate for preventing or restricting the participation in proceedings of the Parliament of a member with an interest defined for the purposes of subsection (2)(a) or (b) in a matter to which the proceedings relate.

(4) Provision shall be made prohibiting a member of the Parliament from—

    (a) advocating or initiating any cause or matter on behalf of any person, by any means specified in the provision, in consideration of any payment or benefit in kind of a description so specified, or

    (b) urging, in consideration of any such payment or benefit in kind, any other member on behalf of any person by any such means.

(5) Provision made in pursuance of subsections (2) to (4) shall include any provision which the Parliament considers appropriate for excluding from proceedings of the Parliament any member who fails to comply with, or contravenes, any provision made in pursuance of those subsections.

(6) Any member of the Parliament who—

    (a) takes part in any proceedings of the Parliament without having complied with, or in contravention of, any provision made in pursuance of subsection (2) or (3), or

    (b) contravenes any provision made in pursuance of subsection (4), is guilty of an offence.

(7) A person guilty of an offence under subsection (6) is liable on summary conviction to a fine not exceeding level 5 on the standard scale.

(8) In this section—

(a) "provision" means provision made by or under an Act of the Scottish Parliament,

(b) references to members of the Parliament include references to the Lord Advocate and the Solicitor General for Scotland, whether or not they are such members.

Legal issues

40 ★ ★ ★ ★ ★

41 Defamatory statements

(1) For the purposes of the law of defamation—

(a) any statement made in proceedings of the Parliament, and

(b) the publication under the authority of the Parliament of any statement, shall be absolutely privileged.

(2) In subsection (1), "statement" has the same meaning as in the Defamation Act 1996.

42 Contempt of court

(1) The strict liability rule shall not apply in relation to any publication—

(a) made in proceedings of the Parliament in relation to a Bill or subordinate legislation, or

(b) to the extent that it consists of a fair and accurate report of such proceedings made in good faith.

(2) In subsection (1), "the strict liability rule" and "publication" have the same meanings as in the Contempt of Court Act 1981.

43 Corrupt practices

The Parliament shall be a public body for the purposes of the Prevention of Corruption Acts 1889 to 1916.

PART II   THE SCOTTISH ADMINISTRATION

Ministers and their staff

44 The Scottish Executive

(1) There shall be a Scottish Executive, whose members shall be—

(a) the First Minister,

(b) such Ministers as the First Minister may appoint under section 47, and

(c) the Lord Advocate and the Solicitor General for Scotland.

(2) The members of the Scottish Executive are referred to collectively as the Scottish Ministers.

(3) A person who holds a Ministerial office may not be appointed a member of the Scottish Executive; and if a member of the Scottish Executive is appointed to a Ministerial office he shall cease to hold office as a member of the Scottish Executive.

(4) In subsection (3), references to a member of the Scottish Executive include a junior Scottish Minister and "Ministerial office" has the same meaning as in section 2 of the House of Commons Disqualification Act 1975.

45 The First Minister

(1) The First Minister shall be appointed by Her Majesty from among the members of the Parliament and shall hold office at Her Majesty's pleasure.

(2) the First Minister may at any time tender his resignation to Her Majesty and shall do so if the Parliament resolves that the Scottish Executive no longer enjoys the confidence of the Parliament.

(3) The First Minister shall cease to hold office if a person is appointed in his place.

(4) If the office of First Minister is vacant or he is for any reason unable to act, the

functions exercisable by him shall be exercisable by a person designated by the Presiding Officer.

(5) A person shall be so designated only if—

(a) he is a member of the Parliament, or

(b) if the Parliament has been dissolved, he is a person who ceased to be a member by virtue of the dissolution.

(6) Functions exercisable by a person by virtue of subsection (5)(a) shall continue to be exercisable by him even if the Parliament is dissolved.

(7) The First Minister shall be the Keeper of the Scottish Seal.

46 Choice of the First Minister

(1) If one of the following events occurs, the Parliament shall within the period allowed nominate one of its members for appointment as First Minister.

(2) The events are—

(a) the holding of a poll at a general election,

(b) the First Minister tendering his resignation to Her Majesty,

(c) the office of First Minister becoming vacant (otherwise than in consequence of his so tendering his resignation),

(d) the First Minister ceasing to be a member of the Parliament otherwise than by virtue of a dissolution.

(3) The period allowed is the period of 28 days which begins with the day on which the event in question occurs; but—

(a) if another of those events occurs within the period allowed, that period shall be extended (subject to paragraph (b)) so that it ends with the period of 28 days beginning with the day on which that other event occurred, and

(b) the period shall end if the Parliament passes a resolution under section 3(1)(a) or when Her Majesty appoints a person as First Minister.

(4) The Presiding Officer shall recommend to Her Majesty the appointment of any member of the Parliament who is nominated by the Parliament under this section.

47 Ministers

(1) The First Minister may, with the approval of Her Majesty, appoint Ministers from among the members of the Parliament.

(2) The First Minister shall not seek Her Majesty's approval for any appointment under this section without the agreement of the Parliament.

(3) A Minister appointed under this section—

(a) shall hold office at her Majesty's pleasure,

(b) may be removed from office by the First Minister,

(c) may at any time resign and shall do so if the Parliament resolves that the Scottish Executive no longer enjoys the confidence of the Parliament,

(d) if he resigns, shall cease to hold office immediately, and

(e) shall cease to hold office if he ceases to be a member of the Parliament otherwise than by virtue of a dissolution.

48 The Scottish Law Officers

(1) It is for the First Minister to recommend to Her Majesty the appointment or removal of a person as Lord Advocate or Solicitor General for Scotland; but he shall not do so without the agreement of the Parliament.

(2) The Lord Advocate and the Solicitor General for Scotland may at any time resign and shall do so if the Parliament resolves that the Scottish Executive no longer enjoys the confidence of the Parliament.

(3) Where the Lord Advocate resigns in consequence of such a resolution, he shall be deemed to continue in office until the warrant of appointment of the person succeeding to the office of Lord Advocate is granted, but only of the purpose of exercising his retained functions.

(4) Subsection (3) is without prejudice to section 287 of the Criminal Procedure (Scotland) Act 1995 (demission of office by Lord Advocate).

(5) Any decision of the Lord Advocate in his capacity as head of the systems of criminal prosecution and investigation of deaths in Scotland shall continue to be taken by him independently of any other person.

(6) ★ ★ ★ ★ ★

49 Junior Scottish Ministers

(1) The First Minister may, with the approval of Her Majesty, appoint persons from among the members of the Parliament to assist the Scottish Ministers in the exercise of their functions.

(2) They shall be known as junior Scottish Ministers.

(3) The First Minister shall not seek Her Majesty's approval for any appointment under this section without the agreement of the Parliament.

(4) A junior Scottish Minister—

    (a) shall hold office at Her Majesty's pleasure,

    (b) may be removed from office by the First Minister,

    (c) may at any time resign and shall do so if the Parliament resolves that the Scottish Executive no longer enjoys the confidence of the Parliament,

    (d) if he resigns, shall cease to hold office immediately, and

    (e) shall cease to hold office if he ceases to be a member of the Parliament otherwise than by virtue of a dissolution.

50 Validity of acts of Scottish Ministers etc.

The validity of any act of a member of the Scottish Executive or junior Scottish Minister is not affected by any defect in his nomination by the Parliament or (as the case may be) in the Parliament's agreement to his appointment.

51 The Civil Service

(1) The Scottish Ministers may appoint persons to be members of the staff of the Scottish Administration.

(2) Service as—

    (a) the holder of any office in the Scottish Administration which is not a ministerial office, or

    (b) a member of the staff of the Scottish Administration,

shall be service in the Home Civil Service.

(3) Subsection (1) and the other enactments conferring power to appoint such persons shall have effect subject to any provision made in relation to the Home Civil Service by or under any Order in Council.

(4)–(9) ★ ★ ★ ★ ★

Ministerial functions

52 ★ ★ ★ ★ ★

53 General transfer of functions

(1) The functions mentioned in subsection (2) shall, so far as they are exercisable within devolved competence, be exercisable by the Scottish Ministers instead of by a Minister of the Crown.

(2) Those functions are—

    (a) those of Her Majesty's prerogative and other executive functions which are exercisable on behalf of Her Majesty by a Minister of the Crown,

    (b) other functions conferred on a Minister of the Crown by a prerogative instrument, and

(c) functions conferred on a Minister of the Crown by any pre-commencement enactment,

but do not include any retained functions of the Lord Advocate.

(3), (4) ★ ★ ★ ★ ★

54 Devolved competence

(1) References in this Act to the exercise of a function being within or outside devolved competence are to be read in accordance with this section.

(2) It is outside devolved competence—

(a) to make any provision by subordinate legislation which would be outside the legislative competence of the Parliament if it were included in an Act of the Scottish Parliament, or

(b) to confirm or approve any subordinate legislation containing such provision.

(3) In the case of any function other than a function of making, confirming or approving subordinate legislation, it is outside devolved competence to exercise the function (or exercise it in any way) so far as a provision of an Act of the Scottish Parliament conferring the function (or, as the case may be, conferring it so as to be exercisable in that way) would be outside the legislative competence of the Parliament.

55, 56 ★ ★ ★ ★ ★

57 Community law and Convention rights

(1) Despite the transfer to the Scottish Ministers by virtue of section 53 of functions in relation to observing and implementing obligations under Community law, any function of a minister of the Crown in relation to any matter shall continue to be exercisable by him as regards Scotland for the purposes specified in section 2(2) of the European Communities Act 1972.

(2) A member of the Scottish Executive has no power to make any subordinate legislation, or to do any other act, so far as the legislation or act is incompatible with any of the Convention rights or with Community law.

(3) Subsection (2) does not apply to an act of the Lord Advocate—

(a) in prosecuting any offence, or

(b) in his capacity as head of the systems of criminal prosecution and investigation of deaths in Scotland,

which, because of subsection (2) of section 6 of the Human Rights Act 1998, is not unlawful under subsection (1) of that section.

58 Power to prevent or require action

(1) If the Secretary of State has reasonable grounds to believe that any action proposed to be taken by a member of the Scottish Executive would be incompatible with any international obligations, he may by order direct that the proposed action shall not be taken.

(2) If the Secretary of State has reasonable grounds to believe that any action capable of being taken by a member of the Scottish Executive is required for the purpose of giving effect to any such obligations, he may by order direct that the action shall be taken.

(3) In subsections (1) and (2), "action" includes making, confirming or approving subordinate legislation and, in subsection (2), includes introducing a Bill in the Parliament.

(4) If any subordinate legislation made or which could be revoked by a member of the Scottish Executive contains provisions—

(a) which the Secretary of State has reasonable grounds to believe to be incompatible with any international obligations or the interests of defence or national security, or

(b) which make modifications of the law as it applies to reserved matters and which the Secretary of State has reasonable grounds to believe to have an adverse effect on the operation of the law as it applies to reserved matters, the Secretary of State may by order revoke the legislation.

(5) An order under this section must state the reasons for making the order.

59–72 ★ ★ ★ ★ ★

73 Power to fix basic rate for Scottish taxpayers

(1) Subject to section 74, this section applies for any year of assessment for which income tax is charged if—

(a) the Parliament has passed a resolution providing for the percentage determined to be the basic rate for that year to be increased or reduced for Scottish taxpayers in accordance with the resolution,

(b) the increase or reduction provided for is confined to an increase or reduction by a number not exceeding three which is specified in the resolution and is either a whole number or half of a whole number, and

(c) the resolution has not been cancelled by a subsequent resolution of the Parliament.

(2) Where this section applies for any year of assessment the Income Tax Acts (excluding this Part) shall have effect in relation to the income of Scottish taxpayers as if any rate determined by the Parliament of the United Kingdom to be the basic rate for that year were increased or reduced in accordance with the resolution of the Scottish Parliament.

(3) In subsection (2) the reference to the income of Scottish taxpayers does not include a reference to any income of Scottish taxpayers which had it been income for the year 1998–99, would have been income to which section 1A of the Income and Corporation Taxes act 1988 (income from savings and distributions) applied for that year.

(4), (5) ★ ★ ★ ★ ★

74 Supplemental provision with respect to resolutions

(1) This section applies to any resolution of the Parliament ("a tax-varying resolution") which—

(a) provides, in accordance with section 73, for an increase or reduction for Scottish taxpayers of the basic rate for any year of assessment, or

(b) cancels a previous resolution of the Parliament providing for such an increase or reduction.

(2) Subject to subsection (3), a tax-varying resolution—

(a) must be expressed so as to relate to no more than a single year of assessment beginning after, but no more than twelve months after, the passing of the resolution, but

(b) shall have effect in relation to a determination by the Parliament of the United Kingdom of the rate to be the basic rate for that year irrespective of whether that determination had been made at the time of the passing of the resolution.

(3), (4) ★ ★ ★ ★ ★

(5) Standing orders shall ensure that only a member of the Scottish Executive may move a motion for a tax-varying resolution.

(6) A tax-varying resolution shall not be passed so as to have effect in relation to any year of assessment before the year 2000–01.

75–90 ★ ★ ★ ★ ★

Miscellaneous

91 Maladministration

(1) The Parliament shall make provision for the investigation of relevant complaints made to its members in respect of any action taken by or on behalf of—

(a) a member of the Scottish Executive in the exercise of functions conferred on the Scottish Ministers, or

    (b) any other office-holder in the Scottish Administration.

(2) For the purposes of subsection (1), a complaint is a relevant complaint if it is a complaint of a kind which could be investigated under the Parliamentary Commissioner Act 1967 if it were made to a member of the House of Commons in respect of a government department or other authority to which that Act applies.

(3) The Parliament may make provision for the investigation of complaints in respect of—

    (a) any action taken by or on behalf of an office-holder in the Scottish Administration,

    (b) any action taken by or on behalf of the Parliamentary corporation,

    (c) any action taken by or on behalf of a Scottish public authority with mixed functions or no reserved functions, or

    (d) any action concerning Scotland and not relating to reserved matters which is taken by or on behalf of a cross-border public authority.

(4) In making provision of the kind required by subsection (1), the Parliament shall have regard (among other things) to the Act of 1967.

(5), (6) ★ ★ ★ ★ ★

92   Queen's Printer for Scotland

(1) There shall be a Queen's Printer for Scotland who shall—

    (a) exercise the Queen's Printer functions in relation to Acts of the Scottish Parliament and subordinate legislation to which this section applies, and

    (b) exercise any other functions conferred on her by this Act or any other enactment.

(2) In subsection (1), "the Queen's Printer functions" means the printing functions in relation to Acts of Parliament and subordinate legislation of the Queen's Printer of Acts of Parliament.

(3) The Queen's Printer for Scotland shall also on behalf of Her Majesty exercise Her rights and privileges in connection with—

    (a) Crown copyright in Acts of the Scottish Parliament,

    (b) Crown copyright in subordinate legislation to which this section applies,

    (c) Crown copyright in any existing or future works (other than subordinate legislation) made in the exercise of a function which is exercisable by any office-holder in, or member of the staff of, the Scottish Administration (or would be so exercisable if the function had not ceased to exist),

    (d) other copyright assigned to Her Majesty in works made in connection with the exercise of functions by any such office-holder or member.

(4)–(6) ★ ★ ★ ★ ★

93, 94   ★ ★ ★ ★ ★

95   Appointment and removal of judges

(1) It shall continue to be for the Prime Minister to recommend to Her Majesty the appointment of a person as Lord President of the Court of Session or Lord Justice Clerk.

(2) The Prime Minister shall not recommend to Her Majesty the appointment of any person who has not been nominated by the First Minister for such appointment.

(3) Before nominating persons for such appointment the First Minister shall consult the Lord President and the Lord Justice Clerk (unless, in either case, the office is vacant).

(4) It is for the First Minister, after consulting the Lord President, to recommend to Her Majesty the appointment of a person as—

    (a) a judge of the Court of Session (other than the Lord President or the Lord Justice Clerk), or

    (b) a sheriff principal or a sheriff.

(5) the First Minister shall comply with any requirement in relation to—

    (a) a nomination under subsection (2), or

(b) a recommendation under subsection (4),
imposed by virtue of any enactment.

(6) A judge of the Court of Session and the Chairman of the Scottish Land Court may be removed from office only by Her Majesty; and any recommendation to Her Majesty for such removal shall be made by the First Minister.

(7) The First Minister shall make such a recommendation if (and only if) the Parliament, on a motion made by the First Minister, resolves that such a recommendation should be made.

(8) Provision shall be made for a tribunal constituted by the First Minister to investigate and report on whether a judge of the Court of Session or the Chairman of the Scottish Land Court is unfit for office by reason of inability, neglect of duty or misbehaviour and for the report to be laid before the Parliament.

(9) Such provision shall include provision—

(a) for the constitution of the tribunal by the First Minister when requested by the Lord President to do so and in such other circumstances as the First Minister thinks fit, and

(b) for the appointment to chair the tribunal of a member of the Judicial Committee who holds or has held any of the offices referred to in section 103(2),

and may include provision for suspension from office.

(10) The First Minister may make a motion under subsection (7) only if—

(a) he has received from a tribunal constituted in pursuance of subsection (8) a written report concluding that the person in question is unfit for office by reason or inability, neglect of duty or misbehaviour and giving reasons for that conclusion,

(b) where the person in question is the Lord President or the Lord Justice Clerk, he has consulted the Prime Minister, and

(c) he has complied with any other requirement imposed by virtue of any enactment.

(11) In subsections (8) to (10)—

"provision" means provision by or under an Act of the Scottish Parliament,

"tribunal" means a tribunal of at least three persons.

96   Provision of information to the Treasury

(1) The Treasury may require the Scottish Ministers to provide within such period as the Treasury may reasonably specify, such information, in such form and prepared in such manner, as the Treasury may reasonably specify.

(2) If the information is not in their possession or under their control, their duty under subsection (1) is to take all reasonable steps to comply with the requirement.

97   Assistance for opposition parties

(1) Her Majesty may by Order in Council provide for the Parliamentary corporation to make payments to registered political parties for the purpose of assisting members of the Parliament who are connected with such parties to perform their Parliamentary duties.

(2) The corporation shall not make any payment to a party in pursuance of such an Order if any of the members of the Parliament who are connected with the party are also members of the Scottish Executive or junior Scottish Ministers.

(3) But such an Order may, in any circumstances specified in the Order, require the fact that any members who are connected with a party are also members of the Scottish Executive or junior Scottish Ministers to be disregarded.

(4) Such an Order may determine the circumstances in which a member of the Parliament and a registered political party are to be regarded for the purposes of this section as connected.

Juridical

98   Devolution issues

Schedule 6 (which makes provision in relation to devolution issues) shall have effect.

99   Rights and liabilities of the Crown in different capacities

(1) Rights and liabilities may arise between the Crown in right of Her Majesty's Government in the United Kingdom and the Crown in right of the Scottish Administration by virtue of a contract, by operation of law or by virtue of an enactment as they may arise between subjects.

(2) Property and liabilities may be transferred between the Crown in one of those capacities and the Crown in the other capacity as they may be transferred between subjects; and they may together create, vary or extinguish any property or liability as subjects may.

(3) Proceedings in respect of—

(a) any property or liabilities to which the Crown in one of those capacities is entitled or subject under subsection (1) or (2), or

(b) the exercise of, or failure to exercise, any function exercisable by an office-holder of the Crown in one of those capacities,

may be instituted by the Crown in either capacity; and the Crown in the other capacity may be a separate party in the proceedings.

(4) This section applies to a unilateral obligation as it applies to a contract.

(5) In this section—

"office-holder", in relation to the Crown in right of Her Majesty's Government in the United Kingdom, means any minister of the Crown or other office-holder under the Crown in that capacity and, in relation to the Crown in right of the Scottish Administration, means any office-holder in the Scottish Administration,

"subject" means a person not acting on behalf of the Crown.

100   Human rights

(1) This Act does not enable a person—

(a) to bring any proceedings in a court or tribunal on the ground that an act is incompatible with the Convention rights, or

(b) to rely on any of the Convention rights in any such proceedings, unless he would be a victim for the purposes of Article 34 of the Convention (within the meaning of the Human Rights Act 1998) if proceedings in respect of the act were brought in the European Court of Human Rights.

(2) Subsection (1) does not apply to the Lord Advocate, the Advocate General, the Attorney General or the Attorney General for Northern Ireland.

(3) This Act does not enable a court or tribunal to award any damages in respect of an act which is incompatible with any of the Convention rights which it could not award if section 8(3) and (4) of the Human Rights Act 1998 applied.

(4) In this section "act" means—

(a) making any legislation,

(b) any other act or failure to act, if it is the act or failure of a member of the Scottish Executive.

101   Interpretation of Acts of the Scottish Parliament etc.

(1) This section applies to—

(a) any provision of an Act of the Scottish Parliament, or of a Bill for such an Act, and

(b) any provision of subordinate legislation made, confirmed or approved, or purporting to be made, confirmed or approved, by a member of the Scottish Executive, which could be read in such a way as to be outside competence.

(2) Such a provision is to be read as narrowly as is required for it to be within competence, if such a reading is possible, and is to have effect accordingly.

(3) In this section "competence"—

(a) in relation to an Act of the Scottish Parliament, or a Bill for such an Act, means the legislative competence of the Parliament, and

(b) in relation to subordinate legislation, means the powers conferred by virtue of this Act.

102   Powers of courts or tribunals to vary retrospective decisions

(1) This section applies where any court or tribunal decides that—

(a) an Act of the Scottish Parliament or any provision of such an Act is not within the legislative competence of the Parliament, or

(b) a member of the Scottish Executive does not have the power to make, confirm or approve a provision of subordinate legislation that he has purported to make, confirm or approve.

(2) The court or tribunal may make an order—

(a) removing or limiting any retrospective effect of the decision, or

(b) suspending the effect of the decision for any period and on any conditions to allow the defect to be corrected.

(3) In deciding whether to make an order under this section, the court or tribunal shall (among other things) have regard to the extent to which persons who are not parties to the proceedings would otherwise be adversely affected.

(4) Where a court or tribunal is considering whether to make an order under this section, it shall order intimation of that fact to be given to—

(a) the Lord Advocate, and

(b) the appropriate law officer, where the decision mentioned in subsection (1) relates to a devolution issue (within the meaning of Schedule 6),

unless the person to whom the intimation would be given is a party to the proceedings.

(5) A person to whom intimation is given under subsection (4) may take part as a party in the proceedings so far as they relate to the making of the order.

(6), (7) ★ ★ ★ ★ ★

103   The Judicial Committee

(1) Any decision of the Judicial Committee in proceedings under this Act shall be stated in open court and shall be binding in all legal proceedings (other than proceedings before the Committee).

(2) No member of the Judicial Committee shall sit and act as a member of the Committee in proceedings under this Act unless he holds or has held—

(a) the office of a Lord of Appeal in Ordinary, or

(b) high judicial office as defined in section 25 of the Appellate Jurisdiction Act 1876 (ignoring for this purpose section 5 of the Appellate Jurisdiction Act 1887).

(3) Her Majesty may by Order in Council—

(a) confer on the Judicial Committee in relation to proceedings under this Act such powers as Her Majesty considers necessary or expedient,

(b) apply the Judicial Committee Act 1833 in relation to proceedings under this Act with exceptions or modifications,

(c) make rules for regulating the procedure in relation to proceedings under this Act before the Judicial Committee.

(4) In this section "proceedings under this Act" means proceedings on a question referred to the Judicial Committee under section 33 or proceedings under Schedule 6.

104–106   ★ ★ ★ ★ ★

107   Legislative power to remedy ultra vires acts

Subordinate legislation may make such provision as the person making the legislation considers necessary or expedient in consequence of—

(a) an Act of the Scottish Parliament or any provision of an Act of the Scottish Parliament which is not, or may not be, within the legislative competence of the Parliament, or

(b) any purported exercise by a member of the Scottish Executive of his functions which is not, or may not be, an exercise or a proper exercise of those functions.

★ ★ ★ ★ ★

Section 29 and 53(4)   SCHEDULE 4
ENACTMENTS ETC. PROTECTED FROM MODIFICATION
PART I   THE PROTECTED PROVISIONS

Particular enactments

1.—(1) An Act of the Scottish Parliament cannot modify, or confer power by subordinate legislation to modify, any of the following provisions.

(2) The provisions are—
  (a) Articles 4 and 6 of the Union with Scotland Act 1706 and of the Union with England Act 1707 so far as they relate to freedom of trade,
  (b) the Private Legislation Procedure (Scotland) Act 1936,
  (c) the following provisions of the European Communities Act 1972—
      Section 1 and Schedule 1,
      Section 2, other than subsection (2), the words following "such Community obligation" in subsection (3) and the words "subject to Schedule 2 to this Act" in subsection (4),
      Section 3(1) and (2),
      Section 11(2),
  (d) paragraphs 5(3)(b) and 15(4)(b) of Schedule 32 to the Local Government, Planning and Land Act 1980 (designation of enterprise zones),
  (e) sections 140A to 140G of the Social Security Administration Act 1992 (rent rebate and rent allowance subsidy and council tax benefit),
  (f) the Human Rights Act 1998.

The law on reserved matters

2.—(1) An Act of the Scottish Parliament cannot modify, or confer power by subordinate legislation to modify, the law on reserved matters.

(2) In this paragraph, "the law on reserved matters" means—
  (a) any enactment the subject-matter of which is a reserved matter and which is comprised in an Act of Parliament or subordinate legislation under an Act of Parliament, and
  (b) any rule of law which is not contained in an enactment and the subject-matter of which is a reserved matter,
and in this sub-paragraph "Act of Parliament" does not include this Act.

(3) Sub-paragraph (1) applies in relation to a rule of Scots private law or Scots criminal law (whether or not contained in an enactment) only to the extent that the rule in question is special to a reserved matter or the subject-matter of the rule is—
  (a) interest on sums due in respect of taxes or excise duties and refunds of such taxes or duties,
  (b) the obligations, in relation to occupational or personal pension schemes, of the trustees or managers,
  [(c) the obligations under an order made by virtue of section 12A(2) or (3) of the Family Law (Scotland) Act 1985 (order relating to pensions lump sums) of the person responsible for a pension arrangement other than an occupational or personal pension scheme; or
  (d) the obligations under Chapter I of Part IV of the Welfare Reform and Pensions Act 1999 (sharing of rights under pension arrangements) of the person responsible for such a pension arrangement; or

(e) the effect of Chapter II of Part IV of that Act of 1999 (sharing of rights in state pension schemes) as read with Part II of the Social Security Contributions and Benefits Act 1992 (contributory benefits).]

[(4) In sub-paragraph (3)(c) "pension arrangement" and "person responsible for a pension arrangement" have the same meaning as in section 27(1) of the Family Law (Scotland) Act 1985.]

3.—(1) Paragraph 2 does not apply to modifications which—

(a) are incidental to, or consequential on, provision made (whether by virtue of the Act in question or another enactment) which does not relate to reserved matters, and

(b) do not have a greater effect on reserved matters than is necessary to give effect to the purpose of the provision.

(2) In determining for the purposes of sub-paragraph (1)(b) what is necessary to give effect to the purpose of a provision, any power to make laws other than the power of the Parliament is to be disregarded.

This Act

4.—(1) An Act of the Scottish Parliament cannot modify, or confer power by subordinate legislation to modify, this Act.

(2) This paragraph does not apply to modifying sections 1(4), 17(5), 19(7), 21(5), 24(2), 28(5), 39(7), 40 to 43, 50, 69(3), 85, [93 and 97] and paragraphs 4(1) to (3) and 6(1) of Schedule 2.

(3) This paragraph does not apply to modifying any provision of this Act (other than sections 64(7), 66(2), 71(7), 77, 78 and 119) which—

(a) charges any sum on the Scottish Consolidated fund,

(b) requires any sum to be paid out of that Fund without further approval, or

(c) requires or authorises the payment of any sum into the Fund.

(4) This paragraph does not apply to any modifications of Part III which are necessary or expedient for the purpose or in consequence of the establishment of a new fund, in addition to the Scottish Consolidated fund, out of which loans may be made by the Scottish Ministers.

(5) This paragraph does not apply to—

(a) modifying so much of any enactment as is modified by this Act,

(b) repealing so much of any provision of this Act as amends any enactment, if the provision ceases to have effect in consequence of any enactment comprised in or made under an Act of the Scottish Parliament.

Enactments modified by this Act

5. An Act of the Scottish Parliament cannot modify, or confer power by subordinate legislation to modify—

(a) the effect of section 119(3) in relation to any provision of an Act of Parliament relating to judicial salaries,

(b) so much of any enactment as—

(i)   is amended by paragraph 2, 7 or 32 of Schedule 8, and

(ii) relates to the Advocate General,

(c) so much of any enactment as is amended by paragraph 9(b) or 29 of Schedule 8.

Shared powers

6. An Act of the Scottish Parliament cannot modify, or confer power by subordinate legislation to modify, any enactment so far as the enactment relates to powers exercisable by a Minister of the Crown by virtue of section 56.

PART II GENERAL EXCEPTIONS

Restatement, etc.

7.—(1) Part I of this Schedule does not prevent an Act of the Scottish Parliament—

(a) restating the law (or restating it with such modifications as are not prevented by that Part), or

(b) repealing any spent enactment,

or conferring power by subordinate legislation to do so.

(2) For the purposes of paragraph 2, the law on reserved matters includes any restatement in an Act of the Scottish Parliament, or subordinate legislation under such an Act, of the law on reserved matters if the subject-matter of the restatement is a reserved matter.

Effect of Interpretation Act 1978

8. Part I of this Schedule does not prevent the operation of any provision of the Interpretation Act 1978.

Change of title etc.

9.—(1) Part I of this Schedule does not prevent an Act of the Scottish Parliament amending, or conferring power by subordinate legislation to amend, any enactment by changing—

(a) any of the titles referred to in sub-paragraph (2), or

(b) any reference to a declarator, in consequence of any provision made by or under an Act of the Scottish Parliament.

(2) The titles are those of—

(a) any court or tribunal or any judge, chairman or officer of a court or tribunal,

(b) any holder of an office in the Scottish Administration which is not a ministerial office or any member of the staff of the Scottish Administration,

(c) any register.

10.–14. ★ ★ ★ ★ ★

Section 30

SCHEDULE 5
RESERVED MATTERS

PART I GENERAL RESERVATIONS

The Constitution

1. The following aspects of the constitution are reserved matters, that is—

(a) the Crown, including succession to the Crown and a regency,

(b) the Union of the Kingdoms of Scotland and England,

(c) the Parliament of the United Kingdom,

(d) the continued existence of the High Court of Justiciary as a criminal court of first instance and of appeal,

(e) the continued existence of the Court of Session as a civil court of first instance and of appeal.

2.—(1) Paragraph 1 does not reserve—

(a) Her Majesty's prerogative and other executive functions,

(b) functions exercisable by any person acting on behalf of the Crown, or

(c) any office in the Scottish Administration.

(2) Sub-paragraph (1) does not affect the reservation by paragraph 1 of honours and dignities or the functions of the Lord Lyon King of Arms so far as relating to the granting of arms; but this sub-paragraph does not apply to the Lord Lyon King of Arms in his judicial capacity.

(3) Sub-paragraph (1) does not affect the reservation by paragraph 1 of the management (in accordance with any enactment regulating the use of land) of the Crown Estate.

(4) Sub-paragraph (1) does not affect the reservation by paragraph 1of the functions of the Security Service, the Secret Intelligence Service and the Government Communications Headquarters.

[(5) Sub-paragraph 1 does not affect the reservation by paragraph 1 of the functions exercisable through the Export Credits Guarantee Department.]

3.—(1) Paragraph 1 does not reserve property belonging to Her Majesty in right of the Crown or belonging to any person acting on behalf of the Crown or held in trust for Her Majesty for the purposes of any person acting on behalf of the Crown.

(2) Paragraph 1 does not reserve the ultimate superiority of the Crown or the superiority of the Prince and Steward of Scotland.

(3) Sub-paragraph (1) does not affect the reservation by paragraph 1 of—
- (a) the hereditary revenues of the Crown, other than revenues from bona vacantia, ultimus haeres and treasure trove,
- (b) the royal arms and standard,
- (c) the compulsory acquisition of property held or used by a Minister of the Crown or government department.

4.—(1) Paragraph 1 does not reserve property held by Her Majesty in Her private capacity.

(2) Sub-paragraph (1) does not affect the reservation by paragraph 1 of the subject-matter of the Crown Private Estates Acts 1800 to 1873.

5. Paragraph 1 does not reserve the use of the Scottish Seal.

Political parties

6. The registration and funding of political parties is a reserved matter [but this paragraph does not reserve making payments to any political party for the purpose of assisting members of the Parliament who are connected with the party to perform their Parliamentary duties].

Foreign affairs etc.

7.—(1) International relations, including relations with territories outside the United Kingdom, the European Communities (and their institutions) and other international organisations, regulation of international trade, and international development assistance and co-operation are reserved matters.

(2) Sub-paragraph (1) does not reserve—
- (a) observing and implementing international obligations, obligations under the Human Rights Convention and obligations under Community law,
- (b) assisting Ministers of the Crown in relation to any matter to which that sub-paragraph applies.

Public service

8.—(1) the Civil Service of the State is a reserved matter.

(2) Sub-paragraph (1) does not reserve the subject-matter of—
- (a) Part I of the Sheriff Courts and Legal Officers (Scotland) Act 1927 (appointment of sheriff clerks and procurators fiscal etc.),
- (b) Part III of the Administration of Justice (Scotland) Act 1933 (officers of the High Court of Justiciary and of the Court of Session).

Defence

9.—(1) The following are reserved matters—
- (a) the defence of the realm,

  (b) the naval, military or air forces of the Crown, including reserve forces,
  (c) visiting forces,
  (d) international headquarters and defence organisations,
  (e) trading with the enemy and enemy property.
  (2) Sub-paragraph (1) does not reserve—
    (a) the exercise of civil defence functions by any person otherwise than as a member of any force or organisation referred to in sub-paragraph (1)(b) to (d) or any other force or organisation reserved by virtue of sub-paragraph (1)(a),
    (b) the conferral of enforcement powers in relation to sea fishing.

Treason

10. Treason (including constructive treason), treason felony and misprision of treason are reserved matters.

PART II   SPECIFIC RESERVATIONS

Preliminary

1. The matters to which any of the Sections in this Part apply are reserved matters for the purposes of this Act.

2. A Section applies to any matter described or referred to in it when read with any illustrations, exceptions or interpretation provisions in that Section.

3. Any illustrations, exceptions or interpretation provisions in a Section relate only to that Section (so that an entry under the heading "exceptions" does not affect any other Section).

Reservations

Head A – Financial and Economic Matters

Section A1   A1. Fiscal, economic and monetary policy
Fiscal, economic and monetary policy, including the issue and circulation of money, taxes and excise duties, government borrowing and lending, control over United Kingdom public expenditure, the exchange rate and the Bank of England.

Exception
Local taxes to fund local authority expenditure (for example, council tax and non-domestic rates).

Section A2   A2. The currency
Coinage, legal tender and bank notes.

Section A3   A3. Financial services
Financial services, including investment business, banking and deposit-taking, collective investment schemes and insurance.

Exception
The subject-matter of section 1 of the Banking and Financial Dealings Act 1971 (bank holidays).

Section A4   A4. Financial markets
Financial markets, including listing and public offers of securities and investments, transfer of securities and insider dealing.

Section A5   A5. Money laundering
The subject-matter of the Money Laundering Regulations 1993, but in relation to any type of business.

★ ★ ★ ★ ★

Note: The text of remaining headings is omitted for reasons of space. The other headings are categorised as follows:
Head B – Home Affairs
Head C – Trade and Industry
Head D – Energy
Head E – Transport
Head F – Social Security
Head G – Regulation of the Professions
Head H – Employment
Head J – Health and Medicines
Head K – Media and Culture
Head L – Miscellaneous

Section 98   SCHEDULE 6
                          DEVOLUTION ISSUES
                          PART I   PRELIMINARY

1. In this Schedule "devolution issue" means—
   (a) a question whether an Act of the Scottish Parliament or any provision of an Act of the Scottish Parliament is within the legislative competence of the Parliament,
   (b) a question whether any function (being a function which any person has purported, or is proposing, to exercise) is a function of the Scottish Ministers, the First Minister or the Lord Advocate.
   (c) a question whether the purported or proposed exercise of a function by a member of the Scottish Executive is, or would be, within devolved competence,
   (d) a question whether a purported or proposed exercise of a function by a member of the Scottish Executive is, or would be incompatible with any of the Convention rights or with Community law,
   (e) a question whether a failure to act by a member of the Scottish Executive is incompatible with any of the Convention rights or with Community law,
   (f) any other question about whether a function is exercisable within devolved competence or in or as regards Scotland and any other question arising by virtue of this Act about reserved matters.
   2. A devolution issue shall not be taken to arise in any proceedings merely because of any contention of a party to the proceedings which appears to the court or tribunal before which the proceedings take place to be frivolous or vexatious.

PART II   PROCEEDINGS IN SCOTLAND

Application of Part II

3. This Part of this Schedule applies in relation to devolution issues in proceedings in Scotland.

Institution of proceedings

4.—(1) Proceedings for the determination of a devolution issue may be instituted by the Advocate General or the Lord Advocate.

(2) The Lord Advocate may defend any such proceedings instituted by the Advocate General.

(3) This paragraph is without prejudice to any power to institute or defend proceedings exercisable apart from this paragraph by any person.

Intimation of devolution issue

5. Intimation of any devolution issue which arises in any proceedings before a court or tribunal shall be given to the Advocate General and the Lord Advocate (unless the person to whom the intimation would be given is a party to the proceedings).

6. A person to whom intimation is given in pursuance of paragraph 5 may take part as a party in the proceedings, so far as they relate to a devolution issue.

Reference of devolution issue to higher court

7. A court, other than the House of Lords or any court consisting of three or more judges of the Court of Session, may refer any devolution issue which arises in proceedings (other than criminal proceedings) before it to the Inner House of the Court of Session

8. A tribunal from which there is no appeal shall refer any devolution issue which arises in proceedings before it to the Inner House of the Court of Session; and any other tribunal may make such a reference.

9. A court, other than any court consisting of two or more judges of the High Court of Justiciary, may refer any devolution issue which arises in criminal proceedings before it to the High Court of Justiciary.

References from superior courts to Judicial Committee

10. Any court consisting of three or more judges of the Court of Session may refer any devolution issue which arises in proceedings before it (otherwise than on a reference under paragraph 7 or 8) to the Judicial Committee.

11. Any court consisting of two or more judges of the High Court of Justiciary may refer any devolution issue which arises in proceedings before it (otherwise than on a reference under paragraph 9) to the Judicial Committee.

Appeals from superior courts to Judicial Committee

12. An appeal against a determination of a devolution issue by the Inner House of the Court of Session on a reference under paragraph 7 or 8 shall lie to the Judicial Committee.

13. An appeal against a determination of a devolution issue by—
   (a) a court of two or more judges of the High Court of Justiciary (whether in the ordinary course of proceedings or on a reference under paragraph 9), or
   (b) a court of three or more judges of the Court of Session from which there is no appeal to the House of Lords,

shall lie to the Judicial Committee, but only with leave of the court concerned or, failing such leave, with special leave of the Judicial Committee.

PART III   PROCEEDINGS IN ENGLAND AND WALES

Application of Part III

14. This Part of this Schedule applies in relation to devolution issues in proceedings in England and Wales.

Institution of proceedings

15.—(1) Proceedings for the determination of a devolution issue may be instituted by the Attorney General.

(2) The Lord Advocate may defend any such proceedings.

(3) This paragraph is without prejudice to any power to institute or defend proceedings exercisable apart from this paragraph by any person.

Notice of devolution issue

16. A court or tribunal shall order notice of any devolution issue which arises in any proceedings before it to be given to the Attorney General and the Lord Advocate (unless the person to whom the notice would be given is a party to the proceedings),

17. A person to whom notice is given in pursuance of paragraph 16 may take part as a party in the proceedings, so far as they relate to a devolution issue.

Reference of devolution issue to High Court or Court of Appeal

18. A magistrates' court may refer any devolution issue which arises in proceedings (other than criminal proceedings) before it to the High Court.

19.–(1) A court may refer any devolution issue which arises in proceedings (other than criminal proceedings) before it to the Courts of Appeal.

(2) Sub-paragraph (1) does not apply to—

(a) a magistrates' court, the Court of Appeal or the House of Lords, or

(b) the High Court if the devolution issue arises in proceedings on a reference under paragraph 18.

20. A tribunal from which there is no appeal shall refer any devolution issue which arises in proceedings before it to the Court of Appeal; and any other tribunal may make such a reference.

21. A court, other than the House of Lords or the Court of Appeal, may refer any devolution issue which arises in criminal proceedings before it to—

(a) the High Court (if the proceedings are summary proceedings), or

(b) the Court of Appeal (if the proceedings are proceedings on indictment).

References from Court of Appeal to Judicial Committee

22. The Court of Appeal may refer any devolution issue which arises in proceedings before it (otherwise than on a reference under paragraph 19, 20 or 21) to the Judicial Committee.

Appeals from superior courts to Judicial Committee

23. An appeal against a determination of a devolution issue by the High Court or the Court of Appeal on a reference under paragraph 18, 19, 20 or 21 shall lie to the Judicial Committee, but only with leave of the High Court or (as the case may be) the Court of Appeal or, failing such leave, with special leave of the Judicial Committee.

24–31 ★ ★ ★ ★ ★

(Equivalent provisions for issues arising in Northern Ireland)

PART V   GENERAL

Proceedings in the House of Lords

32. Any devolution issue which arises in judicial proceedings in the House of Lords shall

be referred to the Judicial Committee unless the House considers it more appropriate, having regard to all the circumstances, that it should determine the issue.

Direct references to Judicial Committee

33. The Lord Advocate, the Advocate General, the Attorney General or the Attorney General for Northern Ireland may require any court or tribunal to refer to the Judicial Committee any devolution issue which has arisen in proceedings before it to which he is a party.

34. The Lord Advocate, the Attorney General, the Advocate General or the Attorney General for Northern Ireland may refer to the Judicial Committee any devolution issue which is not the subject of proceedings.

35.—(1) This paragraph applies where a reference is made under paragraph 34 in relation to a devolution issue which relates to the proposed exercise of a function by a member of the Scottish Executive.

(2) The person making the reference shall notify a member of the Scottish Executive of that fact.

(3) No member of the Scottish Executive shall exercise the function in the manner proposed during the period beginning with the receipt of the notification under sub-paragraph (2) and ending with the reference being decided or otherwise disposed of.

(4) Proceedings relating to any possible failure by a member of the Scottish Executive to comply with sub-paragraph (3) may be instituted by the Advocate General.

(5) Sub-paragraph (4) is without prejudice to any power to institute proceedings exercisable apart from that sub-paragraph by any person.

Expenses

36.—(1) A court or tribunal before which any proceedings take place may take account of any additional expense of the kind mentioned in sub-paragraph (3) in deciding any question as to costs or expenses.

(2) In deciding any such question, the court or tribunal may award the whole or part of the additional expense as costs or (as the case may be) expenses to the party who incurred it (whatever the decision on the devolution issue).

(3) The additional expense is any additional expense which the court or tribunal considers that any party to the proceedings has incurred as a result of the participation of any person in pursuance of paragraph 6, 17 or 27.

Procedure of courts and tribunals

37. Any power to make provision for regulating the procedure before any court or tribunal shall include power to make provision for the purposes of this Schedule including, in particular, provision—

- (a) for prescribing the stage in the proceedings at which a devolution issue is to be raised or referred,
- (b) for the sisting or staying of proceedings for the purpose of any proceedings under this Schedule, and
- (c) for determining the manner in which and the time within which any intimation or notice is to be given.

Interpretation

38. Any duty or power conferred by this Schedule to refer a devolution issue to a court shall be construed as a duty or (as the case may be) power to refer the issue to the court for decision.

★ ★ ★ ★ ★

Access to Justice Act 1999
(1999, c. 22)

An Act to establish the Legal Services Commission, the Community Legal Service and the Criminal Defence Service; to amend the law of legal aid in Scotland; to make further provision about legal services; to make provision about appeals, courts, judges and court proceedings; to amend the law about magistrates and magistrates' courts; and to make provision about immunity from action and costs and indemnities for certain officials exercising judicial functions.   [27 July 1999]

Territorial extent: England and Wales

★ ★ ★ ★ ★

PART III   PROVISION OF LEGAL SERVICES

Legal Services Complaints Commissioner

51 Commissioner

(1) The Lord Chancellor may appoint a person as Legal Services Complaints Commissioner.

(2) Any appointment of a person as Commissioner shall be for a period of not more than three years; and a person appointed as Commissioner shall hold and vacate office in accordance with the terms of his appointment.

(3) At the end of his term of appointment the Commissioner shall be eligible for re-appointment.

(4) The Commissioner shall not be an authorised advocate, authorised litigator, licensed conveyancer or authorised practitioner (within the meaning of the Courts and Legal Services Act 1990) or a notary.

(5) Schedule 8 (which makes further provision about the Commissioner) has effect.

52 Commissioner's functions

(1) If it appears to the Lord Chancellor that complaints about members of any professional body are not being handled effectively and efficiently, he may by direction require the Legal Services Complaints Commissioner to consider exercising in relation to the body such of the powers in subsection (2) as are specified in the direction.

(2) Those powers are—

(a) to require a professional body to provide information, or make reports, to the Commissioner about the handling of complaints about its members,

(b) to investigate the handling of complaints about the members of a professional body,

(c) to make recommendations in relation to the handling of complaints about the members of a professional body,

(d) to set targets in relation to the handling of complaints about the members of a professional body, and

(e) to require a professional body to submit to the Commissioner a plan for the handling of complaints about its members.

(3) Where the Commissioner requires a professional body to submit to him a plan for the handling of compliants about its members but the body—

(a) fails to submit to him a plan which he considers adequate for securing that such complaints are handled effectively and efficiently, or

(b) submits to him such a plan but fails to handle complaints in accordance with it,

he may require the body to pay a penalty.

(4) Before requiring a professional body to pay a penalty under subsection (3) the Commissioner shall afford it a reasonable opportunity of appearing before him to make representations.

(5) The Lord Chancellor shall by order made by statutory instrument specify the maximum amount of any penalty under subsection (3).

(6) In determining the amount of any penalty which a professional body is to be required to pay under subsection (3) the Commissioner shall have regard to all the circumstances of the case, including in particular–
    (a) the total number of complaints about members of the body and, where the penalty is imposed in respect of a failure to handle complaints in accordance with a plan, the number of complaints not so handled, and
    (b) the assets of the body and the number of its members.

(7) A penalty under subsection (3) shall be paid to the Commissioner who shall pay it to the Lord Chancellor.

(8) Where a direction under subsection (1) in relation to a professional body has been given (and not revoked), section 24(1) of the Courts and Legal Services Act 1990 (power of Legal Services Ombudsman to make recommendations about arrangements for investigation of complaints) shall not have effect in relation to the body.

(9) No order shall be made under subsection (5) unless a draft of the order has been laid before, and approved by a resolution of, each House of Parliament.

(10) In this section "professional body" has the same meaning as in section 22 of the Courts and Legal Services Act 1990.

★ ★ ★ ★ ★

Greater London Authority Act 1999
(1999, c. 29)

An Act to establish and make provision about the Greater London Authority, the Mayor of London and the London Assembly; to make provision in relation to London borough councils and the Common Council of the City of London with respect to matters consequential or the establishment of the Greater London Authority; to make provision with respect to the functions of other local authorities and statutory bodies exercising functions in Greater London; to make provision about transport and road traffic in and around Greater London; to make provision about policing in Greater London and to make an adjustment of the metropolitan police district; and for connected purposes.   [11 November 1999]

Territorial extent: England, Scotland and Wales (but necessarily the substantive provisions apply only to London)

PART I   THE GREATER LONDON AUTHORITY

The Authority

1   The Authority
    (1) There shall be an authority for Greater London, to be known as the Greater London Authority.
    (2) The Authority shall be a body corporate.
    (3) The Authority shall have the functions which are transferred to, or conferred or imposed on, the Authority by or under this Act or any other Act.

Membership

2 Membership of the Authority and the Assembly

(1) The Authority shall consist of—
- (a) the Mayor of London; and
- (b) an Assembly for London, to be known as the London Assembly.

(2) The Assembly shall consist of twenty five members, of whom–
- (a) fourteen shall be members of Assembly constituencies ("constituency members"); and
- (b) eleven shall be members for the whole of Greater London ("London Members").

(3) There shall be one constituency member for each Assembly constituency.

(4) The Assembly constituencies shall be the areas, and shall be known by the names, specified in an order made by the Secretary of State.

(5)–(11) ★ ★ ★ ★ ★

3-19 ★ ★ ★ ★ ★

Qualifications and disqualifications

20 Qualification to be the Mayor or an Assembly member

(1) Subject to any disqualification by virtue of this Act or any other enactment, a person is qualified to be elected and to be the Mayor or an Assembly member if he satisfies the requirements of subsections (2) to (4) below.

(2) The person must be—
- (a) a Commonwealth citizen;
- (b) a citizen of the Republic of Ireland; or
- (c) a relevant citizen of the Union.

(3) On the relevant day, the person must have attained the age of 21 years.

(4) The person must satisfy at least one of the following conditions–
- (a) on the relevant day he is, and from that day continues to be, a local government elector for Greater London;
- (b) he has, during the whole of the twelve months preceding that day, occupied as owner or tenant any land or other premises in Greater London;
- (c) his principal or only place of work during that twelve months has been in Greater London;
- (d) he has during the whole of that twelve months resided in Greater London.

(5)–(8) ★ ★ ★ ★ ★

21-29 ★ ★ ★ ★ ★

PART II   GENERAL FUNCTIONS AND PROCEDURE

The general and subsidiary powers of the Authority

30 The general power of the Authority

(1) The Authority shall have power to do anything which it considers will further any one or more of its principal purposes.

(2) Any reference in this Act to the principal purposes of the Authority is a reference to the purposes of—
- (a) promoting economic development and wealth creation in Greater London;
- (b) promoting social development in Greater London; and
- (c) promoting the improvement of the environment in Greater London.

(3) In determining whether or how to exercise the power conferred by subsection (1)

above to further any one or more of its principal purposes, the Authority shall have regard to the desirability of so exercising that power as to—

    (a) further the remaining principal purpose or purposes, so far as reasonably practicable to do so; and

    (b) secure, over a period of time, a reasonable balance between furthering each of its principal purposes.

(4) In determining whether or how to exercise the power conferred by subsection (1) above, the Authority shall have regard to the effect which the proposed exercise of the power would have on—

    (a) the health of persons in Greater London; and

    (b) the achievement of sustainable development in the United Kingdom.

(5) Where the Authority exercises the power conferred by subsection (1) above, it shall do so in the way which it considers best calculated–

    (a) to promote improvements in the health of persons in Greater London, and

    (b) to contribute towards the achievement of sustainable development in the United Kingdom,

        except to the extent that the Authority considers that any action that would need to be taken by virtue of paragraph (a) or (b) above is not reasonably practicable in all the circumstances of the case.

(6) In subsection (5)(a) above, the reference to promoting improvements in health includes a reference to mitigating any detriment to health which would otherwise be occasioned by the exercise of the power.

(7)–(10) ★ ★ ★ ★ ★

31 Limits of the general power

(1) The Authority shall not by virtue of section 30(1) above incur expenditure in doing anything which may be done by a functional body other than the London Development Agency.

(2) In determining whether to exercise the power conferred by section 30(1) above, the Authority shall seek to secure that it does not incur expenditure in doing anything which is being done by the London Development Agency.

(3) The Authority shall not by virtue of section 30(1) above incur expenditure in providing—

    (a) any housing,

    (b) any education services,

    (c) any social services, or

    (d) any health services,

in any case where the provision in question may be made by a London borough council, the Common Council or any other public body.

(4), (5) ★ ★ ★ ★ ★

(6) Nothing in subsections (1) to (5) above shall be taken to prevent the Authority incurring expenditure in co-operating with, or facilitating or co-ordinating the activities of, the bodies mentioned in those subsections.

(7) The Secretary of State may by order amending this section make further provision for preventing the authority from doing by virtue of section 30(1) above anything—

    (a) which may be done by a London borough council, the Common Council or a public body, and

    (b) which is specified, or is of a description specified, in the order.

(8) The Secretary of State may by order impose limits on the expenditure which may be incurred by the Authority by virtue of section 30(1) above.

(9) The Secretary of State may by order amending this section make provision removing or restricting any prohibitions or limitations imposed by this section on what may be done by the Authority by virtue of section 30(1) above.

32 Consultation

(1) The power conferred by section 30(1) above is exercisable only after consultation with such bodies or persons as the Authority may consider appropriate in the particular case.

(2) In determining what consultation (if any) is appropriate under subsection (1) above, the bodies which, and persons whom, the Authority considers consulting must include—

    (a) any London borough council;

    (b) the Common Council; and

    (c) bodies of each of the descriptions specified in subsection (3) below.

(3) Those descriptions are—

    (a) voluntary bodies some or all of whose activities benefit the whole or part of Greater London;

    (b) bodies which represent the interests of different racial, ethnic or national groups in Greater London;

    (c) bodies which represent the interests of different religious groups in Greater London;

    (d) bodies which represent the interests of persons carrying on business in Greater London.

(4), (5) ★ ★ ★ ★ ★

33 Equality of opportunity

(1) The Authority shall make appropriate arrangements with a view to securing that—

    (a) in the exercise of the power conferred on the Authority by section 30 above,

    (b) in the formulation of the policies and proposals to be included in any of the strategies mentioned in section 41(1) below, and

    (c) in the implementation of any of those strategies, there is due regard to the principle that there should be equality of opportunity for all people.

(2) After each financial year the Authority shall publish a report containing—

    (a) a statement of the arrangements made in pursuance of subsection (1) above which had effect during that financial year; and

    (b) an assessment of how effective those arrangements were in promoting equality of opportunity.

(3) The functions conferred or imposed on the Authority under or by virtue of this section shall be functions of the Authority which are exercisable by the Mayor acting on behalf of the Authority.

34 Subsidiary powers of the Authority

(1) The Authority, acting by the Mayor, by the Assembly, or by both jointly, may do anything (including the acquisition or disposal of any property or rights) which is calculated to facilitate, or is conducive or incidental to, the exercise of any functions of the Authority exercisable by the Mayor or, as the case may be, by the Assembly or by both acting jointly.

(2) The Authority shall not by virtue of this section raise money (whether by precepts, borrowing or otherwise) or lend money, except in accordance with the enactments relating to those matters.

35–51 ★ ★ ★ ★ ★

Meetings and procedure of the Assembly

52 Meetings of the whole Assembly

(1) The Assembly may hold, in addition to any meetings required to be held by or under this section or any other enactment, such other meetings as it may determine.

(2) Before the expiration of the period of ten days following the day of the poll at an ordinary election, there shall be a meeting of the Assembly to elect—

    (a) the Chair of the Assembly; and

(b) the Deputy Chair of the Assembly.

(3) On such ten occasions in each calendar year as the Assembly may determine, there shall be a meeting of the Assembly—

(a) to consider the written report submitted for the meeting by the Mayor under section 45 above,

(b) to enable Assembly members to put–
(i) oral or written questions to the Mayor, and
(ii) oral questions to any employees of the Authority who are required to attend such meetings and answer questions put to them by Assembly members; and

(c) to transact any other business on the agenda for the meeting.

(4)–(7) ★ ★ ★ ★ ★

(8) An extraordinary meeting of the Assembly may be called at any time by the chair of the Assembly.

(9) If—

(a) the Chair of the Assembly refuses to call an extraordinary meeting of the Assembly after a requisition for that purpose, signed by five Assembly members, has been presented to him, or

(b) if, without so refusing, the Chair of the Assembly does not call an extraordinary meeting within seven days after such a requisition has been presented to him,

any five Assembly members may forthwith call an extraordinary meeting of the Assembly.

(10) Section 54 below shall not apply in relation to any function of the Assembly under this section.

53   Assembly procedure

(1) All questions coming before, or to be decided by, the Assembly shall be decided by a majority of the members of the Assembly present and voting at a meeting of the Assembly.

(2) In the case of an equality of votes, the person chairing the meeting of the Assembly shall have a second or casting vote.

(3) Subsections (1) and (2) above are subject to any provision to the contrary contained in this or any other enactment.

(4) The Assembly may determine its own procedure and that of its committees and sub-committees (including quorum).

(5) ★ ★ ★ ★ ★

54   Discharge of functions by committees or single members

(1) The Assembly may arrange for any of the functions exercisable by it to be discharged on its behalf—

(a) by a committee or sub-committee of the Assembly; or

(b) by a single member of the Assembly.

(2) The Assembly may arrange for a member of staff of the Authority appointed under section 67(2) below to exercise on the Assembly's behalf any function exercisable by the Assembly under section 67(2) or 70(2) below.

(3) Where by virtue of this section any functions exercisable by the Assembly may be discharged by a committee of the Assembly, then, unless the Assembly otherwise directs, the committee may arrange for the discharge of any of those functions by a sub-committee or by a single member of the Assembly.

(4) Where by virtue of this section any functions exercisable by the Assembly may be discharged by a sub-committee of the Assembly, then, unless the Assembly or the committee concerned otherwise directs, the sub-committee may arrange for the discharge of any of those functions by a single member of the Assembly.

(5)–(8) ★ ★ ★ ★ ★

55 Assembly committees and sub-committees

(1) For the purpose of discharging, in pursuance of arrangements under section 54(1)(a) above, any functions exercisable by the Assembly—

(a) the Assembly may appoint a committee of the Assembly (an "ordinary committee"); and

(b) an ordinary committee may appoint one or more sub-committees ("ordinary sub-committees").

(2) Subject to the provisions of this section—

(a) the number of members, and

(b) their term of office,

shall be fixed in the case of an ordinary committee by the Assembly or, in the case of an ordinary sub-committee, by the appointing committee.

(3) An ordinary committee or sub-committee must not include any person who is not an Assembly member.

(4) The Assembly may appoint one or more committees ("advisory committees") to advise it on any matter relating to the discharge of its functions.

(5) An advisory committee—

(a) may consist of such persons (whether Assembly members of not) appointed for such term as may be determined by the Assembly; and

(b) may appoint one or more sub-committees ("advisory sub-committees") to advise the committee with respect to any matter on which the committee has been appointed to advise.

56 Minutes

(1) Minutes of the proceedings of a meeting of the Assembly, or of any committee or sub-committee of the Assembly, shall be kept in such form as the Assembly may determine.

(2)–(5) ★ ★ ★ ★ ★

57 Political composition of Assembly committees

(1) Sections 15 to 17 of, and Schedule 1 to, the Local Government and Housing Act 1989 (political balance on committees etc.) shall have effect in relation to the Assembly, so far as relating to the appointment of members of its committees, as if the Assembly were a relevant authority and its ordinary committees and advisory committees were ordinary or, as the case may be, advisory committees within the meaning of those provisions (and accordingly bodies to which section 15 of that Act applies).

(2) In the case of any committee of the Assembly, the first appointment of members of the committee shall be an occasion on which the duty imposed by subsection (1) of section 15 of that Act arises in relation to the committee.

58 Openness

(1) Part VA of the Local Government Act 1972 (access to meetings and documents of certain authorities, committees and sub-committees) shall have effect as if–

(a) the Assembly were a principal council, and

(b) any committee or sub-committee of the Assembly were a committee or sub-committee of a principal council, within the meaning of that Part,

but with the following modifications.

(2)–(11) ★ ★ ★ ★ ★

59–65 ★ ★ ★ ★ ★

66 . . .

67–76 ★ ★ ★ ★ ★

Bills in Parliament

77   Power of Authority to promote or oppose Bills in Parliament

(1) The Authority may—

(a) promote a local Bill in Parliament for any purpose which is for the public benefit of the inhabitants of, or of any part of, Greater London; or

(b) oppose any local Bill in Parliament which affects any such inhabitants.

(2) Section 70 of the Local Government Act 1972 (prohibition on promoting Bills for changing local government areas etc.) shall have effect in relation to the Authority as it has effect in relation to a local authority.

(3) The functions conferred on the Authority by subsection (1) above shall be functions of the Authority which are exercisable by the Mayor acting on behalf of the Authority.

(4) The functions conferred on the Authority by subsection (1)(a) above are exercisable subject to, and in accordance with, the provisions of Schedule 5 to this Act.

(5) Before exercising the functions conferred on the Authority by subsection (1)(b) above, the Mayor shall consult the Assembly.

(6) No payment shall be made by the Authority (whether acting by the Mayor, the Assembly or the Mayor and Assembly acting jointly) to the Mayor or an Assembly member for acting as counsel or agent in promoting or opposing a Bill under this section.

(7) A London borough council or the Common Council may contribute towards the expenses of the Authority in promoting a local Bill in Parliament.

78   Power to request provisions in Bills promoted by London local authorities

(1) A local Bill promoted in Parliament by a London local authority may include provisions requested by the Authority.

(2) Subsection (1) above applies only if the Authority confirms the request in writing as soon as practicable after the expiration of 14 days after the Bill has been deposited in Parliament.

(3)–(9) ★ ★ ★ ★ ★

79   Authority's consent to inclusion of certain provisions in local Bills

(1) A local Bill promoted in Parliament by a London local authority may include provisions which affect the exercise of statutory functions by the Authority or any of the functional bodies.

(2) Subsection (1) above applies only if the Authority–

(a) gives its written consent; and

(b) confirms that consent in writing as soon as practicable after the expiration of 14 days after the Bill has been deposited in Parliament.

(3–(8)) ★ ★ ★ ★ ★

House of Lords Act 1999

(1999, c. 34)

An Act to restrict membership of the House of Lords by virtue of a hereditary peerage; to make related provision about disqualifications for voting at elections to and for membership of the House of Commons; and for connected purposes.   [11 November 1999]

Territorial extent: United Kingdom

1   Exclusion of hereditary peers

No-one shall be a member of the House of Lords by virtue of a hereditary peerage.

2 Exception from section 1

(1) Section 1 shall not apply in relation to anyone excepted from it by or in accordance with Standing Orders of the House.

(2) At any time 90 people shall be excepted from section 1; but anyone excepted as holder of the office of Earl Marshal, or as performing the office of Lord Great Chamberlain, shall not count towards that limit.

(3) Once excepted from section 1, a person shall continue to be so throughout his life (until an Act of Parliament provides to the contrary).

(4) Standing Orders shall make provision for filling vacancies among the people excepted from section 1; and in any case where—

    (a) the vacancy arises on a death occurring after the end of the first Session of the next Parliament after that in which this Act is passed, and

    (b) the deceased person was excepted in consequence of an election, that provision shall require the holding of a by-election.

(5) A person may be excepted from section 1 by or in accordance with Standing Orders made in anticipation of the enactment or commencement of this section.

(6) Any question whether a person is excepted from section 1 shall be decided by the Clerk of the Parliaments, whose certificate shall be conclusive.

3 Removal of disqualifications in relation to the House of Commons

(1) The holder of a hereditary peerage shall not be disqualified by virtue of that peerage for–

    (a) voting at elections to the House of Commons, or

    (b) being, or being elected as, a member of that House.

(2) Subsection (1) shall not apply in relation to anyone excepted from section 1 by virtue of section 2.

4 ★ ★ ★ ★ ★

5 Commencement and transitional provision

(1) Sections 1 to 4 (including Schedules 1 and 2) shall come into force at the end of the Session of Parliament in which this Act is passed.

(2) Accordingly, any writ of summons issued for the present Parliament in right of a hereditary peerage shall not have effect after that Session unless it has been issued to a person who, at the end of the Session, is excepted from section 1 by virtue of section 2.

6 Interpretation and short title

(1) In this Act "hereditary peerage" includes the principality of Wales and the earldom of Chester.

(2) This Act may be cited as the House of Lords Act 1999.

Immigration and Asylum Act 1999
(1999, c. 33)

An Act to make provision about immigration and asylum; to make provision about procedures in connection with marriage on superintendent registrar's certificate; and for connected purposes.
[11 November 1999]

Territorial extent: United Kingdom

★ ★ ★ ★ ★

10 Removal of certain persons unlawfully in the United Kingdom

(1) A person who is not a British citizen may be removed from the United Kingdom, in

accordance with directions given by an immigration officer, if—

   (a) having only a limited leave to enter or remain, he does not observe a condition attached to the leave or remains beyond the time limited by the leave;

   (b) he has obtained leave to remain by deception; or

   (c) directions ("the first directions") have been given for the removal, under this section, of a person ("the other person") to whose family he belongs.

(2) Directions may not be given under subsection (1)(a) if the person concerned has made an application for leave to remain in accordance with regulations made under section 9.

(3) Directions may not be given under subsection (1)(c) unless the Secretary of State has given the person concerned written notice, not more than eight weeks after the other person left the United Kingdom in accordance with the first directions, that he intends to remove the person concerned from the United Kingdom.

(4) If such a notice is sent by the Secretary of State by first class post, addressed to the person concerned's last known address, it is to be taken to have been received by that person on the second day after the day on which it was posted.

(5) Directions for the removal of a person under subsection (1)(c) cease to have effect if he ceases to belong to the family of the other person.

(6)–(9) ★ ★ ★ ★ ★

11 Removal of asylum claimants under standing arrangements with Member States

(1) In determining whether a person in relation to whom a certificate has been issued under subsection (2) may be removed from the United Kingdom, a member State is to be regarded as—

   (a) a place where a person's life and liberty is not threatened by reason of his race, religion, nationality, membership of a particular social group, or political opinion; and

   (b) a place from which a person will not be sent to another country otherwise than in accordance with the Refugee Convention.

(2) Nothing in section 15 prevents a person who has made a claim for asylum ("the claimant") from being removed from the United Kingdom to a Member State if—

   (a) the Secretary of State has certified that—

      (i) the Member State has accepted that, under standing arrangements, it is the responsible State in relation to the claimant's claim for asylum; and

      (ii) in his opinion, the claimant is not a national or citizen of the Member State to which he is to be sent;

   (b) the certificate has not been set aside on an appeal under section 65.

(3), (4) ★ ★ ★ ★ ★

12–14 ★ ★ ★ ★ ★

15 Protection of claimants from removal or deportation

(1) During the period beginning when a person makes a claim for asylum and ending when the Secretary of State gives him notice of the decision on the claim, he may not be removed from, or required to leave, the United Kingdom.

(2) Subsection (1) does not prevent–

   (a) directions for his removal being given during that period;

   (b) a deportation order being made against him during that period.

(3) But no such direction or order is to have effect during that period.

(4) This section is to be treated as having come into force on 26 July 1993.

16–31 ★ ★ ★ ★ ★

PART II   CARRIERS' LIABILITY

Clandestine entrants

32   Penalty for carrying clandestine entrants

(1) A person is a clandestine entrant if—

(a) he arrives in the United Kingdom concealed in a vehicle, ship or aircraft,

(b) he passes, or attempts to pass, through immigration control concealed in a vehicle, or

(c) he arrives in the United Kingdom on a ship or aircraft, having embarked—

(i) concealed in a vehicle; and

(ii) at a time when the ship or aircraft was outside the United Kingdom, and claims, or indicated that he intends to seek, asylum in the United Kingdom or evades, or attempts to evade, immigration control.

(2) The person (or persons) responsible for a clandestine entrant is (or are together) liable to—

(a) a penalty of the prescribed amount in respect of the clandestine entrant; and

(b) an additional penalty of that amount in respect of each person who was concealed with the clandestine entrant in the same [rail freight wagon].

(3) A penalty imposed under this section must be paid to the Secretary of State before the end of the prescribed period.

(4) Payment of the full amount of a penalty by one or more of the persons responsible for the clandestine entrant discharges the liability of each of the persons responsible for that entrant.

[(5) Each of the following persons is responsible for a clandestine entrant who arrives in the United Kingdom concealed in a train–

(a) the railway operator who, at its last scheduled stop before arrival in the United Kingdom, had the duty of certifying the train as fit to travel to the United Kingdom;

(b) any other railway operator who has entered into an arrangement with that operator under which they share profits or liabilities arising from that train's journey from the last scheduled stop into the United Kingdom.]

(6) In the case of a clandestine entrant to whom subsection (1)(b) or (c) applies, each of the following is a responsible person—

(a) if the transporter is a detached trailer, the owner, hirer or operator of the trailer;

(b) if it is not, the owner, hirer or driver of the vehicle.

(7) Subject to any defence provided by section 34, it is immaterial whether a responsible person knew or suspected—

(a) that the clandestine entrant was concealed in the [rail freight wagon]; or

(b) that there were one or more other persons concealed with the clandestine entrant in the same [rail freight wagon].

(8) Subsection (9) applies if a transporter ("the carried transporter") is itself being carried in or on another transporter.

(9) If a person is concealed in the carried transporter, the question whether any other person is concealed with that person in the same transporter is to be determined by reference to the carried transporter and not by reference to the transporter in or on which it is carried.

(10) "Immigration control" means United Kingdom immigration control and includes any United Kingdom immigration control operated in a prescribed control zone outside the United Kingdom.

33 ★ ★ ★ ★ ★

34   Defences to claim that penalty is due under section 32

(1) This section applies if it is alleged that a person ("the carrier") is liable to a penalty under section 32.

(2) It is a defence for the carrier to show that he, or an employee of his who was directly responsible for allowing the clandestine entrant to be concealed, was acting under duress.

(3) It is also a defence for the carrier to show that—

  (a) he did not know, and had no reasonable grounds for suspecting, that a clandestine entrant was, or might be, concealed in the [rail freight wagon];

  (b) an effective system for preventing the carriage of clandestine entrants was in operation in relation to the [rail freight wagon]; and

  (c) that on the occasion in question the person or persons responsible for operating that system did so properly.

(4) In determining, for the purposes of this section, whether a particular system is effective, regard is to be had to the code of practice issued by the Secretary of State under section 33.

(5) If there are two or more persons responsible for a clandestine entrant, the fact that one or more of them has a defence under subsection (3) does not affect the liability of the others.

(6) But if a person responsible for a clandestine entrant has a defence under subsection (2), the liability of any other person responsible for that entrant is discharged.

35   Procedure

(1) If the Secretary of State decides that a person ("P") is liable to one or more penalties under section 32, he must notify P of his decision.

(2) A notice under subsection (1) (a "penalty notice") must—

  (a) state the Secretary of State's reasons for deciding that P is liable to the penalty (or penalties);

  (b) state the amount of the penalty (or penalties) to which P is liable;

  (c) specify the date before which, and the manner in which, the penalty (or penalties) must be paid; and

  (d) include an explanation of the steps–

   (i) that P must take if he objects to the penalty;

   (ii) that the Secretary of State may take under this Part to recover any unpaid penalty.

(3) Subsection (4) applies if more than one person is responsible for a clandestine entrant.

(4) If a penalty notice is served on one of the responsible persons, the Secretary of State is to be taken to have served the required penalty notice on each of them.

(5) The Secretary of State must nevertheless take reasonable steps, while the penalty remains unpaid, to secure that the penalty notice is actually served on each of those responsible persons.

(6) If a person on whom a penalty notice is served, . . . alleges that he is not liable for one or more, or all, of the penalties specified in the penalty notice, he may give written notice of his allegation to the Secretary of State.

(7) Notice under subsection (6) ("a notice of objection") must—

  (a) give reasons for the allegation; and

  (b) be given before the end of such period as may be prescribed.

(8) If a notice of objection is given before the end of the prescribed period, the Secretary of State must consider it and determine whether or not any penalty to which it relates is payable.

(9) The Secretary of State may by regulations provide, in relation to detached trailers, for a penalty notice which is served in such manner as may be prescribed to have effect as a penalty notice properly served on the responsible person or persons concerned under this section.

(10) Any sum payable to the Secretary of State as a penalty under section 32 may be recovered by the Secretary of State as a debt due to him.

36   Power to detain vehicles etc. in connection with penalties under section 32

(1) If a penalty notice has been given under section 35, a senior officer may detain any relevant [transporter] until all penalties to which the notice relates, and any expenses reasonably incurred by the Secretary of State in connection with the detention, have been paid.

[(1A) For those purposes "transporter" means the rail freight wagon in which the clandestine entrant arrived in the United Kingdom.]

(2) That power—

    (a) may be exercised only if, in the opinion of the senior officer concerned, there is a significant risk that the penalty (or one or more of the penalties) will not be paid before the end of the prescribed period if the transporter is not detained; and

    (b) may not be exercised if alternative security which the Secretary of State considers is satisfactory, has been given.

(3) If a transporter is detained under this section, the owner, consignor or any other person who has an interest in any freight or other thing carried in or on the transporter may remove it, or arrange for it to be removed, at such time and in such way as is reasonable.

(4) The detention of a transporter under this section is lawful even though it is subsequently established that the penalty notice on which the detention was based was ill-founded in respect of all or any of the penalties to which it related.

(5) But subsection (4) does not apply if the Secretary of State was acting unreasonably in issuing the penalty notice.

37–39 ★ ★ ★ ★ ★

Passengers without proper documents

40   Charges in respect of passengers without proper documents

(1) This section applies if a person requiring leave to enter the United Kingdom arrives in the United Kingdom by ship, aircraft, road passenger vehicle or train and, on being required to do so by an immigration officer, fails to produce—

    (a) a valid passport with photograph or some other document satisfactorily establishing his identity and nationality or citizenship; and

    (b) if he requires a visa, a valid visa of the required kind.

(2) The Secretary of State may charge the owner of the ship, aircraft or vehicle or the train operator, in respect of that person, the sum of £2,000 or such other sum as may be prescribed.

(3) The charge is payable to the Secretary of State on demand.

(4) No charge is payable in respect of any person who is shown by the owner or train operator to have produced the required document or documents to him or his representative when embarking—

    (a) on the ship or aircraft for the voyage or flight to the United Kingdom; or

    (b) on the vehicle or train for the journey to the United Kingdom.

41–58 ★ ★ ★ ★ ★

59   Leave to enter the United Kingdom

(1) A person who is refused leave to enter the United Kingdom under any provision of the 1971 Act may appeal to an adjudicator against—

    (a) the decision that he requires leave; or

    (b) the refusal.

(2) A person who, on an application duly made, is refused a certificate of entitlement or an entry clearance may appeal to an adjudicator against the refusal.

(3) Subsection (4) applies if a person appeals under this section on being refused leave to enter the United Kingdom and—

    (a) before he appeals, directions have been given for his removal from the United Kingdom; or

(b) before or after he appeals, the Secretary of State or an immigration officer serves on him notice that any directions which may be given for his removal as a result of the refusal will be for his removal to a country or one of several countries specified in the notice.

(4) The appellant may—

(a) object to the country to which he would be removed in accordance with the directions, or

(b) object to the country specified in the notice (or to one or more of those specified), and claim that he ought to be removed (if at all) to a different country specified by him.

60   Limitations on rights of appeal under section 59

(1) Section 59 does not entitle a person to appeal, on the ground that he has a right of abode in the United Kingdom, against a decision that he requires leave to enter the United Kingdom if he does not hold—

(a) a United Kingdom passport describing him as a British citizen or as a citizen of the United Kingdom and Colonies having the right of abode in the United Kingdom; or

(b) a certificate of entitlement.

(2) Section 59 does not entitle a person to appeal, on the ground that he does not require leave to enter the United Kingdom, against a decision that he does require such leave if he is required by immigration rules or an order under section 8(2) of the 1971 Act to hold a specified document but does not do so.

(3) Section 59 does not entitle a person to appeal against a refusal of leave to enter while he is in the United Kingdom unless, at the time of the refusal, he held a current entry clearance or was a person named in a current work permit.

(4) Subsection (5) applies to a person who seeks to enter the United Kingdom—

(a) as a visitor;

(b) in order to follow a course of study of not more than six months' duration for which he has been accepted;

(c) with the intention of studying but without having been accepted for any course of study; or

(d) as a dependant of a person within paragraph (a), (b) or (c).

(5) That person—

(a) is not entitled to appeal under section 59 against a refusal of an entry clearance unless he is a family visitor; and

(b) is not entitled to appeal against a refusal of leave to enter if he does not hold a current entry clearance at the time of the refusal.

(6)–(8) ★ ★ ★ ★ ★

(9) Section 59 does not entitle a person to appeal against a refusal of leave to enter, or against a refusal of an entry clearance, if—

(a) the Secretary of State certifies that directions have been given by the Secretary of State (and not by a person acting under his authority) for the appellant not to be given entry to the United Kingdom on the ground that his exclusion is conducive to the public good; or

(b) the leave to enter, or entry clearance, was refused in compliance with any such directions.

(10) "Family visitor" has such meaning as may be prescribed.

61, 62 ★ ★ ★ ★ ★

Deportation

63   Deportation orders

(1) A person may appeal to an adjudicator against—

(a) a decision of the Secretary of State to make a deportation order against him under section 5(1) of the 1971 Act as a result of his liability to deportation under section 3(5) of that Act; or

(b) a refusal by the Secretary of State to revoke a deportation order made against him.

(2) A deportation order is not to be made against a person under section 5(1) of the 1971 Act while an appeal may be brought against the decision to make it.

(3) Subsection (4) applies if—

(a) a person appeals under this section; and

(b) before or after he appeals, the Secretary of State serves on him notice that any directions which may be given for his removal as a result of the deportation order will be for his removal to a country or one of several countries specified in the notice.

(4) The appellant may object to the country specified in the notice (or to one or more of those specified), and claim that he ought to be removed (if at all) to a different country specified by him.

64   Limitations on rights of appeal under section 63

(1) Section 63 does not entitle a person to appeal against a decision to make a deportation order against him if the ground of the decision was that his deportation is conducive to the public good as being in the interests of national security or of the relations between the United Kingdom and any other country or for other reasons of a political nature.

(2) Section 63 does not entitle a person to appeal against a refusal to revoke a deportation order, if—

(a) the Secretary of State has certified that the appellant's exclusion from the United Kingdom would be conducive to the public good; or

(b) revocation was refused on that ground by the Secretary of State (and not by a person acting under his authority).

(3) Section 63 does not entitle a person to appeal against a refusal to revoke a deportation order while he is in the United Kingdom, whether because he has not complied with the requirement to leave or because he has contravened the prohibition on entering.

(4) Subsection (5) applies to—

(a) an appeal against a decision to make a deportation order against a person as belonging to the family of another person; or

(b) an appeal against a refusal to revoke a deportation order so made.

(5) The appellant is not to be allowed, for the purpose of showing that he does not or did not belong to another person's family, to dispute any statement made with a view to obtaining leave for the appellant to enter or remain in the United Kingdom (including any statement made to obtain an entry clearance).

(6) But subsection (5) does not apply if the appellant shows—

(a) that the statement was not so made by him or by any person acting with his authority; and

(b) that, when he took the benefit of the leave, he did not know any such statement had been made to obtain it or, if he did know, he was under the age of eighteen.

Human rights

65   Acts made unlawful by section 6(1) of the Human Rights Act 1998

(1) A person who alleges that an authority has, in taking any decision under the Immigration Acts relating to that person's entitlement to enter or remain in the United Kingdom, [racially discriminated against him or] acted in breach of his human rights may appeal to an adjudicator against that decision unless he has grounds for bringing an appeal against the decision under the Special Immigration Appeals Commission Act 1997.

(2) For the purposes of this Part,

[(a) an authority racially discriminates against a person if he acts, or fails to act, in relation to that other person in a way which is unlawful by virtue of section 19B of the Race Relations Act 1976; and

(b)] an authority acts in breach of a person's human rights if he acts, or fails to act, in relation to that other person in a way which is made unlawful by section 6(1) of the Human Rights Act 1998.

(3) Subsections (4) and (5) apply if, in proceedings before an adjudicator or the Immigration Appeal Tribunal on an appeal, a question arises as to whether an authority has, in taking any decision under the Immigration Acts relating to the appellant's entitlement to enter or remain in the United Kingdom [racially discriminated against him or], acted in breach of the appellant's human rights.

(4) The adjudicator, or the Tribunal, has jurisdiction to consider the question.

(5) If the adjudicator, or the Tribunal, decides that the authority concerned

[(a) racially discriminated against the appellant; or

(b)] acted in breach of the appellant's human rights, the appeal may be allowed on [the ground in question.]

★ ★ ★ ★ ★

Local Government Act 1999
(1999, c. 27)

An Act to make provision imposing on local and certain other authorities requirements relating to economy, efficiency and effectiveness; and to make provision for the regulation of council tax and precepts. [27 July 1999]

Territorial extent: England and Wales (subject to certain modifications in Wales)

PART I   BEST VALUE

Best value authorities

1   Best value authorities

(1) For the purposes of this Part each of these is a best value authority—

(a) a local authority;

(b) a National Park authority;

(c) the Broads Authority;

(d) a police authority;

(e) a fire authority constituted by a combination scheme and a metropolitan county fire and civil defence authority;

(f) the London Fire and Emergency Planning Authority;

(g) a waste disposal authority;

(h) a metropolitan county passenger transport authority;

(i) Transport for London;

(j) the London Development Agency.

(2) In relation to England "local authority" in subsection (1)(a) means—

(a) a county council, a district council, a London borough council, a parish council or a parish meeting of a parish which does not have a separate parish council;

(b) the Council of the Isles of Scilly;

(c) the Common Council of the City of London in its capacity as a local authority;

(d) the Greater London Authority so far as it exercises its functions through the Mayor.

(3) In relation to Wales "local authority" in subsection (1)(a) means a county council, a county borough council or a community council.

(4) In subsection (1)(d) "police authority" means—
  (a) a police authority established under section 3 of the Police Act 1996;
  (b) the Common Council of the City of London in its capacity as a police authority;
  (c) The Metropolitan Police Authority.

(5) In subsection (1)(g) "waste disposal authority" means an authority which—
  (a) is a waste disposal authority for the purposes of Part II of the Environmental Protection Act 1990, or
  (b) is established under section 10 of the Local Government Act 1985 (joint arrangements).

2 ★ ★ ★ ★ ★

Duties

3 The general duty

(1) A best value authority must make arrangements to secure continuous improvement in the way in which its functions are exercised, having regard to a combination of economy, efficiency and effectiveness.

(2) For the purpose of deciding how to fulfil the duty arising under subsection (1) an authority must consult—
  (a) representatives of persons liable to pay any tax, precept or levy to or in respect of the authority,
  (b) representatives of persons liable to pay non-domestic rates in respect of any area within which the authority carries out functions,
  (c) representatives of persons who use or are likely to use services provided by the authority, and
  (d) representatives of persons appearing to the authority to have an interest in any area within which the authority carries out functions.

(3) For the purposes of subsection (2) "representatives" in relation to a group of persons means persons who appear to the authority to be representative of that group.

(4) In deciding on—
  (a) the persons to be consulted, and
  (b) the form, content and timing of consultations, an authority must have regard to any guidance issued by the Secretary of State.

4 Performance indicators and standards

(1) The Secretary of State may by order specify—
  (a) factors ("performance indicators") by reference to which a best value authority's performance in exercising functions can be measured;
  (b) standards ("performance standards") to be met by best value authorities in relation to performance indicators specified under paragraph (a).

(2) An order may specify different performance indicators or standards—
  (a) for different functions;
  (b) for different authorities;
  (c) to apply at different times.

(3) Before specifying performance indicators or standards the Secretary of State shall consult—
  (a) persons appearing to him to represent the best value authorities concerned, and

(b) such other persons (if any) as he thinks fit.

(4) In specifying performance indicators and standards, and in deciding whether to do so, the Secretary of State—

(a) shall aim to promote improvement of the way in which the functions of best value authorities are exercised, having regard to a combination of economy, efficiency and effectiveness, and

(b) shall have regard to any recommendations made to him by the Audit Commission.

(5) In exercising a function a best value authority must meet any applicable performance standard specified under subsection (1)(b).

★ ★ ★ ★ ★

Youth Justice and Criminal Evidence Act 1999
(1999, c. 23)

An Act to provide for the referral of offenders under 18 to youth offender panels; to make provision in connection with the giving of evidence or information for the purposes of criminal proceedings; to amend section 51 of the Criminal Justice and Public Order Act 1994; to make pre-consolidation amendments relating to youth justice; and for connected purposes.   [27 July 1999]

Territorial extent: England and Wales and, in relation to service courts, to Scotland, but the provisions of Part II Chapter IV extend also to Scotland and Northern Ireland

★ ★ ★ ★ ★

PART II   GIVING OF EVIDENCE OR INFORMATION FOR PURPOSES OF CRIMINAL PROCEEDINGS

CHAPTER I   SPECIAL MEASURES DIRECTIONS IN CASE OF VULNERABLE AND INTIMIDATED WITNESSES

Preliminary

16   Witnesses eligible for assistance on grounds of age or incapacity

(1) For the purposes of this Chapter a witness in criminal proceedings (other than the accused) is eligible for assistance by virtue of this section—

(a) if under the age of 17 at the time of the hearing; or

(b) if the court considers that the quality of evidence given by the witness is likely to be diminished by reason of any circumstances falling within subsection (2).

(2) The circumstances falling within this subsection are—

(a) that the witness—

(i) suffers from mental disorder within the meaning of the Mental Health Act 1983, or

(ii) otherwise has a significant impairment of intelligence and social functioning;

(b) that the witness has a physical disability or is suffering from a physical disorder.

(3) In subsection (1)(a) "the time of the hearing", in relation to a witness, means the time when it falls to the court to make a determination for the purposes of section 19(2) in relation to the witness.

(4) In determining whether a witness falls within subsection (1)(b) the court must consider any views expressed by the witness.

(5) In this Chapter references to the quality of a witness's evidence are to its quality in terms of completeness, coherence and accuracy; and for this purpose "coherence" refers to a witness's ability in giving evidence to give answers which address the questions put to the witness and can be understood both individually and collectively.

17   Witnesses eligible for assistance on grounds of fear or distress about testifying

(1) For the purposes of this Chapter a witness in criminal proceedings (other than the accused) is eligible for assistance by virtue of this subsection if the court is satisfied that the quality of evidence given by the witness is likely to be diminished by reason of fear or distress on the part of the witness in connection with testifying in the proceedings.

(2) In determining whether a witness falls within subsection (1) the court must take into account, in particular—

    (a) the nature and alleged circumstances of the offence to which the proceedings relate;

    (b) the age of the witness;

    (c) such of the following matters as appear to the court to be relevant, namely—

        (i)   the social and cultural background and ethnic origins of the witness,

        (ii) the domestic and employment circumstances of the witness, and

        (iii) any religious beliefs or political opinions of the witness;

    (d) any behaviour towards the witness on the part of—

        (i)   the accused,

        (ii) members of the family or associates of the accused, or

        (iii) any other person who is likely to be an accused or a witness in the proceedings.

(3) In determining that question the court must in addition consider any views expressed by the witness.

(4) Where the complainant in respect of a sexual offence is a witness in proceedings relating to that offence (or to that offence and any other offences), the witness is eligible for assistance in relation to those proceedings by virtue of this subsection unless the witness has informed the court of the witness's wish not to be so eligible by virtue of this subsection.

18   ★ ★ ★ ★ ★

Special measures directions

19   Special measures direction relating to eligible witness

(1) This section applies where in any criminal proceedings—

    (a) a party to the proceedings makes an application for the court to give a direction under this section in relation to a witness in the proceedings other than the accused, or

    (b) the court of its own motion raises the issue whether such a direction should be given.

(2) Where the court determines that the witness is eligible for assistance by virtue of section 16 or 17, the court must then—

    (a) determine whether any of the special measures available in relation to the witness (or any combination of them) would, in its opinion, be likely to improve the quality of evidence given by the witness; and

    (b) if so—

        (i)   determine which of those measures (or combination of them) would, in its opinion, be likely to maximise so far as practicable the quality of such evidence; and

        (ii) give a direction under this section providing for the measure or measures so determined to apply to evidence given by the witness.

(3) In determining for the purposes of this Chapter whether any special measure or measures would or would not be likely to improve, or to maximise so far as practicable, the quality of evidence given by the witness, the court must consider all the circumstances of the case, including in particular—

    (a) any views expressed by the witness; and

    (b) whether the measure or measures might tend to inhibit such evidence being effectively tested by a party to the proceedings.

(4) A special measures direction must specify particulars of the provision made by the direction in respect of each special measure which is to apply to the witness's evidence.

(5), (6) ★ ★ ★ ★ ★

20 Further provisions about directions: general

(1) Subject to subsection (2) and section 21(8), a special measures direction has binding effect from the time it is made until the proceedings for the purposes of which it is made are either—

    (a) determined (by acquittal, conviction or otherwise), or

    (b) abandoned,

in relation to the accused or (if there is more than one) in relation to each of the accused.

(2) The court may discharge or vary (or further vary) a special measures direction if it appears to the court to be in the interests of justice to do so, and may do so either—

    (a) on an application made by a party to the proceedings, if there has been a material change of circumstances since the relevant time, or

    (b) of its own motion.

(3)–(6) ★ ★ ★ ★ ★

21, 22 ★ ★ ★ ★ ★

Special measures

23 Screening witness from accused

(1) A special measures direction may provide for the witness, while giving testimony or being sworn in court, to be prevented by means of a screen or other arrangement from seeing the accused.

(2) But the screen or other arrangement must not prevent the witness from being able to see, and to be seen by—

    (a) the judge or justices (or both) and the jury (if there is one);

    (b) legal representatives acting in the proceedings; and

    (c) any interpreter or other person appointed (in pursuance of the direction or otherwise) to assist the witness.

(3) ★ ★ ★ ★ ★

24 Evidence by live link

(1) A special measures direction may provide for the witness to give evidence by means of a live link.

(2) Where a direction provides for the witness to give evidence by means of a live link, the witness may not give evidence in any other way without the permission of the court.

(3) The court may give permission for the purposes of subsection (2) if it appears to the court to be in the interests of justice to do so, and may do so either—

    (a) on an application by a party to the proceedings, if there has been a material change of circumstances since the relevant time, or

    (b) of its own motion.

(4)–(8) ★ ★ ★ ★ ★

25 Evidence given in private

(1) A special measures direction may provide for the exclusion from the court, during the giving of the witness's evidence, of persons of any description specified in the direction.

(2) The persons who may be so excluded do not include—

(a) the accused,

(b) legal representatives acting in the proceedings, or

(c) any interpreter or other person appointed (in pursuance of the direction or otherwise) to assist the witness.

(3) A special measures direction providing for representatives of news gathering or reporting organisations to be so excluded shall be expressed not to apply to one named person who—

(a) is a representative of such an organisation, and

(b) has been nominated for the purpose by one or more such organisations, unless it appears to the court that no such nomination has been made.

(4) A special measures direction may only provide for the exclusion of persons under this section where—

(a) the proceedings relate to a sexual offence; or

(b) it appears to the court that there are reasonable grounds for believing that any person other than the accused has sought, or will seek, to intimidate the witness in connection with testifying in the proceedings.

(5) Any proceedings from which persons are excluded under this section (whether or not those persons include representatives of news gathering or reporting organisations) shall nevertheless be taken to be held in public for the purposes of any privilege or exemption from liability available in respect of fair, accurate and contemporaneous reports of legal proceedings held in public.

26-31 ★ ★ ★ ★ ★

Supplementary

32 Warning to jury

Where on a trial on indictment evidence has been given in accordance with a special measures direction, the judge must give the jury such warning (if any) as the judge considers necessary to ensure that the fact that the direction was given in relation to the witness does not prejudice the accused.

33 ★ ★ ★ ★ ★

CHAPTER II PROTECTION OF WITNESSES FROM CROSS-EXAMINATION BY ACCUSED IN PERSON

General prohibitions

34 Complainants in proceedings for sexual offences

No person charged with a sexual offence may in any criminal proceedings cross-examine in person a witness who is the complainant, either—

(a) in connection with that offence, or

(b) in connection with any other offence (of whatever nature) with which that person is charged in the proceedings.

35 ★ ★ ★ ★ ★

Prohibition imposed by court

36 Direction prohibiting accused from cross-examining particular witness

(1) This section applies where, in a case where neither of sections 34 and 35 operates

to prevent an accused in any criminal proceedings from cross-examining a witness in person—

   (a) the prosecutor makes an application for the court to give a direction under this section in relation to the witness, or

   (b) the court of its own motion raises the issue whether such a direction should be given.

(2) If it appears to the court—

   (a) that the quality of evidence given by the witness on cross-examination—

      (i) is likely to be diminished if the cross-examination (or further cross-examination (or further cross-examination) is conducted by the accused in person, and

      (ii) would be likely to be improved if a direction were given under this section, and

   (b) that it would not be contrary to the interests of justice to give such a direction, the court may give a direction prohibiting the accused from cross-examining (or further cross-examining) the witness in person.

(3) In determining whether subsection (2)(a) applies in the case of a witness the court must have regard, in particular, to—

   (a) any views expressed by the witness as to whether or not the witness is content to be cross-examined by the accused in person;

   (b) the nature of the questions likely to be asked, having regard to the issues in the proceedings and the defence case advanced so far (if any);

   (c) any behaviour on the part of the accused at any stage of the proceedings, both generally and in relation to the witness;

   (d) any relationship (of whatever nature) between the witness and the accused;

   (e) whether any person (other than the accused) is or has at any time been charged in the proceedings with a sexual offence or an offence to which section 35 applies, and (if so) whether section 34 or 35 operates or would have operated to prevent that person from cross-examining the witness in person;

   (f) any direction under section 19 which the court has given, or proposes to give, in relation to the witness.

(4) For the purposes of this section—

   (a) "witness", in relation to an accused, does not include any other person who is charged with an offence in the proceedings; and

   (b) any reference to the quality of a witness's evidence shall be construed in accordance with section 16(5).

37 ★ ★ ★ ★ ★

Cross-examination on behalf of accused

38 Defence representation for purposes of cross-examination

(1) This section applies where an accused is prevented from cross-examining a witness in person by virtue of section 34, 35 or 36.

(2) Where it appears to the court that this section applies, it must—

   (a) invite the accused to arrange for a legal representative to act for him for the purpose of cross-examining the witness; and

   (b) require the accused to notify the court, by the end of such period as it may specify, whether a legal representative is to act for him for that purpose.

(3) If by the end of the period mentioned in subsection (2)(b) either—

   (a) the accused has notified the court that no legal representative is to act for him for the purpose of cross-examining the witness, or

(b) no notification has been received by the court and it appears to the court that no legal representative is to so act,

the court must consider whether it is necessary in the interests of justice for the witness to be cross-examined by a legal representative appointed to represent the interests of the accused.

(4) If the court decides that it is necessary in the interests of justice for the witness to be so cross-examined, the court must appoint a qualified legal representative (chosen by the court) to cross-examine the witness in the interests of the accused.

(5) A person so appointed shall not be responsible to the accused.

(6)–(8) ★ ★ ★ ★ ★

39 Warning to jury

(1) Where on a trial on indictment an accused is prevented from cross-examining a witness in person by virtue of section 34, 35 or 36, the judge must give the jury such warning (if any) as the judge considers necessary to ensure that the accused is not prejudiced—

(a) by any inferences that might be drawn from the fact that the accused has been prevented from cross-examining the witness in person;

(b) where the witness has been cross-examined by a legal representative appointed under section 38(4), by the fact that the cross-examination was carried out, by such a legal representative and not by a person acting as the accused's own legal representative.

(2) Subsection (8)(a) of section 38 applies for the purposes of this section as it applies for the purposes of section 38.

40 ★ ★ ★ ★ ★

CHAPTER III   PROTECTION OF COMPLAINANTS IN PROCEEDINGS
FOR SEXUAL OFFENCES

41 Restriction on evidence or questions about complainant's sexual history

(1) If at a trial a person is charged with a sexual offence, then, except with the leave of the court—

(a) no evidence may be adduced, and

(b) no question may be asked in cross-examination,

by or on behalf of any accused at the trial, about any sexual behaviour of the complainant.

(2) The court may give leave in relation to any evidence or question only on an application made by or on behalf of an accused, and may not give such leave unless it is satisfied—

(a) that subsection (3) or (5) applies, and

(b) that a refusal of leave might have the result of rendering unsafe a conclusion of the jury or (as the case may be) the court on any relevant issue in the case.

(3) This subsection applies if the evidence or question relates to a relevant issue in the case and either—

(a) that issue is not an issue of consent; or

(b) it is an issue of consent and the sexual behaviour of the complainant to which the evidence or question relates is alleged to have taken place at or about the same time as the event which is the subject matter of the charge against the accused; or

(c) it is an issue of consent and the sexual behaviour of the complainant to which the evidence or question relates is alleged to have been, in any respect, so similar—

(i) to any sexual behaviour of the complainant which (according to evidence adduced or to be adduced by or on behalf of the accused) took place as part of the event which is the subject matter of the charge against the accused, or

(ii) to any other sexual behaviour of the complainant which (according to such evidence) took place at or about the same time as that event,

that the similarity cannot reasonably be explained as a coincidence.

(4) For the purposes of subsection (3) no evidence or question shall be regarded as relating

to a relevant issue in the case if it appears to the court to be reasonable to assume that the purpose (or main purpose) for which it would be adduced or asked is to establish or elicit material for impugning the credibility of the complainant as a witness.

(5) This subsection applies if the evidence or question—

(a) relates to any evidence adduced by the prosecution about any sexual behaviour of the complainant; and

(b) in the opinion of the court, would go no further than is necessary to enable the evidence adduced by the prosecution to be rebutted or explained by or on behalf of the accused.

(6) For the purposes of subsections (3) and (5) the evidence or question must relate to a specific instance (or specific instances) of alleged sexual behaviour on the part of the complainant (and accordingly nothing in those subsections is capable of applying in relation to the evidence or question to the extent that it does not so relate).

(7), (8) ★ ★ ★ ★ ★

42, 43 ★ ★ ★ ★ ★

CHAPTER IV   REPORTING RESTRICTIONS

Reports relating to persons under 18

44   Restrictions on reporting alleged offences involving persons under 18

(1) This section applies (subject to subsection (3)) where a criminal investigation has begun in respect of—

(a) an alleged offence against the law of—

(i)   England and Wales, or

(ii) Northern Ireland; or

(b) an alleged civil offence (other than an offence falling within paragraph (a)) committed (whether or not in the United Kingdom) by a person subject to service law.

(2) No matter relating to any person involved in the offence shall while he is under the age of 18 be included in any publication if it is likely to lead members of the public to identify him as a person involved in the offence.

(3) The restrictions imposed by subsection (2) cease to apply once there are proceedings in a court (whether a court in England and Wales, a service court or a court in Northern Ireland) in respect of the offence.

(4) For the purposes of subsection (2) any reference to a person involved in the offence is to—

(a) a person by whom the offence is alleged to have been committed; or

(b) if this paragraph applies to the publication in question by virtue of subsection (5)—

(i)   a person against or in respect of whom the offence is alleged to have been committed, or

(ii) a person who is alleged to have been a witness to the commission of the offence;

except that paragraph (b)(i) does not include a person in relation to whom section 1 of the Sexual Offences (Amendment) Act 1992 (anonymity of victims of certain sexual offences) applies in connection with the offence.

(5)–(13) ★ ★ ★ ★ ★

45   Power to restrict reporting of criminal proceedings involving persons under 18

(1) This section applies (subject to subsection (2)) in relation to—

(a) any criminal proceedings in any court (other than a service court) in England and Wales or Northern Ireland; and

(b) any proceedings (whether in the United Kingdom or elsewhere) in any service court.

(2) This section does not apply in relation to any proceedings to which section 49 of the Children and Young Persons Act 1933 applies.

(3) The court may direct that no matter relating to any person concerned in the proceedings shall while he is under the age of 18 be included in any publication if it is likely to lead members of the public to identify him as a person concerned in the proceedings.

(4) The court or an appellate court may by direction ("an excepting direction") dispense, to any extent specified in the excepting direction, with the restrictions imposed by a direction under subsection (3) if it is satisfied that it is necessary in the interests of justice to do so.

(5) The court or an appellate court may also by direction ("an excepting direction") dispense, to any extent specified in the excepting direction, with the restrictions imposed by a direction under subsection (3) if it is satisfied—

    (a) that their effect is to impose a substantial and unreasonable restriction on the reporting of the proceedings, and

    (b) that it is in the public interest to remove or relax that restriction; but no excepting direction shall be given under this subsection by reason only of the fact that the proceedings have been determined in any way or have been abandoned.

    (6)–(11) ★ ★ ★ ★ ★

Reports relating to adult witnesses

46 Power to restrict reports about certain adult witnesses in criminal proceedings

(1) This section applies where—

    (a) in any criminal proceedings in any court (other than a service court) in England and Wales or Northern Ireland, or

    (b) in any proceedings (whether in the United Kingdom or elsewhere) in any service court,

a party to the proceedings makes an application for the court to give a reporting direction in relation to a witness in the proceedings (other than the accused) who has attained the age of 18.

In this section "reporting direction" has the meaning given by subsection (6).

(2) If the court determines—

    (a) that the witness is eligible for protection, and

    (b) that giving a reporting direction in relation to the witness is likely to improve—

        (i) the quality of evidence given by the witness, or

        (ii) the level of co-operation given by the witness to any party to the proceedings in connection with that party's preparation of its case,

the court may give a reporting direction in relation to the witness.

(3) For the purposes of this section a witness is eligible for protection if the court is satisfied—

    (a) that the quality of evidence given by the witness, or

    (b) the level of co-operation given by the witness to any party to the proceedings in connection with that party's preparation of its case,

is likely to be diminished by reason of fear or distress on the part of the witness in connection with being identified by members of the public as a witness in the proceedings.

(4) In determining whether a witness is eligible for protection the court must take into account, in particular—

    (a) the nature and alleged circumstances of the offence to which the proceedings relate;

    (b) the age of the witness;

    (c) such of the following matters as appear to the court to be relevant, namely—

        (i) the social and cultural background and ethnic origins of the witness,

     (ii) the domestic and employment circumstances of the witness, and
     (iii) any religious beliefs or political opinions of the witness;
  (d) any behaviour towards the witness on the part of—
     (i) the accused,
     (ii) members of the family or associates of the accused, or
     (iii) any other person who is likely to be an accused or a witness in the proceedings.

    (5) In determining that question the court must in addition consider any views expressed by the witness.

    (6) For the purposes of this section a reporting direction in relation to a witness is a direction that no matter relating to the witness shall during the witness's lifetime be included in any publication if it is likely to lead members of the public to identify him as being a witness in the proceedings.

    (7)–(12) ★ ★ ★ ★ ★

★ ★ ★ ★ ★

Freedom of Information Act 2000
(2000, c. 36)

An Act to make provision for the disclosure of information held by public authorities or by persons providing services for them and to amend the Data Protection Act 1998 and the Public Records Act 1958; and for connected purposes.   [30 November 2000]

Territorial extent: England and Wales, Northern Ireland. The Act applies also to a limited extent to public bodies which operate also in Scotland, but not to purely Scottish public authorities such as the Scottish Parliament or Executive.

PART I   ACCESS TO INFORMATION HELD BY PUBLIC AUTHORITIES

Right to information

1   General right of access to information held by public authorities
    (1) Any person making a request for information to a public authority is entitled—
  (a) to be informed in writing by the public authority whether it holds information of the description specified in the request, and
  (b) if that is the case, to have that information communicated to him.

    (2) Subsection (1) has effect subject to the following provisions of this section and to the provisions of sections 2, 9, 12 and 14.

    (3) Where a public authority—
  (a) reasonably requires further information in order to identify and locate the information requested, and
  (b) has informed the applicant of that requirement, the authority is not obliged to comply with subsection (1) unless it is supplied with that further information.

    (4) The information—
  (a) in respect of which the applicant is to be informed under subsection (1)(a), or
  (b) which is to be communicated under subsection (1)(b),
is the information in question held at the time when the request is received, except that account may be taken of any amendment or deletion made between that time and the time

when the information is to be communicated under subsection (1)(b), being an amendment or deletion that would have been made regardless of the receipt of the request.

(5) A public authority is to be taken to have complied with subsection (1)(a) in relation to any information if it has communicated the information to the applicant in accordance with subsection (1)(b).

(6) In this Act, the duty of a public authority to comply with subsection (1)(a) is referred to as "the duty to confirm or deny".

2   Effect of the exemptions in Part II

(1) Where any provision of Part II states that the duty to confirm or deny does not arise in relation to any information, the effect of the provision is that where either—

(a) the provision confers absolute exemption, or

(b) in all the circumstances of the case, the public interest in maintaining the exclusion of the duty to confirm or deny outweighs the public interest in disclosing whether the public authority holds the information,

section 1(1)(a) does not apply.

(2) In respect of any information which is exempt information by virtue of any provision of Part II, section 1(1)(b) does not apply if or to the extent that—

(a) the information is exempt information by virtue of a provision conferring absolute exemption, or

(b) in all the circumstances of the case, the public interest in maintaining the exemption outweighs the public interest in disclosing the information.

(3) For the purposes of this section, the following provisions of Part II (and no others) are to be regarded as conferring absolute exemption—

(a) section 21,

(b) section 23,

(c) section 32,

(d) section 34,

(e) section 36 so far as relating to information held by the House of Commons or the House of Lords,

(f) in section 40—

(i) subsection (1), and

(ii) subsection (2) so far as relating to cases where the first condition referred to in that subsection is satisfied by virtue of subsection (3)(a)(i) or (b) of that section,

(g) section 41, and

(h) section 44.

3   Public authorities

(1) In this Act "public authority" means—

(a) subject to section 4(4), any body which, any other person who, or the holder of any office which—

(i) is listed in Schedule 1, or

(ii) is designated by order under section 5, or

(b) a publicly-owned company as defined by section 6.

(2) For the purposes of this Act, information is held by a public authority if—

(a) it is held by the authority, otherwise than on behalf of another person, or

(b) it is held by another person on behalf of the authority.

4, 5   ★ ★ ★ ★ ★

6   Publicly-owned companies

(1) A company is a "publicly-owned company" for the purposes of section 3(1)(b) if—

(a) it is wholly owned by the Crown, or

(b) it is wholly owned by any public authority listed in Schedule 1 other than—
  (i) a government department, or
  (ii) any authority which is listed only in relation to particular information.
(2), (3) ★ ★ ★ ★ ★

7 ★ ★ ★ ★ ★

8 Request for information
(1) In this Act any reference to a "request for information" is a reference to such a request which—
  (a) is in writing,
  (b) states the name of the applicant and an address for correspondence, and
  (c) describes the information requested.
(2) For the purposes of subsection (1)(a), a request is to be treated as made in writing where the text of the request—
  (a) is transmitted by electronic means,
  (b) is received in legible form, and
  (c) is capable of being used for subsequent reference.

9 Fees
(1) A public authority to whom a request for information is made may, within the period for complying with section 1(1), give the applicant a notice in writing (in this Act referred to as a "fees notice") stating that a fee of an amount specified in the notice is to be charged by the authority for complying with section 1(1).
(2) Where a fees notice has been given to the applicant, the public authority is not obliged to comply with section 1(1) unless the fee is paid within the period of three months beginning with the day on which the fees notice is given to the applicant.
(3) Subject to subsection (5), any fee under this section must be determined by the public authority in accordance with regulations made by the Secretary of State.
(4), (5) ★ ★ ★ ★ ★

10 Time for compliance with request
(1) Subject to subsections (2) and (3), a public authority must comply with section 1(1) promptly and in any event not later than the twentieth working day following the date of receipt.
(2) Where the authority has given a fees notice to the applicant and the fee is paid in accordance with section 9(2), the working days in the period beginning with the day on which the fees notice is given to the applicant and ending with the day on which the fee is received by the authority are to be disregarded in calculating for the purposes of subsection (1) the twentieth working day following the date of receipt.
(3)–(5) ★ ★ ★ ★ ★

11 Means by which communication to be made
(1) Where, on making his request for information, the applicant expresses a preference for communication by any one or more of the following means, namely—
  (a) the provision to the applicant of a copy of the information in permanent form or in another form acceptable to the applicant,
  (b) the provision to the applicant of a reasonable opportunity to inspect a record containing the information, and
  (c) the provision to the applicant of a digest or summary of the information in permanent form or in another form acceptable to the applicant,
the public authority shall so far as reasonably practicable give effect to that preference.
(2) In determining for the purposes of this section whether it is reasonably practicable to communicate information by particular means, the public authority may have regard to all the circumstances, including the cost of doing so.

(3) Where the public authority determines that it is not reasonably practicable to comply with any preference expressed by the applicant in making his request, the authority shall notify the applicant of the reasons for its determination.

(4) Subject to subsection (1), a public authority may comply with a request by communicating information by any means which are reasonable in the circumstances.

12 Exemption where cost of compliance exceeds appropriate limit

(1) Section 1(1) does not oblige a public authority to comply with a request for information if the authority estimates that the cost of complying with the request would exceed the appropriate limit.

(2) Subsection (1) does not exempt the public authority from its obligation to comply with paragraph (a) of section 1(1) unless the estimated cost of complying with that paragraph alone would exceed the appropriate limit.

(3) In subsections (1) and (2) "the appropriate limit" means such amount as may be prescribed, and different amounts may be prescribed in relation to different cases.

(4) The Secretary of State may by regulations provide that, in such circumstances as may be prescribed, where two or more requests for information are made to a public authority—

    (a) by one person, or

    (b) by different persons who appear to the public authority to be acting in concert or in pursuance of a campaign,

the estimated cost of complying with any of the requests is to be taken to be the estimated total cost of complying with all of them.

(5) The Secretary of State may by regulations make provision for the purposes of this section as to the costs to be estimated and as to the manner in which they are to be estimated.

13 ★ ★ ★ ★ ★

14 Vexatious or repeated requests

(1) Section 1(1) does not oblige a public authority to comply with a request for information if the request is vexatious.

(2) Where a public authority has previously complied with a request for information which was made by any person, it is not obliged to comply with a subsequent identical or substantially similar request from that person unless a reasonable interval has elapsed between compliance with the previous request and the making of the current request.

15 ★ ★ ★ ★ ★

16 Duty to provide advice and assistance

(1) It shall be the duty of a public authority to provide advice and assistance, so far as it would be reasonable to expect the authority to do so, to persons who propose to make, or have made, requests for information to it.

(2) Any public authority which, in relation to the provision of advice or assistance in any case, conforms with the code of practice under section 45 is to be taken to comply with the duly imposed by subsection (1) in relation to that case.

Refusal of request

17 Refusal of request

(1) A public authority which, in relation to any request for information, is to any extent relying on a claim that any provision of Part II relating to the duty to confirm or deny is relevant to the request or on a claim that information is exempt information must, within the time for complying with section 1(1), give the applicant a notice which—

    (a) states that fact,

    (b) specifies the exemption in question, and

    (c) states (if that would not otherwise be apparent) why the exemption applies.

(2) ★ ★ ★ ★ ★

(3) A public authority which, in relation to any request for information, is to any extent relying on a claim that subsection (1)(b) or (2)(b) of section 2 applies must, either in the notice under subsection (1) or in a separate notice given within such time as is reasonable in the circumstances, state the reasons for claiming—

  (a) that, in all the circumstances of the case, the public interest in maintaining the exclusion of the duty to confirm or deny outweighs the public interest in disclosing whether the authority holds the information, or

  (b) that, in all the circumstances of the case, the public interest in maintaining the exemption outweighs the public interest in disclosing the information.

(4) A public authority is not obliged to make a statement under subsection (1)(c) or (3) if, or to the extent that, the statement would involve the disclosure of information which would itself be exempt information.

(5) A public authority which, in relation to any request for information, is relying on a claim that section 12 or 14 applies must, within the time for complying with section 1(1), give the applicant a notice stating that fact.

(6), (7) ★ ★ ★ ★ ★

The Information Commissioner and the Information Tribunal

18   The Information Commissioner and the Information Tribunal

(1) The Data Protection Commissioner shall be known instead as the Information Commissioner.

(2) The Data Protection Tribunal shall be known instead as the Information Tribunal.

(3) In this Act—

  (a) the Information Commissioner is referred to as "the Commissioner", and

  (b) the Information Tribunal is referred to as "the Tribunal".

(4)–(7) ★ ★ ★ ★ ★

Publication schemes

19   Publication schemes

(1) It shall be the duty of every public authority—

  (a) to adopt and maintain a scheme which relates to the publication of information by the authority and is approved by the Commissioner (in this Act referred to as a "publication scheme"),

  (b) to publish information in accordance with its publication scheme, and

  (c) from time to time to review its publication scheme.

(2) A publication scheme must—

  (a) specify classes of information which the public authority publishes or intends to publish,

  (b) specify the manner in which information of each class is, or is intended to be, published, and

  (c) specify whether the material is, or is intended to be, available to the public free of charge or on payment.

(3) in adopting or reviewing a publication scheme, a public authority shall have regard to the public interest—

  (a) in allowing public access to information held by the authority, and

  (b) in the publication of reasons for decisions made by the authority.

(4) A public authority shall publish its publication scheme in such manner as it thinks fit.

(5) The Commissioner may, when approving a scheme, provide that his approval is to expire at the end of a specified period.

(6) Where the Commissioner has approved the publication scheme of any public

authority, he may at any time give notice to the public authority revoking his approval of the scheme as from the end of the period of six months beginning with the day on which the notice is given.

(7) Where the Commissioner—

(a) refuses to approve a proposed publication scheme, or

(b) revokes his approval of a publication scheme,

he must give the public authority a statement of his reasons for doing so.

20 Model publication schemes

(1) The Commissioner may from time to time approve, in relation to public authorities falling within particular classes, model publication schemes prepared by him or by other persons.

(2) Where a public authority falling within the class to which an approved model scheme relates adopts such a scheme without modification, no further approval of the Commissioner is required so long as the model scheme remains approved; and where such an authority adopts such a scheme with modifications, the approval of the Commissioner is required only in relation to the modifications.

(3)–(7) ★ ★ ★ ★ ★

PART II EXEMPT INFORMATION

21 Information accessible to applicant by other means

(1) Information which is reasonably accessible to the applicant otherwise than under section 1 is exempt information.

(2) For the purposes of subsection (1)—

(a) information may be reasonably accessible to the applicant even though it is accessible only on payment, and

(b) information is to be taken to be reasonably accessible to the applicant if it is information which the public authority or any other person is obliged by or under any enactment to communicate (otherwise than by making the information available for inspection) to members of the public on request, whether free of charge or on payment.

(3) For the purposes of subsection (1), information which is held by a public authority and does not fall within subsection (2)(b) is not to be regarded as reasonably accessible to the applicant merely because the information is available from the public authority itself on request, unless the information is made available in accordance with the authority's publication scheme and any payment required is specified in, or determined in accordance with, the scheme.

22 Information intended for future publication

(1) Information is exempt information if—

(a) the information is held by the public authority with a view to its publication, by the authority or any other person, at some future date (whether determined or not),

(b) the information was already held with a view to such publication at the time when the request for information was made, and

(c) it is reasonable in all the circumstances that the information should be withheld from disclosure until the date referred to in paragraph (a).

(2) The duty to confirm or deny does not arise if, or to the extent that, compliance with section 1(1)(a) would involve the disclosure of any information (whether or, not already recorded) which falls within subsection (1).

23 Information supplied by, or relating to, bodies dealing with security matters

(1) Information held by a public authority is exempt information if it was directly or

indirectly supplied to the public authority by, or relates to, any of the bodies specified in subsection (3).

(2) A certificate signed by a Minister of the Crown certifying that the information to which it applies was directly or indirectly supplied by, or relates to, any of the bodies specified in subsection (3) shall, subject to section 60, be conclusive evidence of that fact.

(3) The bodies referred to in subsections (1) and (2) are—

    (a) the Security Service,

    (b) the Secret Intelligence Service,

    (c) the Government Communications Headquarters,

    (d) the special forces,

    (e) the Tribunal established under section 65 of the Regulation of Investigatory Powers Act 2000,

    (f) the Tribunal established under section 7 of the Interception of Communications Act 1985,

    (g) the Tribunal established under section 5 of the Security Service Act 1989,

    (h) the Tribunal established under section 9 of the Intelligence Services Act 1994,

    (i) the Security Vetting Appeals Panel,

    (j) the Security Commission,

    (k) the National Criminal Intelligence Service, and

    (l) the Service Authority for the National Criminal Intelligence Service.

(4), (5) ★ ★ ★ ★ ★

24 National security

(1) Information which does not fall within section 23(1) is exempt information if exemption from section 1(1)(b) is required for the purpose of safeguarding national security.

(2) The duty to confirm or deny does not arise if, or to the extent that, exemption from section 1(1)(a) is required for the purpose of safeguarding national security.

(3) A certificate signed by a Minister of the Crown certifying that exemption from section 1(1)(b), or from section 1(1)(a) and (b), is, or at any time was, required for the purpose of safeguarding national security shall, subject to section 60, be conclusive evidence of that fact.

(4) A certificate under subsection (3) may identify the information to which it applies by means of a general description and may be expressed to have prospective effect.

25 ★ ★ ★ ★ ★

26 Defence

(1) Information is exempt information if its disclosure under this Act would, or would be likely to, prejudice—

    (a) the defence of the British Islands or of any colony, or

    (b) the capability, effectiveness or security of any relevant forces.

(2) In subsection (1)(b) "relevant forces" means—

    (a) the armed forces of the Crown, and

    (b) any forces co-operating with those forces,

or any part of any of those forces.

(3) The duty to confirm or deny does not arise if, or to the extent that, compliance with section 1(1)(a) would, or would be likely to, prejudice any of the matters mentioned in subsection (1).

27 International relations

(1) Information is exempt information if its disclosure under this Act would, or would be likely to, prejudice—

    (a) relations between the United Kingdom and any other State,

    (b) relations between the United Kingdom and any international organisation or international court,

    (c) the interests of the United Kingdom abroad, or

    (d) the promotion or protection by the United Kingdom of its interests abroad.

(2) Information is also exempt information if it is confidential information obtained from a State other than the United Kingdom or from an international organisation or international court.

(3) For the purposes of this section, any information obtained from a State, organisation or court is confidential at any time while the terms on which it was obtained require it to be held in confidence or while the circumstances in which it was obtained make it reasonable for the State, organisation or court to expect that it will be so held.

(4) The duty to confirm or deny does not arise if, or to the extent that, compliance with section 1(1)(a)—

    (a) would, or would be likely to, prejudice any of the matters mentioned in subsection (1), or

    (b) would involve the disclosure of any information (whether or not already recorded) which is confidential information obtained from a State other than the United Kingdom or from an international organisation or international court.

    (5) ★ ★ ★ ★ ★

28 Relations within the United Kingdom

(1) Information is exempt information if its disclosure under this Act would, or would be likely to, prejudice relations between any administration in the United Kingdom and any other such administration.

(2) In subsection (1) "administration in the United Kingdom" means—

    (a) the government of the United Kingdom,

    (b) the Scottish Administration,

    (c) the Executive Committee of the Northern Ireland Assembly, or

    (d) the National Assembly for Wales.

(3) The duty to confirm or deny does not arise if, or to the extent that, compliance with section 1(1)(a) would, or would be likely to, prejudice any of the matters mentioned in subsection (1).

29 The economy

(1) Information is exempt information if its disclosure under this Act would, or would be likely to, prejudice—

    (a) the economic interests of the United Kingdom or of any part of the United Kingdom, or

    (b) the financial interests of any administration in the United Kingdom, as defined by section 28(2).

(2) The duty to confirm or deny does not arise if, or to the extent that, compliance with section 1(1)(a) would, or would be likely to, prejudice any of the matters mentioned in subsection (1).

30 Investigations and proceedings conducted by public authorities

(1) Information held by a public authority is exempt information if it has at any time been held by the authority for the purposes of—

    (a) any investigation which the public authority has a duty to conduct with a view to it being ascertained—

        (i) whether a person should be charged with an offence, or

        (ii) whether a person charged with an offence is guilty of it,

    (b) any investigation which is conducted by the authority and in the circumstances may lead to a decision by the authority to institute criminal proceedings which the authority has power to conduct, or

(c) any criminal proceedings which the authority has power to conduct.

(2) Information held by a public authority is exempt information if—

(a) it was obtained or recorded by the authority for the purposes of its functions relating to—

(i)   investigations falling within subsection (1)(a) or (b),

(ii) criminal proceedings which the authority has power to conduct,

(iii) investigations (other than investigations falling within subsection (1)(a) or (b)) which are conducted by the authority for any of the purposes specified in section 31(2) and either by virtue of Her Majesty's prerogative or by virtue of powers conferred by or under any enactment, or

(iv) civil proceedings which are brought by or on behalf of the authority and arise out of such investigations, and

(b) it relates to the obtaining of information from confidential sources.

(3) The duty to confirm or deny does not arise in relation to information which is (or if it were held by the public authority would be) exempt information by virtue of subsection (1) or (2).

(4)–(6) ★ ★ ★ ★ ★

31 Law enforcement

(1) Information which is not exempt information by virtue of section 30 is exempt information if its disclosure under this Act would, or would be likely to, prejudice—

(a) the prevention or detection of crime,

(b) the apprehension or prosecution of offenders,

(c) the administration of justice,

(d) the assessment or collection of any tax or duty or of any imposition of a similar nature,

(e) the operation of the immigration controls,

(f) the maintenance of security and good order in prisons or in other institutions where persons are lawfully detained,

(g) the exercise by any public authority of its functions for any of the purposes specified in subsection (2),

(h) any civil proceedings which are brought by or on behalf of a public authority and arise out of an investigation conducted, for any of the purposes specified in subsection (2), by or on behalf of the authority by virtue of Her Majesty's prerogative or by virtue of powers conferred by or under an enactment, or

(i) any inquiry held under the Fatal Accidents and Sudden Deaths Inquiries (Scotland) Act 1976 to the extent that the inquiry arises out of an investigation conducted, for any of the purposes specified in subsection(2), by or on behalf of the authority by virtue of Her Majesty's prerogative or by virtue of powers conferred by or under an enactment.

(2) The purposes referred to in subsection (1)(g) to (i) are—

(a) the purpose of ascertaining whether any person has failed to comply with the law

(b) the purpose of ascertaining whether any person is responsible for any conduct which is improper,

(c) the purpose of ascertaining whether circumstances which would justify regulatory action in pursuance of any enactment exist or may arise,

(d) the purpose of ascertaining a person's fitness or competence in relation to the management of bodies corporate or in relation to any profession or other activity which he is, or seeks to become, authorised to carry on,

(e) the purpose of ascertaining the cause of an accident,

(f) the purpose of protecting charities against misconduct or mismanagement (whether by trustees or other persons) in their administration,

(g) the purpose of protecting the property of charities from loss or misapplication,

(h) the purpose of recovering the property of charities,

(i) the purpose of securing the health, safety and welfare of persons at work, and

(j) the purpose of protecting persons other than persons at work against risk to health or safety arising out of or in connection with the actions of persons at work.

(3) The duty to confirm or deny does not arise if, or to the extent that, compliance with section 1(1)(a) would, or would be likely to, prejudice any of the matters mentioned in subsection (1).

32 Court records, etc.

(1) Information held by a public authority is exempt information if it is held only by virtue of being contained in—

(a) any document filed with, or otherwise placed in the custody of, a court for the purposes of proceedings in a particular cause or matter,

(b) any document served upon, or by, a public authority for the purposes of proceedings in a particular cause or matter, or

(c) any document created by—

(i) a court, or

(ii) a member of the administrative staff of a court,

for the purposes of proceedings in a particular cause or matter.

(2)–(4) ★ ★ ★ ★ ★

33 Audit functions

(1) This section applies to any public authority which has functions in relation to—

(a) the audit of the accounts of other public authorities, or

(b) the examination of the economy, efficiency and effectiveness with which other public authorities use their resources in discharging their functions.

(2) Information held by a public authority to which this section applies is exempt information if its disclosure would, or would be likely to, prejudice the exercise of any of the authority's functions in relation to any of the matters referred to in subsection (1).

(3) The duty to confirm or deny does not arise in relation to a public authority to which this section applies if, or to the extent that, compliance with section 1(1)(a) would, or would be likely to, prejudice the exercise of any of the authority's functions in relation to any of the matters referred to in subsection (1).

34 Parliamentary privilege

(1) Information is exempt information if exemption from section 1(1)(b) is required for the purpose of avoiding an infringement of the privileges of either House of Parliament.

(2) The duty to confirm or deny does not apply if, or to the extent that, exemption from section 1(1)(a) is required for the purpose of avoiding an infringement of the privileges of either House of Parliament.

(3) A certificate signed by the appropriate authority certifying that exemption from section 1(1)(b), or from section 1(1)(a) and (b), is, or at any time was, required for the purpose of avoiding an infringement of the privileges of either House of Parliament shall be conclusive evidence of that fact.

(4) In subsection (3) "the appropriate authority" means—

(a) in relation to the House of Commons, the Speaker of that House, and

(b) in relation to the House of Lords, the Clerk of the Parliaments.

35 Formulation of government policy, etc.

(1) Information held by a government department or by the National Assembly for Wales is exempt information if it relates to—

(a) the formulation or development of government policy,

(b) Ministerial communications,

(c) the provision of advice by any of the Law Officers or any request for the provision of such advice, or

(d) the operation of any Ministerial private office.

(2) Once a decision as to government policy has been taken, any statistical information used to provide an informed background to the taking of the decision is not to be regarded—

(a) for the purposes of subsection (1)(a), as relating to the formulation or development of government policy, or

(b) for the purposes of subsection (1)(b), as relating to Ministerial communications.

(3) The duty to confirm or deny does not arise in relation to information which is (or if it were held by the public authority would be) exempt information by virtue of subsection (1).

(4) In making any determination required by section 2(1)(b) or (2)(b) in relation to information which is exempt information by virtue of subsection (1)(a), regard shall be had to the particular public interest in the disclosure of factual information which has been used, or is intended to be used, to provide informed background to decision-taking.

(5) ★ ★ ★ ★ ★

36 Prejudice to effective conduct of public affairs

(1) This section applies to—

(a) information which is held by a government department or by the National Assembly for Wales and is not exempt information by virtue of section 35, and

(b) information which is held by any other public authority.

(2) Information to which this section applies is exempt information if, in the reasonable opinion of a qualified person, disclosure of the information under this Act—

(a) would, or would be likely to, prejudice—

(i) the maintenance of the convention of the collective responsibility of Ministers of the Crown, or

(ii) the work of the Executive Committee of the Northern Ireland Assembly, or

(iii) the work of the executive committee of the National Assembly for Wales,

(b) would, or would be likely to, inhibit–

(i) the free and frank provision of advice, or

(ii) the free and frank exchange of views for the purposes of deliberation, or

(c) would otherwise prejudice, or would be likely otherwise to prejudice, the effective conduct of public affairs.

(3) The duty to confirm or deny does not arise in relation to information to which this section applies (or would apply if held by the public authority) if, or to the extent that, in the reasonable opinion of a qualified person, compliance with section 1(1)(a) would, or would be likely to, have any of the effects mentioned in subsection (2).

(4) In relation to statistical information, subsections (2) and (3) shall have effect with the omission of the words "in the reasonable opinion of a qualified person".

(5) In subsections (2) and (3) "qualified person"—

(a) in relation to information held by a government department in the charge of a Minister of the Crown, means any Minister of the Crown,

(b) in relation to information held by a Northern Ireland department, means the Northern Ireland Minister in charge of the department,

(c) in relation to information held by any other government department, means the commissioners or other person in charge of that department,

(d) in relation to information held by the House of Commons, means the Speaker of that House,

(e) in relation to information held by the House of Lords, means the Clerk of the Parliaments,

(f) in relation to information held by the Northern Ireland Assembly, means the Presiding Officer,

(g) in relation to information held by the National Assembly for Wales, means the Assembly First Secretary,

(h)–(o) ★ ★ ★ ★ ★

(6), (7) ★ ★ ★ ★ ★

37 Communications with Her Majesty, etc. and honours

(1) Information is exempt information if it relates to—

(a) communications with Her Majesty, with other members of the Royal Family or with the Royal Household, or

(b) the conferring by the Crown of any honour or dignity.

(2) The duty to confirm or deny does not arise in relation to information which is (or if it were held by the public authority would be) exempt information by virtue of subsection (1).

38–41 ★ ★ ★ ★ ★

42 Legal professional privilege

(1) Information in respect of which a claim to legal professional privilege or, in Scotland, to confidentiality of communications could be maintained in legal proceedings is exempt information.

(2) The duty to confirm or deny does not arise if, or to the extent that, compliance with section 1(1)(a) would involve the disclosure of any information (whether or not already recorded) in respect of which such a claim could be maintained in legal proceedings.

43 ★ ★ ★ ★ ★

44 Prohibitions on disclosure

(1) Information is exempt information if its disclosure (otherwise than under this Act) by the public authority holding it—

(a) is prohibited by or under any enactment,

(b) is incompatible with any Community obligation, or

(c) would constitute or be punishable as a contempt of court.

(2) The duty to confirm or deny does not arise if the confirmation or denial that would have to be given to comply with section 1(1)(a) would (apart from this Act) fall within any of paragraphs (a) to (c) of subsection (1).

PART III   GENERAL FUNCTIONS OF SECRETARY OF STATE, LORD CHANCELLOR AND INFORMATION COMMISSIONER

45   Issue of code of practice by Secretary of State

(1) The Secretary of State shall issue, and may from time to time revise, a code of practice providing guidance to public authorities as to the practice which it would, in his opinion, be desirable for them to follow in connection with the discharge of the authorities' functions under Part I.

(2) The code of practice must, in particular, include provision relating to—

(a) the provision of advice and assistance by public authorities to persons who propose to make, or have made, requests for information to them,

(b) the transfer of requests by one public authority to another public authority by which the information requested is or may be held,

(c) consultation with persons to whom the information requested relates or persons whose interests are likely to be affected by the disclosure of information,

(d) the inclusion in contracts entered into by public authorities of terms relating to the disclosure of information, and

(e) the provision by public authorities of procedures for dealing with complaints about the handling by them of requests for information.

(3) The code may make different provision for different public authorities.

(4) Before issuing or revising any code under this section, the Secretary of State shall consult the Commissioner.

(5) The Secretary of State shall lay before each House of Parliament any code or revised code made under this section.

46 ★ ★ ★ ★ ★

47   General functions of Commissioner

(1) It shall be the duty of the Commissioner to promote the following of good practice by public authorities and, in particular, so to perform his functions under this Act as to promote the observance by public authorities of—

(a) the requirements of this Act, and

(b) the provisions of the codes of practice under sections 45 and 46.

(2) The Commissioner shall arrange for the dissemination in such form and manner as he considers appropriate of such information as it may appear to him expedient to give to the public—

(a) about the operation of this Act,

(b) about good practice, and

(c) about other matters within the scope of his functions under this Act, and may give advice to any person as to any of those matters.

(3) The Commissioner may, with the consent of any public authority, assess whether that authority is following good practice.

(4)–(6) ★ ★ ★ ★ ★

48, 49 ★ ★ ★ ★ ★

PART IV   ENFORCEMENT

50   Application for decision by Commissioner

(1) Any person (in this section referred to as "the complainant") may apply to the Commissioner for a decision whether, in any specified respect, a request for information made by the complainant to a public authority has been dealt with in accordance with the requirements of Part I.

(2) On receiving an application under this section, the Commissioner shall make a decision unless it appears to him—

(a) that the complainant has not exhausted any complaints procedure which is provided by the public authority in conformity with the code of practice under section 45,

(b) that there has been undue delay in making the application,

(c) that the application is frivolous or vexatious, or

(d) that the application has been withdrawn or abandoned.

(3) Where the Commissioner has received an application under this section, he shall either—

(a) notify the complainant that he has not made any decision under this section as a result of the application and of his grounds for not doing so, or

(b) serve notice of his decision (in this Act referred to as a "decision notice") on the complainant and the public authority.

(4) Where the Commissioner decides that a public authority—

(a) has failed to communicate information, or to provide confirmation or denial, in a case where it is required to do so by section 1(1), or

(b) has failed to comply with any of the requirements of sections 11 and 17, the decision notice must specify the steps which must be taken by the authority for complying with that requirement and the period within which they must be taken.

(5) A decision notice must contain particulars of the right of appeal conferred by section 57.

(6), (7) ★ ★ ★ ★ ★

★ ★ ★ ★ ★

Local Government Act 2000
(2000, c. 22)

An Act to make provision with respect to the functions and procedures of local authorities and provision with respect to local authority elections; to make provision with respect to grants and housing benefit in respect of certain welfare services; to amend section 29 of the Children Act 1989; and for connected purposes. [28 July 2000]

Territorial extent: England and Wales

PART I PROMOTION OF ECONOMIC, SOCIAL OR ENVIRONMENTAL WELL-BEING ETC.

Interpretation

1 Meaning of "local authority" in Part I
In this Part "local authority" means—
(a) in relation to England—
   (i) a county council,
   (ii) a district council,
   (iii) a London borough council,
   (iv) the Common Council of the City of London in its capacity as a local authority,
   (v) the Council of the Isles of Scilly,
(b) in relation to Wales, a county council or a county borough council.

Promotion of well-being

2 Promotion of well-being
(1) Every local authority are to have power to do anything which they consider is likely to achieve any one or more of the following objects–
(a) the promotion or improvement of the economic well-being of their area.
(b) the promotion or improvement of the social well-being of their area, and
(c) the promotion or improvement of the environmental well-being of their area.
(2) The power under subsection (1) may be exercised in relation to or for the benefit of—
(a) the whole or any part of a local authority's area, or
(b) all or any persons resident or present in a local authority's area.
(3) In determining whether or how to exercise the power under subsection (1), a local authority must have regard to their strategy under section 4.
(4) The power under subsection (1) includes power for a local authority to—
(a) incur expenditure,
(b) give financial assistance to any person,
(c) enter into arrangements or agreements with any person,

(d) co-operate with, or facilitate or co-ordinate the activities of, any person,

(e) exercise on behalf of any person any functions of that person, and

(f) provide staff, goods, services or accommodation to any person.

(5), (6) ★ ★ ★ ★ ★

3 Limits on power to promote well-being

(1) The power under section 2(1) does not enable a local authority to do anything which they are unable to do by virtue of any prohibition, restriction or limitation on their powers which is contained in any enactment (whenever passed or made).

(2) The power under section 2(1) does not enable a local authority to raise money (whether by precepts, borrowing or otherwise).

(3) The Secretary of State may by order make provision preventing local authorities from doing, by virtue of section 2(1), anything which is specified, or is of a description specified, in the order.

(4) Before making an order under subsection (3), the Secretary of State must consult such representatives of local government and such other persons (if any) as he considers appropriate.

(5) Before exercising the power under section 2(1), a local authority must have regard to any guidance for the time being issued by the Secretary of State about the exercise of that power.

(6)–(8) ★ ★ ★ ★ ★

4 Strategies for promoting well-being

(1) Every local authority must prepare a strategy (referred to in this section as a community strategy) for promoting or improving the economic, social and environmental well-being of their area and contributing to the achievement of sustainable development in the United Kingdom.

(2) A local authority may from time to time modify their community strategy.

(3) In preparing or modifying their community strategy, a local authority–

(a) must consult and seek the participation of such persons as they consider appropriate, and

(b) must have regard to any guidance for the time being issued by the Secretary of State.

(4)–(5) ★ ★ ★ ★ ★

5 Power to amend or repeal enactments

(1) If the Secretary of State thinks that an enactment (whenever passed or made) prevents or obstructs local authorities from exercising their power under section 2(1) he may by order amend, repeal, revoke or disapply that enactment.

(2) The power under subsection (1) may he exercised in relation to—

(a) all local authorities,

(b) particular local authorities, or

(c) particular descriptions of local authority.

(3) The power under subsection (1) to amend or disapply an enactment includes a power to amend or disapply an enactment for a particular period.

6–9 ★ ★ ★ ★ ★

PART II ARRANGEMENTS WITH RESPECT TO EXECUTIVES ETC.

Executive arrangements

10 Executive arrangements

(1) In this Part "executive arrangements" means arrangements by a local authority—

(a) for and in connection with the creation and operation of an executive of the authority, and

(b) under which certain functions of the authority are the responsibility of the executive.

(2) Executive arrangements by a local authority must conform with any provisions made by or under this Part which relate to such arrangements.

Local authority executives

11   Local authority executives

(1) The executive of a local authority must take one of the forms specified in subsections (2) to (5).

(2) It may consist of—

(a) an elected mayor of the authority, and

(b) two or more councillors of the authority appointed to the executive by the elected mayor.

Such an executive is referred to in this Part as a mayor and cabinet executive.

(3) It may consist of—

(a) a councillor of the authority (referred to in this Part as the executive leader) elected as leader of the executive by the authority, and

(b) two or more councillors of the authority appointed to the executive by one of the following—

(i) the executive leader, or

(ii) the authority.

Such an executive is referred to in this Part as a leader and cabinet executive.

(4) It may consist of—

(a) an elected mayor of the authority, and

(b) an officer of the authority (referred to in this Part as the council manager) appointed to the executive by the authority.

Such an executive is referred to in this Part as a mayor and council manager executive.

(5) It may take any such form as may be prescribed in regulations made by the Secretary of State.

(6) Regulations under subsection (5) may, in particular, provide for—

(a) a form of executive some or all of the members of which are elected by the local government electors for the authority's area to a specified post in the executive associated with the discharge of particular functions,

(b) a form of executive some or all of the members of which are elected by those electors but not to any such post,

(c) the system of voting that will be used for elections under paragraph (a) or (b).

(7) A local authority executive may not include the chairman or vice-chairman of the authority.

(8) The number of members of a mayor and cabinet executive or a leader and cabinet executive may not exceed 10.

(9), (10) ★ ★ ★ ★ ★

12   ★ ★ ★ ★ ★

Executive functions

13   Functions which are the responsibility of an executive

(1) This section has effect for the purposes of determining the functions of a local authority which are the responsibility of an executive of the authority under executive arrangements.

(2) Subject to any provision made by this Act or by any enactment which is passed or made after the day on which this Act is passed, any function of a local authority which is not specified in regulations under subsection (3) is to be the responsibility of an executive of the authority under executive arrangements.

(3) The Secretary of State may by regulations make provision for any function of a local authority specified in the regulations—

(a) to be a function which is not to be the responsibility of an executive of the authority under executive arrangements,

(b) to be a function which may be the responsibility of such an executive under such arrangements, or

(c) to be a function which—

(i) to the extent provided by the regulations is to be the responsibility of such an executive under such arrangements, and

(ii) to the extent provided by the regulations is not to be the responsibility of such an executive under such arrangements.

(4)–(8) ★ ★ ★ ★ ★

(9) Any function which is the responsibility of an executive of a local authority under executive arrangements—

(a) is to be regarded as exercisable by the executive on behalf of the authority, and

(b) may be discharged only in accordance with any provisions made by or under this Part which apply to the discharge of any such function by that form of executive.

(10) Accordingly any function which is the responsibility of an executive of a local authority under executive arrangements—

(a) may not be discharged by the authority,

(b) is not to be a function to which section 101(1) of the Local Government Act 1972 applies, and

(c) may be the subject of arrangements made under section 101(5) of that Act only if permitted by any provision made under section 20.

(11) Subject to any provision made under subsection (12), any function which, under executive arrangements, is not the responsibility of an executive of a local authority is to be discharged in any way which would be permitted or required apart from the provisions made by or under this Part.

(12)–(14) ★ ★ ★ ★ ★

Provisions with respect to executive arrangements

14 Discharge of functions: mayor and cabinet executive

(1) Subject to any provision made under section 18, 19 or 20, any functions which, under executive arrangements. are the responsibility of a mayor and cabinet executive are to be discharged in accordance with this section.

(2) The elected mayor—

(a) may discharge any of those functions, or

(b) may arrange for the discharge of any of those functions—

(i) by the executive,

(ii) by another member of the executive,

(iii) by a committee of the executive, or

(iv) by an officer of the authority.

(3) Where by virtue of this section any functions may be discharged by a local authority executive, then, unless the elected mayor otherwise directs, the executive may arrange for the discharge of any of those functions—

(a) by a committee of the executive, or

(b) by an officer of the authority.

(4) Where by virtue of this section any functions may be discharged by a member of a local authority executive, then, unless the elected mayor otherwise directs, that member may arrange for the discharge of any of those functions by an officer of the authority.

(5), (6) ★ ★ ★ ★ ★

15–21 ★ ★ ★ ★ ★

22 Access to information etc.

(1) Meetings of a local authority executive, or a committee of such an executive, are to be open to the public or held in private.

(2) Subject to regulations under subsection (9), it is for a local authority executive to decide which of its meetings, and which of the meetings of any committee of the executive, are to be open to the public and which of those meetings are to be held in private.

(3) A written record must be kept of prescribed decisions made at meetings of local authority executives, or committees of such executives, which are held in private.

(4) A written record must be kept of prescribed decisions made by individual members of local authority executives.

(5) Written records under subsection (3) or (4) must include reasons for the decisions to which they relate.

(6) Written records under subsections (3) and (4), together with such reports, background papers or other documents as may be prescribed, must be made available to members of the public in accordance with regulations made by the Secretary of State.

(7) Regulations under subsection (6) may make provision for or in connection with preventing the whole or part of any record or document containing prescribed information from being made available to members of the public.

(8)–(13) ★ ★ ★ ★ ★

23–49 ★ ★ ★ ★ ★

50 Model code of conduct

(1) The Secretary of State may by order issue a model code as regards the conduct which is expected of members and co-opted members of relevant authorities in England and police authorities in Wales (referred to in this Part as a model code of conduct).

(2) The National Assembly for Wales may by order issue a model code as regards the conduct which is expected of members and co-opted members of relevant authorities in Wales other than police authorities (also referred to in this Part as a model code of conduct).

(3)–(7) ★ ★ ★ ★ ★

51 Duty of relevant authorities to adopt codes of conduct

(1) It is the duty of a relevant authority, before the end of the period of six months beginning with the day on which the first order under section 50 which applies to them is made, to pass a resolution adopting a code as regards the conduct which is expected of members and co-opted members of the authority (referred to in this Part as a code of conduct).

(2) It is the duty of a relevant authority, before the end of the period of six months beginning with the day on which any subsequent order under section 50 which applies to them is made, to pass a resolution—

    (a) adopting a code of conduct in place of their existing code of conduct under this section, or

    (b) revising their existing code of conduct under this section.

(3) A relevant authority may by resolution—

    (a) adopt a code of conduct in place of their existing code of conduct under this section, or

    (b) revise their existing code of conduct under this section.

(4) A code of conduct or revised code of conduct—

(a) must incorporate any mandatory provisions of the model code of conduct which for the time being applies to that authority,

(b) may incorporate any optional provisions of that model code, and

(c) may include other provisions which are consistent with that model code.

(5)–(9) ★ ★ ★ ★ ★

52   Duty to comply with code of conduct

(1) A person who is a member or co-opted member of a relevant authority at a time when the authority adopt a code of conduct under section 51 for the first time—

(a) must, before the end of the period of two months beginning with the date on which the code of conduct is adopted, give to the authority a written undertaking that in performing his functions he will observe the authority's code of conduct for the time being under section 51, and

(b) if he fails to do so, is to cease to be a member or co-opted member at the end of that period.

(2)–(4) ★ ★ ★ ★ ★

Standards committees

53   Standards committees

(1) Subject to subsection (2), every relevant authority must establish a committee (referred to in this Part as a standards committee) which is to have the functions conferred on it by or under this Part.

(2) Subsection (1) does not apply to a parish council or community council.

(3) The number of members of a standards committee of a relevant authority in England or a police authority in Wales and their term of office are to be fixed by the authority (subject to any provision made by virtue of subsection (6)(a)).

(4) A standards committee of a relevant authority in England or a police authority in Wales must include—

(a) at least two members of the authority, and

(b) at least one person who is not a member, or an officer, of that or any other relevant authority.

(5) A standards committee of a relevant authority in England which are operating executive arrangements—

(a) may not include the elected mayor or executive leader, and

(b) may not be chaired by a member of the executive.

(6)–(12) ★ ★ ★ ★ ★

54   Functions of standards committees

(1) The general functions of a standards committee of a relevant authority are—

(a) promoting and maintaining high standards of conduct by the members and co-opted members of the authority, and

(b) assisting members and co-opted members of the authority to observe the authority's code of conduct.

(2) Without prejudice to its general functions, a standards committee of a relevant authority has the following specific functions—

(a) advising the authority on the adoption or revision of a code of conduct,

(b) monitoring the operation of the authority's code of conduct, and

(c) advising, training or arranging to train members and co-opted members of the authority on matters relating to the authority's code of conduct.

(3) A relevant authority may arrange for their standards committee to exercise such other functions as the authority consider appropriate.

(4)–(7) ★ ★ ★ ★ ★

55–56 ★ ★ ★ ★ ★

CHAPTER II   INVESTIGATIONS ETC: ENGLAND

Standards Board for England

57   Standards Board for England

(1) There is to be a body corporate known as the Standards Board for England.

(2) The Standards Board for England is to consist of not less than three members appointed by the Secretary of State.

(3) The Standards Board for England is to have the functions conferred on it by this Part and such other functions as may be conferred on it by order made by the Secretary of State under this subsection.

(4) In exercising its functions the Standards Board for England must have regard to the need to promote and maintain high standards of conduct by members and co-opted members of relevant authorities in England.

(5) The Standards Board for England—

    (a)   must appoint employees known as ethical standards officers who are to have the functions conferred on them by this Part,

    (b)   may issue guidance to relevant authorities in England and police authorities in Wales on matters relating to the conduct of members and co-opted members of such authorities,

    (c)   may issue guidance to relevant authorities in England and police authorities in Wales in relation to the qualifications or experience which monitoring officers should possess, and

    (d)   may arrange for any such guidance to be made public.

(6) Schedule 4 makes further provision in relation to the Standards Board for England.

58   Written allegations

(1) A person may make a written allegation to the Standards Board for England that a member or co-opted member (or former member or co-opted member) of a relevant authority in England has failed, or may have failed, to comply with the authority's code of conduct.

(2) If the Standards Board for England considers that a written allegation under subsection (1) should be investigated, it must refer the case to one of its ethical standards officers.

(3) ★ ★ ★ ★ ★

Functions of ethical standards officers

59   Functions of ethical standards officers

(1) The functions of ethical standards officers are to investigate—

    (a)   cases referred to them by the Standards Board for England under section 58(2), and

    (b)   other cases in which any such officer considers that a member or co-opted member (or former member or co-opted member) of a relevant authority in England has failed, or may have failed, to comply with the authority's code of conduct and which have come to the attention of any such officer as a result of an investigation under paragraph (a).

(2) The Standards Board for England may make arrangements in relation to the assignment of investigations under this section to particular ethical standards officers.

(3) The purpose of an investigation under this section is to determine which of the findings mentioned in subsection (4) is appropriate.

(4) Those findings are—

    (a)   that there is no evidence of any failure to comply with the code of conduct of the relevant authority concerned,

    (b)   that no action needs to be taken in respect of the matters which are the subject of the investigation,

(c) that the matters which are the subject of the investigation should be referred to the monitoring officer of the relevant authority concerned, or

(d) that the matters which are the subject of the investigation should be referred to the president of the Adjudication Panel for England for adjudication by a tribunal falling within section 76(1).

(5) ★ ★ ★ ★ ★

60–63 ★ ★ ★ ★ ★

Reports etc.

64 Reports etc.

(1) Where an ethical standards officer determines in relation to any case that a finding under section 59(4)(a) or (b) is appropriate—

(a) he may produce a report on the outcome of his investigation,

(b) he may provide a summary of any such report to any newspapers circulating in the area of the relevant authority concerned,

(c) he must send to the monitoring officer of the relevant authority concerned a copy of any such report, and

(d) where he does not produce any such report, he must inform the monitoring officer of the relevant authority concerned of the outcome of the investigation.

(2) Where an ethical standards officer determines in relation to any case that a finding under section 59(4)(c) is appropriate he must—

(a) produce a report on the outcome of his investigation,

(b) subject to subsection (4)(b), refer the matters which are the subject of the investigation to the monitoring officer of the relevant authority concerned, and

(c) send a copy of the report to the monitoring officer, and the standards committee, of the relevant authority concerned.

(3) Where an ethical standards officer determines in relation to any case that a finding under section 59(4)(d) is appropriate he must—

(a) produce a report on the outcome of his investigation,

(b) refer the matters which are the subject of the investigation to the president of the Adjudication Panel for England for adjudication by a tribunal falling within section 76(1), and

(c) send a copy of the report to the monitoring officer of the relevant authority concerned and to the president of the Adjudication Panel for England.

(4)–(6) ★ ★ ★ ★ ★

65–74 ★ ★ ★ ★ ★

Adjudication Panels

75 Adjudication Panels

(1) There is to be a panel of persons, known as the Adjudication Panel for England, eligible for membership of tribunals drawn from the Panel.

(2) There is to be a panel of persons, known as the Adjudication Panel for Wales or Panel Dyfarnu Cymru, eligible for membership of tribunals drawn from the Panel.

(3) The members of the Adjudication Panel for England are to be appointed by the Lord Chancellor.

(4) The Lord Chancellor—

(a) must appoint one of the members of the Adjudication Panel for England as president of the Panel, and

(b) may appoint one of those members as deputy president of the Panel.

(5) The members of the Adjudication Panel for Wales are to be appointed by the National Assembly for Wales on such terms and conditions as it may determine.

(6) The National Assembly for Wales—

(a) must appoint one of the members of the Adjudication Panel for Wales as president of the Panel, and

(b) may appoint one of those members as deputy president of the Panel.

(7) Such members of the Adjudication Panel for England as the Lord Chancellor thinks fit must possess such qualifications as may be determined by the Lord Chancellor.

(8) Such members of the Adjudication Panel for Wales as the National Assembly for Wales thinks fit must possess such qualifications as may be determined by the National Assembly for Wales.

(9)–(11) ★ ★ ★ ★ ★

Case tribunals and interim case tribunals

76 Case tribunals and interim case tribunals

(1) Adjudications in respect of matters referred to the president of the relevant Adjudication Panel under section 64(3) or 71(3) are to be conducted by tribunals (referred to in this Part as case tribunals) consisting of not less than three members of the Panel.

(2) Adjudications in respect of matters referred to the president of the relevant Adjudication Panel under section 65(4) or 72(4) are to be conducted by tribunals (referred to in this Part as interim case tribunals) consisting of not less than three members of the Panel.

(3) The president of the relevant Adjudication Panel (or in his absence the deputy president) is to appoint the members of any case tribunal or interim case tribunal.

(4)–(14) ★ ★ ★ ★ ★

Adjudications

77 Adjudications

(1) A person who is the subject of an adjudication conducted by a case tribunal or interim case tribunal may appear before the tribunal in person or be represented by—

(a) counsel or a solicitor, or

(b) any other person whom he desires to represent him.

(2) The Secretary of State may by regulations make such provision as appears to him to be necessary or expedient with respect to adjudications by case tribunals or interim case tribunals drawn from the Adjudication Panel for England.

(3) The president of the Adjudication Panel for England may, after consultation with the Secretary of State, give directions as to the practice and procedure to be followed by tribunals drawn from the Panel.

(4) The National Assembly for Wales may by regulations make such provision as appears to it to be necessary or expedient with respect to adjudications by case tribunals or interim case tribunals drawn from the Adjudication Panel for Wales.

(5) The president of the Adjudication Panel for Wales may, after consultation with the National Assembly for Wales, give directions as to the practice and procedure to be followed by tribunals drawn from the Panel.

(6) Regulations under this section may, in particular, include provision—

(a) for requiring persons to attend adjudications to give evidence and produce documents and for authorising the administration of oaths to witnesses,

(b) for requiring persons to furnish further particulars,

(c) for prescribing the procedure to be followed in adjudications, including provision as to the persons entitled to appear and to be heard on behalf of persons giving evidence,

(d) for the award of costs or expenses (including provision with respect to interest and provision with respect to the enforcement of any such award),

(e) for taxing or otherwise settlinr any such costs or expenses (and for enabling such costs to be taxed in a county court),

(f) for the registration and proof of decisions and awards of tribunals.

(7) A person who without reasonable excuse fails to comply with any requirement imposed by virtue of subsection (6)(a) or (b) is guilty of an offence and liable on summary conviction to a fine not exceeding level 3 on the standard scale.

(8) In this section any reference to documents includes a reference to information held by means of a computer or in any other electronic form.

78   Decisions of interim case tribunals

(1) An interim case tribunal which adjudicates on any matters which are the subject of an interim report must reach one of the following decisions—

(a) that the person to whom the recommendation mentioned in section 65(3) or 72(3) relates should not be suspended or partially suspended from being a member or co-opted member of the relevant authority concerned,

(b) that that person should be suspended or partially suspended from being a member or co-opted member of the authority concerned for a period which does not exceed six months or (if shorter) the remainder of the person's term of office.

(2) An interim case tribunal must give notice of its decision to the standards committee of the relevant authority concerned.

(3) If the decision of an interim case tribunal is that a person should be suspended or partially suspended from being a member or co-opted member of the relevant authority concerned—

(a) the notice must give details of the suspension or partial suspension and specify the date on which the suspension or partial suspension is to begin, and

(b) the relevant authority must suspend or partially suspend the person in accordance with the notice.

(4)–(9) ★ ★ ★ ★ ★

(10) A person who is suspended or partially suspended under this section may appeal to the High Court—

(a) against the suspension or partial suspension, or

(b) against the length of the suspension or partial suspension.

79   Decisions of case tribunals

(1) A case tribunal which adjudicates on any matter must decide whether or not any person to which that matter relates has failed to comply with the code of conduct of the relevant authority concerned.

(2) Where a case tribunal decides that a person has not failed to comply with the code of conduct of the relevant authority concerned, it must give notice to that effect to the standards committee of the relevant authority concerned.

(3) Where a case tribunal decides that a person has failed to comply with the code of conduct of the relevant authority concerned, it must decide whether the nature of the failure is such that the person should be suspended or disqualified in accordance with subsection (4).

(4) A person may be—

(a) suspended or partially suspended from being a member or co-opted member of the relevant authority concerned, or

(b) disqualified for being, or becoming (whether by election or otherwise), a member of that or any other relevant authority.

(5) Where a case tribunal makes such a decision as is mentioned in subsection (4)(a), it must decide the period for which the person should be suspended or partially suspended (which must not exceed one year or, if shorter, the remainder of the person's term of office).

(6) Where a case tribunal makes such a decision as is mentioned in subsection (4)(b), it must decide the period for which the person should be disqualified (which must not exceed five years).

(7) Where a case tribunal decides that a person has failed to comply with the code of conduct of the relevant authority concerned but should not be suspended or disqualified as mentioned in subsection (4), it must give notice to the standards committee of the relevant authority concerned—

    (a) stating that the person has failed to comply with that code of conduct, and

    (b) specifying the details of that failure.

(8)–(14) ★ ★ ★ ★ ★

(15) Where a case tribunal decides under this section that a person has failed to comply with the code of conduct of the relevant authority concerned, that person may appeal to the High Court against that decision, or any other decision under this section which relates to him.

80 ★ ★ ★ ★ ★

Disclosure and registration of Members' interests etc.

81 Disclosure and registration of Members' interests etc.

(1) The monitoring officer of each relevant authority must establish and maintain a register of interests of the members and co-opted members of the authority.

(2) The mandatory provisions of the model code applicable to each relevant authority ("the mandatory provisions") must require the members and co-opted members of each authority to register in that authority's register maintained under subsection (1) such financial and other interests as are specified in the mandatory provisions.

(3) The mandatory provisions must also—

    (a) require any member or co-opted member of a relevant authority who has an interest specified in the mandatory provisions under subsection (2) to disclose that interest before taking part in any business of the authority relating to that interest,

    (b) make provision for preventing or restricting the participation of a member or co-opted member of a relevant authority in any business of the authority to which an interest disclosed under paragraph (a) relates.

(4) Any participation by a member or co-opted member of a relevant authority in any business which is prohibited by the mandatory provisions is not a failure to comply with the authority's code of conduct if the member or co-opted member has acted in accordance with a dispensation from the prohibition granted by the authority's standards committee in accordance with regulations made under subsection (5).

(5) The Secretary of State may prescribe in regulations the circumstances in which standards committees may grant dispensations under subsection (4).

(6)–(8) ★ ★ ★ ★ ★

Code of conduct for local government employees

82 Code of conduct for local government employees

(1) The Secretary of State may by order issue a code as regards the conduct which is expected of qualifying employees of relevant authorities in England and police authorities in Wales.

(2) The National Assembly for Wales may by order issue a code as regards the conduct which is expected of qualifying employees of relevant authorities in Wales (other than police authorities).

(3) The power under subsection (1) or (2) to issue a code includes power—

    (a) to issue a separate code for council managers (within the meaning of Part II of this Act), and

(b) to revise any code which has been issued.

(4)–(6) ★ ★ ★ ★ ★

(7) The terms of appointment or conditions of employment of every qualifying employee of a relevant authority (whether appointed or employed before or after the commencement of this section) are to be deemed to incorporate any code for the time being under this section which is applicable.

(8) In this section "qualifying employee", in relation to a relevant authority, means an employee of the authority other than an employee falling within any description of employee specified in regulations under this subsection.

(9) The power to make regulations under subsection (8) is to be exercised—

(a) in relation to England. by the Secretary of State, and

(b) in relation to Wales, by the National Assembly for Wales.

83–91 ★ ★ ★ ★ ★

Maladministration etc.

92   Payments in cases of maladministration etc.

(1) Where a relevant authority consider—

(a) that action taken by or on behalf of the authority in the exercise of their functions amounts to, or may amount to, maladministration, and

(b) that a person has been, or may have been, adversely affected by that action, the authority may, if they think appropriate, make a payment to, or provide some other benefit for, that person.

(2) Any function which is conferred on the Greater London Authority under this section is to be exercisable by the Mayor of London and the London Assembly acting jointly on behalf of the Authority.

(3) In this section—

"action" includes failure to act,

"relevant authority" has the same meaning as in Part III of this Act.

★ ★ ★ ★ ★

Police (Northern Ireland) Act 2000

(2000, c. 32)

An Act to make provision about policing in Northern Ireland, and for connected purposes.

[23 November 2000]

Territorial extent: Northern Ireland

1   Name of the police in Northern Ireland

(1) The body of constables known as the Royal Ulster Constabulary shall continue in being as the Police Service of Northern Ireland (incorporating the Royal Ulster Constabulary).

(2) The body of constables referred to in subsection (1) shall be styled for operational purposes the "Police Service of Northern Ireland".

(3) The body of constables known as the Royal Ulster Constabulary Reserve shall continue in being as the Police Service of Northern Ireland Reserve (incorporating the Royal Ulster Constabulary Reserve).

(4) The body of constables referred to in subsection (3) shall be styled for operational purposes "The Police Service of Northern Ireland Reserve".

2 The Northern Ireland Policing Board

(1) There shall be a body corporate to be known as the Northern Ireland Policing Board (in this Act referred to as "the Board").

(2) Schedule 1 shall have effect in relation to the Board.

(3) The Police Authority for Northern Ireland is hereby dissolved.

(4) Schedule 2 (which contains provisions for the transfer of the functions, assets, liabilities and staff of the Police Authority for Northern Ireland to the Board and other supplementary provisions) shall have effect.

3 General functions of the Board

(1) The Board shall secure the maintenance of the police in Northern Ireland.

(2) The Board shall secure that—

  (a) the police,

  (b) the police support staff, and

  (c) traffic wardens appointed by the Board under section 71, are efficient and effective.

(3) In carrying out its functions under subsections (1) and (2) the Board shall—

  (a) in accordance with the following provisions of this Act, hold the Chief Constable to account for the exercise of his functions and those of the police, police support staff and traffic wardens;

  (b) monitor the performance of the police in—

   (i) carrying out the general duty under section 32(1);

   (ii) complying with the Human Rights Act 1998;

   (iii) carrying out the policing plan;

  (c) keep itself informed as to—

   (i) the workings of Part VII of the 1998 Act (police complaints and disciplinary proceedings) and trends and patterns in complaints under that Part;

   (ii) the manner in which complaints from members of the public against traffic wardens are dealt with by the Chief Constable under section 71;

   (iii) trends and patterns in crimes committed in Northern Ireland;

   (iv) trends and patterns in recruitment to the police and the police support staff;

   (v) the extent to which the membership of the police and the police support staff is representative of the community in Northern Ireland;

  (d) assess—

   (i) the effectiveness of measures taken to secure that the membership of the police and the police support staff is representative of that community;

   (ii) the level of public satisfaction with the performance of the police and of district policing partnerships;

   (iii) the effectiveness of district policing partnerships in performing their functions and, in particular, of arrangements made under Part III in obtaining the views of the public about matters concerning policing and the co-operation of the public with the police in preventing crime;

   (iv) the effectiveness of the code of ethics issued under section 52;

  (e) make arrangements for obtaining the co-operation of the public with the police in the prevention of crime.

(4) In carrying out its functions, the Board shall have regard to—

  (a) the principle that the policing of Northern Ireland is to be conducted in an impartial manner;

  (b) the policing plan;

  (c) any code of practice issued by the Secretary of State under section 27, and

  (d) the need—

   (i) to co-ordinate its activities with those of other statutory authorities; and

  (ii) to co-operate with such authorities.

4–53 ★ ★ ★ ★ ★

54 Regulations as to emblems and flags
  (1) The Secretary of State may make regulations—
    (a) prescribing the design of an emblem for the police; and
    (b) regulating the use of that or any other emblem—
      (i) on equipment or property used for the purposes of the police; or
      (ii) otherwise in connection with the police.
  (2) The Secretary of State may make regulations—
    (a) prescribing the design of a flag for the police; and
    (b) regulating the flying or carrying of that or any other flag—
      (i) on land or buildings used for the purposes of the police; or
      (ii) otherwise in connection with the police.
  (3) ★ ★ ★ ★ ★

★ ★ ★ ★ ★

Political Parties, Elections and Referendums Act 2000
(2000, c. 41)

An Act to establish an Electoral Commission; to make provision about the registration and finances of political parties; to make provision about donations and expenditure for political purposes; to make provision about election and referendum campaigns and the conduct of referendums; to make provision about election petitions and other legal proceedings in connection with elections; to reduce the qualifying periods set out in sections 1 and 3 of the Representation of the People Act 1985; to make pre-consolidation amendments relating to European Parliamentary Elections; and for connected purposes. [30 November 2000]

Territorial extent: United Kingdom, except that ss 50–69 do not apply to Northern Ireland (see SI 2001 No 446).

1 Establishment of the Electoral Commission
  (1) There shall be a body corporate to be known as the Electoral Commission or, in Welsh, Comisiwn Etholiadol (in this Act referred to as "the Commission").
  (2) The Commission shall consist of members to be known as Electoral Commissioners.
  (3) There shall be not less than five, but not more than nine, Electoral Commissioners.
  (4) The Electoral Commissioners shall be appointed by Her Majesty (in accordance with section 3).
  (5) Her Majesty shall (in accordance with section 3) appoint one of the Electoral Commissioners to be the chairman of the Commission.
  (6) Schedule 1, which makes further provision in relation to the Commission, shall have effect.

2 Speaker's Committee
  (1) There shall be a Committee (to be known as "the Speaker's Committee") to perform the functions conferred on the Committee by this Act.
  (2) The Speaker's Committee shall consist of the Speaker of the House of Commons, who shall be the chairman of the Committee, and the following other members, namely—
    (a) the Member of the House of Commons who is for the time being the Chairman of the Home Affairs Select Committee of the House of Commons;

(b) the Secretary of State for the Home Department (whether or not a Member of the House of Commons);

(c) a Member of the House of Commons who is a Minister of the Crown with responsibilities in relation to local government; and

(d) five Members of the House of Commons who are not Ministers of the Crown.

(3) The member of the Committee mentioned in subsection (2)(c) shall be appointed to membership of the Committee by the Prime Minister.

(4) The members of the Committee mentioned in subsection (2)(d) shall be appointed to membership of the Committee by the Speaker of the House of Commons.

(5), (6) ★ ★ ★ ★ ★

3–21 ★ ★ ★ ★ ★

22 Parties to be registered in order to field candidates at elections

(1) Subject to subsection (4), no nomination may be made in relation to a relevant election unless the nomination is in respect of—

(a) a person who stands for election in the name of a qualifying registered party; or

(b) a person who does not purport to represent any party; or

(c) a qualifying registered party, where the election is one for which registered parties may be nominated.

(2) For the purposes of subsection (1) a party (other than a minor party) is "qualifying registered party" in relation to a relevant election if—

(a) the constituency, local government area or electoral region in which the election is held—

(i) is in England, Scotland or Wales, or

(ii) is the electoral region of Scotland or Wales,

and the party was, on the last day for publication of notice of the election, registered in respect of that part of Great Britain in the Great Britain register maintained by the Commission under section 23, or

(b) the constituency, district electoral area or electoral region in which the election is held—

(i) is in Northern Ireland, or

(ii) is the electoral region of Northern Ireland,

and the party was, on that day, registered in the Northern Ireland register maintained by the Commission under that section.

(3) For the purposes of subsection (1) a person does not purport to represent any party if either—

(a) the description of the candidate given in his nomination paper, is—

(i) "Independent", or

(ii) where the candidate is the Speaker of the House of Commons seeking re-election, "The Speaker seeking re-election"; or

(b) no description of the candidate is given in his nomination paper.

(4) Subsection (1) does not apply in relation to any parish or community election.

(5) The following elections are relevant elections for the purposes of this Part—

(a) parliamentary elections,

(b) elections to the European Parliament,

(c) elections to the Scottish Parliament,

(d) elections to the National Assembly for Wales,

(e) elections to the Northern Ireland Assembly,

(f) local government elections, and

(g) local elections in Northern Ireland.

(6) For the purposes of this Act a person stands for election in the name of a registered

party if his nomination paper includes a description authorised by a certificate issued by or on behalf of the registered nominating officer of the party.

23 The new registers

(1) In place of the register of political parties maintained by the registrar of companies under the Registration of Political Parties Act 1998, there shall be the new registers of political parties mentioned in subsection (2) which—

  (a) shall be maintained by the Commission, and

  (b) (subject to the provisions of this section) shall be so maintained in such form as the Commission may determine.

(2) The new registers of political parties are—

  (a) a register of parties that intend to contest relevant elections in one or more of England, Scotland and Wales (referred to in this Act as "the Great Britain register"); and

  (b) a register of parties that intend to contest relevant elections in Northern Ireland (referred to in this Act as "the Northern Ireland register").

(3) Each party registered in the Great Britain register shall be so registered in respect of one or more of England, Scotland and Wales; and the entry for each party so registered shall be marked so as to indicate—

  (a) the part or parts of Great Britain in respect of which it is registered; and

  (b) if the party is a minor party, that it is such a party.

(4) A party may be registered under this Part in both of the new registers, but where a party is so registered—

  (a) the party as registered in the Great Britain register, and

  (b) the party as registered in the Northern Ireland register,

shall constitute two separate registered parties.

  (5), (6) ★ ★ ★ ★ ★

24–36 ★ ★ ★ ★ ★

37 Party political broadcasts

(1) A broadcaster shall not include in its broadcasting services any party political broadcast made on behalf of a party which is not a registered party.

(2) In this Act "broadcaster" means—

  (a) the holder of a licence under the Broadcasting Act 1990 or 1996,

  (b) the British Broadcasting Corporation, or

  (c) Sianel Pedwar Cymru.

38–50 ★ ★ ★ ★ ★

51 Sponsorship

(1) For the purposes of this Part sponsorship is provided in relation to a registered party if—

  (a) any money or other property is transferred to the party or to any person for the benefit of the party, and

  (b) the purpose (or one of the purposes) of the transfer is (or must, having regard to all the circumstances, reasonably be assumed to be)–

    (i) to help the party with meeting, or to meet, to any extent any defined expenses incurred or to be incurred by or on behalf of the party, or

    (ii) to secure that to any extent any such expenses are not so incurred.

(2) In subsection (1) "defined expenses" means expenses in connection with—

  (a) any conference, meeting or other event organised by or on behalf of the party;

  (b) the preparation, production or dissemination of any publication by or on behalf of the party; or

(c) any study or research organised by or on behalf of the party.

(3) The following do not, however, constitute sponsorship by virtue of sub-section (1)—

(a) the making of any payment in respect of—

(i) any charge for admission to any conference, meeting or other event, or

(ii) the purchase price of, or any other charge for access to, any publication;

(b) the making of any payment in respect of the inclusion of an advertisement in publication where the payment is made at the commercial rate payable for the inclusion of such an advertisement in any such publication;

and subsection (1) also has effect subject to section 52(3).

(4) The Secretary of State may by order made on the recommendation of the Commission amend subsection (2) or (3).

(5) In this section "publication" means a publication made available in whatever form and by whatever means (whether or not to the public at large or any section of the public).

52, 53 ★ ★ ★ ★ ★

54 Permissible donors

(1) A donation received by a registered party must not be accepted by the party if—

(a) the person by whom the donation would be made is not, at the time of its receipt by the party, a permissible donor; or

(b) the party is (whether because the donation is given anonymously or by reason of any deception or concealment or otherwise) unable to ascertain the identity of that person.

(2) For the purposes of this Part the following are permissible donors—

(a) an individual registered in an electoral register;

(b) a company—

(i) registered under the Companies Act 1985 or the Companies (Northern Ireland) Order 1986, and

(ii) incorporated within the United Kingdom or another member State, which carries on business in the United Kingdom;

(c) a registered party;

(d) a trade union entered in the list kept under the Trade Union and Labour Relations (Consolidation) Act 1992 or the Industrial Relations (Northern Ireland) Order 1992;

(e) a building society (within the meaning of the Building Societies Act 1986);

(f) a limited liability partnership registered under the Limited Liability Partnerships Act 2000, or any corresponding enactment in force in Northern Ireland, which carries on business in the United Kingdom;

(g) a friendly society registered under the Friendly Societies Act 1974 or a society registered (or deemed to be registered) under the Industrial and Provident Societies Act 1965 or the Industrial and Provident Societies Act (Northern Ireland) 1969; and

(h) any unincorporated association of two or more persons which does not fall within any of the preceding paragraphs but which carries on business or other activities wholly or mainly in the United Kingdom and whose main office is there.

(3) In relation to a donation in the form of a bequest subsection (2)(a) shall be read as referring to an individual who was, at any time within the period of five years ending with the date of his death, registered in an electoral register.

(4) Where any person ("the principal donor") causes an amount ("the principal donation") to be received by a registered party by way of a donation—

(a) on behalf of himself and one or more other persons, or

(b) on behalf of two or more other persons,

then for the purposes of this Part each individual contribution by a person falling within paragraph (a) or (b) of more than £200 shall be treated as if it were a separate donation received from that person.

(5) In relation to each such separate donation, the principal donor must ensure that, at the time when the principal donation is received by the party, the party is given—

(a) (except in the case of a donation which the principal donor is treated as making) all such details in respect of the person treated as making the donation as are required by virtue of paragraph 2 of Schedule 6 to be given in respect of the donor of a recordable donation; and

(b) (in any case) all such details in respect of the donation as are required by virtue of paragraph 4 of Schedule 6 to be given in respect of a recordable donation.

(6) Where—

(a) any person ("the agent") causes an amount to be received by a registered party by way of a donation on behalf of another person ("the donor"), and

(b) the amount of that donation is more than £200,

the agent must ensure that, at the time when the donation is received by the party, the party is given all such details in respect of the donor as are required by virtue of paragraph 2 of Schedule 6 to be given in respect of the donor of a recordable donation.

(7) A person commits an offence if, without reasonable excuse, he fails to comply with subsection (5) or (6).

(8) ★ ★ ★ ★ ★

55 ★ ★ ★ ★ ★

56 Acceptance or return of donations: general

(1) Where—

(a) a donation is received by a registered party, and

(b) it is not immediately decided that the party should (for whatever reason) refuse the donation,

all reasonable steps must be taken forthwith by or on behalf of the party to verify (or, so far as any of the following is not apparent, ascertain) the identity of the donor, whether he is a permissible donor, and (if that appears to be the case) all such details in respect of him as are required by virtue of paragraph 2 of Schedule 6 to be given in respect of the donor of a recordable donation.

(2) If a registered party receives a donation which it is prohibited from accepting by virtue of section 54(1), or which it is decided that the party should for any other reason refuse, then—

(a) unless the donation falls within section 54(1)(b), the donation, or a payment of an equivalent amount, must be sent back to the person who made the donation or any person appearing to be acting on his behalf,

(b) if the donation falls within that provision, the required steps (as defined by section 57(1)) must be taken in relation to the donation,

within the period of 30 days beginning with the date when the donation is received by the party.

(3) Where—

(a) subsection (2)(a) applies in relation to a donation, and

(b) the donation is not dealt with in accordance with that provision, the party and the treasurer of the party are each guilty of an offence.

(4) Where—

(a) subsection (2)(b) applies in relation to a donation, and

(b) the donation is not dealt with in accordance with that provision, the treasurer of the party is guilty of an offence.

(5), (6) ★ ★ ★ ★ ★

57 Return of donations where donor unidentifiable

(1) For the purposes of section 56(2)(b) the required steps are as follows—

   (a) if the donation mentioned in that provision was transmitted by a person other than the donor, and the identity of that person is apparent, to return the donation to that person;

   (b) if paragraph (a) does not apply but it is apparent that the donor has, in connection with the donation, used any facility provided by an identifiable financial institution, to return the donation to that institution; and

   (c) in any other case, to send the donation to the Commission.

(2) In subsection (1) any reference to returning or sending a donation to any person or body includes a reference to sending a payment of an equivalent amount to that person or body.

(3) Any amount sent to the Commission in pursuance of subsection (1)(c) shall be paid by them into the Consolidated Fund.

58   Forfeiture of donations made by impermissible or unidentifiable donors

(1) This section applies to any donation received by a registered party—

   (a) which, by virtue of section 54(1)(a) or (b), the party are prohibited from accepting, but

   (b) which has been accepted by the party.

(2) The court may, on an application made by the Commission, order the forfeiture by the party of an amount equal to the value of the donation.

(3) The standard of proof in proceedings on an application under this section shall be that applicable to civil proceedings.

(4) An order may be made under this section whether or not proceedings are brought against any person for an offence connected with the donation.

(5) In this section "the court" means—

   (a) in relation to England and Wales, a magistrates' court;

   (b) in relation to Scotland, the sheriff; and

   (c) in relation to Northern Ireland, a court of summary jurisdiction;

and proceedings on an application under this section to the sheriff shall be civil proceedings.

59–100   ★ ★ ★ ★ ★

101   Referendums to which this Part applies

(1) Subject to the following provisions of this section, this Part applies to any referendum held throughout—

   (a) the United Kingdom;

   (b) one or more of England, Scotland, Wales and Northern Ireland; or

   (c) any region in England specified in Schedule 1 to the Regional Development Agencies Act 1998.

(2) In this Part—

   (a) "referendum" means a referendum or other poll held, in pursuance of any provision made by or under an Act of Parliament, on one or more questions specified in or in accordance with any such provision;

   (b) "question" includes proposition (and "answer" accordingly includes response).

(3)–(5) ★ ★ ★ ★ ★

102–103   ★ ★ ★ ★ ★

104   Referendum questions

(1) Subsection (2) applies where a Bill is introduced into Parliament which—

   (a) provides for the holding of a poll that would be a referendum to which this Part applies, and

   (b) specifies the wording of the referendum question.

(2) The Commission shall consider the wording of the referendum question, and

shall publish a statement of any views of the Commission as to the intelligibility of that question—

(a) as soon as reasonably practicable after the Bill is introduced, and

(b) in such manner as they may determine.

(3) Subsections (4) and (5) apply where the wording of the referendum question in the case of any poll that would be a referendum to which this Part applies falls to be specified in subordinate legislation within the meaning of the Interpretation Act 1978.

(4) If a draft of the instrument in question is to be laid before Parliament for approval by each House, the Secretary of State—

(a) shall consult the Commission on the wording of the referendum question before any such draft is so laid, and

(b) shall, at the time when any such draft is so laid, lay before each House a report stating any views as to the intelligibility of that question which the Commission have expressed in response to that consultation.

(5) If the instrument in question is to be subject to annulment in pursuance of a resolution of either House of Parliament, the Secretary of State—

(a) shall consult the Commission on the wording of the referendum question before making the instrument; and

(b) shall, at the time when the instrument is laid before Parliament, lay before each House a report stating any views as to the intelligibility of that question which the Commission have expressed in response to that consultation.

(6), (7) ★ ★ ★ ★ ★

105 Permitted participants

(1) In this Part "permitted participant", in relation to a particular referendum to which this Part applies, means—

(a) a registered party by whom a declaration has been made under section 106 in relation to the referendum; or

(b) any of the following by whom a notification has been given under section 106 in relation to the referendum, namely—

(i)   any individual resident in the United Kingdom or registered in an electoral register (as defined by section 54(8)), or

(ii) any body falling within any of paragraphs (b) and (d) to (h) of section 54(2).

(2) In this Part "responsible person" means—

(a) if the permitted participant is a registered party—

(i)   the treasurer of the party, or

(ii) in the case of a minor party, the person for the time being notified to the Commission by the party in accordance with section 106(2)(b);

(b) if the permitted participant is an individual, that individual; and

(c) otherwise, the person or officer for the time being notified to the Commission by the permitted participant in accordance with section 106(4)(b)(ii).

106 Declarations and notifications for purposes of section 105

(1) For the purposes of section 105(1) a registered party makes a declaration to the Commission under this section if the party makes a declaration to the Commission which identifies—

(a) the referendum to which it relates, and

(b) the outcome or outcomes for which the party proposes to campaign.

(2) A declaration under this section—

(a) must be signed by the responsible officers of the party (within the meaning of section 64); and

(b) if made by a minor party, must be accompanied by a notification which states the name of the person who will be responsible for compliance on the part of the party with the provisions of Chapter II.

(3) For the purposes of section 105(1) an individual or body gives a notification to the Commission under this section if he or it gives the Commission a notification which identifies—

(a) the referendum to which it relates, and

(b) the outcome or outcomes for which the giver of the notification proposes to campaign.

(4) A notification under this section must—

(a) if given by an individual, state—

(i) his full name, and

(ii) his home address in the United Kingdom, or (if he has no such address in the United Kingdom) his home address elsewhere,

and be signed by him;

(b) if given by a body falling within any of paragraphs (b) and (d) to (h) of section 54(2), state—

(i) all such details in respect of the body as are required by virtue of any of sub-paragraphs (4) and (6) to (10) of paragraph 2 of Schedule 6 to be given in respect of such a body as the donor of a recordable donation, and

(ii) the name of the person or officer who will be responsible for compliance on the part of the body with the provisions of Chapter II,

and be signed by the body's secretary or a person who acts in a similar capacity in relation to the body.

(5)–(7) ★ ★ ★ ★ ★

107 Register of declarations and notifications for purposes of section 105

(1) The Commission shall maintain a register of—

(a) all declarations made to them under section 106; and

(b) all notifications given to them under that section.

(2) The register shall be maintained by the Commission in such form as they may determine and shall contain, in the case of each such declaration or notification all of the information supplied to the Commission in connection with it in pursuance of section 106.

(3) Where any declaration or notification is made or given to the Commission under section 106, they shall cause—

(a) the information mentioned in subsection (2) to be entered in the register, or

(b) in the case of a notification under section 106(5), any change required as a consequence of the notification to be made in the register,

as soon as is reasonably practicable.

(4) The information to be entered in the register in respect of a permitted participant who is an individual shall, however, not include his home address.

108 Designation of organisations to whom assistance is available

(1) The Commission may, in respect of any referendum to which this Part applies, designate permitted participants as organisations to whom assistance is available in accordance with section 110.

(2) Where there are only two possible outcomes, in the case of a referendum to which this Part applies, the Commission—

(a) may, in relation to each of those outcomes, designate one permitted participant as representing those campaigning for the outcome in question; but

(b) otherwise shall not make any designation in respect of the referendum.

(3) Where there are more than two possible outcomes in the case of a referendum to which this Part applies, the Secretary of State may, after consulting the Commission, by order

specify the possible outcomes in relation to which permitted participants may be designated in accordance with subsection (4).

(4) In such a case the Commission—

(a) may, in relation to each of two or more outcomes specified in any such order, designate one permitted participant as representing those campaigning for the outcome in question; but

(b) otherwise shall not make any designation in respect of the referendum.

109 ★ ★ ★ ★ ★

110   Assistance available to designated organisations

(1) Where the Commission have made any designations under section 108 in respect of a referendum, assistance shall be available to the designated organisations in accordance with this section.

(2) The Commission shall make to each designated organisation a grant of the same amount, which shall be an amount not exceeding £600,000 determined by the Commission.

(3) A grant under subsection (2) may be made subject to such conditions as the Commission consider appropriate.

(4) Each designated organisation (or, as the case may be, persons authorised by the organisation) shall have the rights conferred by or by virtue of Schedule 12, which makes provision as to—

(a) the sending of referendum addresses free of charge;

(b) the use of rooms free of charge for holding public meetings; and

(c) referendum campaign broadcasts.

(5) In this section and Schedule 12 "designated organisation", in relation to a referendum, means a person or body designated by the Commission under section 108 in respect of that referendum.

111–126 ★ ★ ★ ★ ★

127   Referendum campaign broadcasts

(1) A broadcaster shall not include in its broadcasting services any referendum campaign broadcast made on behalf of any person or body other than one designated in respect of the referendum in question under section 108.

(2) In this section "referendum campaign broadcast" means any broadcast whose purpose (or main purpose) is or may reasonably be assumed to be—

(a) to further any campaign conducted with a view to promoting or procuring a particular outcome in relation to any question asked in a referendum to which this Part applies, or

(b) otherwise to promote or procure any such outcome.

★ ★ ★ ★ ★

Public Finance and Accountability (Scotland) Act 2000
(2000, asp. 1)

An Act of the Scottish Parliament to make provision about public resources and finances and, for the purposes of section 70 of the Scotland Act 1998, about accountability for their use; and for connected purposes.   [17 January 2000]

Territorial extent: Scotland

PART I PUBLIC RESOURCES AND FINANCES

Use of resources

1 Use of resources

(1) The use of resources by—

(a) the Scottish Administration, and

(b) each body or office-holder (other than an office-holder in the Scottish Administration) whose expenditure is payable out of the Scottish Consolidated Fund ("the Fund") under any enactment,

for any purpose in any financial year must be authorised for that year by Budget Act and must not exceed any amount so authorised in relation to that purpose.

(2) The use of resources accruing to the Scottish Administration or any such body or office-holder in a financial year ("accruing resources") for any purpose in that financial year must be so authorised separately from the use of other resources.

(3) In this Act a reference to the use of resources is a reference to their expenditure, consumption or reduction in value.

2 Emergency arrangements

(1) This section applies where, at the beginning of any financial year ("the current financial year"), the use of resources mentioned in section 1(1) has not been authorised for that year by Budget Act.

(2) Until there is in force a Budget Act authorising that use of resources for the current financial year—

(a) any purpose for which the use of resources was authorised for the previous financial year by Budget Act shall be taken to be a purpose for which the use of resources is authorised for the current financial year, and

(b) the use of resources for any purpose for each calendar month of the current financial year must not exceed whichever is the greater of—

(i) one-twelfth of any amount authorised in relation to that purpose by Budget Act for the previous financial year, and

(ii) the amount of resources used for that purpose in the corresponding calendar month of the previous financial year;

and section 1 has effect accordingly.

(3) Subsection (2) is subject to any provision made by Budget Act for the current financial year.

3 Contingencies

(1) This section applies where it is proposed that resources be used for any purpose in any financial year by the Scottish Administration or a body or office-holder referred to in section 1(1)(b) other than in accordance with that section (whether or not as modified by section 2).

(2) The resources may be so used only with the authority of the Scottish Ministers.

(3) The Scottish Ministers may authorise the use of resources only if they consider that—

(a) the use is necessarily required in the public interest, and

(b) it is not reasonably practicable, for reasons of urgency, for the requirements of section 1 in relation to the use to be satisfied by a Budget Act.

(4) The aggregate amount of the resources which the Scottish Ministers may authorise to be used under this section in any financial year must not exceed 0.5% of the aggregate amount of the resources which, at the beginning of that year, were authorised to be used in that year by virtue of section 1.

(5) Where the Scottish Ministers authorise the use of resources under this section they must, as soon as possible, lay before the Parliament a report setting out the circumstances of the authorisation and why they considered it to be necessary.

★ ★ ★ ★ ★

Regulation of Investigatory Powers Act 2000
(2000, c. 23)

An Act to make provision for and about the interception of communications, the acquisition and disclosure of data relating to communications, the carrying out of surveillance, the use of covert human intelligence sources and the acquisition of the means by which electronic data protected by encryption or passwords may be decrypted or accessed; to provide for Commissioners and a tribunal with functions and jurisdiction in relation to those matters, to entries on and interferences with property or with wireless telegraphy and to the carrying out of their functions by the Security Service, the Secret Intelligence Service and the Government Communications Headquarters; and for connected purposes.   [28 July 2000]

Territorial extent: United Kingdom

1   Unlawful interception

(1) It shall be an offence for a person intentionally and without lawful authority to intercept, at any place in the United Kingdom, any communication in the course of its transmission by means of—

(a) a public postal service; or

(b) a public telecommunication system.

(2) It shall be an offence for a person—

(a) intentionally and without lawful authority, and

(b) otherwise than in circumstances in which his conduct is excluded by subsection (6) from criminal liability under this subsection,

to intercept, at any place in the United Kingdom, any communication in the course of its transmission by means of a private telecommunication system.

(3) Any interception of a communication which is carried out at any place in the United Kingdom by, or with the express or implied consent of, a person having the right to control the operation or the use of a private telecommunication system shall be actionable at the suit or instance of the sender or recipient, or intended recipient, of the communication if it is without lawful authority and is either—

(a) an interception of that communication in the course of its transmission by means of that private system; or

(b) an interception of that communication in the course of its transmission, by means of a public telecommunication system, to or from apparatus comprised in that private telecommunication system.

(4) Where the United Kingdom is a party to an international agreement which—

(a) relates to the provision of mutual assistance in connection with, or in the form of, the interception of communications,

(b) requires the issue of a warrant, order or equivalent instrument in cases in which assistance is given, and

(c) is designated for the purposes of this subsection by an order made by the Secretary of State,

it shall be the duty of the Secretary of State to secure that no request for assistance in accordance with the agreement is made on behalf of a person in the United Kingdom to the competent authorities of a country or territory outside the United Kingdom except with lawful authority.

(5) Conduct has lawful authority for the purposes of this section if, and only if—

(a) it is authorised by or under section 3 or 4;

(b) it takes place in accordance with a warrant under section 5 ("an interception warrant"); or

(c) it is in exercise, in relation to any stored communication, of any statutory power that is exercised (apart from this section) for the purpose of obtaining information or of taking possession of any document or other property;

and conduct (whether or not prohibited by this section) which has lawful authority for the purposes of this section by virtue of paragraph (a) or (b) shall also be taken to be lawful for all other purposes.

(6) The circumstances in which a person makes an interception of a communication in the course of its transmission by means of a private telecommunication system are such that his conduct is excluded from criminal liability under subsection (2) if—

(a) he is a person with a right to control the operation or the use of the system, or

(b) he has the express or implied consent of such a person to make the interception.

(7) A person who is guilty of an offence under subsection (1) or (2) shall be liable—

(a) on conviction on indictment, to imprisonment for a term riot exceeding two years or to a fine, or to both;

(b) on summary conviction, to a fine not exceeding the statutory maximum.

(8) No proceedings for any offence which is an offence by virtue of this section shall be instituted—

(a) in England and Wales, except by or with the consent of the Director of Public Prosecutions;

(b) in Northern Ireland, except by or with the consent of the Director of Public Prosecutions for Northern Ireland.

2 Meaning and location of "interception" etc.

(1) In this Act—

"postal service" means any service which—

(a) consists in the following, or in any one or more of them, namely, the collection, sorting, conveyance, distribution and delivery (whether in the United Kingdom or elsewhere) of postal items; and

(b) is offered or provided as a service the main purpose of which, or one of the main purposes of which, is to make available, or to facilitate, a means of transmission from place to place of postal items containing communications;

"private telecommunication system" means any telecommunication system which, without itself being a public telecommunication system, is a system in relation to which the following conditions are satisfied–

(a) it is attached, directly or indirectly and whether or not for the purposes of the communication in question, to a public telecommunication system; and

(b) there is apparatus comprised in the system which is both located in the United Kingdom and used (with or without other apparatus) for making the attachment to the public telecommunication system;

"public postal service" means any postal service which is offered or provided to, or to a substantial section of, the public in any one or more parts of the United Kingdom;

"public telecommunications service" means any telecommunications service which is offered or provided to, or to a substantial section of, the public in any one or more parts of the United Kingdom;

"public telecommunication system" means any such parts of a telecommunication system by means of which any public telecommunications service is provided as are located in the United Kingdom;

"telecommunications service" means any service that consists in the provision of access to, and of facilities for making use of, any telecommunication system (whether or not provided by the person providing the service); and

"telecommunication system" means any system (including the apparatus comprised in it) which exists (whether wholly or partly in the United Kingdom or elsewhere) for the purpose of facilitating the transmission of communications by any means involving the use of electrical or electro-magnetic energy.

(2)–(11) ★ ★ ★ ★ ★

3   Lawful interception without an interception warrant

(1) Conduct by any person consisting in the interception of a communication is authorised by this section if the communication is one which, or which that person has reasonable grounds for believing, is both—

(a) a communication sent by a person who has consented to the interception; and

(b) a communication the intended recipient of which has so consented.

(2) Conduct by any person consisting in the interception of a communication is authorised by this section if—

(a) the communication is one sent by, or intended for, a person who has consented to the interception; and

(b) surveillance by means of that interception has been authorised under Part II.

(3) Conduct consisting in the interception of a communication is authorised by this section if–

(a) it is conduct by or on behalf of a person who provides a postal service or a telecommunications service; and

(b) it takes place for purposes connected with the provision or operation of that service or with the enforcement, in relation to that service, of any enactment relating to the use of postal services or telecommunications services.

(4), (5) ★ ★ ★ ★ ★

4   Power to provide for lawful interception

(1) Conduct by any person ("the interceptor") consisting in the interception of a communication in the course of its transmission by means of a telecommunication system is authorised by this section if—

(a) the interception is carried out for the purpose of obtaining information about the communications of a person who, or who the interceptor has reasonable grounds for believing, is in a country or territory outside the United Kingdom;

(b) the interception relates to the use of a telecommunications service provided to persons in that country or territory which is either—

(i) a public telecommunications service; or

(ii) a telecommunications service that would be a public telecommunications service if the persons to whom it is offered or provided were members of the public in a part of the United Kingdom;

(c) the person who provides that service (whether the interceptor or another person) is required by the law of that country or territory to carry out, secure or facilitate the interception in question;

(d) the situation is one in relation to which such further conditions as may be prescribed by regulations made by the Secretary of State are required to be satisfied before conduct may be treated as authorised by virtue of this subsection; and

(e) the conditions so prescribed are satisfied in relation to that situation.

(2) Subject to subsection (3), the Secretary of State may by regulations authorise any such conduct described in the regulations as appears to him to constitute a legitimate practice reasonably required for the purpose, in connection with the carrying on of any business, of monitoring or keeping a record of–

(a) communications by means of which transactions are entered into in the course of that business; or

(b) other communications relating to that business or taking place in the course of its being carried on.

(3) Nothing in any regulations under subsection (2) shall authorise the interception of any communication except in the course of its transmission using apparatus or services provided by or to the person carrying on the business for use wholly or partly in connection with that business.

(4)–(9) ★ ★ ★ ★ ★

5   Interception with a warrant

(1) Subject to the following provisions of this Chapter, the Secretary of State may issue a warrant authorising or requiring the person to whom it is addressed, by any such conduct as may be described in the warrant, to secure any one or more of the following—

(a) the interception in the course of their transmission by means of a postal service or telecommunication system of the communications described in the warrant,

(b) the making, in accordance with an international mutual assistance agreement, of a request for the provision of such assistance in connection with, or in the form of, an interception of communications as may be so described;

(c) the provision, in accordance with an international mutual assistance agreement, to the competent authorities of a country or territory outside the United Kingdom of any such assistance in connection with, or in the form of, an interception of communications as may be so described;

(d) the disclosure, in such manner as may be so described, of intercepted material obtained by any interception authorised or required by the warrant, and of related communications data.

(2) The Secretary of State shall not issue an interception warrant unless he believes—

(a) that the warrant is necessary on grounds falling within subsection (3); and

(b) that the conduct authorised by the warrant is proportionate to what is sought to be achieved by that conduct.

(3) Subject to the following provisions of this section, a warrant is necessary on grounds falling within this subsection if it is necessary—

(a) in the interests of national security;

(b) for the purpose of preventing or detecting serious crime;

(c) for the purpose of safeguarding the economic well-being of the United Kingdom; or

(d) for the purpose, in circumstances appearing to the Secretary of State to be equivalent to those in which he would issue a warrant by virtue of paragraph (b), of giving effect to the provisions of any international mutual assistance agreement.

(4) The matters to be taken into account in considering whether the requirements of subsection (2) are satisfied in the case of any warrant shall include whether the information which it is thought necessary to obtain under the warrant could reasonably be obtained by other means.

(5) A warrant shall not be considered necessary on the ground falling within subsection (3)(c) unless the information which it is thought necessary to obtain is information relating to the acts or intentions of persons outside the British Islands.

(6) The conduct authorised by an interception warrant shall be taken to include—

(a) all such conduct (including the interception of communications not identified by the warrant) as it is necessary to undertake in order to do what is expressly authorised or required by the warrant;

(b) conduct for obtaining related communications data; and

(c) conduct by any person which is conduct in pursuance of a requirement imposed by or on behalf of the person to whom the warrant is addressed to be provided with assistance with giving effect to the warrant.

15 General safeguards

(1) Subject to subsection (6), it shall be the duty of the Secretary of State to ensure, in relation to all interception warrants, that such arrangements are in force as he considers necessary for securing—

(a) that the requirements of subsections (2) and (3) are satisfied in relation to the intercepted material and any related communications data; and

(b) in the case of warrants in relation to which there are section 8(4) certificates, that the requirements of section 16 are also satisfied.

(2) The requirements of this subsection are satisfied in relation to the intercepted material and any related communications data if each of the following—

(a) the number of persons to whom any of the material or data is disclosed or otherwise made available,

(b) the extent to which any of the material or data is disclosed or otherwise made available,

(c) the extent to which any of the material or data is copied, and

(d) the number of copies that are made, is limited to the minimum that is necessary for the authorised purposes.

(3) The requirements of this subsection are satisfied in relation to the intercepted material and any related communications data if each copy made of any of the material or data (if not destroyed earlier) is destroyed as soon as there are no longer any grounds for retaining it as necessary for any of the authorised purposes.

(4)–(8) ★ ★ ★ ★ ★

16–58 ★ ★ ★ ★ ★

59 Intelligence Services Commissioner

(1) The Prime Minister shall appoint a Commissioner to be known as the Intelligence Services Commissioner.

(2) Subject to subsection (4), the Intelligence Services Commissioner shall keep under review, so far as they are not required to be kept under review by the Interception of Communications Commissioner—

(a) the exercise by the Secretary of State of his powers under sections 5 to 7 of the Intelligence Services Act 1994 (warrants for interference with wireless telegraphy, entry and interference with property etc.);

(b) the exercise and performance by the Secretary of State, in connection with or in relation to—

(i) the activities of the intelligence services, and

(ii) the activities in places other than Northern Ireland of the officials of the Ministry of Defence and of members of Her Majesty's forces,

of the powers and duties conferred or imposed on him by Parts II and III of this Act;

(c) the exercise and performance by members of the intelligence services of the powers and duties conferred or imposed on them by or under Parts II and III of this Act;

(d) the exercise and performance in places other than Northern Ireland, by officials of the Ministry of Defence and by members of Her Majesty's forces, of the powers and duties conferred or imposed on such officials or members of Her Majesty's forces by or under Parts II and III; and

(e) the adequacy of the arrangements by virtue of which the duty imposed by section 55 is sought to be discharged—

(i) in relation to the members of the intelligence services; and

(ii) in connection with any of their activities in places other than Northern

Ireland, in relation to officials of the Ministry of Defence and members of Her Majesty's forces.

(3) The Intelligence Services Commissioner shall give the Tribunal all such assistance (including his opinion as to any issue falling to be determined by the Tribunal) as the Tribunal may require—

(a) in connection with the investigation of any matter by the Tribunal; or

(b) otherwise for the purposes of the Tribunal's consideration or determination of any matter.

(4) It shall not be the function of the Intelligence Services Commissioner to keep under review the exercise of any power of the Secretary of State to make, amend or revoke any subordinate legislation.

(5) A person shall not be appointed under this section as the Intelligence Services Commissioner unless he holds or has held a high judicial office (within the meaning of the Appellate Jurisdiction Act 1876).

(6)–(10) ★ ★ ★ ★ ★

60   Co-operation with and reports by s. 59 Commissioner

(1) It shall be the duty of—

(a) every member of an intelligence service,

(b) every official of the department of the Secretary of State, and

(c) every member of Her Majesty's forces,

to disclose or provide to the Intelligence Services Commissioner all such documents and information as he may require for the purpose of enabling him to carry out his functions under section 59.

(2) As soon as practicable after the end of each calendar year, the Intelligence Services Commissioner shall make a report to the Prime Minister with respect to the carrying out of that Commissioner's functions.

(3) The Intelligence Services Commissioner may also, at any time, make any such other report to the Prime Minister on any matter relating to the carrying out of the Commissioner's functions as the Commissioner thinks fit.

(4) The Prime Minister shall lay before each House of Parliament a copy of every annual report made by the Intelligence Services Commissioner under subsection (2), together with a statement as to whether any matter has been excluded from that copy in pursuance of subsection (5).

(5) If it appears to the Prime Minister, after consultation with the Intelligence Services Commissioner, that the publication of any matter in an annual report would be contrary to the public interest or prejudicial to—

(a) national security,

(b) the prevention or detection of serious crime,

(c) the economic well-being of the United Kingdom, or

(d) the continued discharge of the functions of any public authority whose activities include activities that are subject to review by that Commissioner,

the Prime Minister may exclude that matter from the copy of the report as laid before each House of Parliament.

(6) ★ ★ ★ ★ ★

61–64 ★ ★ ★ ★ ★

65

(1) There shall, for the purpose of exercising the jurisdiction conferred on them by this section, be a tribunal consisting of such number of members as Her Majesty may by Letters Patent appoint.

(2) The jurisdiction of the Tribunal shall be—

(a) to be the only appropriate tribunal for the purposes of section 7 of the Human Rights Act 1998 in relation to any proceedings under subsection (1)(a) of that section (proceedings for actions incompatible with Convention rights) which fall within subsection (3) of this section;

(b) to consider and determine any complaints made to them which, in accordance with subsection (4), are complaints for which the Tribunal is the appropriate forum;

(c) to consider and determine any reference to them by any person that he has suffered detriment as a consequence of any prohibition or restriction, by virtue of section 17, on his relying in, or for the purposes of, any civil proceedings on any matter; and

(d) to hear and determine any other such proceedings falling within subsection (3) as may be allocated to them in accordance with provision made by the Secretary of State by order.

(3) Proceedings fall within this subsection if—

(a) they are proceedings against any of the intelligence services;

(b) they are proceedings against any other person in respect of any conduct, or proposed conduct, by or on behalf of any of those services;

(c) they are proceedings brought by virtue of section 55(4); or

(d) they are proceedings relating to the taking place in any challengeable circumstances of any conduct falling within subsection (5).

(4) The Tribunal is the appropriate forum for any complaint if it is a complaint by a person who is aggrieved by any conduct falling within subsection (5) which he believes—

(a) to have taken place in relation to him, to any of his property, to any communications sent by or to him, or intended for him, or to his use of any postal service, telecommunications service or telecommunication system; and

(b) to have taken place in challengeable circumstances or to have been carried out by or on behalf of any of the intelligence services.

(5) Subject to subsection (6), conduct falls within this subsection if (whenever it occurred) it is—

(a) conduct by or on behalf of any of the intelligence services;

(b) conduct for or in connection with the interception of communications in the course of their transmission by means of a postal service or telecommunication system;

(c) conduct to which Chapter II of Part I applies;

(d) conduct to which Part II applies;

(e) the giving of a notice under section 49 or any disclosure or use of a key to protected information;

(f) any entry on or interference with property or any interference with wireless telegraphy.

(6) For the purposes only of subsection (3), nothing mentioned in paragraph (d) or (f) of subsection (5) shall be treated as falling, within that subsection unless it is conduct by or on behalf of a person holding any office, rank or position with—

(a) any of the intelligence services;

(b) any of Her Majesty's forces;

(c) any police force;

(d) the National Criminal Intelligence Service;

(e) the National Crime Squad; or

(f) the Commissioners of Customs and Excise;

and section 48(5) applies for the purposes of this subsection as it applies for the purposes of Part II.

(7) For the purposes of this section conduct takes place in challengeable circumstances if–

(a) it takes place with the authority, or purported authority, of anything falling within subsection (8); or

(b) the circumstances are such that (whether or not there is such authority) it would not have been appropriate for the conduct to take place without it, or at least without proper consideration having been given to whether such authority should be sought;

but conduct does not take place in challengeable circumstances to the extent that it is authorised by, or takes place with the permission of, a judicial authority.

(8) The following fall within this subsection—

(a) an interception warrant or a warrant under the Interception of Communications Act 1985;

(b) an authorisation or notice under Chapter II of Part I of this Act;

(c) an authorisation under Part II of this Act or under any enactment contained in or made under an Act of the Scottish Parliament which makes provision equivalent to that made by that Part;

(d) a permission for the purposes of Schedule 2 to this Act;

(e) a notice under section 49 of this Act; or

(f) an authorisation under section 93 of the Police Act 1997.

(9)–(11) ★ ★ ★ ★ ★

Terrorism Act 2000
(2000, c. 11)

An Act to make provision about terrorism; and to make temporary provision for Northern Ireland about the prosecution and punishment of certain offences, the preservation of peace and the maintenance of order.   [20 July 2000]

Territorial extent: United Kingdom (with certain limited exceptions)

PART I   INTRODUCTORY

1   Terrorism: interpretation

(1) In this Act "terrorism" means the use or threat of action where—

(a) the action falls within subsection (2),

(b) the use or threat is designed to influence the government or to intimidate the public or a section of the public, and

(c) the use or threat is made for the purpose of advancing a political, religious or ideological cause.

(2) Action falls within this subsection if it—

(a) involves serious violence against a person,

(b) involves serious damage to property,

(c) endangers a person's life, other than that of the person committing the action,

(d) creates a serious risk to the health or safety of the public or a section of the public, or

(e) is designed seriously to interfere with or seriously to disrupt an electronic system.

(3) The use or threat of action falling within subsection (2) which involves the use of firearms or explosives is terrorism whether or not subsection (1)(b) is satisfied.

(4) In this section—

(a) "action" includes action outside the United Kingdom,

(b) a reference to any person or to property is a reference to any person, or to property, wherever situated,

(c) a reference to the public includes a reference to the public of a country other than the United Kingdom, and

(d) "the government" means the government of the United Kingdom, of a Part of the United Kingdom or of a country other than the United Kingdom.

(5) In this Act a reference to action taken for the purposes of terrorism includes a reference to action taken for the benefit of a proscribed organisation.

2 ★ ★ ★ ★ ★

PART II   PROSCRIBED ORGANISATIONS

Procedure

3 Proscription

(1) For the purposes of this Act an organisation is proscribed if—

(a) it is listed in Schedule 2, or

(b) it operates under the same name as an organisation listed in that Schedule.

(2) Subsection (1)(b) shall not apply in relation to an organisation listed in Schedule 2 if its entry is the subject of a note in that Schedule.

(3) The Secretary of State may by order—

(a) add an organisation to Schedule 2;

(b) remove an organisation from that Schedule,

(c) amend that Schedule in some other way.

(4) The Secretary of State may exercise his power under subsection (3)(a) in respect of an organisation only if he believes that it is concerned in terrorism.

(5) For the purposes of subsection (4) an organisation is concerned in terrorism if it—

(a) commits or participates in acts of terrorism,

(b) prepares for terrorism,

(c) promotes or encourages terrorism, or

(d) is otherwise concerned in terrorism.

4 Deproscription: application

(1) An application may be made to the Secretary of State for the exercise of his power under section 3(3)(b) to remove an organisation from Schedule 2.

(2) An application may be made by—

(a) the organisation, or

(b) any person affected by the organisation's proscription.

(3) The Secretary of State shall make regulations prescribing the procedure for applications under this section.

(4) The regulations shall, in particular—

(a) require the Secretary of State to determine an application within a specified period of time, and

(b) require an application to state the grounds on which it is made.

5 Deproscription: appeal

(1) There shall be a commission, to be known as the Proscribed Organisations Appeal Commission.

(2) Where an application under section 4 has been refused, the applicant may appeal to the Commission.

(3) The Commission shall allow an appeal against a refusal to deproscribe an organisation if it considers that the decision to refuse was flawed when considered in the light of the principles applicable on an application for judicial review.

(4) Where the Commission allows an appeal under this section by or in respect of an organisation, it may make an order under this subsection.

(5) Where an order is made under subsection (4) the Secretary of State shall as soon as is reasonably practicable—
  (a) lay before Parliament, in accordance with section 123(4), the draft of an order under section 3(3)(b) removing the organisation from the list in Schedule 2, or
  (b) make an order removing the organisation from the list in Schedule 2 in pursuance of section 123(5).
(6) Schedule 3 (constitution of the Commission and procedure) shall have effect.

6 Further appeal

(1) A party to an appeal under section 5 which the, Proscribed Organisations Appeal Commission has determined may bring a further appeal on a question of law to—
  (a) the Court of Appeal, if the first appeal was heard in England and Wales,
  (b) the Court of Session, if the first appeal was heard in Scotland, or
  (c) the Court of Appeal in Northern Ireland, if the first appeal was heard in Northern Ireland.
(2) An appeal under subsection (1) may be brought only with the permission—
  (a) of the Commission, or
  (b) where the Commission refuses permission, of the court to which the appeal would be brought.
(3) An order under section 5(4) shall not require the Secretary of State to take any action until the final determination or disposal of an appeal under this section (including any appeal to the House of Lords).

7–9 ★ ★ ★ ★ ★

10 Immunity

(1) The following shall not be admissible as evidence in proceedings for an offence under any of sections 11 to 13, 15 to 19 and 56—
  (a) evidence of anything done in relation to an application to the Secretary of State under section 4,
  (b) evidence of anything done in relation to proceedings before the Proscribed Organisations Appeal Commission under section 5 above or section 7(1) of the Human Rights Act 1998,
  (c) evidence of anything done in relation to proceedings under section 6 (including that section as applied by section 9(2)), and
  (d) any document submitted for the purposes of proceedings mentioned in any of paragraphs (a) to (c).
(2) But subsection (1) does not prevent evidence from being adduced on behalf of the accused.

Offences

11 Membership

(1) A person commits an offence if he belongs or professes to belong to a proscribed organisation.
(2) It is a defence for a person charged with an offence under subsection (1) to prove—
  (a) that the organisation was not proscribed on the last (or only) occasion on which he became a member or began to profess to be a member, and
  (b) that he has not taken part in the activities of the organisation at any time while it was proscribed.
(3) A person guilty of an offence under this section shall be liable—
  (a) on conviction on indictment, to imprisonment for a term not exceeding ten years, to a fine or to both, or

(b) on summary conviction, to imprisonment for a term not exceeding six months, to a fine not exceeding the statutory maximum or to both.

(4) ★ ★ ★ ★ ★

12 Support

(1) A person commits an offence if—

(a) he invites support for a proscribed organisation, and

(b) the support is not, or is not restricted to, the provision of money or other property (within the meaning of section 15).

(2) A person commits an offence if he arranges, manages or assists in arranging or managing a meeting which he knows is—

(a) to support a proscribed organisation,

(b) to further the activities of a proscribed organisation, or

(c) to be addressed by a person who belongs or professes to belong to a proscribed organisation.

(3) A person commits an offence if he addresses a meeting and the purpose of his address is to encourage support for a proscribed organisation or to further its activities.

(4) Where a person is charged with an offence under subsection (2)(c) in respect of a private meeting it is a defence for him to prove that he had no reasonable cause to believe that the address mentioned in subsection (2)(c) would support a proscribed organisation or further its activities.

(5) In subsections (2) to (4)—

(a) "meeting" means a meeting of three or more persons, whether or not the public are admitted, and

(b) a meeting is private if the public are not admitted.

(6) A person guilty of an offence under this section shall be liable—

(a) on conviction on indictment, to imprisonment for a term not exceeding ten years, to a fine or to both, or

(b) on summary conviction, to imprisonment for a term not exceeding six months, to a fine not exceeding the statutory maximum or to both.

13 Uniform

(1) A person in a public place commits an offence if he—

(a) wears an item of clothing, or

(b) wears, carries or displays an article, in such a way or in such circumstances as to arouse reasonable suspicion that he is a member or supporter of a proscribed organisation.

(2) A constable in Scotland may arrest a person without a warrant if he has reasonable grounds to suspect that the person is guilty of an offence under this section.

(3) A person guilty of an offence under this section shall be liable on summary conviction to—

(a) imprisonment for a term not exceeding six months,

(b) a fine not exceeding level 5 on the standard scale, or

(c) both.

14 ★ ★ ★ ★ ★

Offences

15 Fund-raising

(1) A person commits an offence if he—

(a) invites another to provide money or other property, and

(b) intends that it should be used, or has reasonable cause to suspect that it may be used, for the purposes of terrorism.

(2) A person commits an offence if he—

    (a) receives money or other property, and

    (b) intends that it should be used, or has reasonable cause to suspect that it may be used, for the purposes of terrorism.

(3) A person commits an offence if he—

    (a) provides money or other property, and

    (b) knows or has reasonable cause to suspect that it will or may be used for the purposes of terrorism.

(4) In this section a reference to the provision of money or other property is a reference to its being given, lent or otherwise made available, whether or not for consideration.

16–18 ★ ★ ★ ★ ★

19 Disclosure of information: duty

(1) This section applies where a person—

    (a) believes or suspects that another person has committed an offence under any of sections 15 to 18, and

    (b) bases his belief or suspicion on information which comes to his attention in the course of a trade, profession, business or employment.

[(1A) But this section does not apply if the information came to the person in the course of a business in the regulated sector.]

(2) The person commits an offence if he does not disclose to a constable as soon as is reasonably practicable—

    (a) his belief or suspicion, and

    (b) the information on which it is based.

(3) It is a defence for a person charged with an offence under subsection (2) to prove that he had a reasonable excuse for not making the disclosure.

(4) Where—

    (a) a person is in employment,

    (b) his employer has established a procedure for the making of disclosures of the matters specified in subsection (2), and

    (c) he is charged with an offence under that subsection, it is a defence for him to prove that he disclosed the matters specified in that subsection in accordance with the procedure.

(5) Subsection (2) does not require disclosure by a professional legal adviser of—

    (a) information which he obtains in privileged circumstances, or

    (b) a belief or suspicion based on information which he obtains in privileged circumstances.

(6) For the purpose of subsection (5) information is obtained by an adviser in privileged circumstances if it comes to him, otherwise than with a view to furthering a criminal purpose—

    (a) from a client or a client's representative, in connection with the provision of legal advice by the adviser to the client,

    (b) from a person seeking legal advice from the adviser, or from the person's representative, or

    (c) from any person, for the purpose of actual or contemplated legal proceedings.

(7)–(8) ★ ★ ★ ★ ★

20–21B ★ ★ ★ ★ ★

22 Penalties

A person guilty of an offence under any of sections 15 to 18 shall be liable—

    (a) on conviction on indictment, to imprisonment for a term not exceeding 14 years, to a fine or to both, or

(b) on summary conviction, to imprisonment for a term not exceeding six months, to a fine not exceeding the statutory maximum or to both.

23–40 ★ ★ ★ ★ ★

PART V   COUNTER-TERRORIST POWERS

Suspected terrorists

40 Terrorist: interpretation

(1) In this Part "terrorist" means a person who—

(a) has committed an offence under any of sections 11, 12, 15 to 18, 54 and 56 to 63, or

(b) is or has been concerned in the commission, preparation or instigation of acts of terrorism.

(2) The reference in subsection (1)(b) to a person who has been concerned in the commission, preparation or instigation of acts of terrorism includes a reference to a person who has been, whether before or after the passing of this Act, concerned in the commission, preparation or instigation of acts of terrorism within the meaning given by section 1.

41 Arrest without warrant

(1) A constable may arrest without a warrant a person whom he reasonably suspects to be a terrorist.

(2) Where a person is arrested under this section the provisions of Schedule 8 (detention: treatment, review and extension) shall apply.

(3) Subject to subsections (4) to (7), a person detained under this section shall (unless detained under any other power) be released not later than the end of the period of 48 hours beginning—

(a) with the time of his arrest under this section, or

(b) if he was being detained under Schedule 7 when he was arrested under this section, with the time when his examination under that Schedule began.

(4) If on a review of a person's detention under Part II of Schedule 8 the review officer does not authorise continued detention, the person shall (unless detained in accordance with subsection (5) or (6) or under any other power) be released.

(5) Where a police officer intends to make an application for a warrant under paragraph 29 of Schedule 8 extending a person's detention, the person may be detained pending the making of the application.

(6) Where an application has been made under paragraph 29 or 36 of Schedule 8 in respect of a person's detention, he may be detained pending the conclusion of proceedings on the application.

(7) Where an application under paragraph 29 or 36 of Schedule 8 is granted in respect of a person's detention, he may be detained, subject to paragraph 37 of that Schedule, during the period specified in the warrant.

(8) The refusal of an application in respect of a person's detention under paragraph 29 or 36 of Schedule 8 shall not prevent his continued detention in accordance with this section.

(9) A person who has the powers of a constable in one Part of the United Kingdom may exercise the power under subsection (1) in any Part of the United Kingdom.

42 Search of premises

(1) A justice of the peace may on the application of a constable issue a warrant in relation to specified premises if he is satisfied that there are reasonable grounds for suspecting that a person whom the constable reasonably suspects to be a person falling within section 40(1)(b) is to be found there.

(2) A warrant under this section shall authorise any constable to enter and search the

specified premises for the purpose of arresting the person referred to in subsection (1) under section 41.

(3) In the application of subsection (1) to Scotland—

    (a) "justice of the peace" includes the sheriff, and

    (b) the justice of the peace or sheriff can be satisfied as mentioned in that subsection only by having heard evidence on oath.

43   Search of persons

(1) A constable may stop and search a person whom he reasonably suspects to be a terrorist to discover whether he has in his possession anything which may constitute evidence that he is a terrorist.

(2) A constable may search a person arrested under section 41 to discover whether he has in his possession anything which may constitute evidence that he is a terrorist.

(3) A search of a person under this section must be carried out by someone of the same sex.

(4) A constable may seize and retain anything which he discovers in the course of a search of a person under subsection (1) or (2) and which he reasonably suspects may constitute evidence that the person is a terrorist.

(5) A person who has the powers of a constable in one Part of the United Kingdom may exercise a power under this section in any Part of the United Kingdom.

44–58   ★ ★ ★ ★ ★

Inciting terrorism overseas

59   England and Wales

(1) A person commits an offence if—

    (a) he incites another person to commit an act of terrorism wholly or partly outside the United Kingdom, and

    (b) the act would, if committed in England and Wales, constitute one of the offences listed in subsection (2).

(2) Those offences are—

    (a) murder,

    (b) an offence under section 18 of the Offences against the Person Act 1861 (wounding with intent),

    (c) an offence under section 23 or 24 of that Act (poison),

    (d) an offence under section 28 or 29 of that Act (explosions), and

    (e) an offence under section 1(2) of the Criminal Damage Act 1971 (endangering life by damaging property).

(3) A person guilty of an offence under this section shall be liable to any penalty to which he would be liable on conviction of the offence listed in subsection (2) which corresponds to the act which he incites.

(4) For the purposes of subsection (1) it is immaterial whether or not the person incited is in the United Kingdom at the time of the incitement.

(5) Nothing in this section imposes criminal liability on any person acting on behalf of, or holding office under, the Crown.

60, 61   ★ ★ ★ ★ ★

Terrorist bombing and finance offences

62   Terrorist bombing: jurisdiction

(1) If—

    (a) a person does anything outside the United Kingdom as an act of terrorism or for the purposes of terrorism, and

(b) his action would have constituted the commission of one of the offences listed in subsection (2) if it had been done in the United Kingdom,

he shall be guilty of the offence.

(2) The offences referred to in subsection (1)(b) are—

(a) an offence under section 2, 3 or 5 of the Explosive Substances Act 1883 (causing explosions, &c.),

(b) an offence under section 1 of the Biological Weapons Act 1974 (biological weapons), and

(c) an offence under section 2 of the Chemical Weapons Act 1996 (chemical weapons).

63-113 ★ ★ ★ ★ ★

PART VIII   GENERAL

114   Police powers

(1) A power conferred by virtue of this Act on a constable—

(a) is additional to powers which he has at common law or by virtue of any other enactment, and

(b) shall not be taken to affect those powers.

(2) A constable may if necessary use reasonable force for the purpose of exercising a power conferred on him by virtue of this Act (apart fromparagraphs 2 and 3 of Schedule 7).

(3) Where anything is seized by a constable under a power conferred by virtue of this Act, it may (unless the contrary intention appears) be retained for so long as is necessary in all the circumstances.

115 ★ ★ ★ ★ ★

116   Powers to stop and search

(1) A power to search premises conferred by virtue of this Act shall be taken to include power to search a container.

(2) A power conferred by virtue of this Act to stop a person includes power to stop a vehicle (other than an aircraft which is airborne).

(3) A person commits an offence if he fails to stop a vehicle when required to do so by virtue of this section.

(4) A person guilty of an offence under subsection (3) shall be liable on summary conviction to—

(a) imprisonment for a term not exceeding six months,

(b) a fine not exceeding level 5 on the standard scale, or

(c) both.

★ ★ ★ ★ ★

SCHEDULE 2   PROSCRIBED ORGANISATIONS

The Irish Republican Army.

Cumann na mBan.

Fianna na hEireann.

The Red Hand Commando.

Saor Eire.

The Ulster Freedom Fighters.

The Ulster Volunteer Force.

The Irish National Liberation Army
The Irish People's Liberation Organisation
The Ulster Defence Association
The Loyalist Volunteer Force
The Continuity Army Council
The Orange Volunteers
The Red Hand Defenders
Al-Qa'ida
Egyptian Islamic Jihad
Al-Gama'at al-Islamiya
Armed Islamic Group (Groupe Islamique Armée) (GIA)
Salafist Group for Call and Combat (Groupe Salafiste pour la Prédication et le Combat) (GSPC)
Babbar Khalsa
International Sikh Youth Federation
Harakat Mujahideen
Jaish e Mohammed
Lashkar e Tayyaba
Liberation Tigers of Tamil Eelam (LTTE)
Hizballah External Security Organisation
Hamas-Izz al-Din al-Qassem Brigades
Palestinian Islamic Jihad—Shaqaqi
Abu Nidal Organisation
Islamic Army of Aden
Mujaheddin e Khalq
Kurdistan Workers' Party (Partiya Karkeren Kurdistan) (PKK)
Revolutionary Peoples' Liberation Party—Front (Devrimci Halk Kurtulus Partisi-Cephesi) (DHKP-C)
Basque Homeland and Liberty (Euskadi ta Askatasuna) (ETA)
17 November Revolutionary Organisation (N17)

SCHEDULE 3   THE PROSCRIBED ORGANISATIONS APPEAL COMMISSION

Constitution and administration

1.—(1) The Commission shall consist of members appointed by the Lord Chancellor.
(2) The Lord Chancellor shall appoint one of the members as chairman.
(3) A member shall hold and vacate office in accordance with terms of his appointment.
(4) A member may resign at any time by notice in writing to the Lord Chancellor.
2.   The Lord Chancellor may appoint officers and servants for the Commission.
3.   The Lord Chancellor—
  (a) may pay sums by way of remuneration, allowances, pensions and gratuities to or in respect of members, officers and servants,
  (b) may pay compensation to a person who ceases to be a member of the Commission if the Lord Chancellor thinks it appropriate because of special circumstances, and
  (c) may pay sums in respect of expenses of the Commission.

Procedure

4.—(1) The Commission shall sit at such times and in such places as the Lord Chancellor may direct.
(2) The Commission may sit in two or more divisions.

(3) At each sitting of the Commission—
- (a) three members shall attend,
- (b) one of the members shall be a person who holds or has held high judicial office (within the meaning of the Appellate Jurisdiction Act 1876), and
- (c) the chairman or another member nominated by him shall preside and report the Commission's decision.

5.—(1) The Lord Chancellor may make rules—
- (a) regulating the exercise of the right of appeal to the Commission;
- (b) prescribing practice and procedure to be followed in relation to proceedings before the Commission;
- (c) providing for proceedings before the Commission to be determined without an oral hearing in specified circumstances;
- (d) making provision about evidence in proceedings before the Commission (including provision about the burden of proof and admissibility of evidence);
- (e) making provision about proof of the Commission's decisions.

(2) In making the rules the Lord Chancellor shall, in particular, have regard to the need to secure—
- (a) that decisions which are the subject of appeals are properly reviewed, and
- (b) that information is not disclosed contrary to the public interest.

(3) The rules shall make provision permitting organisations to be legally represented in proceedings before the Commission.

(4) The rules may, in particular—
- (a) provide for full particulars of the reasons for proscription or refusal to deproscribe to be withheld from the organisation or applicant concerned and from any person representing it or him;
- (b) enable the Commission to exclude persons (including representatives) from all or part of proceedings;
- (c) enable the Commission to provide a summary of evidence taken in the absence of a person excluded bv virtue of paragraph (b);
- (d) permit preliminary or incidental functions to be discharged by a single member;
- (e) permit proccedings for permission to appeal under section 6 to be determined by a single member;
- (f) make provision about the functions of persons appointed under paragraph 7;
- (g) make different provision for different parties or descriptions of party.

(5) Rules under this paragraph—
- (a) shall be made by statutory instrument, and
- (b) shall not be made unless a draft has been laid before and approved by resolution of each House of Parliament.

(6) In this paragraph a reference to proceedings before the Commission includes a reference to proceedings arising out of proceedings before the Commission.

6.—(1) This paragraph applies to—
- (a) proceedings brought by an organisation before the Commission, and
- (b) proceedings arising out of proceedings to which paragraph (a) applies.

(2) Proceedings shall be conducted on behalf of the organisation by a person designated by the Commission (with such legal representation as he may choose to obtain).

(3) In paragraphs 5 and 8 of this Schedule a reference to an organisation includes a reference to a person designated under this paragraph.

SCHEDULE 3A–5 ★ ★ ★ ★ ★

SCHEDULE 6   FINANCIAL INFORMATION

Orders

1.—(1) Where an order has been made under this paragraph in relation to a terrorist investigation, a constable named in the order may require a financial institution [to which the order applies] to provide customer information for the purposes of the investigation.

[(1A)] ★ ★ ★ ★ ★

(2) The information shall be provided—

(a) in such manner and within such time as the constable may specify, and

(b) notwithstanding any restriction on the disclosure of information imposed by statute or otherwise.

(3) An institution which fails to comply with a requirement under this paragraph shall be guilty of an offence.

(4) It is a defence for an institution charged with an offence under sub-paragraph (3) to prove—

(a) that the information required was not in the institution's possession, or

(b) that it was not reasonably practicable for the institution to comply with the requirement.

(5) An institution guilty of an offence under sub-paragraph (3) shall be liable on summary conviction to a fine not exceeding level 5 on the standard scale.

Procedure

2. An order under paragraph 1 may be made only on the application of—

(a) in England and Wales or Northern Ireland, a police officer of at least the rank of superintendent, or

(b) in Scotland, the procurator fiscal.

3. An order under paragraph 1 may be made only by—

(a) in England and Wales, a Circuit judge,

(b) in Scotland, the sheriff, or

(c) in Northern Ireland, a [Crown Court judge].

4.—(1) Crown Court Rules may make provision about the procedure for an application under paragraph 1.

(2) The High Court of Justiciary may, by Act of Adjournal, make provision about the procedure for an application under paragraph 1.

Criteria for making order

5. An order under paragraph 1 may be made only if the person making it is satisfied that—

(a) the order is sought for the purposes of a terrorist investigation,

(b) the tracing of terrorist property is desirable for the purposes of the investigation, and

(c) the order will enhance the effectiveness of the investigation.

★ ★ ★ ★ ★

Anti-terrorism, Crime and Security Act 2001
(2001, c. 24)

An Act to amend the Terrorism Act 2000; to make further provision about terrorism and security; to provide for the freezing of assets; to make provision about immigration and asylum; to amend or extend the criminal law and powers for preventing crime and enforcing that law: to make provision about the control of pathogens and toxins; to provide for the retention of communications data; to provide for implementation of Title VI of the Treaty on European Union; and for connected purposes.   [14 December 2001]

Territorial extent: United Kingdom (provisions reproduced here).

1–3 ★ ★ ★ ★ ★

PART 2   FREEZING ORDERS

Orders

4   Power to make order
(1) The Treasury may make a freezing order if the following two conditions are satisfied.
(2) The first condition is that the Treasury reasonably believe that—
(a) action to the detriment of the United Kingdom's economy (or part of it) has been or is likely to be taken by a person or persons, or
(b) action constituting a threat to the life or property of one or more nationals of the United Kingdom or residents of the United Kingdom has been or is likely to be taken by a person or persons.
(3) If one person is believed to have taken or to be likely to take the action the second condition is that the person is—
(a) the government of a country or territory outside the United Kingdom, or
(b) a resident of a country or territory outside the United Kingdom.
(4) If two or more persons are believed to have taken or to be likely to take the action the second condition is that each of them falls within paragraph (a) or (b) of subsection (3); and different persons may fall within different paragraphs.

5   Contents of order
(1) A freezing order is an order which prohibits persons from making funds available to or for the benefit of a person or persons specified in the order.
(2) The order must provide that these are the persons who are prohibited—
(a) all persons in the United Kingdom, and
(b) all persons elsewhere who are nationals of the United Kingdom or are bodies incorporated under the law of any part of the United Kingdom or are Scottish partnerships.
(3) The order may specify the following (and only the following) as the person or persons to whom or for whose benefit funds are not to be made available—
(a) the person or persons reasonably believed by the Treasury to have taken or to be likely to take the action referred to in section 4;
(b) any person the Treasury reasonably believe has provided or is likely to provide assistance (directly or indirectly) to that person or any of those persons.
(4) A person may be specified under subsection (3) by—
(a) being named in the order, or
(b) falling within a description of persons set out in the order.
(5) The description must be such that a reasonable person would know whether he fell within it.

(6) Funds are financial assets and economic benefits of any kind.

6 ★ ★ ★ ★ ★

7 Review of order

The Treasury must keep a freezing order under review.

8 Duration of order

A freezing order ceases to have effect at the end of the period of 2 years starting with the day on which it is made.

9 ★ ★ ★ ★ ★

Orders: procedure etc.

10 Procedure for making freezing orders

(1) A power to make a freezing order is exercisable by statutory instrument.

(2) A freezing order—

    (a) must be laid before Parliament after being made;

    (b) ceases to have effect at the end of the relevant period unless before the end of that period the order is approved by a resolution of each House of Parliament (but without that affecting anything done under the order or the power to make a new order).

(3) The relevant period is a period of 28 days starting with the day on which the order is made.

(4) In calculating the relevant period no account is to be taken of any time during which Parliament is dissolved or prorogued or during which both Houses are adjourned for more than 4 days.

(5) If the Treasury propose to make a freezing order in the belief that the condition in section 4(2)(b) is satisfied, they must not make the order unless they consult the Secretary of State.

11–14 ★ ★ ★ ★ ★

15 The Crown

(1) A freezing order binds the Crown, subject to the following provisions of this section.

(2) No contravention by the Crown of a provision of a freezing order makes the Crown criminally liable; but the High Court or in Scotland the Court of Session may, on the application of a person appearing to the Court to have an interest, declare unlawful any act or omission of the Crown which constitutes such a contravention.

(3) Nothing in this section affects Her Majesty in her private capacity; and this is to be construed as if section 38(3) of the Crown Proceedings Act 1947 (meaning of Her Majesty in her private capacity) were contained in this Act.

16–20 ★ ★ ★ ★ ★

PART 4   IMMIGRATION AND ASYLUM

Suspected international terrorists

21 Suspected international terrorist: certification

(1) The Secretary of State may issue a certificate under this section in respect of a person if the Secretary of State reasonably—

    (a) believes that the person's presence in the United Kingdom is a risk to national security, and

    (b) suspects that the person is a terrorist.

(2) In subsection (1)(b) "terrorist" means a person who—

   (a) is or has been concerned in the commission, preparation or instigation of acts of international terrorism,

   (b) is a member of or belongs to an international terrorist group, or

   (c) has links with an international terrorist group.

(3) A group is an international terrorist group for the purposes of subsection (2)(b) and (c) if—

   (a) it is subject to the control or influence of persons outside the United Kingdom, and

   (b) the Secretary of State suspects that it is concerned in the commission, preparation or instigation of acts of international terrorism.

(4) For the purposes of subsection (2)(c) a person has links with an international terrorist group only if he supports or assists it.

(5) In this Part—

"terrorism" has the meaning given by section 1 of the Terrorism Act 2000, and

"suspected international terrorist" means a person certified under subsection (1).

(6) Where the Secretary of State issues a certificate under subsection (1) he shall as soon as is reasonably practicable—

   (a) take reasonable steps to notify the person certified, and

   (b) send a copy of the certificate to the Special Immigration Appeals Commission.

(7) The Secretary of State may revoke a certificate issued under subsection (1).

(8) A decision of the Secretary of State in connection with certification under this section may be questioned in legal proceedings only under section 25 or 26.

(9) An action of the Secretary of State taken wholly or partly in reliance on a certificate under this section may be questioned in legal proceedings only by or in the course of proceedings under—

   (a) section 25 or 26, or

   (b) section 2 of the Special Immigration Appeals Commission Act 1997 (appeal).

22 ★ ★ ★ ★ ★

23 Detention

(1) A suspected international terrorist may be detained under a provision specified in subsection (2) despite the fact that his removal or departure from the United Kingdom is prevented (whether temporarily or indefinitely) by—

   (a) a point of law which wholly or partly relates to an international agreement, or

   (b) a practical consideration.

(2) The provisions mentioned in subsection (1) are—

   (a) paragraph 16 of Schedule 2 to the Immigration Act 1971 (detention of persons liable to examination or removal), and

   (b) paragraph 2 of Schedule 3 to that Act (detention pending deportation).

24 ★ ★ ★ ★ ★

25 Certification: appeal

(1) A suspected international terrorist may appeal to the Special Immigration Appeals Commission against his certification under section 21.

(2) On an appeal the Commission must cancel the certificate if—

   (a) it considers that there are no reasonable grounds for a belief or suspicion of the kind referred to in section 21(1)(a) or (b), or

   (b) it considers that for some other reason the certificate should not have been issued.

(3) If the Commission determines not to cancel a certificate it must dismiss the appeal.

(4) Where a certificate is cancelled under subsection (2) it shall be treated as never having been issued.

(5) An appeal against certification may be commenced only—

(a) within the period of three months beginning with the date on which the certificate is issued, or

(b) with the leave of the Commission, after the end of that period but before the commencement of the first review under section 26.

26   Certification: review

(1) The Special Immigration Appeals Commission must hold a first review of each certificate issued under section 21 as soon as is reasonably practicable after the expiry of the period of six months beginning with the date on which the certificate is issued.

(2)–(7) ★ ★ ★ ★ ★

27   Appeal and review: supplementary

(1) The following provisions of the Special Immigration Appeals Commission Act 1997 shall apply in relation to an appeal or review under section 25 or 26 as they apply in relation to an appeal under section 2 of that Act—

(a) section 6 (person to represent appellant's interests),

(b) section 7 (further appeal on point of law), and

(c) section 7A (pending appeal).

(2)–(10) ★ ★ ★ ★ ★

28   ★ ★ ★ ★ ★

29   Duration of sections 21 to 23

(1) Sections 21 to 23 shall, subject to the following provisions of this section, expire at the end of the period of 15 months beginning with the day on which this Act is passed.

(2) The Secretary of State may by order—

(a) repeal sections 21 to 23;

(b) revive those sections for a period not exceeding one year;

(c) provide that those sections shall not expire in accordance with subsection (1) or an order under paragraph (b) or this paragraph, but shall continue in force for a period not exceeding one year.

(3) An order under subsection (2)—

(a) must be made by statutory instrument, and

(b) may not be made unless a draft has been laid before and approved by resolution of each House of Parliament.

(4) An order may be made without compliance with subsection (3)(b) if it contains a declaration by the Secretary of State that by reason of urgency it is necessary to make the order without laying a draft before Parliament; in which case the order—

(a) must be laid before Parliament, and

(b) shall cease to have effect at the end of the period specified in subsection (5) unless the order is approved during that period by resolution of each House of Parliament.

(5)–(7) ★ ★ ★ ★ ★

30   Legal proceedings: derogation

(1) In this section "derogation matter" means—

(a) a derogation by the United Kingdom from Article 5(1) of the Convention on Human Rights which relates to the detention of a person where there is an intention to remove or deport him from the United Kingdom, or

(b) the designation under section 14(1) of the Human Rights Act 1998 of a derogation within paragraph (a) above.

(2) A derogation matter may be questioned in legal proceedings only before the Special Immigration Appeals Commission; and the Commission—

(a) is the appropriate tribunal for the purpose of section 7 of the Human Rights Act 1998 in relation to proceedings all or part of which call a derogation matter into question; and

(b) may hear proceedings which could, but for this subsection, be brought in the High Court or the Court of Session.

(3)–(7) ★ ★ ★ ★ ★

★ ★ ★ ★ ★

PART 6 WEAPONS OF MASS DESTRUCTION

★ ★ ★ ★ ★

Nuclear weapons

47 Use etc. of nuclear weapons

(1) A person who—

(a) knowingly causes a nuclear weapon explosion;

(b) develops or produces, or participates in the development or production of, a nuclear weapon;

(c) has a nuclear weapon in his possession;

(d) participates in the transfer of a nuclear weapon; or

(e) engages in military preparations, or in preparations of a military nature, intending to use, or threaten to use, a nuclear weapon, is guilty of an offence.

(2) Subsection (1) has effect subject to the exceptions and defences in sections 48 and 49.

48 Exceptions

(1) Nothing in section 47 applies—

(a) to an act which is authorised under subsection (2); or

(b) to an act done in the course of an armed conflict.

(2) The Secretary of State may—

(a) authorise any act which would otherwise contravene section 47 in such manner and on such terms as he thinks fit; and

(b) withdraw or vary any authorisation given under this subsection.

(3) Any question arising in proceedings for an offence under section 47 as to whether anything was done in the course of an armed conflict shall be determined by the Secretary of State.

49 Defences

(1) In proceedings for an offence under section 47(1)(c) or (d) relating to an object it is a defence for the accused to show that he did not know and had no reason to believe that the object was a nuclear weapon.

(2) But he shall be taken to have shown that fact if—

(a) sufficient evidence is adduced to raise an issue with respect to it; and

(b) the contrary is not proved by the prosecution beyond reasonable doubt.

(3) In proceedings for such an offence it is also a defence for the accused to show that he knew or believed that the object was a nuclear weapon but, as soon as reasonably practicable after he first knew or believed that fact, he took all reasonable steps to inform the Secretary of State or a constable of his knowledge or belief.

★ ★ ★ ★ ★

SCHEDULES
SCHEDULE 1 FORFEITURE OF TERRORIST CASH
PART 1 INTRODUCTORY

Terrorist cash

1 (1) This Schedule applies to cash ("terrorist cash") which—

(a) is within subsection (1)(a) or (b) of section 1, or

(b) is property earmarked as terrorist property.

(2) "Cash" means—

(a) coins and notes in any currency,

(b) postal orders,

(c) cheques of any kind, including travellers' cheques,

(d) bankers' drafts,

(e) bearer bonds and bearer shares,

found at any place in the United Kingdom.

(3) Cash also includes any kind of monetary instrument which is found at any place in the United Kingdom, if the instrument is specified by the Secretary of State by order.

(4) The power to make an order under sub-paragraph (3) is exercisable by statutory instrument, which is subject to annulment in pursuance of a resolution of either House of Parliament.

PART 2 SEIZURE AND DETENTION

Seizure of cash

2 (1) An authorised officer may seize any cash if he has reasonable grounds for suspecting that it is terrorist cash.

(2) An authorised officer may also seize cash part of which he has reasonable grounds for suspecting to be terrorist cash if it is not reasonably practicable to seize only that part.

Detention of seized cash

3 (1) While the authorised officer continues to have reasonable grounds for his suspicion, cash seized under this Schedule may be detained initially for a period of 48 hours.

(2) The period for which the cash or any part of it may be detained may be extended by an order made by a magistrates' court or (in Scotland) the sheriff; but the order may not authorise the detention of any of the cash—

(a) beyond the end of the period of three months beginnging with the date of the order, and

(b) in the case of any further order under this paragraph, beyond the end of the period of two years beginning with the date of the first order.

(3) A justice of the peace may also exercise the power of a magistrates' court to make the first order under sub-paragraph (2) extending the period.

(4) An order under sub-paragraph (2) must provide for notice to be given to persons affected by it.

(5) An application for an order under sub-paragraph (2)—

(a) in relation to England and Wales and Northern Ireland, may be made by the Commissioners of Customs and Excise or an authorised officer,

(b) in relation to Scotland, may be made by a procurator fiscal,

and the court, sheriff or justice may make the order if satisfied, in relation to any cash to be further detained, that one of the following conditions is met.

(6) The first condition is that there are reasonable grounds for suspecting that the cash is intended to be used for the purposes of terrorism and that either—

(a) its continued detention is justified while its intended use is further investigated or consideration is given to bringing (in the United Kingdom or elsewhere) proceedings against any person for an offence with which the cash is connected, or

(b) proceedings against any person for an offence with which the cash is connected have been started and have not been concluded.

(7) The second condition is that there are reasonable grounds for suspecting that the cash consists of resources of an organisation which is a proscribed organisation and that either—

(a) its continued detention is justified while investigation is made into whether or not it consists of such resources or consideration is given to bringing (in the United Kingdom or elsewhere) proceedings against any person for an offence with which the cash is connected, or

(b) proceedings against any person for an offence with which the cash is connected have been started and have not been concluded.

(8) The third condition is that there are reasonable grounds for suspecting that the cash is property earmarked as terrorist property and that either—

(a) its continued detention is justified while its derivation is further investigated or consideration is given to bringing (in the United Kingdom or elsewhere) proceedings against any person for an offence with which the cash is connected, or

(b) proceedings against any person for an offence with which the cash is connected have been started and have not been concluded.

4 ★ ★ ★ ★ ★

Release of detained cash

5 (1) This paragraph applies while any cash is detained under this Schedule.

(2) A magistrates' court or (in Scotland) the sheriff may direct the release of the whole or any part of the cash if satisfied, on an application by the person from whom it was seized, that the conditions in paragraph 3 for the detention of cash are no longer met in relation to the cash to be released.

(3) A authorised officer or (in Scotland) a procurator fiscal may, after notifying the magistrates' court, sheriff or justice under whose order cash is being detained, release the whole or any part of it if satisfied that the detention of the cash to be released is no longer justified.

(4) But cash is not to be released—

(a) if an application for its forfeiture under paragraph 6, or for its release under paragraph 9, is made, until any proceedings in pursuance of the application (including any proceedings on appeal) are concluded.

(b) if (in the United Kingdom or elsewhere) proceedings are started against any person for an offence with which the cash is connected, until the proceedings are concluded.

PART 3   FORFEITURE

Forfeiture

6 (1) While cash is detained under this Schedule, an application for the forfeiture of the whole or any part of it may be made—

(a) to a magistrates' court by the Commissioners of Customs and Excise or an authorised officer,

(b) (in Scotland) to the sheriff by the Scottish Ministers.

(2) The court or sheriff may order the forfeiture of the cash or any part of it if satisfied that the cash or part is terrorist cash.

(3) In the case of property earmarked as terrorist property which belongs to joint tenants one of whom is an excepted joint owner, the order may not apply to so much of it as the court or sheriff thinks is attributable to the excepted joint owner's share.

(4) An excepted joint owner is a joint tenant who obtained the property in circumstances

in which it would not (as against him) be earmarked; and references to his share of the earmarked property are to so much of the property as would have been his if the joint tenancy had been severed.

Appeal against forfeiture

7 (1) Any party to proceedings in which an order is made under paragraph 6 ("a forfeiture order") who is aggrieved by the order may appeal—

  (a) in relation to England and Wales, to the Crown Court,

  (b) in relation to Scotland, to the Court of Session,

  (c) in relation to Northern Ireland, to a county court.

  (2) An appeal under sub-paragraph (1) must be made—

  (a) within the period of 30 days beginning with the date on which the order is made, or

  (b) if sub-paragraph (6) applies, before the end of the period of 30 days beginning with the date on which the order under section 3(3)(b) of the Terrorism Act 2000 referred to in that sub-paragraph comes into force.

  (3) The appeal is to be by way of a rehearing.

  (4) The court hearing the appeal may make any order it thinks appropriate.

  (5) If the court upholds the appeal, it may order the release of the cash.

  (6) ★ ★ ★ ★ ★

★ ★ ★ ★ ★

SCHEDULE 3
FREEZING ORDERS

★ ★ ★ ★ ★

Compensation

10 (1) A freezing order may include provision for the award of compensation to or on behalf of a person on the grounds that he has suffered loss as a result of—

  (a) the order;

  (b) the fact that a licence has not been granted under the order;

  (c) the fact that a licence under the order has been granted on particular terms rather than others;

  (d) the fact that a licence under the order has been varied or revoked.

  (2) In particular, the order may include—

  (a) provision about the person who may make a claim for an award;

  (b) provision about the person to whom a claim for an award is to be made (which may be provision that it is to be made to the High Court or, in Scotland, the Court of Session);

  (c) provision about the procedure for making and deciding a claim;

  (d) provision that no compensation is to be awarded unless the claimant has behaved reasonably (which may include provision requiring him to mitigate his loss, for instance by applying for a licence);

  (e) provision that compensation must be awarded in specified circumstances or may be awarded in specified circumstances (which may include provision that the circumstances involve negligence or other fault);

  (f) provision about the amount that may be awarded;

  (g) provision about who is to pay any compensation awarded (which may include provision that it is to be paid or reimbursed by the Treasury);

  (h) provision about how compensation is to be paid (which may include provision for payment to a person other than the claimant).

Treasury's duty to give reasons

11 A freezing order must include provision that if—

(a) a person is specified in the order as a person to whom or for whose benefit funds are not to be made available, and

(b) he makes a written request to the Treasury to give him the reason why he is so specified,

as soon as is practicable the Treasury must give the person the reason in writing.

★ ★ ★ ★ ★

Convention Rights (Compliance) (Scotland) Act 2001
(2001 asp 7)

An Act of the Scottish Parliament to amend certain enactments relating to the sentencing and release of life prisoners, the constitution and powers of the Parole Board, legal advice and assistance and legal aid, homosexual offences and the appointment and removal of the procurator fiscal of the Lyon Court which are or may be incompatible with the European Convention on Human Rights; and to enable further changes in the law where it is or may be incompatible with the Convention.
[5 July 2001]

Territorial extent: Scotland

★ ★ ★ ★ ★

PART 6   POWER TO MAKE REMEDIAL ORDERS

12 **Remedial orders**

(1) In the circumstances set out in subsection (2) below, the Scottish Ministers may, by order (in this Part of this Act, a "remedial order"), make such provision as they consider necessary or expedient in consequence of—

(a) an Act of Parliament or an Act of the Scottish Parliament;

(b) any subordinate legislation made under any such Act;

(c) any provision of any such Act or subordinate legislation; or

(d) any exercise or purported exercise of functions by a member of the Scottish Executive, which is or may be incompatible with any of the Convention rights.

(2) Those circumstances are that the Scottish Ministers are of the opinion that there are compelling reasons for making a remedial order as distinct from taking any other action.

(3) A remedial order may—

(a) make different provision for different purposes;

(b) relate to—

(i) all cases to which the power to make it extends;

(ii) those cases subject to specified exceptions; or

(iii) any particular case or class of case;

(c) make—

(i) any supplementary, incidental or consequential provision; or

(ii) any transitory, transitional or saving provision, which the Scottish Ministers consider necessary or expedient;

(d) modify any enactment or prerogative instrument or any other instrument or document relating to the exercise of purported exercise of functions by the Scottish Ministers;

(e) make provision (other than provision creating criminal offences or increasing the punishment for criminal offences) which has retrospective effect;

(f)   provide for the delegation of functions.

(4)   A remedial order shall not, however, create any criminal offence punishable—

(a)   on summary conviction, with imprisonment for a period exceeding three months or with a fine exceeding the amount specified as level 5 on the standard scale;

(b)   on conviction on indictment, with a period of imprisonment exceeding two years.

(5)   The conferring by subsection (1) above of the power to make remedial orders does not prejudice the extent of any other power.

13   Procedure for remedial orders: general

(1)   A remedial order shall be made by statutory instrument.

(2)   No remedial order shall be made unless laid in draft before and approved by resolution of the Scottish Parliament.

(3)   Before laying a draft remedial order for the purposes of subsection (2) above, the Scottish Ministers shall—

(a)   lay a copy of the proposed draft order, together with a statement of their reasons for proposing to make the order, before the Scottish Parliament;

(b)   give such public notice of the contents of the proposed draft order as they consider appropriate and invite persons wishing to make observations on the draft order to do so, in writing, within the period of 60 days beginning with the day on which that public notice was given or the day on which the draft order was laid under this subsection, whichever is earlier, or, if both those actions occurred on the same day, that day;

(c)   have regard to any written observations submitted within that period.

(4), (5)   ★ ★ ★ ★ ★

14   Procedure for remedial orders: urgent cases

(1)   Where it appears to the Scottish Ministers that, for reasons of urgency, it is necessary to make a remedial order without following the procedure under section 13(2) to (4) above, they may do so.

(2)   After so making a remedial order, the Scottish Ministers shall forthwith—

(a)   give such public notice of the contents of the order as they consider appropriate and invite persons wishing to make observations on the order to do so, in writing, within the period of 60 days beginning with the day on which it was made;

(b)   lay the order, together with a statement of their reasons for having made it, before the Scottish Parliament.

(3)   The Scottish Ministers shall have regard to any written observations submitted within the period mentioned in subsection (2)(a) above.

(4)   As soon as practicable after the end of that period, the Scottish Ministers shall lay before the Scottish Parliament a statement—

(a)   summarising all the observations to which they had to have regard under subsection (3) above; and

(b)   specifying the modifications (if any) which they consider it appropriate to make to the remedial order.

(5)   If modifications have been specified under subsection (4)(b) above, the Scottish Ministers shall—

(a)   make a remedial order by virtue of this subsection giving effect to those modifications and replacing the remedial order made under subsection (1) above; and

(b)   lay the remedial order made by virtue of this subsection before the Scottish Parliament,

or (where the modification specified consists only of the proposed revocation of the remedial order), by order, simply revoke the remedial order made under subsection (1) above.

(6)   If, at the end of the period of 120 days beginning with the day on which a remedial

order was made under subsection (1) above, the Scottish Parliament has not, by resolution, approved the order or any remedial order made by virtue of subsection (5) above replacing it, then the remedial order or, as the case may be the replacement remedial order ceases to have effect (but without that affecting anything done under that order or the power to make a fresh remedial order, whether under the procedure set out in section 13 above or this section).

★ ★ ★ ★ ★

Criminal Justice and Police Act 2001
(2001, c. 16)

An Act to make provision for combating crime and disorder; to make provision about the disclosure of information relating to criminal matters and about powers of search and seizure; to amend the Police and Criminal Evidence Act 1984, the Police and Criminal Evidence (Northern Ireland) Order 1989 and the Terrorism Act 2000; to make provision about the police, the National Criminal Intelligence Service, and the National Crime Squad; to make provision about the powers of the Courts in relation to criminal matters; and for connected purposes.   [11 May 2001]

Territorial extent: England and Wales but Parts 2, 5 (National Criminal Intelligence Service) extend to the United Kingdom.

1   Offences leading to penalties on the spot
(1) For the purposes of this Chapter "penalty offence" means an offence committed under any of the provisions mentioned in the first column of the following Table and described, in general terms, in the second column:

Offence creating provision	Description of offence
Section 12 of the Licensing Act 1872 (c. 94)	Being drunk in a highway, other public place or licensed premises
Section 80 of the Explosives Act 1875 (c. 17)	Throwing fireworks in a thoroughfare
Section 31 of the Fire Services Act 1947 (c. 41)	Knowingly giving a false alarm to a fire brigade
Section 55 of the British Transport Commission Act 1949 (c. xxix)	Trespassing on a railway
Section 56 of the British Transport Commission Act 1949 (c. xxix)	Throwing stones etc. at trains or other things on railways
Section 169C(3) of the Licensing Act 1964 (c. 26)	Buying or attempting to buy alcohol for consumption in a bar in licensed premises by a person under 18
Section 91 of the Criminal Justice Act 1967 (c. 80)	Disorderly behaviour while drunk in a public place
Section 5(2) of the Criminal Law Act 1967 (c. 58)	Wasting police time or giving false report
Section 43(1)(b) of the Telecommunications Act 1984 (c. 12)	Using public telecommunications system for sending message known to be false in order to cause annoyance
Section 12 of this Act	Consumption of alcohol in designated public place

(2) The Secretary of State may by order amend an entry in the Table or add or remove an entry.

(3)–(5) ★ ★ ★ ★ ★

Penalty notices and penalties

2   Penalty notices

(1) A constable who has reason to believe that a person aged 18 or over has committed a penalty offence may give him a penalty notice in respect of the offence.

(2) Unless the notice is given in a police station, the constable giving it must be in uniform.

(3) At a police station, a penalty notice may be given only by an authorised constable.

(4) In this Chapter "penalty notice" means a notice offering the opportunity, by paying a penalty in accordance with this Chapter, to discharge any liability to be convicted of the offence to which the notice relates.

(5) "Authorised constable" means a constable authorised, on behalf of the chief officer of police for the area in which the police station is situated, to give penalty notices.

3   Amount of penalty and form of penalty notice

(1) The penalty payable in respect of a penalty offence is such amount as the Secretary of State may specify by order.

(2) But the Secretary of State may not specify an amount which is more than a quarter of the amount of the maximum fine for which a person is liable on conviction of the offence.

(3) A penalty notice must—
  (a) be in the prescribed form;
  (b) state the alleged offence;
  (c) give such particulars of the circumstances alleged to constitute the offence as are necessary to provide reasonable information about it;
  (d) specify the suspended enforcement period (as to which see section 5) and explain its effect;
  (e) state the amount of the penalty;
  (f) state the justices' chief executive to whom, and the address at which, the penalty may be paid; and
  (g) inform the person to whom it is given of his right to ask to be tried for the alleged offence and explain how that right may be exercised.

(4)–(6) ★ ★ ★ ★ ★

4   Effect of penalty notice

(1) This section applies if a penalty notice is given to a person ("A") under section 2.

(2) If A asks to be tried for the alleged offence, proceedings may be brought against him.

(3) Such a request must be made by a notice given by A—
  (a) in the manner specified in the penalty notice; and
  (b) before the end of the period of suspended enforcement (as to which see section 5).

(4) A request which is made in accordance with subsection (3) is referred to in this Chapter as a "request to be tried".

(5) If, by the end of the suspended enforcement period–
  (a) the penalty has not been paid in accordance with this Chapter, and
  (b) A has not made a request to be tried,
a sum equal to one and a half times the amount of the penalty may be registered under section 8 for enforcement against A as a fine.

5   General restriction on proceedings

(1) Proceedings for the offence to which a penalty notice relates may not be brought until

the end of the period of 21 days beginning with the date on which the notice was given ("the suspended enforcement period").

(2) If the penalty is paid before the end of the suspended enforcement period, no proceedings may be brought for the offence.

(3) Subsection (1) does not apply if the person to whom the penalty notice was given has made a request to be tried.

6   Secretary of State's guidance

The Secretary of State may issue guidance—

   (a) about the exercise of the discretion given to constables by this Chapter;
   (b) about the issuing of penalty notices;
   (c) with a view to encouraging good practice in connection with the operation of provisions of this Chapter.

7–38   ★ ★ ★ ★ ★

39   Intimidation of witnesses

   (1) A person commits an offence if—
   (a) he does an act which intimidates, and is intended to intimidate, another person ("the victim");
   (b) he does the act—
       (i) knowing or believing that the victim is or may be a witness in any relevant proceedings; and
       (ii) intending, by his act, to cause the course of justice to be obstructed, perverted or interfered with;
and
   (c) the act is done after the commencement of those proceedings.

   (2) For the purposes of subsection (1) it is immaterial—
   (a) whether or not the act that is done is done in the presence of the victim;
   (b) whether that act is done to the victim himself or to another person; and
   (c) whether or not the intention to cause the course of justice to be obstructed, perverted or interfered with is the predominating intention of the person doing the act in question.

   (3) If, in proceedings against a person for an offence under this section, it is proved—
   (a) that he did any act that intimidated, and was intended to intimidate, another person, and
   (b) that he did that act knowing or believing that that other person was or might be a witness in any relevant proceedings that had already commenced,
he shall be presumed, unless the contrary is shown, to have done the act with the intention of causing the course of justice to be obstructed, perverted or interfered with.

   (4) A person guilty of an offence under this section shall be liable—
   (a) on conviction on indictment, to imprisonment for a term not exceeding five years or to a fine, or to both;
   (b) on summary conviction, to imprisonment for a term not exceeding six months or to a fine not exceeding the statutory maximum, or to both.

   (5) References in this section to a witness, in relation to any proceedings, include references to a person who provides, or is able to provide, any information or any document or other thing which might be used as evidence in those proceedings or which (whether or not admissible as evidence in those proceedings)—
   (a) might tend to confirm evidence which will be or might be admitted in those proceedings;
   (b) might be referred to in evidence given in those proceedings by another witness; or

(c) might be used as the basis for any cross examination in the course of those proceedings.

(6) References in this section to doing an act include references to issuing any threat (whether against a person or his finances or property or otherwise), or making any other statement.

(7) This section is in addition to, and not in derogation of, any offence subsisting at common law.

40   Harming witnesses etc.

(1) A person commits an offence if, in circumstances falling within subsection (2)—
    (a) he does an act which harms, and is intended to harm, another person; or
    (b) intending to cause another person to fear harm, he threatens to do an act which would harm that other person.

(2) The circumstances fall within this subsection if—
    (a) the person doing or threatening to do the act does so knowing or believing that some person (whether or not the person harmed or threatened or the person against whom harm is threatened) has been a witness in relevant proceedings; and
    (b) he does or threatens to do that act because of that knowledge or belief.

(3) If, in proceedings against a person for an offence under this section, it is proved that, within the relevant period—
    (a) he did an act which harmed, and was intended to harm, another person, or
    (b) intending to cause another person to fear harm, he threatened to do an act which would harm that other person,
and that he did the act, or (as the case may be) threatened to do the act, with the knowledge or belief required by paragraph (a) of subsection (2), he shall be presumed, unless the contrary is shown, to have done the act, or (as the case may be) threatened to do the act, because of that knowledge or belief.

(4) For the purposes of this section it is immaterial—
    (a) whether or not the act that is done or threatened, or the threat that is made, is or would be done or is made in the presence of the person who is or would be harmed or of the person who is threatened;
    (b) whether or not the motive mentioned in subsection (2)(b) is the predominating motive for the act or threat; and
    (c) whether the harm that is done or threatened is physical or financial or is harm to a person or to his property.

(5) A person guilty of an offence under this section shall be liable—
    (a) on conviction on indictment, to imprisonment for a term not exceeding five years or to a fine, or to both;
    (b) on summary conviction, to imprisonment for a term not exceeding six months or to a fine not exceeding the statutory maximum, or to both.

(6) In this section "the relevant period", in relation to an act done, or threat made, with the knowledge or belief that a person has been a witness in any relevant proceedings, means the period that begins with the commencement of those proceedings and ends one year after they are finally concluded.

(7), (8) ★ ★ ★ ★ ★

41   Relevant proceedings

(1) A reference in section 39 or 40 to relevant proceedings is a reference to any proceedings in or before the Court of Appeal, the High Court, the Crown Court or any county court or magistrates' court which—
    (a) are not proceedings for an offence; and
    (b) were commenced after the coming into force of that section.

(2)–(5) ★ ★ ★ ★ ★

42 Police directions stopping the harassment etc of a person in his home

(1) Subject to the following provisions of this section, a constable who is at the scene may give a direction under this section to any person if—

(a) that person is present outside or in the vicinity of any premises that are used by any individual ("the resident") as his dwelling;

(b) that constable believes, on reasonable grounds, that that person is present there for the purpose (by his presence or otherwise) of representing to the resident or another individual (whether or not one who uses the premises as his dwelling), or of persuading the resident or such another individual—

(i) that he should not do something that he is entitled or required to do; or

(ii) that he should do something that he is not under any obligation to do; and

(c) that constable also believes, on reasonable grounds, that the presence of that person (either alone or together with that of any other persons who are also present)—

(i) amounts to, or is likely to result in, the harassment of the resident; or

(ii) is likely to cause alarm or distress to the resident.

(2) A direction under this section is a direction requiring the person to whom it is given to do all such things as the constable giving it may specify as the things he considers necessary to prevent one or both of the following—

(a) the harassment of the resident; or

(b) the causing of any alarm or distress to the resident.

(3) A direction under this section may be given orally; and where a constable is entitled to give a direction under this section to each of several persons outside, or in the vicinity of, any premises, he may give that direction to those persons by notifying them of his requirements either individually or all together.

(4) The requirements that may be imposed by a direction under this section include a requirement to leave the vicinity of the premises in question (either immediately or after a specified period of time).

(5) A direction under this section may make exceptions to any requirement imposed by the direction, and may make any such exception subject to such conditions as the constable giving the direction thinks fit; and those conditions may include–

(a) conditions as to the distance from the premises in question at which, or otherwise as to the location where, persons who do not leave their vicinity must remain; and

(b) conditions as to the number or identity of the persons who are authorised by the exception to remain in the vicinity of those premises.

(6) The power of a constable to give a direction under this section shall not include–

(a) any power to give a direction at any time when there is a more senior-ranking police officer at the scene; or

(b) any power to direct a person to refrain from conduct that is lawful under section 220 of the Trade Union and Labour Relations (Consolidation) Act 1992 (c. 52) (right peacefully to picket a work place);

but it shall include power to vary or withdraw a direction previously given under this section.

(7) Any person who knowingly contravenes a direction given to him under this section shall be guilty of an offence and liable, on summary conviction, to imprisonment for a term not exceeding three months or to a fine not exceeding level 4 on the standard scale, or to both.

(8) A constable in uniform may arrest without warrant any person he reasonably suspects is committing an offence under this section.

(9) In this section "dwelling" has the same meaning as in Part 1 of the Public Order Act 1986 (c. 64).

43–49 ★ ★ ★ ★ ★

PART 2   POWERS OF SEIZURE

Additional powers of seizure

50   Additional powers of seizure from premises

(1) Where—

  (a) a person who is lawfully on any premises finds anything on those premises that he has reasonable grounds for believing may be or may contain something for which he is authorised to search on those premises,

  (b) a power of seizure to which this section applies or the power conferred by subsection (2) would entitle him, if he found it, to seize whatever it is that he has grounds for believing that thing to be or to contain, and

  (c) in all the circumstances, it is not reasonably practicable for it to be determined, on those premises—

    (i) whether what he has found is something that he is entitled to seize, or

    (ii) the extent to which what he has found contains something that he is entitled to seize,

that person's powers of seizure shall include power under this section to seize so much of what he has found as it is necessary to remove from the premises to enable that to be determined.

(2) Where—

  (a) a person who is lawfully on any premises finds anything on those premises ("the seizable property") which he would be entitled to seize but for its being comprised in something else that he has (apart from this subsection) no power to seize,

  (b) the power under which that person would have power to seize the seizable property is a power to which this section applies, and

  (c) in all the circumstances it is not reasonably practicable for the seizable property to be separated, on those premises, from that in which it is comprised,

that person's powers of seizure shall include power under this section to seize both the seizable property and that from which it is not reasonably practicable to separate it.

(3) The factors to be taken into account in considering, for the purposes of this section, whether or not it is reasonably practicable on particular premises for something to be determined, or for something to be separated from something else, shall be confined to the following—

  (a) how long it would take to carry out the determination or separation on those premises;

  (b) the number of persons that would be required to carry out that determination or separation on those premises within a reasonable period;

  (c) whether the determination or separation would (or would if carried out on those premises) involve damage to property;

  (d) the apparatus or equipment that it would be necessary or appropriate to use for the carrying out of the determination or separation; and

  (e) in the case of separation, whether the separation–

    (i) would be likely, or

    (ii) if carried out by the only means that are reasonably practicable on those premises, would be likely,

to prejudice the use of some or all of the separated seizable property for a purpose for which something seized under the power in question is capable of being used.

(4) ★ ★ ★ ★ ★

(5) This sectionapplies toeachof the powers of seizure specifiedinPart 1of Schedule 1.

(6) ★ ★ ★ ★ ★

51   Additional powers of seizure from the person

(1) Where—

(a) a person carrying out a lawful search of any person finds something that he has reasonable grounds for believing may be or may contain something for which he is authorised to search,

(b) a power of seizure to which this section applies or the power conferred by subsection (2) would entitle him, if he found it, to seize whatever it is that he has grounds for believing that thing to be or to contain, and

(c) in all the circumstances it is not reasonably practicable for it to be determined, at the time and place of the search–

   (i) whether what he has found is something that he is entitled to seize, or

   (ii) the extent to which what he has found contains something that he is entitled to seize,

that person's powers of seizure shall include power under this section to seize so much of what he has found as it is necessary to remove from that place to enable that to be determined.

52–53 ★ ★ ★ ★ ★

54 Obligation to return items subject to legal privilege

(1) If, at any time after a seizure of anything has been made in exercise of a power of seizure to which this section applies—

(a) it appears to the person for the time being having possession of the seized property in consequence of the seizure that the property—

   (i) is an item subject to legal privilege, or

   (ii) has such an item comprised in it,

   and

(b) in a case where the item is comprised in something else which has been lawfully seized, it is not comprised in property falling within subsection (2),

it shall be the duty of that person to secure that the item is returned as soon as reasonably practicable after the seizure.

(2) Property in which an item subject to legal privilege is comprised falls within this subsection if—

(a) the whole or a part of the rest of the property is property falling within subsection (3) or property the retention of which is authorised by section 56; and

(b) in all the circumstances, it is not reasonably practicable for that item to be separated from the rest of that property (or, as the case may be, from that part of it) without prejudicing the use of the rest of that property, or that part of it, for purposes for which (disregarding that item) its use, if retained, would be lawful.

Remedies and safeguards

59 Application to the appropriate judicial authority

(1) This section applies where anything has been seized in exercise, or purported exercise, of a relevant power of seizure.

(2) Any person with a relevant interest in the seized property may apply to the appropriate judicial authority, on one or more of the grounds mentioned in subsection (3), for the return of the whole or a part of the seized property.

(3) Those grounds are—

(a) that there was no power to make the seizure;

(b) that the seized property is or contains an item subject to legal privilege that is not comprised in property falling within section 54(2);

(c) that the seized property is or contains any excluded material or special procedure material which—

   (i) has been seized under a power to which section 55 applies;

   (ii) is not comprised in property falling within section 55(2) or (3); and

(iii) is not property the retention of which is authorised by section 56;

(d) that the seized property is or contains something seized under section 50 or 51 which does not fall within section 53(3);

and subsections (5) and (6) of section 55 shall apply for the purposes of paragraph (c) as they apply for the purposes of that section.

(4) Subject to subsection (6), the appropriate judicial authority, on an application under subsection (2), shall—

(a) if satisfied as to any of the matters mentioned in subsection (3), order the return of so much of the seized property as is property in relation to which the authority is so satisfied; and

(b) to the extent that that authority is not so satisfied, dismiss the application.

(5)–(7) ★ ★ ★ ★ ★

60–63 ★ ★ ★ ★ ★

64 Meaning of "appropriate judicial authority"

(1) Subject to subsection (2), in this Part "appropriate judicial authority" means—

(a) in relation to England and Wales and Northern Ireland, a judge of the Crown Court;

(b) in relation to Scotland, a sheriff.

(2) ★ ★ ★ ★ ★

★ ★ ★ ★ ★

International Criminal Court Act 2001
(2001, c. 17)

An Act to give effect to the Statute of the International Criminal Court; to provide for offences under the law of England and Wales and Northern Ireland corresponding to offences within the jurisdiction of that Court; and for connected purposes. [11 May 2001]

Territorial extent: The United Kingdom (but not in relation to all provisions: see e.g., s. 51 below).

PART 1   THE INTERNATIONAL CRIMINAL COURT

1   The ICC and the ICC Statute

(1) In this Act—

"the ICC" means the International Criminal Court established by the Statute of the International Criminal Court, done at Rome on 17th July 1998;

"the ICC Statute" means that Statute; and

"ICC crime" means a crime (other than the crime of aggression) over which the ICC has jurisdiction in accordance with the ICC Statute.

(2) References in this Act to articles are, unless otherwise indicated, to articles of the ICC Statute.

(3) Schedule 1 to this Act contains supplementary provisions relating to the ICC.

PART 2   ARREST AND DELIVERY OF PERSONS

Proceedings on request

2   Request for arrest and surrender

(1) Where the Secretary of State receives a request from the ICC for the arrest and sur-render of a person alleged to have committed an ICC crime, or to have been convicted by the ICC, he shall transmit the request and the documents accompanying it to an appropriate judicial officer.

(2) If it appears to the Secretary of State that the request should be considered by an appropriate judicial officer in Scotland, he shall transmit the request and the documents accompanying it to the Scottish Ministers who shall transmit them to an appropriate judicial officer.

(3) If the request is accompanied by a warrant of arrest and the appropriate judicial officer is satisfied that the warrant appears to have been issued by the ICC, he shall endorse the warrant for execution in the United Kingdom.

(4) If in the case of a person convicted by the ICC the request is not accompanied by a warrant of arrest, but is accompanied by—

(a) a copy of the judgment of conviction,

(b) information to demonstrate that the person sought is the one referred to in the judgment of conviction, and

(c) where the person sought has been sentenced, a copy of the sentence imposed and a statement of any time already served and the time remaining to be served,

the officer shall issue a warrant for the arrest of the person to whom the request relates.

(5) In this Part a warrant endorsed or issued under this section is referred to as a "section 2 warrant".

3   Request for provisional arrest

(1) This section applies where the Secretary of State receives from the ICC a request for the provisional arrest of a person alleged to have committed an ICC crime or to have been convicted by the ICC.

(2) If it appears to the Secretary of State that application for a warrant should be made in England and Wales—

(a) he shall transmit the request to a constable and direct the constable to apply for a warrant for the arrest of that person, and

(b) on an application by a constable stating on oath that he has reason to believe—

(i) that a request has been made on grounds of urgency by the ICC for the arrest of a person, and

(ii) that the person is in, or on his way to, the United Kingdom, an appropriate judicial officer shall issue a warrant for the arrest of that person.

(3), (4) ★ ★ ★ ★ ★

(5) In this Part a warrant issued under this section is referred to as a "provisional warrant".

4   Dealing with person arrested under provisional warrant

(1) A person arrested under a provisional warrant shall be brought before a competent court as soon as is practicable.

(2) If there is produced to the court a section 2 warrant in respect of that person, the court shall proceed as if he had been arrested under that warrant.

(3) If no such warrant is produced, the court shall remand him pending the production of such a warrant.

(4)–(7) ★ ★ ★ ★ ★

5 Proceedings for delivery order

(1) A person arrested under a section 2 warrant shall be brought before a competent court as soon as is practicable.

(2) If the competent court is satisfied—
   (a) that the warrant—
      (i) is a warrant of the ICC and has been duly endorsed under section 2(3), or
      (ii) has been duly issued under section 2(4), and
   (b) that the person brought before the court is the person named or described in the warrant,

it shall make a delivery order.

(3) A "delivery order" is an order that the person be delivered up—
   (a) into the custody of the ICC, or
   (b) if the ICC so directs in the case of a person convicted by the ICC, into the custody of the state of enforcement,

in accordance with arrangements made by the Secretary of State.

(4) In the case of a person alleged to have committed an ICC crime, the competent court may adjourn the proceedings pending the outcome of any challenge before the ICC to the admissibility of the case or to the jurisdiction of the ICC.

(5) In deciding whether to make a delivery order the court is not concerned to enquire—
   (a) whether any warrant issued by the ICC was duly issued, or
   (b) in the case of a person alleged to have committed an ICC crime, whether there is evidence to justify his trial for the offence he is alleged to have committed.

(6) Whether or not it makes a delivery order, the competent court may of its own motion, and shall on the application of the person arrested, determine—
   (a) whether the person was lawfully arrested in pursuance of the warrant, and
   (b) whether his rights have been respected.

(7) In making a determination under subsection (6) the court shall apply the principles which would be applied on an application for judicial review.

(8) If the court determines—
   (a) that the person has not been lawfully arrested in pursuance of the warrant, or
   (b) that the person's rights have not been respected,

it shall make a declaration or declarator to that effect, but may not grant any other relief.

(9) The court shall notify the Secretary of State (and, where the proceedings are in Scotland, the Scottish Ministers) of any declaration or declarator under subsection (8) and the Secretary of State shall transmit that notification to the ICC.

6–22 ★ ★ ★ ★ ★

Supplementary provisions

23 Provisions as to state or diplomatic immunity

(1) Any state or diplomatic immunity attaching to a person by reason of a connection with a state party to the ICC Statute does not prevent proceedings under this Part in relation to that person.

(2) Where—
   (a) state or diplomatic immunity attaches to a person by reason of a connection with a state other than a state party to the ICC Statute, and
   (b) waiver of that immunity is obtained by the ICC in relation to a request for that person's surrender,

the waiver shall be treated as extending to proceedings under this Part in connection with that request.

(3) A certificate by the Secretary of State—

(a) that a state is or is not a party to the ICC Statute, or

(b) that there has been such a waiver as is mentioned in subsection (2),

is conclusive evidence of that fact for the purposes of this Part.

(4) The Secretary of State may in any particular case, after consultation with the ICC and the state concerned, direct that proceedings (or further proceedings) under this Part which, but for subsection (1) or (2), would be prevented by state or diplomatic immunity attaching to a person shall not be taken against that person.

(5), (6) ★ ★ ★ ★ ★

24-27 ★ ★ ★ ★ ★

28 Questioning

(1) This section applies where the Secretary of State receives a request from the ICC for assistance in questioning a person being investigated or prosecuted.

(2) The person concerned shall not be questioned in pursuance of the request unless—

(a) he has been informed of his rights under article 55, and

(b) he consents to be interviewed.

(3) The provisions of article 55 are set out in Schedule 3 to this Act.

(4) Consent for the purposes of subsection (2)(b) may be given—

(a) by the person himself, or

(b) in circumstances in which it is inappropriate for the person to act for himself, by reason of his physical or mental condition or his youth, by an appropriate person acting on his behalf.

(5) Such consent may be given orally or in writing, but if given orally it shall be recorded in writing as soon as is reasonably practicable.

29-50 ★ ★ ★ ★ ★

51 Genocide, crimes against humanity and war crimes

(1) It is an offence against the law of England and Wales for a person to commit genocide, a crime against humanity or a war crime.

(2) This section applies to acts committed—

(a) in England or Wales, or

(b) outside the United Kingdom by a United Kingdom national, a United Kingdom resident or a person subject to UK service jurisdiction.

★ ★ ★ ★ ★

SCHEDULE 3   RIGHTS OF PERSONS DURING INVESTIGATION: ARTICLE 55

Article 55

Rights of persons during an investigation

In respect of an investigation under this Statute, a person:

(a) Shall not be compelled to incriminate himself or herself or to confess guilt;

(b) Shall not be subjected to any form of coercion, duress or threat, to torture or to any other form of cruel, inhuman or degrading treatment or punishment;

(c) Shall, if questioned in a language other than a language the person fully understands and speaks, have, free of any cost, the assistance of a competent interpreter and such translations as are necessary to meet the requirements of fairness; and

(d) Shall not be subjected to arbitrary arrest or detention, and shall not be deprived of his or her liberty except on such grounds and in accordance with such procedures as are established in this Statute.

Where there are grounds to believe that a person has committed a crime within the jurisdiction of the Court and that person is about to be questioned either by the Prosecutor, or by national authorities pursuant to a request made under Part 9, that person shall also have the following rights of which he or she shall be informed prior to being questioned:

(a) To be informed, prior to being questioned, that there are grounds to believe that he or she has committed a crime within the jurisdiction of the Court;

(b) To remain silent, without such silence being a consideration in the determination of guilt or innocence;

(c) To have legal assistance of the person's choosing, or, if the person does not have legal assistance, to have legal assistance assigned to him or her, in any case where the interests of justice so require, and without payment by the person in any such case if the person does not have sufficient means to pay for it; and

(d) To be questioned in the presence of counsel unless the person has voluntarily waived his or her right to counsel.

★ ★ ★ ★ ★

British Overseas Territories Act 2002
(2002, c. 8)

An Act to make provision about the name "British overseas territories" and British citizenship so far as relating to the British overseas territories. [26 February 2002]

Territorial extent: United Kingdom

Change of names

1 British overseas territories
(1) As the territories mentioned in Schedule 6 to the British Nationality Act 1981 (c.61) are now known as "British overseas territories"—

(a) in section 50(1) of that Act (definitions), at the appropriate place insert—
" 'British overseas territory' means a territory mentioned in Schedule 6;",

(b) for "dependent territory" (or "dependent territories"), wherever occurring in that Act, substitute "British overseas territory" (or "British overseas territories"), and

(c) in the heading to that Schedule, for "British Dependent Territories" substitute "British Overseas Territories".

(2) In any other enactment passed or made before the commencement of this section (including an enactment comprised in subordinate legislation), any reference to a dependent territory within the meaning of the British Nationality Act 1981 shall be read as a reference to a British overseas territory.

(3) In the Interpretation Act 1978 (c.30), at the appropriate place in Schedule 1 (list of definitions) insert—
" 'British overseas territory' has the same meaning as in the British Nationality Act 1981;".

2 British overseas territories citizenship
(1) Pursuant to section 1, British Dependent Territories citizenship is renamed "British overseas territories citizenship"; and a person having that citizenship is a "British overseas territories citizen".

(2), (3) ★ ★ ★ ★ ★

British citizenship

3 Conferral on British overseas territories citizens
(1) Any person who, immediately before the commencement of this section, is a British

overseas territories citizen shall, on the commencement of this section, become a British citizen.

(2) Subsection (1) does not apply to a person who is a British overseas territories citizen by virtue only of a connection with the Sovereign Base Areas of Akrotiri and Dhekelia.

(3) A person who is a British citizen by virtue of this section is a British citizen by descent for the purposes of the British Nationality Act 1981 if, and only if—

(a) he was a British overseas territories citizen by descent immediately before the commencement of this section, and

(b) if at that time he was a British citizen as well as a British overseas territories citizen, he was a British citizen by descent.

European Communities (Amendment) Act 2002
(2002, c. 3)

An Act to make provision consequential on the Treaty signed at Nice on 26th February 2001 amending the Treaty on European Union, the Treaties establishing the European Communities and certain related Acts.   [26 February 2002]

Territorial extent: United Kingdom

Note: This Act amends s. 1 of the European Communities Act 1972 by adding to the list of Treaties Articles 2 to 10 of the Treaty of Nice, and the other provisions of the Treaty so far as relating to those Articles, and the Protocols adopted on the occasion of the signing of the Treaty. That Treaty is also declared by s. 3 of the Act to be approved for the purpose of s. 6 of the European Parliamentary Elections Act 1978.

Office of Communications Act 2002
(2002, c. 11)

An Act to establish a body corporate to be known as the Office of Communications; and to confer functions in relation to proposals about the regulation of communications on that body, on certain existing regulators and on the Secretary of State.   [19 March 2002]

Territorial extent: United Kingdom

1   The Office of Communications

(1) There shall be a body corporate to be known as the Office of Communications (in this Act referred to as "OFCOM").

(2) OFCOM shall consist of such number of members as the Secretary of State may determine; but he shall not determine a membership for OFCOM of less than three or more than six.

(3) The membership of OFCOM shall comprise—

(a) a chairman appointed by the Secretary of State;

(b) such number of other members appointed by the Secretary of State as he may determine; and

(c) the executive members.

(4) The executive members of OFCOM shall comprise—

(a) the chief executive of OFCOM; and

(b) such other persons (if any) as may be appointed by the Secretary of OFCOM from amongst their employees.

(5) It shall be for the members of OFCOM mentioned in subsection (3)(a) and (b), after consulting the chief executive of OFCOM—

    (a) to determine whether there should be any executive members falling within subsection (4)(b) and (subject to subsections (2) and (6)(a)) how many; and

    (b) to make any appointments of executive members required for the purposes of any such determination.

(6) The Secretary of State—

    (a) may, by a direction to OFCOM, set a maximum and a minimum number for the executive members of OFCOM; and

    (b) shall exercise his powers under this section to secure that the number of executive members of OFCOM is, so far as practicable, at all times less than the number of other members.

(7)–(10) ★ ★ ★ ★ ★

2 Initial function of OFCOM

(1) It shall be the function of OFCOM (subject to subsection (5)) to do such things as they consider appropriate for facilitating the implementation of, or for securing the modification of, any relevant proposals about the regulation of communications.

(2) It shall be the duty of OFCOM to carry out their function under subsection (1) in such manner as—

    (a) appears to them to ensure, so far as they are facilitating the implementation of any such proposals, that there is effective co-operation in relation to the implementation of the proposals between themselves and both the existing regulators and the Secretary of State; and

    (b) does not interfere—

        (i) with the effective carrying out by the existing regulators of the functions conferred on them otherwise than by this Act; or

        (ii) with the effective carrying out by the Secretary of State of his functions relating to wireless telegraphy.

(3) In this Act references to relevant proposals about the regulation of communications are references to the following proposals (whether or not Parliament has given any approval on which the implementation of the proposals depends)—

    (a) any proposals by the Secretary of State for the conferring on OFCOM (whether by transfers from the existing regulators or otherwise) of any functions relating to telecommunications, wireless telegraphy, broadcasting, radio and television services or other activities connected with the communications industry; and

    (b) any other proposals by the Secretary of State made in association with any proposals falling within paragraph (a) and relating to the subject-matter of those proposals, to any matters that are incidental or supplemental to those proposals or to any consequential or transitional matters.

(4) Subject to subsections (5) and (6), OFCOM shall have power, for the purpose of carrying out their function under subsection (1), to do such things as appear to them to be incidental or conducive to the carrying out of that function.

(5) Nothing in this section shall be taken, in relation to proposals that have not yet been approved by Parliament—

    (a) as dispensing with the need for any Parliamentary approval otherwise required for the implementation of the proposals; or

    (b) as authorising OFCOM, before any such approval is given, to engage in any activities other than activities which are connected with, or consist in, either—

        (i) the formulation of the proposals; or

        (ii) the taking of preparatory steps towards their implementation when approved.

(6) OFCOM shall not have any power, for the purposes of or in connection with their

function under this section, to borrow money from any person other than the Secretary of State.

3   Management of OFCOM

OFCOM shall, in managing their affairs, have regard—

    (a) to such general guidance concerning the management of the affairs of public bodies as OFCOM consider appropriate; and

    (b) subject to any such guidance and only to the extent that they may reasonably be regarded as applicable in relation to a statutory corporation, to generally accepted principles of good corporate governance.

4   Functions of existing regulators

(1) The functions of each of the existing regulators shall (subject to subsection (4)) include—

    (a) a duty to do everything that is necessary for facilitating the implementation of any relevant proposals about the regulation of communications;

    (b) a duty to carry out all that regulator's functions in such manner as appears to that regulator best to secure that OFCOM—

        (i) is able effectively to carry out their function under section 2(1); and

        (ii) will be able effectively to carry out any functions which will become functions of OFCOM in consequence of the implementation of any such proposals;

    (c) a power to do all such other things as that regulator considers appropriate for facilitating the implementation of, or for securing the modification of, any relevant proposals about the regulation of communications;

    (d) a power to carry out the functions of that regulator in a manner that promotes the interests of OFCOM.

(2) It shall be the duty of each of the existing regulators to comply with any direction by the Secretary of State, in relation to the carrying out of that regulator's functions under this Act, that requires that regulator—

    (a) to prepare a draft scheme setting out, in the manner required by the Secretary of State, the regulator's proposals for any such transfers of property, rights and liabilities from that regulator to OFCOM as may be specified or described in the direction;

    (b) to consult with OFCOM about those proposals; and

    (c) to submit that draft scheme, in such form as he may require, to the Secretary of State.

(3)–(5) ★ ★ ★ ★ ★

5   Winding up of OFCOM on abandonment etc. of proposals

(1) If, in consequence of the abandonment or modification of any relevant proposals about the regulation of communications it appears to the Secretary of State that it is no longer necessary for OFCOM to continue to exist, he may by order provide for the winding up and dissolution of OFCOM.

(2) If, in consequence of the abandonment or modification of any relevant proposals about the regulation of communications, it appears to the Secretary of State at any time after the end of 2003 that it is no longer necessary for OFCOM to continue to exist, it shall be the Secretary of State's duty to lay before Parliament a draft of an order under subsection (1) providing for OFCOM to be wound up and dissolved as soon as reasonably practicable.

(3) The power to make an order under this section shall be exercisable by statutory instrument, and no such order shall be made unless a draft of the order has been laid before Parliament and has been approved by a resolution of each House.

(4)–(7) ★ ★ ★ ★ ★

6   Interpretation

(1) In this Act—

"existing regulator" means any of the following—

(a) the Broadcasting Standards Commission;

(b) the Director General of Telecommunications;

(c) the Independent Television Commission;

(d) the Radio Authority;

★ ★ ★ ★ ★

SCHEDULE   FURTHER PROVISION ABOUT OFCOM

Qualification for membership of non-executive members

1   (1) Before appointing a person to be the chairman or another non-executive member of OFCOM, the Secretary of State shall satisfy himself that that person will have no such financial or other interest as is likely to affect prejudicially the carrying out by him of his functions as a member of OFCOM.

(2) The Secretary of State shall also satisfy himself from time to time with respect to the chairman and every other non-executive member of OFCOM that that member has no such interest.

(3) Every person who—

(a) is a person whom the Secretary of State proposes to appoint to be the chairman or another non-executive member of OFCOM, or

(b) is the chairman or another non-executive member of OFCOM,

shall, whenever requested by the Secretary of State to do so, furnish him with such information as the Secretary of State considers necessary for the performance by him of his duties under sub-paragraphs (1) and (2).

(4) For the purposes of this paragraph and paragraph 2 a person shall not be taken to have an interest that is likely to affect prejudicially the carrying out by him of his functions as a member of OFCOM by reason only that he is or has been—

(a) the Director General of Telecommunications;

(b) a member of another existing regulator;

(c) a member of the staff of any of the existing regulators; or

(d) a person engaged on the Secretary of State's behalf in any activities connected with the carrying out of the Secretary of State's functions relating to wireless telegraphy.

★ ★ ★ ★ ★

Scottish Public Services Ombudsman Act 2002

(2002 asp 11)

An Act of the Scottish Parliament to make provision (including provision for the purposes of section 91 of the Scotland Act 1998) for the appointment and functions of the Scottish Public Services Ombudsman; and for connected purposes.   [23 April 2002]

Territorial extent: Scotland

The Scottish Public Services Ombudsman

1   The Scottish Public Services Ombudsman

(1) For the purposes of this Act there is to be an officer known as the Scottish Public

Services Ombudsman (in this Act referred to as the "Ombudsman") who is to be an individual appointed by Her Majesty on the nomination of the Scottish Parliament.

(2) Her Majesty may, on the nomination of the Parliament, appoint individuals to be deputy Scottish Public Services Ombudsmen; and in this Act references to a deputy Ombudsman are to any such deputy.

(3) There are to be no more than three deputy Ombudsmen at any time.

(4) The Ombudsman's functions may be exercised by a deputy Ombudsman if—

(a) the office of Ombudsman is vacant (unless there is an acting Ombudsman appointed under paragraph 5(1) of schedule 1), or

(b) the Ombudsman is for any reason unable to act,

and while exercising those functions the deputy Ombudsman is to be treated for all purposes, except those of paragraphs 3(a), 4, 7 and 8 of schedule 1, as the Ombudsman.

(5) ★ ★ ★ ★ ★

Investigations by the Ombudsman

2   Power of investigation

(1) The Ombudsman may investigate any matter, whenever arising, if—

(a) the matter consists of action taken by or on behalf of a person liable to investigation under this Act,

(b) the matter is one which the Ombudsman is entitled to investigate, and

(c) a complaint in respect of the matter has been duly made to the Ombudsman.

(2) The Ombudsman may investigate any matter, whenever arising, if—

(a) paragraphs (a) and (b) of subsection (1) are satisfied, and

(b) the person liable to investigation has requested the Ombudsman to investigate the matter.

(3) Without prejudice to paragraph 2(2) of schedule 1, it is for the Ombudsman to decide whether to initiate, continue or discontinue an investigation under subsection (1) or (2).

(4) The Ombudsman may take such action in connection with the complaint or request as the Ombudsman thinks may be of assistance in reaching any such decision.

(5) Such action may, in particular, include action with a view to resolving the complaint or request.

3   Persons liable to investigation

(1) The persons liable to investigation under this Act are the persons specified, or of a class specified, in Parts 1 and 2 of schedule 2; and references in this Act to a listed authority are references to any such person.

(2) Her Majesty may by Order in Council amend Part 2 of that schedule so as to—

(a) modify any entry in it,

(b) remove any entry from it, or

(c) subject to subsections (3) to (6) and section 4, add any entry to it.

(3) An entry may be added to that Part of that schedule only if the entry relates to a person who, or a class of persons each of whom, is—

(a) a Scottish public authority with mixed functions or no reserved functions,

(b) a publicly-owned company, or

(c) a person who is neither a Scottish public authority nor a publicly-owned company but who appears to Her Majesty to exercise functions of a public nature.

(4), (5) ★ ★ ★ ★ ★

(6) No entry is to be added to Part 2 of schedule 2 in relation to—

(a) a person whose sole activity is, or whose main activities are—

(i) the provision of education, or the provision of training otherwise than under the Industrial Training Act 1982,

(ii) the development of curricula, the conduct of examinations or the validation of educational courses,

(iii) the control of entry to any profession or the regulation of the conduct of members of any profession, or

(iv) the investigation of complaints by members of the public regarding the actions of any person or the supervision or review of such investigations or of steps taken following them, or

(b) a person operating in an exclusively or predominantly commercial manner or a person carrying on under national ownership an industry or undertaking or part of an industry or undertaking.

4 ★ ★ ★ ★ ★

5 Matters which may be investigated

(1) The matters which the Ombudsman is entitled to investigate are—

(a) in relation to a listed authority other than one to whom paragraph (b), (d) or (e) applies, any action taken by or behalf of the authority (other than action consisting of a service failure) in the exercise of administrative functions of the authority,

(b) in relation to a health service body or an independent provider, any action taken by or on behalf of the body or provider (other than action consisting of a service failure),

(c) in relation to a listed authority other than one to whom paragraph (d) or (e) applies, any service failure,

(d) in relation to a family health service provider, any action taken by or on behalf of the provider in connection with any family health services provided by that provider,

(e) in relation to a registered social landlord, any action taken by or on behalf of the landlord.

(2) In subsection (1), "service failure", in relation to a listed authority, means—

(a) any failure in a service provided by the authority,

(b) any failure of the authority to provide a service which it was a function of the authority to provide.

(3) The Ombudsman may investigate a matter falling within subsection (1) pursuant to a complaint only if a member of the public claims to have sustained injustice or hardship in consequence of—

(a) where the matter is such action as is mentioned in paragraph (a), (b) or (e) of that subsection, maladministration in connection with the action in question,

(b) where the matter is such failure or other action as is mentioned in paragraph (c) or (d), the failure or other action in question.

(4) A person making such a claim is referred to in this Act as the "person aggrieved".

(5) The Ombudsman may investigate a matter falling within subsection (1) pursuant to a request only if the Ombudsman is satisfied that—

(a) it has been alleged publicly (whether or not by a person aggrieved) that one or more members of the public have sustained injustice or hardship as mentioned in subsection (3), and

(b) the listed authority in question has taken all reasonable steps to deal with the matter to which the allegation relates.

(6) In this section "member of the public" means any individual or body of persons (whether incorporated or not) other than—

(a) the Parliamentary corporation,

(b) a local authority or other authority or body constituted for purposes of the public service or of local government,

(c) an authority or body constituted for the purposes of carrying on under national ownership an industry or undertaking or part of an industry or undertaking,

(d) any other authority or body—

      (i)   whose members are appointed by Her Majesty or by any Minister of the Crown or government department or by a member of the Scottish Executive, or

      (ii) whose revenues consist wholly or mainly of money provided by the Parliament of the United Kingdom or sums payable out of the Scottish Consolidated Fund (whether directly or indirectly).

(7) This section is subject to sections 6 to 8.

6 ★ ★ ★ ★ ★

7 Matters which may be investigated: restrictions

(1) The Ombudsman is not entitled to question the merits of a decision taken without maladministration by or on behalf of a listed authority in the exercise of a discretion vested in that authority.

(2) Subsection (1) does not apply to the merits of a decision taken by or on behalf of a health service body, a family health service provider or an independent provider to the extent that the decision was taken in consequence of the exercise of clinical judgement.

(3) The Ombudsman must not investigate action taken by or on behalf of a member of the Scottish Executive unless the action was taken in the exercise of functions conferred on the Scottish Ministers or of functions conferred on the First Minister alone.

(4) For the purposes of subsection (3), functions conferred on the Scottish Ministers include functions exercised by them on behalf of a Minister of the Crown or government department by virtue of section 93 (agency arrangements) of the Scotland Act 1998 (c.46).

(5)–(7) ★ ★ ★ ★ ★

(8) The Ombudsman must not investigate any matter in respect of which the person aggrieved has or had—

      (a) a right of appeal to a Minister of the Crown or the Scottish Ministers,

      (b) a right of appeal, reference or review to or before any tribunal constituted by or under any enactment or by virtue of Her Majesty's prerogative, or

      (c) a remedy by way of proceedings in any court of law,

unless the Ombudsman is satisfied that, in the particular circumstances, it is not reasonable to expect the person aggrieved to resort or have resorted to the right or remedy.

(9) Subsection (10) applies where a matter in respect of which a complaint is made under this Act—

      (a) is a matter in respect of which a complaint can be made, or a review can be requested, by the person aggrieved under a procedure operated by any listed authority (whether or not the listed authority in relation to whom the complaint under this Act is made), and

      (b) is not a matter of the kind mentioned in subsection (8) or paragraph 12 of schedule 4.

(10) In such a case, the Ombudsman must not investigate the matter unless the Ombudsman is satisfied that—

      (a) the other procedure has been invoked and exhausted, or

      (b) in the particular circumstances it is not reasonable to expect the procedure to be invoked or, as the case may be, exhausted.

8 Excluded matters

(1) The Ombudsman must not investigate any matter specified in schedule 4.

(2) Her Majesty may by Order in Council amend schedule 4 so as to—

      (a) modify any entry in it,

      (b) remove any entry from it,

      (c) add any entry to it.

(3) Nothing in section 7 or schedule 4 prevents the Ombudsman conducting an

investigation in respect of action taken by a listed authority in operating a procedure established to examine complaints or review decisions.

9   Complaints: who may complain

(1) A complaint may be made to the Ombudsman—
   (a) by the person aggrieved, or
   (b) by a person authorised in writing for the purpose by the person aggrieved.

(2) The persons who may be authorised for the purpose of subsection (1)(b) include, in particular—
   (a) a member of the Scottish Parliament,
   (b) a listed authority,
   (c) a member, officer or member of staff of a listed authority.

(3) Despite subsection (1)—
   (a) where an individual by whom a complaint might have been made has died or is for any reason unable to act, the complaint may be made by—
      (i) any person authorised for the purpose of subsection (1)(b) before the individual's death or inability to act,
      (ii) the individual's personal representatives or a member of the individual's family, or
      (iii) any other person suitable to represent the individual,
   (b) where a body by whom a complaint might have been made is for any reason unable to act for itself, the complaint may be made by another person suitable to represent it.

(4) Except where subsection (5) applies, the person aggrieved must be resident in the United Kingdom at the time the complaint is made (or, if the person has died, must have been so resident at the time of death).

(5) This subsection applies where the complaint relates to action taken—
   (a) in relation to the person while the person was present—
      (i) in the United Kingdom, or
      (ii) on an installation in a designated area within the meaning of the Continental Shelf Act 1964, a ship registered in the United Kingdom or an aircraft so registered, or
   (b) in relation to rights or obligations which accrued or arose in the United Kingdom or on such an installation, ship or aircraft.

10   Complaints: time limits and procedure

(1) The Ombudsman must not consider a complaint made more than 12 months after the day on which the person aggrieved first had notice of the matter complained of, unless the Ombudsman is satisfied that there are special circumstances which make it appropriate to consider a complaint made outwith that period.

(2) ★ ★ ★ ★ ★

(3) A complaint must be made in writing or electronically unless the Ombudsman is satisfied that there are special circumstances which make it appropriate to consider a complaint made orally.

(4) It is for the Ombudsman to determine whether a complaint has been duly made.

11   ★ ★ ★ ★ ★

12   Investigation procedure

(1) An investigation under section 2 must be conducted in private.

(2) Where the investigation is pursuant to a complaint, the Ombudsman must give—
   (a) the listed authority in question, and
   (b) any other person who is alleged in the complaint to have taken the action complained of,

an opportunity to comment on any allegations contained in the complaint.

(3) In other respects the procedure for conducting the investigation is to be such as the Ombudsman thinks fit.

(4) The Ombudsman may, in particular—

(a) obtain information from such persons and in such manner, and make such inquiries, as the Ombudsman thinks fit,

(b) determine whether any person may be represented, by counsel or solicitor or otherwise, in the investigation.

(5) The Ombudsman may pay to—

(a) the person by whom the complaint was made (where an investigation is pursuant to a complaint), and

(b) any other person who attends or supplies information for the purposes of an investigation (whether or not pursuant to a complaint),

such allowances in respect of expenses properly incurred by the person and by way of compensation for loss of time as the Parliamentary corporation may determine.

(6) The conduct of an investigation does not affect—

(a) any action taken by the listed authority in question,

(b) any power or duty of the listed authority to take further action with respect to any matter being investigated.

13   Evidence

(1) For the purposes of an investigation, the Ombudsman may require the listed authority in question and any of the persons mentioned in subsection (2) to supply information or produce documents relevant to the investigation.

(2) Those persons are—

(a) any member, officer or member of staff of the listed authority, and

(b) any other person,

who in the Ombudsman's opinion is able to supply such information or to produce such documents.

(3) Where the listed authority in question is an office-holder in the Scottish Administration, the persons referred to in subsection (2)(a) include, in particular—

(a) any other office-holder in the Scottish Administration,

(b) any member of the staff of the Scottish Administration assigned to assist the office-holder under investigation in the exercise of the office-holder's functions.

(4) For the purposes of any such investigation the Ombudsman has the same powers as the Court of Session in respect of—

(a) the attendance and examination of witnesses (including the administration of oaths and the examination of witnesses abroad), and

(b) the production of documents.

(5) No obligation to maintain secrecy or other restriction on the disclosure of information obtained by or supplied to persons in Her Majesty's service, whether imposed by any enactment or by any rule of law, applies to the disclosure of information for the purposes of an investigation by the Ombudsman.

(6) The Crown (whether in right of Her Majesty's Government in the United Kingdom or in right of the Scottish Administration) is not entitled in relation to any investigation by the Ombudsman to any such privilege in respect of the production of documents or the giving of evidence as is allowed by law in legal proceedings.

(7) No person is or may be required or authorised by virtue of this Act to supply any information or answer any question relating to proceedings of the Scottish Cabinet or of any committee of the Scottish Cabinet, or to produce so much of any document as relates to such proceedings.

(8) For the purposes of subsection (7), a certificate issued by the most senior member of

the staff of the Scottish Administration, with the approval of the First Minister, and certifying that any information, question, document or part of a document so relates is conclusive.

(9) Subject to subsections (5) and (6), no person is compelled, for the purposes of an investigation by the Ombudsman, to give any evidence or produce any document which that person could not be compelled to give or to produce in civil proceedings before the Court of Session.

14 ★ ★ ★ ★ ★

15 Reports on investigations

(1) After conducting an investigation, the Ombudsman must—

    (a) if the investigation is pursuant to a complaint, send a report of the investigation to the persons specified in section 11(2) and to the Scottish Ministers,

    (b) if the investigation is pursuant to a request, send a report of the investigation to the persons specified in section 11(4) and to the Scottish Ministers,

and must lay a copy of the report before the Parliament.

(2) Subsection (3) of section 11 applies for the purposes of subsection (1)(a) of this section as it does for the purposes of subsection (2)(d) of that section.

(3) Apart from identifying the listed authority in question, the report must not—

    (a) mention the name of any person, or

    (b) contain any particulars which, in the Ombudsman's opinion, are likely to identify any person and can be omitted without impairing the effectiveness of the report,

unless the Ombudsman determines that it is necessary to do so.

(4) The listed authority in question must, unless the Ombudsman otherwise directs—

    (a) make arrangements, having effect for a period of at least 3 weeks, for allowing any person to—

        (i) inspect the report at any reasonable time,

        (ii) obtain a copy of it, or any part of it (whether or not on payment of a reasonable fee), and

    (b) publicise those arrangements.

(5)–(7) ★ ★ ★ ★ ★

16 Special reports

(1) This section applies where a report under section 15 finds that the person aggrieved has sustained injustice or hardship as is mentioned in section 5(3).

(2) If, following the making of the report, it appears to the Ombudsman that the injustice or hardship has not been, or will not be, remedied, the Ombudsman may make a special report on the case.

(3) The Ombudsman must—

    (a) send a special report made under subsection (2) to the persons to whom the report under section 15 was sent, and

    (b) lay a copy of the report before the Parliament.

(4) Section 15(3) applies in relation to a special report as it applies in relation to a report under that section.

(5) The Ombudsman may make arrangements for the special report to be available to the public in such manner (whether or not on payment of a reasonable fee) as the Ombudsman thinks fit.

(6) The listed authority to whom the special report relates is liable to reimburse the Ombudsman in respect of any expenses incurred by the Ombudsman by virtue of subsection (5).

★ ★ ★ ★ ★

SCHEDULE 4   MATTERS WHICH THE OMBUDSMAN MUST NOT INVESTIGATE

1. Action taken—
   (a) by or with the authority of a member of the Scottish Executive, or
   (b) by any police authority or any joint police board constituted by an amalgamation scheme made or approved under the Police (Scotland) Act 1967 (c. 77),
for the purposes of or in connection with the investigation or prevention of crime or the protection of the security of the State.

2. The commencement or conduct of—
   (a) civil or criminal proceedings before any court of law, or
   (b) proceedings before any international court or tribunal.

3. Action taken by any office-holder in, or member of the staff of, the Scottish Administration appointed to be an officer, or a member of the administrative staff, of any court or tribunal, so far as that action is taken at the direction, or on the authority (whether express or implied), of any person acting in a judicial capacity or in the capacity of a member of the tribunal.

4. Action taken by a member of the administrative staff of any tribunal specified in schedule 3 so far as that action is taken at the direction, or on the authority (whether express or implied), of any person acting in the capacity of a member of the tribunal.

5. Action taken by a person appointed under section 5(3)(c) of the Criminal Injuries Compensation Act 1995, so far as that action is taken at the direction, or on the authority (whether express or implied), of any person acting in the capacity of an adjudicator appointed under that section to determine appeals.

6. Any exercise of the prerogative of mercy or of the power of a member of the Scottish Executive to make a reference in respect of any person to the High Court of Justiciary.

7. (1) Action taken in matters relating to contractual or other commercial transactions of a listed authority.

(2) The action referred to in sub-paragraph (1) does not include any action taken by or on behalf of a health service body, a family health service provider or an independent provider in matters—
   (a) relating to NHS contracts (as defined by section 17A of the National Health Service (Scotland) Act 1978),
   (b) arising from arrangements between a health service body and an independent provider for the provision of services by the provider,
   (c) arising from arrangements between a family health service provider and an independent provider for the provision of services by the independent provider.

(3) The transactions referred to in sub-paragraph (1) include, in particular, transactions relating to the operation of public passenger transport, the carrying on of a dock or harbour undertaking, the provision of entertainment, or the provision and operation of industrial establishments and of markets.

(4) The transactions referred to in sub-paragraph (1) do not include—
   (a) any transaction relating to the acquisition or disposal of land,
   (b) any transaction (not being a transaction mentioned in sub-paragraph (3)) in the discharge of functions exercisable under any public general Act, other than a transaction required for the procurement of the goods or services necessary to discharge those functions.

8. Action taken in respect of appointments or removals, pay, discipline, superannuation or other personnel matters.

9. The grant of honours, awards or privileges within the gift of the Crown, including the grant of Royal Charters.

10. Action concerning—
(a) the giving of instruction, whether secular or religious, or
(b) conduct, curriculum or discipline,
in any educational establishment under the management of an education authority.
11–15. ★ ★ ★ ★ ★
★ ★ ★ ★ ★

Sex Discrimination (Election Candidates) Act 2002
(2002, c. 2)

An Act to exclude from the operation of the Sex Discrimination Act 1975 and the Sex Discrimination (Northern Ireland) Order 1976 certain matters relating to the selection of candidates by political parties.   [26 February 2002]

Territorial extent: Great Britain (s. 1), United Kingdom (s. 3).

1   Exclusion of candidate selection from 1975 Act
At the beginning of Part 5 of the Sex Discrimination Act 1975 insert—

"**42A   Selection of candidates**
(1) Nothing in Parts 2 to 4 shall—
(a) be construed as affecting arrangements to which this section applies, or
(b) render unlawful anything done in accordance with such arrangements.
(2) This section applies to arrangements made by a registered political party which—
(a) regulate the selection of the party's candidates in a relevant election, and
(b) are adopted for the purpose of reducing inequality in the numbers of men and women elected, as candidates of the party, to be members of the body concerned.
(3) The following elections are relevant elections for the purposes of this section—
(a) parliamentary elections;
(b) elections to the European Parliament;
(c) elections to the Scottish Parliament;
(d) elections to the National Assembly for Wales;
(e) local government elections within the meaning of section 191, 203 or 204 of the Representation of the People Act 1983 (excluding any election of the Mayor of London).
(4) In this section "registered political party" means a party registered in the Great Britain register under Part 2 of the Political Parties, Elections and Referendums Act 2000.".

2   ★ ★ ★ ★ ★

3   Expiry
(1) This Act shall expire at the end of 2015 unless an order is made under this section.
(2) At any time before this Act expires the Secretary of State may by order provide that subsection (1) shall have effect with the substitution of a later time for the time specified there (whether originally or by virtue of a previous order).
(3) An order under this section shall be made by statutory instrument; but no order shall be made unless a draft has been laid before, and approved by resolution of, each House of Parliament.

4   ★ ★ ★ ★ ★

PART II

Other Constitutional Materials

The Constitution of the United States

We the People of the United States, in order to form a more perfect Union, establish Justice, ensure Domestic Tranquillity, provide for the common Defence, promote the general Welfare, and secure the Blessings of Liberty to ourselves and our Posterity, do ordain and establish this CONSTITUTION for the United States of America.

Articles I–VII

★ ★ ★ ★ ★

AMENDMENTS TO THE CONSTITUTION

Article I
Congress shall make no law respecting an establishment of religion, or prohibiting the free exercise thereof; or abridging the freedom of speech or of the press; or the right of the people peaceably to assemble, and to petition the government for a redress of grievances.

Article II
A well-regulated militia being necessary to the security of a free state, the right of the people to keep and bear arms shall not be infringed.

Article III
No soldier shall, in time of peace, be quartered in any house without the consent of the owner, nor in time of war but in a manner to be prescribed by law.

Article IV
The right of the people to be secure in their persons, houses, papers, and effects, against unreasonable searches and seizures, shall not be violated, and no warrants shall issue but upon probable cause, supported by oath or affirmation, and particularly describing the place to be searched, and the persons or things to be seized.

Article V
No person shall be held to answer for a capital or other infamous crime unless on a presentment or indictment of a grand jury, except in cases arising in the land or naval forces, or in the militia, when in actual service, in time of war or public danger; nor shall any person be subject for the same offence to be twice put in jeopardy of life or limb; nor shall be compelled in any criminal case to be a witness against himself, nor be deprived of life, liberty, or property, without due process of law; nor shall private property be taken for public use without just compensation.

Article VI
In all criminal prosecutions, the accused shall enjoy the right to a speedy and public trial, by an impartial jury of the state and district wherein the crime shall have been committed, which

district shall have been previously ascertained by law, and to be informed of the nature and cause of the accusation; to be confronted with the witnesses against him; to have compulsory process for obtaining witnesses in his favor, and to have the assistance of counsel for his defence.

Article VII

In suits at common law, where the value in controversy shall exceed twenty dollars, the right of trial by jury shall be preserved, and no fact tried by a jury shall be otherwise re-examined in any court of the United States than according to the rules of the common law.

Article VIII

Excessive bail shall not be required, nor excessive fines imposed, nor cruel and unusual punishments inflicted.

Article IX

The enumeration in the constitution of certain rights shall not be construed to deny or disparage others retained by the people.

Article X

The powers not delegated to the United States by the constitution, nor prohibited by it to the states, are reserved to the states respectively, or to the people.

[*The foregoing ten amendments were adopted at the first session of Congress, and were declared to be in force, December 15, 1791.*]

Articles XI–XIII

★ ★ ★ ★ ★

Article XIV

1. All persons born or naturalized in the United States, and subject to the jurisdiction thereof, are citizens of the United States and of the state wherein they reside. No state shall make or enforce any law which shall abridge the privileges or immunities of citizens of the United States; nor shall any state deprive any person of life, liberty, or property without due process of law; nor deny to any person within its jurisdiction the equal protection of the law.

2.–4.   ★ ★ ★ ★ ★

5. The Congress shall have power to enforce, by appropriate legislation, the provisions of this article.

[*Declared in force, July 28, 1868.*]

★ ★ ★ ★ ★

European Convention for the Protection of Human Rights and Fundamental Freedoms (1950)

[*The European Convention on Human Rights*]

The Governments signatory hereto, being Members of the Council of Europe,

Considering the Universal Declaration of Human Rights proclaimed by the General Assembly of the United Nations on 10 December 1948;

Considering that this Declaration aims at securing the universal and effective recognition and observance of the Rights therein declared;

Considering that the aim of the Council of Europe is the achievement of greater unity between its Members and that one of the methods by which the aim is to be pursued is the maintenance and further realization of Human Rights and Fundamental Freedoms;

Reaffirming their profound belief in those Fundamental Freedoms which are the foundation of justice and peace in the world and are best maintained on the one hand by an effective political democracy and on the other by a common understanding and observance of the Human Rights upon which they depend;

Being resolved, as the Governments of European countries which are like-minded and have a common heritage of political traditions, ideals, freedom and the rule of law to take the first steps for the collective enforcement of certain of the Rights stated in the Universal Declaration;

Have agreed as follows:

Article 1 Obligation to respect human rights
The High Contracting Parties shall secure to everyone within their jurisdiction the rights and freedoms defined in Section I of this Convention.

SECTION I RIGHTS AND FREEDOMS

Article 2 Right to life
1. Everyone's right to life shall be protected by law. No one shall be deprived of his life intentionally save in the execution of a sentence of a court following his conviction of a crime for which this penalty is provided by law.
2. Deprivation of life shall not regarded as inflicted in contravention of this article when it results from the use of force which is no more than absolutely necessary:
   (a) in defence of any person from unlawful violence;
   (b) in order to effect a lawful arrest or to prevent the escape of a person lawfully detained;
   (c) in action lawfully taken for the purpose of quelling a riot or insurrection.

Article 3 Prohibition of torture
No one shall be subjected to torture or to inhuman or degrading treatment or punishment.

Article 4 Prohibition of slavery and forced labour
1. No one shall be held in slavery or servitude.
2. No one shall be required to perform forced or compulsory labour.
3. For the purpose of this article the term "forced or compulsory labour' shall not include:
   (a) any work required to be done in the ordinary course of detention imposed according to the provisions of Article 5 of this Convention or during conditional release from such detention;
   (b) any service of a military character or, in case of conscientious objectors in countries where they are recognized, service exacted instead of compulsory military service;
   (c) any service exacted in case of an emergency or calamity threatening the life or well-being of the community;
   (d) any work or service which forms part of normal civic obligations.

Article 5 Right to liberty and security
1. Everyone has the right to liberty and security of person.
No one shall be deprived of his liberty save in the following cases and in accordance with a procedure prescribed by law:
   (a) the lawful detention of a person after conviction by a competent court;
   (b) the lawful arrest or detention of a person for non-compliance with the lawful

order of a court or in order to secure the fulfilment of any obligation prescribed by law;

(c) the lawful arrest or detention of a person effected for the purpose of bringing him before the competent legal authority on reasonable suspicion of having committed an offence or when it is reasonably considered necessary to prevent his committing an offence or fleeing after having done so;

(d) the detention of a minor by lawful order for the purpose of educational supervision or his lawful detention for the purpose of bringing him before the competent legal authority;

(e) the lawful detention of persons for the prevention of the spreading of infectious diseases, of persons of unsound mind, alcoholics or drug addicts, or vagrants;

(f) the lawful arrest or detention of a person to prevent his effecting an unauthorized entry into the country or of a person against whom action is being taken with a view to deportation or extradition.

2.   Everyone who is arrested shall be informed promptly, in a language which he understands, of the reasons for his arrest and of any charge against him.

3.   Everyone arrested or detained in accordance with the provisions of paragraph 1(c) of this article shall be brought promptly before a judge or other officer authorized by law to exercise judicial power and shall be entitled to trial within a reasonable time or to release pending trial. Release may be conditioned by guarantees to appear for trial.

4.   Everyone who is deprived of his liberty by arrest or detention shall be entitled to take proceedings by which the lawfulness of his detention shall be decided speedily by a court and his release ordered if the detention is not lawful.

5.   Everyone who has been the victim of arrest or detention in contravention of the provisions of this article shall have an enforceable right to compensation.

Article 6   Right to a fair trial

1.   In the determination of his civil rights and obligations or of any criminal charge against him, everyone is entitled to a fair and public hearing within a reasonable time by an independent and impartial tribunal established by law. Judgment shall be pronounced publicly but the press and public may be excluded from all or part of the trial in the interest of morals, public order or national security in a democratic society, where the interests of juveniles or the protection of the private life of the parties so require, or to the extent strictly necessary in the opinion of the court in special circumstances where publicity would prejudice the interests of justice.

2.   Everyone charged with a criminal offence shall be presumed innocent until proved guilty according to law.

3.   Everyone charged with a criminal offence has the following minimum rights:

(a) to be informed promptly, in a language which he understands and in detail, of the nature and cause of the accusation against him;

(b) to have adequate time and facilities for the preparation of his defence;

(c) to defend himself in person or through legal assistance of his own choosing or, if he has not sufficient means to pay for legal assistance, to be given it free when the interests of justice so require;

(d) to examine or have examined witnesses against him and to obtain the attendance and examination of witnesses on his behalf under the same conditions as witnesses against him;

(e) to have the free assistance of an interpreter if he cannot understand or speak the language used in court.

Article 7   No punishment without law

1.   No one shall be held guilty of any criminal offence on account of any act or omission which did not constitute a criminal offence under national or international law at the time

when it was committed. Nor shall a heavier penalty be imposed than the one that was applicable at the time the criminal offence was committed.

2.   This article shall not prejudice the trial and punishment of any person for any act or omission which, at the time when it was committed, was criminal according to the general principles of law recognized by civilized nations.

Article 8   Right to respect for private and family life

1.   Everyone has the right to respect for his private and family life, his home and his correspondence.

2.   There shall be no interference by a public authority with the exercise of this right except such as is in accordance with the law and is necessary in a democratic society in the interests of national security, public safety or the economic well-being of the country, for the prevention of disorder or crime, for the protection of health or morals, or for the protection of the rights and freedoms of others.

Article 9   Freedom of thought, conscience and religion

1.   Everyone has the right to freedom of thought, conscience and religion; this right includes freedom to change his religion or belief, and freedom, either alone or in community with others and in public or private, to manifest his religion or belief, in worship, teaching, practice and observance.

2.   Freedom to manifest one's religion or beliefs shall be subject only to such limitations as are prescribed by law and are necessary in a democratic society in the interests of public safety, for the protection of public order, health or morals, or for the protection of the rights and freedoms of others.

Article 10   Freedom of expression

1.   Everyone has the right to freedom of expression. This right shall include freedom to hold opinions and to receive and impart information and ideas without interference by public authority and regardless of frontiers. This article shall not prevent States from requiring the licensing of broadcasting, television or cinema enterprises.

2.   The exercise of these freedoms, since it carries with it duties and responsibilities, may be subject to such formalities, conditions, restrictions or penalties as are prescribed by law and are necessary in a democratic society, in the interests of national security, territorial integrity or public safety, for the prevention of disorder or crime, for the protection of health or morals, for the protection of the reputation or rights of others, for preventing the disclosure of information received in confidence, or for maintaining the authority and impartiality of the judiciary.

Article 11   Freedom of assembly and association

1.   Everyone has the right to freedom of peaceful assembly and to freedom of association with others, including the right to form and to join trade unions for the protection of his interests.

2.   No restrictions shall be placed on the exercise of these rights other than such as are prescribed by law and are necessary in a democratic society in the interests of national security or public safety, for the prevention of disorder or crime, of the protection of health or morals or for the protection of the rights and freedoms of others. This article shall not prevent the imposition of lawful restrictions on the exercise of these rights by members of the armed forces, of the police or of the administration of the State.

Article 12   Right to marry

Men and women of marriageable age have the right to marry and to found a family, according to the national laws governing the exercise of this right.

Article 13   Right to an effective remedy

Everyone whose rights and freedoms as set forth in this Convention are violated shall have an effective remedy before a national authority notwithstanding that the violation has been committed by persons acting in an official capacity.

Article 14   Prohibition of discrimination
The enjoyment of the rights and freedoms set forth in this Convention shall be secured without discrimination on any ground such as sex, race, colour, language, religion, political or other opinion, national or social origin, association with a national minority, property, birth or other status.

Article 15   Derogation in time of emergency
1.   In time of war or other public emergency threatening the life of the nation any High Contracting Party may take measures derogating from its obligations under this Convention to the extent strictly required by the exigencies of the situation, provided that such measures are not inconsistent with its other obligations under international law.

2.   No derogation from Article 2, except in respect of deaths resulting from lawful acts of war, or from Articles 3, 4 (paragraph 1) and 7 shall be made under this provision.

3.   Any High Contracting Party availing itself of this right of derogation shall keep the Secretary-General of the Council of Europe fully informed of the measures which it has taken and the reasons therefor. It shall also inform the Secretary-General of the Council of Europe when such measures have ceased to operate and the provisions of the Convention are again being fully executed.

Article 16   Restrictions on political activity of aliens
Nothing in Articles 10, 11, and 14 shall be regarded as preventing the High Contracting Parties from imposing restrictions on the political activity of aliens.

Article 17   Prohibition of abuse of rights
Nothing in this Convention may be interpreted as implying for any State, group or person any right to engage in any activity or perform any act aimed at the destruction of any of the rights and freedoms set forth herein or at their limitation to a greater extent than is provided for in the Convention.

Article 18   Limitation on use of restrictions on rights
The restrictions permitted under this Convention to the said rights and freedoms shall not be applied for any purpose other than those for which they have been prescribed.

SECTION II   EUROPEAN COURT OF HUMAN RIGHTS

Article 19   Establishment of the court
To ensure the observance of the engagements undertaken by the High Contracting Parties in the Convention and the protocols thereto, there shall be set up a European Court of Human Rights, hereinafter referred to as "the Court". It shall function on a permanent basis.

Article 20   Number of judges
The Court shall consist of a number of judges equal to that of the High Contracting Parties.

Article 21   Criteria for office
1.   The judges shall be of high moral character and must either possess the qualifications required for appointment to high judicial office or be jurisconsults of recognised competence.

2.   The judges shall sit on the Court in their individual capacity.

3.   During their term of office the judges shall not engage in any activity which is incompatible with their independence, impartiality or with the demands of a full-time office; all questions arising from the application of this paragraph shall be decided by the Court.

Article 22 Election of judges

1. The judges shall be elected by the Parliamentary Assembly with respect to each High Contracting Party by a majority of votes cast from a list of three candidates nominated by the High Contracting Party.

2. The same procedure shall be followed to complete the Court in the event of the accession of new High Contracting Parties and in filling casual vacancies.

Article 23 Terms of office

1. The judges shall be elected for a period of six years. They may be re-elected. However, the terms of office of one-half of the judges elected at the first election shall expire at the end of three years.

2. The judges whose terms of office are to expire at the end of the initial period of three years shall be chosen by lot by the Secretary General of the Council of Europe immediately after their election.

3. In order to ensure that, as far as possible, the terms of office of one-half of the judges are renewed every three years, the Parliamentary Assembly may decide, before proceeding to any subsequent election, that the term or terms of office of one or more judges to be elected shall be for a period other than six years but not more than nine and not less than three years.

4. In cases where more than one term of office is involved and where the Parliamentary Assembly applies the preceding paragraph, the allocation of the terms of office shall be effected by a drawing of lots by the Secretary General of the Council of Europe immediately after the election.

5. A judge elected to replace a judge whose term of office has not expired shall hold office for the remainder of his predecessor's term.

6. The terms of office of judges shall expire when they reach the age of 70.

7. The judges shall hold office until replaced. They shall, however, continue to deal with such cases as they already have under consideration.

Article 24 Dismissal

No judge may be dismissed from his office unless the other judges decide by a majority of two-thirds that he has ceased to fulfil the required conditions.

Article 25 Registry and legal secretaries

The Court shall have a registry, the functions and organisation of which shall be laid down in the rules of the Court. The Court shall be assisted by legal secretaries.

Article 26 Plenary court

The plenary court shall:
- (a) elect its President and one or two Vice-Presidents for a period of three years; they may be re-elected;
- (b) set up Chambers, constituted for a fixed period of time;
- (c) elect the Presidents of the Chambers of the Court; they may be re-elected;
- (d) adopt the rules of the Court; and
- (e) elect the Registrar and one or more Deputy Registrars.

Article 27 Committees, Chambers and Grand Chamber

1. To consider cases brought before it, the Court shall sit in committees of three judges, in Chambers of seven judges and in a Grand Chamber of seventeen judges. The Court's Chambers shall set up committees for a fixed period of time.

2. There shall sit as an *ex officio* member of the Chamber and the Grand Chamber the judge elected in respect of the State Party concerned or, if there is none or if he is unable to sit, a person of its choice who shall sit in the capacity of judge.

3. The Grand Chamber shall also include the President of the Court, the Vice-Presidents, the Presidents of the Chambers and other judges chosen in accordance with the rules of the

Court. When a case is referred to the Grand Chamber under Article 43, no judge from the Chamber which rendered the judgment shall sit in the Grand Chamber, with the exception of the President of the Chamber and the judge who sat in respect of the State Party concerned.

Article 28   Declarations of inadmissibility by committees

A committee may, by a unanimous vote, declare inadmissible or strike out of its list of cases an individual application submitted under Article 34 where such a decision can be taken without further examination. The decision shall be final.

Article 29   Decisions by Chambers on admissibility and merits

1.   If no decision is taken under Article 28, a Chamber shall decide on the admissibility and merits of individual applications submitted under Article 34.

2.   A Chamber shall decide on the admissibility and merits of inter-State applications submitted under Article 33.

3.   The decision on admissibility shall be taken separately unless the court, in exceptional cases, decides otherwise.

Article 30   Relinquishment of jurisdiction to the Grand Chamber

Where a case pending before a Chamber raises a serious question affecting the interpretation of the Convention or the protocols thereto, or where the resolution of a question before the Chamber might have a result inconsistent with a judgment previously delivered by the Court, the Chamber may, at any time before it has rendered its judgment, relinquish jurisdiction in favour of the Grand Chamber, unless one of the parties to the case objects.

Article 31   Powers of the Grand Chamber

The Grand Chamber shall:

(a) determine applications submitted either under Article 33 or Article 34 when a Chamber has relinquished jurisdiction under Article 30 or when the case has been referred to it under Article 43; and

(b) consider requests for advisory opinions submitted under Article 47.

Article 32   Jurisdiction of the Court

1.   The jurisdiction of the Court shall extend to all matters concerning the interpretation and application of the Convention and the protocols thereto which are referred to it as provided in Articles 33, 34 and 47.

2.   In the event of dispute as to whether the Court has jurisdiction, the Court shall decide.

Article 33   Inter-state cases

Any High Contracting Party may refer to the Court any alleged breach of the provisions of the Convention and the protocols thereto by another High Contracting Party.

Article 34   Individual applications

The Court may receive applications from any person, non-governmental organisation or group of individuals claiming to be the victim of a violation by one of the High Contracting Parties of the rights set forth in the Convention or the protocols thereto. The High Contracting Parties undertake not to hinder in any way the effective exercise of this right.

Article 35   Admissibility criteria

1.   The Court may only deal with the matter after all domestic remedies have been exhausted, according to the generally recognised rules of international law, and within a period of six months from the date on which the final decision was taken.

2.   The Court shall not deal with any individual application submitted under Article 34 that:

(a) is anonymous; or

(b) is substantially the same as a matter that has already been examined by the Court or has already been submitted to another procedure of international investigation or settlement and contains no relevant new information.

3. The Court shall declare inadmissible any individual application submitted under Article 34 which it considers incompatible with the provisions of the Convention or the protocols thereto, manifestly ill-founded, or an abuse of the right of application.

4. The Court shall reject any application which it considers inadmissible under this Article. It may do so at any stage of the proceedings.

Article 36 Third-party intervention

1. In all cases before a Chamber or the Grand Chamber, a High Contracting Party one of whose nationals is an applicant shall have the right to submit written comments and to take part in hearings.

2. The President of the Court may, in the interest of the proper administration of justice, invite any High Contracting Party which is not a party to the proceedings or any person concerned who is not the applicant to submit written comments or take part in hearings.

Article 37 Striking out applications

1. The Court may at any stage of the proceedings decide to strike an application out of its list of cases where the circumstances lead to the conclusion that:
   (a) the applicant does not intend to pursue his application; or
   (b) the matter has been resolved; or
   (c) for any other reason established by the Court, it is no longer justified to continue the examination of the application.
However, the Court shall continue the examination of the application if respect for human rights as defined in the Convention and the protocols thereto so requires.

2. The Court may decide to restore an application to its list of cases if it considers that the circumstances justify such a course.

Article 38 Examination of the case and friendly settlement proceedings

1. If the Court declares the application admissible, it shall:
   (a) pursue the examination of the case, together with the representatives of the parties, and if need be, undertake an investigation, for the effective conduct of which the States concerned shall furnish all necessary facilities;
   (b) place itself at the disposal of the parties concerned with a view to securing a friendly settlement of the matter on the basis of respect of human rights as defined in the Convention and the protocols thereto.

2. Proceedings conducted under paragraph 1(b) shall be confidential.

Article 39 Finding of a friendly settlement

If a friendly settlement is effected, the Court shall strike the case out of its list by meansof a decision which shall be confinedtoa brief statement of the facts and of the solution reached.

Article 40 Public hearings and access to documents

1. Hearings shall be public unless the Court in exceptional circumstances decides otherwise.

2. Documents deposited with the Registrar shall be accessible to the public unless the President of the Court decides otherwise.

Article 41 Just satisfaction

If the Court finds that there has been a violation of the Convention or the protocols thereto, and if the internal law of the High Contracting Party concerned allows only partial reparation to be made, the Court shall, if necessary, afford just satisfaction to the injured party.

Article 42   Judgments of Chambers

Judgments of Chambers shall become final in accordance with the provisions of Article 44, paragraph 2.

Article 43   Referral to the Grand Chamber

1. Within a period of three months from the date of the judgment of the Chamber, any party to the case may, in exceptional cases, request that the case be referred to the Grand Chamber.

2. A panel of five judges of the Grand Chamber shall accept the request if the case raises a serious question affecting the interpretation or application of the Convention or the protocols thereto, or a serious issue of general importance.

3. If the panel accepts the request, the Grand Chamber shall decide the case by means of a judgment.

Article 44   Final judgments

1. The judgment of the Grand Chamber shall be final.

2. The judgment of a Chamber shall become final:
   (a) when the parties declare that they will not request that the case be referred to the Grand Chamber; or
   (b) three months after the date of the judgment, if reference of the case to the Grand Chamber has not been requested; or
   (c) when the panel of the Grand Chamber rejects the request to refer under Article 43.

3. The final judgment shall be published.

Article 45   Reasons for judgments and decisions

1. Reasons shall be given for judgments as well as for decisions declaring applications admissible or inadmissible.

2. If a judgment does not represent, in whole or in part, the unanimous opinion of the judges, any judge shall be entitled to deliver a separate opinion.

Article 46   Binding force and execution of judgments

1. The High Contracting Parties undertake to abide by the final judgment of the Court in any case to which they are parties.

2. The final judgment of the Court shall be transmitted to the Committee of Ministers, which shall supervise its execution.

Article 47   Advisory opinions

1. The Court may, at the request of the Committee of Ministers, give advisory opinions on legal questions concerning the interpretation of the Convention and the protocols thereto.

2. Such opinions shall not deal with any question relating to the content or scope of the rights or freedoms defined in Section I of the Convention and the protocols thereto, or with any other question which the Court or the Committee of Ministers might have to consider in consequence of any such proceedings as could be instituted in accordance with the Convention.

3. Decisions of the Committee of Ministers to request an advisory opinion of the Court shall require a majority vote of the representatives entitled to sit on the Committee.

Article 48   Advisory jurisdiction of the Court

The Court shall decide whether a request for an advisory opinion submitted by the Committee of Ministers is within its competence as defined in Article 47.

Article 49   Reasons for advisory opinions

1. Reasons shall be given for advisory opinions of the Court.

2. If the advisory opinion does not represent, in whole or in part, the unanimous opinion of the judges, any judge shall be entitled to deliver a separate opinion.

3. Advisory opinions of the Court shall be communicated to the Committee of Ministers.

Article 50   Expenditure on the Court
The expenditure on the Court shall be borne by the Council of Europe.

Article 51   Privileges and immunities of judges
The judges shall be entitled, during the exercise of their functions, to the privileges and immunities provided for in Article 40 of the Statute of the Council of Europe and in the agreements made thereunder.

SECTION III   MISCELLANEOUS PROVISIONS

Article 52

★ ★ ★ ★ ★

Article 53   Safeguard for existing human rights
Nothing in this Convention shall be construed as limiting or derogating from any of the human rights and fundamental freedoms which may be ensured under the laws of any High Contracting Party or under any other agreement to which it is a Party.

Articles 54–56

★ ★ ★ ★ ★

Article 57   Reservations
1. Any State may, when signing this Convention or when depositing its instrument of ratification, make a reservation in respect of any particular provision of the Convention to the extent that any law then in force in its territory is not in conformity with the provision. Reservations of a general character shall not be permitted under this article.
2. Any reservation made under this article shall contain a brief statement of the law concerned.

★ ★ ★ ★ ★

PROTOCOLS

Enforcement of certain Rights and Freedoms not included in Section I of the Convention

The Governments signatory hereto, being Members of the Council of Europe,

Being resolved to take steps to ensure the collective enforcement of certain rights and freedoms other than those already included in Section I of the Convention for the Protection of Human Rights and Fundamental Freedoms signed at Rome on 4th November 1950 (hereinafter referred to as 'the Convention'),

Have agreed as follows:

Article 1   Protection of property
Every natural or legal person is entitled to the peaceful enjoyment of his possessions. No one shall be deprived of his possessions except in the public interest and subject to the conditions provided for by law and by the general principles of international law.

The preceding provisions shall not, however, in any way impair the right of a State to enforce such laws as it deems necessary to control the use of property in accordance with the general interest or to secure the payment of taxes or other contributions or penalties.

Article 2   Right to education

No person shall be denied the right to education. In the exercise of any functions which it assumes in relation to education and to teaching, the State shall respect the right of parents to ensure such education and teaching in conformity with their own religious and philosophical convictions.

Article 3   Right to free elections

The High Contracting Parties undertake to hold free elections at reasonable intervals by secret ballot, under conditions which will ensure the free expression of the opinion of the people in the choice of the legislature.

★ ★ ★ ★ ★

4. Protecting certain Additional Rights

The Governments signatory hereto, being Members of the Council of Europe.

Being resolved to take steps to ensure the collective enforcement of certain rights and freedoms other than those already included in Section I of the Convention for the Protection of Human Rights and Fundamental Freedoms signed at Rome on 4 November 1950 (hereinafter referred to as 'the Convention') and in Articles 1 to 3 of the First Protocol to the Convention, signed at Paris on 20 March 1952,

Have agreed as follows:

Article 1   Prohibition of imprisonment for debt

No one shall be deprived of his liberty merely on the ground of inability to fulfil a contractual obligation.

Article 2   Freedom of movement

1. Everyone lawfully within the territory of a State shall, within that territory, have the right to liberty of movement and freedom to choose his residence.

2. Everyone shall be free to leave any country, including his own.

3. No restrictions shall be placed on the exercise of these rights other than such as are in accordance with law and are necessary in a democratic society in the interests of national security or public safety, for the maintenance of 'order public', for the prevention of crime, for the protection of the rights and freedoms of others.

4. The rights set forth in paragraph 1 may also be subject, in particular areas, to restrictions imposed in accordance with law and justified by the public interest in a democratic society.

Article 3   Prohibition of expulsion of nationals

1. No one shall be expelled, by means either of an individual or of a collective measure, from the territory of the State of which he is a national.

2. No one shall be deprived of the right to enter the territory of the State of which he is a national.

Article 4   Prohibition of collective expulsion of aliens

Collective expulsion of aliens is prohibited.

★ ★ ★ ★ ★

Note: This Protocol has not yet been ratified by the United Kingdom.

6. Concerning the Abolition of the Death Penalty

The member States of the Council of Europe, signatory to this Protocol to the Convention for the Protection of Human Rights and Fundamental Freedoms, signed at Rome on 4 November 1950 (hereinafter referred to as 'the Convention').

Considering that the evolution that has occurred in several member States of the Council of Europe expresses a general tendency in favour of abolition of the death penalty.
Have agreed as follows:

Article 1   Abolition of the death penalty
The death penalty shall be abolished. No one shall be condemned to such penalty or executed.

Article 2   Death penalty in time of war
A state may make provision in its law for the death penalty in respect of acts committed in time of war or of imminent threat of war; such penalty shall be applied only in the instance laid down in the law and in accordance with its provisions. The State shall communicate to the Secretary General of the Council of Europe the relevant provisions of that law.

Article 3   Prohibition of derogations
No derogation from the provision of this Protocol shall be made under Article 15 of the Convention.

Article 4   Prohibition of reservations
No reservation may be made under Article 57 of the Convention in respect of the provisions of this Protocol.
Note: Protocol 7 is not included as it is not yet in force and has not been ratified by the UK.

Treaty Establishing the European Community (Treaty of Rome)
(25 March 1957)

Note: The Treaty is printed as amended with effect from 1 May 1999 by the Amsterdam Treaty. Amendments contained in the Nice Treaty have not yet been added pending ratification by all Member States (the United Kingdom has passed the necessary legislation: see the European Communities (Amendment) Act 2002, but the Treaty cannot come into force until ratified by all Member States).

EC TREATY (AMSTERDAM VERSION) PART ONE   (PRINCIPLES)

Article 1
By this Treaty, the High Contracting Parties establish among themselves a EUROPEAN COMMUNITY.

Article 2
The Community shall have as its task, by establishing a common market and an economic and monetary union and by implementing the common policies or activities referred to in Articles 3 and 4, to promote throughout the Community a harmonious, balanced and sustainable development of economic activities, a high level of employment and of social protection, equality between men and women, sustainable and non-inflationary growth, a high degree of competitiveness and convergence of economic performance, a high level of protection and improvement of the quality of the environment, the raising of the standard of living and quality of life, and economic and social cohesion and solidarity among Member States.

Article 3
1.   For the purposes set out in Article 2, the activities of the Community shall include, as provided in this Treaty and in accordance with the timetable set out therein:
(a) the prohibition, as between Member States, of customs duties and quantitative

restrictions on the import and export of goods, and of all other measures having equivalent effect;

(b) a common commercial policy;

(c) an internal market characterised by the abolition, as between Member States, of obstacles to the free movement of goods, persons, services and capital;

(d) measures concerning the entry and movement of persons as provided for in Title IV;

(e) a common policy in the sphere of agriculture and fisheries;

(f) a common policy in the sphere of transport;

(g) a system ensuring that competition in the internal market is not distorted;

(h) the approximation of the laws of Member States to the extent required for the functioning of the common market;

(i) the promotion of co-ordination between employment policies of the Member States with a view to enhancing their effectiveness by developing a co-ordinated strategy for employment;

(j) a policy in the social sphere comprising a European Social Fund;

(k) the strengthening of economic and social cohesion;

(l) a policy in the sphere of the environment;

(m) the strengthening of the competitiveness of Community industry;

(n) the promotion of research and technological development;

(o) encouragement for the establishment and development of trans-European networks;

(p) a contribution to the attainment of a high level of health protection;

(q) a contribution to education and training of quality and to the flowering of the cultures of the Member States;

(r) a policy in the sphere of development cooperation;

(s) the association of the overseas countries and territories in order to increase trade and promote jointly economic and social development;

(t) a contribution to the strengthening of consumer protection;

(u) measures in the spheres of energy, civil protection and tourism.

2.   In all the activities referred to in this Article, the Community shall aim to eliminate inequalities, and to promote equality between men and women.

Article 4

1.   For the purposes set out in Article 2, the activities of the Member States and the Community shall include, as provided in this Treaty and in accordance with the timetable set out therein, the adoption of an economic policy which is based on the close coordination of Member States' economic policies, on the internal market and on the definition of common objectives, and conducted in accordance with the principle of an open market economy with free competition.

2.   Concurrently with the foregoing, and as provided in this Treaty and in accordance with the timetable and the procedures set out therein, these activities shall include the irrevocable fixing of exchange rates leading to the introduction of a single currency, the ECU, and the definition and conduct of a single monetary policy and exchange-rate policy the primary objective of both of which shall be to maintain price stability and, without prejudice to this objective, to support the general economic policies in the Community, in accordance with the principle of an open market economy with free competition.

3.   These activities of the Member States and the Community shall entail compliance with the following guiding principles: stable prices, sound public finances and monetary conditions and a sustainable balance of payments.

Article 5

The Community shall act within the limits of the powers conferred upon it by this Treaty and of the objectives assigned to it therein.

In areas which do not fall within its exclusive competence, the Community shall take action, in accordance with the principle of subsidiarity, only if and in so far as the objectives of the proposed action cannot be sufficiently achieved by the Member States and can therefore, by reason of the scale or effects of the proposed action, be better achieved by the Community.

Any action by the Community shall not go beyond what is necessary to achieve the objectives of this Treaty.

Article 6

Environmental protection requirements must be integrated into the definition and implementation of the Community policies and activities referred to in Article 3, in particular with a view to promoting sustainable development.

Article 7

1.   The tasks entrusted to the Community shall be carried out by the following institutions:
- — a EUROPEAN PARLIAMENT,
- — a COUNCIL,
- — a COMMISSION,
- — a COURT OF JUSTICE,
- — a COURT OF AUDITORS.

Each institution shall act within the limits of the powers conferred upon it by this Treaty.

2.   The Council and the Commission shall be assisted by an Economic and Social Committee and a Committee of the Regions acting in an advisory capacity.

Articles 8, 9   ★ ★ ★ ★ ★

Article 10

Member States shall take all appropriate measures, whether general or particular, to ensure fulfilment of the obligations arising out of this Treaty or resulting from action taken by the institutions of the Community. They shall facilitate the achievement of the Community's tasks.

They shall abstain from any measure which could jeopardise the attainment of the objectives of this Treaty.

Article 11

1.   Member States which intend to establish closer cooperation between themselves may be authorised, subject to Articles 43 and 44 of the Treaty on European Union, to make use of the institutions, procedures and mechanisms laid down by this Treaty, provided that the cooperation proposed:
- (a) does not concern areas which fall within the exclusive competence of the Community;
- (b) does not affect Community policies, actions or programmes;
- (c) does not concern the citizenship of the Union or discriminate between nationals of Member States;
- (d) remains within the limits of the powers conferred upon the Community by this Treaty; and
- (e) does not constitute a discrimination or a restriction of trade between Member States and does not distort the conditions of competition between the latter.

2.   The authorisation referred to in paragraph 1 shall be granted by the Council, acting by a qualified majority on a proposal from the Commission and after consulting the European Parliament.

If a member of the Council declares that, for important and stated reasons of national policy, it intends to oppose the granting of an authorisation by qualified majority, a vote shall not be taken. The Council may, acting by a qualified majority, request that the matter be referred to the Council, meeting in the composition of the Heads of State or Government, for decision by unanimity.

Member States which intend to establish closer cooperation as referred to in paragraph 1 may address a request to the Commission, which may submit a proposal to the Council to that effect. In the event of the Commission not submitting a proposal, it shall inform the Member States concerned of the reasons for not doing so.

3. Any Member State which wishes to become a party to cooperation set up in accordance with this Article shall notify its intention to the Council and to the Commission, which shall give an opinion to the Council within three months of receipt of that notification. Within four months of the date of the notification, the Commission shall decide on it and on such specific arrangements as it may deem necessary.

4. The acts and decisions necessary for the implementation of cooperation activities shall be subject to all the relevant provisions of this Treaty, save as otherwise provided for in this Article and in Articles 43 and 44 of the Treaty on European Union.

5. This Article is without prejudice to the provisions of the Protocol integrating the Schengen acquis into the framework of the European Union.

Article 12
Within the scope of application of this Treaty, and without prejudice to any special provisions contained therein, any discrimination on grounds of nationality shall be prohibited.

The Council, acting in accordance with the procedure referred to in Article 189c, may adopt rules designed to prohibit such discrimination.

Article 13
Without prejudice to the other provisions of this Treaty and within the limits of the powers conferred by it upon the Community, the Council, acting unanimously on a proposal from the Commission and after consulting the European Parliament, may take appropriate action to combat discrimination based on sex, racial or ethnic origin, religion or belief, disability, age or sexual orientation.

Article 14
1. The Community shall adopt measures with the aim of progressively establishing the internal market over a period expiring on 31 December 1992, in accordance with the provisions of this Article and of Articles 15, 26, 47(2), 49, 80, 93 and 95 and without prejudice to the other provisions of this Treaty.

2. The internal market shall comprise an area without internal frontiers in which the free movement of goods, persons, services and capital is ensured in accordance with the provisions of this Treaty.

3. The Council, acting by a qualified majority on a proposal from the Commission, shall determine the guidelines and conditions necessary to ensure balanced progress in all the sectors concerned.

Article 15
When drawing up its proposals with a view to achieving the objectives set out in Article 14, the Commission shall take into account the extent of the effort that certain economies showing differences in development will have to sustain during the period of establishment of the internal market and it may propose appropriate provisions.

If these provisions take the form of derogations, they must be of a temporary nature and must cause the least possible disturbance to the functioning of the common market.

Article 16
Without prejudice to Articles 73, 86 and 87, and given the place occupied by services of general economic interest in the shared values of the Union as well as their role in promoting social and territorial cohesion, the Community and the Member States, each within their

respective powers and within the scope of application of this Treaty, shall take care that such services operate on the basis of principles and conditions which enable them to fulfil their missions.

PART TWO   (CITIZENSHIP OF THE UNION)

Article 17
1. Citizenship of the Union is hereby established.
Every person holding the nationality of a Member State shall be a citizen of the Union.
2. Citizens of the Union shall enjoy the rights conferred by this Treaty and shall be subject to the duties imposed thereby.

★ ★ ★ ★ ★

CHAPTER 2—(PROHIBITION OF QUANTITATIVE RESTRICTIONS BETWEEN MEMBER STATES)

Article 28
Quantitative restrictions on imports and all measures having equivalent effect shall be prohibited between Member States.

★ ★ ★ ★ ★

Article 30
The provisions of Articles 28 and 29 shall not preclude prohibitions or restrictions on imports, exports or goods in transit justified on grounds of public morality, public policy or public security; the protection of health and life of humans, animals or plants; the protection of national treasures possessing artistic, historic or archaeological value; or the protection of industrial and commercial property. Such prohibitions or restrictions shall not, however, constitute a means of arbitrary discrimination or a disguised restriction on trade between Member States.

★ ★ ★ ★ ★

TITLE III   FREE MOVEMENT OF PERSONS, SERVICES AND CAPITAL

CHAPTER 1—(WORKERS)

Article 39
1. Freedom of movement for workers shall be secured within the Community.
2. Such freedom of movement shall entail the abolition of any discrimination based on nationality between workers of the Member States as regards employment, remuneration and other conditions of work and employment.
3. It shall entail the right, subject to limitations justified on grounds of public policy, public security or public health:
    (a) to accept offers of employment actually made;
    (b) to move freely within the territory of Member States for this purpose;
    (c) to stay in a Member State for the purpose of employment in accordance with the provisions governing the employment of nationals of that State laid down by law, regulation or administrative action;
    (d) to remain in the territory of a Member State after having been employed in that

State, subject to conditions which shall be embodied in implementing regulations to be drawn up by the Commission.

4. The provisions of this Article shall not apply to employment in the public service.

★ ★ ★ ★ ★

CHAPTER 2—(RIGHT OF ESTABLISHMENT)

Article 48

Companies or firms formed in accordance with the law of a Member State and having their registered office, central administration or principal place of business within the Community shall, for the purposes of this Chapter, be treated in the same way as natural persons who are nationals of Member States.

"Companies or firms" means companies or firms constituted under civil or commercial law, including co-operative societies, and other legal persons governed by public or private law, save for those which are non-profit-making.

CHAPTER 3—(SERVICES)

Article 49

Within the framework of the provisions set out below, restrictions on freedom to provide services within the Community shall be prohibited in respect of nationals of Member States who are established in a State of the Community other than that of the person for whom the services are intended.

The Council may, acting by a qualified majority on a proposal from the Commission, extend the provisions of the Chapter to nationals of a third country who provide services and who are established within the Community.

Article 50

Services shall be considered to be "services" within the meaning of this Treaty where they are normally provided for remuneration, in so far as they are not governed by the provisions relating to freedom of movement for goods, capital and persons.

"Services" shall in particular include:

    (a) activities of an industrial character;
    (b) activities of a commercial character;
    (c) activities of craftsmen;
    (d) activities of the professions.

Without prejudice to the provisions of the Chapter relating to the right of establishment, the person providing a service may, in order to do so, temporarily pursue his activity in the State where the service is provided, under the same conditions as are imposed by that State on its own nationals.

★ ★ ★ ★ ★

Article 51

Within the framework of the provisions set out below, restrictions on the freedom of establishment of nationals of a Member State in the territory of another Member State shall be prohibited. Such prohibition shall also apply to restrictions on the setting up of agencies, branches or subsidiaries by nationals of any Member State established in the territory of any Member State.

Freedom of establishment shall include the right to take up and pursue activities as self-employed persons and to set up and manage undertakings, in particular companies or firms within the meaning of the second paragraph of Article 58, under the conditions laid down for its own nationals by the law of the country where such establishment is effected, subject to the provisions of the Chapter relating to capital.

★ ★ ★ ★ ★

TITLE VI   COMMON RULES ON COMPETITION, TAXATION AND APPROXIMATION OF LAWS

CHAPTER 1—(RULES ON COMPETITION)

Section 1—Rules applying to undertakings

Article 81

1. The following shall be prohibited as incompatible with the common market: all agreements between undertakings, decisions by associations of undertakings and concerted practices which may affect trade between Member States and which have as their object or effect the prevention, restriction or distortion of competition within the common market, and in particular those which:

(a) directly or indirectly fix purchase or selling prices or any other trading conditions;

(b) limit or control production, markets, technical development, or investment;

(c) share markets or sources of supply;

(d) apply dissimilar conditions to equivalent transactions with other trading parties, thereby placing them at a competitive disadvantage;

(e) make the conclusion of contracts subject to acceptance by the other parties of supplementary obligations which, by their nature or according to commercial usage, have no connection with the subject of such contracts.

2. Any agreements or decisions prohibited pursuant to this Article shall be automatically void.

3. The provisions of paragraph 1 may, however, be declared inapplicable in the case of:

— any agreement or category of agreements between undertakings;

— any decision or category of decisions by associations of undertakings;

— any concerted practice or category of concerted practices;

which contributes to improving the production or distribution of goods or to promoting technical or economic progress, while allowing consumers a fair share of the resulting benefit, and which does not:

(a) impose on the undertakings concerned restrictions which are not indispensable to the attainment of these objectives;

(b) afford such undertakings the possibility of eliminating competition in respect of a substantial part of the products in question.

Article 82

Any abuse by one or more undertakings of a dominant position within the common market or in a substantial part of it shall be prohibited as incompatible with the common market in so far as it may affect trade between Member States.

Such abuse may, in particular, consist in:

(a) directly or indirectly imposing unfair purchase or selling prices or other unfair trading conditions;

(b) limiting production, markets or technical development to the prejudice of consumers;

(c) applying dissimilar conditions to equivalent transactions with other trading parties, thereby placing them at a competitive disadvantage;

(d) making the conclusion of contracts subject to acceptance by the other parties of supplementary obligations which, by their nature or according to commercial usage, have no connection with the subject of such contracts.

★ ★ ★ ★ ★

CHAPTER 3—(APPROXIMATION OF LAWS)

Article 94

The Council shall, acting unanimously on a proposal from the Commission and after consulting the European Parliament and the Economic and Social Committee, issue directives for the approximation of such laws, regulations or administrative provisions of the Member States as directly affect the establishment or functioning of the common market.

Article 95

1. By way of derogation from Article 94 and save where otherwise provided in this Treaty, the following provisions shall apply for the achievement of the objectives set out in Article 14. The Council shall, acting in accordance with the procedure referred to in Article 251 and after consulting the Economic and Social Committee, adopt the measures for the approximation of the provisions laid down by law, regulation or administrative action in Member States which have as their object the establishment and functioning of the internal market.

2. Paragraph 1 shall not apply to fiscal provisions, to those relating to the free movement of persons nor to those relating to the rights and interests of employed persons.

3. The Commission, in its proposals envisaged in paragraph 1 concerning health, safety, environmental protection and consumer protection, will take as a base a high level of protection, taking into account in particular any new development based on scientific facts within their relevant powers, the European Parliament and Council will also seek to achieve this objective.

4. If, after the adoption by the Council or the Commission of a harmonisation measure a Member State deems it necessary to apply national provisions on grounds of major needs referred to in Article 30, or relating to protection of the environment or the working environment, it shall notify the Commission of these provisions as well as the grounds for maintaining them.

★ ★ ★ ★ ★

TITLE XI   SOCIAL POLICY, EDUCATION, VOCATIONAL TRAINING AND YOUTH

Article 136

The Community and the Member States, having in mind fundamental social rights such as those set out in the European Social Charter signed at Turin on 18 October 1961 and in the 1989 Community Charter of the Fundamental Social Rights of Workers, shall have as their objectives the promotion of employment, improved living and working conditions, so as to make possible their harmonisation while the improvement is being maintained, proper social protection, dialogue between management and labour, the development of human resources with a view to lasting high employment and the combating of exclusion.

To this end the Community and the Member States shall implement measures which take account of the diverse forms of national practices, in particular in the field of contractual relations, and the need to maintain the competitiveness of the Community economy.

They believe that such a development will ensue not only from the functioning of the common market, which will favour the harmonisation of social systems, but also from the procedures provided for in this Treaty and from the approximation of provisions laid down by law, regulation or administrative action.

Article 137

1.   With a view to achieving the objectives of Article 136, the Community shall support and complement the activities of the Member States in the following fields:
— improvement in particular of the working environment to protect workers' health and safety;
— working conditions;
— the information and consultation of workers;
— the integration of persons excluded from the labour market, without prejudice to Article 150;
— equality between men and women with regard to labour market opportunities and treatment at work.

2.   To this end, the Council may adopt, by means of directives, minimum requirements for gradual implementation, having regard to the conditions and technical rules obtaining in each of the Member States. Such directives shall avoid imposing administrative, financial and legal constraints in a way which would hold back the creation and development of small and medium-sized undertakings.

The Council shall act in accordance with the procedure referred to in Article 251 after consulting the Economic and Social Committee and the Committee of the Regions.

The Council, acting in accordance with the same procedure, may adopt measures designed to encourage cooperation between Member States through initiatives aimed at improving knowledge, developing exchanges of information and best practices, promoting innovative approaches and evaluating experiences in order to combat social exclusion.

3.   However, the Council shall act unanimously on a proposal from the Commission, after consulting the European Parliament, the Economic and Social Committee and the Committee of the Regions in the following areas:
— social security and social protection of workers;
— protection of workers where their employment contract is terminated;
— representation and collective defence of the interests of workers and employers, including co-determination, subject to paragraph 6;
— conditions of employment for third-country nationals legally residing in Community territory;
— financial contributions for promotion of employment and job-creation, without prejudice to the provisions relating to the Social Fund.

4.   A Member State may entrust management and labour, at their joint request, with the implementation of directives adopted pursuant to paragraphs 2 and 3.

In this case, it shall ensure that, no later than the date on which a directive must be transposed in accordance with Article 249, management and labour have introduced the necessary measures by agreement, the Member State concerned being required to take any necessary measure enabling it at any time to be in a position to guarantee the results imposed by that directive.

5.   The provisions adopted pursuant to this Article shall not prevent any Member State from maintaining or introducing more stringent protective measures compatible with this Treaty.

6.   The provisions of this Article shall not apply to pay, the right of association, the right to strike or the right to impose lock-outs.

Article 138

1.   The Commission shall have the task of promoting the consultation of management and labour at Community level and shall take any relevant measure to facilitate their dialogue by ensuring balanced support for the parties.

2. To this end, before submitting proposals in the social policy field, the Commission shall consult management and labour on the possible direction of Community action.

3. If, after such consultation, the Commission considers Community action advisable, it shall consult management and labour on the content of the envisaged proposal. Management and labour shall forward to the Commission an opinion or, where appropriate, a recommendation.

4. On the occasion of such consultation, management and labour may inform the Commission of their wish to initiate the process provided for in Article 139. The duration of the procedure shall not exceed nine months, unless the management and labour concerned and the Commission decide jointly to extend it.

Article 139

1. Should management and labour so desire, the dialogue between them at Community level may lead to contractual relations, including agreements.

2. Agreements concluded at Community level shall be implemented either in accordance with the procedures and practices specific to management and labour and the Member States or, in matters covered by Article 137, at the joint request of the signatory parties, by a Council decision on a proposal from the Commission.

The Council shall act by qualified majority, except where the agreement in question contains one or more provisions relating to one of the areas referred to in Article 137(3), in which case it shall act unanimously.

Article 140

With a view to achieving the objectives of Article 136 and without prejudice to the other provisions of this Treaty, the Commission shall encourage cooperation between the Member States and facilitate the coordination of their action in all social policy fields under this chapter, particularly in matters relating to:

— employment;
— labour law and working conditions;
— basic and advanced vocational training;
— social security;
— prevention of occupational accidents and diseases;
— occupational hygiene;
— the right of association and collective bargaining between employers and workers.

To this end, the Commission shall act in close contact with Member States by making studies, delivering opinions and arranging consultations both on problems arising at national level and on those of concern to international organisations.

Before delivering the opinions provided for in this Article, the Commission shall consult the Economic and Social Committee.

Article 141

1. Each Member State shall ensure that the principle of equal pay for male and female workers for equal work or work of equal value is applied.

2. For the purpose of this Article 'pay' means the ordinary basic or minimum wage or salary and any other consideration, whether in cash or in kind, which the worker receives directly or indirectly, in respect of his employment, from his employer.

Equal pay without discrimination based on sex means:

(a) that pay for the same work at piece rates shall be calculated on the basis of the same unit of measurement;

(b) that pay for work at time rates shall be the same for the same job.

3. The Council, acting in accordance with the procedure referred to in Article 251, and after consulting the Economic and Social Committee, shall adopt measures to ensure the application of the principle of equal opportunities and equal treatment of men and women in

matters of employment and occupation, including the principle of equal pay for equal work or work of equal value.

4.   With a view to ensuring full equality in practice between men and women in working life, the principle of equal treatment shall not prevent any Member State from maintaining or adopting measures providing for specific advantages in order to make it easier for the under-represented sex to pursue a vocational activity or to prevent or compensate for disadvantages in professional careers.

★ ★ ★ ★ ★

TITLE XVI   INDUSTRY

Article 157

1.   The Community and the Member States shall ensure that the conditions necessary for the competitiveness of the Community's industry exist.

For that purpose, in accordance with a system of open and competitive markets, their action shall be aimed at:

— speeding up the adjustment of industry to structural changes;
— encouraging an environment favourable to initiative and to the development of undertakings throughout the Community, particularly small and medium-sized undertakings;
— encouraging an environment favourable to co-operation between undertakings;
— fostering better exploitation of the industrial potential of policies of innovation, research and technological development.

2.   The Member States shall consult each other in liaison with the Commission and, where necessary, shall co-ordinate their action. The Commission may take any useful initiative to promote such co-ordination.

3.   The Community shall contribute to the achievement of the objectives set out in paragraph 1 through the policies and activities it pursues under other provisions of this Treaty. The Council, acting unanimously on a proposal from the Commission, after consulting the European Parliament and the Economic and Social Committee, may decide on specific measures in support of action taken in the Member States to achieve the objectives set out in paragraph 1.

This Title shall not provide a basis for the introduction by the Community of any measure which could lead to a distortion of competition.

★ ★ ★ ★ ★

PART FIVE   (INSTITUTIONS OF THE COMMUNITY)
TITLE I   PROVISIONS GOVERNING THE INSTITUTIONS

CHAPTER 1—(THE INSTITUTIONS)

Section 1—The European Parliament

Article 189

The European Parliament, which shall consist of representatives of the peoples of the States brought together in the Community, shall exercise the powers conferred upon it by this Treaty. The number of Members of the European Parliament shall not exceed seven hundred.

Article 190

1.   The representatives in the European Parliament of the peoples of the States brought together in the Community shall be elected by direct universal suffrage.

1. The number of representatives elected in each Member State is as follows:

Belgium	25
Denmark	16
Germany	99
Greece	25
Spain	64
France	87
Ireland	15
Italy	87
Luxembourg	6
Netherlands	31
Austria	21
Portugal	25
Finland	16
Sweden	22
United Kingdom	87

In the event of amendments to this paragraph, the number of representatives elected in each Member State must ensure appropriate representation of the peoples of the States brought together in the Community.

3. Representatives shall be elected for a term of five years.

4. The European Parliament shall draw up a proposal for elections by direct universal suffrage in accordance with a uniform procedure in all Member States or in accordance with principles common to all Member States.

The Council shall, acting unanimously after obtaining the assent of the European Parliament, which shall act by a majority of its component members, lay down the appropriate provisions, which it shall recommend to Member States for adoption in accordance with their respective constitutional requirements.

5. The European Parliament shall, after seeking an opinion from the Commission and with the approval of the Council acting unanimously, lay down the regulations and general conditions governing the performance of the duties of its Members.

Article 191

Political parties at European level are important as a factor for integration within the Union. They contribute to forming a European awareness and to expressing the political will of the citizens of the Union.

Article 192

In so far as provided in this Treaty, the European Parliament shall participate in the process leading up to the adoption of Community acts by exercising its powers under the procedures laid down in Articles 251 and 253 and by giving its assent or delivering advisory opinions.

The European Parliament may, acting by a majority of its Members, request the Commission to submit any appropriate proposal on matters on which it considers that a Community act is required for the purpose of implementing this Treaty.

Article 193

In the course of its duties, the European Parliament may, at the request of a quarter of its Members, set up a temporary Committee of Inquiry to investigate, without prejudice to the powers conferred by this Treaty on other institutions or bodies, alleged contraventions or maladministration in the implementation of Community law, except where the alleged facts are being examined before a court and while the case is still subject to legal proceedings.

The temporary Committee of Inquiry shall cease to exist on the submission of its report.

The detailed provisions governing the exercise of the right of inquiry shall be determined by common accord of the European Parliament, the Council and the Commission.

Article 194
Any citizen of the Union, and any natural or legal person residing or having its registered office in a Member State, shall have the right to address, individually or in association with other citizens or persons, a petition to the European Parliament on a matter which comes within the Community's fields of activity and which affects him, her or it directly.

Article 195
1. The European Parliament shall appoint an Ombudsman empowered to receive complaints from any citizen of the Union or any natural or legal person residing or having its registered office in a Member State concerning instances of maladministration in the activities of the Community institutions or bodies, with the exception of the Court of Justice and the Court of First Instance acting in their judicial role.

In accordance with his duties, the Ombudsman shall conduct inquiries for which he finds grounds, either on his own initiative or on the basis of complaints submitted to him direct or through a member of the European Parliament, except where the alleged facts are or have been the subject of legal proceedings. Where the Ombudsman establishes an instance of maladministration, he shall refer the matter to the institution concerned, which shall have a period of three months in which to inform him of its views.

The Ombudsman shall then forward a report to the European Parliament and the institution concerned. The person lodging the complaint shall be informed of the outcome of such inquiries.

The Ombudsman shall submit an annual report to the European Parliament on the outcome of his inquiries.

2. The Ombudsman shall be appointed after each election of the European Parliament for the duration of its term of office. The Ombudsman shall be eligible for re-appointment.

The Ombudsman may be dismissed by the Court of Justice at the request of the European Parliament if he no longer fulfils the conditions required for the performance of his duties or if he is guilty of serious misconduct.

3. The Ombudsman shall be completely independent in the performance of his duties. In the performance of those duties he shall neither seek nor take instructions from any body.

The Ombudsman may not, during his term of office, engage in any other occupation, whether gainful or not.

4. The European Parliament shall, after seeking an opinion from the Commission and with the approval of the Council acting by a qualified majority, lay down the regulations and general conditions governing the performance of the Ombudsman's duties.

Article 196
The European Parliament shall hold an annual session. It shall meet, without requiring to be convened, on the second Tuesday in March.

The European Parliament may meet in extraordinary session at the request of a majority of its members or at the request of the Council or of the Commission.

Article 197
The European Parliament shall elect its President and its officers from among its members.

Members of the Commission may attend all meetings and shall, at their request, be heard on behalf of the Commission.

The Commission shall reply orally or in writing to questions put to it by the European Parliament or by its members.

The Council shall be heard by the European Parliament in accordance with the conditions laid down by the Council in its rules of procedure.

Article 198

Save as otherwise provided in this Treaty, the European Parliament shall act by an absolute majority of the votes cast.

The Rules of Procedure shall determine the quorum.

Article 199

The European Parliament shall adopt its Rules of Procedure, acting by a majority of its Members.

The proceedings of the European Parliament shall be published in the manner laid down in its Rules of Procedure.

Article 200

The European Parliament shall discuss in open session the annual general report submitted to it by the Commission.

Article 201

If a motion of censure on the activities of the Commission is tabled before it, the European Parliament shall not vote thereon until at least three days after the motion has been tabled and only by open vote.

If the motion of censure is carried by a two-third majority of the votes cast, representing a majority of the members of the European Parliament, the members of the Commission shall resign as a body. They shall continue to deal with current business until they are replaced in accordance with Article 214. In this case, the term of office of the members of the Commission appointed to replace them shall expire on the date on which the term of office of the members of the Commission obliged to resign as a body would have expired.

Section 2—The Council

Article 202

To ensure that the objectives set out in the Treaty are attained, the Council shall, in accordance with the provisions of this Treaty:

— ensure co-ordination of the general economic policies of the Member States;
— have power to take decisions;
— confer on the Commission, in the acts which the Council adopts, powers for the implementation of the rules which the Council lays down. The Council may impose certain requirements in respect of the exercise of these powers. The Council may also reserve the right, in specific cases, to exercise directly implementing powers itself. The procedures referred to above must be consonant with principles and rules to be laid down in advance by the Council, acting unanimously on a proposal from the Commission and after obtaining the Opinion of the European Parliament.

★ ★ ★ ★ ★

Article 205

1.   Save as otherwise provided in this Treaty, the Council shall act by a majority of its members.

2.   Where the Council is required to act by a qualified majority, the votes of its members shall be weighted as follows:

Belgium	5
Denmark	3
Germany	10
Greece	5
Spain	8

```
France.....................................  10
Ireland ...................................   3
Italy .....................................  10
Luxembourg ...............................    2
Netherlands...............................    5
Austria ...................................    4
Portugal ..................................    5
Finland...................................    3
Sweden....................................    4
United Kingdom ...........................   10
```

For their adoption, acts of the Council shall require at least:
- — 62 votes in favour where this Treaty requires them to be adopted on a proposal from the Commission,
- — 62 votes in favour, cast by at least 10 members, in other cases.

3. Abstentions by members present in person or represented shall not prevent the adoption by the Council of acts which require unanimity.

★ ★ ★ ★ ★

Section 3—The Commission

Article 211

In order to ensure the proper functioning and development of the common market, the Commission shall:
- — ensure that the provisions of this Treaty and the measures taken by the institutions pursuant thereto are applied;
- — formulate recommendations or deliver opinions on matters dealt with in this Treaty, if it expressly so provides or if the Commission considers it necessary;
- — have its own power of decision and participate in the shaping of measures taken by the Council and by the European Parliament in the manner provided for in this Treaty;
- — exercise the powers conferred on it by the Council for the implementation of the rules laid down by the latter.

★ ★ ★ ★ ★

Section 4—The Court of Justice

Article 220

The Court of Justice shall ensure that in the interpretation and application of this Treaty the law is observed.

Article 221

The Court of Justice shall consist of 15 Judges.

The Court of Justice shall sit in plenary session. It may, however, form chambers, each consisting of three, five or seven Judges, either to undertake certain preparatory inquiries or to adjudicate on particular categories of cases in accordance with rules laid down for these purposes.

The Court of Justice shall sit in plenary session when a Member State or a Community institution that is a party to the proceedings so requests.

Should the Court of Justice so request, the Council may, acting unanimously, increase the number of Judges and make the necessary adjustments to the second and third paragraphs of this Article and to the second paragraph of Article 223.

Article 222

The Court of Justice shall be assisted by eight Advocates General. However a ninth Advocate-General shall be appointed as from 1 January 1995 until 6 October 2000.

It shall be the duty of the Advocate-General, acting with complete impartiality and independence, to make, in open court, reasoned submissions on cases brought before the Court of Justice, in order to assist the Court in the performance of the task assigned to it in Article 220.

Should the Court of Justice so request, the Council may, acting unanimously, increase the number of Advocates General and make the necessary adjustments to the third paragraph of Article 223.

Article 223

The Judges and Advocates General shall be chosen from persons whose independence is beyond doubt and who possess the qualifications required for appointment to the highest judicial offices in their respective countries or who are jurisconsults of recognised competence; they shall be appointed by common accord of the Governments of the Member States for a term of six years.

Every three years there shall be a partial replacement of the Judges. Eight and seven Judges shall be replaced alternately.

Every three years there shall be a partial replacement of the Advocates General. Four Advocates General shall be replaced on each occasion.

Retiring Judges and Advocates General shall be eligible for reappointment.

The Judges shall elect the President of the Court of Justice from among their number for a term of three years. He may be re-elected.

Article 224

The Court of Justice shall appoint its Registrar and lay down the rules governing his service.

Article 225

1.   A Court of First Instance shall be attached to the Court of Justice with jurisdiction to hear and determine at first instance, subject to a right of appeal to the Court of Justice on points of law only and in accordance with the conditions laid down by the Statute, certain classes of action or proceeding defined in accordance with the conditions laid down in paragraph 2. The Court of First Instance shall not be competent to hear and determine questions referred for a preliminary ruling under Article 234.

2.   At the request of the Court of Justice and after consulting the European Parliament and the Commission, the Council, acting unanimously, shall determine the classes of action or proceeding referred to in paragraph 1 and the composition of the Court of First Instance and shall adopt the necessary adjustments and additional provisions to the Statute of the Court of Justice. Unless the Council decides otherwise, the provisions of this Treaty relating to the Court of Justice, in particular the provisions of the Protocol on the Statute of the Court of Justice, shall apply to the Court of First Instance.

3.   The members of the Court of First Instance shall be chosen from persons whose independence is beyond doubt and who possess the ability required for appointment to judicial office; they shall be appointed by common accord of the governments of the Member States for a term of six years. The membership shall be partially renewed every three years. Retiring members shall be eligible for re-appointment.

4.   The Court of First Instance shall establish its rules of procedure in agreement with the Court of Justice. Those rules shall require the unanimous approval of the Council.

Article 226

If the Commission considers that a Member State has failed to fulfil an obligation under this Treaty, it shall deliver a reasoned opinion on the matter after giving the State concerned the opportunity to submit its observations.

If the State concerned does not comply with the opinion within the period laid down by the Commission, the latter may bring the matter before the Court of Justice.

Article 227
A Member State which considers that another Member State has failed to fulfil an obligation under this Treaty may bring the matter before the Court of Justice.

Before a Member State brings an action against another Member State for an alleged infringement of an obligation under this Treaty, it shall bring the matter before the Commission.

The Commission shall deliver a reasoned opinion after each of the States concerned has been given the opportunity to submit its own case and its observations on the other party's case both orally and in writing.

★ ★ ★ ★ ★

Article 228
1. If the Court of Justice finds that a Member State has failed to fulfil an obligation under this Treaty, the State shall be required to take the necessary measures to comply with the judgment of the Court of Justice.

2. If the Commission considers that the Member State concerned has not taken such measures it shall, after giving that State the opportunity to submit its observations, issue a reasoned opinion specifying the points on which the Member State concerned has not complied with the judgment of the Court of Justice.

If the Member State concerned fails to take the necessary measures to comply with the Court's judgment within the time-limit laid down by the Commission, the latter may bring the case before the Court of Justice. In so doing it shall specify the amount of the lump sum or penalty payment to be paid by the Member State concerned which it considers appropriate in the circumstances.

If the Court of Justice finds that the Member State concerned has not complied with its judgment it may impose a lump sum or penalty payment on it.

This procedure shall be without prejudice to Article 227.

Article 229
Regulations adopted jointly by the European Parliament and the Council, and by the Council, pursuant to the provisions of this Treaty, may give the Court of Justice unlimited jurisdiction with regard to the penalties provided for in such regulations.

Article 230
The Court of Justice shall review the legality of acts adopted jointly by the European Parliament and the Council, of acts of the Council, of the Commission and of the ECB, other than recommendations and opinions, and of acts of the European Parliament intended to produce legal effects *vis-à-vis* third parties.

It shall for this purpose have jurisdiction in actions brought by a Member State, the Council or the Commission on grounds of lack of competence, infringement of an essential procedural requirement, infringement of this Treaty or of any rule of law relating to its application, or misuse of powers.

The Court shall have jurisdiction under the same conditions in actions brought by the European Parliament by the Court of Auditors and by the ECB for the purpose of protecting their prerogatives. Any natural or legal person may, under the same conditions, institute proceedings against a decision addressed to that person or against a decision which, although in the form of a regulation or a decision addressed to another person, is of direct and individual concern to the former.

The proceedings provided for in this Article shall be instituted within two months of the publication of the measure, or of its notification to the plaintiff, or, in the absence thereof, of the day on which it came to the knowledge of the latter, as the case may be.

Article 231

If the action is well founded, the Court of Justice shall declare the act concerned to be void.

In the case of a regulation, however, the Court of Justice shall, if it considers this necessary, state which of the effects of the regulation which it has declared void shall be considered as definitive.

★ ★ ★ ★ ★

Article 234

The Court of Justice shall have jurisdiction to give preliminary rulings concerning:

(a) the interpretation of this Treaty;

(b) the validity and interpretation of acts of the institutions of the Community and of the ECB;

(c) the interpretation of the statutes of bodies established by an act of the Council, where those statutes so provide.

Where such a question is raised before any court or tribunal of a Member State, that court or tribunal may, if it considers that a decision on the question is necessary to enable it to give judgment, request the Court of Justice to give a ruling thereon.

Where any such question is raised in a case pending before a court or tribunal of a Member State against whose decisions there is no judicial remedy under national law, that court or tribunal shall bring the matter before the Court of Justice.

CHAPTER 2—(PROVISIONS COMMON TO SEVERAL INSTITUTIONS)

Article 249

In order to carry out their task and in accordance with the provisions of this Treaty, the European Parliament acting jointly with the Council, the Council and the Commission shall make regulations and issue directives, take decisions, make recommendations or deliver opinions.

A regulation shall have general application. It shall be binding in its entirety and directly applicable in all Member States.

A directive shall be binding, as to the result to be achieved, upon each Member State to which it is addressed, but shall leave to the national authorities the choice of form and methods.

A decision shall be binding in its entirety upon those to whom it is addressed. Recommendations and opinions shall have no binding force.

Article 250

1. Where, in pursuance of this Treaty, the Council acts on a proposal from the Commission, unanimity shall be required for an act constituting an amendment to that proposal, subject to Article 251(4) and (5).

2. As long as the Council has not acted, the Commission may alter its proposal at any time during the procedures leading to the adoption of a Community act.

Article 251

1. Where reference is made in this Treaty to this Article for the adoption of an act, the following procedure shall apply.

2. The Commission shall submit a proposal to the European Parliament and the Council.

The Council, acting by a qualified majority after obtaining the opinion of the European Parliament,

— if it approves all the amendments contained in the European Parliament's opinion, may adopt the proposed act thus amended;

— if the European Parliament does not propose any amendments, may adopt the proposed act;

— shall otherwise adopt a common position and communicate it to the European Parliament. The Council shall inform the European Parliament fully of the reasons which led it to adopt its common position. The Commission shall inform the European Parliament fully of its position.

If, within three months of such communication, the European Parliament:

(a) approves the common position or has not taken a decision, the act in question shall be deemed to have been adopted in accordance with that common position;

(b) rejects, by an absolute majority of its component members, the common position, the proposed act shall be deemed not to have been adopted;

(c) proposes amendments to the common position by an absolute majority of its component members, the amended text shall be forwarded to the Council and to the Commission, which shall deliver an opinion on those amendments.

3.   If, within three months of the matter being referred to it, the Council, acting by a qualified majority, approves all the amendments of the European Parliament, the act in question shall be deemed to have been adopted in the form of the common position thus amended; however, the Council shall act unanimously on the amendments on which the Commission has delivered a negative opinion. If the Council does not approve all the amendments, the President of the Council, in agreement with the President of the European Parliament, shall within six weeks convene a meeting of the Conciliation Committee.

4.   The Conciliation Committee, which shall be composed of the members of the Council or their representatives and an equal number of representatives of the European Parliament, shall have the task of reaching agreement on a joint text, by a qualified majority of the members of the Council or their representatives and by a majority of the representatives of the European Parliament. The Commission shall take part in the Conciliation Committee's proceedings and shall take all the necessary initiatives with a view to reconciling the positions of the European Parliament and the Council. In fulfilling this task, the Conciliation Committee shall address the common position on the basis of the amendments proposed by the European Parliament.

5.   If, within six weeks of its being convened, the Conciliation Committee approves a joint text, the European Parliament, acting by an absolute majority of the votes cast, and the Council, acting by a qualified majority, shall have a period of six weeks from that approval in which to adopt the act in question in accordance with the joint text. If either of the two institutions fails to approve the proposed act, it shall be deemed not to have been adopted.

6.   Where the Conciliation Committee does not approve a joint text, the proposed act shall be deemed not to have been adopted.

7.   The periods of three months and six weeks referred to in this Article may be extended by a maximum of one month and two weeks respectively at the initiative of the European Parliament or the Council.

Article 252

Where reference is made in this Treaty to this Article for the adoption of an act, the following procedure shall apply:

(a) The Council, acting by a qualified majority on a proposal from the Commission and after obtaining the Opinion of the European Parliament, shall adopt a common position.

(b) The Council's common position shall be communicated to the European Parliament. The Council and the Commission shall inform the European Parliament fully of the reasons which led the Council to adopt its common position and also of the Commission's position.

If, within three months of such communication, the European Parliament approves this common position or has not taken a decision within that period, the Council shall definitively adopt the act in question in accordance with the common position.

   (c) The European Parliament may, within the period of three months referred to in point (b), by an absolute majority of its component Members, propose amendments to the Council's common position.

The European Parliament may also, by the same majority, reject the Council's common position. The result of the proceedings shall be transmitted to the Council and the Commission.

If the European Parliament has rejected the Council's common position, unanimity shall be required for the Council to act on a second reading.

   (d) The Commission shall, within a period of one month, re-examine the proposal on the basis of which the Council adopted its common position, by taking into account the amendments proposed by the European Parliament.

The Commission shall forward to the Council, at the same time as its re-examined proposal, the amendments of the European Parliament which it has not accepted, and shall express its opinion on them. The Council may adopt these amendments unanimously.

   (e) The Council, acting by a qualified majority, shall adopt the proposal as re-examined by the Commission.

Unanimity shall be required for the Council to amend the proposal as re-examined by the Commission.

   (f) In the cases referred to in points (c), (d) and (e), the Council shall be required to act within a period of three months. If no decision is taken within this period, the Commission proposal shall be deemed not to have been adopted.

   (g) The periods referred to in points (b) and (f) may be extended by a maximum of one month by common accord between the Council and the European Parliament.

★ ★ ★ ★ ★

CHAPTER 3—(THE ECONOMIC AND SOCIAL COMMITTEE)

Article 257

An Economic and Social Committee is hereby established. It shall have advisory status.

The Committee shall consist of representatives of the various categories of economic and social activity, in particular, representatives of producers, farmers, carriers, workers, dealers, craftsmen, professional occupations and representatives of the general public.

Article 258

The number of members of the Committee shall be as follows:

Belgium	12
Denmark	9
Germany	24
Greece	12
Spain	21
France	24
Ireland	9
Italy	24
Luxembourg	6
Netherlands	12
Austria	12

The members of the Committee shall be appointed by the Council, acting unanimously, for four years. Their appointments shall be renewable. The members of the Committee may not be bound by any mandatory instructions. They shall be completely independent in the performance of their duties, in the general interest of the Community. The Council, acting by a qualified majority, shall determine the allowances of members of the Committee.

★ ★ ★ ★ ★

Article 308
If action by the Community should prove necessary to attain, in the course of the operation of the common market, one of the objectives of the Community and this Treaty has not provided the necessary powers, the Council shall, acting unanimously on a proposal from the Commission and after consulting the European Parliament, take the appropriate measures.

★ ★ ★ ★ ★

Article 311
The Protocols annexed to this Treaty by common accord of the Member States shall form an integral part thereof.

Article 312
This Treaty is concluded for an unlimited period.

Treaty on European Union

ADOPTED BY THE EU MEMBER STATES
(Done at Maastricht) 7 February 1992

Entry into force: 1 November 1993

Territorial application: EU Member States

TITLE I   COMMON PROVISIONS

Article 1
By this Treaty, the HIGH CONTRACTING PARTIES establish among themselves a EUROPEAN UNION, hereinafter called the Union.

This Treaty marks a new stage in the process of creating an ever closer union among the peoples of Europe, in which decisions are taken as openly as possible and as closely as possible to the citizen.

The Union shall be founded on the European Communities, supplemented by the policies and forms of co-operation established by this Treaty. Its task shall be to organise, in a manner demonstrating consistency and solidarity, relations between the Member States and between their peoples.

Article 2
The Union shall set itself the following objectives:

— to promote economic and social progress and a high level of employment and to achieve balanced and sustainable development, in particular through the creation of an area without internal frontiers, through the strengthening of economic and social cohesion and through the establishment of economic and monetary union, ultimately including a single currency in accordance with the provisions of this Treaty;

— to assert its identity on the international scene, in particular through the implementation of a common foreign and security policy including the framing of a common defence policy, which might in time lead to a common defence in accordance with the provisions of Article 17;

— to strengthen the protection of the rights and interests of the nationals of its Member States through the introduction of a citizenship of the Union;

— to maintain and develop the Union as an area of freedom, security and justice, in which the free movement of persons is assured in conjunction with appropriate measures with respect to external border controls, asylum, immigration and the prevention and combating of crime;

— to maintain in full the "*acquis communautaire*" and build on it with a view to considering to what extent the policies and forms of co-operation introduced by this Treaty may need to be revised with the aim of ensuring the effectiveness of the mechanisms and the institutions of the Community.

The objectives of the Union shall be achieved as provided in this Treaty and in accordance with the conditions and the timetable set out therein while respecting the principle of subsidiarity as defined in Article 5 of the Treaty establishing the European Community.

Article 3
The Union shall be served by a single institutional framework which shall ensure the consistency and the continuity of the activities carried out in order to attain its objectives while respecting and building upon the "*acquis communautaire*".

The Union shall in particular ensure the consistency of its external activities as a whole in the context of its external relations, security, economic and development policies. The Council and the Commission shall be responsible for ensuring such consistency and shall co-operate to this end. They shall ensure the implementation of these policies, each in accordance with its respective powers.

Article 4
The European Council shall provide the Union with the necessary impetus for its development and shall define the general political guidelines thereof.

The European Council shall bring together the Heads of State or of Government of the Member States and the President of the Commission.

They shall be assisted by the Ministers for Foreign Affairs of the Member States and by a Member of the Commission. The European Council shall meet at least twice a year, under the chairmanship of the Head of State or of Government of the Member State which holds the Presidency of the Council.

The European Council shall submit to the European Parliament a report after each of its meetings and a yearly written report on the progress achieved by the Union.

Article 5
The European Parliament, the Council, the Commission, the Court of Justice and the Court of Auditors shall exercise their powers under the conditions and for the purposes provided for, on the one hand, by the provisions of the Treaties establishing the European Communities and of the subsequent Treaties and Acts modifying and supplementing them and, on the other hand, by the other provisions of this Treaty.

Article 6

1. The Union is founded on the principles of liberty, democracy, respect for human rights and fundamental freedoms and the rule of law, principles which are common to Member States.

2. The Union shall respect fundamental rights, as guaranteed by the European Convention for the Protection of Human Rights and Fundamental Freedoms signed in Rome on 4 November 1950 and as they result from the constitutional traditions common to the Member States, as general principles of Community law.

3. The Union shall respect the national identities of its Member States.

4. The Union shall provide itself with the means necessary to attain its objectives and carry through its policies.

★ ★ ★ ★ ★

TITLE VI   PROVISIONS ON POLICE AND JUDICIAL COOPERATION IN CRIMINAL MATTERS

Article 29

Without prejudice to the powers of the European Community, the Union's objective shall be to provide citizens with a high level of safety within an area of freedom, security and justice by developing common action among the Member States in the fields of police and judicial cooperation in criminal matters and by preventing and combating racism and xenophobia.

That objective shall be achieved by preventing and combating crime, organised or otherwise, in particular terrorism, trafficking in persons and offences against children, illicit drug trafficking and illicit arms trafficking, corruption and fraud, through:

— closer cooperation between police forces, customs authorities and other competent authorities in the Member States, both directly and through the European Police Office (Europol), in accordance with the provisions of Articles 30 and 32;

— closer cooperation between judicial and other competent authorities of the Member States in accordance with the provisions of Articles 31(a) to (d) and 32;

— approximation, where necessary, of rules on criminal matters in the Member States, in accordance with the provisions of Article 31(e).

Article 30

1. Common action in the field of police cooperation shall include:

    (a) operational cooperation between the competent authorities, including the police, customs and other specialised law enforcement services of the Member States in relation to the prevention, detection and investigation of criminal offences;

    (b) the collection, storage, processing, analysis and exchange of relevant information, including information held by law enforcement services on reports on suspicious financial transactions, in particular through Europol, subject to appropriate provisions on the protection of personal data;

    (c) cooperation and joint initiatives in training, the exchange of liaison officers, secondments, the use of equipment, and forensic research;

    (d) the common evaluation of particular investigative techniques in relation to the detection of serious forms of organised crime.

2. The Council shall promote cooperation through Europol and shall in particular, within a period of five years after the date of entry into force of the Treaty of Amsterdam:

    (a) enable Europol to facilitate and support the preparation, and to encourage the coordination and carrying out, of specific investigative actions by the competent authorities of the Member States, including operational actions of joint teams comprising representatives of Europol in a support capacity;

(b) adopt measures allowing Europol to ask the competent authorities of the Member States to conduct and coordinate their investigations in specific cases and to develop specific expertise which may be put at the disposal of Member States to assist them in investigating cases of organised crime;

(c) promote liaison arrangements between prosecuting/investigating officials specialising in the fight against organised crime in close cooperation with Europol;

(d) establish a research, documentation and statistical network on cross-border crime.

★ ★ ★ ★ ★

Police and Criminal Evidence Act 1984 Revised Codes of Practice A–C

Note: For the legal status of the Codes and other issues relating to them, see ss. 66 and 67 of the Police and Criminal Evidence Act 1984 (*supra*). The Codes were revised in accordance with s. 67(7) of the Act with effect from 9 April 1995. A further revised Code A was approved to come into effect in 1997 and a further revision was introduced with effect from 1 March 1999. The most recent revised version of each Code is printed below (except for Codes D and E which are not reproduced).

PACE—Code of Practice for the Exercise By Police Officers of Statutory Powers of Stop and Search (Code A)

Note: The Notes for Guidance are not reproduced here.

1   General

1.1–1.4   ★ ★ ★ ★ ★

1.5   This code applies to stops and searches under powers:

(a) requiring reasonable grounds for suspicion that articles unlawfully obtained or possessed are being carried;

(b) authorised under section 60 of the Criminal Justice and Public Order Act 1994, (as amended by section 8 of the Knives Act 1997), based upon a reasonable belief that incidents involving serious violence may take place or that people are carrying dangerous instruments or offensive weapons within any locality in the police area;

(c) authorised under section 13A of the Prevention of Terrorism (Temporary Provisions) Act 1989, (as amended by section 81 of the Criminal Justice and Public Order Act 1994 and section 1 of the Prevention of Terrorism (Additional Powers) Act 1996);

(d) authorised under section 13B of the Prevention of Terrorism (Temporary Provisions) Act 1989, (as inserted by section 1 of the Prevention of Terrorism (Additional Powers) Act 1996);

(e) exercised under paragraph 4(2) of Schedule 5 to the Prevention of Terrorism (Temporary Provisions) Act 1989.

(a) Powers requiring reasonable suspicion

1.6   Whether a reasonable ground for suspicion exists will depend on the circumstances in each case, but there must be some objective basis for it. An officer will need to consider the nature of the article suspected of being carried in the context of other factors such as the time and the place, and the behaviour of the person concerned or those with him. Reasonable suspicion may exist, for example, where information has been received such as a description of an article being carried or of a suspected offender; a person is seen acting covertly or warily or attempting to hide something; or a person is carrying a certain type of article at an unusual time or in a place where a number of burglaries or thefts are known to have taken place recently. But the decision to stop and search must be based on all the facts which bear on the likelihood that an article of a certain kind will be found.

1.6A   For example, reasonable suspicion may be based upon reliable information or intelligence which indicates that members of a particular group or gang, or their associates, habitually carry knives unlawfully or weapons or controlled drugs.

1.7   Subject to the provision in paragraph 1.7AA below, reasonable suspicion can never be supported on the basis of personal factors alone without supporting intelligence or information. For example, a person's colour, age, hairstyle or manner of dress, or the fact that he is known to have a previous conviction for possession of an unlawful article, cannot be used alone or in combination with each other as the sole basis on which to search that person. Nor may it be founded on the basis of stereotyped images of certain persons or groups as more likely to be committing offences.

1.7AA   However, where there is reliable information or intelligence that members of a group or gang who habitually carry knives unlawfully or weapons or controlled drugs, and wear a distinctive item of clothing or other means of identification to indicate membership of it, the members may be identified by means of that distinctive item of clothing or other means of identification.

1.7A   Where a police officer has reasonable grounds to suspect that a person is in innocent possession of a stolen or prohibited article or other item for which he is empowered to search, the power of stop and search exists notwithstanding that there would be no power of arrest. However every effort should be made to secure the person's co-operation in the production of the article before resorting to the use of force.

(b) Authorisation under section 60 of the Criminal Justice and Public Order Act 1994, as amended by section 8 of the Knives Act 1997

1.8   Authority to exercise the powers of stop and search under section 60 of the Criminal Justice and Public Order Act 1994, as amended by section 8 of the Knives Act 1997, may be given where it is reasonably believed that incidents involving serious violence may take place in any locality in the police area, and it is expedient to use these powers to prevent their occurrence, or that persons are carrying dangerous instruments or offensive weapons without good reason in any locality in any police area. Authorisation may only be given by an officer of the rank of inspector or above, in writing, specifying the grounds on which it was given, the locality in which the powers may be exercised and the period of time for which they are in force. The period authorised shall be no longer than appears reasonably necessary to prevent, or try to prevent incidents of serious violence, or to deal with the problem of carrying dangerous instruments or offensive weapons and it may not exceed 24 hours. If an inspector gives an authorisation, he must, as soon as practicable, inform an officer of or above the rank of superintendent. An officer of or above the rank of superintendent may direct that the period shall be extended for a further 24 hours if violence or the carrying of dangerous instruments or offensive weapons has occurred or is suspected to have occurred and the continued use of the powers is considered necessary to prevent or deal with further such activity. That direction must also be given in writing at the time or as soon as practicable afterwards.

(c) Authorisation under section 13A of the Prevention of Terrorism (Temporary Provisions) Act 1989, as inserted by section 81 of the Criminal Justice and Public Order Act 1994 and amended by the Prevention of Terrorism (Additional Powers) Act 1996

1.8A   . . .

2   Action before a search is carried out

(a) Searches requiring reasonable suspicion

2.1   Where an officer has the reasonable grounds for suspicion necessary to exercise a power of stop and search, he may detain the person concerned for the purposes of and with a view to searching him. There is no power to stop or detain a person against his will in order to find grounds for a search.

2.2   Before carrying out a search the officer may question the person about his behaviour or his presence in circumstances which gave rise to the suspicion, since he may have a satisfactory explanation which will make a search unnecessary. If, as a result of any questioning preparatory to a search, or other circumstances which come to the attention of the officer, there cease to be reasonable grounds for suspecting that an article is being carried of a kind for which there is a power of stop and search, no search may take place.

2.3   The reasonable grounds for suspicion which are necessary for the exercise of the initial power to detain may be confirmed or eliminated as a result of the questioning of a person detained for the purposes of a search (or such questioning may reveal reasonable grounds to suspect the possession of a different kind of unlawful article from that originally suspected); but the reasonable grounds for suspicion without which any search or detention for the purposes of a search is unlawful cannot be retrospectively provided by such questioning during his detention or by his refusal to answer any question put to him.

(b) All searches

2.4   Before any search of a detained person or attended vehicle takes place the officer must take reasonable steps to give the person to be searched or in charge of the vehicle the following information:
>   (i)   his name (except in the case of enquiries linked to the investigation of terrorism, in which case he shall give his warrant or other identification number) and the name of the police station to which he is attached;
>   (ii)   the object of the search; and
>   (iii)   his grounds or authorisation for undertaking it.

2.5   If the officer is not in uniform he must show his warrant card. In doing so in the case of enquiries linked to the investigation of terrorism, the officer need not reveal his name. Stops and searches under the powers mentioned in paragraphs 1.5 (b) and (c) may be undertaken only by a constable in uniform.

2.6   Unless it appears to the officer that it will not be practicable to make a record of the search, he must also inform the person to be searched (or the owner or person in charge of a vehicle that is to be searched, as the case may be) that he is entitled to a copy of the record of the search if he asks for it within a year. If the person wishes to have a copy and is not given one on the spot, he shall be advised to which police station he should apply.

2.7   If the person to be searched, or in charge of a vehicle to be searched, does not appear to understand what is being said, or there is any doubt about his ability to understand English, the officer must take reasonable steps to bring the information in paragraphs 2.4 and 2.6 to his attention. If the person is deaf or cannot understand English and has someone with him then the officer must try to establish whether the person can interpret or otherwise help him to give the required information.

3   Conduct of the search

3.1   Every reasonable effort must be made to reduce to the minimum the embarrassment that a person being searched may experience.

3.2   The co-operation of the person to be searched shall be sought in every case, even if he initially objects to the search. A forcible search may be made only if it has been established that the person is unwilling to co-operate (e.g. by opening a bag) or resists. Although force may only be used as a last resort, reasonable force may be used if necessary to conduct a search or to detain a person or vehicle for the purposes of a search.

3.3   The length of time for which a person or vehicle may be detained will depend on the circumstances, but must in all circumstances, be reasonable and not extend beyond the time taken for the search. Where the exercise of the power requires reasonable suspicion, the thoroughness and extent of a search must depend on what is suspected of being carried, and by whom. If the suspicion relates to a particular article which is seen to be slipped into a person's pocket, then, in the absence of other grounds for suspicion or an opportunity for the article to be moved elsewhere, the search must be confined to that pocket. In the case of a small article which can readily be concealed, such as a drug, and which might be concealed anywhere on the person, a more extensive search may be necessary. In the case of searches mentioned in paragraph 1.5(b), (c), (d) and (e), which do not require reasonable grounds for suspicion, the officer may make any reasonable search to find what he is empowered to search for.

3.4   The search must be conducted at or nearby the place where the person or vehicle was first detained.

3.5   Searches in public must be restricted to superficial examination of outer clothing. There is no power to require a person to remove any clothing in public other than an outer coat, jacket or gloves (other than under sections 13A and 13B of the Prevention of Terrorism (Temporary Provisions) Act 1989, which grant a constable in addition the power to require a person to remove in public any headgear and footwear, or under section 60 of the Criminal Justice and Public Order Act 1994 as amended by the Crime and Disorder Act 1998, which grants a constable power to require the removal of any item worn to conceal identity). Where on reasonable grounds it is considered necessary to conduct a more thorough search (e.g. by requiring a person to take off a T-shirt), this shall be done out of public view for example, in a police van or police station if there is one nearby. Any search involving the removal of more than an outer coat, jacket, gloves, headgear or footwear, or any other item concealing identity, may only be made by an officer of the same sex as the person searched and may not be made in the presence of anyone of the opposite sex unless the person being searched specifically requests it. [See Note 3A and 3C]. No search involving exposure of intimate parts of the body may take place in a police van. All searches involving exposure of intimate parts of the body shall be conducted in accordance with paragraph 11 of Annex A to Code C. The other provisions of Code C do not apply to persons at police stations for the purposes of searches under stop and search powers.

3.5A   The powers under sections 13A and 13B of the Prevention of Terrorism (Temporary Provisions) Act 1989 allow a constable to search only for articles which could be used for terrorist purposes. The powers must not be used for any other purpose (for example to search for drugs in the absence of reasonable grounds for suspicion). However, this would not prevent a search being carried out under other powers if, in course of exercising powers under sections 13A or 13B, the police officer formed reasonable grounds for suspicion.

4   ★ ★ ★ ★ ★

Code of Practice for the Searching of Premises by Police Officers and the Seizure of Property Found by Police Officers on Persons or Premises (Code B)

Note: See note to Code A (*supra*). The Notes for Guidance are not reproduced.

1   General

1.1   This code of practice must be readily available at all police stations for consultation by police officers, detained persons and members of the public.

1.2   The notes for guidance included are not provisions of this code, but are guidance to police officers and others about its application and interpretation.

1.3   This code applies to the following searches of premises:
(a) undertaken for the purposes of an investigation into an alleged offence, with the occupier's consent, other than searches made in the following circumstances:
— routine searches of crime scenes –calls to a fire or a burglary made by or on behalf of an occupier or searches following the activation of fire or burglar alarms
— searches to which paragraph 4.4 applies
— bomb threat calls;
(b) under powers conferred by sections 17, 18 and 32 of the Police and Criminal Evidence Act 1984;
(c) undertaken in pursuance of a search warrant issued in accordance with section 15 of, or Schedule 1 to the Police and Criminal Evidence Act 1984, or section 15 of, or Schedule 7 to the Prevention of Terrorism (Temporary Provisions) Act 1989.

★ ★ ★ ★ ★

1.3A   Any search of a person who has not been arrested which is carried out during a search of premises shall be carried out in accordance with Code A.

1.3B   This code does not apply to the exercise of a statutory power to enter premises or to inspect goods, equipment or procedures if the exercise of that power is not dependent on the existence of grounds for suspecting that an offence may have been committed and the person exercising the power has no reasonable grounds for such suspicion.

2   Search warrants and production orders

(a) Action to be taken before an application is made

2.1   Where information is received which appears to justify an application, the officer concerned must take reasonable steps to check that the information is accurate, recent and has not been provided maliciously or irresponsibly. An application may not be made on the basis of information from an anonymous source where corroboration has not been sought.

2.2   The officer shall ascertain as specifically as is possible in the circumstances the nature of the articles concerned and their location.

2.3   The officer shall also make reasonable enquiries to establish what, if anything, is known about the likely occupier of the premises and the nature of the premises themselves; and whether they have been previously searched and if so how recently; and to obtain any other information relevant to the application.

2.4   No application for a search warrant may be made without the authority of an officer of at least the rank of inspector (or, in a case of urgency where no officer of this rank is readily available, the senior officer on duty). No application for a production order or warrant under Schedule 1 to the Police and Criminal Evidence Act 1984, or under Schedule 7 to the Prevention of Terrorism (Temporary Provisions) Act 1989, may be made without the authority of an officer of at least the rank of superintendent.

2.5   Except in a case of urgency, if there is reason to believe that a search might have an adverse effect on relations between the police and the community then the local police community liaison officer shall be consulted before it takes place. In urgent cases, the local police community liaison officer should be informed of the search as soon as practicable after it has been made.

(b) Making an application

2.6   An application for a search warrant must be supported by an information in writing, specifying:
    (i)   the enactment under which the application is made;
    (ii) as specifically as is reasonably practicable the premises to be searched and the object of the search; and
    (iii) the grounds on which the application is made (including, where the purpose of the proposed search is to find evidence of an alleged offence, an indication of how the evidence relates to the investigation).

2.7   An application for a search warrant under paragraph 12(a) of Schedule 1 to the Police and Criminal Evidence Act 1984, or under Schedule 7 to the Prevention of Terrorism (Temporary Provisions) Act 1989, shall also, where appropriate, indicate why it is believed that service of notice of an application for a production order may seriously prejudice the investigation.

2.8   If an application is refused, no further application may be made for a warrant to search those premises unless supported by additional grounds.

3   ★ ★ ★ ★ ★

4   Search with consent

4.1   Subject to paragraph 4.4 below, if it is proposed to search premises with the consent of a person entitled to grant entry to the premises the consent must, if practicable, be given in writing on the notice of Powers and Rights before the search takes place. The officer must make enquiries to satisfy himself that the person is in a position to give such consent.

4.2   ★ ★ ★ ★ ★

4.3   An officer cannot enter and search premises or continue to search premises under 4.1 above if the consent has been given under duress or is withdrawn before the search is completed.

4.4   ★ ★ ★ ★ ★

5   Searching of premises: general considerations

(a) Time of searches

5.1   Searches made under warrant must be made within one calendar month from the date of issue of the warrant.

5.2   Searches must be made at a reasonable hour unless this might frustrate the purpose of the search.

5.3   A warrant authorises an entry on one occasion only.

(b) Entry other than with consent

5.4–5.6   ★ ★ ★ ★ ★

(c) Notice of powers and rights

5.7   If an officer conducts a search to which this code applies he shall, unless it is impracticable to do so, provide the occupier with a copy of a notice in a standard format:
    (i)   specifying whether the search is made under warrant, or with consent, or in the

exercise of the powers described in 3.1 to 3.3 above (the format of the notice shall provide for authority or consent to be indicated where appropriate – see 3.3 and 4.1 above);

(ii) summarising the extent of the powers of search and seizure conferred in the Act;

(iii) explaining the rights of the occupier, and of the owner of property seized in accordance with the provisions of 6.1 to 6.5 and 6.8 below, set out in the Act and in this code;

(iv) explaining that compensation may be payable in appropriate cases for damage caused in entering and searching premises, and giving the address to which an application for compensation should be directed; and

(v) stating that a copy of this code is available to be consulted at any police station.

5.8   If the occupier is present, copies of the notice mentioned above, and of the warrant (if the search is made under warrant) should if practicable be given to the occupier before the search begins, unless the officer in charge of the search reasonably believes that to do so would frustrate the object of the search or endanger the officers concerned or other persons. If the occupier is not present, copies of the notice, and of the warrant where appropriate, should be left in a prominent place on the premises or appropriate part of the premises and endorsed with the name of the officer in charge of the search (except in the case of inquiries linked to the investigation of terrorism, in which case the officer's warrant or other identification number should be given), the name of the police station to which he is attached and the date and time of the search. The warrant itself should be endorsed to show that this has been done.

5.9–5.14   ★ ★ ★ ★ ★

6   Seizure and retention of property

(a) Seizure

6.1   Subject to paragraph 6.2 below, an officer who is searching any premises under any statutory power or with the consent of the occupier may seize:

(a)   anything covered by a warrant; and

(b)   anything which he has reasonable grounds for believing is evidence of an offence or has been obtained in consequence of the commission of an offence.

Items under (b) may only be seized where this is necessary to prevent their concealment, alteration, loss, damage or destruction.

6.2   No item may be seized which is subject to legal privilege (as defined in section 10 of the Police and Criminal Evidence Act 1984).

6.3   An officer who decides that it is not appropriate to seize property because of an explanation given by the person holding it, but who has reasonable grounds for believing that it has been obtained in consequence of the commission of an offence by some person, shall inform the holder of his suspicions and shall explain that, if he disposes of the property, he may be liable to civil or criminal proceedings.

6.4   An officer may photograph or copy, or have photographed or copied, any document or other article which he has power to seize in accordance with paragraph 6.1 above.

6.5   Where an officer considers that a computer may contain information that could be used in evidence, he may require the information to be produced in a form that can be taken away and in which it is visible and legible.

(b) Retention

6.6   Subject to paragraph 6.7 below, anything which has been seized in accordance with the above provisions may be retained only for as long as is necessary in the circumstances. It may be retained, among other purposes:

(i)   for use as evidence at a trial for an offence;

(ii) for forensic examination or for other investigation in connection with an offence; or

(iii) where there are reasonable grounds for believing that it has been stolen or obtained by the commission of an offence, in order to establish its lawful owner.

6.7   Property shall not be retained in accordance with 6.6 (i) and (ii) (i.e., for use as evidence or for the purposes of investigation) if a photograph or copy would suffice for those purposes.

6.8–6.9   ★ ★ ★ ★ ★

7   Action to be taken after searches

7.1   Where premises have been searched in circumstances to which this code applies, other than in the circumstances covered by paragraph 1.3(a), the officer in charge of the search shall, on arrival at a police station, make or have made a record of the search. The record shall include:

(i)   the address of the premises searched;

(ii)   he date, time and duration of the search;

(iii) the authority under which the search was made. Where the search was made in the exercise of a statutory power to search premises without warrant, the record shall include the power under which the search was made; and where the search was made under warrant, or with written consent, a copy of the warrant or consent shall be appended to the record or kept in a place identified in the record;

(iv)   the names of all the officers who conducted the search (except in the case of enquiries linked to the investigation of terrorism, in which case the record shall state the warrant or other identification number and duty station of each officer concerned);

(v)   the names of any persons on the premises if they are known;

(vi)   either a list of any articles seized or a note of where such a list is kept and, if not covered by a warrant, the reason for their seizure;

(vii) whether force was used, and, if so, the reason why it was used;

(viii) details of any damage caused during the search, and the circumstances in which it was caused.

7.2   Where premises have been searched under warrant, the warrant shall be endorsed to show:

(i)   whether any articles specified in the warrant were found;

(ii)   whether any other articles were seized;

(iii) the date and time at which it was executed;

(iv)   the names of the officers who executed it (except in the case of enquiries linked to the investigation of terrorism, in which case the warrant or other identification number and duty station of each officer concerned shall be shown);

(v)   whether a copy, together with a copy of the notice of powers and rights was handed to the occupier; or whether it was endorsed as requested by paragraph 5.8, and left on the premises together with the copy notice and, if so, where.

7.3   Any warrant which has been executed or which has not been executed within one calendar month of its issue shall be returned, if it was issued by a justice of the peace, to the clerk to the justices for the petty sessions area concerned or, if issued by a judge, to the appropriate officer of the court from which he issued it.

8   ★ ★ ★ ★ ★

Code of Practice for the Detention, Treatment and Questioning of Persons by Police Officers (Code C)

Note: See note above Code A (*supra*). The Notes for Guidance are not reproduced.

1 General

1.1   All persons in custody must be dealt with expeditiously, and released as soon as the need for detention has ceased to apply.

1.1A   A custody officer is required to perform the functions specified in this code as soon as is practicable. A custody officer shall not be in breach of this code in the event of delay provided that the delay is justifiable and that every reasonable step is taken to prevent unnecessary delay. The custody record shall indicate where a delay has occurred and the reason why.

1.2   This code of practice must be readily available at all police stations for consultation by police officers, detained persons and members of the public.

1.3   The notes for guidance included are not provisions of this code, but are guidance to police officers and others about its application and interpretation. Provisions in the annexes to this code are provisions of this code.

1.4   If an officer has any suspicion, or is told in good faith, that a person of any age may be mentally disordered or mentally handicapped, or mentally incapable of under-standing the significance of questions put to him or his replies, then that person shall be treated as a mentally disordered or mentally handicapped person for the purposes of this code.

1.5   If anyone appears to be under the age of 17 then he shall be treated as a juvenile for the purposes of this code in the absence of clear evidence to show that he is older.

1.6   If a person appears to be blind or seriously visually handicapped, deaf, unable to read, unable to speak or has difficulty orally because of a speech impediment, he should be treated as such for the purposes of this code in the absence of clear evidence to the contrary.

1.7   In this code "the appropriate adult" means:

    (a)   in the case of a juvenile:

        (i)   his parent or guardian (or, if he is in care, the care authority or voluntary organisation. The term "in care" is used in this code to cover all cases in which a juvenile is "looked after" by a local authority under the terms of the Children Act 1989);

        (ii)   a social worker; or

        (iii)   failing either of the above, another responsible adult aged 18 or over who is not a police officer or employed by the police.

    (b)   in the case of a person who is mentally disordered or mentally handicapped:

        (i)   a relative, guardian or other person responsible for his care or custody;

        (ii)   someone who has experience of dealing with mentally disordered or mentally handicapped persons but is not a police officer or employed by the police (such as an approved social worker as defined by the Mental Health Act 1983 or a specialist social worker); or

        (iii)   failing either of the above, some other responsible adult aged 18 or over who is not a police officer or employed by the police.

1.8   Whenever this code requires a person to be given certain information he does not have to be given it if he is incapable at the time of understanding what is said to him or is violent or likely to become violent or is in urgent need of medical attention, but he must be given it as soon as practicable.

1.9   Any reference to a custody officer in this code includes an officer who is performing the functions of a custody officer.

1.10   Subject to paragraph 1.12, this code applies to people who are in custody at police stations in England and Wales whether or not they have been arrested for an offence and to those who have been removed to a police station as a place of safety under section 135 and 136 of the Mental Health Act 1983. Section 15 (reviews and extensions of detention) however applies solely to people in police detention, for example those who have been brought to a police station under arrest for an offence or have been arrested at a police station for an offence after attending there voluntarily.

1.11–1.12   ★ ★ ★ ★ ★

2   Custody records

2.1   A separate custody record must be opened as soon as practicable for each person who is brought to a police station under arrest or is arrested at the police station having attended there voluntarily. All information which has to be recorded under this code must be recorded as soon as practicable in the custody record unless otherwise specified. Any audio or video recording made in the custody area is not part of the custody record.

2.2   In the case of any action requiring the authority of an officer of a specified rank, his name and rank must be noted in the custody record. The recording of names does not apply to officers dealing with persons detained under the Prevention of Terrorism (Temporary Provisions) Act 1989. Instead the record shall state the warrant or other identification number and duty station of such officers.

2.3   The custody officer is responsible for the accuracy and completeness of the custody record and for ensuring that the record or a copy of the record accompanies a detained person if he is transferred to another police station. The record shall show the time of and reason for transfer and the time a person is released from detention.

2.4   A solicitor or appropriate adult must be permitted to consult the custody record of a person detained as soon as practicable after their arrival at the police station. When a person leaves police detention or is taken before a court, he or his legal representative or his appropriate adult shall be supplied on request with a copy of the custody record as soon as practicable. This entitlement lasts for 12 months after his release.

2.5   ★ ★ ★ ★ ★

2.6   All entries in custody records must be timed and signed by the maker. In the case of a record entered on a computer this shall be timed and contain the operator's identification. Warrant or other identification numbers shall be used rather than names in the case of detention under the Prevention of Terrorism (Temporary Provisions) Act 1989.

2.7   The fact and time of any refusal by a person to sign a custody record when asked to do so in accordance with the provisions of this code must itself be recorded.

3   Initial action

(a) Detained persons: normal procedure

3.1   When a person is brought to a police station under arrest or is arrested at the police station having attended there voluntarily the custody officer must tell him clearly of the following rights and of the fact that they are continuing rights which may be exercised at any stage during the period in custody.

  (i)   the right to have someone informed of his arrest in accordance with section 5 below;

  (ii)   the right to consult privately with a solicitor in accordance with section 6 below, and the fact that independent legal advice is available free of charge; and

  (iii)   the right to consult this and the other codes of practice.

3.2   In addition the custody officer must give the person a written notice setting out the above three rights, the right to a copy of the custody record in accordance with paragraph 2.4 above and the caution in the terms prescribed in section 10 below. The notice must also explain the arrangements for obtaining legal advice. The custody officer must also give the person an additional written notice briefly setting out his entitlements while in custody. The custody officer shall ask the person to sign the custody record to acknowledge receipt of these notices and any refusal to sign must be recorded on the custody record.

3.3   ★ ★ ★ ★ ★

3.4   The custody officer shall note on the custody record any comment the person may make in relation to the arresting officer's account but shall not invite comment. If the custody officer authorises a person's detention he must inform him of the grounds as soon as practicable and in any case before that person is then questioned about any offence. The custody officer shall note any comment the person may make in respect of the decision to detain him but, again, shall not invite comment. The custody officer shall not put specific questions to the person regarding his involvement in any offence, nor in respect of any comments he may make in response to the arresting officer's account or the decision to place him in detention. . . .

3.5   The custody officer shall ask the detained person whether at this time he would like legal advice (see paragraph 6.5). The person shall be asked to sign the custody record to confirm his decision. The custody officer is responsible for ensuring that in confirming any decision the person signs in the correct place.

3.5A   If video cameras are installed in the custody area, notices which indicate that cameras are in use shall be prominently displayed. Any request by a detained person or other person to have video cameras switched off shall be refused.

(b) Detained persons: special groups

3.6   If the person appears to be deaf or there is doubt about his hearing or speaking ability or ability to understand English, and the custody officer cannot establish effective communication, the custody officer must as soon as practicable call an interpreter, and ask him to provide the information required above. [See Section 13]

3.7   If the person is a juvenile, the custody officer must, if it is practicable, ascertain the identity of a person responsible for his welfare. That person may be his parent or guardian (or, if he is in care, the care authority or voluntary organisation) or any other person who has, for the time being, assumed responsibility for his welfare. That person must be informed as soon as practicable that the juvenile has been arrested, why he has been arrested and where he is detained. This right is in addition to the juvenile's right in section 5 of the code not to be held incommunicado.

3.8   In the case of a juvenile who is known to be subject to a supervision order, reasonable steps must also be taken to notify the person supervising him.

3.9   If the person is a juvenile, is mentally handicapped or appears to be suffering from a mental disorder, then the custody officer must, as soon as practicable, inform the appropriate adult (who in the case of a juvenile may or may not be a person responsible for his welfare, in accordance with paragraph 3.7 above) of the grounds for his detention and his whereabouts, and ask the adult to come to the police station to see the person.

3.10   It is imperative that a mentally disordered or mentally handicapped person who has been detained under section 136 of the Mental Health Act 1983 should be assessed as soon as possible. If that assessment is to take place at the police station, an approved social worker and a registered medical practitioner should be called to the police station as soon as possible in order to interview and examine the person. Once the person has been interviewed and examined and suitable arrangements have been made for his treatment or care, he can no longer be detained under section 136. The person should not be released until he has been seen by both the approved social worker and the registered medical practitioner.

3.11   If the appropriate adult is already at the police station, then the provisions of paragraphs 3.1 to 3.5 above must be complied with in his presence. If the appropriate adult is not at the police station when the provisions of paragraphs 3.1 to 3.5 above are complied with, then these provisions must be complied with again in the presence of the appropriate adult once that person arrives.

3.12   The person should be advised by the custody officer that the appropriate adult (where applicable) is there to assist and advise him and that he can consult privately with the appropriate adult at any time.

3.13   If, having been informed of the right to legal advice under paragraph 3.11 above, either the appropriate adult or the person detained wishes legal advice to be taken, then the provisions of section 6 of this code apply.

3.14   If the person is blind or seriously visually handicapped or is unable to read, the custody officer should ensure that his solicitor, relative, the appropriate adult or some other person likely to take an interest in him (and not involved in the investigation) is available to help in checking any documentation. Where this code requires written consent or signification, then the person who is assisting may be asked to sign instead if the detained person so wishes.

(c) Persons attending a police station voluntarily

3.15   Any person attending a police station voluntarily for the purpose of assisting with an investigation may leave at will unless placed under arrest. If it is decided that he should not be allowed to do so then he must be informed at once that he is under arrest and brought before the custody officer, who is responsible for ensuring that he is notified of his rights in the same way as other detained persons. If he is not placed under arrest but is cautioned in accordance with section 10 below, the officer who gives the caution must at the same time inform him that he is not under arrest, that he is not obliged to remain at the police station but that if he remains at the police station he may obtain free legal advice if he wishes. The officer shall point out that the right to legal advice includes the right to speak with a solicitor on the telephone and ask him if he wishes to do so.

3.16   If a person who is attending the police station voluntarily (in accordance with paragraph 3.15) asks about his entitlement to legal advice, he should be given a copy of the notice explaining the arrangements for obtaining legal advice.

(d) Documentation

3.17   The grounds for a person's detention shall be recorded, in his presence if practicable.

3.18   Action taken under paragraphs 3.6 to 3.14 shall be recorded.

4   Detained persons' property

(a) Action

4.1   The custody officer is responsible for:
- (a) ascertaining:
    - (i) what property a detained person has with him when he comes to the police station (whether on arrest, re-detention on answering to bail, commitment to prison custody on the order or sentence of a court, on lodgement at the police station with a view to his production in court from such custody, on arrival at a police station on transfer from detention at another station or from hospital or on detention under section 135 or 136 of the Mental Health Act 1983);
    - (ii) what property he might have acquired for an unlawful or harmful purpose while in custody.
- (b) the safekeeping of any property which is taken from him and which remains at the police station.

To these ends the custody officer may search him or authorise his being searched to the extent that he considers necessary (provided that a search of intimate parts of the body or involving the removal of more than outer clothing may only be made in accordance with Annex A to this code). A search may only be carried out by an officer of the same sex as the person searched.

4.2   A detained person may retain clothing and personal effects at his own risk unless the custody officer considers that he may use them to cause harm to himself or others, interfere with evidence, damage property or effect an escape or they are needed as evidence. In this event the custody officer may withhold such articles as he considers necessary. If he does so he must tell the person why.

4.3   Personal effects are those items which a person may lawfully need or use or refer to while in detention but do not include cash and other items of value.

(b) Documentation

4.4   The custody officer is responsible for recording all property brought to the police station that a detained person had with him, or had taken from him on arrest. The detained person shall be allowed to check and sign the record of property as correct. Any refusal to sign should be recorded.

4.5   If a detained person is not allowed to keep any article of clothing or personal effects the reason must be recorded.

5   Right not to be held incommunicado

(a) Action

5.1   Any person arrested and held in custody at a police station or other premises may on request have one person known to him or who is likely to take an interest in his welfare informed at public expense as soon as practicable of his whereabouts. If the person cannot be contacted the person who has made the request may choose up to two alternatives. If they too cannot be contacted the person in charge of detention or of the investigation has discretion to allow further attempts until the information has been conveyed.

5.2   ★ ★ ★ ★ ★

5.3   The above right may be exercised on each occasion that a person is taken to another police station.

5.4   The person may receive visits at the custody officer's discretion.

5.5   Where an enquiry as to the whereabouts of the person is made by a friend, relative or person with an interest in his welfare, this information shall be given, if he agrees and if Annex B does not apply.

5.6   Subject to the following condition, the person should be supplied with writing materials on request and allowed to speak on the telephone for a reasonable time to one person. Where an officer of the rank of inspector or above considers that the sending of a letter or the making of a telephone call may result in:

(a)   any of the consequences set out in the first and second paragraph of Annex B and the person is detained in connection with an arrestable or a serious arrestable offence, for which purpose, any reference to a serious arrestable offence in Annex B includes an arrestable offence; or

(b)   either of the consequences set out in paragraph 8 of Annex B and the person is detained under the Prevention of Terrorism (Temporary Provisions) Act 1989,

that officer can deny or delay the exercise of either or both these privileges. However, nothing in this section permits the restriction or denial of the rights set out in sections 5.1 and 6.1.

5.7   Before any letter or message is sent, or telephone call made, the person shall be informed that what he says in any letter, call or message (other than in the case of a communi-cation to a solicitor) may be read or listened to as appropriate and may be given in evidence. A telephone call may be terminated if it is being abused. The costs can be at public expense at the discretion of the custody officer.

(b) Documentation

5.8   A record must be kept of:
   (a) any request made under this section and the action taken on it;
   (b) any letters, messages or telephone calls made or received or visits received; and
   (c) any refusal on the part of the person to have information about himself or his whereabouts given to an outside enquirer. The person must be asked to counter-sign the record accordingly and any refusal to sign should be recorded.

6   Right to legal advice

(a) Action

6.1   Subject to the provisos in Annex B all people in police detention must be informed that they may at any time consult and communicate privately, whether in person, in writing or by telephone with a solicitor, and that independent legal advice is available free of charge from the duty solicitor.

6.2–6.5   ★ ★ ★ ★ ★

6.6   A person who wants legal advice may not be interviewed or continue to be interviewed until he has received it unless:
   (a) Annex B applies; or
   (b) an officer of the rank of superintendent or above has reasonable grounds for believing that:
      (i) delay will involve an immediate risk of harm to persons or serious loss of, or damage to, property; or
      (ii) where a solicitor, including a duty solicitor, has been contacted and has agreed to attend, awaiting his arrival would cause unreasonable delay to the process of investigation; or
   (c) the solicitor nominated by the person, or selected by him from a list:
      (i) cannot be contacted; or
      (ii) has previously indicated that he does not wish to be contacted; or
      (iii) having been contacted, has declined to attend;
   and the person has been advised of the Duty Solicitor Scheme (where one is in oper-ation) but has declined to ask for the duty solicitor, or the duty solicitor is unavailable. (In these circumstances the interview may be started or continued without further delay provided that an officer of the rank of inspector or above has given agreement for the interview to proceed in those circumstances.)
   (d) the person who wanted legal advice changes his mind.
   In these circumstances the interview may be started or continued without further delay provided that the person has given his agreement in writing or on tape to being interviewed without receiving legal advice and that an officer of the rank of Inspector or above, having inquired into the person's reasons for his change of mind, has given authority for the interview to proceed. Confirmation of the person's agreement, his change of mind, his reasons where given and the name of the authorising officer shall be recorded in the taped or written interview record at the beginning or recommence-ment of interview.

6.7   Where 6.6(b)(i) applies, once sufficient information to avert the risk has been obtained, questioning must cease until the person has received legal advice or 6.6(a), (b)(ii), (c) or (d) apply.

6.8   Where a person has been permitted to consult a solicitor and the solicitor is available (i.e., present at the station or on his way to the station or easily contactable by telephone) at the time the interview begins or is in progress, he must be allowed to have his solicitor present while he is interviewed.

6.9   The solicitor may only be required to leave the interview if his conduct is such that the investigating officer is unable properly to put questions to the suspect.

6.10   If the investigating officer considers that a solicitor is acting in such a way, he will stop the interview and consult an officer not below the rank of superintendent, if one is readily available, and otherwise an officer not below the rank of inspector who is not connected with the investigation. After speaking to the solicitor, the officer who has been consulted will decide whether or not the interview should continue in the presence of that solicitor. If he decides that it should not, the suspect will be given the opportunity to consult another solicitor before the interview continues and that solicitor will be given an opportunity to be present at the interview.

6.11   The removal of a solicitor from an interview is a serious step and, if it occurs, the officer of superintendent rank or above who took the decision will consider whether the incident should be reported to the Law Society. If the decision to remove the solicitor has been taken by an officer below the rank of superintendent, the facts must be reported to an officer of superintendent rank or above who will similarly consider whether a report to the Law Society would be appropriate. Where the solicitor concerned is a duty solicitor, the report should be both to the Law Society and to the Legal Aid Board.

6.12–6.15   ★ ★ ★ ★ ★

(b) Documentation

6.16   Any request for legal advice and the action taken on it shall be recorded.

6.17   If a person has asked for legal advice and an interview is begun in the absence of a solicitor or his representative (or the solicitor or his representative has been required to leave an interview), a record shall be made in the interview record.

7   ★ ★ ★ ★ ★

8   Conditions of Detention

(a) Action

8.1   So far as is practicable, not more than one person shall be detained in each cell.

8.2   Cells in use must be adequately heated, cleaned and ventilated. They must be adequately lit, subject to such dimming as is compatible with safety and security to allow people detained overnight to sleep. No additional restraints shall be used within a locked cell unless absolutely necessary, and then only suitable handcuffs. In the case of a mentally handicapped or mentally disordered person, particular care must be taken when deciding whether to use handcuffs.

8.3   Blankets, mattresses, pillows and other bedding supplied should be of a reasonable standard and in a clean and sanitary condition.

8.4   Access to toilet and washing facilities must be provided.

8.5   If it is necessary to remove a person's clothes for the purposes of investigation, for hygiene or health reasons or for cleaning, replacement clothing of a reasonable standard of comfort and cleanliness shall be provided. A person may not be interviewed unless adequate clothing has been offered to him.

8.6   At least two light meals and one main meal shall be offered in any period of 24 hours. Drinks should be provided at mealtimes and upon reasonable request between mealtimes. Whenever necessary, advice shall be sought from the police surgeon on medical or dietary matters. As far as practicable, meals provided shall offer a varied diet and meet any special dietary needs or religious beliefs that the person may have; he may also have meals supplied by his family or friends at his or their own expense.

8.7 Brief outdoor exercise shall be offered daily if practicable.

8.8 A juvenile shall not be placed in a police cell unless no other secure accommodation is available and the custody officer considers that it is not practicable to supervise him if he is not placed in a cell or the custody officer considers that a cell provides more comfortable accommodation than other secure accommodation in the police station. He may not be placed in a cell with a detained adult.

8.9 Reasonable force may be used if necessary for the following purposes:

    (i)   to secure compliance with reasonable instructions, including instructions given in pursuance of the provisions of a code of practice; or

    (ii) to prevent escape, injury, damage to property or the destruction of evidence.

8.10 People detained shall be visited every hour, and those who are drunk, at least every half hour. A person who is drunk shall be roused and spoken to on each visit. Should the custody officer feel in any way concerned about the person's condition, for example because he fails to respond adequately when roused, then the officer shall arrange for medical treatment in accordance with paragraph 9.2 of this code.

(b) Documentation

8.11 A record must be kept of replacement clothing and meals offered.

8.12 If a juvenile is placed in a cell, the reason must be recorded.

9 Treatment of Detained Persons

(a) General

9.1 If a complaint is made by or on behalf of a detained person about his treatment since his arrest, or it comes to the notice of any officer that he may have been treated improperly, a report must be made as soon as practicable to an officer of the rank of inspector or above who is not connected with the investigation. If the matter concerns a possible assault or the possibility of the unnecessary or unreasonable use of force then the police surgeon must also be called as soon as practicable.

(b) Medical Treatment

9.2 The custody officer must immediately call the police surgeon (or, in urgent cases,— for example, where a person does not show signs of sensibility or awareness,—must send the person to hospital or call the nearest available medical practitioner) if a person brought to a police station or already detained there:

    (a) appears to be suffering from physical illness or a mental disorder; or

    (b) is injured; or

    (c) [Not Used]

    (d) fails to respond normally to questions or conversation (other than through drunkenness alone); or

    (e) otherwise appears to need medical attention. This applies even if the person makes no request for medical attention and whether or not he has recently had medical treatment elsewhere (unless brought to the police station direct from hospital).

9.3 If it appears to the custody officer, or he is told, that a person brought to the police station under arrest may be suffering from an infectious disease of any significance he must take steps to isolate the person and his property until he has obtained medical directions as to where the person should be taken, whether fumigation should take place and what precautions should be taken by officers who have been or will be in contact with him.

9.4   If a detained person requests a medical examination the police surgeon must be called as soon as practicable. He may in addition be examined by a medical practitioner of his own choice at his own expense.

9.5–9.9   ★ ★ ★ ★ ★

10   Cautions

(a) When a caution must be given

10.1   A person whom there are grounds to suspect of an offence must be cautioned before any questions about it (or further questions if it is his answers to previous questions which provide the grounds for suspicion) are put to him regarding his involvement or suspected involvement in that offence if his answers or his silence (i.e., failure or refusal to answer a question or to answer satisfactorily) may be given in evidence to a court in a prosecution. He therefore need not be cautioned if questions are put for other purposes, for example, solely to establish his identity or his ownership of any vehicle or to obtain information in accordance with any relevant statutory requirement (see paragraph 10.5C) or in furtherance of the proper and effective conduct of a search (for example to determine the need to search in the exercise of powers of stop and search or to seek co-operation while carrying out a search), or to seek verification of a written record in accordance with paragraph 11.13.

10.2   Whenever a person who is not under arrest is initially cautioned or is reminded that he is under caution (see paragraph 10.5) he must at the same time be told that he is not under arrest and is not obliged to remain with the officer (see paragraph 3.15).

10.3   A person must be cautioned upon arrest for an offence unless:
   (a) it is impracticable to do so by reason of his condition or behaviour at the time; or
   (b) he has already been cautioned immediately prior to arrest in accordance with paragraph 10.1 above.

(b) Action: general

10.4   The caution shall be in the following terms:
You do not have to say anything. But it may harm your defence if you do not mention when questioned something which you later rely on in court. Anything you do say may be given in evidence.

10.5   When there is a break in questioning under caution the interviewing officer must ensure that the person being questioned is aware that he remains under caution. If there is any doubt the caution should be given again in full when the interview resumes.

Special warnings under sections 36 and 37 of the Criminal Justice and Public Order Act 1994

10.5A   When a suspect who is interviewed after arrest fails or refuses to answer certain questions, or to answer them satisfactorily, after due warning, a court or jury may draw such inferences as appear proper under sections 36 and 37 of the Criminal Justice and Public Order Act 1994. This applies when:
   (a) a suspect is arrested by a constable and there is found on his person, or in or on his clothing or footwear, or otherwise in his possession, or in the place where he was arrested, any objects, marks or substances, or marks on such objects, and the person fails or refuses to account for the objects, marks or substances found; or
   (b) an arrested person was found by a constable at a place at or about the time the offence for which he was arrested, is alleged to have been committed, and the person fails or refuses to account for his presence at that place.

10.5B   For an inference to be drawn from a suspect's failure or refusal to answer a question about one of these matters or to answer it satisfactorily, the interviewing officer must first tell him in ordinary language:

(a) what offence he is investigating;

(b) what fact he is asking the suspect to account for;

(c) that he believes this fact may be due to the suspect's taking part in the commission of the offence in question;

(d) that a court may draw a proper inference if he fails or refuses to account for the fact about which he is being questioned;

(e) that a record is being made of the interview and that it may be given in evidence if he is brought to trial.

10.5C   Where, despite the fact that a person has been cautioned, failure to co-operate may have an effect on his immediate treatment, he should be informed of any relevant consequences and that they are not affected by the caution. Examples are when his refusal to provide his name and address when charged may render him liable to detention, or when his refusal to provide particulars and information in accordance with a statutory requirement, for example, under the Road Traffic Act 1988, may amount to an offence or may make him liable to arrest.

(c) Juveniles, the mentally disordered and the mentally handicapped

10.6   If a juvenile or a person who is mentally disordered or mentally handicapped is cautioned in the absence of the appropriate adult, the caution must be repeated in the adult's presence.

(d) Documentation

10.7   A record shall be made when a caution is given under this section, either in the officer's pocket book or in the interview record as appropriate.

11   Interviews: general

11.1A, 11.1, 11.2   ★ ★ ★ ★ ★

11.2A At the beginning of an interview carried out in a police station, the interviewing officer, after cautioning the suspect, shall put to him any significant statement or silence which occurred before his arrival at the police station, and shall ask him whether he confirms or denies that earlier statement or silence and whether he wishes to add anything. A 'significant' statement or silence is one which appears capable of being used in evidence against the suspect, in particular a direct admission of guilt, or failure or refusal to answer a question or to answer it satisfactorily, which might give rise to an inference under Part III of the Criminal Justice and Public Order Act 1994.

11.3   No police officer may try to obtain answers to questions or to elicit a statement by the use of oppression. Except as provided for in paragraph 10.5C, no police officer shall indicate, except in answer to a direct question, what action will be taken on the part of the police if the person being interviewed answers questions, makes a statement or refuses to do either. If the person asks the officer directly what action will be taken in the event of his answering questions, making a statement or refusing to do either, then the officer may inform the person what action the police propose to take in that event provided that action is itself proper and warranted.

11.4   As soon as a police officer who is making enquiries of any person about an offence believes that a prosecution should be brought against him and that there is sufficient evidence for it to succeed, he should ask the person if he has anything further to say. If the person indicates that he has nothing more to say the officer shall without delay cease to question him about that offence. This should not, however, be taken to prevent officers in revenue cases or acting under the confiscation provisions of the Criminal Justice Act 1988 or the Drug Trafficking Offences Act 1986 from inviting suspects to complete a formal question and answer record after the interview is concluded.

(b) Interview records

    11.5 (a) An accurate record must be made of each interview with a person suspected of an offence, whether or not the interview takes place at a police station.

        (b) The record must state the place of the interview, the time it begins and ends, the time the record is made (if different), any breaks in the interview and the names of all those present; and must be made on the forms provided for this purpose or in the officer's pocket-book or in accordance with the code of practice for the tape-recording of police interviews with suspects.

        (c) The record must be made during the course of the interview, unless in the investigating officer's view this would not be practicable or would interfere with the conduct of the interview, and must constitute either a verbatim record of what has been said or, failing this, an account of the interview which adequately and accurately summarises it.

    11.6 ★ ★ ★ ★ ★

    11.7 If an interview record is not made during the course of the interview it must be made as soon as practicable after its completion.

    11.8 Written interview records must be timed and signed by the maker.

    11.9 If an interview record is not completed in the course of the interview the reason must be recorded in the officer's pocket book.

    11.10 Unless it is impracticable the person interviewed shall be given the opportunity to read the interview record and to sign it as correct or to indicate the respects in which he considers it inaccurate. If the interview is tape-recorded the arrangements set out in the relevant code of practice apply. If the person concerned cannot read or refuses to read the record or to sign it, the senior police officer present shall read it over to him and ask him whether he would like to sign it as correct (or make his mark) or to indicate the respects in which he considers it inaccurate. The police officer shall then certify on the interview record itself what has occurred.

    11.11 If the appropriate adult or the person's solicitor is present during the interview, he should also be given an opportunity to read and sign the interview record (or any written statement taken down by a police officer).

    11.12 Any refusal by a person to sign an interview record when asked to do so in accordance with the provisions of this code must itself be recorded.

    11.13–11.16 ★ ★ ★ ★ ★

12 Interviews in police stations

(a) Action

    12.1 If a police officer wishes to interview, or conduct enquiries which require the presence of a detained person the custody officer is responsible for deciding whether to deliver him into his custody.

    12.2 In any period of 24 hours a detained person must be allowed a continuous period of at least 8 hours for rest, free from questioning, travel or any interruption by police officers in connection with the investigation concerned. This period should normally be at night. The period of rest may not be interrupted or delayed, except at the request of the person, his appropriate adult or his legal representative, unless there are reasonable grounds for believing that it would:

(i) involve a risk of harm to persons or serious loss of, or damage to, property;

(ii) delay unnecessarily the person's release from custody; or

(iii) otherwise prejudice the outcome of the investigation.

If a person is arrested at a police station after going there voluntarily, the period of 24 hours runs from the time of his arrest and not the time of arrival at the police station. Any action which is required to be taken in accordance with section 8 of this code, or in accordance with medical advice or at the request of the detained person, his appropriate adult or his legal representative, does not constitute an interruption to the rest period such that a fresh period must be allowed.

12.3   A detained person may not be supplied with intoxicating liquor except on medical directions. No person who is unfit through drink or drugs to the extent that he is unable to appreciate the significance of questions put to him and his answers may be questioned about an alleged offence in that condition except in accordance with Annex C.

12.4   As far as practicable interviews shall take place in interview rooms which must be adequately heated, lit and ventilated.

12.5   Persons being questioned or making statements shall not be required to stand.

12.6   Before the commencement of an interview each interviewing officer shall identify himself and any other officers present by name and rank to the person being interviewed, except in the case of persons detained under the Prevention of Terrorism (Temporary Provisions) Act 1989 when each officer shall identify himself by his warrant or other identification number and rank rather than his name.

12.7   Breaks from interviewing shall be made at recognised meal times. Short breaks for refreshment shall also be provided at intervals of approximately two hours, subject to the interviewing officer's discretion to delay a break if there are reasonable grounds for believing that it would:

(i) involve a risk of harm to persons or serious loss of, or damage to, property;

(ii) delay unnecessarily the person's release from custody; or

(iii) otherwise prejudice the outcome of the investigation.

12.8   If in the course of the interview a complaint is made by the person being questioned or on his behalf concerning the provisions of this code then the interviewing officer shall:

(i) record it in the interview record; and

(ii) inform the custody officer, who is then responsible for dealing with it in accordance with section 9 of this code.

(b) Documentation

12.9–12.13   ★ ★ ★ ★ ★

13–15   ★ ★ ★ ★ ★

16   Charging of detained persons

(a) Action

16.1   When an officer considers that there is sufficient evidence to prosecute a detained person, and that there is sufficient evidence for a prosecution to succeed, and that the person has said all that he wishes to say about the offence, he should without delay (and subject to the following qualification) bring him before the custody officer who shall then be responsible for considering whether or not he should be charged. When a person is detained in respect of more than one offence it is permissible to delay bringing him before the custody officer until the above conditions are satisfied in respect of all the offences (but see paragraph 11.4). Any resulting action should be taken in the presence of the appropriate adult if the person is a juvenile or mentally disordered or mentally handicapped.

16.2   When a detained person is charged with or informed that he may be prosecuted for an offence he shall be cautioned in the terms:

You do not have to say anything. But it may harm your defence if you do not mention now something which you later rely on in court. Anything you do say may be given in evidence.

16.3   At the time a person is charged he shall be given a written notice showing particulars of the offence with which he is charged and including the name of the officer in the case (in terrorist cases, the officer's warrant or other identification number instead), his police station and the reference number for the case. So far as possible the particulars of the charge shall be stated in simple terms, but they shall also show the precise offence in law with which he is charged. The notice shall begin with the following words:

You are charged with the offence(s) shown below. You do not have to say anything. But it may harm your defence if you do not mention now something which you later rely on in court. Anything you do say may be given in evidence.

If the person is a juvenile or is mentally disordered or mentally handicapped the notice shall be given to the appropriate adult.

16.4   If at any time after a person has been charged with or informed he may be prosecuted for an offence, a police officer wishes to bring to the notice of the person any written statement made by another person or the content of an interview with another person, he shall hand to that person a true copy of any such written statement or bring to his attention the content of the interview record, but shall say or do nothing to invite any reply or comment save to warn him that he does not have to say anything but that anything he does say may be given in evidence and to remind him of his right to legal advice in accordance with paragraph 6.5 above. If the person cannot read then the officer may read it to him. If the person is a juvenile or mentally disordered or mentally handicapped the copy shall also be given to, or the interview record brought to the attention of, the appropriate adult.

16.5   Questions relating to an offence may not be put to a person after he has been charged with that offence, or informed that he may be prosecuted for it, unless they are necessary for the purpose of preventing or minimising harm or loss to some other person or to the public or for clearing up an ambiguity in a previous answer or statement, or where it is in the interests of justice that the person should have put to him and have an opportunity to comment on information concerning the offence which has come to light since he was charged or informed that he might be prosecuted. Before any such questions are put to him, he shall be warned that he does not have to say anything but that anything he does say may be given in evidence and reminded of his right to legal advice in accordance with paragraph 6.5 above.

16.6   Where a juvenile is charged with an offence and the custody officer authorises his continued detention he must try to make arrangements for the juvenile to be taken into the care of a local authority to be detained pending appearance in court unless he certifies that it is impracticable to do so, or, in the case of a juvenile of at least 12 years of age, no secure accommodation is available and there is a risk to the public of serious harm from that juvenile, in accordance with section 38(6) of the Police and Criminal Evidence Act 1984, as amended by Section 59 of the Criminal Justice Act 1991 and section 24 of the Criminal Justice and Public Order Act 1994.

(b) Documentation

16.7   A record shall be made of anything a detained person says when charged.

16.8   Any questions put after charge and answers given relating to the offence shall be contemporaneously recorded in full on the forms provided and the record signed by that person or, if he refuses, by the interviewing officer and any third parties present. If the questions are tape-recorded the arrangements set out in Code E apply.

16.9   If it is not practicable to make arrangements for the transfer of a juvenile into local authority care in accordance with paragraph 16.6 above the custody officer must record the reasons and make out a certificate to be produced before the court together with the juvenile.

[17]   ★ ★ ★ ★ ★

ANNEX A   ★ ★ ★ ★ ★

ANNEX B   DELAY IN NOTIFYING ARREST OR ALLOWING ACCESS TO LEGAL ADVICE

A   Persons detained under the Police and Criminal Evidence Act 1984

(a) Action

1.   The rights set out in sections 5 or 6 of the code or both may be delayed if the person is in police detention in connection with a serious arrestable offence, has not yet been charged with an offence and an officer of the rank of superintendent or above has reasonable grounds for believing that the exercise of either right:

(i)   will lead to interference with or harm to evidence connected with a serious arrestable offence or interference with or physical injury to other persons; or

(ii)   will lead to the alerting of other persons suspected of having committed such an offence but not yet arrested for it; or

(iii)   will hinder the recovery of property obtained as a result of such an offence.

2.   These rights may also be delayed where the serious arrestable offence is either:

(i)   a drug trafficking offence and the officer has reasonable grounds for believing that the detained person has benefited from drug trafficking, and that the recovery of the value of that person's proceeds of drug trafficking will be hindered by the exercise of either right; or

(ii)   an offence to which Part VI of the Criminal Justice Act 1988 (covering confiscation orders) applies and the officer has reasonable grounds for believing that the detained person has benefited from the offence, and that the recovery of the value of the property obtained by that person from or in connection with the offence or if the pecuniary advantage derived by him from or in connection with it will be hindered by the exercise of either right.

3.   Access to a solicitor may not be delayed on the grounds that he might advise the person not to answer any questions or that the solicitor was initially asked to attend the police station by someone else, provided that the person himself then wishes to see the solicitor. In the latter case the detained person must be told that the solicitor has come to the police station at another person's request, and must be asked to sign the custody record to signify whether or not he wishes to see the solicitor.

4.   These rights may be delayed only for as long as is necessary and, subject to paragraph 9 below, in no case beyond 36 hours after the relevant time as defined in section 41 of the Police and Criminal Evidence Act 1984. If the above grounds cease to apply within this time, the person must as soon as practicable be asked if he wishes to exercise either right, the custody record must be noted accordingly, and action must be taken in accordance with the relevant section of the code.

5.   A detained person must be permitted to consult a solicitor for a reasonable time before any court hearing.

(b) Documentation

6.   The grounds for action under this Annex shall be recorded and the person informed of them as soon as practicable.

7. Any reply given by a person under paragraphs 4 or 9 must be recorded and the person asked to endorse the record in relation to whether he wishes to receive legal advice at this point.

8.–11. ★ ★ ★ ★ ★

ANNEX C–E ★ ★ ★ ★ ★

Note: Codes D (identification) and E (tape recording) are not reproduced.

Civil Procedure Rules 1998

PART 54   JUDICIAL REVIEW

54.1 Scope and Interpretation
(1) This Part contains rules about judicial review.
(2) In this Part—
  (a) a "claim for judicial review" means a claim to review the lawfulness of—
    (i) an enactment; or
    (ii) a decision, action or failure to act in relation to the exercise of a public function;
  (b) an order of mandamus is called a "mandatory order";
  (c) an order of prohibition is called a "prohibiting order";
  (d) an order of certiorari is called a "quashing order";
  (e) "the judicial review procedure" means the Part 8 procedure as modified by this Part;
  (f) "interested party" means any person (other than the claimant and defendant) who is directly affected by the claim; and
  (g) "court" means the High Court, unless otherwise stated. (Rule 8.1(6)(b) provides that a rule or practice direction may, in relation to a specified type of proceedings, disapply or modify any of the rules set out in Part 8 as they apply to those proceedings)

54.2 When This Part Must Be Used
The judicial review procedure must be used in a claim for judicial review where the claimant is seeking—
  (a) a mandatory order;
  (b) a prohibiting order;
  (c) a quashing order; or
  (d) an injunction under section 30 of the Supreme Court Act 1981 (restraining a person from acting in any office in which he is not entitled to act).

54.3 When this Part May Be Used
(1) The judicial review procedure may be used in a claim for judicial review where the claimant is seeking—
  (a) a declaration; or
  (b) an injunction. (Section 31(2) of the Supreme Court Act 1981 sets out the circumstances in which the court may grant a declaration or injunction in a claim for judicial review)
(Where the claimant is seeking a declaration or injunction in addition to one of the remedies listed in rule 54.2, the judicial review procedure must be used)
(2) A claim for judicial review may include a claim for damages but may not seek damages alone.

(Section 31(4) of the Supreme Court Act 1981 sets out the circumstances in which the court may award damages on a claim for judicial review)

54.4   Permission Required

The court's permission to proceed is required in a claim for judicial review whether started under this Part or transferred to the Administrative Court.

54.5   Time Limit for Filing Claim Form

(1) The claim form must be filed—

    (a) promptly; and

    (b) in any event not later than 3 months after the grounds to make the claim first arose.

(2) The time limit in this rule may not be extended by agreement between the parties.

(3) This rule does not apply when any other enactment specifies a shorter time limit for making the claim for judicial review.

54.6   Claim Form

(1) In addition to the matters set out in rule 8.2 (contents of the claim form) the claimant must also state—

    (a) the name and address of any person he considers to be an interested party;

    (b) that he is requesting permission to proceed with a claim for judicial review;

    (c) any remedy (including any interim remedy) he is claiming.

(Part 25 sets out how to apply for an interim remedy)

(2) The claim form must be accompanied by the documents required by the relevant practice direction.

54.7   Service of Claim Form

The claim form must be served on—

    (a) the defendant; and

    (b) unless the court otherwise directs, any person the claimant considers to be an interested party,

within 7 days after the date of issue.

54.8   Acknowledgment of Service

(1) Any person served with the claim form who wishes to take part in the judicial review must file an acknowledgment of service in the relevant practice form in accordance with the following provisions of this rule.

(2) Any acknowledgment of service must be—

    (a) filed not more than 21 days after service of the claim form; and

    (b) served on—

        (i) the claimant; and

        (ii) subject to any direction under rule 54.7(b), any other person named in the claim form, as soon as practicable and, in any event, not later than 7 days after it is filed.

(3) The time limits under this rule may not be extended by agreement between the parties.

(4) The acknowledgment of service—

    (a) must—

        (i) where the person filing it intends to contest the claim, set out a summary of his grounds for doing so; and

        (ii) state the name and address of any person the person filing it considers to be an interested party; and

    (b) may include or be accompanied by an application for directions.

(5) Rule 10.3(2) does not apply.

54.9–54.16   ★ ★ ★ ★ ★

54.17   Court's Powers to Hear Any Person

(1) Any person may apply for permission—
  (a) to file evidence; or
  (b) make representations at the hearing of the judicial review.

(2) An application under paragraph (1) should be made promptly.

54.18   Judicial Review May be Decided Without a Hearing

The court may decide the claim for judicial review without a hearing where all the parties agree.

54.19   Court's Powers in Respect of Quashing Orders

(1) This rule applies where the court makes a quashing order in respect of the decision to which the claim relates.

(2) The court may—
  (a) remit the matter to the decision-maker; and
  (b) direct it to reconsider the matter and reach a decision in accordance with the judgment of the court.

(3) Where the court considers that there is no purpose to be served in remitting the matter to the decision-maker it may, subject to any statutory provision, take the decision itself.

(Where a statutory power is given to a tribunal, person or other body it may be the case that the court cannot take the decision itself.)

54.20   Transfer

The court may—
  (a) order a claim to continue as if it had not been started under this Part; and
  (b) where it does so, give directions about the future management of the claim. (Part 30 (transfer) applies to transfers to and from the Administrative Court.)

INDEX